TRANSFORMING RELATIONS

Michael A. Signer
March 29, 1945–January 10, 2009
Courtesy of the University of Notre Dame Archives

TRANSFORMING
RELATIONS

Essays on Jews and Christians throughout History

IN HONOR OF MICHAEL A. SIGNER

Foreword by John Van Engen

Edited by Franklin T. Harkins

University of Notre Dame Press
Notre Dame, Indiana

Published in the United States of America

Stanza 4 from "My Parents' Lodging Place," in Yehuda Amichai,
Open Closed Open, copyright © 2000 by Yehuda Amichai, English translation
copyright © 2000 by Chana Bloch and Chana Kronfeld, is reprinted by
permission of Houghton Mifflin Harcourt Publishing Company.

The Press and the volume editor gratefully acknowledge the generous financial
support for the publication of this volume provided by

Friends of the Hebrew Union College–Jewish Institute of Religion,
with special appreciation to David Ellenson, President

Department of Theology, University of Notre Dame,
with special appreciation to John Cavadini, Chair

Library of Congress Cataloging-in-Publication Data

Transforming relations : essays on Jews and Christians throughout history in
honor of Michael A. Signer / edited by Franklin T. Harkins.
p.   cm. — (From the Helen Kellogg Institute for International Studies)
Includes bibliographical references and index.
ISBN-13: 978-0-268-03090-2 (pbk. : alk. paper)
ISBN-10: 0-268-03090-1 (pbk. : alk. paper)
1. Judaism—Relations—Christianity.   2. Christianity and other religions—
Judaism.   I. Signer, Michael Alan.   II. Harkins, Franklin T.
BM535.T64   2010
296.3'9609—dc22   2010004293

Lines Written after Reading Celan

for Michael

Your name wanders through night and day.
Uncompanionably, it may find you, though
You will neither have gone nor arrived. Its touch
So pure, you will never know that you were known.

Your name drips from the small hands of the clock.
Incomprehensibly, it may find you, though
You were lost in the infinite labyrinth of doubt. Its touch
So violent, you will never know that you are gone.

The leaves copper in August covering up why.
Their rustle shouts down the almost
Impossibly diffident conversation between you
And you across the acres of hurt, borderlands
To keep promise promise and outcome itself.

Easiest to be in love with what should be.
Admittedly, you did not hit the mark of you.
But what you have become is the apple love's
Arrow throws in its way to pierce, remind it
Of how imperfectly it is.

Easiest to hate the promiser who did not keep
Faith with the setting out. But remember the angel
Judges harshly because he sees too much and not enough.
Love reaches backward as well as forward. It burns
The electric flesh into any word it now finds.

Cyril O'Regan

Contents

II. MODERN PERSPECTIVES: THEOLOGY, PRAXIS, AND PERCEPTIONS OF THE OTHER

Foreword

Graced with a capacious intelligence, a generous humanity, and an easy eloquence, Michael Signer forged his own distinct way as a Reform rabbi and a medieval professor, a person of humane letters and of covenantal allegiance who self-consciously reached out across scholarly and religious divides. Gifted with wit and compassion, and capable both of a mordant turn of phrase and of tender care, he touched countless lives over more than a generation of teaching.

Students, colleagues, and friends conceived this volume as a celebratory offering to honor his thirty-five years of teaching, half of them at Hebrew Union College in Los Angeles, his hometown and home community, and half at the University of Notre Dame, where he served with distinction as the first Abrams Chair for Jewish Thought and Culture—all this with, it was fully expected, many more years to come. The volume appears now, grievously, as a memorial tribute. Faced with an implacable and unrelenting illness, Michael Signer fought back bravely, even optimistically, making plans for a return to teaching while continuing to guide students and converse with colleagues. He learned of this volume's making and had the opportunity to see its list of contributors and leaf through its pages: pages written under his inspiration. The results speak for themselves. In the introduction, Franklin Harkins, a former student of Michael's, has set out the essentials of his unique contribution to Jewish-Christian relations, in both their historical and present-day dimensions, and has delineated the main lines of each contributor's essay. My few words here aim at something different: to offer, however fleetingly, a glimpse of the person.

Except for his beloved life's companion, Betty Roseman Signer, no single one of his colleagues and friends could pretend to understand the richly variegated dimensions of Michael Signer's life. There was the boy of German-Jewish heritage, who grew up a single child in sunny southern California, ever loyal to his people and religious community, Reform, not Orthodox, and discrete about Zionism. There was the honors student in Hebrew literature at the University of California, Los Angeles, who also took classes about the medieval church. And there was the rabbinical student in Cincinnati and Jerusalem, who honed a lifelong instinctive pastoral sense of how to care and guide. This young rabbi then went off to study things medieval at the Pontifical Institute for Mediaeval Studies in Toronto and found in Leonard Boyle, a Dominican priest and future prefect of the Vatican library, an influential mentor and dear friend. Back in Los Angeles as a rabbinical professor, he shaped numerous young people for the rabbinate, while also serving as an adjunct professor among former and new teachers at UCLA and reaching out to Catholic priests in dialogue. As the first chaired professor of Jewish studies in a midwestern Catholic university with hardly a Jewish undergraduate on its roster, he sustained his medieval scholarly work but moved laterally to meet student needs and the blind spots he perceived. He set up highly effective courses on, among other things, the Holocaust, and led young suburban Catholics to sites such as Auschwitz. As a colleague, he kept trying to bring people together across intellectual and religious divides of all sorts. As a preacher, he continued to teach in congregations large and small. As a writer, he could address both a specialist medieval crowd and the most general of Jewish and Christian audiences. As a networker, he was at ease with colleagues in Toronto, New York, Germany, France, and Israel, as well as in Los Angeles, Cincinnati, and Notre Dame. As a man of faith, he could make space for those people who saw Jesus of Nazareth as the Anointed One, while always himself defending and upholding the Jewish covenant. The longer I knew Michael Signer, the more I sensed the layered complexity of his formation and the deep foundations laid at Hebrew Union College in Cincinnati and Los Angeles, which are movingly captured in the eulogy penned by his friend Rabbi David Ellenson.

Michael and I first met under notable circumstances roughly thirty years ago, at a medieval conference sponsored by the University of the South. He was presenting the results of his dissertation on Andrew of St. Victor, I asked to serve as moderator of the session, and Beryl Smalley herself, the inspiration for one important dimension of his scholarly work, offered the commentary. Neither Michael nor I knew then that, a good fifteen years later, we would be staging our own conference on Christians and Jews in twelfth-century Europe. Michael and I shared connections that crisscrossed in surprising and affecting ways: student days and teachers at UCLA (he as an undergraduate, I later as a graduate student); sensitivity to the plight of German Jewish émigré scholars and recognition of their deep influence upon our own work; an abiding fascination with the intricate richness of high medieval Latin Christian culture, including twelfth-century exegesis (on which we both wrote dissertations); a love of medieval studies in all its interdisciplinary abundance, along with the brilliance and quirkiness of many of its scholars; and our place as medievalists working at a Catholic university, although not ourselves Catholic. In this setting our work was always generously fostered and appreciated, but we could on occasion find ourselves in an alien-seeming universe—the more so as the Church moved in restorationist directions, away from the more open spirit fostered by the Second Vatican Council that we had first come to know and that remained central to Michael's ecumenical efforts.

As an observer of human history and communities, Michael followed his own inner rhythms. For a young student of Hebrew literature to seek out a history course on the medieval church, and even to begin to learn Latin, was quite remarkable, especially for someone already eyeing the rabbinate. His teacher of medieval church history at UCLA (Gerhart Ladner) came from a Viennese Jewish family, a part of its assimilated bourgeoisie, a family that vacationed with the Freuds. In the early 1930s, after flirting with the Stefan George circle, Ladner, moved initially by medieval art, music, and liturgy, converted to Catholicism. He escaped Europe in 1938 and eventually settled at UCLA. Ladner (my *Doktorvater*) went on to explore in depth the theological core of his adopted community, so effectively that his *The Idea of Reform* (1959), which explored historic Christian notions of human holiness and God-likeness remade, laid some of the foundations for the calling of the Second Vatican Council. At HUC-Cincinnati, Michael then came equally or more under the influence of another refugee scholar (Ben-Zion Wacholder), a distinguished Talmudist who compellingly set out the historic core of Jewish tradition. These men, along with Arnold Band, his teacher of Hebrew literature, and other teachers at UCLA, such as Amos Funkenstein—an amazing student of Jewish history and of the history of ideas, as well as someone oriented to things German—became Michael's paradigms of the scholarly life. But the life stories of some émigré scholars also gave rise to deep-brooding questions. How had some Jewish men of learning become so closely bound to their German culture, even to lean politically toward the right wing? Why had some found historic Christian culture so appealing or satisfying, even to the point of crossing over to it? In the aftermath of the Shoah, how could a young scholar in the German Reform tradition, one not inclined to radical Orthodoxy or Zionism, understand their intellectual aspirations and choices, yet still share in and carry forward the best of their ideals? He and I touched on these matters and others like them more than once in conversation, gingerly, quietly. Firm in his Jewish covenantal allegiance, Michael nonetheless openly and sincerely engaged German and Christian scholars, especially Catholics, and was beloved by them. (Some of these friends, in a teasing document penned in Latin to celebrate his sixtieth birthday, named him to the cardinalate for meritorious service.) At the same time, in a contrariety of another sort, he also lived with, if occasionally chafed under, the status of Reform rabbis amid an Orthodox establishment in Israel.

Michael Signer studied at Toronto just as medieval studies was in full flourish there. He could have gone forward in Jewish history at Columbia University, but instead chose, as nearer to his own purposes, an open-ended but religiously oriented interdisciplinary program. At the heart of the Toronto enterprise was a powerful focus on texts and their transmission in handwritten codices. For Michael, this focus would become second nature. It was what he expected of his own students and what he himself did with aplomb, eventually producing an exemplary edition of a Latin biblical commentary on Ezekiel. I remember vividly, in what turned out to be the last doctoral exam we conducted together, that a student was asked about a proposed edition and stumbled over certain basics. Michael, with a gleam in his eye (I was sitting across from him), leaped in and with utter crispness and clarity laid out the way to proceed. All this Michael had absorbed quite especially from Leonard Boyle, whose photo stood prominently in Michael's office. Under Boyle's patronage, Michael eventually organized an exhibit of Hebrew manuscripts held in the Vatican Library—I think, a first for the Vatican. Father Boyle spent six weeks at Notre Dame toward the end of his life and offered for one last time an abbreviated version of his famous diplomatics course, the study of medieval documentary materials. Michael, by then a senior professor with students of his own, sat in on the course, and I remember him coming out of the seminar room one day with a glow on his face, partly from the thrill of the subject matter for him, more perhaps from the satisfaction of watching his friend and teacher at work with yet another set of young students.

Some editors of texts fail to rise much above the editorial project itself—one reason, beyond matters of competence in language and script, why the making of editions has largely disappeared as a dissertation project. But for Michael it was always about more, about meaning: what those texts, once recovered and set out, had to tell us about past peoples and, in this case, past approaches to and understandings of Scripture. In the introduction to his own edition of Andrew of St. Victor's commentary on Ezekiel, he moved such interpretative matters importantly forward. That edition is now essential reading. Over against those scholars who found that most Christian talk of the Hebrew letter and of Jewish interpreters cast up only literary and dialectical straw men, Michael held to the reality of the encounter and the importance of this medieval Christian grappling with the Hebrew letter and learning from Jewish interlocutors. But over against those who cast all this in a vaguely ecumenical haze, Michael pointed out with clarity that Christians—including the Victorines and their heirs—still expected that Jews would be gathered in at the end of time, and on Christian terms. Again, he sought to work out and articulate a position somewhere between two worlds.

Michael's search for meaning in texts went further still, partly inspired by another Toronto professor, Brian Stock. How we interpret texts and how we elicit meaning from them—be they sacred or school texts, be they seemingly straightforward or dizzyingly difficult—in short, this matter of hermeneutics, became in many ways the central theme of Michael's medieval teaching and scholarly writing. This drew him closer to literary approaches than is the case for most biblical scholars or theologians. And, while it built on the work of others on both the Jewish and Christian sides, it yielded his own vision of medieval exegesis in the twelfth century. Others in this volume touch upon some of its features. Here, I would like to step back a little and offer my own observations about scholarly dispositions that arose from the depths of Michael's character.

For Michael, the sacred text did not become submerged, as the inherited traditions tended to have it, in the intricacies of law and practice (Talmud) or of theology and practice (Church doctrine), nor could it be reduced to a labyrinth of historical-philological puzzles (as in much modern biblical work). For him, it was not fundamentally text, either in the philological sense of some of his medievalist training, or in the theological sense of proof-texting, or indeed as a point of departure for legal debate. It was story, or "narrative," to use the scholarly term. As Michael perceived it, twelfth-century scholars, first Rashi on the Jewish side and later the Victorines in Paris on the Christian side, wanted to get back to the biblical "letter" in this sense, to the stories and the words that made them up and then to the meanings and resonances of those stories. Thus the impulse to reclaim the "letter" was not merely recovery of "plain sense" in some modern sense. This was the implicit direction of Beryl Smalley's influential work, whereas Michael conceived a more contextually nuanced medieval meaning. Without articulating it as such, he probably was instinctively thinking in consonance with haggadic interpretation. Any effort to get back to the story, Michael understood, was itself an act of creating meaning. Moreover, he saw that in the twelfth century both the Jewish and the Christian interpreters sought to reconstruct the sacred text's "plain" story with half an eye cocked toward their Christian or Jewish rivals and occasional interlocutors.

This was the complex—and alternative—dynamic he envisioned, and longingly hoped to capture within the covers of a single book. Virtually all of Michael's graduate classes, accordingly, focused on one or another of the biblical stories or characters, often the early ones. From them he elicited for his students the richness of narrative and community meaning with which twelfth-century interpreters, Jewish and Christian, endowed those stories. One of my own deep regrets is that our vague aspirations to co-teach a course on Jewish and Christian exegesis in the twelfth century never materialized, owing, as usual, to the busyness of our respective lives and departmental obligations. Engaging an issue from both sides was exactly why Michael went to Toronto and to Notre Dame. Such engagement, which he saw first happening in twelfth-century northern France, he saw as fundamental to European intellectual history and fundamental as well for both the Jewish and the Christian religious communities.

Michael's broad medievalist approach was ingenious on another count, and spoke to larger matters of interpretation. Law played a crucial role in medieval Christian culture, just as Jewish medieval culture produced its own theologies and pieties, although for the most part, neither would have recognized these aspects in the other—quite the contrary. They shared Scripture, however, at least the Hebrew Bible, and to varying degrees they self-consciously and polemically jostled with one another over its meaning. This common engagement provided the deeper background for another aspect of Michael's life and work, that is, his commitment to dialogue. This he practiced superbly well, as few others could, with clarity, without fudging prickly issues, yet with civility, good will, sometimes humor, and sometimes biting wit. This was a side of him that I saw less of in actual practice, although we talked about it. With me he could be almost apologetic about all the time spent on contemporary exchange rather than medieval scholarship, the looming shadow there, once again, of his scholarly paradigms, whereas, as I said more than once, he doubtless accomplished more good than did many medieval scholars. In the last years he spoke more than once of virtually having reinvented himself. He was not simply practicing dialogue. He was writing about it in ever greater depth and becoming a kind of theologian. He foresaw gathering these materials into a book even before he completed the "big medieval book." Here too Michael was making his own way and drawing upon that ability to navigate more than one world with surprising ease, at least to the public eye.

Where there were dialogue partners as serious and clear-headed as he, he could enter fully into a give-and-take and concede space in both Jewish and Christian directions, as well as finding space for both. Where Christian groups needed reminding of the heavy burden of past policy and practice, he could be firm, particularly against any backsliding and any fudging of the truth, himself in some sense representing the Jewish victim and insisting on the plain facts of the past. Alternatively, with Jewish audiences, he could present to them a Christianity that they often likely knew little or nothing of, and encourage them to read the New Testament, to see for themselves how little of early Christian belief and practice was intelligible apart from the Hebrew Bible. He could even present Jews and Christians as ultimately worshiping the same One, beyond name and distinction. It was a role at which he was preternaturally gifted and, in some deep and authentic sense, one he truly enjoyed. I can see him still, asked, fairly frequently, to say the grace before a meeting of faculty or of scholars gathered at Notre Dame. He would draw his yarmulke from his jacket pocket and offer a prayer in Hebrew. Only one or two of his listeners might understand the words or know their origin. But it was then, I sometimes thought, that he seemed very much himself, doing what he was meant to be doing and speaking most in his own voice.

Michael was instinctively pastoral. I saw this as it related to students and colleagues. His vision of medieval exegesis attracted many fine students. But especially those students, no matter the interest, who happened to struggle, those whom other teachers might give up on or become impatient with, these Michael regularly took in hand, showed them kindness, tried to help them find a workable topic, was patient as they labored to produce chapters, and encouraged them when things went well. With colleagues too, inside and especially outside the university, he had an eye for those who somehow found themselves at odds with the prevailing winds. He saw the potential in their work, the insights or innovative directions that others might have looked past. These were the ones he wanted to invite for talks or conferences, and to encourage and support, to patronize (in the proper and noble sense of that term). Perhaps it was simply his humanity, perhaps that in his own life he too had known personal sorrow and some difficulty, including the early loss of his father (another experience we shared). He was also strikingly clear-eyed about people who got themselves into their own trouble, although he was never in my experience judgmental. Whether he was compassionate with himself, however, is another matter. While often lively and engaging, Michael also seemed heavy-hearted at times about not accomplishing what, in his mind, he should have accomplished, despite all that he achieved on so many fronts.

Community was likewise a matter, so it seemed to me, with which he struggled at times—an affliction of many scholars. Seminary or departmental communities could seem too all-consuming, all too narrow at times, and almost claustrophobic for someone of broad vision and varied interests. A scholarly rabbi resident in a small midwestern town and a Catholic university could find his options severely limited. Hence the importance of travel, and even more particularly, I sensed, of friends abroad—indeed, the importance of friends *tout court*. These friendships took in a wide range of people: the rabbis who delivered his eulogy in Los Angeles and at Notre Dame, the Catholic priests in Europe who were his most intense dialogue partners, the scholars who shared his passion for twelfth-century exegesis, the students whose intellectual growth he nurtured, and many others, most importantly his wife-companion and closest friend, Betty.

For myself, among many things, I look back especially on lunches we shared on a regular basis at a local Mexican restaurant, a little hint and taste for a moment of southern California. There we could talk about everything—life and work, the world and the university, the state of our writing projects and quality of our classes, ourselves and our families, the past and the present, even teasingly about our common weakness for heart-stoppingly rich cheeses. (Michael once proposed that we form a "cheese-aholics anonymous" group.) He had almost perfect pitch for any interlocutor and could converse in their own language. Also, like an accomplished story-teller, he, as a student of sacred story and sacred storytelling, could speak compellingly in his own, spinning out his own story.

That story ended far too early and abruptly. His friendship, his words, his twinkling humor, his incisive commentary, his quiet insights—all are sorely missed. He lived and worked as a scholarly rabbi. This volume testifies eloquently to that, offering an echo of his words and insight and vision.

John Van Engen

Acknowledgments

A project of this magnitude does not come to fruition without the cooperation of many people and friends. I wish to begin by thanking Barbara Hanrahan of the University of Notre Dame Press for her support and enthusiasm for this project which honors the work and accomplishments of Michael A. Signer, and Rebecca DeBoer and Carole Roos at the Press for their excellent editorial work. I am much obliged to my Fordham colleague Nina Rowe for locating the historiated initial of *Synagoga* and *Ecclesia* in MS Dijon, Bibliothèque municipale 198 f. 3v, which appears as the cover image for the book, and to the staff at the Bibliothèque municipale in Dijon for granting permission to reprint this image. I also thank my graduate assistants at Fordham University, Nathaniel Wood and Erica Olson, who helped in many ways. A very special word of gratitude to both David Ellenson and Hebrew Union College–Jewish Institute of Religion and John Cavadini and the Theology Department at the University of Notre Dame for their generous support of this Festschrift. Betty Signer truly deserves special recognition for her support and encouragement throughout this process and during all of the years that I have known her. I am indebted to my wife, Angela, not only for her practical assistance in various ways, but more importantly for her constant encouragement and love, without which this project would not have reached completion. Finally, I remain forever grateful to my excellent teacher and wonderful friend, Michael Signer, whose life, accomplishments, and friendship inspired the work collected in this volume and touched deeply the lives of each of the contributors. My hope is that this collection of essays will continue Michael's transformative work in Jewish-Christian relations. May Michael's name be for a blessing.

Bronx, New York
October 2009

Contributors

ARNOLD J. BAND is Professor Emeritus of Hebrew and Comparative Literature at the University of California, Los Angeles.

JEREMY COHEN is the Spiegel Family Foundation Professor of European Jewish History at Tel Aviv University in Israel.

BOYD TAYLOR COOLMAN is Assistant Professor of Theology at Boston College in Chestnut Hill, Massachusetts.

DALE M. COULTER is Associate Professor of Historical Theology at Regent University School of Divinity in Virginia Beach, Virginia.

DAVID ELLENSON is President of Hebrew Union College–Jewish Institute of Religion and is the I. H. and Anna Grancell Professor of Jewish Religious Thought at HUC-JIR in Los Angeles.

DEBORAH L. GOODWIN is Associate Professor of Religion at Gustavus Adolphus College in Saint Peter, Minnesota.

ANGELA KIM HARKINS is Assistant Professor of Religious Studies at Fairfield University in Fairfield, Connecticut.

FRANKLIN T. HARKINS is Assistant Professor of Theology at Fordham University in New York City.

HANSPETER HEINZ is Professor Emeritus of Pastoral Theology at the University of Augsburg in Germany and President of the Discussion Group "Jews and Christians" of the Central Committee of German Catholics (*Zentralkomitee der deutschen Katholiken*).

SARA JAPHET is the Yehezkel Kaufmann Professor of Bible, Emerita, at the Hebrew University of Jerusalem, and President of the World Union of Jewish Studies.

E. ANN MATTER is the William R. Kenan, Jr., Professor of Religious Studies and Associate Dean for Arts and Letters at the University of Pennsylvania in Philadelphia.

DAVID NOVAK holds the J. Richard and Dorothy Shiff Chair of Jewish Studies as Professor of the Study of Religion and Professor of Philosophy at the University of Toronto.

PETER OCHS is the Edgar M. Bronfman Professor of Modern Judaic Studies in the Department of Religious Studies at the University of Virginia in Charlottesville.

CYRIL O'REGAN is the Huisking Professor of Theology at the University of Notre Dame in Notre Dame, Indiana.

PETER VON DER OSTEN-SACKEN is Professor Emeritus of New Testament and Christian-Jewish Studies at Humboldt University of Berlin, and former Director of the Institute for Church and Judaism at Humboldt University.

JOHN T. PAWLIKOWSKI, O.S.M. is Professor of Ethics and Director of the Catholic-Jewish Studies Program at Catholic Theological Union in Chicago. He is also President Emeritus of the International Council of Christians and Jews.

DAVID FOX SANDMEL is the Crown Ryan Associate Professor of Jewish Studies at Catholic Theological Union in Chicago.

LESLEY SMITH is Fellow in Politics and Senior Tutor at Harris Manchester College in the University of Oxford.

ARJO VANDERJAGT is Professor Emeritus of the History of Ideas, Faculty of Philosophy, at the University of Groningen in the Netherlands.

ISRAEL JACOB YUVAL is the Academic Head of Scholion—Interdisciplinary Research Center in Jewish Studies, and a Professor in the Department of History of the Jewish People in the Mandel Institute of Jewish Studies at the Hebrew University of Jerusalem.

GROVER A. ZINN is the William H. Danforth Professor of Religion, Emeritus, and former Associate Dean of the College of Arts and Sciences at Oberlin College in Oberlin, Ohio.

Introduction

The Transformative Work of Michael A. Signer

Franklin T. Harkins

The essays collected in this volume are dedicated to Michael A. Signer by a select group of his colleagues, students, and friends. Their collective purpose is to honor him, on the occasion of his thirty-fifth anniversary of teaching, as a scholar and teacher of Judaism, Christianity, and Jewish-Christian relations in antiquity, the Middle Ages, and modernity. As Professor of Jewish History at Hebrew Union College–Jewish Institute of Religion (1974–1992) and Abrams Professor of Jewish Thought and Culture at the University of Notre Dame (1992–present), Michael Signer, through his excellent teaching and wide-ranging scholarship, has contributed profoundly to the diverse fields of rabbinic Judaism, Jewish history, medieval studies, the history of scriptural exegesis, and Jewish-Christian relations. This book consists of entirely new work in one or more of these areas written specifically to honor Signer and his many contributions.

Michael Signer's education at Hebrew Union College in Cincinnati and at the University of Toronto's Centre for Medieval Studies, along with his training and experience as an ordained Reform rabbi have equipped him with a combination of scholarly expertise and pastoral gifts rarely found in the academy. Furthermore, from the time he wrote his dissertation (a critical edition of Andrew of St. Victor's commentary on Ezekiel) at Toronto under the direction of the late Father Leonard Boyle, O.P., Signer has acquired and honed his skills as a scholar and religious leader in conversation and interaction with Christian scholars, pastors, and lay persons. Thus, Signer's firm conviction that Judaism and Christianity are, in fact, and must always be recognized as "two living traditions," a principle that pervades his scholarly and pedagogical work, grows out of his own personal experiences with the Christian other.[1] For over three decades, Michael Signer has conducted his scholarship while training both laity and clergy in Jewish and Catholic communities. As such he epitomizes the scholar-teacher who is not only well versed in his academic field, but also able to mediate between that field and the broader contemporary world.[2]

Signer's academic career is squarely situated in the midst of and has contributed significantly to the transforming relations between Jews and Christians since the Second Vatican Council. Paragraph four of *Nostra Aetate*, the conciliar *Declaration on the Relation of the Church to Non-Christian Religions*, effectively reversed the "teaching of contempt" for Jews and Judaism that had characterized Catholic teaching, proclamation, and practice for nearly two millennia. The council fathers acknowledged the strong "spiritual ties" that bind Christians to the Jewish people, rejected the deicide charge and supersessionism (along with their putative New Testament foundations), deplored all anti-Semitism, and encouraged the Christian faithful to recognize their Jewish neighbors as fellow human beings created in the image of God. Furthermore, the bishops sought to further "mutual understanding and appreciation" between Jews and Christians by advocating "biblical and theological enquiry and . . . friendly discussions."[3]

Throughout his career, Signer has engaged passionately and productively in precisely such interreligious study and amiable deliberation. For example, during his tenure at Hebrew Union College, he participated for over a decade in the Los Angeles Priest-Rabbi Dialogue. This group of seminary professors, pastors, and rabbis not only reflected on such theological issues as liturgy, covenant, and the Kingdom of God, but also initiated a professor-exchange program between Hebrew Union College and St. John's Seminary in Camarillo. In 1988, Signer wrote about the personally transformative potential of such interreligious dialogue and mutual exchange, affirming, "I believe that the next twenty years of *Nostra Aetate* lie in this transformation of the individual Catholic or Jew."[4]

In the two decades since penning these words, Signer has worked tirelessly to provide his students, both Jewish and Christian, with unique opportunities to engage in face-to-face Jewish-Christian dialogue and be transformed by encountering the other. For example, approximately every other autumn since 2000, Signer, in his capacity as Director of the Notre Dame Holocaust Project, has accompanied about a dozen of his Christian students from Notre Dame to international Jewish-Christian symposia in such places central to the Shoah in Poland and Germany as Oswieçim (Auschwitz), Kraków, and Nuremberg.[5] These symposia bring Jewish and Christian students and faculty from Poland, Germany, Israel, and the United States together: (1) to see places where the Nazis devised and executed their plan to destroy Europe's Jewish population, such as the Nazi Party rally grounds in Nuremberg or the concentration camp at Auschwitz-Birkenau, for example; (2) to hear historical lectures on such topics as Nazi ideology, Jewish life and culture in Germany prior to the Shoah, and Jewish-Catholic relations in Poland before and during World War II; (3) to read and study official Catholic documents such as "We Remember: A Reflection on the Shoah" (1998) and Jewish statements such as "*Dabru Emet:* A Jewish Statement on Christians and Christianity" (2000); and (4) to dialogue about what they have seen, heard, and read.[6] Through these profound experiences, the Jew and the Christian together confront the long history of Christian anti-Judaism and triumphalism that paved the way for Nazi anti-Semitism and Jewish annihilation. They encounter one another as members of different religious communities that share certain things in common: they worship the same God, seek authority from the same book (namely, the *Tanakh* or Old Testament), accept the moral principles of Torah, and are called to work together for a more just and peaceful world. They learn the profundity of Signer's convictions that "the renewed relationship between Christians and Jews has a human face," and "friendship and experience can have unprecedented consequences."[7] In short, inspired by Signer's learned and passionate leadership, they themselves engage actively in transforming relations.

That Jews and Christians worship the same God, share authoritative Scriptures, recognize the inherent and inalienable dignity of every human being, and have an obligation to cooperate in bringing about the kingdom of God are significant affirmations that Michael Signer and several other prominent Jewish scholars, together constituting the National Jewish Scholars Project, have jointly contributed to the dialogue in "*Dabru Emet:* A Jewish Statement on Christians and Christianity" (2000).[8] Many quarters of the Jewish community in the United States and elsewhere have been reluctant, for various valid reasons, to engage in dialogue with their Christian counterparts or even recognize the sea change that has taken place in Christian teaching on Jews and Judaism since Vatican II. *Dabru Emet,* which first appeared as a full-page advertisement in the *New York Times* on 10 September 2000 and gained the signatures of more than two hundred rabbis and Jewish scholars, marks the first major response from the Jewish community to Christian gestures of repentance and efforts at reformulating a more positive theology of Judaism. As a means of introducing a Jewish audience to Christian thinking on themes growing out of *Dabru Emet* (e.g., God, Scripture, commandment, Israel, worship, redemption, image of God), Signer and his National Jewish Scholars Project colleagues also edited a collection of essays published in 2000 entitled *Christianity in Jewish Terms.*[9] This volume is significant in that it represents the first Jewish theological exploration of the renewed relationship between Jews and Christians.[10]

Signer's own essay in *Christianity in Jewish Terms,* "Searching the Scriptures: Jews, Christians, and the Book," stands as a kind of snapshot of his scholarly work in the history of Jewish and Christian biblical exegesis and the motivations that underlie it.[11] His point of departure here is what he describes as "a significant point of contact between Jews and Christians," namely, seeking the meaning of God's word for their lives in authoritative Scripture.[12] Yet, throughout the history of the Common Era, this has been more a point of divergence than convergence.[13] The Jewish and Christian communities have distinguished themselves from one another by means of mutually exclusive and antagonistic exegeses. Indeed, Signer notes that while scholars are still engaged in explaining the initial "parting of the ways" between Jews and Christians, they are in agreement that "the interpretation of Scripture was at the heart of the separation."[14] The many scholarly articles that Signer has produced astutely demonstrate that "[t]he history of scriptural interpretation provides a significant point of entry for understanding the nature of the relationship between Judaism and Christianity during the past two millennia."[15]

Signer has broadened our understanding of the interreligious encounter considerably by highlighting the mutually disapproving, divisive, and destructive nature of much historical Christian and Jewish exegeses, on the one hand, and by unearthing resources within the interpretive tradition of both communities that might be used to promote a more positive relationship in the present and future. First, Signer never shies away from the polemical side of the historical and exegetical Jewish-Christian encounter. In fact, because he believes that our blazing a new trail together necessitates knowing the path we have hitherto trod, his work takes every opportunity to invite the reader into the worlds of ancient and medieval interpretive confrontation, sometimes to the reader's surprise. For example, in his overview of rabbinic literature in the *Handbook of Patristic Exegesis,* Signer explains that the development of midrash during the Amoraic period in Eretz Israel may partially be the result of Jewish efforts to confront their Christian counterparts.[16] *Genesis Rabbah* on the Akedah or sacrifice of Isaac (Gen. 22:1–18; *Gen. Rab.* 56.1–2) is the example of rabbinic response to Christianity that Signer offers. This midrash explains that once Abraham and Isaac see the "place" (Gen. 22:4; *maqom,* also a euphemism for God) where the former is to sacrifice the latter, Abraham commands the two young men accompanying them to "remain here with the ass" (Gen. 22:5) precisely because they do not see the place. Noting that other Jewish sources describe the Gentiles as "a nation resembling an ass," Signer explains this midrash as affirming that Christians are like the ass, incapable of perceiving God. Furthermore, he situates this polemical reading within the vigorous Jewish-Christian debates of the third and fourth centuries concerning the verifiability of divine revelation and the possibility of God's having revealed Himself to non-Jews at all.[17] This reading of *Genesis Rabbah* on the Akedah illustrates how Signer uses Jewish-Christian relations as a lens through which to re-examine long-standing views in new, thought-provoking, and fruitful ways.

Signer's scholarship has also contributed much to our understanding of the myriad ways that Christian thinkers and exegetes in late antiquity and the Middle Ages interpreted scriptural revelation over against Jews and Judaism. In his article, "The *Glossa ordinaria* and the Transmission of Medieval Anti-Judaism," for example, Signer demonstrates how the standard scriptural gloss used by twelfth- and thirteenth-century schoolmen conveys and even intensifies certain themes found in the ancient *Adversus Iudaeos* tradition.[18] For instance, he skillfully shows how the author of the

Glossa on the Pentateuch introduces into the Abraham narrative the malicious Johannine depiction of the Jews as children of the devil filled with vice. By means of interlinear glosses, the author interprets the Lord's call to Abram to leave his country and his father's house and journey to the land that the Lord will show him (Gen. 12:1) as *really* signifying the call from God the Father to the incarnate Christ to depart from the sins of the Jewish people from which he is descended as a human and from the home of the devil, and to enter into the land of the Gentiles of which the Lord would give him knowledge through the apostles.[19] Additionally, Signer illustrates how the glossator on the Pentateuch, again by interlinear glosses, brings terms that had for centuries been integral to the patristic anti-Jewish arsenal of accusations such as *perditio, caecitas, duritia,* and *perfidia* into the very text of the Hebrew Bible.[20] Comparison with other twelfth-century commentaries such as Hugh of St. Victor's *Adnotationes* on the Pentateuch, Andrew of St. Victor's exegetical notes, Richard of St. Victor's *Liber exceptionum,* and Peter Comestor's *Historia scholastica* highlights the ardently anti-Jewish character of the *Glossa ordinaria.* Signer's careful and contextual reading of the *Gloss* on the Pentateuch exemplifies the critical contributions he has made to our understanding of Christian anti-Jewish exegesis and polemic in the Middle Ages.

At the same time, Signer has shown that the history of Jewish and Christian interaction around the scriptural text is by no means entirely antagonistic.[21] In fact, much of his work seeks points of contact between the ancient and medieval Jewish-Christian exegetical encounter, on the one hand, and actual or desired efforts at cooperative study and dialogue since Vatican II, on the other. Indeed, according to Signer, "the most productive dialogue between Jews and Christians is grounded on face-to-face studies of texts in the Hebrew Bible through the lenses of pre-modern interpretations in both traditions."[22] Signer has devoted much of his career to studying what he identifies as an important historical model for modern Jewish-Christian interaction around the biblical text, namely, the exegetical encounters in northern France in the twelfth century between the school of Rabbi Solomon ben Isaac of Troyes (more commonly known as Rashi, 1040–1105) and Christian scholars associated with the Parisian Abbey of St. Victor.[23] Advancing the work of Sarah Kamin, Frank Talmage, and other scholars who have demonstrated mutual influence between the school of

Rashi and the school of St. Victor, Signer has established a common emphasis on *peshato shel Miqra* or *sensus litteralis,* the plain sense or simple meaning of the scriptural text.[24] At the heart of this emphasis on the "letter" lies the search for what Signer has dubbed a "sequential narrative," which he understands as a novel contribution to the exegetical tradition of both the Jewish and Christian communities.[25] He explains:

> The innovation of Rashi and the Victorines, I would argue, is the use of the narrative framework of Scripture as the basis of their commentaries in order to avoid the fragmentation or diffusion of the biblical text that they found in the literary forms of biblical commentary in their respective traditions. Their commentaries reveal a unity of theme or content where the biblical verse may seem disjointed. In order to realize this narrative unity, their commentaries develop exegetical techniques whereby biblical lemmata become embedded in the commentary. This process of embedding the biblical verse into the commentary itself provides the opportunity to "fill in the gaps" for the reader. In this manner Rashi would differ from the earlier midrashim, where the paradigmatic reading dominated. The Victorines differed from patristic commentary where the sequence of the verse was subordinated to a meditation on a single word or phrase.[26]

Signer's scholarship reveals that while neither Rashi nor the Victorines denigrated or dispensed with traditional midrashic, figural, or allegorical interpretation, both believed these meanings must be built on or into the fundamental narrative of divine redemption that is emplotted in the biblical text.[27] Having this redemptive narrative or *historia* as the *fundamentum* of all scriptural reading enabled both the Jewish and Christian communities to locate themselves within God's continuing covenant. Thus, Signer has deftly shown that an emphasis on sequential narrative and plain meaning served the needs of each religious community as it accommodated to life in the rapidly changing world of northern France during the twelfth-century renaissance.[28]

Signer has also well noted and thoroughly examined the ways in which Jewish and Christian efforts to understand the letter of Scripture enabled each religious community to understand the other more profoundly. For example, in his essay, "Polemic and Exegesis: The Varieties of Twelfth-Century Hebraism," he shows how Christian scholars throughout the twelfth century, from Stephen Harding to Hugh and Andrew of St. Victor to Herbert of Bosham, gained insights into the Hebrew text of Scripture and its literal sense through scholarly interactions with their living Jewish counterparts.[29] Indeed, contact with actual Jews is what appears to constitute the core of twelfth-century Christian Hebraism, Signer maintains. His emphasis on the centrality of Christian interaction with actual Jews around the scriptural text provides a necessary complement to Jeremy Cohen's work on the so-called "hermeneutical Jew" within medieval Christianity. In his *Living Letters of the Law: Ideas of the Jew in Medieval Christianity*,[30] Cohen analyzes how Christian exegetes from Augustine to Thomas Aquinas constructed an imaginary "hermeneutical Jew" from the scriptural text for their specific, most often anti-Jewish, theological purposes. Signer's work lucidly illustrates how, by contrast, interaction with actual Jews enabled Christian scholars in the twelfth century to gain greater insight into the text of Hebrew Scripture, the Jewish tradition as living and diverse, and their own religious community and its history.

The essays in this volume seek to honor Michael Signer and the many ways his scholarship and teaching has contributed to the ongoing history of transforming relations between Jews and Christians. The volume is divided into two parts, which correspond to the two major historical periods in which Signer has studied the interreligious relationship. In Part One, "Ancient and Medieval Perspectives: Exegesis, Polemic, and Cultural Exchange," Signer's colleagues and students present studies of Jewish and Christian encounters with the scriptural text and with one another in antiquity and the Middle Ages. The essays in Part Two, "Modern Perspectives: Theology, Praxis, and Perceptions of the Other," both reveal the recent positive strides that Jews and Christians have made together and suggest roadblocks, either actual or potential, that may serve to delay contemporary interreligious progress.

Arnold Band, who taught Signer as an undergraduate student at UCLA, offers a brief introductory essay to Part One that provides a personal window onto Signer's early formation in the reading and interpretation of religious texts, both Jewish and Christian, that would become the foundation of his scholarly work. By recounting some of his own interactions with Signer as teacher and student, Band highlights the profound care for the student that would become so characteristic of Signer's own pedagogical work.

Following Band's introductory piece, essays by David Novak and Israel Jacob Yuval analyze Jewish-Christian relations in the ancient period and underscore points of convergence between modes of thought and discourse in the two communities that are significant yet have been generally overlooked. In his essay, David Novak considers the divine law as a point of fundamental division between Jews and Christians from the ancient beginnings of their mutual encounter. He argues, however, that the law was and remains a point of contact between the two religious traditions. Indeed, the Rabbis and Paul, the most original theological authorities in Judaism and Christianity, respectively, shared an understanding of the pre-covenantal aspect of the law that might be called the "minimal law of God." Furthermore, Novak demonstrates that even regarding the divine law that follows from the Sinai covenant, which has deeply divided Jews and Christians for two millennia, reconsidering the Rabbis and Paul can enable the two communities to come to a better understanding of themselves and the other.

In a similar vein, Israel Jacob Yuval examines the possibility of the influence of early Christian texts on the self-understanding of Judaism and the polemical presentation of Christianity found in the Talmud and Midrashim. Yuval sets his own approach here against what he understands as a principled outlook in modern Jewish research, epitomized by the work of Saul Lieberman and Ephraim Elimelech Urbach, that "systematically ignores the possibility of points of contact between Christianity and Judaism." In an effort to overcome this traditional posture of "parallelophobia," the scholarly fear of seriously considering the possibility of mutual influence between the two communities, Yuval advocates "parallelomania," that is, searching for parallel and dialogic developments in the ancient literature. Using James Scott's idea of "hidden transcripts" in conjunction with the anthropological theory of Fredrik Barth, Yuval argues that, although rabbinic Judaism created a highly developed world of halakhic texts and their meaning that was closed off from its surroundings, one can find within this world and its literature hidden polemics against Christianity that reveal dialogue and mutual influence.

The next seven essays in Part One treat various aspects of Christian and Jewish scriptural exegesis in twelfth-century northern France, a field of study that has benefited much from the scholarly endeavors of Michael Signer. Grover A. Zinn introduces these essays with a consideration of the various ways the Psalms were used in the life, theological education, and spiritual formation of the canons at the Parisian Abbey of St. Victor. Beyond various liturgical uses, the Victorine canons encountered the Psalms in and through hearing such patristic works as Augustine's *Expositions on the Psalms* read regularly in the refectory, training their memories in the *schola* or classroom, receiving instruction in moral formation as novices, learning the proper way to pray, discovering and setting out on the road of love that leads to God, and progressing from ascetic discipline to contemplative experience of the divine presence. Such multivalent, intersecting, and mutually enriching uses of the Psalter illustrate how the scriptural text served as the foundation for the holistic vision of education and spiritual formation at St. Victor.

From this broad view of Victorine engagement with Sacred Scripture, we move to the hermeneutical specifics. Dale Coulter investigates the literal approach that characterized the interpretive enterprise of the Victorines and their Jewish counterparts by reconstructing the "theoretical framework" for Hugh of St. Victor's method. The foundation of this framework is *historia*, which Hugh takes to be the meaning attached to a series or narration of events (what Coulter designates "history I") and the primary meaning or referent of a word (what Coulter designates "history II"). Through a careful consideration of a variety of passages from Hugh's corpus related to exegetical theory and practice, Coulter highlights the multivalence, even ambiguity, of the Victorine master's understanding of *historia* and literal reading. It is precisely this indeterminate aspect of Hugh's theory, Coulter concludes, that enabled his students to receive and appropriate his thought on historical or literal interpretation differently. That this is so is demonstrated in the following essays by Boyd Taylor Coolman and Franklin T. Harkins, which analyze the exegetical practice of Richard of St. Victor and Andrew of St. Victor, respectively. Coolman considers Richard's reading of Isaiah 7:14, "Behold a virgin will conceive . . . ," the controversial text that prompted the Victorine's *De Emmanuele,* in the context of the renewed interest among both Christian and Jewish exegetes in the scriptural letter and the larger narrative in which a particular text is situated. Coolman argues that Richard's christological interpretation of Isaiah's prophecy emerges in relation to various similar and dissimilar correspondences between the content of the prophecy and the overarching narrative of Christian salvation history. According to Richard, Jewish exegetes read Isaiah's prophecy within a narrative framework that is simply too narrow, namely, that of Isaiah 7–8; by expanding the context to the significantly larger narrative of creation, fall, and restoration, Richard aims to provide a more reasonable reading of this pivotal text. In so doing, Coolman concludes, Richard draws on Hugh's understanding of the relationship between narrative and reason.

Andrew of St. Victor was another of Hugh's students who, through face-to-face encounters with Jewish biblical scholars in his Parisian context, converted his master's theory into a distinctive practice of literal reading. By considering the respective readings of the story of Esau and Jacob (Gen. 25 and 27) found in the *Glossa ordinaria* and in Andrew of St. Victor, Franklin T. Harkins highlights the way in which the biblical text, as read in the Christian schools of twelfth-century Northern France, served as a springboard for both "polemical and partnering" trajectories in Jewish-Christian relations. More specifically, Harkins demonstrates that whereas the *Glossa* canonized the traditional Christian allegorical reading of the siblings as the Jewish people and the Church, respectively, Andrew followed his ancient and contemporary sources—including the *Glossa* itself—"with unequal step" in the production of an alternative reading that was informed by and further opened the way to positive interreligious relations.

Deborah L. Goodwin hones in on a particular aspect of the scriptural story of Esau and Jacob over which medieval exegetes—both Jewish and Christian—spilled much ink, namely, Rebekah's seemingly duplicitous actions in securing Isaac's blessings for her younger beloved son, Jacob. Goodwin takes Rebekah's action in the narrative of Genesis 25–27 as a prism through which to analyze and compare the exegetical approaches of two skilled twelfth-century readers of the sacred text, one Jewish and one Christian: Rabbi Samuel ben Meir (Rashbam) and Peter Comestor. Goodwin argues that whereas both Rashbam and Comester were practitioners of the literal or historical methodology that had recently come to characterize their respective communities, each exegete read Rebekah's actions in such a way that served his own theological and polemical goals. In Rashbam and Comester, then, Goodwin finds further evidence for a foundational presupposition of Michael Signer's own scholarly work, namely, that for Jewish and Christian exegetes in twelfth-century Europe the biblical text served simultaneously as a point of contact and of contention.

Sara Japhet seeks to shed new light on the exegetical method and intellectual milieu of Rashbam by studying the introductions to two of his commentaries on biblical books, namely, the Song of Songs and Lamentations. These introductions provide a unique window onto Rashbam and the context of Jewish exegesis in which he worked precisely because the sages of the Peshat school of Northern France generally did not compose introductions to their commentaries. Furthermore, Japhet here presents and discusses Rashbam's introduction to Lamentations for the first time. Her study reveals that in the scope of his interests as well as in his literary acumen, Rashbam stood alone among Jewish biblical commentators of the twelfth century.

Moving from Jewish and Christian exegetical practice in the twelfth century to a popular medieval Christian theological construct of Jews, E. Ann Matter traces the development of the image of the Wandering Jew in the High and Late Middle Ages. Matter shows that the legend of the Wandering Jew, a trope on the story of the *Via crucis* that assumed a seemingly ubiquitous status in western Christian literature of the thirteenth through fifteenth century, has its roots in the twelfth-century emphasis, exemplified by Honorius Augustodunensis and Andrew of St. Victor, on the conversion of the Jews as one of the signs of the End Times. The earliest extant versions of the legend depict the Wandering Jew as having been cursed by Christ to roam the earth until the latter's second advent as a punishment for having insulted the Savior on the way to his sacrificial death. In different interpretations of the story, however, the Wanderer appears in different times and places, in various guises, and for a whole range of purposes, both good and evil. According to a fifteenth-century Italian account, for example, in the winter of 1411 the Wanderer mysteriously appeared in Florence wearing a Franciscan habit, where he rescued travelers from a sudden snowstorm. Matter demonstrates that the various portraits of the Wandering Jew together reveal the fundamentally ambivalent attitude of medieval Christians—indeed, medieval Christendom—toward the Jewish people: on the one hand, they are fugitives on account of their scornful treatment of Jesus; on the other hand, they testify to the truth of Christianity until the end of the world.

In an effort to honor Michael Signer and his fruitful work with others, Lesley Smith offers a study of the collaborative work of the thirteenth-century Dominican master and administrator Hugh of St. Cher. Smith here reconsiders the question, much contested among modern scholars, of the authorship of Hugh's most well-known work, the *Postilla in totam bibliam*. The commonly accepted scholarly view is that the *Postilla*, a multi-volume commentary on the entire Bible, is simply too massive a work for Hugh to have written by himself. As such, Hugh is seen not as a brilliant individual thinker, but rather a mere collaborator, the director of a group of Dominican brothers at St. Jacques who together produced the *Postilla*. Against this reading, Smith argues that collaboration was the common mode of work among Mendicant scholars in the thirteenth century and that modern historians have erred in preferring not to think of the great scholars of this period (including Albert the Great and Thomas Aquinas) as anything other than solitary geniuses. She helpfully reminds us of the need to study medieval scholars and their work not only within their larger religious context but also according to their own standards.

Within two centuries of the collaborative exegetical work of Hugh of St. Cher, scholastic modes of thought and discourse had begun to wane in many European religious circles and were being replaced by what has been dubbed a "theology of piety," whose principal purpose was devotional rather than speculative. It is within this context that Arjo Vanderjagt situates and studies the northern humanist of Groningen, Wessel Gansfort (1419–1489), and his use of Hebrew. After providing a brief biographical sketch of Gansfort, Vanderjagt analyzes how he makes use of Hebrew in three of his major works, namely, *De oratione Dominica, De causis incarnationis: de magnitudine et amaritudine Dominicae passionis,* and *De sacramento Eucharistiae.* Vanderjagt argues that, as the titles of these works intimate, Gansfort cited texts from and explored terms in the Hebrew Bible in order to deepen his own and his Christian readers' knowledge of and

devotion to Jesus, not as a means of dialoguing with his Jewish counterparts. In fact, Gansfort often used Hebrew texts simultaneously to bolster
Christian doctrines such as the Trinity and to variously polemicize against
the Jews.

In the final essay in Part One, Jeremy Cohen provides a unique window onto the changing nature of the Jewish-Christian encounter in early
sixteenth-century Europe by considering a story from Solomon ibn Verga's
work, *Shevet Yehudah* (The Staff of Judah), about the rescue of Jews from a
slanderous libel owing to the sleeplessness of their king. *Shevet Yehudah,*
containing some six dozen stories of Jewish tribulation and survival from
the destruction of the Second Temple in the first century CE to the persecution of Spanish-Portuguese Jewry in ibn Verga's own day, was one of the
most popular Hebrew books of the sixteenth century. By means of a thorough investigation of one of the book's stories in which Jewish exoneration
from the charge of ritual murder hangs on the correct interpretation of
the Psalmist's words, "See, the guardian of Israel neither dozes nor sleeps"
(Ps. 121:4), Cohen shows how *Shevet Yehudah* serves as a bridge between
Jewish self-understanding in the Middle Ages and in the early modern
period. More specifically, Cohen argues that the tale under consideration
expresses ibn Verga's and his religious community's determination to leave
the Jewish-Christian encounter of the Middle Ages behind and move into
a qualitatively new era.

Part Two of the present volume consists of essays that treat various
aspects of the qualitatively different relationship that has come to prevail
between Jews and Christians in the modern period, particularly since the
middle of the twentieth century. In his brief introductory essay, Peter von
der Osten-Sacken reads the dictum of a late nineteenth-century rabbi in
the German army, "What we need is to get to know, to understand, and
to respect each other," as a helpful guideline for the contemporary Jewish-
Christian relationship. Careful to nuance the military chaplain's words in
light of both the past and recent history of the two communities, von der
Osten-Sacken rightly recognizes the limits of and potential pitfalls involved
in mutual understanding. Here he draws, for example, on Martin Buber's
notion that in dialogue Jews and Christians are centered around a mystery
whose status as mystery remains ultimately unaltered by the interreligious

encounter and that each partner should therefore strive to recognize the other in the mystery as he or she is.

Angela Kim Harkins illustrates the potential dangers of failing to understand the other religious community on its own terms in her essay on the Second Vatican Council's use of the phrase "the people of God." While recognizing the importance of *populus Dei* as a post-conciliar ecclesial model, Harkins maintains that the expression as it is used in the Council's Dogmatic Constitution on the Church (*Lumen Gentium*) is problematic from the perspective of contemporary Jewish-Christian relations. The problem, as she sees it, is twofold, namely: (1) "the people of God" is not a phrase that ancient Israel used to describe itself; rather it is a Christian theological construct that the bishops impose upon biblical Judaism; and (2) *Lumen Gentium* describes ancient Israel with scriptural references that highlight exclusivity and thereby set up Israel as a contrasting type to the Church, the new and more inclusive "people of God." Furthermore, Harkins argues, the expression "the people of God" is complicated by the difficult social and political context in which the phrase first appeared in modern biblical scholarship. In light of the terrible history of the "hermeneutical Jew" and the *Adversus Iudaeos* tradition generally, Harkins concludes: "It is important that bishops and Christian theologians draw upon a sound historical understanding of actual Jews and Jewish self-understandings when they construct their theologies of Jews and Judaism or of the Church in relation to the Jewish people."

David Ellenson considers one modern instantiation of Jewish teaching on Christianity and its adherents by analyzing the pertinent responsa of Rabbi Hayim David Halevi (1924–1998), Chief Sephardic Rabbi of Tel Aviv–Jaffa and one of the most famous rabbinic authorities in Israel during the twentieth century. Ellenson focuses on a particular responsum, "Concerning the Relationships between Jews and Non-Jews," which appears in Rabbi Halevi's nine-volume collection of responsa entitled *'Aseh l'kha rav*. In order to highlight the mature thought of Rabbi Halevi on Christians and Christianity, Ellenson reads this responsum against the backdrop of some of his other responsa as well as those of one of his major rivals, Rabbi Ovadiah Yosef, former Chief Sephardic Rabbi of Israel and founder and head of the Israeli Shas party. Ellenson shows how Rabbi Halevi's approach to traditional Jewish legal material on Christians is, in the words of Avi Ravitsky, one of "conservative audacity." Acknowledging, for example, that the Talmud and rabbinic tradition speak strongly against "idolatry" and associate it with Christian Trinitarianism, Rabbi Halevi maintained that these statements do not refer to Christians in the modern context. Additionally, Rabbi Halevi further opened the way to respectful relations with the Christian "other" by affirming that ethical human obligations constitute a meta-principle informing the entire Jewish legal tradition.

The next two essays, by Peter Ochs and John T. Pawlikowski, engage the scholarly work of Michael Signer directly. According to Peter Ochs, Signer's scholarship on plain-sense exegesis in medieval Judaism and Christianity reveals a general theological philosophy of the plain sense, a philosophy that introduces a model for text-historical studies and for reparative work in the area of contemporary Jewish-Christian relations. By providing an overview of Signer's work and through closer readings of several of his essays, Ochs seeks to provide evidence of this philosophy and to outline its defining features. The basic elements of Signer's philosophy as identified by Ochs are (1) presupposition of the plain sense; (2) presupposition of the limits of plain sense and the need for interpreted senses; (3) recognition of the need to "return" to the plain sense without losing the interpreted sense; (4) observation of parallels between the reparative strategies of both medieval Jewish and Christian plain-sense commentaries; and (5) acknowledgment of the reparative potential of plain-sense reading for both intracommunal divisions and Jewish-Christian relations. Ochs concludes his piece by highlighting the ways in which Signer's theological philosophy is a "reparative hermeneutic," that is, a practice of reading both signs on a page and signs in the world toward the ultimate end of repairing relations within and between religious communities.

The precise nature of the theological relationship or bond between Jews and Christians is the focus of John T. Pawlikowski's dialogue with Michael Signer. After providing a brief overview of Signer's understanding of the theological nexus between Jews and Christians as it is found in a number of essays on various aspects of the interreligious relationship, Pawlikowski—in the spirit of mutual respect that is so central to the ongoing dialogue—raises several important questions that may be addressed to

Signer and notes several areas where his perspective may require further elaboration. First, Pawlikowski inquires whether Signer's emphasis on studying how Jews and Christians have traditionally interpreted their common biblical texts (Hebrew Scriptures–Old Testament) as a means of recognizing a certain bondedness through difference reveals an overly optimistic approach to classical modes of interpretation. Second, Pawlikowski maintains that Signer's understanding of the Jewish-Christian relationship must give greater consideration to the New Testament and to the portrayals of Jesus provided there, which would enable a deeper appreciation of the theological rift that separates the two faith communities. But do the Church's christological proclamations make viewing Jesus as a limited bond between Jews and Christians virtually impossible? In Pawlikowski's view, the new scholarly understanding of the gradual nature of the Jewish-Christian separation in the first centuries of the Common Era as well as the reaffirmation of Christianity's profound Jewish roots raise a number of pressing questions for Signer's understanding of the relationship. Finally, Pawlikowski asks whether the experience of the Holocaust has undermined covenantal certitude on both sides of the interreligious divide and invites Signer to grapple in a more comprehensive way with the implications of the Shoah for contemporary Jewish-Christian bonding.

The last two essays in the volume, by David Fox Sandmel and Hanspeter Heinz, consider from very different angles how the contemporary churches—both Protestant and Catholic—understand the bond or relationship between themselves and the Jewish people. David Fox Sandmel investigates the ways in which the relatively recent dramatic changes in Christian perceptions of Jews and Judaism are reflected in what he calls the "Christian reclamation of Judaism." Here he presents some examples of this complex phenomenon, suggests factors contributing to it, and reflects on its implications for Jewish-Christian relations now and in the future. Sandmel notes at the outset that whereas the primary participants in the dialogue historically have been Jews, Roman Catholics, and mainline Protestants, the general trend toward the incorporation of Jewish traditions and practices into Christian worship and spirituality is most pronounced in the evangelical community. Among the elements of Judaism that increasing numbers of evangelical churches are incorporating and appropriating are (1) Hebrew terms and songs; (2) Jewish ritual items such as menorahs, shofars, and mezuzot; (3) the bar or bat mitzvah; and (4) the Passover seder. Some of the factors influencing these modes of reclamation include the increasing appreciation by Christians of the Jewishness of Jesus, a claim to kinship with the Jewish people, the impact of the Holocaust on Christian self-understanding, the existence of the State of Israel, the emergence of Christian Zionism, and the influence of Jews for Jesus and similar "messianic Jewish" organizations. Sandmel suggests that, while some Jews might welcome this Christian reclamation of Judaism as indicative of a positive attitudinal shift among Christians, for most it represents a step backward toward traditional Christian supersessionism and, as such, poses serious challenges to the future of Jewish-Christian relations.

Hanspeter Heinz brings this volume in honor of Michael Signer to a fitting close by recounting the ways in which his friendship and inter-religious work with Signer has profoundly transformed his own understanding of Judaism and Christianity's bond with it. Heinz describes the strides that have been made in the Jewish-Catholic dialogue since *Nostra Aetate*, often in spite of considerable obstacles that have threatened to slow progress. The particular focus of his essay is what Heinz dubs "the latest setback," Pope Benedict XVI's *motu proprio* rescript entitled *Summorum Pontificum* pertaining to the Tridentine rite and its wider re-admission. Heinz describes the work of the discussion group "Jews and Christians" of the Central Committee of German Catholics (*Zentralkomitee der deutschen Katholiken*), of which he is the president and Signer a member, in anticipation of and in reaction to the *motu proprio*. From the time of its announcement just before Easter in 2007, the discussion group voiced its objection to the promulgation of a *motu proprio* that would more generally allow the celebration of the pre-conciliar Mass of the 1962 *Missale Romanum*. In short, the group "Jews and Christians" claimed that the re-introduction of the Good Friday Intercession "for the conversion of the Jews" and of other elements of the Tridentine rite favors contempt for the Jews and disregard for the Old Testament, and contradicts the ecclesiology of the Second Vatican Council. What Heinz finds most troubling about the *motu proprio* that Pope Benedict issued on 7 July 2007 is that it suggests little or no concern for the relationship between the Catholic Church and the Jewish people and how this fragile relationship might be damaged by the rescript itself. Heinz concludes his contribution by affirming his own and the discussion group's firm commitment, in the face of this recent obstacle from Rome, to continue to work toward a better relationship between Jews and Christians. All of us, as contributors to this volume, hope that these essays will complement and continue the passionate and transformative work of Michael Signer, our esteemed colleague, teacher, and friend.

Notes

1. See, e.g., Michael A. Signer, "The Role of the Local Bishop in Catholic-Jewish Relations," in *Unfailing Patience and Sound Teaching: Reflections on Episcopal Ministry in Honor of Rembert G. Weakland, O.S.B.,* ed. David A. Stosur (Collegeville, MN: Liturgical Press, 2003), 133–49; and *"Speculum Concilii:* Through the Mirror Brightly," in *Unanswered Questions: Theological Views of Jewish-Catholic Relations,* ed. Roger Brooks (Notre Dame, IN: University of Notre Dame Press, 1988), 105–27, especially 116 where Michael takes the phrase from the title of Samuel Sandmel, *Two Living Traditions: Essays on Religion and the Bible* (Detroit: Wayne State University Press, 1972).

2. Samuel Sandmel contrasts the "scholar-teacher" with the "scholar-antiquarian" in his essay, "Antiquarianism and Contemporaneity: The Relevance of Studies in Religion," in *Two Living Traditions,* 20–27. Whereas the "scholar-antiquarian" is focused narrowly on his academic field and the analytic skills that it requires, the "scholar-teacher" possesses an openness to the world along with the synthetic skills to connect scholarly analysis and practical experience. Michael Signer has described his own interest in this nexus between theory and practice, scholarship and lay-pastoral reality, as having been motivated in part by Sandmel's essay. See Michael A. Signer, *"Communitas et Universitas:* From Theory to Practice in Judaeo-Christian Studies," in *When Jews and Christians Meet,* ed. Jakob J. Petuchowski (Albany: State University of New York Press, 1988), 59–83, especially 60–61.

3. *Vatican Council II: The Basic Sixteen Documents—Constitutions, Decrees, Declarations,* ed. Austin Flannery, O.P. (Northport, NY: Costello, 1996), 569–74, quotation from 573.

4. Signer, *"Speculum Concilii,"* 114.

5. As Michael's graduate student and teaching assistant at the University of Notre Dame, I had the distinct privilege of attending three of these symposia, namely: "Theology at the Edge of Auschwitz," Oświęcim, Poland, 29 September–5 October 2002; "Building Toward the Future: Jewish-Christian Dialogue in Intercultural Context," Kraków, Poland, 14–20 September 2003; and "Memory and

Reconciliation: Jewish-Christian Relations in Cultural Context," Nuremberg, Germany, 11–17 September 2005.

6. The 1998 Vatican document "We Remember" can be found together with numerous national Catholic episcopal conference statements occasioned by the fiftieth anniversary of the liberation of Auschwitz in the volume issued by the Secretariat for Ecumenical and Interreligious Affairs of the U.S. Catholic Conference of Catholic Bishops entitled *Catholics Remember the Holocaust* (Washington, DC: United States Catholic Conference, 1998), 47–56. *Dabru Emet* can be found in *Christianity in Jewish Terms*, ed. Tikva Frymer-Kensky, David Novak, Peter Ochs, David Fox Sandmel, and Michael A. Signer (Boulder, CO: Westview Press, 2000), xv–xviii.

7. Signer, "The Role of the Local Bishop," 134.

8. The five scholars at the heart of the National Jewish Scholars Project are Tikva Frymer-Kensky, David Novak, Peter Ochs, David Sandmel, and Michael Signer.

9. For full citation, see n. 6 above.

10. For Signer's own discussion of this volume in the context of the dialogue, see his "Trinity, Unity, Idolatry? Medieval and Modern Perspectives on *Shittuf*," in *Lesarten des jüdisch-christlichen Dialoges: Festschrift zum 70. Geburtstag von Clemens Thoma*, ed. Silvia Käppeli (Bern: Peter Lang, 2002), 275–84.

11. See Frymer-Kensky et al., *Christianity in Jewish Terms*, 85–98.

12. Signer, "Searching the Scriptures," in *Christianity in Jewish Terms*, 85–86.

13. For Michael, the canonical shape of Hebrew Scripture itself within Judaism and Christianity reveals a "dialectic of community–non-community" that has come to characterize the relationship between the Church and Synagogue. See, e.g., Michael A. Signer, "The Aims and Objectives of Judaeo-Christian Studies— A Jewish Response," in *Defining a Discipline: The Aims and Objectives of Judaeo-Christian Studies—Papers Presented at the First Bronstein Colloquium, November 7–8, 1983*, ed. Jakob J. Petuchowski (Cincinnati, OH: Hebrew Union College–Jewish Institute of Religion, 1984), 73–82, quotation from 76. Elsewhere, Michael elucidates the divisive potential and reality of biblical exegesis, maintaining: "Scripture . . . might have been [the area] most conjunctive for Jews and Christians during the Middle Ages, but because of the exclusivity of truth in revelation claimed by Jews and Christians [it] was the most disjunctive" (Michael A. Signer, "The Land of Israel in Medieval Jewish Exegetical and Polemical Literature," in *The Land of Israel: Jewish Perspectives*, ed. Lawrence A. Hoffman [Notre Dame, IN: University of Notre Dame Press, 1986], 210–233, quotation from 214).

14. Signer, "Searching the Scriptures," 89.

15. Ibid., 87.

16. Michael A. Signer and Susan L. Graham, "Rabbinic Literature," a special contribution in Charles Kannengiesser, *Handbook of Patristic Exegesis: The Bible in Ancient Christianity*, vol. 1 (Leiden: Brill, 2004), 120–44.

17. Ibid., 130–31.

18. Michael A. Signer, "The *Glossa ordinaria* and the Transmission of Medieval Anti-Judaism," in *A Distinct Voice: Medieval Studies in Honor of Leonard E. Boyle, O.P.*, ed. Jacqueline Brown and William P. Stoneman (Notre Dame, IN: University of Notre Dame Press, 1997), 591–605.

19. Ibid., 593–94.

20. Ibid., 597–98.

21. In Michael's view, "To continue the agenda of revealing the continuity of anti-Judaism within Christianity without adding elements in which Christianity drew upon Judaism is to draw a false dichotomy in the relationship" ("The Aim and Objectives of Judaeo-Christian Studies," 75).

22. Michael A. Signer, "Tradition in Transition: Approaches to Jewish-Christian Relations," in *Jews and Christians in Conversation: Crossing Cultures and Generations*, ed. Edward Kessler, John Pawlikowski, Judith Herschcopf Banki, and Barbara Ellen Bowe (Cambridge: Orchard Academic, 2002), 123–40, quotation from 134. See also Michael A. Signer, "The Rift That Binds: Hermeneutical Approaches to the Jewish-Christian Relationship," in *Ecumenism: Present Realities and Future Prospects*, ed. Lawrence Cunningham (Notre Dame, IN: University of Notre Dame Press, 1990), 95–115; and Michael A. Signer, "One Covenant or Two: Can We Sing a New Song?" in *Reinterpreting Revelation and Tradition: Jews and Christians in Conversation*, ed. John T. Pawlikowski and Hayim Goren Perelmuter (Franklin, WI: Sheed and Ward, 2000), 3–23.

23. See Signer, "*Speculum Concilii*," where he specifically affirms: "The 'dialogue' at St. Victor did not reveal a post-Vatican II tolerance, but it does provide a significant historical precedent" (122).

24. See, e.g., Michael A. Signer, "*Peshat, Sensus Litteralis*, and Sequential Narrative: Jewish Exegesis and the School of St. Victor in the Twelfth Century," in *The Frank Talmage Memorial Volume*, ed. Barry Walfish (Haifa: Haifa University Press, 1993), 203–16; Michael A. Signer, "Restoring the Narrative: Jewish and Christian Exegesis in the Twelfth Century," in *With Reverence for the Word: Medieval Exegesis in Judaism, Christianity, and Islam*, ed. Jane Dammen McAuliffe, Barry D. Walfish, and Joseph W. Goering (New York: Oxford University Press, 2003), 70–82; and Michael A. Signer, "Consolation and Confrontation: Jewish and Christian Interpretation of the Prophetic Books," in *Scripture and Pluralism: Reading the Bible in the Religiously Plural Worlds of the Middle Ages and Renaissance*, ed. Thomas J. Heffernan and Thomas E. Burman (Leiden: Brill, 2005), 77–93.

25. On his term "sequential narrative" in Jewish exegesis of the period, see Signer, "The Land of Israel," especially 213.

26. Signer, "Restoring the Narrative," 71–72.

27. For example, in Michael A. Signer, "Do Jews Read the 'Letter'? Reflections on the Sign (אות) in Medieval Jewish Biblical Exegesis," in *The Quest for Context and*

Meaning: Studies in Biblical Intertextuality in Honor of James A. Sanders, ed. Craig A. Evans and Shemaryahu Talmon (Leiden: Brill, 1997), 613–24, he demonstrates that medieval Jewish exegesis reveals a greater sensitivity to figural language in the biblical text than Christian exegetes have traditionally imagined.

28. See Signer, "*Peshat, Sensus Litteralis,* and Sequential Narrative"; and Signer, "Restoring the Narrative," where he concludes: "For the Jewish people in the late eleventh century, their lowly status and the growing strength of the Christian Church were the source of some anxiety about the possibilities of future redemption. Christians were experiencing confusion about the future directions of their sense of religious community and the fragmentation of theological knowledge. The resolution for each community . . . may have rested in the shift from a metaphoric to a metonymic reading of scripture. To domesticate a narrative by limiting the potential expansions of its meanings provides a center from which members may diverge, but still define themselves. The lives of Jews and Christians in northern France diverged in their rites, rituals, and theology, but not in their goal—the discovery of a narrative that fused biblical text and ancient traditions for members of their communities" (p. 79).

29. Michael A. Signer, "Polemic and Exegesis: The Varieties of Twelfth-Century Hebraism," in *Hebraica Veritas? Christian Hebraists and the Study of Judaism in Early Modern Europe,* ed. Allison P. Coudert and Jeffrey S. Shoulson (Philadelphia: University of Pennsylvania Press, 2004), 21–32.

30. Jeremy Cohen, *Living Letters of the Law: Ideas of the Jew in Medieval Christianity* (Berkeley: University of California Press, 1999).

I. ANCIENT AND MEDIEVAL PERSPECTIVES:
EXEGESIS, POLEMIC, AND CULTURAL EXCHANGE

CHAPTER ONE

The Making of a Medievalist

Arnold J. Band

The standard brief biography of Michael Signer's career usually attached to his articles cites his training at Hebrew Union College and the Centre for Medieval Studies at the University of Toronto. Such brief biographies, however, do not really satisfy one's curiosity regarding the intellectual formation of the author we are reading. How, for instance, does this brief citation of two academic institutions explain the interests and training of such a widely acclaimed scholar of medieval Jewish and Christian texts, of one who can work in both Hebrew and Latin exegetical commentaries on the Bible, on Rashi and Hugh of St. Victor? While one might argue that each institution provided Signer with specific training in the texts in which he specializes, one wonders how he conceived of the possibility of such fruitful comparative work in two religious traditions which have produced so few scholars who can work in both at the same time. On a more personal level, one should ask how Michael Signer, born and reared in Los Angeles, a city not steeped in historical consciousness, developed such keen interests in the medieval European past. The genesis and development of a historian is, to be sure, of prime historical concern.

Missing from the usual biographical account is the crucial period he spent as an undergraduate student at UCLA before his graduate studies in Cincinnati and Toronto. Signer, however, testifies that "my intellectual world was utterly transformed during the years 1962–66. . . ." His description of that period in his life can be found in an article he wrote for a Festschrift edited in my honor in 2002 by two of my former students, William Cutter and David C. Jacobson.[1] In tribute to me, his teacher during those under-graduate years, Signer's article is entitled, "*Dor dor vedorshav:* Of Fathers and Sons." This title is never explicitly explained in the four pages of his brief preface, though intimations are scattered throughout. The title invites exegesis. Note that its first part is a famous rabbinic dictum suggesting that every generation has its specific scholarly exegetes, while the second part is the title of the well-known novel by Turgenev, the paradigm of the examination of the cultural schism between generations. If these two statements stood apart from any following text, it would be difficult to reconcile the apparent contradiction between the two parts: change is normal in the first statement, yet disruptive in the second. But the title is the preface to a personal, autobiographical essay in which Mike Signer narrates his version of the special relationship that has developed between us over the past forty-five years, and the only coherent exegesis one should offer to the enigmatic title must be based on the content of the essay that it introduces. While the author discusses these formative years lucidly and eloquently, he does not furnish some of the basic historical contexts that I will provide here.

In September 1963 when I returned from a year's research in Jerusalem to my teaching at UCLA, I found waiting for me a group of students who had to be examined for placement in our Hebrew language courses. The test format was simple: I would pull a book off the shelf in my office and ask the student to read, preferably an unvocalized text. Among the more advanced students I found one, Mike Signer, who was intriguing since his background was so different from that of the other advanced students who were either the children of Israelis or the products of Orthodox Day Schools. He had been brought up in a Reform Temple and his Hebrew was acquired in its religious school. While he had had less exposure to the language than the others and he had to struggle with the unvocalized text, I felt that his answers to my questions exhibited a greater sense of grammar than did the others (he had already learned some Latin). In addition, he expressed an interest in becoming a Reform rabbi and I felt that the encounter with my Orthodox students would be interesting. Finally, he had a quick wit and a winning smile. I thought I could do something with this student for whom the class was much more than a convenient way to discharge the university language requirement, and I admitted him into the third-year Hebrew language class which I was assigned to teach.

We plunged into a variety of texts, mostly modern ones with a supplement I provided of passages from Bialik's *Sefer ha-agada,* the well-known anthology of rabbinic texts. Since the class was relatively small and intimate, each student was called upon daily to participate in the lesson. At first, Mike found the pace too fast. Whenever he expressed doubts about his ability to compete with his colleagues, especially those with Orthodox Day School training, I assured him that by the time he graduated from UCLA, he could read most texts in Hebrew and would know more than most applicants to rabbinical school. Of course, I did not tell him when I said "read" I meant something very specific, certainly not the basic understanding of the language of the text.

Unlike most of the students, however, Mike learned almost immediately that for me learning to read was not merely a matter of grammar or vocabulary, but that reading is the interpretation of texts, one of the most challenging and rewarding human enterprises. Trained as both a Classical Philologist and a New Critic, I would fuse both approaches, the study of texts in their historical contexts and the close reading of the text for its rhetorical devices. Few students were capable of responding to the subtleties of this method of reading, but Mike was astonishingly receptive and that made the class worth teaching. He quickly realized that the intellectual history of Judaism was shaped by the sophisticated reading of its texts which were often refractions of previous texts. In those days the term "intertextuality" had not yet arrived from France, but what we were discussing was a pervasive system of intertextuality. These readings inevitably led to discussions about the authors and their worldviews, particularly those of the modern Hebrew authors which preoccupied me: Agnon, Bialik, and Berdiczewski, masters of the problematics of Jewish spiritual existence in the modern period. These discussions, however, always began and ended with a demanding reading of a text. What Mike reminds me, however, in his eloquent preface mentioned above is how I conveyed a strong sense of values while teaching these texts: "A student of Arnold Band's must surely remember his tirades against the twin demons of 'bourgeois thinking' and 'revivalism.' These warnings have become part of the 'hermeneutics of suspicion' that interrupts the flow of my thoughts and restrains my intellectual exuberance."[2]

Mike was open to suggestions that he study with other professors to hear other approaches. I recall sending him off to study Russian literature in translation with my colleague, Vladimir Markov. I do not know how he got to Gerhart Ladner, the famous historian of the medieval church, but I do recall how Ladner was so thrilled to have in his class an undergraduate student who could read Hebrew and Latin. Studying with Ladner was crucial for Mike since those were the days of the Second Vatican Council, of *Nostra Aetate*. Ladner's courses provided Mike, the future rabbinical student, with the basis for a proper understanding of the profound implications of these momentous events in the Church. I would argue, however, that had Mike not studied at UCLA, he would not have become the medievalist he is, equally at home in Jewish and Christian texts.

In addition, during the 1960s Jewish Studies became more accepted as a legitimate academic discipline in North American universities and Michael Signer, in fact, was a paradigmatic student of the new period. Ten years earlier there were few universities in this country where one could be exposed to a thorough study of Hebrew texts of all periods. While the various Jewish seminaries did teach Hebrew texts, they spent little if any time on the Christian intellectual milieux. A happy convergence of historical factors allowed Signer to become the scholar he is, but it is he who took advantage of the situation. Other students exposed to the same forces did not do so.

The academic year 1966–67 was also crucial in Signer's development. During that year he was officially a first-year rabbinical student at Hebrew Union College, and he spent the year as required in Jerusalem. While most first-year rabbinical students had to invest most of their efforts in learning the Hebrew language, Mike could already take substantive courses in Hebrew at the Hebrew University. Coincidentally, I was spending that year in Jerusalem finishing my work on my Agnon book. I would meet with Mike as usual either in my apartment or at the university and was delighted to share his excitement with his courses there. The Jerusalem experience surely confirmed his desire to make Jewish Studies his life's work. His subsequent time in Cincinnati and Toronto could be so rewarding precisely because the years 1962–1967 were so formative. Signer was a product of the sixties, but not of the upheavals in the universities that have recast so many attitudes since then.

Upon completing his doctoral studies at the Centre for Medieval Studies at the University of Toronto, Signer returned to Los Angeles as a faculty member at Hebrew Union College where he served until 1992 when he was invited to join the faculty of the University of Notre Dame. He returned to Los Angeles as a rabbi and with a doctorate, no longer my student, but my colleague and friend.

I have mentioned that Michael Signer's brief preface to the Festschrift edited in my honor dwells upon the transmission of knowledge from one generation to the next, from fathers to sons, through the reading of texts. I would like to demonstrate this process by explicating a poem by the modern Israeli poet Yehudah Amichai (1923–2000), certainly the most popular Israeli poet to date. This popularity owes much both to Amichai's linguistic accessibility: Amichai's language is really not too difficult and translates easily into English and other western languages. This does not mean that his poetry is thin or simple, but that it is closer to the Hebrew an educated Israeli would speak and read than that of poets like Bialik or Alterman who preceded him. If, in fact, you can read a Hebrew newspaper, you can read Amichai. And, to the extent that his poetry recasts previous Hebrew texts, they are usually texts that someone who has gone to a decent Israeli high school would know. Just as his language speaks to the average educated Israeli, the themes that obsess him are those that engage any sensitive human being: the wonders of the sensuous world around us; the love for a partner, for the family, for children; meditations on the meaning of life and death, on fathers and sons; and the sheer delight in the play of words. These topics may seem to be ordinary, but it is precisely because they are ordinary—and not the demanding social and national issues of his predecessors—that his poetic treatment of them was so innovative in the 1950s and 1960s. Amichai taught poets and readers that there is profound poetry in the seemingly mundane aspects of life, and that there is a resonant elegance in everyday Hebrew when used to convey the profundity of the mundane. Having lived through the great events of Jewish life—*aliyah* from Germany in the 1930s, six years in the British Army, several years in the Palmah, over fifty years in Jerusalem with all its tensions—there is in Amichai's poetry no anger or rancor, but rather a wise, often bemused and humorous acceptance of what life has to offer.

In the last volume Amichai published, *Patuah Sagur Patuah* (*Open Closed Open*) (2002), we find an untitled poem in which he returns to one of his favorite themes: his father. It opens with a stunning declarative statement: "My father was God and didn't know it" ("אָבִי הָיָה אֱלֹהִים וְלֹא יָדַע"). While one might read this as a blasphemous line, it is just the opposite. Building on the model of the Ten Commandments which are treated with whimsical respect throughout the poem, he emphasizes the lessons about life that he learned from his father, a pious man who appears as a loving and beloved figure throughout his poetry. Throughout this poem, we notice the subtle use of texts which performs this tribute to his father. In a sense, the poem is a study in intertextuality. In English translation, the poem reads as follows:

> My father was God and didn't know it. He gave me
> the Ten Commandments not in thunder and not in anger,
> not in fire and not in a cloud, but gently
> and with love. He added caresses and tender words,
> "would you" and "please." And chanted "remember" and "keep"
> with the same tune, and pleaded and wept quietly
> between one commandment and the next: Thou shalt not
> take the name of thy Lord in vain, shalt not take, not in vain,
> please don't bear false witness against your neighbor.
> And he hugged me tight and whispered in my ear,
> Thou shalt not steal, shalt not commit adultery, shalt not kill.
> And he lay the palms of his wide-open hands on my head
> With the Yom Kippur blessing: Honor, love, that thy days
> may be long upon this earth. And the voice of my father—
> white as his hair. Then he turned his face to me one last time,
> as on the day he died in my arms, and said, I would like to add
> two more commandments:
> the Eleventh Commandment, "Thou shalt not change,"

and the Twelfth Commandment, "Thou shalt change. You will change."
Thus spoke my father, and he turned and walked away
and disappeared into his strange distances.[3]

The poem is energized by the contrast between the direct, harsh commandments which we all know from their source in the Tanakh and the softening of this harshness by the poet's rendition of his father's version of these commandments which are thus significantly modified. From the very beginning we are introduced to this transformation since we learn: "My father was God and didn't know it." The irony is compounded when we realize that this new God, his father, didn't even know he was God—ironic since God is supposed to be omniscient. He gave the poet, Yehudah Amichai, the Ten Commandments, not in a thunderous, threatening revelation, but "gently and with love." Instead of the stern "Thou shalt, or thou shalt not," he always added, "please," or beseeched, "would you." The play with texts moves from the Bible itself to the *piyyut,* "Lekha Dodi," sung on Sabbath eves where we find "The terms 'remembering' and 'observing' used variously in one commandment" which Amichai converts here to "'remembering' and 'observing' in one tune" ("זָכוֹר וְשָׁמוֹר בְּנִגּוּן אֶחָד,") and again softening the severity of the commandment which here the father chants—God does not declare or command.

When Amichai actually comes to the presentation of individual commandments, he either deconstructs them as in the Third, "Thou shalt not take the name of thy Lord in vain"—"לֹא תִשָּׂא שֵׁם אֱלֹהֶיךָ לַשָּׁוְא," where Amichai repeats "תִשָּׂא" and "לַשָּׁוְא" as plaintive echoes—or softens them as in the Ninth, "Thou shalt not bear false witness against your neighbor," where he precedes it with "please" ("אָנָּא"). And when he comes to the three short commandments forbidding stealing, adultery, and murder, his father would hug him tight and whisper them in his ear.

The most radical—and revealing—departure from the biblical text is found in the echo of the Fifth Commandment where we are ordered to honor our father and mother. Amichai changes it to "Honor, love, so that your days may be long upon this earth" ("כַּבֵּד, אֱהַב, לְמַעַן יַאֲרִיכוּן יָמֶיךָ עַל פְּנֵי הָאֲדָמָה"). Note that here, in this paean of love to his father he doesn't mention honor of parents, but honor and love in general, and this advice is coupled with the reward "that your days may be long upon this earth," perhaps a hopeful prayer by a man who knew that his days were, indeed, numbered. Love, respect, and tolerance of others are hallmarks of Amichai's temperament.

His father's real innovation comes in the addition of two new commandments: an Eleventh and Twelfth, which his father uttered as "he turned his face to [him] one last time as on the day he died in [his] arms." The Eleventh: "Thou shalt not change" ("לֹא תִּשְׁתַּנֶּה"), and the Twelfth: "Thou shalt change. You will change" ("הִשְׁתַּנֵּה, תִּשְׁתַּנֶּה"). It is with this seeming paradox calling for no change and change at the same time that Amichai's father—or rather Amichai himself—leaves us at the end of the poem. When the father says, "Thou shalt not change," he clearly means to tell the son that he should be the person he has already become: sensitive, loving, independent, but not raging in rebellion. He has his own way of interpreting reality, just as his father had his own subtle variations on the Ten Commandments. His father loves him just the way he is. Yet the father knows that life involves change, that his son must grow in experience, must live his own life. Neither of these two commandments are in the Ten Commandments, but together comprise the father's final advice to the son, and in turn, Amichai's advice to us, his readers. "Thou shalt not change," "Thou shalt change. You will change."

While this is the overt final message, there is another one embedded in the very text of the poem itself. The poem, with its intricate yet accessible weave of texts, is a remarkable achievement in the development of Hebrew culture. When we contemplate the construction of meaning through these old yet new words, this verbal play of "don't change" and "change," of tradition and innovation, we cannot escape the echoes of a keen sense of intertextuality, of the immersion in a sensibility that is aware of the hybridity of the text which is both traditional and innovative, precisely the insight Michael Signer has gained in considering his career: "As my own scholarly project in the history of medieval Jewish and Christian biblical interpretation has evolved, it becomes clearer that it is precisely the theme of rewriting the tradition for 'a new generation' that is at the foundation of the entire endeavor."[4]

Notes

1. Michael A. Signer, "*Dor dor vedorshav:* Of Fathers and Sons," in *History and Literature: New Readings of Jewish Texts in Honor of Arnold J. Band,* ed. William Cutter and David C. Jacobson (Providence, RI: Program of Judaic Studies, Brown University, 2002), xxxiii–xxxvi, quote taken from xxxiii.

2. Ibid., xxxiii.

3. The English translation is from Yehuda Amichai, *Open Closed Open: Poems,* trans. Chana Bloch and Chana Kronfeld (New York: Harcourt, 2000), 58, and is reprinted by permission of Houghton Mifflin Publishing Company. The Hebrew may be found in Yehuda Amichai, *Patuah Sagur Patuah* (Jerusalem: Schocken, 1998). All subsequent quotations from the English and Hebrew versions of this poem are taken from p. 58 of these volumes, respectively.

4. Signer, "*Dor dor vedorshav,*" in *History and Literature,* xxxiv.

CHAPTER TWO

The End of the Law

A Significant Difference between Judaism and Christianity

David Novak

Beyond Legalism and Antinomianism

On the issue of the law of God, which seems to divide Jews and Christians profoundly, there is nonetheless some significant commonality. This commonality can be seen by going back to the most original theological authorities in our respective traditions: the Rabbis and Paul.[1] The commonality between them is that both for the Rabbis and for Paul there is an aspect of the law of God that must precede the revelation and acceptance of the Covenant, be it the Covenant of Sinai or the Covenant of Calvary. Furthermore, this aspect of the law of God in both of our traditions is the necessary (but not sufficient) condition of the Covenant, and it is one that still functions intact within the Covenant. Finally, this pre-covenantal aspect of the law of God, what might be called the *minimal law of God,* is quite similarly constituted by the Rabbis and by Paul. Both the Rabbis and Paul speak about a law known to the Gentiles before revelation. This commonality about the minimal (but not maximal) law of God can be developed dialogically in the present by the Jewish disciples of the Rabbis with the Christian disciples of Paul.

It is over the issue of the law of God that follows from the Covenant of Sinai, however, that we are most deeply divided. Yet even here, if we cannot have commonality, then at least we can have a clearer understanding of our differences. When there is confusion about what the differences between Jews and Christians truly are, we not only misunderstand the other community, we misunderstand ourselves. That is because Judaism and Christianity are historically interrelated like no other religious traditions in human history. Indeed, the case can be made that much Jewish self-understanding can be seen as the Jewish attempt to further distinguish Judaism from Christianity, especially in the face of repeated Christian attempts to absorb Judaism into itself by claiming Christianity to be the fulfillment of Judaism. An even better case can be made that virtually all Christian self-understanding can be seen as the Christian attempt to simultaneously affirm its Jewish roots yet prevent Christianity from simply being reabsorbed into Judaism. In both traditions, we can best pinpoint this disagreement as a disagreement over the meaning of the law of God.

Initially, any such quest for accuracy should avoid the two most usual characterizations of each other's community, which became quite popular in the nineteenth and early twentieth centuries, namely, the characterization of Judaism as "legalism" and of Christianity as "antinomianism." Thus it became usual for many modern Christians to characterize Judaism as "legalistic," charging that Jews observe the commandments of the Torah ("the works of the Law") as ends in themselves, that they are only concerned with praxis per se, thus ignoring what these commandments ultimately intend.[2] On the other hand, it became usual for some modern Jews to characterize Christianity as "antinomian," charging that Christians have dispensed with law altogether, and that they are only concerned with faith as an "otherworldly" pursuit, whose content is "dogmatic" rather than ethical.[3]

The inaccuracy of both of these characterizations entails misunderstanding one's own tradition and the other's tradition as well. When Christians are convinced that Judaism is in essence legalism and pursue that characterization systematically, they inevitably so underestimate the role of law in their own tradition that they become ripe targets for the truly antinomian forces in history.[4] And when Jews are convinced that Christianity is in essence antinomian and pursue that characterization systematically, they inevitably overestimate the role of law in their own tradition. Accordingly, they underestimate the theological foundations of their own law and become ripe targets for the truly atheistic forces in history.[5]

Here again, going back to the Rabbis and to Paul will help us demarcate our respective positions more accurately and thus not let us fall into a misunderstanding of the other tradition. Proper historical-theological research and reflection demonstrate that the Rabbis did not see Christianity as being antinomian and that Paul did not see Judaism as being legalistic.

For the Rabbis and their heirs, any community that has accepted the Noahide Commandments is considered to be a lawful Gentile community, worthy of Jewish respect. This is even more so when that community has accepted these commandments as divine commandments. And this is superlatively so when that Gentile community has accepted these commandments (or their equivalent) as the law of God revealed through the Mosaic Torah.[6] Most rabbinic authorities judged Christians to be a community that affirms a moral law that is both divine and revealed in Scripture. Indeed, Christianity is the only religious tradition apart from Judaism that fulfills all three criteria.[7] One, it has a body of norms that include what Jews have seen to be the Noahide Commandments; two, it affirms that moral law comes from God; three, it finds its moral law in the Mosaic legislation. That is frequently as surprising to many Jews as it is even more surprising to many more Christians.

What is perhaps most surprising, certainly to many Christians, is that Paul did not differ from Pharisaic-Rabbinic Judaism because he thought it was legalistic.[8] In his most intense reflection on Judaism in the Letter to the Romans, Paul writes: "They have zeal for God, but not with proper acknowledgment [*ou kat' epignōsin*]. For they do not acknowledge the righteousness of God. . . . For Christ is the end of the Law [*telos gar nomou*] so that everyone who believes might become righteous [*eis dikaiōsynēn*]" (Rom. 10:2–4). Note that Paul does not say that the Jews are zealous for the Law for its own sake. He acknowledges they are zealous for God and observe the commandments in the context of their covenantal relationship with God. As such, they are clearly interested in the source of the Law, not just with their own behavior. Moreover, Paul does not say that the Jews are unconcerned with the end of the Law. When he states that Christ is the *telos* of the Law, it is clear that such an assertion presupposes that his hearers—including his Jewish hearers—are vitally concerned with the end of the Law. Thus they certainly do not deny *that* the Law has a true end, that is, it intends a purpose beyond its own observance. Instead, it is that the Jews do not acknowledge, that they choose to reject, the One *whom*, for Paul, the Law from its very beginning has always intended.[9] Hence Paul's argument with Pharisaic-Rabbinic Judaism is a theological argument that could not possibly have been made against "legalists," that is, against the type of people today we call "legal positivists."

We see that Paul specifically locates the fundamental difference between Christians and Jews in the issue of the law of God, not whether there is a law or not, and not whether that law is from God or not, and not whether that law has a purpose or not. Instead, the point of fundamental difference here is *what* or *who* is the true *telos* of the law of God. For Christians, the answer is Jesus Christ. But for Jews, *what* or *who* is the true *telos* of God's law revealed in the Torah? The formulation of an answer to this question is considerably stimulated by the challenge of Christianity, particularly the challenge posed by Paul, who was the early Christian who probably knew Judaism best from within.

Three Types of Divine Law

Before one discusses how rabbinic Jews view the end of God's law, one must analyze the various terms used to designate that law. These terms are all biblical, but they will be defined here in accordance with their usage by the Rabbis. By this analysis we will begin to see how each of the separate normative entities so designated intends its own specific end. In conclusion, I shall try to show how all these specific ends are truly interrelated aspects of one overall end.

The two most general terms used for the law of God in classical rabbinic Judaism are *Torah* (what Paul, following the Septuagint, called *nomos*) and *Mitsvah* (what Paul called "works"). *Torah*, which literally means "instruction," is used to designate the law of God as it is to be known, as the object of intellectual pursuit.[10] *Mitsvah*, which literally means "commandment," is used to designate the law of God as it is to be done, as the object of practical pursuit.[11] One of the great debates among the Rabbis of the first century of this era was whether *Torah* has value in and of itself, over and above its necessity for informing Jews how to perform a *mitsvah*.[12] The decision that *Torah* is more than just the means for immediate action re-affirmed the truth that God's word is more than law in the sense of being praxis alone. The priority of *Torah* over *Mitsvah* certainly reinforces the conviction that the Law has both a source and an end, both of which (or *whom*) go beyond human deeds.

In Scripture itself three distinct terms are used to designate specific aspects of the Law. The use of all three terms in tandem can be seen in the following passage: "In the future, when your son shall ask you saying: 'What are the commemorations [*'edot*] and the decrees [*huqqim*] and the ordinances [*mishpatim*] that the Lord our God has commanded you,' you shall say to your son: 'We were slaves of Pharaoh in Egypt and the Lord commanded us to do all these decrees, to fear the Lord our God for our good [*le-tov lanu*] always, to keep us alive as we are today'" (Deut. 6:20–22, 24). In rabbinic tradition, *'edot* ("commemorations") refer to those commandments that commemorate the mighty acts of God in history, such as the commandment to celebrate Passover in remembrance of the Exodus from Egypt.[13] *Huqqim* ("decrees") refer to those commandments that seem to have no known purpose other than obedience to God's will, such as the prohibition of eating pork and the prohibition of wearing clothes made of wool and linen. *Mishpatim* ("laws") refer to those commandments that have an obvious social purpose, such as the prohibitions of murder and robbery.[14]

One may now ask whether these three aspects of the law of God are arranged in any hierarchal order. One can discern in the history of Judaism three different orderings of them.

First, from the passage in Deuteronomy just quoted, one could infer that the primary meaning of the Torah and its commandments is to enable us to actively commemorate the mighty acts of God in history. It is this active experience that inspires the fear of God and the reverent observance of all the other commandments, which are thus seen as divine decrees (*huqqim*). Israel's acceptance of the Torah and its commandments is seen as their response to what God has done for them in past history, and that they anticipate more such good in future history. Thus all of God's laws are for Israel's good, even if some of them do not seem to be based on God's mighty acts in history. As for the laws whose evident purpose is social, one could infer that the reference to collective good and collective life in the scriptural passage quoted above includes the welfare of the body politic (*bonum commune*).

Second, one can also infer from the designation of all the commandments as "decrees" (*ḥuqqim*), based on the fear of God, that the primary meaning of the Torah and its commandments is to enable Israel to respond to the ever-present authority of God, which is to be experienced immediately in the present. Accordingly, the reference to the Exodus is not the basis of the commandments, but rather the Exodus is the most vivid example of God's authority not being limited to the present alone. In other words, the commemoration of the event is for the sake of the commandments; the commandments are not for the sake of commemorating any event. This can be seen in the interpretation of the following scriptural verse by Rashi, the most influential of the medieval biblical commentators, who had the extraordinary ability to condense centuries of rabbinic teaching into a sentence or two. The verse reads: "You shall remember that you were a slave in Egypt, so you shall keep and do all these decrees [*ha-ḥuqqim*]" (Deut. 16:12). From this verse itself it would seem that the purpose of performing all the decrees of the Torah is in order to remember being a slave in Egypt and to be actively grateful for God's liberation of every Jew from this terrible bondage. However, totally consistent with much of the earlier rabbinic tradition, Rashi writes: "For this reason [*'al menat ken*] I liberated you [from Egypt], in order that you keep and do these decrees."[15] Experience is for the sake of action; action is not for the sake of commemorating experience. Thus the commemoration of experience is the content of the commemorative commandments [*'edot*], but it does not constitute their *telos*. Like all the other commandments, their *telos* is to respond to the authoritative Source of the Law. And as for the laws whose social benefit is quite evident, they too are essentially divine decrees. Even their evident benefit is still secondary to their essential normativity, which is because they are the direct commandments of God.

Third, one can infer that the purpose of the commandments is the enhancement of human life, especially human life in community. Thus Maimonides, the leading Jewish rationalist theologian in the Middle Ages, assumes that one of the two main purposes of the entire Torah is the "good care of the body" [*tiqqun ha-guf*], especially the body politic.[16] Accordingly, he writes concerning the commandment to remember being a slave in Egypt: "Man should remember states of distress at a time when he prospers. . . . For there was a fear of the moral qualities that are generally acquired by all those brought up in prosperity—I mean conceit, vanity, and neglect of the correct opinions."[17] Even the historically conditioned commandments are seen as being for the sake of the fulfillment of general human needs. Their function is thus natural. As Maimonides writes elsewhere: "The *festivals* are all for rejoicings and pleasurable gatherings, which in most cases are indispensable for man; they are also useful in the establishment of friendship, which must exist among people living in political societies."[18] In fact, he even goes so far as to interpret some of the so-called "decrees without reasons" (*ḥuqqim*) in terms of natural teleology. So, for example, he gives health reasons (that is, for reasons of "care of the body") for the dietary prohibitions of eating pork and eating meat and milk together.[19]

The Eschatological Horizon

As we have seen, Paul's divergence from Pharisaic-Rabbinic Judaism is not over the Law itself but, rather, over the true *telos* of the Law. But, as we have also seen, there are three types of law in the Torah: commemorative commandments, immediate divine decrees, and social laws. Now we must locate and analyze the type of teleology involved in these three types of Torah law. For reasons I hope will become apparent at the conclusion of this essay, let us begin by looking at the decrees (*ḥuqqim*) first, the social laws (*mishpaṭim*) second, and the commemorative commandments (*'edot*) third.

At first glance it would seem that the decrees have no distinct teleology at all. As one rabbinic text puts it: "I have decreed a decree; I have enjoined an enactment [*gezerah*]; you have no right to violate them!"[20] Here it seems the only essential factor is the proper acknowledgment of the divine source of the commandment.[21] Nevertheless, even when the Torah itself does not present any end for which a specific commandment is to be performed, the Rabbis clearly believed that the performance of the commanded act entails significant consequences. Here they are affirming the numerous promises in Scripture of reward for faithfulness in keeping the commandments and punishment for not keeping them. Furthermore, one of the most fundamental distinctions between Pharisaic and Sadducean Judaism— unanimously confirmed by the Rabbis, Josephus, and the New Testament— is that keeping the commandments has positive consequences for the faithful, primarily in the world-to-come (*'olam ha-ba'*) and, conversely, negative consequences elsewhere for transgressors.[22]

Here we see a very interesting teleology at work. Normally one would say that in order for an act to have teleological significance, the actor or agent must have a clear idea of what he or she is intending by the act. Along these lines, Aristotle, the greatest philosophical proponent of teleological ethics, argues that if it can only be known *what* well-being (*eudaimonia*) is after one's death, then one cannot say that all human action intelligently strives for that end here and now. Such an "end" (*telos*) cannot be a purpose at all.[23] Yet the Mishnah states: "Be as careful [*zahir*] when performing an easy commandment as when performing a hard commandment, for you do not know what the reward is for the performance of the commandments."[24] Indeed, other rabbinic texts state that the reason why the specific supernatural consequences of keeping the commandments are not made known is to prevent one from calculating the positive commandments, choosing to do those whose reward is great and neglecting those whose reward is paltry.[25] The performance of the commandments would then be consequential, there being an evaluative calculus, thus enabling one to do as it were a "cost-benefit" assessment whenever confronted by a positive commandment. (The negative commandments, conversely, all have their respective punishments stipulated in the Torah or by rabbinic exegesis of the Torah.)[26]

In this view, there is a fundamental distinction between ends as purposes and ends as consequences. When an end functions as a purpose, it is clear that the commandment itself is subordinate to its end: it is a means thereto. But when an end functions as a consequence, especially as an unknown consequence, the end is subordinate to the "means," just like an effect is subordinate to its cause. The reason for insisting that these consequences are unknown, I think, is to thereby assert that these commandments

as acts have real effects extending beyond the personal experience of the
actor or agent. These real effects are seen to be factors somehow in God's
future redemption (*ge'ulah*) of the entire cosmos, beginning with Israel.
Confining the significance of these acts to their subjective *meaning*, rather
than extending that significance to their objective *truth*, frequently cannot
ascribe to these acts their ultimate importance as components of God's
law, which is the same law whereby God governs the entire created universe.[27] And, especially at times of persecution and suffering, the subjective
meaning of the commandments can even be negative for the one who keeps
the commandments.[28] In these cases virtue is often not its own reward.[29]

At this level, then, the essence of the commandments is that they are
to be obeyed as God's will. In the phenomenological structure of the commandments as divine decrees (*ḥuqqim*), that consideration is primary. The
consideration of consequences is secondary to it, although a necessary consideration (a corollary, if you will) as we have just seen.

Consequences that cannot be the object of specific intention are not
"teleological" in the sense which that term has had since it was radically
reinterpreted by Aristotle. They are, instead, "eschatological" in the sense
of being the general results of faithfulness to the Covenant: what is hoped
for at the endtime (*eschaton*).[30] As Scripture puts it: "Refrain your voice
from weeping and your eyes from tears; there is reward [*sekhar*] for your
labor . . . and there is hope for the final end [*tiqvah l'aḥareetekh*], says the
Lord" (Jer. 31:16–17, MT).

The teleology of the social laws (*mishpatim*) is most apparent. Clearly,
the consequences of keeping these commandments are their inherent ends
for which they were initially commanded. They are their "original intent,"
if you will. Indeed, the basic standard of justice (*mishpat*), which lies behind
all of these laws, is what determines their essential meaning. This can be seen
even before the revelation of the Torah and its commandments at Sinai.
Thus when God informs Abraham of his intent to destroy the wicked cities
of Sodom and Gomorrah, that is done so that Abraham "might command
his children and household after him to keep the way of the Lord to perform righteousness [*tsedaqah*] and justice [*mishpat*]" (Gen. 18:19). However,
it seems as though Abraham already had an idea of what that divine justice is to be inasmuch as he challenges God's proposal as being inherently

unjust: "Shall the judge [*ha-shofeṭ*] of the whole earth not do justice [*mishpaṭ*]?!" (Gen. 18:25). But if justice is simply what God was now proposing to do (that is, destroy everyone in the two cities), then Abraham would have no real basis from which to question God. Accordingly, permitting him to question God's particular proposal at this time, on the basis of God's general standard of justice, will better enable Abraham to properly interpret the social laws to be put into practice in his human domain.

The intended teleological consequences of the social laws certainly cannot be regarded as having been fulfilled in this world as yet. There is too little justice in the city of man, and the city of God has not yet been established on earth. Even God's minimal law is hardly ubiquitous in the political and economic order. It is more often a goal than a real presupposition. So, these laws call for political fulfillment in the future. And because one understands the ends of these laws (all of them being *mishpaṭim*), that future is not a mysterious, transcendent *eschaton*. Instead, the implementation of that realm is a practical task having some chance of success even in the imperfect present and immediate future.

All of this sounds quite similar to Plato's political theory in the *Republic*. It is to be noted, moreover, that Plato assumed that this optimal human society could be actually brought into existence by a philosopher-king.[31] For some Jewish thinkers, this sounded similar enough to the Prophets' vision of the Messiah-king. Thus Maimonides, who deeply internalized the political philosophy of Plato (which he learned from the works of the Muslim philosopher Alfarabi), combined these two visions in his own political thought. He saw the practical teleology of the commandments of the Torah, primarily characterized by the social laws, as being fulfilled by the program of the Messiah-king. Thus he writes: "The Messiah-king is to arise in the future and restore the Davidic monarchy to its former splendor, to its original authority. He will build the Temple, gather the dispersed of Israel, and restore all the laws [*kol ha-mishpaṭim*] in his days as they originally were."[32] He furthermore emphasizes that this Messiah-king is not a supernatural figure, but only an extraordinary political leader of the Jewish people.[33] Because of this emphasis, I might add, Maimonides has been the prime inspiration of religious, as opposed to secular, Zionism in modern times.[34]

Even though Maimonides applied Plato's political philosophy to his messianic Jewish theology, he also retained and emphasized the original prophetic vision of the universal implications of the reign of the Messiah-king. In this Jewish version, as Maimonides puts it, the Messiah-king "will structure [*ve-yitaqen*] the whole world to serve the Lord altogether."[35]

Nevertheless, Maimonides' teleology of the Torah is not truly eschatological. For him, the Messiah-king's realm is not truly redemptive. It does not constitute the ultimate transformation of human life as it does in the more apocalyptic visions of the Prophets and the Rabbis. In Maimonides' theology of history, the true *telos* of the Torah *and* the reign of the Messiah-king together is to make it possible for the faithful of Israel and the righteous Gentiles "to be able to merit the life of the world-to-come [*'olam ha-ba'*]."[36] Furthermore, for Maimonides, the "world-to-come" is not the culmination of history, neither that of Israel nor that of humankind. Instead, it is an eternal realm, which can be apprehended even in the embodied life of this world (*ha'olam ha-zeh*), and one that can be ultimately attained after the death of the body and the final ascent of the soul.[37] Therefore, the Torah intends two ends.[38] First, there is the social *telos* of the exalted, but wholly natural, reign of the Messiah-king, a reign in which the Torah is the complete law for all Israel, and then the basic law for all humankind. This *telos* is temporal, but it is not eschatological. Second, there is the spiritual *telos* of the world-to-come, which Maimonides understands to be *the-world-beyond.* It seems to be what some have called "beatitude," which is a wholly transparent and everlasting experience of God as God truly is eternally.[39] As such, the temporal *telos* is not ultimate, and the ultimate *telos* is not temporal. It is eternal.

It must be said at this point that a number of Jewish theologians were very much troubled by what they saw as Maimonides' radical departure from classical Jewish eschatology.[40] Nevertheless, his teleology had many supporters, support that grew after his death.

The Primacy of the Commemorative Commandments

We have now seen that a primary emphasis on the divine decrees (*ḥuqqim*) leads to an eschatology without a teleology, and that a primary emphasis on the social laws (*mishpatim*) leads to a teleology without an eschatology. I shall now try to show how a primary emphasis on the commemorative commandments (*'edot*) leads to both an eschatology and a teleology functioning in tandem.

The eschatological implications of the commemorative commandments are most evident in the celebration of Passover, which is the historical festival par excellence in Judaism. Based on the five promises of redemption in Exodus 6:2–8, the Rabbis ordained that four cups of wine be drunk at the celebration of the Exodus during the table liturgy called the *seder* (literally, "the order," indicating that each ritual act is part of an intentional order).[41] But a fifth cup is poured that is not drunk by the participants in the *seder*. This last cup is left on the table in anticipation of the arrival of Elijah the Prophet, who is the harbinger of the coming of the Messiah-king. At a late point in the liturgy the door is opened and all rise to greet the Prophet—who, unfortunately, still has not yet come. That absence indicates that the fifth promise of final redemption (*ge'ulah shlemah*) has not yet been fulfilled.[42]

Being the final promise, the suggestion here is that it is the *telos* of the earlier promises which, having been fulfilled, can be celebrated through prescribed acts (*mitsvot*). This final redemption, now still only promised but not yet fulfilled, is the future horizon to which all the earlier events point, and which their prescribed celebrations ultimately intend. Being their *telos*, these commandments can already anticipate it. And being their *telos*, this event does not obliterate these commemorative commandments; instead, it places them in their ultimate context. These commandments envision this final end for they celebrate God's deliverance of His people, and with them the redemption of the whole world.[43] As such, the following rabbinic text, a slightly shorter version of which appears in the narrative (*haggadah*) recited during the *seder*, is quite informative: "Ben Zoma said to the Rabbis: 'Is the Exodus from Egypt to be recounted during the days of the Messiah?' . . . They said to him that its celebration will not be uprooted from its place in Jewish observance, but that it will supplement the downfall of the worldly kingdom [*malkhiyot*] which will be the root [*'iqqar*] and the celebration of the Exodus from Egypt will be secondary [*tefelah*] to it."[44]

The rabbinic insistence that partially redeemed history will still be an acknowledged part of wholly redeemed history implies that the future, no matter how supernatural, is not to completely transcend the past; the past is not totally overcome. This implication is closely related to a major implication of the doctrine of the resurrection of the dead (*tehiyyat ha-metim*). This doctrine, along with the doctrines of the world-to-come and the Messiah-king, comprises classical Jewish eschatology. All three are aspects of the Kingdom of God (*malkhut shamayim*). The doctrine of the resurrection of the dead implies that no matter how much better immortal human life is than mortal human life, it is nonetheless inconceivable without the body.[45]

The primary emphasis of the commemorative commandments, with their teleological eschatology or eschatological teleology, enables Jews to best understand the broken condition of the history of Israel—and, by extension, all of human history. Primary emphasis of the divine decrees, however, too easily suggests that God is already King and all that this kingship needs is universal enforcement. Surely, that is too simple and leads to a too simple eschatology, one having authoritarian, imperialist overtones of which the experience of tyranny, both ancient and modern, should make us quite suspicious. Also, primary emphasis on the social laws too easily suggests that universal justice is at hand, and that proper political organization can bring it about quickly enough. Surely, though, that is too simple and entails a too simple teleology, of which our modern experience of the failure of totalizing political ideologies, which proclaimed their ability to bring about complete social justice imminently, should also make us quite suspicious.

The primary emphasis on the commemorative commandments, however, needs the complementary emphasis on the divine decrees and the social laws. Without an emphasis on the divine decrees, intending as they do God's transcendent authority, the covenantal intimacy of historical experience could too easily suggest some sort of symbiosis of God and man, thus eclipsing the transcendence of God, even God's transcendence of the Covenant with Israel.[46] And without the emphasis on social justice, the Covenant lacks its moral pre-conditions in the law of God that preceded the revelation of the Torah at Sinai. As such, the Covenant would lose its universal dimension, its concern for all humankind.

Finally, this concern with what God has accomplished in history, which is celebrated by the commemorative commandments, is most closely associated with God's election of Israel, which lies at the core of the Covenant. In the commemorative commandments the people Israel celebrates her election by God more directly and more intensely than she does through the other kinds of commandments.

The eschatological horizon of the Covenant, with the teleology of the commandments that ultimately intend it, also promises that God's redemption beginning with Israel does not end with her. That ultimate redemption will finally include the whole world. Surely, the presence of Christianity in the world shows to some Jews that our election into the Covenant has already begun to bless the world and more forcefully anticipate its full and final redemption.[47] At least until that time, and perhaps even afterward, we Jews must keep all of God's commandments revealed in the Torah and explicated and supplemented by our normative tradition. Paul has not persuaded us otherwise.[48]

Notes

1. See David Novak, "Before Revelation: The Rabbis, Paul, and Karl Barth," *Journal of Religion* 71 (1991): 50–66.

2. For a fairly recent example of this charge of "Jewish legalism," see the Lutheran theologian Helmut Thielecke, *Theological Ethics,* trans. J. W. Doberstein (Grand Rapids, MI: Eerdmans, 1979), 1:20, 69.

3. See Leo Baeck, "Romantic Religion," trans. W. Kaufmann, in his *Judaism and Christianity,* ed. W. Kaufmann (Philadelphia: Jewish Publication Society of America, 1958), 189–292. Baeck (d. 1956), who was the leader of German Jewry during the years of the Nazi horror, might well be considered the last great Jewish polemicist against Christianity. The first version of "Romantische Religion" was published in 1922; the final version was published in 1938. During those years too many (but not all, thank God) German Christian theologians were providing theological arguments for the inferiority of Judaism, arguments that were readily utilized by the German anti-Semites who came to power in 1933 and who were hell-bent on destroying both Judaism and the Jews. To be sure, there is much to disagree with theologically in Baeck's essay, but one can still appreciate the poignancy of his ethical critique of Christianity when considering the historical context in which this essay was written and rewritten.

4. For an example of this, see Joseph Fletcher, *Morals and Medicine* (Boston: Beacon Press, 1954), 211–55.

5. For an example of this, see Haim H. Cohn, "Secularization of Divine Law," *Jewish Law in Ancient and Modern Israel* (New York: KTAV, 1971), 1–49.

6. See Maimonides, *Mishneh Torah,* Kings 8.11–9.1.

7. See David Novak, *Jewish-Christian Dialogue* (New York: Oxford University Press, 1989), 42–56.

8. See E. P. Sanders, *Paul and Palestinian Judaism* (Philadelphia: Fortress Press, 1977), 550–51.

9. See Martin Luther, *Commentary on Romans,* trans. J. T. Mueller (London: Zondervan, 1954), 130.

10. See e.g., *Mishnah Avot* 2.11.

11. See e.g., *Mishnah Kiddushin* 1.7.

12. Babylonian Talmud *Kiddushin* 39b and parallels. See David Weiss Halivni, *Peshat and Derash* (New York: Oxford University Press, 1991), 101–25; also, David Novak, "The Dialectic between Theory and Practice in Rabbinic Thought" in *Study and Knowledge in Jewish Thought,* ed. H. Kreisel (Beer Sheva: Ben-Gurion University of the Negev Press, 2006), 121–35.

13. See Nahmanides, *Commentary on the Torah,* Exodus 13:16.

14. See Babylonian Talmud *Yoma* 67b re Lev. 18:4.

15. Compare Nahmanides, *Commentary on the Torah,* Deut. 16:12; Deut. 5:15.

16. *Guide of the Perplexed,* 3.27.

17. Ibid., 3.39, trans. S. Pines (Chicago: University of Chicago Press, 1963), 552.

18. Ibid., 3.43, 570.

19. Ibid., 3.48.

20. *Bemidbar Rabbah* 19.1 re Num. 19.2.

21. See *Beresheet Rabbah* 44.1 re Ps. 18:31.

22. See e.g., *Mishnah Avot* 2.16; Josephus, *Antiquities of the Jews,* 18.12; Matthew 6:1–5.

23. *Nicomachean Ethics* 1.10.1100a10–1101a21.

24. *Mishnah Avot* 2.1.

25. See Palestinian Talmud *Peah* 1.1/15d.

26. See *Mishnah Sanhedrin* 7.1–9.1, 11.1; *Makkot* 3.1–10.

27. See *Beresheet Rabbah* 1.1; also, Harry A. Wolfson, *Philo* (Cambridge, MA: Harvard University Press, 1947), 2:165–200.

28. See e.g., Babylonian Talmud *Hullin* 142a.

29. Compare Spinoza, *Ethics,* 5.P42.

30. However, the Rabbis were very critical of those who attempted to actually calculate the end-time. See Babylonian Talmud *Sanhedrin* 97b.

31. *Republic* 473D.

32. *Mishneh Torah,* Kings 11.1.

33. Ibid., 12.3.

34. See Louis Jacobs, *Principles of the Jewish Faith* (New York: Basic Books, 1964), 386–87.

35. *Mishneh Torah*, Kings 11.4.

36. Ibid., 12.4.

37. *Mishneh Torah*, Repentance 3.8.

38. *Guide of the Perplexed*, 2.40 and 3.27.

39. Compare Thomas Aquinas, *Summa theologiae*, IaIIae q. 69 a. 2.

40. See note of Abraham ben David of Posquières on *Mishneh Torah*, Repentance 3.8; also, David Novak, *The Election of Israel* (Cambridge: Cambridge University Press, 1995), 200–7 for a critique of Maimonides on the question of temporality in Jewish theology.

41. *Mishnah Pesaḥim* 10.1; Palestinian Talmud *Pesaḥim* 10.1/37b–c.

42. See *Haggadah Shlemah*, 3rd ed., ed. M.M. Kasher (Jerusalem: Torah Shelema Institute, 1967), sec. 1, pp. 90–95.

43. See Babylonian Talmud *Berakhot* 57b, where the experience of the Sabbath in this world anticipates the experience of the complete Sabbath of the world-to-come.

44. *Tosefta Berakhot* 1.10; see, also, *Haggadah Shlemah*, sec. 2, p. 18.

45. See Reinhold Niebuhr, *The Nature and Destiny of Man* (New York: Charles Scribner's Sons, 1943), 2:294–98.

46. The *ḥuqqim* are observed out of fear of God, whereas the *'edot* are observed out of love of God. Love without fear could lead to a symbiosis *with* God; fear without love could lead to estrangement *from* God. See Palestinian Talmud *Berakhot* 9.7/14b; Obadiah Bertinoro, *Commentary on the Mishnah: Avot* 1.3.

47. See Maimonides, *Mishneh Torah*, Kings 11.2 (uncensored ed.); also, Novak, *Jewish-Christian Dialogue*, 59–66.

48. See David Novak, "Law and Eschatology: A Jewish-Christian Intersection" in *The Last Things: Biblical and Theological Perspectives on Eschatology*, ed. C.E. Braaten and R.W. Jenson (Grand Rapids, MI: Eerdmans, 2002), 90–112.

CHAPTER THREE

ǀ

Christianity in Talmud and Midrash

Parallelomania or Parallelophobia?

Israel Jacob Yuval

לזכרו של רעי, מיכאל, אוהב האדם

ומרבה שלום בין דתות ואומות

One of the best-known statements about identity from ancient times is doubtless that made by Paul in the Epistle to the Galatians 3:28 regarding the equality and cooperation among all those who believe in Jesus. Paul says: "There is neither Jew nor Greek, there is neither slave nor free, there is neither male nor female; for you are all one in Christ Jesus."[1] This universal declaration is in striking contrast to an opposite Jewish expression. In the Morning Blessings, it states: "Blessed art Thou, O Lord our God, King of the Universe, who has not made me a Gentile . . . who has not made me a slave . . . who has not made me a woman." I would like to begin with these two positions regarding the question of identity as a way of introducing the issue of polemics. Is Jewish self-identity, which seems here to be for-mulated in a manner diametrically opposed to that of Paul, expressed in deliberate polemics with it, or was the Jewish formula already known to Paul, and was it he who turned it topsy-turvy?

The picture becomes more complex upon examining the history of the Jewish formula. Its present form is relatively late, its source being the Babylonian Talmud.[2] In the tannaitic literature,[3] we find a somewhat different wording: instead of "who has not made me a slave," there is the phrase "who has not made me an ignoramus." Thus, that formula which precisely inverts Paul's words only appears in the later textual witnesses, strengthening the possibility that there alone was the blessing formulated in opposition to the Pauline formulation.

Texts similar to the Jewish declaration cited above also appear in ancient Greek literature.[4] Plutarch states that Plato gave thanks for three things: that he was born a human being and not an animal, a Greek and not a barbarian, and that he was born in the generation of Socrates.[5] The biographer of the Greek philosophers, Diogenes Laertius, mentions Hermippus, who attributes to Thales a statement attributed by others to Socrates: namely, that he gave thanks to fate that he was born a human and not beast, a man and not a woman, a Greek and not a barbarian.[6]

What is the relationship among the Greek, the Pauline, and the rabbinic statements?[7] At first glance, it seems most reasonable to assume that Paul's words relate to the Greek saying, against which they wish to present the opposite approach. In light of this, one might argue that the early Jewish blessing also echoes the ancient Greek saying, adapted to the particularly Jewish context. According to this hypothesis, the common Greek source explains the similarity between the two independent later versions, the Pauline and the rabbinic, leaving no basis to speak of a polemic between them. But even according to this assumption, it is possible that in its later development—i.e., as it took shape in the Morning Blessings of the Babylonian Talmud—the Jewish declaration acquired an additional function: namely, to confute the view of Paul; it was from this that the version that precisely inverts his words was born. If this is the case, one may state that, in reaction to the challenge posed by Pauline Christianity in the guise of a universal religion, Judaism established a sectarian outlook infused with consciousness of chosenness and distinctiveness. Whereas Paul based human salvation upon belief in Jesus and saw the execution of the laws of the Torah as an obligation whose time had passed, the definition of Jewish identity made the fulfillment of the commandments the exclusive condition for attaining salvation. These three blessings thus express a feeling of gratitude for the fact that one is not numbered among one of the three groups that are exempt from the *mitzvot*, whether in a full or partial sense.[8] This being so, the debate with Paul regarding the Morning Blessings touches upon the fundamentals of Jewish faith.

It is also possible to read the later development of the Jewish declaration as an internal Jewish development that did not at all know or take into consideration Paul's words. In this spirit one may also understand the substitution of the word "slave" for "ignoramus." The ignoramus also does not fulfill *mitzvot*, for "an ignoramus cannot be God-fearing,"[9] but he falls under the rubric of those who are obligated to perform them. It may be that the preference for "slave" was intended to create a category for those who not only fail to perform the commandments but who are also exempt from them. It may be for this reason that Rav Acha bar Yaakov asked his son to change the early tannaitic formula of "ignoramus" to "slave."[10]

Moreover, one may not exclude an even more far-reaching possibility, according to which Paul was already familiar with the earlier form of the Jewish declaration, such that his declaration ought to be seen not in opposition to the Greek outlook but rather as a rejection of the particularistic consciousness of Jewish election. According to this view, Paul felt the inherent contradiction between the monotheistic faith in one God who created the whole world, on the one hand, and a religion that champions a God who chooses for Himself one special people out of all the nations, on the other.

Indeed, the scales seem balanced so that the question of who influenced whom or who polemicized against whom remains open. This case exemplifies in an incisive manner the complexity of the possibilities even when confronting a rabbinic text that has such a clear parallel to Paul's words. In deciding this case, it would appear that the consideration of probability ought to be the decisive one, and that among the multitude of factors considered as reasonable one will find the historical outlook held by each scholar regarding his period. It is my position that the most likely possibility is that which assumes that the Jewish formulation, at least in its later development, sought to confute Paul and debate the validity of the Christian ecumenical approach. However, it is clear that for many researchers the question of probability may lead to entirely different conclusions.[11]

I have not begun this essay with the above example in order to decide matters one way or another, but rather to exemplify how the great scholars approached this problem—and, in particular, the greatest Talmud scholar of the last generation, Saul Lieberman, who devoted a detailed discussion to this issue in his monumental work, *Tosefta ke-Peshuta*.[12] Like his distinguished predecessors—Luther and Schopenhauer—he also noted the similarity between the Jewish blessings and the Greek aphorism. But, in his words, "These ought not to be seen as betraying external influence, as the blessings themselves are concerned with the benefits that the Almighty bestows upon human beings, which it is the nature of every person to feel." Here that approach which emphasizes internal and "authentic" development, free of every kind of external "influence"—an approach particularly beloved by many scholars of the previous generation, and even by several major scholars in our own day—was victorious.[13]

What is interesting in Lieberman's words is not only what he says, but primarily what he does not say. Lieberman, a Talmudic scholar who seemingly saw and knew everything, does not so much as mention the famous words of Paul! His argument refuting "external influence" is directed toward the Greek statement alone, not to the Pauline one. We may reasonably assume that this silence was the result of a certain sense of disquiet that he felt about gathering Christian material for purposes of comparison with its Jewish-Talmudic counterpart. This position was shared by many Jewish scholars who discussed this issue and did not seriously weigh the possibility that the later Jewish blessing sought to confront that of Paul.

It seems to me that what we find here is a principled outlook in Jewish research, one that systematically ignores the possibility of points of contact between Christianity and Judaism.[14] In 1939 the then-young scholar Ephraim Elimelech Urbach published a strongly worded criticism against Yitzhak (Fritz) Baer,[15] who at the time was viewed in Jerusalem as the leading historian and as founder of historical studies at the Hebrew University. Urbach attacked Baer for the comparison he drew between the founder of medieval Ashkenazic Pietism, R. Judah he-Hasid, and St. Francis of Assisi.[16] Urbach dismissed the evidence of similarity between Ashkenazic Hasidism and Franciscanism with a single sentence that became a slogan for members of his generation: "Similar conditions produce similar results." That is, the comparison does not indicate any connections, but only a common *Zeitgeist.* This debate is reminiscent of the debates among scholars of Christianity regarding the relation between the origins of Christianity and the pagan religions that precede it, in which the question raised was whether the parallel phenomena are to be seen as "analogies or genealogies."[17]

Baer himself, who did not hesitate to note the depth of the symbiosis between Jewish and Christian culture in the Middle Ages, was reluctant to do so once he began dealing with the rabbinic literature of late antiquity. In his studies written after 1950, he engaged in a move that "bypassed" Christianity, representing Second Temple Judaism as a kind of proto-Talmudic culture—all in order to bolster its "authenticity" and to argue that it predated Christianity.[18] By contrast, the influence of "Greek wisdom" upon Jewish culture did not bother him at all. On the contrary, he portrayed Second Temple Judaism as having undergone a decisive transformation from the biblical period, specifically due to Greco-Hellenistic influence. Baer is exceptional in the extremes represented by his solution, but in his approach to the Talmudic material he and most of the scholars of the previous generation shared the same qualms about Christianity. They preferred to relate the Talmud to Greek and Roman culture as opposed to the possibility that the Talmud was born in a cultural environment in which there was a striking Christian presence.[19] Notwithstanding Urbach's criticism of the comparison drawn by Baer between R. Judah he-Hasid and Francis of Assisi, he himself changed his tune when he came to discuss rabbinic literature. While he drew many comparisons between rabbinic literature and that of early Christianity, he nevertheless saw these resemblances as testimony to Christianity being influenced by Judaism, and not vice versa.[20]

Over the last generation the picture has changed somewhat. Today one hears more strongly the dialogical tendency to interpret parallels between rabbinic literature and Christian literature as testimony to the lively dialogue between the two religions, although there is much dispute regarding both its timing and its intensity.[21] There is also greater awareness that similarities between rabbinic literature and Christian literature derive, on more than one occasion, from Jewish absorption of Christian ideas. It also seems doubtless that the efforts of scholars in Israel, Europe, and America to find a Christian context for the world of the Talmud derives from, among other factors, adoption of the contemporary cultural ideal that tends to reduce the tensions between Judaism and Christianity, as well as from the multicultural trends that are today predominant. In Israel, there may also operate a hidden longing to "return" to Europe and its culture. The Talmud as seen through Christian lenses provides entry to a Western world with a Jewish "kosher" stamp.

But in spite of all this, the advocates of the "authenticist" tendency have not been silenced, and their voices have recently been joined by that of Alon Goshen-Gottstein.[22] The comparative and dialogic approaches to which Goshen-Gottstein refers using the term "polemomania"—a reworking of the term "parallelomania" coined by Samuel Sandmel—are intended to indicate the path of those scholars who are affected by a "pathological" quest for parallels and influences, even in those places where the parallels may be seen as the result of parallel internal development.[23]

For the sake of transparency, I must confess to being among those "afflicted by this disease." I would nevertheless argue that the alternative to parallelomania is likely to be parallelophobia. Parallelophobia with regard to Christianity is a deeply rooted cultural phenomenon within the Jewish tradition. It begins with the midrashic and Talmudic literature and continues down to our own day. Its expressions include a hidden desire to conceal the threatening, close presence of the sister religion.

There is a seemingly weighty claim in support of the parallelophobic position: namely, that rabbinic literature in general, and Palestinian literature in particular, makes very little mention of Christians and Christianity. How should this silence be interpreted? In order to answer this question, I would like to make use of James Scott's concept, "hidden transcripts,"[24] to argue that rabbinic Judaism created a closed, almost hermetically sealed language of a highly developed and sophisticated halakhic world, of halakhic texts with their own inner logic, of liturgical ceremonies and social taboos intended to create a separation between itself and its surroundings. But behind this wall a profound dialogue was being conducted with the community on the other side of the wall. Scott spoke of a hidden language used by those in a position of inferiority vis-à-vis the superior dominant force. Such was not the situation of the Sages in relation to the Christian religion, certainly not during the first centuries of the Common Era. I therefore prefer to use the term "hidden language" or "transcript" in a different sense, as implying the refusal to admit the very need for struggle, of one who denies the very existence of his opponent.

Regarding this point I am influenced by the theory of the Norwegian anthropologist, Fredrik Barth, who dealt with ethnic groups that live alongside and at times even within one another. In his opinion, the boundaries between different peoples or ethnic groups do not only signify the differences between them; the selfsame differences—in language, appearance, way of life—may also serve as a vehicle for mutual exchange of cultural influences. As a result, what initially may be perceived as particularism and as a barrier intended to preserve ethnic uniqueness may, in fact, serve as an intermediary that stimulates dialogue with the other culture.[25]

I would like to apply these distinctions to the relations between Jews and Christians during the formative period of the two religions. Just as certain modern Jewish scholars—including the best among them—feel uncomfortable openly discussing the possibility of Christian influence on Judaism, so too did the Sages of the Talmud and Midrash refrain from doing so. Christianity is absent from the explicit language of the Talmud and the Midrash not because the Sages made light of the threat it posed, but because they did not wish to openly admit the danger posed by it. Anyone traveling today in the remnants of the Jewish cities of Tiberias and Zippori (Sepphoris) in the Galilee cannot but be impressed by the massive penetration of Christianity in these areas during the first centuries CE. The only synagogue discovered to date in the archaeological excavations at Zippori, from the fifth century CE, is small in size and located near the wall of the city—that is, at its periphery. By contrast, in the center of the town, at the intersection of the *cardo* and the *decumanus,* two large and impressive churches were discovered. Above Jewish Tiberias on Mount Bereniki, a church of huge and even threatening dimensions was built during the first half of the sixth century.[26] Quite recently a fourth-century church has been discovered in the center of the city.[27] In the face of this massive penetration of Christianity into the centers of Jewish settlement, the Sages adopted a tactic of ignoring it. The polemic with Christianity that gradually came to dominate the Land of Israel was not conducted openly, but in a convoluted and allusive manner. The Talmuds and midrashim do not explicitly state the name of the rival with whom they are struggling, but the shadow of Christianity nevertheless looms in these rabbinic texts. One is reminded of the words of Karl Popper: "Every genuine test of a theory is an attempt to falsify it or to refute it."[28] And long before Popper, the Talmud (*b. San-hedrin* 78a) set forth this rule regarding laws of testimony: "Any testimony that cannot be confuted is not valid testimony." Indeed, I must admit that in terms of the laws of proof the parallelomaniacs are in the weaker position.

Nevertheless, historical plausibility works in its favor. Can we imagine the emergence of a rival religion that appropriated to itself all the components of Judaism's own identity without this arousing opposition? In the discussion that follows, I will present two specific cases to illustrate the advantages and drawbacks of the approach that wishes to uncover hidden polemic. I will begin with a vague, marginal, and almost unknown biblical figure: Doeg the Edomite, a figure who in rabbinic thought enjoyed the dramatic status of an arch-villain. I will attempt to illustrate that internal literary exegesis need not come at the expense of the comparative historical context.

Doeg the Edomite as a Type of Jesus

The mishnah in Sanhedrin chapter 10 begins with the sweeping declaration, "All Israel have a share in the World to Come." This declaration, evidently a late addition, is reminiscent of Paul's words in Romans 11:26, "All Israel shall be saved." On another occasion, I argued that this statement does not relate to Paul's original intention, whatever that might have been, but rather to the later exegesis given it by the Church, which reduced the concept "Israel" to "spiritual Israel," and delimited those who were to be saved by the well-known dictum, "extra Ecclesiam nulla salus est." The mishnah formulates a comparable rule, giving *carte blanche* to every Jew as such to enjoy the World to Come, thereby setting forth a position analogous but opposite to that of the Church's doctrine of salvation. Only those born as Jews, "carnal Israel," will merit the Life to Come. Further on, the mishnah enumerates several heretical views whose adherents are also denied a share in the World to Come: one who reads "external books," one who "whispers over a wound," and one who pronounces the Ineffable Divine Name (i.e., the Tetragrammaton) as written. My argument was that each of these three deviations were seen as characteristic, in the eyes of the Sages, of Jewish Christians. According to this interpretation, this mishnah deals directly with Christians, without mentioning them by name.[29]

Here I wish to focus on the sequel to this mishnah which lists four biblical figures who have no share in the World to Come—Balaam, Doeg, Ahithophel, and Gehazi. I will concentrate on only one of these figures, Doeg. Why did he, of all people, receive this dubious distinction?

Doeg the Edomite was an officer in the court of King Saul.[30] While fleeing from Saul, David arrived together with his entourage at the priestly city of Nob. They were hungry, and in order to satisfy their hunger David begged the priest Ahimelech to give him and his lads some of the holy shewbread. The latter acceded to this request only after David assured him that the young men were ritually pure. The entire event was observed by Doeg the Edomite who, after David had fled to the land of the Philistines, denounced Ahimelech to the king. Saul ordered Doeg to kill Ahimelech along with the eighty-five priests who were with him at the time of this incident. A later echo of this story appears in Psalm 52, a chapter devoted to a description of Doeg's treachery, where he is presented as a base and deceitful person. Concerning his punishment, it is stated there that God would uproot him "from the land of the living." This expression was understood by the Rabbis as bearing an eschatological meaning, from which they reached the conclusion that he had no portion in the World to Come.

This chapter is familiar to everyone who reads the New Testament. Jesus' well-known permission to pluck ears of grain on the Sabbath in a pericope common to all three Synoptic gospels—in Mark 2, Luke 6, and Matthew 12—is based on this incident.[31] Jesus infers from the story of David that, just as his hunger and that of his entourage overrides the prohibition against eating the shewbread, so too did Jesus' distress and that of his disciples override the Shabbat. According to the Matthean account, Jesus also infers the permission to pluck grain on Shabbat from the practice in the Temple of offering sacrifices on the Sabbath. This latter proof of Matthew is superior to the former one in three respects: first, that it infers from one case relating to the Shabbat to another one, also dealing with the Shabbat; second, that it places the Temple and Jesus on the same level thus, just as the Shabbat is pushed aside for purposes of the Temple service, so too is it pushed aside for the needs of Jesus; third, whereas the former proof justifies violation of the Shabbat only in order to save a life or in an emergency situation, the second homily presents a principled and sweeping permission.

Let us now turn to the figure of Doeg and to the surprising function that he plays in the following brief Talmudic story: "An incident involving Doeg son of Joseph, whose father [left him] as a small child to his mother. Every day his mother would weigh him on the scales and give his weight in gold to the Temple. When the enemies became stronger, she slaughtered him and ate him. And concerning this Jeremiah keened: *Should women eat their offspring, the children of their tender care?* [Lam. 2:20]. The Holy Spirit answered and said, *Should priest and prophet be slain in the Sanctuary of the Lord?* [Lam. 2:20]."[32]

As Avigdor Shinan has already shown, this little story is pregnant with meaning.[33] The name Doeg son of Joseph is an invention that has no basis in Scripture, where he is known simply as Doeg or Doeg the Edomite. According to the extant version, Doeg son of Joseph is the name of the son. His father died, leaving his mother alone to raise him. But according to the parallel version in *Lamentations Rabbah,* Doeg son of Joseph is the name of the father who died. Both versions portray the mother's intense love for her son and her great wealth. She would measure his weight every day and give that amount in gold to the Temple, presumably on the assumption that this would save her son's life. The midrash here makes a wordplay in Hebrew: the verse in Lamentations speaks of *'ollei tipuhim,* "lovingly reared children," but it sounds similar to *tefah,* the measure used by the mother to weigh the child as long as the Temple existed.

During the Roman War, the great wealth that existed prior to the Destruction of the Temple was transformed into terrible hunger and deprivation, and the loving mother literally consumed her own offspring's flesh. The author's homily is based on Lamentations 2:20: "Should women eat their offspring, the children of their tender care? Should priest and prophet be slain in the Sanctuary of the Lord?" According to the literal meaning of this verse, two complementary complaints are lodged against God: first, that mothers eat the flesh of their own children; second, that priest and prophet were murdered in the Temple. Our midrashic author transforms the two halves of the verse into a dialogue: "Should women eat their offspring, the children of their tender care?" is the complaint regarding the grave punishment, to which this explanation comes in response: "Should priest and prophet be slain in the Sanctuary of the Lord?" That is, the punishment came about because of the grave sin of murdering priest and prophet in the Temple. The version found in the Babylonian Talmud does not elaborate on the nature of this sin. Here we are helped by the version in *Lamentations Rabbah:* "[T]his refers to Zechariah son of Jehoiada." The grave punishment of the destruction of Temple and city, which led mothers to eat their beloved children, was precipitated by the murder of the prophet Zechariah ben Jehoyada. But the verse speaks not only of the murder of the prophet, but also of that of the priest. Hence Doeg is introduced into the story to allude to the murder of the priests of Nob.

Again there is a familiar echo from the New Testament, from Matthew 23:29–35. The Jews are presented there as murderers of prophets, whose measure of guilt is about to overflow, causing them to be punished for all the murders from the past, from that of the innocent Abel down to that of the prophet Zechariah. The connection between the destruction of the Temple and the murder of Zechariah is thus common to both Matthew and *Lamentations Rabbah.* Both texts allude to what is related in 2 Chronicles 24:21–22 concerning the murder of the prophet Zechariah ben Jehoyada at the behest of King Joash. At the time of his death the prophet said: "May the Lord see and avenge!" This demand for vengeance was realized: according to the midrash, in the destruction of the First Temple; and according to Matthew, in the destruction of the Second Temple. There may thus be a connection between this reading of the story of Zechariah and the declaration placed in the mouth of the Jews by Matthew 27:25: "His blood be on us and on our children!"

I will not analyze here the dramatic midrashic texts that depict in bold colors the boiling blood of Zechariah, who refused to rest or to be quiet until Nebuzaradan—the destroyer of Jerusalem—killed more than one million people, including many women and children, in punishment for the murder of the prophet Zechariah. I have argued elsewhere that these midrashim are to be read as a hidden polemic against Matthew.[34] Matthew claims that in the future the crime of the murder of Zechariah will be combined with that of the murder of Jesus and his believers until the cup will overflow and heavy punishment will come—the destruction of the

Second Temple. By contrast, the midrash asserts that this sin was already atoned for by the Destruction of the First Temple and that the blood of Zechariah had already rested. A similar motif appears in the midrash concerning Doeg son of Joseph. Doeg dies at his mother's hand, atoning by his death for the murder of Zechariah. The name "son of Joseph" as well as the removal of the father from the story (according to one version) bring the figure of Doeg closer to that of Jesus, albeit with an opposite tendency: the death of the son is presented as a punishment that atones for the murder of the prophets.

Let us now turn to another image of Doeg, that in the Jerusalem Talmud, *Sanhedrin* 10.1 [29a]: "Doeg was a great Torah scholar. Israel came and asked David: Does the shewbread override the Shabbat? He said to them: Its arrangement overrides the Shabbat, but its kneading and its shaping do not override the Shabbat. Doeg was there and he said: Who is this that rules on halakhic matters in my presence? They told him: David son of Jesse. Immediately he went and took counsel with Saul king of Israel to kill Nob the city of priests. Of this it is written: *And the king said to the guard who stood about him, 'Turn and kill the priests of the Lord because their hand is also with David'* [1 Sam. 22:17]."

This story seeks to answer a simple question: Why did Doeg betray the priests of Nob into the vengeful hands of Saul? The answer given is derived directly from the mental world of the Sages, who transform King David and Doeg into two sages debating with one another over halakhic matters. Even though Doeg is the greater of the two, the people turn specifically to David with their halakhic question, thereby hurting Doeg's pride, who takes vengeance on them by denouncing them to Saul.

The question they asked David was: "Does the shewbread override the Shabbat?" This is a very strange question. From whence did the Rabbis get the idea of connecting the preparation of the shewbread in the Temple with the biblical story of David and the eating of the shewbread? In the biblical narrative, the halakhic difficulty regarding the eating of shewbread arises only in the context of ritual purity, not in connection with laws of Shabbat. And why should they ask specifically whether the shewbread overrides Shabbat? Do not all aspects of the Temple ritual override the Shabbat?

Interestingly, the only one to draw a connection between the permission to eat shewbread and the permission to override the Shabbat in the Temple is Matthew! True, in Matthew as well one is dealing with two separate responses, but it is he who, by presenting Jesus' two homilies in conjunction with one another, draws a connection between the eating of the shewbread and the overriding of the Shabbat. It therefore seems quite likely that the author of this passage in the Yerushalmi, who formulated this question, had this passage in Matthew in mind.

The Gospel of Matthew was known among Jews, whether in its Aramaic or Hebrew version, as may be seen from a quotation from it cited in the *Bavli*[35] as well as from the testimony of Epiphanius of Salamis in his *Panarion* (*Adversus Judaeus*).[36] The Jerusalem Talmud ascribes to David the opinion that the kneading of the shewbread does not override the Shabbat, from which one may infer that the plucking of grain is also forbidden—things that seem like polemics against Jesus, whose opinion coincides with that of David. The Yerushalmi does not state Doeg's position, but if we continue the train of thought that Doeg is a metonym for Jesus, it is clear that he permitted the plucking of corn on the Sabbath for purposes of the Temple service,[37] which would coincide with Jesus' position. Perhaps it is for this reason that he is called Doeg *son of Joseph.*

There is yet another expression of this surprising connection between eating the shewbread and the Shabbat. The late midrashic collection *Yalqut Shim'oni* contains a midrash that describes, in connection with the above biblical story, the dialogue between David and Ahimelech regarding the shewbread. David attempts to convince Ahimelech that his youths are pure and hence permitted to eat the bread. Suddenly the discussion changes direction: "And it was the Sabbath. And David saw that they were baking the shewbread on Shabbat, as Doeg had instructed them. He said to them: What are you doing? Its baking does not overrule the Shabbat, but only its arrangement, as is said, *on the Sabbath day they shall set it* [Lev. 24:8]. Since he found nothing there but the shewbread, David said to him: Give it to me, that we not die of starvation, for a doubt of saving life overrides the Shabbat."[38]

After David had convinced Ahimelech that his youths were pure, there was seemingly no obstacle to their partaking of the bread. The midrash nevertheless creates a halakhically problematic situation in which David is confronted with a new difficulty: it is Shabbat, and according to David it is forbidden to bake the shewbread on Shabbat. How then can he eat bread that has been prepared in a forbidden manner? The midrash's solution is simple: it is a matter of saving life. David wishes to benefit from the Shabbat desecration so as not to die of starvation. This transformation of the halakhic dilemma from the prohibition against eating the shewbread by impure people to the question of whether saving a life overrides the Shabbat completely overlaps Jesus' teaching in the gospels, according to which he allowed his hungry disciples to violate the Shabbat. In the midrash this role is played by David, who relaxes the Shabbat prohibitions only in order to save life, whereas Doeg is represented as permitting the desecration of Shabbat.[39]

The possibility that the figure of Doeg is a concealed allusion to Jesus sheds light on another aspect of his inclusion in the mishnah in *Sanhedrin* among those who have no portion in the World to Come. It also explains why, according to another midrash, Doeg was thirty-four years old at the time of his death, an age very close to that of Jesus at his death.[40]

Why was Doeg specifically chosen to represent the archetypal figure of Jesus? There are several possible reasons. First, because Doeg was the enemy of David, from whose seed the Messiah was to spring. The tension between the two was already noted by the author of Psalm 52, which opens with the words "For the Choirmaster, a psalm of David," in which Doeg is presented as a liar who received his punishment. This tendency also finds expression in Pseudo-Philo, who likewise speaks of Doeg's punishment: "For days are coming, when a fiery worm will come on his tongue and make it melt," a description alluding to the eschatological punishment of the evildoers: "For their worm shall not die, their fire shall not be quenched" (Isa. 66:24).[41] The Sages' position, according to which Doeg has no portion in the World to Come, continues this tendency.

It would also seem that his name, Doeg *the Edomite,* further strengthened his negative image, as the Sages used Edom as a synonym for Rome and subsequently for Christianity. According to one midrash, his designation *ha-Edomi* expressed his jealousy of David, who was known as *admoni,* "the red one."[42] Other midrashim draw a connection between *edomi* and *dam,* "blood," as he was held accountable for spilling the blood of the priests or of David. Yet other midrashim draw a connection between *edomi* and *adom,* "red": "for he reddened the faces of all in halakhah," that is, he embarrassed them.[43] A similar claim is articulated against Jesus in the work *Toldot Yeshu*.[44]

There may be another explanation for the connection between Doeg and Jesus, and the Gospel of Matthew may again prove helpful. The biblical Doeg was the first one to destroy the priestly city and temple. This was, as will be remembered, precisely the accusation placed in the Matthean Jesus' mouth: that the destruction of Jerusalem was punishment for the murder of the prophets including his own crucifixion (Matt. 23:37–24:2). This accusation may have elicited the desire of the Rabbis to invent a typological forebear of Jesus in the form of one who destroyed sanctuaries and murdered priests, whom they then adorned with several other qualities reminiscent of Jesus.

In this context, it is worth examining another midrash: "Slay them not, lest my people forget; make them totter by your power and bring them down, O Lord, our shield (Ps. 59:12). The Rabbis explained this verse as referring to Doeg and Ahithophel. David said: 'Slay not' Doeg or Ahithophel, 'lest' the following generations 'forget.' 'Make them totter' [i.e., go about from place to place] 'and bring them down'—bring them down from their greatness."[45]

Is this an attempt to take Augustine's well-known exposition of this verse, originally applied to the Jews,[46] and to turn it around to apply to Christians or to figures symbolically equivalent to Christians? *Bereshit Rabbah* is contemporary with Augustine, and we seem to have returned to our original point of departure: the inability to determine in a definitive way whether what we have here is analogy or genealogy. Here, too, the particular scholar's *a priori* viewpoint and the question of historical likelihood are decisive. It seems likely that, in light of the growing strength of Christianity and of the challenge and threat it presented to the continued existence of a distinctive Jewish identity, we have before us a defensive Jewish response which prefers to conceal the alternative with which it is engaged in dispute.

Competing Kisses: Esau and Judas

I wish to point out the advantage of the comparative, "parallelomania" approach by means of one additional example. To do so, I will turn to one of the most dramatic scenes in the book of Genesis, namely that which concludes the story of Jacob and Esau. The biblical narrative describes the moving scene of the reunion of the two brothers following decades of separation and relations charged with mutual hatred and jealousy. Returning from Aram, Jacob is received by Esau at the head of a military brigade of four hundred men. The tension reaches its height just before the meeting—and then the text relates that Esau ran to meet Jacob "and embraced him, and fell on his neck and kissed him, and they wept" (Gen. 33:4). This is a moving moment by any account. It is difficult not to feel great affection and admiration for Esau.

But this is not how the Sages saw it. In the Masoretic text the word *vayishaqehu* ("and he kissed him") is marked with dots above each letter. In medieval manuscripts, such dots were used to indicate erasure. Esau's kiss of Jacob was seen by the Sages as something unsuitable, inappropriate, and therefore to be expunged. The midrashic explanation of these dots is as follows: "The entire word *vayishakehu* is marked with superscript dots, to indicate that he did not come to kiss him, but to bite him [a wordplay in Hebrew: נשק/נשך]. But Jacob's neck became like marble, and the teeth of that evil one [Esau] were blunted and melted like wax. And why does the text say, *and they wept* [that is, if they did not kiss, why did they weep]? This one wept for his neck, and that one wept for his teeth" (*Cant. Rab.* 7:1). A similar reading appears in *Midrash Proverbs* 26: "There is a dot on *vayishaqehu* to teach that this was not a true kiss of love, but of hatred." Thus the Rabbis changed Esau's kiss of brotherly love to one of deceit. This picture was taken from the Midrash into the traditional biblical commentaries beginning with Rashi, and there is no Jewish child educated in the traditional manner who does not know that Esau's kiss was really one of hatred.

How might we account for this interpretation? The simple explanation is that Jacob was the father of the Jewish people, while Esau was a metonymic figure for Rome and subsequently for Christendom, and the Rabbis did not like this closeness between the two brothers. But it is difficult not to hear an echo of another kiss here as well, equally famous and well known—namely, the kiss of Judas. Already in late antique Christianity, Judas Escariot's kiss of Jesus became an event that exemplified the perfidy of the Jews,[47] while in the Middle Ages it became a widely represented scene in painting, sculpture, and manuscript illumination. The midrash's response was to portray the kiss of Esau, the archetypal father of Christendom, as a kiss of hatred, deceit, and hypocrisy. In opposition to the "Jew" Judas who kissed Jesus, the "Christian" Esau was presented kissing Jacob. The mockery implied in the midrash about Esau's weeping, "that one wept for his teeth," fits well with the previous image, "and he blunted the teeth of that evildoer." The blunting of teeth appears several times in the midrashic literature in the context of a decisive answer to the Christian. Particularly well known is the use of this expression in the Passover haggadah, where it serves as the answer ("and you shall blunt his teeth") to the wicked son who "removes himself from the collectivity and denied the basic principle"—presumably, one suspected of closeness to Christianity.

Conclusion

Do these two examples prove the existence of a hidden polemic against Christianity? Skeptics will continue to answer in the negative. And indeed, there is no proof in the text that Esau's treacherous kiss was a response to Judas' kiss in the gospel accounts of the New Testament. But such a possibility exists, and it passes the test of plausibility. In my opinion, this is sufficient reason to seriously consider the theory of a hidden polemic. The argument of the parallelophobes against the parallelomaniacs is that one does not need the Christian context in order to understand the Jewish sources. My response is that the Christian context gives them a deeper historical significance. The parallelomaniac grabs hold of historical plausibility in order to argue that only by means of it does the full meaning of the text become evident, while the parallelophobe argues that historical plausibility is "recruited" for this purpose—or, to quote Goshen-Gottstein, "One who comes equipped with polemical eyeglasses will find polemics wherever he seeks it."[48]

And indeed, at times it appears that the debate between the parallelomaniacs and the parallelophobes concerns the scope of the historical method. The parallelomaniacs' first priority is to consider what is historically plausible and only then to apply the literary method, whereas the parallelophobes tend to focus first on the textual reading and only later to draw the historical conclusions. In rare cases they are so cautious that they avoid the historical perspective altogether. For example, Morton Smith concluded his 1945 philological dissertation, "Parallels between the Gospels and Tannaitic literature" (written in Hebrew), with the following extraordinary sentence: "I think that these places suffice to demonstrate that, in the Gospels, Jesus appears a number of times in the same position where, in tannaitic literature, God or the Torah appears. This is *the fact,* from which one may easily come to think that, in the *thoughts* of the Gospel authors, Jesus occupied the same place as that occupied by God or Torah in the *thoughts* of the tannaitic authors. But were we to say that, we would again be entering into the realm of historical doubt, because to move from similarity of words to similarity in ideas means: to move from the known world to a world *that cannot be known.*"[49]

Immediately after these words appears the phrase, "The End." Thus concludes a philological work by an outstanding scholar, at the beginning of his career, who deliberately refrained from deriving any conclusions pertaining to the history of ideas from the philological facts. In his eyes, history is a collection of "doubts," belonging to "a world that cannot be known."

A certain reservation concerning the predominance of the historical method has been recently raised by Moshe Idel. In his essay entitled, "The Ascent and Decline of the Historical Jew," Idel writes: "Historians are capable of creating myths no less than any Kabbalist or preacher. . . . Heinrich Graetz invented a meeting between Abraham Abulafia and the pope, and even knew exactly what Abulafia said to his interlocutor! Closer to our time, other historians have invented a wonderful new myth, whose slogan serves as the title of a new book: *The Ways that Never Parted.* This myth seeks to create the impression that over the course of centuries mutual relations between Judaism and Christianity existed continually."[50]

Idel's position is based on his intuition that the routine of religious life fulfills a more important function than great historical expectations. He therefore downplays the centrality of the ideas of exile and redemption as a formative feature in Jewish religious consciousness: "Most human beings live within what is called history. . . . They are far less troubled by historical exile and redemption in some distant age at the end of the world many centuries after their own death. For such people, the concrete reality of a great bodily or spiritual experience is far greater than the influence of external changes, political subjugation, or national catastrophe."[51] In Idel's eyes, Baer and Scholem greatly exaggerated in positing exile and redemption as a formative force with a fixed and central presence in Jewish religious consciousness. By doing so, Baer and Scholem, like Buber and Baron, created the construct that Idel dubs "the historical Jew"—that is to say, one who sees in history and historical consciousness a unifying reality that creates Jewish identity.

In light of Idel's words concerning the marginality of the Jewish-Christian encounter during the first centuries CE, it is no surprise that he conducts his discussion of the centrality or marginality of the experience of exile in Jewish religious consciousness without mentioning Christianity at all. Yet it is clear that the exile burned into the consciousness a sense of religious inferiority vis-à-vis the rival religion to such a degree that confrontation with the option of redemption did not merely pertain to an event that was to occur "in some distant age at the end of the world" many centuries in the future, but rather fulfilled a vital apologetic function in the everyday encounter—in the street, in the courtyard, in the marketplace—in the Christian "other." The alternative that Christianity offered to the Jewish exile dealt a fatal blow to Jewish self-consciousness such that, rather than seeing itself as a congregation chosen and beloved by God, it was seen as rejected, expelled, and accursed. The initial assumptions thus determined the consequences. When one excludes Christianity *ab initio* from discussion of the role of exile and redemption in Jewish consciousness, it should not be surprising that the points of contact between the religions appear like "myths" and an invention of historians.

And indeed, "the historical Jew" is in a state of decline. The comparative moves made by Scholem, Baer, Baron, and many others have multiplied greatly over the last two decades in the works of—among others—Idel himself. And indeed, comparative historical criticism has not revealed the inner face of and the hidden forces within Jewish history as Baer and Scholem had hoped, but rather its eclecticism, its flexibility, its ability to absorb external ideas and to map various options of acculturation. From the high priests of the tribe appointed over its innermost secrets, the historians have became "double agents" acting in the general service of the broad culture.

Their narrative has ceased to be tribal and internal and has been persistent in portraying a fluid Judaism—albeit one that constantly requires a redefinition of its identity in light of its lack of distinct boundaries.

In my opinion, this is the reason for the decline in the status of history as a defining factor in Jewish cultural experience. It derives from the difficulty in accepting a polyphonic and complex cultural narrative. As long as historians provided the fodder for shaping a national collective identity, they were beloved and accepted. But during the last generation history has undergone a process of privatization and no longer serves the general public consciousness. It tends rather to break down and threaten the collective identity, and it is gradually being replaced by inner phenomenological reflections that emphasize the literary, religious, and philosophical significance of the sources.

In a fine chapter on the place of comparison within the study of religions, Jonathan Smith writes: "Comparison does not necessarily tell us how things are. Comparison tells us how things might be conceived."[52] Those of us afflicted with parallelomania may easily identify with these words. The parallelophobic approach views culture as a closed entity that develops specifically under circumstances of separation and isolation from neighboring cultures. But cultural identities never develop wholly internally, but through a dialogical process in which one culture consciously separates itself from another culture to which it is sufficiently close. This is a dynamic process in which there is no rest for even a moment and in which, to return to the formula of Fredrik Barth, ethnic identities do not develop in a situation of lack of mobility, communication, and information concerning their environs, but specifically through ongoing processes of rejection and absorption. Polemics and dialogue are thus intrinsically interwoven.

Notes

1. A similar formulation can be found in Col. 3:11: "Here there cannot be Greek and Jew, circumcised and uncircumcised, barbarian, Scythian, slave, free man, but Christ is all, and in all."

2. *Babylonian Talmud Menahot* 43b–44a.

3. *Tossefta Berakhot* 6.18 (Saul Lieberman edition, New York 1955, p. 38).

4. David Kaufmann, "Das Alter der drei Benedictionen von Israel, vom Freien und von Mann," *Monatsschrift für Geschichte und Wissenschaft des Judentums* 37 (1892): 14–18.

5. Plutarch, *Parallel Lives: The Life of Marius*, 46; Lactantius attributes a similar version of this statement to Plato: Lactantius, *Divine Institutes*, 3.19.17.

6. Diogenes Laertius, *The Lives and Opinions of Eminent Philosophers: Life of Thales*, 7.

7. This question has been discussed considerably in recent literature, including: Yoel H. Kahn, "The Three Morning Blessings 'Who did not Make Me': A Historical Study of a Jewish Liturgical Text," Ph.D. diss., University of Michigan, Ann Arbor, 1999; Joseph Tabory, *Kenishta: Studies in the Synagogue World* (Ramat Gan: Bar-Ilan University Press, 2001), 107–38 ("The Benedictions of Self-Identity and the Changing Status of Women and of Orthodoxy"); and Dalia Sara Marx, "The Early Morning Ritual in Jewish Liturgy: Textual, Historical, and Theological Discussion in *Birkhot Hashakhar* (the Morning Blessings) and an Examination of Their Performative Aspects" [Hebrew], Ph.D. diss., Hebrew University of Jerusalem, 2005, 111–25, 144–48.

8. Marx, "The Early Morning Ritual," 111–16.

9. *Mishnah Avot* 2.5.

10. *Babylonian Talmud Menahot* 43b–44a.

11. Tabory, *Kenishta*, n. 26, discusses the possibility of such Jewish confrontation with Paul, but rejects it as "unlikely," his claim being that "Christianity was not a major concern of the Jews in Babylon and there is very little reaction to Christianity, if any, to be found in this Talmud." He thereby enters into a circular argument, in which claim and proofs are used indiscriminately, without distinguishing between cause and effect. The "assumption" that the [Babylonian] Talmud relates to Christianity is rejected out of hand as unlikely on the basis of the "fact" that it does not relate to Christianity. One need not add that this statement is incorrect.

12. *Seder Zera'im*, Pt. I (New York: Jewish Theological Seminary of America, 1955), 119–21.

13. A typical representative of this viewpoint is Ismar Elbogen, *Jewish Liturgy: A Comprehensive History* (New York: Jewish Theological Seminary of America, 1993), 78. He writes there that a further "parallel" to these blessings appears in the Persian prayer to Ormuzd, "Who created the worshippers as Iranian and members of a good religion, as free men and not slaves, as men and not women." He also sees Paul's words as "parallel" and, after providing a parallel presentation of the Jewish source opposite the Christian one, adds that the parallel derives from the fact that Paul's statement "comes from a Jewish source," though he provides no reference or proof of this claim. The assumption that we have here a parallel is also accepted by Naphtali Wieder, *The Formation of Jewish Liturgy in the East and the West* [Hebrew] (Jerusalem: Mekhon Ben-Tsevi le-heker kehilot Yisrael ba-Mizrah,

Yad Yitshak Ben-Tsevi, and Hebrew University of Jerusalem, 1998), 199–218. Dalia Marx also followed this path ("The Early Morning Ritual," 144–48). Her point of departure is that "it is not necessary to prove a shared common genetic source" among the various Jewish, Greek and Christian blessings—that is, it is possible to speak of influence through necessity alone.

14. On the fear of cultural influence as a widespread phenomenon, see Harold Bloom, *The Anxiety of Influence: A Theory of Poetry* (New York: Oxford University Press, 1973).

15. This criticism appeared in the original version of Urbach's introduction to his edition of *Sefer Arugat ha-Bosem* (Jerusalem: Mekize Nirdamim, 1939), 12–13, n. 1, but was deleted from subsequent editions. See Yaacov Sussmann, "The Scholarly Oeuvre of Professor Ephraim Elimelech Urbach" [Hebrew], in *Ephraim E. Urbach: A Bibliography*, Supplement to *Jewish Studies* 1 (1993): 29–30, 60–61, 118. See also Oded Irshai, "Ephraim E. Urbach and the Study of Judeo-Christian Dialogue in Late Antiquity: Some Preliminary Observations," in *How Should Rabbinic Literature Be Read in the Modern World?* ed. Matthew Kraus (Piscataway, NJ: Gorgias Press, 2006), 173–76, 188–97. At a later date, and in the wake of the Holocaust, Baer retreated from his willingness to admit the great influence of Christianity upon Judaism (see below, n. 18).

16. J. F. Baer, "The Religious-Social Tendency of *Sepher Hassidim*" [Hebrew], in *Zion* 3 (1937–38): 1–50. For an abridged English translation, see "The Socio-Religious Orientation of *Sefer Hasidim*" in *Binah: Jewish Civilization University Series,* ed. Joseph Dan (Jerusalem: International Center for University Teaching of Jewish Civilization, Everyman's University, Israel, 1985).

17. Jonathan Smith, *Drudgery Divine: On the Comparison of Early Christianities and the Religions of Late Antiquity* (Chicago: University of Chicago Press, 1990), 47–50.

18. Israel Yuval, "Yitzhak Baer and the Search for Authentic Judaism," in *The Jewish Past Revisited: Reflections on Modern Jewish Historians,* ed. David N. Myers and David B. Ruderman (New Haven, CT: Yale University Press, 1998), 77–87, here 81.

19. Here one should quote the words of Yaakov Sussman: "And in truth, it would seem the spiritual world of the Sages needs to be examined against the background of their natural milieu environs, the culture of the East, [rather] than against the background of Western culture, and not only in Persian Babylonia but also in Palestine. . . . Seeing the world of the Sages in terms of Western (Greco-Roman) culture has been accepted by modern scholarship at least since the beginning of the nineteenth century, coupled with almost completely ignoring the natural Oriental surrounding in which they lived and were active" (Yaakov Sussmann, "Torah shebealpe" [Hebrew], in *Mehqerei Talmud: Talmudic Studies Dedicated to the Memory of Prof. Ephraim E. Urbach* [Hebrew], ed. Y. Sussman and D. Rosenthal [Jerusalem: Magnes Press, 2005], 209–384, here 351 n. 93).

20. Oded Irshai, "Ephraim E. Urbach," esp. 178–80.

21. According to Neusner, the Sages responded to Christianity only from the beginning of the fourth century CE; see Jacob Neusner, *Judaism and Christianity in the Age of Constantine: History, Messiah, Israel, and the Initial Confrontation* (Chicago: University of Chicago Press, 1987). A similar view is held by Marc Hirshman, *A Rivalry of Genius: Jewish and Christian Biblical Interpretation in Late Antiquity* (Albany: State University of New York Press, 1996), 16. Martin Goodman asserts that the Sages did not display interest in pagan religions in general and in Gentile Christianity in particular. Thus, even such an event as the christianization of the Roman Empire was not of interest to the Sages. See Martin Goodman, "Palestinian Rabbis and the Conversion of Constantine to Christianity," in *The Talmud Yerushalmi and Graeco-Roman Culture,* ed. Peter Schäfer and Catherine Hezser (Tübingen: Mohr Siebeck, 2000), 1–9. Keith Hopkins (in "Christian Number and Its Implications," *Journal of Early Christian Studies* 6 [1998]: 185–226, esp. 216) maintains that according to the conventional figures, by which the total number of Christians prior to 175 CE was three percent of the overall Jewish population of the Roman Empire (i.e., 100,000 Christians out of a total of 3 million Jews), one may conclude that the majority of the Jews remained faithful to their religion, and Christianity remained a marginal phenomena in the eyes of the Jews. Hopkins thinks that until the year 300 CE the Jewish apathy toward Christianity did not change, based upon the absence of explicit references to Christianity in rabbinic literature. By this, he abandons the numerical basis that guides him throughout his study and returns to impressions based on literary silence. But this silence continued also after 300 CE, when the number of Christians in the empire grew steeply, from 6 million in 300 CE to 30 million in 350 CE—half the total population of the Roman Empire. Thus, we cannot learn anything from the quantitative data regarding religion and cultural competition.

22. Alon Goshen-Gottstein, "Polemomania: Methodological Reflections on the Study of the Judeo-Christian Controversy between the Talmudic Sages and Origen over the Interpretation of the Song of Songs" [Hebrew], *Jewish Studies* 42 (2003–4): 119–90. In a similar manner, Adiel Schremer sought to diminish the weight of the dispute with Christianity and to emphasize the confrontation with the pagan Roman empire; see Adiel Schremer, "Midrash and History: God's Power, the Roman Empire, and Hopes for Redemption in Tannaitic Literature" [Hebrew], *Zion* 72 (2006–7): 5–36. Menahem Kister recently presented as a "test case" the rabbinic exegesis of *tohu va-vohu* ("without form and void," Gen. 1:2) compared with the Christian exegesis of the same verse and concluded that, at least in this case, one may not speak of mutual influence, but rather only of "a shared tradition" whose source underlies the Jewish literature of the Second Temple period. See Menahem Kister, "*Tohu wa-Bohu:* Primordial Elements and *Creatio ex Nihilo,*" *Jewish Studies Quar-*

terly 14 (2007): 229–56. It is clear that not every similarity between the Sages and the Church fathers indicates direct influence. The question under consideration pertains to the basic assumptions of the researcher, whether in the absence of an unequivocal proof one way or another his own inclinations draw him toward the comparative-dialogical interpretation or more toward a "joint tradition" having inner authenticity.

23. Samuel Sandmel, "Parallelomania," *Journal of Biblical Literature* 81 (1962): 1–13.

24. James C. Scott, *Domination and the Arts of Resistance* (New Haven, CT: Yale University Press, 1990).

25. Fredrik Barth, *Ethnic Groups and Boundaries: The Social Organization of Culture Difference* (Boston: Little Brown, 1987).

26. Yizhar Hirschfeld, *Excavations at Tiberias, 1989–1994* (Jerusalem: Israel Antiquities Authority, 2004), 220: "The church on the mountaintop symbolized the triumph of Christianity, since the structure was visible from the entire area around the Sea of Galilee."

27. Published by the Israel Antiquities Authority (www.antiquities.org.il) on August 7, 2007. I thank my friend Professor Ze'ev Weiss for this reference.

28. Karl Popper, *Conjectures and Refutations* (London: Routledge and Kegan Paul, 1963), 33–39.

29. Israel J. Yuval, "All Israel Have a Portion in the World to Come," in *Redefining First-Century Jewish and Christian Identities: Essays in Honor of Ed Parish Sanders,* ed. Fabian E. Udoh, Susannah Heschel, Mark A. Chancey, and Gregory Tatum (Notre Dame, IN: University of Notre Dame Press, 2008), 114–38.

30. 1 Sam. 22.

31. Menahem Kister, "Plucking on the Sabbath and Christian-Jewish Polemic," *Immanuel* 24 (1990): 35–51; originally published in Hebrew as: "Plucking of Grain on the Sabbath and the Jewish-Christian Debate," *Jerusalem Studies in Jewish Thought* 3:3 (1983–84), 349–66.

32. *Babylonian Talmud Yoma* 38b; for a similar version, see *Lamentations Rabba* 1.

33. Avigdor Shinan, "The Unfolding of a Rabbinic Legend: The Story of Doeg ben Yosef's Son" [Hebrew], *Mahanayim* 7 (1994): 70–75.

34. Israel J. Yuval, "God Will See the Blood: Sin, Punishment, and Atonement in the Jewish-Christian Discourse," in *Jewish Blood: Reality and Metaphor in History, Religion, and Culture,* ed. Mitchell B. Hart (London: Routledge, 2009), 83–98.

35. *Babylonian Talmud Shabbat* 116a–b.

36. See *The Panarion of Epiphanius of Salamis,* Bk. I, sect. 2, no. 10, 3.7–3.8.

37. R. Travers Herford, in his *Christianity in Talmud and Midrash* (New York: Ktav, 1903), 71, presents the theory that Doeg was identified specifically with Judas

Escariot, who betrayed Jesus. However, he admits that this identification raises great difficulty, as one might have expected the Sages to identify Judas with a sympathetic character rather than with a negative one such as Doeg.

38. *Yalqut Shim 'oni*, §131.

39. *Babylonian Talmud Yebamot* 7a.

40. *Babylonian Talmud Sanhedrin* 106b.

41. Yair Zakovitch, *David: From Shepherd to Messiah* [Hebrew] (Jerusalem: Yad Ben-Zvi, 1995), 155–56.

42. *Midrash Tehillim (Shoher Tov)* §52; *Yalqut Shim'oni*, §131.

43. *Midrash Tehillim (Shoher Tov)* §52; *Yalqut Shim'oni*, §131.

44. Samuel Kraus, *Das Leben Jesu nach jüdischen Quellen* (Berlin, 1902), 66.

45. *Genesis Rabba* 38.11.

46. See Augustine, *Expositiones in Psalmos*, 59:12; *De civitate Dei* 18.46. See Jeremy Cohen, *Living Letters of the Law: Ideas of the Jew in Medieval Christianity* (Berkeley: University of California Press, 1999), 33.

47. An explicit identification between Judas Iscariot and the Jews generally may already be found in the fourth century in, for example, the writings of St. Jerome and of John Chrysostom. See *The Homilies of Saint Jerome*, vol. 1: *On the Psalms*, trans. Roy J. Deferrari, Hermigild Dressler, et al. (Washington, DC: Catholic University of America Press, 1981), 255–59; John Chrysostom, *In proditione Judae homiliae 1–2* (PG 49.373–92). Chaim Maccoby, *Judas Iscariot and the Myth of Jewish Evil* (New York: Free Press, 1992), 81, 101, claims that the discerning reader will already find clear hints of this in the New Testament itself.

48. Goshen-Gottstein, "Polemomania," 188.

49. Morton Smith, "Parallels between the Gospels and the Tannaitic Literature," Ph.D. diss., Hebrew University of Jerusalem, 1945, 159 (emphases mine).

50. Moshe Idel, "The Ascent and Decline of the Historical Jew" [Hebrew], in *The Past and Beyond: Studies in History and Philosophy Presented to Elazar Weinryb*, ed. Amir Horowitz, Ram Ben-Shalom, Ora Limor, and Avriel Bar-Levav (Tel Aviv: Open University of Israel Press, 2006), 171–207, here 205.

51. Idel, "The Ascent and Decline," 194–95.

52. Smith, *Drudgery Divine*, 52.

CHAPTER FOUR

The Psalms at the Abbey of Saint-Victor

From the Novices' schola *to the Heights of* contemplatio

Grover A. Zinn

From the time of the Second Temple the psalms have provided the Jewish and Christian traditions with a rich source of liturgical poetry as well as a wellspring of texts ranging in subject from personal and community laments to high praise of the Holy One to verses of joyful celebration.[1] Whether in the Jerusalem Temple or later in the synagogues of the diaspora, psalms found their place in the liturgy as well as in the personal religious lives of Jewish leaders and people alike. The rabbinic tradition, writers on mysticism, and other Jewish interpreters of the psalms have understood them as having complex levels of meaning that continue to nourish life in the many varieties of Judaism. For Christianity, born within the matrix of Judaism in the first century CE, the psalms have also provided a rich and multifaceted resource for public worship, scholarly commentary, and private devotion. The monastic cycle of the liturgical Hours, medieval mystical treatises, the psalmody of Calvinist churches, and centuries of psalms commentary manifest the diverse presence and wide influence of the psalms in Christianity. Judaism and Christianity hardly agree on the ways in which the psalms are to be used and interpreted in the context of worship, in the historical memory of groups of believers, and in religious ideas derived from long meditation and scholarly reflection on these gems of spiritual insight. One need only participate as a Christian in a Yom Kippur service to discern the profound, and profoundly different, climate of significance and communal memory for the psalms in Judaism as distinct from Christianity. Nevertheless, the psalms have a vital and sustained place in both of the religious traditions that share these ancient texts.

This essay is written in deep consciousness of and gratitude for what this author owes to the honoree of this Festschrift, Michael Signer. Michael and I shared many moments of enlightenment (as well as times of temporary perplexity) as we pursued a long and vigorous conversation about texts and traditions with a continual deepening of scholarly and spiritual insight. In the end, Michael and I remained and affirmed what we were: members of two different religious traditions living somewhere in that Augustinian interface between a material world/body and a spiritual realm of which a person may have only brief glimpses and intimations at best. As individuals, each of us exists in a space-time continuum through which the experiences of life flow. What we offer to each other in the midst of this ever-changing river of life is insight born from specific instances and individual lives—insight that takes form like flying sparks or flickering flames that intimate those deeper truths that draw us onward, deeper, and closer together and closer to the Holy One, Blessed be His Name. The psalms embody in their verses multiple expressive modes, employing the languages of worship, praise, humiliation, anxiety, joy, despair, and other diverse emotions that make them a magnificent mirror in which to view the range of what it means to be human—in relation to others and in relation to that which transcends otherness.

This essay proposes to examine select uses of the psalms in twelfth-century France at the Abbey of Saint-Victor, located on the left bank of Seine River at Paris and home to the Victorine exegetes whom Michael so closely studied.[2] Founded by William of Champeaux in 1108 when he left his position as archdeacon and master of the cathedral school of Notre-Dame in Paris, the Abbey of Saint-Victor quickly became a center for distinctive forms of biblical interpretation, path-breaking theological reflection, creative liturgical development, and a brilliant and widely influential spiritual/ascetic/contemplative tradition.[3]

The uses of the psalms in the liturgy and in Victorine commentaries are beyond the scope of this essay, except as the liturgy and biblical commentaries intersect with other activities and writings involving use of the psalms. From the standpoint of the daily liturgy involving the Office and celebration of Mass, psalms were chanted communally by the canons in a regular repetitive cycle. Thus these texts became deeply engraved in their consciousness and provided both a vocabulary for reflection and a field of ready reference points for individual and group recollection. Significant works of psalms commentary were written by Victorines or by persons influenced by Victorine exegetical practices. Hugh of Saint-Victor's comments on the psalms, gathered in Book Two of his *Miscellanea*,[4] are unfortunately fragmentary and remain relatively unstudied. In striking contrast to his surviving *Notulae* on the Pentateuch, which are concerned with the literal or historical sense, the surviving bits of Hugh's psalms commentary focus not on the grammatical or historical sense of the text but rather on a tropological interpretation or in some cases a theological *divisio*. In addition, Hugh's exploration of the topic of "the Four Daughters of God" indicates a probable use of Jewish sources, as Rebecca Moore has indicated.[5] Richard of Saint-Victor's contribution to psalms commentary is found in a series of "mystical annotations" on selected psalms.[6] Directed toward allegorical and tropological interpretations, these also are relatively unstudied and deserve more attention.

In light of Hugh's use of a psalm verse to provide a topical "outline" for his treatise *De institutione novitiorum* (to be explored below), it is of more than passing interest that Richard also used a psalm as a vehicle for instructing novices. In Richard's case, Psalm 28 provided a vehicle for tropological interpretation and thus moral instruction for novices.[7] Richard's commentary on this psalm often circulated as an independent text, apart from the larger collection of his mystical commentary on selected psalms.[8] Finally, the psalms commentary of Herbert of Bosham (an intellectual disciple of Andrew of Saint-Victor, theological instructor and advisor to Thomas Becket after his consecration as archbishop of Canterbury, and "editor" of Peter Lombard's vastly influential commentary on the psalms) manifests Victorine influence and an almost unique mindset as he explores the "literal" sense of psalms and the messianic-christological meaning (or lack thereof) in psalms with potentially divergent Jewish and Christian interpretations.[9]

Psalms in the Refectory

The first location in the abbey for examining the presence of psalms in the daily life of the canons of Saint-Victor, apart from the church with its daily round of abundant psalmody in the canonical Hours and Mass, is the refectory. As the canons gathered daily in the refectory for food, they ate in silence (like their Benedictine and Cistercian counterparts) while the *lector* read aloud for the canons' edification. He read from texts that were specified in a yearly cycle of readings listed in chapter 48 of the *Liber ordinis* of the community.[10] Occasionally, the *Liber ordinis* gives only general instructions for the reading, such as suggesting that "expositions of the gospels and letters and sermons" appropriate for the liturgical season be read.[11] In general, however, the readings were specified and drawn from the biblical text or writings—usually biblical commentaries or sermons—of major patristic authors. Three of the great authorial figures of ancient and early medieval Christianity dominate the list of readings: Origen, Augustine, and Gregory the Great. Readings included: Origen's sermons on Isaiah, homilies on the Old Testament, and homilies on the Books of Kings; Augustine's *Expositions on the Psalms*, commentary on the Epistle of John, and commentary on the letters of Paul; and Gregory's *Moralia in Iob*.[12] An anonymous exposition on Ezekiel may refer to Gregory's sermons on that book.

Of the specified readings only one addresses the psalms directly, namely Augustine's *Expositions on the Psalms*. Augustine's expositions were assigned to a time period of variable length, whereas the other readings were assigned to fixed periods (e.g., Gregory's *Moralia* was to be read from the kalends of August to the kalends of September). Augustine's *Expositions on the Psalms* were read by the refectory *lector* from the octave of Epiphany until Septuagesima. The length of this liturgical period varied from year to year, depending on how early or late the date of Easter fell. The earliest Septuagesima can occur is January 18; the latest, March 22. The octave of Epiphany is January 14. Hence the time available for reading Augustine's psalms expositions varied from a minimum of four days to a maximum of forty days. Thus, for at least one period of time (of variable length) the canons not only chanted the weekly cycle of the psalms in the abbey church, but they also heard at mealtime one of the major psalms commentaries from late antique Christianity. Both of these experiences of the psalms involved all, or essentially all, of the canons, but they differed in one noteworthy respect. The chanting of the psalms in the liturgy was participatory both vocally and aurally, whereas the experience in the refectory for the community was one of reception (i.e., hearing) only.

The *Expositions* of Augustine would not have been the only vehicle for conveying the psalms and their meanings to the canons in the refectory. The *Liber ordinis* assigns the reading of Gregory the Great's *Moralia in Iob* to the period from the kalends of August to the kalends of September.[13] During this month-long reading, an attentive canon would have heard mention and interpretation of a great number of psalms. Indeed, in the *Moralia* the total number of citations of texts from the psalms surpasses the total citations from any other biblical book except Job, the text on which Gregory is commenting. In the index to the *Corpus Christianorum* edition of the *Moralia,* references to quotations from psalm texts occupy twelve columns (with one citation per line of index); the second-ranking book in terms of total number of citations is the Gospel of Matthew which requires eight and one-third columns in the index.[14] As has been mentioned, beyond Gregory's *Moralia* the commentaries and homilies of other seminal Christian thinkers provided the silent diners in the refectory at Saint-Victor with spiritual nourishment from the psalms. With interwoven threads of relationship, these texts—which included works of biblical commentary, spiritual edification, and doctrinal explication—created a complex fabric of knowledge and experience in combination with the liturgical psalmody of the community and the use of psalm texts in major treatises by Victorine writers. As we will see, psalm texts figured significantly in educational and formative activities at Saint-Victor and in the spiritual writings of the canons. Thus the fabric woven, as it were, through the use of these texts in multiple situations created a set of references that extended to a number of experiential "loci" at the abbey in which psalms were encountered including church, cloister, classroom, personal study, asceticism-discipline, and meditative-contemplative experience.

Psalms, the Novices' *schola,* and the Art of Memory

Novices at Saint-Victor made the acquaintance of the psalms not only in the church and the refectory but also in their classroom or *schola*.[15] First of all, when being instructed in the form of canonical life and prepared in various ways by the master of novices for presentation as a potential member of the community, a novice would be required to acquire and demonstrate to the master of novices and abbot that he had the requisite skills to read (*lectare*), to sing (*cantare*), and to chant the psalms (*psallare*).[16]

Probably the most conspicuous manifestation of the psalms in the Victorine education program, however, is in their use as an *exemplum*. Hugh used the problem of memorizing all the psalms as the *exemplum* for his recommended memory technique in his treatise on the "art of memory," *De tribus maximis circumstantiis gestorum*.[17] This treatise, the first medieval text on the art of memory, was examined for the first time in relation to the classical memory tradition in my 1974 article "Hugh of St. Victor and the Art of Memory."[18] Mary Carruthers has since examined Hugh's work in more detail and placed it in the much broader field of medieval memory techniques, theory, and practice.[19]

After discussing various aspects of memory and memorization techniques in this treatise, Hugh gives a practical example by suggesting how to memorize all 150 psalms.[20] The student should imagine a line of numbers extending from one to 150. The first *versus* (verse or segment)[21] of each psalm, from Psalm 1 to Psalm 150, is "attached" at the proper numerical place on this line. Then each successive verse or segment of an individual psalm is taken as an individual "unit" that is suspended, again in numerical order, beneath the *locus* of the previous verse or segment of the psalm. In this way Hugh develops a two-dimensional grid with a unique memory "place" for each psalm and each verse or segment of a psalm. The result is a memory device with which a canon may call to mind not only the *incipits* of individual psalms in their sequential place among all the psalms, but also particular verses or segments in sequential relationship within a single psalm. As Hugh points out, with this kind of memory system one does not need to thumb back and forth in a large manuscript to find a specific psalm or an individual verse or segment by virtue of the fact that every psalm is present to the trained memory as a text related to a number on a number line.

By using the psalms as an *exemplum* Hugh directs the students' attention to memorization of a primary literary and liturgical text for regular canons. He also points to a technique that could be used to memorize other sequential or ordered data. In *De tribus maximis circumstantiis gestorum,* Hugh passes from principles of memory training to the place of memory in scriptural reading and lays the foundation for the historical or literal interpretation of the biblical text. Hugh envisions the student of Scripture constructing an image in the "ark [*archa*] of the heart" with a timeline traversing the spacious memory image. Along the timeline "persons" are appropriately arranged, while in the area around the line "loci" are indicated "as far as the capacity for abbreviation allows." This image will then form a storehouse of historical information, the "foundation of the foundation" that will undergird and support reading and understanding the biblical text as a historical narrative.[22] Hugh thus effectively moves from the *schola* task of preparing novices for the liturgy to the *schola* task of preparing them to interpret the biblical text and build their "house" of historical, allegorical (theological), and tropological meanings for shaping action and thought throughout their lives.

Psalms in Hugh's *De institutione novitiorum*

De institutione novitiorum is notable with respect to the psalms for two very different reasons.[23] First, Hugh here makes little if any use of citations from individual psalms within his ongoing presentation concerning discipline of the mind and the body. This presentation is conducted under a basic organizing scheme of the rhetorical *topoi* of person, place, time, and action.[24] Second and far more importantly, *De institutione novitiorum* uses a psalm verse as the anchoring "authority" on which the treatise's division of topics is based. This thematic or "framing" use of a psalmic verse is a significant usage that we will find in other Victorine texts. In the case of *De institutione novitiorum,* the psalm that provides the overarching structural outline and the principles for the pedagogical and moral intentions of the treatise is Psalm 118:66: "Teach me goodness, discipline, and knowledge."[25] This verse not only furnishes scriptural warrant for the three general topics proposed for the treatises, but it also provides a referential and memorative device that links the core themes of *De institutione novitiorum* with a psalm used in the liturgy.

In addition to Psalm 118:66, which provides the lapidary formulation of topics, the Prologue draws on two other psalmic verses to establish the novices as those who are traveling along the road (*via*) of life. First, using a verse drawn from the same psalm as the lapidary formula, the novices are like those whom the Psalmist praises as "blessed" (*beati*) because they are "undefiled" on the "road" (*via*) as they "walk in the law of the Lord" (i.e., justice; Psalm 118:1). Second, they are constantly corrected according to the Lord's discipline (*disciplina*) along that road (Psalm 17:36). Indeed the theme of traveling along a road (*via*) toward God and/or the celestial homeland is a central theme in some of Hugh's most powerful works on love or charity, especially *De laude caritatis* and *De substantia dilectionis*. Thus, this evocation of the image of a road and a journey at the outset of *De institutione novitiorum* connects with and calls to mind other spiritual writings within the Hugonian corpus.

Besides that based on Psalm 118:66, the Prologue to *De institutione novitiorum* offers another threefold schematic pattern, this time one of linear connectedness: the search for God is the search for everlasting blessedness (*beatitudo*); blessedness is only achieved through virtue (*virtus*); and virtue can only be achieved through the practice of discipline (*disciplina*).[26] Reversing this order, it may be said that the novice ascends from discipline to the acquisition of virtue and thence to the culmination of life and to the celestial life of blessedness. From the very beginning of the treatise, then, discipline (which has a very distinctive cast in Hugh's formulation) is presented as the starting point of the journey and in a real sense the motive force of transformation.

The treatise itself opens with a consideration of the quest for (1) knowledge (*scientia*) that focuses on learning as the acquisition of the knowledge that will make it possible to lead a virtuous life and (2) discipline (*disciplina*), particularly discipline of the body in terms of posture, gestures, motion, and the like, which is seen as the application of knowledge to achieve virtue and a balanced harmonious life in community.[27] With the goal of establishing the virtues that lead to blessedness, Hugh outlines the kinds of knowledge needed by sketching out the varieties of "situations" for which one must acquire the knowledge necessary for forming one's life in order to be virtuous. The major divisions of situations are: places (church, cloister, refectory); times (day, night); actions (talking, silence); and persons (the rank of the person with whom one is interacting).[28] This pattern of topics for the *divisio* of instruction in virtue and discipline immediately recalls the topics used for organizing memory training and for comprehension of order in the flow of time and history as presented in *De tribus maximis circumstantiis gestorum* and the *Didascalicon*.[29]

The sources of the knowledge needed to advance in virtue are five: reason, instruction (*doctrina*), example (here Hugh offers the metaphor of the formation of a wax seal by the impression of the matrix), meditation on Sacred Scripture, and careful consideration of one's own actions and usual behavior.[30] When dealing with knowledge derived from Scripture study Hugh clearly states that the knowledge is not "theoretical" or "theological" but rather practical and moral, intended to shape life and encourage humility and other virtues.[31] In particular, the treatise makes clear that this knowledge does not lead to classroom disputations as found in secular schools. The second major section of the treatise, on discipline, has attracted considerable attention in scholarly literature because it describes in great detail the regulation of the body (gestures, facial expressions, posture, gait, eating habits, etc.) that is necessary to achieve the goal of a harmonious balanced life that leads to (and reflects) both inner harmony and harmony with the divine order.[32] Jean-Claude Schmitt has called Hugh's treatment of bodily regulation "the most important theoretical text on gestures in the twelfth century."[33]

After analyzing at length both knowledge and virtue, Hugh brings the treatise to a sudden end, leaving the structure set forth by Psalm 118 only two-thirds complete. Goodness (*bonitas*), he declares, is a divine gift, implying that it is not something that can be taught in the Victorine *schola novitiorum* through the formation of mind and body set forth in *De institutione novitiorum*. The treatise concludes: "Brothers, we have said these things to you concerning knowledge and discipline; but as for goodness, pray that God will give it to you. Amen."[34]

Psalms in Hugh's *De virtute orandi*

If *De institutione novitiorum* instructs the brothers to pray, *De virtute orandi* sets out to analyze prayer itself.[35] *De virtute orandi* (also known as *De modo orandi* in the manuscript tradition[36] and so named in Migne) is, as Dominique Poirel has pointed out, an *ars orandi*, the first treatise in the medieval West that treats prayer in terms of rhetorical theory.[37] In analyzing prayer rhetorically, Hugh takes account of the one praying, the *narratio* of the prayer, the objective of the one praying, the persuasive role of prayer, and the one to whom the prayer is addressed (i.e., God). Three types (*species*) of prayer are distinguished from each other according to the absence of a request directed to God (*supplicatio*), the presence of an explicit request (*postulatio*), and the ambiguous presence of a request (*insinuatio*).[38] Each type is further divided into three subcategories, thus yielding a ninefold typology of prayer:[39] **Supplicatio:** *captatio, exactio, oratio pura;* **Postulatio:** *obsecratio, rogatio, postulatio simplex;* **Insinuatio:** *timor, fiducia, contemptus.* In light of the latter part of this treatise in which Hugh counters the view that the only legitimate prayer is one with a petition to God, it should be noted that one of his three types, *supplicatio,* contains no request or petition that is addressed to God. Indeed, Hugh explicitly says that *supplicatio* (1) precedes a petition to God and (2) can be found frequently in Sacred Scripture.[40] In order to enable the canons and other readers to appreciate the variety of names (e.g., "my refuge"), words (e.g., "mercy" or "consider"), and phrases (e.g., "give attention to the voice of my prayer, my King and my God") that may fall under the rubric "supplicatio," Hugh gives illustrations from three psalms, namely 143:2, 17:3, and 5:2–3.[41]

Following this analysis of the three types and nine sub-types of prayer, Hugh turns to consider the psalmody of the Daily Office and Mass at Saint-Victor in relation to the interior affective states that may be evoked in prayer. Taking up the assertion "by some" (who remain nameless) that it is impossible to use the words of Scripture, especially the psalms, to convey to God the very personal matters of individual petitions and the like, Hugh responds that in chanting psalms one may find appropriate interior affections evoked in relation to God while a person is engaged in this communal liturgical action. In his typical way of dividing a subject (in a manner similar to his analysis of types of prayer in the first part of this treatise) Hugh presents nine affections related to prayer.[42] Although Hugh admits that in one sense the affections are beyond categorization because they are infinite in number, he goes on to maintain that certain ones are worthy of praise and acceptable to God. The nine affections identified are: loving, wonder, joy, humility, sorrow, fear, indignation, zeal, and proper presumption. Each is given a brief active description: e.g., the affection of loving (*dilectio*) is "when the mind, seeing or recalling the one whom it loves, is immediately ignited with the fire of love (*amoris igne*)," while the affection of fear is "when the mind is struck by the consideration of punishments that are approaching."[43] Hugh proceeds to group the affections in triads and points out that each group is related to a particular kind of scriptural passage. Love, wonder, and joy are related to and evoked by passages of praise (*laudatio*): e.g., a passage recalling goodness causes the affection of love to arise, while one recalling power and strength summons wonder. Humility, sorrow, and fear are related to and evoked by passages that recall unhappiness and distress (*commemoratio infelicitatis et miserie*), while indignation, zeal, and good presumption are related to and evoked by passages of Scripture that involve criticism and accusations against enemies. Then Hugh offers what he calls an *exemplum* of each affection by associating a psalm (identified by its *incipit*) with each:[44]

Loving: *Diligam te Domine* (Ps. 17:1)
Wonder: *Domine Dominus noster* (Ps. 8:1)
Joy: *Omnes gentes* (Ps. 46:1)
Humility: *In te domine speraui* (Ps. 30:1)
Sorrow: *Usquequo Domine obliuisceris?* (Ps. 12:1)
Fear: *Domine ne in furore* (Ps. 6:1)
Indignation: *Quid gloriaris in malitia* (Ps. 51:1)
Zeal: *Deus ultionum* (Ps. 91:1)
Good presumption: *Iudica me Domine quoniam ego* (Ps. 25:1)

This association of a psalm with an affection is not one in which the psalm is identified as one to be recalled or chanted on an occasion of joy, fear, or another affection. Hugh argues, on the contrary, that a psalm is capable of "triggering" or leading one to experience these affections inwardly as one chants the psalm exteriorly.[45]

In his analysis and typology of prayer and of the affections in relation to the psalms, Hugh's work is part of a turning point in the understanding of the relation between prayer and psalmody. The twelfth century saw a transition from the "objective" purpose of corporate prayer and praise represented particularly by the institution of monastic prayer, with communal celebration of the Daily Office and the concomitant chanting of the Psalter, as it had developed from the ninth century. The twelfth-century transition involved movement to a more "subjective" understanding of prayer as involving personal experiences of a particularly affective kind in relation to the divine. Such a shift can be seen even in the late eleventh century with figures such as Anselm of Canterbury, while in the twelfth century the Victorines (along with the Cistercians) were crucial to this shift.

Psalms, the Road (*via*) to God, and *De laude caritatis*

Hugh's brief treatise *De laude caritatis* is a deeply moving and affective work that praises charity as the road (*via*) by which humans travel up to God and the road by which God travels down to humans.[46] In its use of the motifs of road, travel, running, and companions, *De laude caritatis* shares a thematic (and affective) relationship with Hugh's treatise *De substantia dilectionis*. It also shares with Hugh's great work *De arrha animae* themes of ascent and descent as well as the power of love or charity to draw opposites together and overcome alienation and loneliness.

For our present purposes *De laude caritatis* is noteworthy because, of the few scriptural passages that Hugh invokes in this work, psalm verses significantly outnumber selections from other biblical books. Of the thirteen individual citations, five are from the Psalms, two are from the Gospel of John, and two are from the Song of Songs. Hugh cites Hosea, Romans, 1 Corinthians, and 1 John only once each. Moreover, all but one of the psalm citations are brought into the flow of the treatise at a critical moment, namely when Hugh is moving toward his central affirmation that charity is the road to God, the road along which those who are just run.[47] Here Hugh cites Psalm 118:32 ("I have run the road of your commandments") and the opening verse of this psalm ("Blessed are those who are undefiled on the road, who walk in the law of the Lord"). He then invokes verse 30 of Psalm 118 ("I have chosen the road of truth, I have not forgotten your judgments") along with verses from the Gospel of John and 1 John that link truth and love. Through a series of verbal connections, Hugh brings together the road of justice, love and truth, and the one who runs as just.[48] He then returns to the psalm that directly links justice and love, a psalm that he finds commending both the road of justice and the ardent charity that will impel the runner: "I have run the road of your commandments and you have enlarged my heart" (Psalm 118:32). What, Hugh asks, is a heart that is enlarged? It is one that boils with love and is filled by charity. Justice and love are united on the road to God.

For attentive readers such as the canons of Saint-Victor for whom Hugh composed his treatises, the psalm passages in *De laude caritatis* establish an important scriptural (and thus memorative) link with *De institutione novitiorum* in particular. The first psalm citation in the Prologue to *De institutione novitiorum* is 118:1 ("Blessed are those who are undefiled on the road, who walk in the law of the Lord"). The novices are called to walk in the road of God's commandments, which finally means to walk in the way of discipline (of body and mind) that leads along with knowledge and goodness (Psalm 118:66) to virtue and blessedness. Likewise in *De laude caritatis* the same psalm summons those who love God with true charity to run the road of the divine commandments; and if they recall the threefold topical structure of *De institutione novitiorum* (knowledge, discipline, and goodness) they will more readily establish the link between the praise of love and the discipline of formation in their hearts and actions.

Psalms in Richard's *De duodecim patriarchis*

Richard of St. Victor's treatise *On the Twelve Patriarchs* presents the thirteen stages of the ascetic-contemplative life as an extended moral interpretation of the twelve sons and one daughter of the Patriarch Jacob.[49] The children are borne by his two wives, Leah and Rachel, and the handmaid of each wife, Zelpha and Bala respectively. The tropological interpretation of the father, mothers, sons, and daughter is rooted in texts found in two sections of the book of Genesis: (1) the narrative of the births of the thirteen children of Jacob in Genesis 29:31–30:24 and 35:16–18, and (2) Jacob's deathbed blessing of his sons recorded in Genesis 49. Another biblical narrative on which Richard draws extensively in the final chapters of this treatise is the account of Jesus' Transfiguration in Matthew 17. Finally, as we seek to show, verses from the psalms play decisive interpretive roles in defining and delineating aspects of the interpretation of the texts from Genesis and Matthew.

The names of the children, the sequence of the childrens' births, their mothers' cries as the children are born, and other details set forth in the Genesis texts provide the basic materials for the symbolic representation of the unfolding of the ascetic-contemplative journey that begins with spiritual awakening in the arousal of holy fear and culminates in the final fruition of ecstatic contemplation. However, the treatise opens not with a quotation from Genesis, but rather one from the Psalter, namely Psalm 67:28: "Benjamin a youth in ecstasy of mind."[50]

This quotation sounds several notes and forges important links as Richard launches an intricate presentation concerning the development of the path of discipline leading to ascetic self-mastery and contemplative vision. Benjamin is the last-born son of Jacob; he is the end, the climax, the peak of the unfolding tropological meaning of the literal narrative of the story of Jacob and his family. Thus, the psalm verse at the very beginning of the treatise points to the culmination of Richard's work and the way of life it presents. But before Benjamin—i.e., the attainment of the heights of contemplative experience—can be born, all the other children, emblematic of the stages of progress in the ordering of the virtues and life as a whole, must first be born on the level of history and interpreted with tropological insight. Because the psalm declares that Benjamin is a "young man" (*adolescentulus*), Richard proposes to set the *exemplum* of a young man before other young men (i.e., young canons of Saint-Victor) to inspire them and draw them onward to the contemplative goal of their vocation.[51] Finally, ecstasy of mind, the goal of the life of ascetic discipline of the body and mind or soul, is personified by Benjamin, the youth, whose mother Rachel (interpreted by Richard as reason) dies at his birth.[52]

Thus at the outset of one of his major treatises on the life of contemplative asceticism Richard uses a short psalm verse (describing Benjamin as a young man in ecstasy of mind) as a prelude to his presentation on the nature and structure of the life-long quest for the knowledge of self, knowledge of God, and the experience of divine presence. Richard weaves a rich fabric from experience and learning in order to lead the young canons (and in subsequent times and locales, other readers) on a personal itinerary through the stages of spiritual advancement.[53] His skillfully articulated insights and cautionary injunctions accompany vivid personifications of each stage via images of the four mothers, their birthing experiences, their thirteen children, and the children's names.[54]

One fascinating aspect of this tropological drama of spiritual development is the role that the psalms play in the determination of the moral meaning and spiritual significance of many of the thirteen stages. This important psalmic element in Richard's spiritual teaching appears to have been generally overlooked in the literature on his writings on the ascetic-contemplative life. A brief statistical interlude, however, will underscore the significant presence of the psalms in *De duodecim patriarchis*. If one simply measures the frequency of citation of each biblical book in the treatise, leaving aside the quotations and references to the two sections of Genesis that deal directly with Jacob's children, the most cited book is the Psalter. More indicative than this quantitative measure is a more qualitative one that considers the way in which Richard employs many of the psalm citations. Not only does a verse from the psalms provide the textual rubric under which Richard launches his interpretation of Jacob's children, but the psalms also provide numerous "confirming" or "clarifying" passages in the course of the tropological interpretation of the names, actions, and other aspects of the scriptural account of Jacob's children, his wives, and the wives' handmaids. Richard cites these psalm verses in order to "shape" his interpretation of passages related to the family of Jacob or to provide supporting texts for distinctions and clarifications that he makes while developing his own theories of ascetic discipline, individual experience, and divine leading in the personal quest for ecstatic transformation.

The first four stages of the contemplative quest as outlined in *De duodecim patriarchis* represent the successive acquisition of the virtues of fear, grief, hope, and love, which are personified by the first four children of Leah, who herself personifies the affections.[55] Richard insists, however, that each of these virtues must be established as an *ordered* virtue. Without discipline (i.e., being put in order) and without being acquired in the proper sequence, they are quite simply *disordered*. In order of birth (which corresponds to the order of the stages or virtues) the sons or virtues are: Reuben = fear; Simeon = grief; Levi = hope; Judah = love (*amor*). Richard takes the meaning of the Hebrew name of each child and the mother's exclamation as she gives birth to the child as pointers for developing the moral meaning personified by the offspring. However, in each of these instances Richard's analysis includes not only the material from the Genesis account, but also distinctive applications of psalm verses that define, delimit, and/or determine the primary tropological meaning of each child as a personification of one stage of progress in an individual's journey to acquire spiritual discipline and discernment.

Richard's presentation of Reuben, the first-born, opens not with a citation from Genesis but with Psalm 110:10: "The fear of the Lord is the beginning of wisdom."[56] Since the spiritual quest seeks "the highest wisdom,"[57] this verse from Psalm 110 not only sets the stage for the identification of Reuben (whose name means "son of vision") with fear, but also encapsulates the trajectory of the treatise in a scriptural formulation that presents religious fear as the very beginning of wisdom (not the antithesis of wisdom). Thus fear is here presented as the necessary first step to be taken in the movement toward personal experience of divine Wisdom, a movement finally culminating in the ecstatic experience of the divine presence.[58] Richard resolves the tension between the state of one who is oblivious to sin, is unable to foresee future evils, and possesses neither shame for his depravity nor fear of God's power, yet bears the name "son of vision" and symbolizes the "birth" of fear, by proposing that fear is born of the sudden "seeing" of one's own depraved life and an awareness of divine judgment. A similar exegetical tactic (associated with human and divine "seeing") allies Leah's statement at Reuben's birth with the idea of Reuben as personified fear.[59]

The second stage, grief, is introduced by Richard's comment that the more a person fears punishment the more he laments faults.[60] As Richard quickly points out, "at whatever hour a sinner shall have been converted and shall have mourned, he will be saved, according to this: 'A contrite and humbled heart, O God, you will not despise'" (Ps. 50:19). Thus, before the name of the second son has even been mentioned Richard has launched a psalm verse that evokes divine acceptance of the contrite and humble heart: humbled through fear, contrite through grief, in Richard's compact and lapidary dyadic formulation.[61] Again a psalm citation has been called upon to shape the tropological interpretation given to another son of Jacob and Leah, Simeon, the personification of grief.

Leah's third son Levi, whose name means "added," personifies the third stage, hope for forgiveness.[62] Richard takes "added" to mean that the third stage, like the third son, exists only after the first two. Only after fear and grief can hope for forgiveness be "added," i.e., be realized. After this introduction to "hope" Richard turns to Psalm 93:19 as the confirming scriptural witness: "According to the multitude of griefs in my heart, your comforts have given joy to my soul." This verse is the only biblical text directly quoted in chapter 10.

In treating the birth of the fourth son, Judah, Richard's prose becomes more affective with an outpouring of language that embraces intimacy, longing, and love.[63] Judah, whose name means "confessing," is the personification of love (*amor*) in Richard's spiritual path. But Leah also becomes a manifestation of love in her cry in giving birth to Judah: "Now my husband shall be joined to me."[64] The true spouse of the soul is, of course, God, as Richard points out, and our Victorine spiritual guide celebrates this with language that echoes the Song of Songs in an outpouring of affective prose.[65] To establish an interpretive link between the meaning of Judah's name, "confessing," and the theme of love, Richard proceeds via the person of Leah rather than her son. What, he asks, does Leah render to the Lord for a son such as Judah? Richard responds that whatever a person "approves" is something that she or he loves: "The truth is that one would not love if one did not approve of the object of love." Moreover approval is praise and "praise" is "confession itself."[66] Thus, through this long chain of verbal connections confession is linked to love. Again Richard has summoned psalm verses to provide scriptural warrant. In this case the warrant is one justifying the linking of praise and confession to love (both linked through Leah rather than Judah in this passage, although elsewhere Judah is the subject for analyzing praise, confession, and love):

"I shall confess abundantly to the Lord with my mouth" (Ps. 108:30). Surely and without doubt, you [i.e., Leah, the affective aspect of the soul] truly confess to the Lord not only frequently, but also unceasingly, if you love Him perfectly. "I will bless the Lord at all times; His praise shall always be in my mouth" (Ps. 33:20). Indeed you always praise if you always love and always long.[67]

The nine stages of the ascetic-contemplative quest that follow unfold via the interpretation of the births of the remaining eight sons and one daughter of Jacob. With three exceptions citations from the Psalms are rare in these nine stages. Psalms return to the rhetorical stage as major pointers in the interpretation of Issachar as the personification of "joy" (and his "borderland" experience of the presence and absence of spiritual goods in the midst of material existence) and of Zabulon as the personification of "zeal."[68] However, it is with the presentation of Benjamin, the final child born and the second child of Rachel who represents the last stage of the quest, ecstasy, that the Psalms return in full force. With the birth of the two sons of Rachel, first Joseph (personifying the virtue of discretion) and then Benjamin (personifying ecstasy), the question is no longer one of advancement forward but of ascension, i.e., of being raised up finally to those heavens into which Paul reports he was snatched up in ecstasy (2 Cor. 12:2).[69] To attain self-knowledge is to ascend to the full height of rational knowing, to ascend the mountain, an ascension that Richard first associated with Psalm 63:7–8: "Let man ascend to a high heart, and God shall be exalted."[70] It is not enough to ascend, however. One must *stand* and *stay* on the mountain, a point that brings Richard to underscore his meaning with yet another psalm verse: "Who shall ascend the mountain of the Lord, and who shall stand in His holy place?" (Ps. 23:3).[71] After evoking Jerusalem and the Temple, Richard continues by insisting that the contemplative must learn to live on the mountain in the holy place. Here other psalms as well as repetitions of psalm verses cited earlier pour forth like a cascade, filled with images of ascending the holy mountain, entering and dwelling in the tabernacle, and resting on the holy mountain.[72] Suddenly the holy mountain of the Psalms is transformed in Richard's text into another mountain, namely the Mount of Transfiguration.[73] On this mountain the transforming moment of ecstasy takes place as the disciples who have climbed the mountain behold the light of Jesus' Transfiguration and then fall down fainting: a powerful, evocative image or personification of the death of reason (which has climbed the mountain of self-knowledge) in the moment in which a new knowledge, ecstatic apprehension of the divine presence, is born. This moment, defined by the biblical narrative of the Transfiguration as a potent theophany that overpowered the disciples and struck them senseless, is coupled with another biblical image of transformation, namely the death of Rachel (reason) and the birth of Benjamin (ecstasy), the culmination of the narrative of the births of Jacob's children.[74]

Richard thus offers a rich and complex symbolic representation of the end of the spiritual journey woven from texts in Genesis, the Psalms, and Matthew. This representation superimposes images of two mountains (Jerusalem and the Mount of Transfiguration), two losses of consciousness or life (the fainting of disciples and the death of Rachel), and two manifestations of divine presence (the Jerusalem Temple and the Light of the Transfiguration). The spiritual journey's ecstatic culmination, combining birthing (Benjamin) and death (Rachel) from the book of Genesis, returns the reader in a reflexive movement to the very words Richard so carefully set forth at the beginning of his treatise and thus at the beginning of the spiritual journey: "Benjamin a young man in ecstasy of mind."

As the foregoing analysis has shown, in Richard's presentation of the journey personified by the children of Jacob the psalms serve as constant companions to the images drawn from Genesis and Matthew and greatly enrich his own profound reflection on the dynamics, progression, and perils of the ascetic-contemplative quest. The psalms appear in order to clarify and confirm the contours of the spiritual journey. But they are surely there also as potent memorative markers of spiritual states and longings. The psalms quoted in Richard's text are also chanted in the choir, recalled in the meditative memory, set forth in other Victorine treatises, and read in the refectory as part of ancient and early medieval commentaries and sermons. These intersecting trajectories of psalm usage in multiple settings of the common life of the canons at Saint-Victor mutually support each other and invest each other with deeper meaning: as, for example, the chant in the Daily Office recalls the meaning of ascending the holy mountain in

The Twelve Patriarchs, or individual reflection on the virtue of hope leads to Psalm 93:19 ("According to the multitude of my griefs in my heart your comforts have given joy to my soul") and thence to the birth of Simeon. Set within a community experience of the psalms in liturgy, in refectory readings, in meditation and rumination, in the novices' classroom, and in treatises written to guide canons to the deepest and highest levels of spiritual experience, the psalms conveyed multiple levels of meaning to the members of the community of Saint-Victor. They offered, through their rich repertoire of words and images, yet another avenue by which God might approach humans and humans might approach God on the road of love celebrated by Hugh in several treatises and delineated in its subtle contours in Richard's spiritual writings.

Notes

1. See Robert Alter, *The Psalms: A Translation with Commentary* (New York: W.W. Norton, 2007); and *The Psalms,* trans. Mitchell Dahood. Anchor Bible Commentary vols. 16, 17, 17A (Garden City, NY: Doubleday, 1966–70).

2. See, e.g., *Andreae de Sancto Victore Opera 6: Expositio in Ezechielem,* CCCM 53E (Turnhout: Brepols, 1991); *Jews and Christians in Twelfth-Century Europe,* ed. Michael A. Signer and John Van Engen (Notre Dame, IN: University of Notre Dame Press, 2001); "Andrew of St. Victor's Anti-Jewish Polemics," in *The Bible in the Mirror of Its Interpreters,* ed. Sara Japhet (Jerusalem: Magnes Press, 1993), 412–20; "Restoring the Narrative: Jewish and Christian Exegesis in the Twelfth Century," in *With Reverence for the Word: Medieval Exegesis in Judaism, Christianity, and Islam,* ed. Jane Dammen McAuliffe, Barry D. Walfish, and Joseph W. Goering (New York: Oxford University Press, 2003), 70–82; and "Rabbi and *Magister:* Overlapping Intellectual Models of the Twelfth-Century Renaissance," *Jewish History* 22.1–2 (2008): 115–37.

3. For the early years of the abbey, see Robert-Henri Bautier, "Les origine et les premiers développements de l'abbaye Saint-Victor de Paris," in *L'Abbaye parisienne de Saint-Victor au moyen âge. Communications présentées au XIIIe Colloque d'Humanisme médiéval de Paris (1986–1988),* ed. Jean Longère (Paris-Turnhout: Brepols, 1991), 23–52; and Jean Châtillon, *Théologie, Spiritualité, et Métaphysique dans l'oeuvre oratoire d'Achard de Saint-Victor,* Études de philosophie médiévale 58 (Paris: J. Vrin, 1969), 53–85.

4. PL 177:589A–633A.

5. Rebecca Moore, *Jews and Christians in the Life and Thought of Hugh of St. Victor* (Atlanta: Scholars Press, 1998), 89–92.

6. *Mysticae adnotationes in Psalmos* (PL 196:265/6D–402B).

7. PL 196:285C–322D.

8. See Rudolph Goy, *Die handschriftliche Überlieferung der Werke Richards von St. Viktor im Mittelalter.* Bibliotheca Victorina 18 (Turnhout: Brepols, 2005), entry for *Mysticae adnotationes in Psalmos.*

9. As with so many areas of Victorine exegesis, Beryl Smalley showed the way with Herbert in her influential *The Study of the Bible in the Middle Ages* (Notre Dame, IN: University of Notre Dame Press, 1964), 186–95. For a more recent and fuller treatment of Herbert, his commentary, and other activities, see Deborah L. Goodwin, *Take Hold of the Robe of a Jew: Herbert of Bosham's Christian Hebraism* (Leiden: Brill, 2006).

10. *Liber ordinis sancti victoris parisiensis,* ed. Lucas Jocqué and Ludovicus Milis, CCCM 61 (Turnhout: Brepols, 1984), 212–14 (hereafter *Lo* with chapter and page, and lines where necessary).

11. *Lo,* ch. 48:213, lines 33–35.

12. The designations "exposition," "sermons," etc. are taken from the *Liber ordinis.* I have examined the calendar of readings with a different aim in an article, "The Influence of Augustine's *De doctrina christiana* upon the Writings of Hugh of St. Victor," in *Reading and Wisdom: The* De doctrina christiana *of Augustine in the Middle Ages,* ed. Edward D. English (Notre Dame, IN: University of Notre Dame Press, 1995), 48–60. Valuable contributions by Michael Signer and Margaret Gibson on Victorine topics will be found in this volume, the result of a conference at the University of Notre Dame.

13. *Lo,* ch. 48:214, lines 46–47.

14. See Gregorius Magnus, *Moralia in Iob,* CCSL 143B:1837–43 and 1855–59. (For another basis on which to estimate Gregory's Psalms commentary, see Paterius, PL 79:819B–896A. For interpretations of psalms only see Paterius, cols. 1017C–1025/26A; for interpretations of Matthew see Paterius, cols. 1025A–1052C. Paterius' texts are mostly from the *Moralia* but other Gregorian works are also referenced, e.g., the sermons on Ezekiel and the sermons on the gospels.)

15. The novices' *schola* is mentioned repeatedly in the *Liber ordinis:* see especially *Lo,* ch. 22:103–11 (entitled *De susceptione novitiorum*) where the orientation, instruction, and formation provided by the master of novices are sketched in some detail.

16. *Lo,* ch. 22, lines 244–248. This chapter also stipulates that when a novice sits in the cloister he should hold his Psalter—a comment suggesting both how closely the novitiate and the Psalter were connected and that the novice had a copy of the Psalms that might be considered his own.

17. William M. Green, "Hugo of St. Victor, *De tribus maximis circumstantiis gestorum," Speculum* 18 (1943): 484–93, now translated by Mary Carruthers as "The Three Best Memory Aids for Learning History," in *The Medieval Craft of Memory:*

An Anthology of Texts and Pictures, ed. Mary Carruthers and Jan M. Ziolkowski (Philadelphia: University of Pennsylvania Press, 2002), 32–40.

18. Grover A. Zinn, "Hugh of St. Victor and the Art of Memory," *Viator* 5 (1974): 211–34.

19. See Mary Carruthers, *The Craft of Thought: Meditation, Rhetoric, and the Making of Images, 400–1200* (Cambridge: Cambridge University Press, 2000), 243–46; and *The Book of Memory: A Study of Memory in Medieval Culture,* 2nd ed. (Cambridge: Cambridge University Press, 2008), xiii–xv, 53–55, 101–6, 257–60, 333–35, 339–44, 427–28.

20. Green, "Hugo of St. Victor," 489, line 27 through 490, line 1.

21. *Versus* does not refer to the division of the biblical text into verses as found in modern texts, but rather to a short segment of the text according to the usage of Cassiodorus in his *Expositio psalmorum* (CCSL 97–98).

22. Green, "Hugo of St. Victor," 491, lines 3–33 with attention to line 15 where Hugh speaks of needing a "foundation of the foundation."

23. A Latin edition and French translation of *De institutione novitiorum* is found in *L'oeuvre de Hugues de Saint-Victor,* vol. 1, ed. H.B. Feiss and P. Sicard, trans. D. Poirel, H. Rochais, and P. Sicard (Turnhout: Brepols, 1997), 18–114. *De institutione novitiorum* will be cited hereafter as *Din* according to chapter and pages in this edition with lines as needed.

24. See *Din,* chs. 1–5:23–37. The *topoi* also appear elsewhere in Hugh's writings. They provide a basic set of categories in Hugh's method for the study and interpretation of Scripture in *Didascalicon* VI.3 where the basic elements are the person, deed done, time, and place (see *Didascalicon de studio legendi: Studienbuch,* ed. Thilo Offergeld, Fontes Christiani 27 [Freiburg: Herder, 1997], 360, and for an English translation *The Didascalicon of Hugh of St. Victor: A Medieval Guide to the Arts,* trans. Jerome Taylor [New York: Columbia University Press, 1961], 135–36). The "circumstances" are also central to Hugh's teaching on memory training in *De tribus maximis circumstantiis gestorum* where the keys for memorizing history are time, person, and place (see Green, "Hugo of St. Victor," 489, lines 14–33).

25. *Din,* prol:19–21, lines 27–28.

26. *Din,* prol:18–19, lines 9–11.

27. See *Din,* "Introduction," 15–16.

28. *Din,* chs. 1–5:23–37.

29. See n. 24 above.

30. *Din,* ch. 1:22–23, lines 62–67.

31. *Din,* ch. 6:37–41, esp. lines 268–285.

32. *Din,* chs. 10–20:48–99, of which the opening section is entitled "Quid sit disciplina et quantum valeat." Major studies of Hugh's notion of "disciplina" and its relation to bodily comportment, gestures, and training in the cathedral schools are Jean-Claude Schmitt, *La raison des gestes dans l'Occident médiéval* (Paris: Galli-

mard, 1990); and C. Stephen Jaeger, *The Envy of Angels: Cathedral Schools and Social Ideals in Medieval Europe, 950–1200* (Philadelphia: University of Pennsylvania Press, 1994), esp. ch. 9.

33. Schmitt, *La raison des gestes,* 174.

34. *Din,* ch. 20:98–99, lines 1229–1230: "Hec uobis, fratres, de scientia et disciplina interim nos diximus. Bonitatem uero orate ut uobis det Deus. Amen."

35. A Latin edition and French translation of *De virtute orandi* is found in *L'oeuvre de Hugues de Saint-Victor,* vol. 1, ed. H. B. Feiss and P. Sicard, trans. D. Poirel, H. Rochais, and P. Sicard (Turnhout: Brepols, 1997), 126–71. *De virtute orandi* will be cited hereafter as *Dvo* according to chapter and pages in this edition with lines as needed.

36. For titles given to this treatise in the manuscript tradition, see Rudolf Goy, *Die Überlieferung der Werke Hugos von St. Viktor: Ein Beitrag zur Kommunikationsgeschichte des Mittelalters* (Stuttgart: Anton Hiersemann, 1976), 404–5.

37. *Dvo,* "Introduction," 117.

38. *Dvo,* ch. 6:134–35.

39. *Dvo,* chs. 6–9:134–43.

40. *Dvo,* ch. 7:134–35.

41. *Dvo,* ch. 7:136–39, lines 158–176.

42. *Dvo,* ch. 14:152–55, lines 391–410 (summary).

43. *Dvo,* ch. 14:152–55, lines 396–397 and 404–5.

44. *Dvo,* ch. 14:154–57, lines 425–436.

45. See *Dvo,* "Introduction," 118 and 124–25 where, citing *Dvo,* ch. 12, Poirel notes the difference between Hugh and Alcuin on this issue, observing that the latter understood particular psalms as useful for expressing the feelings already present to individuals. Hugh eloquently sums up his own opposing view in *Dvo,* ch. 12:148–49, lines 314–338.

46. A Latin edition and French translation of *De laude caritatis* is found in *L'oeuvre de Hugues de Saint-Victor,* vol. 1, ed. H. B. Feiss and P. Sicard, trans. D. Poirel, H. Rochais, and P. Sicard (Turnhout: Brepols, 1997), 182–207. *De laude caritatis* will be cited hereafter as *Dlc* according to chapter and pages in this edition with lines as needed.

47. *Dlc,* chs. 7–8:188–93. These are short chapters but they are pivotal. They contain four of the five psalm quotations as well as the quotations from Hosea, the Gospel of John, and 1 John, a fact that underscores the intersection of Hugh's vision of a "road" of ascent and descent with scriptural passages that embody his upward vision in verbal images.

48. See *Dlc,* ch. 8:191, text preceding n. 35 (and also in n. 35 on p. 205).

49. *De duodecim patriarchis* is found in PL 196:1A–64A as *Benjamin minor.* A critical edition and French translation is found in *Les douze patriarches ou Beniamin minor,* ed. and trans. Jean Châtillon, Monique Duchet-Suchaux, and Jean Longère

(Paris: Cerf, 1997). For an English translation see *Richard of St. Victor: The Twelve Patriarchs, the Mystical Ark, Book Three of the Trinity*, trans. Grover A. Zinn (New York: Paulist Press, 1979). *De duodecim patriarchis* will be cited hereafter as *Ddp* according to chapter, columns in PL, and pages in Châtillon and Zinn.

    50. "Beniamin adulescentulus in extasi mentis." In the Vulgate the verse begins "Ibi Beniamin . . . ." For Augustine Psalm 67:28 is a typological foreshadowing of the Apostle Paul's experience on the road to Damascus (Acts 9:4) and his ascent to the "third heaven" (2 Cor. 12:2). Augustine also briefly mentions that "excessus mentis" (i.e., ecstasy) can be caused by fear (*pavor*) or an "unveiling" (*revelatio*). When commenting on this verse from Psalm 67, Cassiodorus also presents the Benjamin-Paul typology but uses it first with "adulescentulus" to relate Benjamin to Paul, the "youth" who witnessed the stoning of Stephen (Acts 7:57). Then, noting that Benjamin is "in pavore" (Cassiodorus' text compared to Augustine's "excessus mentis"), meaning ecstasy, Cassiodorus also parallels Benjamin with Paul's experience on the road to Damascus. See Augustine, *Enarrationes in Psalmos* (CCSL 39:894–95) and Cassiodorus, *Expositio psalmorum* (CCSL 97:598–99). As Châtillon has noted, Richard makes use of traditional materials to create something very new, namely an integrated typology of Jacob's family that reflects a sense of the complexity of the human person, his faculties, and the stages of spiritual advancement. It is perhaps worthy of note that Psalm 67 is associated with the celebration of the election of a new abbot at Saint-Victor. The psalm was chanted as the prior and sub-prior led the newly elected abbot to the church and to his new abbatial seat (see *Lo*, ch. 1:17, lines 47–50).

    51. *Ddp*, ch. 1 (PL 196:1A; Châtillon, 90–91; Zinn, 53).

    52. See Gen. 35:17–18. Richard's interpretation of the death of Rachel and the birth of Benjamin is found in *Ddp*, chs. 73–74 (PL 196:52D–54C; Châtillon, 302–9; Zinn, 130–32).

    53. On the relationship of learning (*scientia*) and experience (*experentia*) see n. 58 below.

    54. See Grover A. Zinn, "Personification Allegory and Visions of Light in Richard of St. Victor's Teaching on Contemplation," *University of Toronto Quarterly* 46 (1977): 190–214.

    55. In Richard's interpretation Leah represents the affections whereas Rachel represents reason. Leah's six sons are the virtues that discipline the will. Rachel's son Joseph personifies the discretion that regulates all of life since only reason can discern and understand. As has been noted, Benjamin, born of Rachel (reason) at the moment of Rachel's (reason's) death, personifies ecstatic contemplation which is beyond reason. The sons of the handmaids govern thoughts (Bala = imagination) and control deeds (Zelpha = senses). Richard gives an important place to Leah's daughter Dinah who personifies shame. See Zinn, *Richard of St. Victor*, "Introduction," 13–22.

56. *Ddp*, ch. 8 (PL 196:6D–7A; Châtillon, 110–13; Zinn, 60–61).

57. *Ddp*, ch. 3 (PL 196:3C; Châtillon, 96–97, lines 15–17; Zinn, 56).

58. On personal experience as opposed to knowledge gained from others, see Richard's remark in *Ddp*, ch. 4 (PL 196:3D–4A; Châtillon, 98–99, lines 1–3; Zinn, 56): "Those who have been taught by experience rather than by hearing will easily recognize. . . ." See also Richard's *De arca mystica* 5.19 (PL 196:192B–C; Zinn, 343), where he remarks that "we are better instructed by the practical knowledge" of those who have advanced to the highest levels of contemplation "not so much by the teaching (*doctrina*) of another person as from . . . [our] own experience." See also the opening lines of *Ddp*, ch. 1 where Richard says that many know who Benjamin is, some by knowledge (i.e., teaching), others by experience (PL 196:1A; Châtillon, 90–91; Zinn, 53). Finally see Grover Zinn, "Exegesis and Spirituality in Richard of St. Victor," in *Doors of Understanding: Conversations in Global Spirituality in Honor of Ewert Cousins*, ed. Steven Chase (Quincy, IL: Franciscan Press, 1997), 127–42, esp. 140–42. For the culmination of the spiritual journey in ecstatic contemplation, see *De arca mystica* 5.5–19 (PL 196:167D–192C; Zinn, 316–43); Zinn, "Personification Allegory"; and Zinn, *Richard of Saint-Victor*, "Introduction," 37–44. For Richard's teaching on contemplative experience, see Steven Chase, *Angelic Wisdom: The Cherubim and the Grace of Contemplation in Richard of St. Victor* (Notre Dame, IN: University of Notre Dame Press, 1995); and Dale M. Coulter, *Per Visibilia ad Invisibilia: Theological Method in Richard of St. Victor (d. 1173)*, Bibliotheca Victorina 19 (Turnhout: Brepols, 2006).

59. *Ddp*, ch. 8 (PL 196:3A; Châtillon, 112–13; Zinn, 61). Leah's cry at birth is "God has seen my abasement" (Gen. 29:32).

60. *Ddp*, ch. 9 (PL196:7AB; Châtillon, 112–15, here p. 112, lines 1–2; Zinn, 64).

61. *Ddp*, ch. 9 (PL 196:7B; Châtillon, 114–15, lines 10–12; Zinn, 61).

62. *Ddp*, ch. 10 (PL 196:7C–8A; Châtillon, 114–117; Zinn, 62).

63. *Ddp*, chs. 11–13 (PL 196:8A–10B; Châtillon 116–27; Zinn, 63–66).

64. Gen. 29:34.

65. *Ddp*, ch. 12 (PL 196:8C–D; Châtillon, 120–21, lines 1–16; Zinn, 63).

66. *Ddp*, ch. 12 (PL 196:8D–9A; Châtillon, 120–23, lines 17–23; Zinn, 63–64).

67. *Ddp*, ch. 12 (PL 196:8D–9A; Châtillon, 120–23, lines 17–21; Zinn, 64).

68. *Ddp*, chs. 37–44 (PL 196:26D–33C; Châtillon, 194–223; Zinn, 91–101).

69. *Ddp*, ch. 74 (PL 196:52D–53D; Châtillon, 302–7; Zinn, 131–32).

70. *Ddp*, ch. 75 (PL 196:53D–54C; Châtillon, 306–9; Zinn, 133).

71. *Ddp*, ch. 76 (PL 196:54C–55B; Châtillon, 310–11, here lines 5–6; Zinn, 134–35, here 134).

72. For example: "Lord, who shall dwell in your tabernacle? And who shall rest on your holy mountain?" (Ps. 14:1); "Who shall ascend the mountain of the Lord, who shall stand in His holy place?" (Ps. 23:3); and "Lord, who shall ascend, who shall stand on your holy mountain? Send forth your light and your truth; they have

led me and brought me to your sacred mountain and into your tabernacle" (Ps. 42:3). Matthew 17:4, the disciples' statement on the Mount of Transfiguration ("It is good for us to be here"), is the only non-psalms passage from Scripture in this chapter.

73. *Ddp*, ch. 78 (PL 196:55D–56A; Châtillon, 316–17; Zinn, 138).

74. *Ddp*, chs. 73–74 (PL 196:52B–53D; Châtillon, 299–307; Zinn, 130–32).

CHAPTER FIVE

Historia and Sensus litteralis

An Investigation into the Approach to Literal Interpretation at the Twelfth-Century School of St. Victor

Dale M. Coulter

Exploring the nature of literal exegesis at St. Victor remains an important enterprise in both the history of biblical interpretation and the medieval contribution to it.[1] As Beryl Smalley noted in her now-classic study of medieval exegesis, the Victorines restated the monastic conception of *lectio divina* and thus "saved the whole structure [of exegesis] by strengthening its basis."[2] It is clear from the work of Smalley, Michael Signer, and others that saving the exegetical enterprise consisted primarily in a return to the literal interpretation of the text for the Victorines as well as their Jewish counterparts.[3] Indeed, for the Victorines, any failure to discern the literal sense led to a failure to discern the remaining spiritual senses correctly. This priority placed on literal interpretation held true whether interpreting a text of Scripture, the pseudo-Athanasian creed, or a *mappa mundi*.[4] The works of Hugh of St. Victor stand at the center of this Victorine approach as the fount from which it flows. While the general outlines of Hugh's understanding of literal interpretation and his commitment to it remains clear, another examination of his works may prove fruitful in illustrating the nuances of how the Victorines sought to strengthen the "base" of the exegetical enterprise.

The current essay attempts to offer a reconstruction of the "theoretical framework" behind Hugh of St. Victor's conception of literal exegesis with the intent of providing further insight into how it functioned. I intentionally use the terms "theoretical" and "framework" to reinforce the notion that Hugh operated with a relatively stable understanding of the exegetical enterprise while also continuously attempting to think more clearly about its details in light of exegetical practice and concerns. In his earliest works, the *Didasalicon* and *De tribus diebus,* the latter probably written between 1115 and 1121 and the former completed before 1125, Hugh makes programmatic statements about literal interpretation and its place within the educational enterprise at St. Victor. However, from 1125 on Hugh began probing the details of the program through a series of works: *Sententiae de divinitate* (a *reportatio* composed between 1125–1130), *Chronicon* (1130–1131), *De scripturis et scriptoribus sacris* (1130s), and the *De sacramentis* (1131–1137).[5] By probing these works, what one discovers are two dominant ways of describing literal interpretation associated with the term *historia* that could, and did, compete with one another at times. Unpacking Hugh's discussion of *historia* will become important for understanding the details of his "framework" and how it functions.

A second and related claim is that Boethius' understanding of language serves as an important, albeit neglected, source for this framework. Much of the recent scholarship on Hugh has focused on the influence of Augustine for any understanding of how literal interpretation functioned at St. Victor.[6] Where the secondary literature does mention Boethius, it primarily concerns his influence on Hugh's *Didascalicon,*[7] or his epistemology as found in Hugh's *De unione animae et corporis.*[8] However, Boethian thought also made a significant impact on discussions about language and its interpretation at St. Victor. In this regard it is important to recall G. R. Evans' point that medieval signification theory rests upon Boethius' commentaries on Aristotle's *De Interpretatione* as much as upon Augustine's *De doctrina christiana.*[9] While Augustine's hand lies behind Hugh's soteriology and his understanding of history as the outworking of the divine plan, I will suggest that taking into consideration Boethian texts fosters a more complete picture of the role of language in Hugh's view of literal interpretation.

Within Hugh's thought, literal interpretation in its broadest sense becomes tantamount to understanding the visible world because human language represents the attempt to order and describe that world through the relationship of terms and their referents (*voces* to *res*) as well as the teleological structure of created realities (*res*) within the divine plan. By teleological structure is meant the orderly or purposeful arrangement of *res* in scripture as it parallels the orderly arrangement of *res* within the world. For example, because of his view of the special status of created reality (*res*), Hugh finds a strong connection between the way divine providence orders all things and the way scripture arranges things in a narrative.[10] To put it succinctly, since Hugh holds that scriptural narratives reveal a broader historical narrative of the divine plan, they parallel cosmic narrative and vice-versa. As we will see, this implies that Hugh's "theoretical framework" involves a rich, multilayered understanding of literal interpretation at the center of which is an attempt to hold together dual authorship of scripture. In short, literal interpretation must involve an analysis of words and their referents as well as the referents themselves, or the *res* comprising the created order. This essay proceeds first by examining Hugh's understanding of *historia* in relation to literal interpretation before turning to Hugh's conception of the process of interpretation. It concludes by pointing to the ongoing tensions within Hugh's framework that Hugh himself never fully resolved.

Historia and Literal Interpretation

Hugh scatters what he means by the term *historia* and his understanding of how literal interpretation should function over several works.[11] *Historia* encompasses the meaning attached to a series or narration of events (history I) and the primary meaning attached to a word or the discovery of the referent (the *res*) to which a word points (history II).[12] While one can find both ideas in Hugh's discussion of *historia* in the *Didascalicon*,[13] he came to summarize these two meanings in a basic definition: "history is the narration of events expressed by the letter's primary meaning."[14]

Viewing *historia* as the meaning connected to a series of events (history I) primarily concerns the historical narratives of scripture, e.g., Judges and Kings, and other historical books, while also serving as the foundation for the theological enterprise by providing "the integrating structural principle of order in the exposition of the truth of the Christian religion."[15] As such, it encompasses the orderly arrangement of *res* within the narrative sequence of a particular text or book (*rerum gestarum narratio* or *series*)[16] and their relationship to the larger narrative of Christian salvation history. Defining *historia* as a series of events occurring in time involves a two-layered meaning that includes a particular historical narrative and the broader narrative of Christian salvation history. The ambiguity between these two ways of understanding a series of events remains an unresolved issue in Hugh that created conflict between two of his disciples, Richard of St. Victor and Andrew of St. Victor, over whether to read Isaiah 7–8 simply in terms of a particular historical narrative or part of a larger narrative encompassing a Christian view of salvation history.

Yet, Hugh's use of the basic definition to synthesize both meanings of *historia* in *De sacramentis, Chronicon,* and *De scripturis* suggests that finding the primary meaning of the terms on the page (history II), which applies to all genres of scripture, also serves as the foundation inasmuch as it grounds the spiritual meaning of a passage. This is the first and most basic step in determining the literal meaning of the text, and it closely aligns literal meaning with the meaning of the human author. The *sensus litteralis* principally involves investigating history I and II, which can be broken down into three components: (1) the referents (*res*) for the terms the human author employed; (2) the meaning of a particular historical narrative that holds together the referents in a coherent arrangement; and (3) the broader narrative of Christian salvation history of which the particular textual narrative forms a part.[17]

Jan W. M. van Zwieten identifies another dimension to Hugh's understanding of the literal interpretation of a passage. He suggests that Hugh differentiates between *sensus historicus* and *lectio historica*.[18] The former points to the interrelationship between literal interpretation and spiritual interpretation in which the literal meaning becomes the ground for the three remaining senses, while the latter indicates only the pursuit of literal interpretation. Both approaches encompass history I and II with the only difference being the ultimate criterion of meaning. The historical reading of a passage (*lectio historica*) reserves as its ultimate criteria the principles of analysis Hugh outlines in the *trivium* and *quadrivium* informed by insights from historical data. Conversely, the sense that the historical reading embodies (*sensus historicus*) uses these principles but leaves the spiritual meaning as the final arbiter in determining which competing literal interpretation the interpreter should choose. As van Zwieten implies, the division between these two approaches breaks down in Hugh's actual practice. In *De scripturis* 5, Hugh discusses *lectio historica* by reference to his distinction between human words and the realities to which they point (*voces* and *res*).[19] The method of *lectio historica* becomes important because one must discover the referents to which terms refer before moving to spiritual interpretation, which is, properly speaking, moving from one kind of entity (*res*) to another kind. As Hugh states, "To not know the letter is to not know what the letter signifies and what is signified by the letter. . . . Consequently, since those things (*res*) that the letter signifies are signs of the spiritual understanding, how can they be signs to you when they are not yet signified for you? . . . The one who proceeds orderly proceeds best."[20] The implication is that *lectio historica* helps discover the proper *res*, which is a necessary part of extracting the sense embodied within the historical (*sensus historicus*) and the foundation of any movement to the other senses.

From these two dimensions of Hugh's view on literal interpretation, discovering the referent of a term (history II) becomes more important than unpacking it as a series of events (history I), at least in terms of the starting point for interpretation. Apart from understanding the proper referent of a term (*vox*), one cannot discern all the details in a narrative sequence. Furthermore, without the identification of this referent, the interpreter cannot be certain about moving to the spiritual interpretation of the passage. Finally, as Hugh's broader definition of *historia*, history II encompasses all of scripture, providing the needed groundwork in every instance of a movement to a mystical interpretation. This would account for the two chapters on literal interpretation in *De scripturis* comprising an explanation of the relationship between words and their referents, which is properly speaking, an account of history II.[21] It also explains why the six circumstances listed in *De scripturis* 14 do not concern terms (*voces*) but the realities (*res*) identified by them. As has been noted by Mary Carruthers, circumstances were taken from ancient rhetoric as a means of classifying material.[22] In the case of Hugh's understanding of interpretation, the six circumstances he identifies (object, person, number, place, time, and deed) function as topics of invention in order to construct a spiritual interpretation because they offer different ways of analyzing the referents of the human author in question. Therefore, interpretation begins with the *trivium*, which concerns identifying the meaning of terms (*significatio vocum*) in order to identify the appropriate referent (history II).

Once the interpreter identifies the referent (*res*), a second move requiring the arts of the *quadrivium* may become necessary because the *quadrivium* concerns the meaning inherent to things (*significatio rerum*).[23] In this case, the *quadrivium* provides a deeper analysis of the referents in question and not what they signify. The point of such analysis is to determine whether the narrative sequence corresponds to reality (the visible world). This does not necessarily mean that the interpreter seeks to determine whether the narrative is historical, but whether the narrative could be historical. Two examples of the *quadrivium* at work in literal exegesis are Hugh's, and his disciple Richard's, use of geometry to resolve difficulties of measurement that directly pertained to whether the structure under discussion—Noah's ark or Ezekiel's temple—could have actually existed.[24] Obviously, if neither structure could have been built according to mathematical principles then there could be no literal meaning.

Hugh's use of the *quadrivium* to verify a literal meaning does not imply that either he or Richard must be committed to the claim that Noah's ark or Ezekiel's temple were real objects existing at a particular moment in time. They do not have to be part of "history" in the modern sense of the term to have a literal interpretation. Instead, as with Ezekiel's temple, they could be part of a prophetic narrative that is literary and still possess a literal interpretation because their existence as part of the visible world is a theoretical possibility. This seems to be why most of Richard's literal commentary on Ezekiel's vision attempts to resolve issues surrounding the architectural design of the temple and its being placed on a steeply inclined mountain.[25] It also adds a dimension to the literal meaning of a passage beyond whether it is historical narrative to include literary narratives that may be prophetic. Ultimately, what seems to be at stake in literal interpretation is whether the facts a narrative sequence purports to set forth are empirically verifiable in some way, not whether they are historical. Following Hugh, the Victorines exert much energy in resolving inconsistencies between the dates of kings, spatial measurements for various objects, and geographical references among other things, which in part requires the mathematics central to the *quadrivium*.[26] If these inconsistencies cannot be resolved then it appears unlikely that a passage possesses a literal meaning.[27] It is a testimony to the success of the program at St. Victor that the Victorines probed more than others into these matters. Upon grasping the referent and determining its correspondence to the visible world, the reader then possesses the full meaning of the text in its literal sense.[28] *Lectio historica* as preparation for *sensus historicus* then concerns understanding a word, its referent, and the characteristics of the referent in order to ascertain the interplay between the two.

There is additional support for the claim that understanding the relationship between terms and their referents (history II) comes prior to a historical series of events (history I) and is in a sense more foundational in literal interpretation for Hugh. In his earlier works, Hugh introduces the triad of word-concept-thing (*vox-intellectus-res*) as a way of explaining how the mind comes to know something. In the *Sententiae de divinitate* he states, "Moreover, it should be kept in mind that although in other books, that is, in pagan books, there are only these three, that is, things, concepts and words—and words signify things through the mediation of concepts—in the divine utterance there is much more."[29] Hugh had made a similar point in the *Didascalicon* with some elaboration. He states, "From this is most surely gathered how profound is the understanding to be sought in the Sacred Writings, in which we come through the word to a concept, through the concept to a thing, through the thing to its idea, and through its idea to arrive at truth."[30] Both statements point to the influence of Boethian language theory on Hugh's understanding of the relationship between terms and their referents, and call for further explanation.

In the first book of *Didascalicon,* Hugh indicates that Boethius claimed the problem with the ancients' (*antiqui*) search for the natures of things (*naturas rerum*) was their failure to correctly understand the role of *voces* and *intellectus*.[31] The search for wisdom was short-circuited at the beginning of the process because the ancients (which seems to mean Epicurus, not all ancient philosophers) failed to test adequately their words and concepts.

Hugh then proceeds to provide a lengthy quotation from Boethius' second commentary on the *Isagoge,* the point of which is to make a case for the need to employ logic to test whether human words and concepts have some correspondence to the visible world. Subsequently, Hugh divides logic in accordance with the *trivium* in which grammar corresponds to linguistic (*sermocinalis*) logic while dialectic and rhetoric correspond to logic concerning the construction of arguments (*dissertiva*).[32] One can see here the connection between logic, as Hugh defines it, and literal interpretation since the *trivium* governs the way in which human language functions to identify the visible world. This underscores why determining the referents identified by terms is foundational for the interpretive enterprise. The process of extracting wisdom from the world, and from a text about the world, is short-circuited without applying the proper tests to human words in order to determine their referents.

Second, although Hugh quotes from the commentary on the *Isagoge* in the *Didascalicon,* Boethius does not discuss the epistemological triad of word-concept-thing in that work.[33] Instead, one must turn to his commentaries on Aristotle's *De Interpretatione* to find it.[34] In both commentaries, Boethius notes that an individual can only conceive a thing (*res*) by a concept (*intellectus*), which is in turn signified by a word (*vox*).[35] Concepts form a bridge between words and their referents.[36] Finally, Boethius indicates that a thing and the concept it generates come by nature (*naturaliter*), whereas a term is a product of convention.[37] This suggests an epistemology in which the mind receives impressions from the objects in the world around it and subsequently creates language to name those objects.

The Boethian influence on Hugh's epistemology not only provides insight into Hugh's distinction between terms and their referents, but also explains how Hugh argues for the special status of created things (*res*) as the language of God to humanity (*vox Dei ad homines*).[38] Hugh may have taken from Boethius the idea that created things and the concepts that they generate produce meaning naturally as the background for his claim. This idea also reinforces Hugh's further claim that scripture holds a special place among writings because, unlike secular writings, in it one created thing can point to and provide meaning for another created thing. In light of these assertions, it seems clear that the Boethian theory of language provides a greater influence on Hugh than Augustine's understanding of language in the *De doctrina christiana*.[39] It is because of Boethius' assertions about the confusion between words, concepts, and their referents that Hugh places primacy on the need to begin with an investigation of words and things (history II) rather than a series of events (history I).

A second point regarding the importance of history II concerns Hugh's desire to ground spiritual interpretation in an analysis of the movement from a term to its referent. In *De scripturis* 5, Hugh chastises those who think that the word lion signifies Christ. A word has no characteristics that can be transferred to Christ; instead the term *leo* only functions as a conventional sign pointing toward the animal or the *res* that, in this instance, is its proper referent. Hugh forcefully states, "For a word (*dictio*) does not sleep with its eyes open, rather the animal does, which the word (*dictio*) signifies. Therefore, realize that when it says a lion signifies Christ, it is not the term 'animal' but the animal itself that is signified."[40] The misguided conclusion of Hugh's opponents that the interpreter can move from the term *leo* to Christ serves to undermine literal interpretation because it disregards the word's proper referent, which is the object of literal interpretation (history II). As Hugh states elsewhere, "If these two words (*voces*), that is, 'devil' and 'lion,' signify one and the same thing (*rem*), the likeness of the same thing to itself is insufficient."[41] To suggest that *leo* and *diabolus* possess the same referent misses an important move in interpretation, the proper things (*res*) to which both terms point. In an important sense, this mistake is analogous to the error of the ancients in not discriminating properly between terms, concepts, and things. Without this move the interpreter cannot continue to an allegorical interpretation of the passage in question because no adequate comparison can be made when both terms are mistakenly understood to signify the same reality (*res*). As such, history II forms the essential first step in literal interpretation.

For Hugh, *historia* encapsulated the meaning he gave to the literal interpretation of a text. It began with the investigation of the referents to which the words on the page pointed and concluded with the relationship between the particular historical narrative and the broader narrative of salvation history. Moreover, sometimes providing a literal interpretation simply meant finding the appropriate referents and then determining whether they could have existed. This would be especially the case in a prophetic narrative like Ezekiel's. Finally, discovering the referent of a term was foundational to the extraction of the wisdom contained in the passage. This is why the *trivium* becomes so important to literal interpretation because without it, one could not be certain as to the meaning of the terms and whether those terms reflected historical realities, let alone other modes of truth. Hugh's "theoretical framework" is best stated with his simple definition of *historia* as "the narration of events expressed by the letter's primary meaning."

The Theoretical Framework and the Interpretation of a Text

If the present analysis is sound, a progression of investigation into a text of scripture may be discerned from Hugh's writings. This progression corresponds to Hugh's differentiation between "initial referents" (*res primae*) and "secondary referents" (*res secundae*).[42] Interpretation begins with identifying initial referents, which are those realities of the created order (*res*) indicated by the primary meanings of the various terms (*voces*) comprising a passage. Presumably engaging in this activity would mean breaking the passage down into its respective component parts or into lemmata. Here the interpreter makes use of the *trivium* in order to identify the correct referents. Upon identifying the *res primae*, a closer analysis of each referent begins. The *quadrivium* may be used to investigate and discover the characteristics and qualities of the entity (*res*) in question, and to resolve any additional difficulties that may be present. The ultimate purpose of this investigation lies in the movement from initial meanings (*res primae*) to secondary meanings (*res secundae*) because it is only by identifying various characteristics of a particular referent (*res*) that likenesses can be drawn forth and comparisons made to another *res*.[43] But this generalized account of the progression within Hugh's thought requires several more detailed steps as the interpreter moves from terms to their initial referents.

The textual analysis of terms involves a further subdivision in the *trivium*. This subdivision corresponds to a differentiation between the *littera*, the *sensus*, and the *sententia* of a passage that Hugh proposed early on in his career.[44] The first step in explaining a text, or moving from terms (*voces*) to their referents, involves the *littera,* which focuses on the syntactical construction of a passage. A comparison of the meaning given to *littera* in *Didascalicon* 3.8 with its meaning in 6.9 suggests that the art of grammar is required for this initial step.[45] In 3.8, Hugh defines *littera* as "the coherent ordering of words, which we also call construction," a definition for grammatical construction or syntax stemming from Priscian and current in twelfth-century grammatical analyses.[46] The examples Hugh provides in *Didascalicon* 6.9 deal with the function of the cases of words or other peculiarities of syntax in a passage confirming this judgment.[47] Therefore, the interpreter first approaches a text with syntactical issues in mind, attempting to bring grammatical clarity where needed.

Once the interpreter finds the syntactical arrangement of a passage coherent, the next step requires an investigation of the *sensus,* or the clear meaning (*aperta significatio*) presented by the text.[48] On the one hand, this seems to be no more than the meaning conveyed after grammatical issues are resolved. On the other hand, Hugh himself suggests that the *sensus* of a passage is not always so clear, which is why some resort to allegory too quickly.[49] This implies that the surface meaning of a passage may remain obscure even with syntactical clarity. Part of the strategy at this stage involves utilizing dialectic and rhetoric to determine the proper referent of the terms comprising a passage. Hugh elsewhere appeals to dialectic when he states, "words (*voces*) are either univocal or equivocal. If univocal they signify one thing; if equivocal, they signify only a few things, that is, two or three or four as are imposed by a person."[50] By reading Hugh's understanding of *sensus* in light of his statements about the problems in determining the referent of a term, it appears that even when the syntactical arrangement of a passage is clear, difficulties remain for the interpreter if a *vox* has more than one meaning, that is, points to more than one *res.* It is interesting to note that Isidore of Seville (d. 636) uses *leo* as an example of an equivocal term indicating that it can identify a real (*verus*) lion, a representation (*pictus*) of a lion, or a constellation (*caelestis*).[51]

Yet, this cannot be everything involved in discovering the *sensus* to a passage. If the *sensus* is the obvious meaning of the letter, then, along with the *littera,* it encompasses both a term's initial referent (history II) and the entire narrative sequence comprising all of the referents signified (history I). Hugh indicates that some places in scripture still have no *sensus* even after the *significatio verborum* becomes clear; that is, a person may understand all of the individual referents to which the words in a passage point (history II) and still not understand the authorial meaning behind the narrative as a whole. Indeed, this is precisely what Hugh claims when he states, "perhaps you cannot understand what the whole taken together intends to signify."[52] The narrative sequence can remain incoherent to the interpreter due to an idiomatic expression or some other reason.[53] In such instances, the interpreter may, as Richard of St. Victor does, appeal to a custom in the land of Palestine. He interprets the phrase, "and the grinders have ceased" (Eccles. 12:3), by suggesting that in Palestine "women customarily sit at the millstone and grind the grain."[54] The information supplied by Palestinian customs provides additional insight into the meaning of the entire phrase without which the *sensus* would have remained somewhat unclear. This is most likely the point at which consultation of contemporary Jewish interpretations of a passage would have been extremely helpful. Thus, as Rainer Berndt affirms, *sensus* "indicates in Hugh the coherence of the collection of significations offered by different terms (*voces*) of which the *littera* is composed."[55]

The potential incoherence of a narrative leads still to a further issue in determining the *sensus* of a passage. As I indicated earlier, history I most likely indicates both the narrative sequence of a particular text and the larger narrative of Christian salvation history. In light of this implicit twofold meaning, Hugh's choice of a prophetic text in *Didascalicon* 6.10 to make his point seems intentional. If an interpreter could not understand the *sensus* of a particular narrative sequence in a clearly historical book like Kings, the only option left would be to remain agnostic about its literal interpretation. The interpreter could not deny that the particular narrative in Kings was *historia* because it formed part of an obviously historical book. However, Hugh's list of historical books does not include prophetic texts like Isaiah. These texts combine prophetic narrative with historical narrative, making it easier to deny a particular narrative sequence as having any correspondence to reality (the visible world) and thus only a spiritual meaning. As a result the *sensus* may finally necessitate an analysis of the referents (*res*) in a passage by reference to the *quadrivium*. Only after moving from a term to its referent and investigating the referent itself would the interpreter discover the *sensus* in a text.

The final step involves determining whether a passage possesses the *sententia* or "deeper meaning," which is the spiritual meaning identified with the remaining senses.[56] As Grover Zinn notes, the basis for this final move to the "deeper meaning" lies in the transference of properties from initial referents (*res primae*) to secondary referents (*res secundae*).[57] This implies that while analogous to the way secular writings are interpreted, the *sententia* of a scriptural passage further seeks the intention of the divine author. Thus Grover Zinn's and Roger Baron's assertions that Hugh follows the procedure of moving from *littera* to *sensus* and finally to *sententia* in his commentary on the *Celestial Hierarchy* should be clarified slightly.[58] The ground for the *sententia* in the Areopagite's work must be something related to a historical reading (*lectio historica*) where principles of analysis provide the ultimate criteria of determining the author's intention, as opposed to the sense embodied within the historical (*sensus historicus*) where theological principles determine the divine intention. Indeed, in this sense secular writings can possess no *sententia*.[59]

The differentiation between *littera, sensus,* and *sententia* provides some clarity to the progression of interpretation. The *littera* and *sensus* of a passage concern what Hugh means by literal interpretation or the term's primary meaning (its referent as determined by the human author) and its coherence in a narrative sequence, while *sententia* concerns the spiritual interpretation. Hugh further specifies that not all of these will be found in every passage.[60] Some passages will only possess the *littera* and the *sensus* or a literal meaning. Other passages will only possess the *littera* and the *sententia* or a spiritual meaning since the *littera* taken by itself cannot be the literal interpretation. In this instance, there can be no clear separation between the intention of the human author and the intention of the divine author with respect to the meaning of the text. Finally, there are passages that possess all three, indicating that they have both a literal and spiritual meaning. The interpreter seeks to move through each stage, noting which tools the respective stage requires and being cautious not to find certain types of meaning where there are none.

Conclusion: On the Meaning of *Historia*

We may now ask again: what does Hugh mean by literal interpretation? As we have seen, close examination of Hugh's writings yields a rich and complex answer. Most importantly, it means the initial referent to which a term points (history II). This seems to be how other Victorines understood it, including the anonymous author of *Speculum de mysteriis ecclesiae* who clearly states that "history is the meaning of words in relation to things" (*historia est significatio vocum ad res*).[61] Breaking down a narrative sequence into lemmata would have allowed the exegete to discover the objects (*res*) to which the terms (*voces*) referred. Yet, these *res* also had to be viewed in terms of the narrative sequence of which they were part. When all of the referents were organized into a coherent whole they could be taken as the *narratio gestarum rerum* or *factum*. The term *factum* (act/event or what happened/what was done) seems to be Hugh's shorthand for the entire narrative sequence (history I).[62] Moreover, the relationship between a particular historical narrative and the broader narrative of salvation history remained part of the enterprise in literal interpretation although Hugh never spelled out the specifics. Finally, an analysis of the entire narrative sequence might include a defense of its possibility, leading to a third meaning of literal exegesis: the possible (literal/historical) existence in the visible world of the objects (*res*) or collection of objects (*res*) described in the narrative sequence. In his use of geometry to determine the feasibility of Noah's ark floating, Hugh implies that a text cannot be taken as literal if what it describes does not correspond to the visible world in some way.

There are additional issues pertaining to Hugh's understanding of *historia* that should be addressed in any complete analysis of literal interpretation but lie beyond the scope of the present inquiry. The two most prominent issues are: (1) the relationship between a Christian view of salvation history and historical knowledge, and (2) the relationship between a particular narrative sequence and the broad sweep of history itself.[63] Does the historical knowledge Hugh requires to be memorized in *Chronicon* not differ from Christian salvation history even though both would be considered part of *historia*? Is Hugh not employing historical knowledge when he says that "there are some things in the books of the Maccabees and in

Daniel that you cannot easily understand unless you first have come to know those who have reigned in the kingdoms of Syria and Egypt after Alexander the Great"?[64] Does insight from Jewish exegetes essentially function as historical knowledge?[65] How does this relate to a Christian interpretation of salvation history as understood through Hugh's division into the works of creation and restoration in *De sacramentis*? It is clear in *De sacramentis* that the grand scheme of salvation history is the "integrating structural principle" as Grover Zinn notes. Are these two implicit distinctions within Hugh's understanding of *historia*? Moreover, how does Hugh understand the relationship between a particular narrative sequence in a book of scripture and the larger narrative of Christian salvation history? Does Hugh even attempt to relate the two? As a subtext to this issue, how does Hugh view the relationship between prophetic books, which combine prophetic and historical narratives, and historical books? These questions only scratch the surface of an array of issues involving the ambiguity that continued to surround Hugh's understanding of *historia* and literal exegesis. What they do reveal is the number of possible ways Hugh's thought could be taken, depending on the priorities of his followers.

Notes

1. All of the major monographs on medieval exegesis in general note the significant contribution of the Victorines. The present essay assumes the more substantial work done by these scholars. See Beryl Smalley, *The Study of the Bible in the Middle Ages* (Notre Dame, IN: University of Notre Dame Press, 1964); C. Spicq, *Esquisse d'une histoire d l'exégèse latin au Moyen Age,* Bibliothéque thomiste 26 (Paris: J. Vrin, 1944); Henri de Lubac, *Exégèse médiévale: les quatre sens de l'Écriture,* 4 vols., Théologie: études publiées sous la direction de la Faculté de théologie S. J. de Lyon-Fourvière 41 (Paris: Editions Montaigne, 1959–64); Henri de Lubac, *Medieval Exegesis: The Four Senses of Scripture,* vol. 1, trans. M. Sebanc (Grand Rapids, MI: Eerdmans, 1998); Henri de Lubac, *Medieval Exegesis: The Four Senses of Scripture,* vol. 2, trans. E. M. Macierowski (Grand Rapids, MI: Eerdmans, 2000); G. R. Evans, *The Language and Logic of the Bible: The Earlier Middle Ages* (Cambridge: Cambridge University Press, 1984).

2. Smalley, *Study of the Bible,* 196.

3. See Michael A. Signer, "*Peshat, Sensus Litteralis,* and Sequential Narrative: Jewish Exegesis and the School of St. Victor in the Twelfth Century," in *The Frank*

Talmage Memorial Volume, ed. Barry Walfish (Haifa: Haifa University Press, 1993), 203–16.

4. Richard of St. Victor's (d. 1173) *De Trinitate* represents his attempt to interpret the pseudo-Athanasian creed which was recited regularly at St. Victor. See *De Trinitate* 1.5 (*De Trinitate: text critique avec introduction, notes et tables,* ed. J. Ribaillier [Paris: J. Vrin, 1958], 90–91; *La Trinité,* ed. G. Salet [Paris: Les Editions du Cerf, 1959], 72, 74 [hereafter, Ribaillier and Salet, respectively]). See also the prologue to Hugh of St. Victor's (d. 1141) *Descriptio mappae mundi* where he indicates that his intention is to provide an analysis of the meanings (*significationes*) by which things are signified. See Patrick Gautier Dalché, *La 'Descriptio mappe mundi' de Hugues de Saint-Victor. Texte inédit avec introduction et commentaire* (Paris: Etudes augustiniennes, 1988), 133, and Dalché's comments, 111–13.

5. For the dates of Hugh's works, the primary source has been Damien van den Eynde, *Essai sur la succession et la date de écrits de Hugues de S. Victor* (Rome: Pontificium Athenaeum Antonianum, 1960). However, van den Eynde's dating is being revised by French scholarship. See Patrice Sicard, *Diagrammes médiévaux et exégèse visuelle. Le 'Libellus de formatione arche' de Hugues de Saint-Victor* (Paris: Brepols, 1993), 132–38; Patrice Sicard, *Hugues de Saint-Victor et son école* (Turnhout: Brepols, 1991), 24; and Dominique Poirel, *Livre de la nature et débat trinitaire au XIIe siècle. Le 'De tribus diebus' de Hugues de Saint-Victor* (Turnhout: Brepols, 2002), 131–54. On the *Chronicon,* see William M. Green, "Hugo of St. Victor, *De tribus maximis circumstantiis gestorum,*" *Speculum* 18 (1943): 484–93, esp. 486.

6. See Grover A. Zinn, "Hugh of St. Victor's *De scripturis et scriptoribus sacris* as an *Accessus* Treatise for the Study of the Bible," *Traditio* (1997): 111–34; Grover A. Zinn, "The Influence of Augustine's *De doctrina christiana* upon the Writings of Hugh of St. Victor," in *Reading and Wisdom: The* De doctrina christiana *of Augustine in the Middle Ages,* ed. Edward D. English (Notre Dame, IN: University of Notre Dame Press, 1995), 48–60; Eileen C. Sweeney, "Hugh of St. Victor: The Augustinian Tradition of Sacred and Secular Reading Revised," in *Reading and Wisdom,* 61–83; Patrice Sicard, *Diagrammes médiévaux et exégèse visuelle. Le Libellus de formatione arche de Hugues de Saint-Victor* (Paris: Brepols, 1993), 157–70; Rainer Berndt, *André de Saint-Victor († 1175). Exégète et théologien* (Paris: Brepols, 1991), 176–94; and Rainer Berndt, "La pratique exégétique d'André de Saint-Victor: Tradition victorine et influence rabbinique," in *L'abbaye parisienne de Saint-Victor au Moyen Age. Communications présentées au XIIIe Colloque d'Humanisme médiéval de Paris (1986–1988),* ed. Jean Longère (Paris: Brepols, 1991), 271–90, esp. 271–77.

7. See Jean Châtillon, *Le mouvement canonial au Moyen Age: réforme de l'église, spiritualité et culture,* ed. Patrice Sicard (Paris: Brepols, 1992), 393–418; and Roger Baron, *Science et sagesse chez Hugues de Saint-Victor* (Paris: P. Lethielleux, 1957), 69–73.

8. See J.-A. Robilliard, "Les six genres de contemplation chez Richard de Saint-Victor et leur origine platonicienne," *Revue des sciences philosophiques et théologiques* 28 (1939): 229–33; and John P. Kleinz, *The Theory of Knowledge of Hugh of St. Victor* (Washington, DC: Catholic University of America Press, 1944), 66–75.

9. Evans, *Language and Logic of the Bible*, 72–73. Boethius' translation of Aristotle's *De Interpretatione* as well as his commentaries on it were part of the *logica vetus*. Martin M. Tweedale mentions that the second commentary may not have been widely used prior to Abelard. See his "Logic (i): From the Late Eleventh Century to the Time of Abelard," in *History of Twelfth-Century Western Philolosophy,* ed. Peter Dronke (Cambridge: Cambridge University Press, 1988), 196–226, esp. 197. However, William of Champeaux (d. c. 1122), the founder of St. Victor, cites Boethius' second commentary on *De Interpretatione* in his *Introductiones dialecticae* 4.5, suggesting its presence within Victorine thought. See Yukio Iwakuma, "The *Introductiones dialecticae secundum Wilgelmum* and *secundum G. Paganellum,*" *Cahiers de l'institute du moyen-age grec et latin* 63 (1993): 45–114.

10. This idea compresses Hugh's two definitions of history as (1) the narration of deeds and events and (2) the first signification of a *vox* to a *res*, with what Wanda Cizewski has called the *littera* of creation or a literal understanding of the *res* comprising the visible world. See Hugh's *De tribus diebus* 1–15 (PL 176.811C–23B); and Wanda Cizewski, "Reading the World as Scripture: Hugh of St. Victor's *De tribus diebus,*" *Florilegium* 9 (1987): 65–88.

11. *Sententiae de divinitate* II.172–210 ("Ugo di San Vittore 'auctor' delle *Sententiae de divinitate,*" ed. A. Piazzoni, *Studi Medievali,* 3rd series 23 [1982]: 861–955, here 918–19 [hereafter, Piazzoni]); *Didascalicon* (hereafter, *Did.*) 5.2–3 (*Hugonis de Sancto Victore Didascalicon de studio legendi,* ed. Charles H. Buttimer [Washington, DC: Catholic University of America Press, 1939], 95–96 [hereafter, Buttimer]; *The Didascalicon of Hugh of St. Victor: A Medieval Guide to the Arts,* trans. Jerome Taylor [New York: Columbia University Press, 1961], 120–22 [hereafter, Taylor]); 6.2–3, 6–10 (Buttimer, 113–17, 123–28; Taylor, 135–39, 145–49); *De scripturis et scriptoribus sacris* 3–5, 14 (PL 175.11D–15A, 20D–21D); *De sacramentis* Prologue.4–5 (PL 176.185A-C; *Hugh of Saint Victor on the Sacraments of the Christian Faith (De sacramentis),* trans. Roy J. Deferrari [Cambridge, MA: Mediaeval Academy of America, 1951], 5 [hereafter, Deferrari]); *De tribus maximis circumstantiis gestorum* or *Chronicon* (Green, "Hugo of Saint Victor").

12. M.-D. Chenu, *La théologie au douzième siècle* (Paris: Vrin, 1957), 65; *Nature, Man, and Society in the Twelfth Century: Essays on New Theological Perspectives in the Latin West,* ed. and trans. Jerome Taylor and Lester K. Little (Toronto: University of Toronto Press, 1997), 166, indicates that *historia* also refers to an intellectual discipline designed to deal with the facts of the narrative (history I). My division between history I and II corresponds to the implicit distinction Hugh at

times himself acknowledges between *littera* and *historia*. See Evans, *Language and Logic of the Bible*, 68–69. De Lubac, *Exégèse médiévale*, 1.2, 425–69; *Medieval Exegesis*, vol. 2, 41–82, sees *littera* and *historia* as interchangeable. Yet, Hugh is also content to use *historia* in reference to both.

13. See *Did.* 6.3 (Buttimer, 116–17; Taylor, 137–38), where Hugh refers to a broader and more narrow way of understanding *historia*.

14. See Hugh, *Chronicon:* "Historia est rerum gestarum narratio per primam litterae significationem expressa" (Green, "Hugo of Saint Victor," 491, lines 4–5). This definition, or slight variations of it, is found in other works and appears to be something Hugh settled upon at the beginning of the 1130s or late 1120s. Cf. *De sacramentis*, Prologue.4 (PL 176.185; Deferrari, 5); *De scripturis* 3 (PL 175.12A). Zinn brought this out in early articles on Hugh. See, e.g., Grover A. Zinn, "*Historia fundamentum est:* The Role of History in the Contemplative Life According to Hugh of St. Victor," in *Contemporary Reflections on the Medieval Christian Tradition: Essays in Honor of Ray C. Petry*, ed. George H. Shriver (Durham, NC: Duke University Press, 1974), 135–58, esp. 140–41.

15. Zinn, "*Historia fundamentum est*," 141. Zinn points out that the *De sacramentis* is set up according to the order and shape of history I. See *De sacramentis*, Prologue.3 (PL 176.184A–D; Deferrari, 4–5); 1.1.29 (PL 176.204C; Deferrari, 27). Hugh provides a list of books that are narrative in genre and therefore indicative of history I. Cf. *Didascalicon* 6.3 (Buttimer, 115; Taylor, 137).

16. While I recognize that the phrase *rerum gestarum narratio* means the narration of deeds/events (things carried out), there is a distinct slippage between Hugh's understanding of the term *res* as a substance having its own existence and his understanding of *res* in *res gesta*. Normally the latter means deeds or acts but Hugh seems so thoroughly committed to the former definition of *res* that I would suggest he reads the phrase with it in mind. One can see this when Hugh posits *gestum* (an action) like Jesus raising Lazarus from the dead as a subcategory of things (*res*), presumably because the action can be broken down into two things (Jesus and Lazarus) and their orderly relation as indicated by the verb "to raise."

17. Hugh divides Christian salvation history into two states, three periods of time, and six stages. Cf. Hugh, *De scripturis* 17 (PL 175.24B–D). The division into two states is the old and new, while the division into three periods of time is the natural law, written law, and grace. The six ages are: (1) Adam to Noah; (2) Noah to Abraham; (3) Abraham to David; (4) David to Babylonian exile; (5) Babylonian exile to Christ; and (6) Christ to the end of the world.

18. Jan W. M. van Zwieten, "Jewish Exegesis within Christian Bounds: Richard of St. Victor's *De Emmanuele* and Victorine Hermeneutics," *Bijdragen, tijdschrift voor filosofie en theologie* 48 (1987): 327–34.

19. There is a difference in the title of the chapter between Migne's edition and the *Indiculum*. The *Indiculum* has the title, *Quam sit necessaria lectio historica,*

whereas Migne has the title, *Quod sit necessaria interpretatio litteralis et historica.* Cf. Zinn, "Hugh of St. Victor's *De scripturis,*" 126 n. 60; and J. de Ghellinck, "La table des matières de la première édition des oeuvres de Hugues de Saint-Victor," *Recherches de Sciences Religieuses* 1 (1910): 270–89, 385–96, esp. 278.

20. *De scripturis* 5: "Litteram autem ignorare est ignorare quid littera significet, et quid significetur a littera. . . . Cum igitur res illae quas littera significat, spiritualis intelligentiae signa sint, quomodo signa tibi esse possunt, quae necdum tibi significata sunt? . . . Ille rectissime incedit, qui incedit ordinate" (PL 175.13D–14A). This means, as van Zwieten says, that *lectio historica* prepares one for *sensus historicus.* See his "Jewish Exegesis," 329.

21. *De scripturis* 5 and 14 (PL 175.13D–15A, 20D–21D).

22. See Mary Carruthers, *The Book of Memory: A Study of Memory in Medieval Culture* (Cambridge: Cambridge University Press, 1990).

23. Hugh identifies the purpose of the *trivium* and *quadrivium* in several places: *Sententiae de divinitate* II.195–200 (Piazzoni, 919); *De scripturis* 13 (PL 175.20B–D); *De sacramentis* Prologue.6 (PL 176.185C–D; Deferrari, 5–6). In *Did.* 2.20, Hugh states that the *trivium* "concerns words which are external and the *quadrivium* concerns concepts which are conceived internally" (*quia trivium de vocibus quae extrinsecus sunt et quadrivium de intellectibus qui intrinsecis conceptis sunt;* Buttimer, 39; Taylor, 75).

24. See Hugh, *De arca Noe morali* 1.3 (PL 176.628C–629C). See also van Zwieten, "Scientific and Spiritual Culture in Hugh of St. Victor," in *Centres of Learning: Learning and Location in Pre-modern Europe and the Near East,* ed. Jan W. Drijvers and Alasdair A. MacDonald (Leiden: E. J. Brill, 1995), 177–86, who discusses Hugh's use of geometry for literal and spiritual interpretation. On Richard, see Walter Cahn, "Architecture and Exegesis: Richard of St.-Victor's Ezekiel Commentary and Its Illustrations," *The Art Bulletin* 76 (1994): 33–68, esp. 53–68; J. Schröder, *Gervasius von Canterbury, Richard von Saint-Victor und die Methodik der Bauerfassung im 12. Jahrhundert,* Band I (Köln: Kleikamp Druck, 2000), 181, 214–16 (hereafter, Schröder); and Patrice Sicard, "L'urbanisme de la Cité de Dieu: constructions et architectures dans la pensée théologique du XIIe siècle," in *L'abbé Suger, le manifeste gothique de Saint-Denis et la pensée victorine,* ed. Dominique Poirel and Alain Erlande-Brandenburg (Turnhout: Brepols, 2001), 109–40.

25. The discrepancies in measurement account for Gregory the Great's rejection of any literal meaning to Ezekiel's vision. See Gregory, *Homiliae in Hiezechielem prophetam,* ed. M. Adriaen, CCSL 142 (Turnhout: Brepols, 1971), 208. A contemporary of Richard's, Robert of Cricklade, agreed with Gregory. Cf. Cahn, "Architecture and Exegesis," 57; Smalley, *Study of the Bible,* 108–9.

26. Berndt, *André de Saint-Victor,* 214, also mentions chronology and geography as two places in Andrew where one can see the influence of the *quadrivium.*

27. See Berndt, "La pratique exégétique d'André de Saint-Victor," 288–89, who indicates that the narrative truth of the story depends upon its internal coherence

and agreement with the facts. I would suggest the broader criterion of correspondence to reality because focusing on whether the narrative could reflect historical realities allows for the literal interpretation of a narrative sequence that is not necessarily historical and thus could not have agreement with historical facts. Ezekiel's temple provides a good example. Its literal interpretation does not depend upon whether it did exist as a *historical* fact but if it could exist as such.

28. G. R. Evans highlights Hugh's point that the interpreter looks for the *veritas rerum* and *forma verborum* when discussing how to read Genesis (*Language and Logic of the Bible*, 69–70). Hugh states, "For just as we know the truth of 'things' by the truth of words, so, conversely, when the truth of 'things' is known, we may more easily know the truth of words. For through that historical narration we are carried on to a deeper understanding of 'things'" ("Quia sicut per veritatem verborum cognoscimus veritatem rerum ita contra, cognita veritate rerum, facilius cognoscimus veritatem verborum; quia per istam historicam narrationem ad altiorum rerum intelligentiam provehimur"; PL 175.32D–3A). In light of this quotation, Evans notes that the distinction between the "'historical' strictly speaking and 'literal' lies close to the heart of the distinction between the significance of words and the significance of 'things' in scripture" (70). I would suggest this also reinforces my claim that understanding things as they are arranged in sequential narrative (history I) and the relationship between a word and a thing (history II) corresponds to understanding the visible world.

29. II.191–94: "Est praetera notandum quod, cum aliis libris, id est in libris ethnicorum, tria tantum sint, id est res, intellectus et voces, et voces significent res mediantibus intellectibus, in divino eloquio multo aliter est" (Piazzoni, 919).

30. *Did.* 5.3: "Ex quo nimirum colligitur, quam profunda in sacris litteris requirenda sit intelligentia, ubi per vocem ad intellectum, per intellectum ad rem, per rem ad rationem, per rationem pervenitur ad veritatem" (Buttimer, 97; Taylor, 122; translation taken from Taylor). Taylor links Hugh's statement to Eriugena but, as will become clear, the parallel with Boethius seems much stronger. See Taylor, 219–20 n. 7.

31. *Did.* 1.11 (Buttimer, 19; Taylor, 58). Sweeney, "Hugh of St. Victor: Augustinian Tradition," 68, recognizes the Boethian link but does not explore it.

32. See also Constant J. Mews, "Logic in the Service of Philosophy: William of Champeaux and His Influence," in *Schrift, Schreiber, Schenker: Studien zur Abtei Sankt Viktor in Paris und den Viktorinern*, ed. Rainer Berndt (Berlin: Akademie Verlag, 2005), 89–96. Mews finds the distinction between *sermocinalis* and *dissertiva* in William of Champeaux and suggests that Hugh may have gotten the distinction from a commentary like William's on Cicero's *De inventione*.

33. The second commentary on the *Isagoge* does discuss the problem of universals in terms of the relationship between *intellectus* and *res*. Cf. Boethius, *Commentaria in Porphyrium a se translatum* II, ed. S. Brandt, CSEL 48 (Leipzig: G.

Freytag, 1906), 159–69. For a translation of the passage, see *Five Texts on the Mediaeval Problem of Universals,* trans. and ed. P. V. Spade (Indianapolis: Hackett, 1994), 20–25. For a discussion of the problem of universals in relation to Hugh, see John P. Kleinz, *The Theory of Knowledge of Hugh of Saint Victor* (Washington, DC: Catholic University of America Press, 1944), 41–62.

34. *In Perihermeneias* I.1.1, ed. C. Meiser (Leipzig: Teubner, 1880), 36–38. While there is currently no evidence for Boethius' commentaries in the library at St. Victor, it is clear that St. Victor possessed a copy of Abelard's logical works (MS Paris BnF lat. 14614), including his comments on Boethius' two commentaries. In addition, in two places the distinction between *vox, intellectus,* and *res* is indicated as being mentioned by William of Champeaux, providing further evidence of the presence of this epistemological triad early on at St. Victor. Cf. fragments 1, 3, 4, and 14, where the view that a *locus* (topic) is a *res,* not a *vox* or an intellectus, is attributed to William in N. J. Green-Pedersen, "William of Champeaux on Boethius' Topics According to Orleans Bibl. Mun. 266," *Cahiers de l'institut du moyen-âge grec et latin* 13 (1974): 13–30; and the *Introductiones dialecticae secundum Wilgelmum* 3–4, which uses the distinction in Iwakuma, "The *Introductiones dialecticae secundum Wilgelmum,*" 72–73.

35. *In Peri.* I.1.1 (Meiser, I 37, 13–15; 38, 21–24); *In Peri.* II.1.1 (Meiser, II 20, 14–25). See also John Magee, *Boethius on Signification and Mind* (Leiden: E. J. Brill, 1989), 64–92, where he gives a detailed explanation of the relevant sections of Boethius' second commentary.

36. Boethius' language parallels Hugh's *Sententiae de divinitate* as quoted above: "in quantum vero vox per intellectuum medietatem subiectas intellectui res demonstrat. . . ." Cf. *In Peri.* II.1 (Meiser, 7, 12–14). There is no direct linguistic parallel with Boethius' first commentary but the section cited in the previous note does discuss the way *intellectus* mediates between *res* and *voces.*

37. *In Peri.* I.1.1 (Meiser, I 37, 24–25); *In Peri.* II.1.1 (Meiser, II 23, 2–5).

38. *Did.* 5.3 (Buttimer, 96; Taylor, 121). In *Sententiae de divinitate* II (Piazzoni, 919), Hugh uses the expression *res vero ex institutione Dei.* See also *De scripturis* 14 (PL 175.20D–21D).

39. Sicard, *Diagrammes médiévaux,* 157–70, does not mention Boethius in his analysis of Hugh's understanding about *vox* and *res.* Steven Chase's work on Richard's *De arca mystica* fails to mention Boethius, even in the bibliography: see *Angelic Wisdom: The Cherubim and the Grace of Contemplation in Richard of St. Victor* (Notre Dame, IN: University of Notre Dame Press, 1995). Nor does Rainer Berndt reference Boethius in his section on *vox* and *res* with regard to Andrew: see *André de Saint-Victor,* 176–94.

40. *De scripturis* 5: "Non enim dictio apertis oculis dormit, sed animal ipsum quod dictio significat. Intellige igitur quod cum leo Christum significare dicit, non nomen animalis, sed animal ipsum significatur" (PL 175.13C–D). There seems to be

a close relationship between *vox* and *dictio* for Hugh. When making a similar statement about the term *leo* in *Did.* 5.3 (Buttimer, 97; Taylor, 122), Hugh uses *vox* instead of *dictio*. Both terms represent spoken language.

41. *Did.* 5.3: "si enim duae hae voces, id est, diabolus et leo, unam et eandem rem significant, incompetens est similitudo eiusdem rei ad seipsam" (Buttimer, 97; Taylor, 122).

42. *De scripturis* 14 (PL 175.20D). Richard sets forth Hugh's position in *Liber exceptionum* 1.2.5 (*Liber exceptionum. Texte critique avec introduction, notes et tables*, ed. Jean Châtillon [Paris, J. Vrin, 1958], 116).

43. It is interesting to note that Frans van Liere's analysis of Andrew of St. Victor's exegetical practice roughly follows this same procedure. Van Liere notes that there are four elements to Andrew's practice: (1) criticism, division, and punctuation of a text; (2) grammatical and linguistic analysis of the text; (3) literary analysis; and (4) application of quadrivium, history, and knowledge of antiquities as these pertain to the facts. Cf. Frans van Liere, "Introduction," *Andreae de Sancto Victore opera, II Expositio hystorica in librum Regum*, CCCM 53A (Turnhout: Brepols, 1996), xli.

44. See Berndt, *André de Saint-Victor*, 177–84; Grover Zinn, "History and Contemplation: The Dimensions of the Restoration of Man in Two Treatises on Noah's Ark by Hugh of St. Victor," Ph.D. diss., Duke University, 1969, 95–101; G. Paré, A. Brunet, P. Tremblay, *La renaissance du XIIe siècle. Les écoles et l'enseignement* (Paris-Ottawa: J. Vrin, 1933), 228–29.

45. *Did.* 3.8 (Buttimer, 58; Taylor, 92); 6.9 (Buttimer, 126; Taylor, 147–48). Taylor (92 n. 54) notes the comparison between the two chapters. See also Berndt, *André de Saint-Victor*, 177–78; and Zinn, "History and Contemplation," 96.

46. "[L]ittera est congrua ordinatio dictionum, quod etiam constructionem vocamus" (Buttimer, 58; Taylor, 92). Note also Hugh's *De grammatica* 4, which states "constructio est dictionum congrua in oratione ordinatio" (*Hugonis de Sancto Victore Opera Propaedeutica*, ed. Roger Baron [Notre Dame, IN: University of Notre Dame Press, 1966], 106 line 917). This follows Priscian's definition: "constructio . . . est congrua dictionum ordinatio" (*Institutionum grammaticarum Libri XVIII* 17.2, Grammatici latini, ed. M. Hertz, vol. 3 [Leipzig, 1855], 108, 1.5–109, 1.3. Although, as Taylor notes (80 n. 84), Hugh does not mention this particular work of Priscian's in the *Did.*, it does not imply that Hugh was unfamiliar with the work, only that he did not wish novices to spend time in lengthy examinations of one particular art or science.

47. Zinn, "History and Contemplation," 97, mentions Jerome's direct translation of Hebraisms as an example of what would produce odd grammatical constructions. See also Paré, Brunet, Tremblay, *La renaissance du XIIe siècle*, 228–29.

48. *Did.* 3.8 (Buttimer, 58; Taylor, 92).

49. *Did.* 6.9 (Buttimer, 126; Taylor, 147–48).

50. *Sententiae de divinitate* II.206–8: "Item voces aut univoce sunt aut equivoce. Si univoce, unum significant; si equivoce pauca tantum, id est duo vel tria vel quattro prout ab homine imposita sunt" (Piazzoni, 919). In the same section Hugh had already stated, "voces enim ex impositione hominum significant." The use of the term *impositio* with its verbal cognate *imposita sunt* points toward the technical expression of imposition taken from dialectic. As G. R. Evans notes, dialecticians used imposition to denote the "flexible attachment of words to the things they signify" (*Language and Logic of the Bible*, 75–80, here 75).

51. Isidore of Seville, *Etymologiarum* 2.26, lines 4–7, vol. 1, books 1–10, ed. W. M. Lindsay (Oxford: Clarendon Press, 1911).

52. *Did.* 6.10: "Sed fortasse quid hoc totum simul significare velit, intelligere non potes" (Buttimer, 127; Taylor, 148).

53. *Did.* 6.10 (Buttimer, 128; Taylor, 149). Hugh explicitly mentions idiomatic expressions.

54. *De meditandis plagis quae circa finem mundi evenient:* "Et otiosae erunt molentes (Eccl. 12.3). . . . Juxta morem terrae Palaestinorum videtur hoc dicere, ubi solent feminae ad molam sedere, et fruges terere" (PL 196.204B). This short tract offers a literal interpretation of Eccles. 12 as it relates to the final tribulation at the end of the world. Richard thinks that if one examines the surface of the letter (*ad litterae superficiem*), as he has done, it will become apparent that Eccles. 12 contains a summary of the great tribulation. See also *In visionem Ezechielis* 8, where Richard speculates that the roof of the gatehouse to the temple must have been flat as opposed to upright based on an appeal to the custom of the buildings in Palestine (PL 196.554D; Schröder, 442).

55. Berndt, *André de Saint-Victor*, 178: "désigne chez Hugues la cohérence d'ensemble des significations offertes par les différents mots (*voces*) dont est composée la *littera.*"

56. For further discussion of the meaning of *sententia*, see Zinn, "History and Contemplation," 96–100; Paré, Brunet, Tremblay, *La renaissance du XIIe siècle*, 228–29, 267–74; and Evans, *Language and Logic of the Bible*, 140–43. The term seems to imply the meaning given by the divine author since *sententia* refers to opinions, verdicts, or judgments.

57. Zinn, "History and Contemplation," 97.

58. See Roger Baron, *Etudes sur Hugues de Saint-Victor* (Paris: Desclée de Brouwer, 1964), 136–39; and Zinn, "History and Contemplation," 96.

59. This illuminates one of the differences between St. Victor and the so-called school of Chartres. The Victorines reject the attempt to discover the *integumentum* of secular *auctores,* as for example William of Conches' *Glossa super Platonem.* Cf. Winthrop Wetherbee, *Platonism and Poetry in the Twelfth Century: The Literary Influence of the School of Chartres* (Princeton, NJ: Princeton University Press, 1972), 36–46.

60. *Did.* 6.8 (Buttimer, 125; Taylor, 147).

61. "[H]istoria est significatio vocum ad res" (PL 177.375A). Printed among the works of Hugh in *Patrologiae latinae,* the work has been determined to be authored by someone within the Victorine community. Cf. Châtillon, *Le mouvement canonial au moyen âge,* 293–323. Châtillon uses it in his reconstruction of Victorine ecclesiology.

62. See Hugh's discussion in *De scripturis* 3 (PL 175.11D–12C).

63. Hugh uses the phrase "the entire sequence and extension of time" (*tota series et porrectio temporis*) to designate the broader sweep of history in contradistinction to his more narrow *series vel narratio gestarum rerum.* Cf. Hugh, *De scripturis* 17 (PL 175.24B). Hugh also uses the phrase *gesta temporum* in reference to the events or deeds occurring over the course of human history. Cf. *Chronicon* Prologue (Green, "Hugo of St. Victor," 491 lines 13–14).

64. *De scripturis* 18: "In libris etiam Machabaeorum et in Daniele quaedam dicuntur, quae non facile intelligere possis, nisi cognoveris primum eos qui post Alexandrum Magnum in regnum Syriae et Aegypti successerunt" (PL 175.25C).

65. Richard uses Jewish contemporaries to resolve chronological issues among the kings of Judah and Israel. Cf. *De concordia temporum regum congrenantium super Judam et super Israel* (PL 196.241B). Andrew does as well. Cf. Michael Signer, "Introduction," in *Andreae de Sancto Victore opera, Expositio in Ezechielem,* CCCM 53E (Turnhout: Brepols, 1991), xxxvi.

CHAPTER SIX

The Harmony of Similar and Dissimilar Things

Narrative and Reason in Richard of St. Victor's De Emmanuele

Boyd Taylor Coolman

Near the beginning of *De doctrina christiana,* Augustine of Hippo compares the Incarnation to a remedy applied to wounded human beings in order to effect their healing: "[J]ust as physicians when they bind up wounds do not do so haphazardly but neatly so that a certain beauty accompanies the utility of the bandages, so the medicine of Wisdom in assuming human nature is harmonized [*coaptare*] to our wounds, healing some by dissimilar things and some by similar things."[1] The bishop provides examples of these similar and dissimilar things. Born of a woman, Christ freed those who had been deceived by a woman; as a human being He freed human beings; as a mortal He freed mortals; in death He freed the dead. Complementing these similar things are certain dissimilarities: ensnared by serpentine wisdom, humans were freed by divine foolishness; humans ill used their immortality, incurring death, but Christ restored life by using his mortality well; from Eve's corrupt spirit came sin, while salvation came from Mary's incorrupt flesh. In these correspondences Augustine espies a beautiful utility in Christ's Incarnation, the salvific aptness of which persuasively reveals divine wisdom.[2]

This inclination to revel in harmonies between humanity's ruin and redemption is ubiquitous in Christian history; Augustine is neither the first nor last. His comments here, however, provide a suitable backdrop from which to consider the exegetical practice of one of the bishop's medieval readers, Richard of St. Victor.[3] As seen below, in his exegesis of Isaiah 7:14, "Behold a virgin will conceive," etc.—the controversial text which prompts Richard's treatise *De Emmanuele*[4]—he argues for a christological interpretation in a manner reminiscent of Augustine's text.[5] For Richard, the correct interpretation of Isaiah's prophecy emerges in relation to various similar and dissimilar correspondences[6] between the content of the prophecy and the larger narrative of Christian salvation history.[7]

At the same time, Richard's interpretation of Isaiah's prophecy is shaped by his twelfth-century context, in particular an increased interaction between Christian and Jewish exegetes at that time. Recently scholars have noted the significant and often parallel developments that occurred in the realm of biblical exegesis within Jewish and Christian communities during the eleventh and twelfth centuries.[8] In their attempts to understand the literal sense of the biblical text, Jewish and Christian exegetes alike were acquiring greater sensitivity to the sequence of textual narrative and the interpretive implications entailed by such narrative frameworks. The twelfth-century context, with its renewed interest in various aspects of scriptural exegesis, provided fertile soil for a fruitful interaction between Jewish and Christian exegetes. Michael Signer has demonstrated the significant and, in many ways, parallel developments that occurred in the realm of biblical exegesis within Jewish and Christian communities during the eleventh and twelfth centuries in Europe. In addition to their increased sensitivity to textual narrative, Jewish and Christian exegetes alike also stressed the experience of the reader, the role of the author, and the order of nature in their attempts to understand the literal sense of the biblical text. On the Christian side, this development is most conspicuous among the scholars at the Abbey of St. Victor in Paris, specifically with Hugh and his pupils Andrew and Richard.[9]

This new sensitivity is pivotal in Richard's interpretation of Isaiah 7:14. Signer has argued that the intramural debate between Andrew and Richard turns on the question of narrative units in the text. He argues that the Jewish exegetes by whom Andrew was influenced in his own exegesis of the Isaiah passage saw chapters 7–8 as constituting one coherent narrative sequence, while Richard, though still concerned with the concept of narrative units, saw them as distinct.[10] As Richard presents it, his disagreement with the Jewish interpretation (reported by his colleague, Andrew of St. Victor, along with his students[11]) concerns the proper narrative framework within which to interpret Isaiah's prophecy. For Richard, the prophecy finds its most reasonable and fitting interpretation when understood within the framework of Christian salvation history, reaching from creation and fall in Genesis to the annunciation and Incarnation in the Gospels. His principal strategy, accordingly, is to locate the prophecy within this context and then to argue for a christological interpretation by employing the principle of similar and dissimilar correspondences between the prophecy and both its antecedents in Eden and its fulfillment in Bethlehem. In so doing, he reveals yet another—perhaps the most important—influence, namely that of Hugh of St. Victor. It is Hugh's theoretical account of such an exegetical method in his *Didascalicon de studio legendi* that Richard appears here to have appropriated.[12]

The Narrative Context of Isaiah 7–8 and the Jewish Interpretation of the Prophecy

At the outset of the *De Emmanuele,* Richard records the Jewish interpretation of the prophecy. The Jewish strategy is to proceed sequentially through the text, finding clues to a coherent interpretation of the prophetic sign in the context of the immediately surrounding verses. The first verses of Isaiah 7 describe how Rasin (Resin), the king of Syria, and Phacee (Pekah), the king of Israel, have aligned themselves for battle against Jerusalem and King Ahaz.[13] God commands Isaiah to take his son and go to Ahaz with a prophecy declaring that they should not fear because the Lord will prevent Rasin and Phacee from accomplishing their purposes and will destroy them instead. Into this situation is given the prophecy, beginning in verse 14: "Therefore the Lord himself shall give you a sign. Behold a virgin shall conceive, and bear a son; and his name shall be called Emmanuel. He shall eat butter and honey, that he may know to refuse evil and to choose the good." Of equally crucial significance are verses 3–4 of chapter 8, where Isaiah says: "And I went to the prophetess, and she conceived and bore a son. Then the Lord said to me, Call his name 'Hasten to take away the spoils, make haste to take away the prey'; for before the child knows how to call 'My Father' or 'My mother,' the strength of Damascus and the spoils of Samaria will be carried away by the king of the Assyrians." The debate between Richard's and Andrew's students concerns these verses.

For their part, the Jews argue that the sign prophesied in chapter 7 finds its fulfillment in the opening verses of chapter 8 and that these two chapters thus provide a sufficient narrative framework for the most reasonable and coherent interpretation of the text. First, on linguistic grounds they argue that the word in the Hebrew text of Isaiah 7:14 is not "virgin" but "young or hidden woman."[14] Accordingly, there is no suggestion of a virgin giving birth, as Christians claim. This bolsters their more substantial claim that the prophecy concerning the birth of a child is fulfilled in the first verses of chapter 8 which records that the prophetess of Isaiah conceived and bore a son from Isaiah himself. It is prophesied in chapter 7 that a woman will conceive, and in chapter 8 a woman conceives. It is prophesied in chapter 7 that a woman will give birth to a son, and in chapter 8 a woman bears a son.[15]

Next, they claim that what was promised through the sign was subsequently fulfilled: "Indeed, does not the fulfillment follow the sign? During the days of the infant son of the young woman, [in which] Judah trembled in the presence of those two kings, the one was killed by the Assyrians, the other lay slaughtered by Hosea the son of Elam. See the sign went out first, the fulfillment followed. Judah was freed from fear, and the sign was given so that this fear would be removed."[16] In short, they argue that a christological interpretation is incoherent within the narrative sequence of Isaiah 7–8 because, from their perspective, it introduces an anachronism: it is impossible for the birth of Jesus of Nazareth, six centuries later, to be the sign which Isaiah foretold in chapter 7 and which was fulfilled in chapter 8. The Jews thus challenge the Christians: "Let that which you yourselves place there be removed from the text and you will see immediately that these things are fittingly [*convenire*] said concerning the son of the prophetess."[17]

Richard's Jewish exegetes accuse the Christians of being "perverters and violent distorters of Scripture" because they focus exclusively on the two verses describing the sign while ignoring the immediate narrative context.[18] From this Jewish perspective, the Christians "proceed according to a difficult method, while [the Jews] proceed in a smooth manner, in which the whole content of the chapter is harmonized [*consonant*]." The Christians, they claim, "adhere to one small verse, while contradicting the whole context of the literal sense," while they themselves "follow the whole chapter from the beginning to the end, in order that it might be better understood."[19] The Jewish argument is succinctly summed up in a statement that Richard records: "See," they say, "everything proceeds rationally, everything which was promised happens."[20]

Richard's Response: The Insufficiency of the Jewish Interpretation

Richard responds to the Jewish interpretation with a two-part strategy. First, he attempts to refute the Jewish interpretation by showing its insufficiency. Second, and more importantly, he tries to show how a christological interpretation yields a more complete and satisfying, and therefore more reasonable, account of all the elements of the prophecy.

Richard's attempt to demonstrate the insufficiency of the Jewish interpretation entails several claims. He argues that for something to be a sign, it has to be unusual and extraordinary. But, in his mind, there is nothing unusual about a young woman who gives birth to a son nor about a child who eats butter and honey.[21] More substantively, from his perspective the subsequent deliverance from the two kings who were attacking Judah occurs too soon after the child's birth for his knowledge of good and evil to be a sign of that deliverance. From Richard's viewpoint, the liberation from these enemies occurred before the sign, rendering it no sign at all.[22] He then treats the philological problem concerning what kind of woman is to give birth. Is she a virgin or young woman? Here, he resorts to Jerome, who had argued that although the Hebrew text does not use the word for virgin (*beculah*), the word which is used (*almah*) can and should be understood to mean a virgin.[23] In short, Richard argues that there is no complete correspondence between the sign given in Isaiah 7:14–15 and the events which are described in the opening verses of chapter 8.

Richard's manner of arguing against the proposed correspondences of the Jewish interpretation merits further attention. He observes that the letter of the biblical text is always ambiguous, always partly revealing and partly obscuring its true meaning.[24] How, then, is the true meaning to be determined? The determining criteria is a principle of similar and dissimilar things, reminiscent of Augustine, and he applies this principle as the lynchpin of his refutation of the Jewish interpretation. He argues that in the purported connection between chapters 7 and 8 there are three kinds of things: similar things, dissimilar things, and, in addition to these two, things altogether contrary:

> Notice that it is said concerning Emmanuel that *before he knows to refuse evil and choose the good, the land will be forsaken of those two kings* [7:16]. This is similar to what is read concerning the son of the prophetess that *before the boy knows to call his father or his mother, the strength of Damascus and the spoils of Samaria will be carried away by the king of the Assyrians* [8:4]. It is said that *his name shall be called Emmanuel* [7:14b]. This is dissimilar to that which was commanded concerning him, *Call his name, Hasten to take away the spoils, make haste to take away the prey* [8:3]. For it does not say, *Call his name Emmanuel* [7:14b]. . . . There [in 7:14a] we read that *a virgin will conceive and bear a son.* This is altogether contrary to what we find here [in ch. 8], that by the approach of her husband the young woman conceived. It does not say *a virgin,* but *a young woman* or *a hidden woman.*[25]

And so Richard concludes: "See how the whole context of the letter is not contradicted by us, as they wish, but is found to refute them."[26]

Here, then, Richard argues that although there are similarities between the prophecy in chapter 7 and the events described in chapter 8, there are certain dissimilarities and certain things altogether contrary, which prohibit any complete correspondence between them. Given the ambiguity and obscurity of the letter and the indeterminacy of the historical sense, the

Jewish interpretation fails for Richard because in it the various textual and prophetic elements fail to cohere sufficiently with the proposed narrative framework. In Richard's mind, another narrative context must be sought.

The Narrative Context of Christian Salvation History

As intimated above, Richard's own approach is to shift the narrative context from Isaiah 7–8 to the entire span of Christian salvation history, from Genesis to the Gospels.[27] Noteworthy at this juncture is how he understands this shift in relation to the literal sense of the text. He explicitly recognizes that, in one sense, by proposing a christological interpretation he is abandoning the literal sense *of the local narrative* of Isaiah 7–8. He informs his opponents that "even if it is never granted to you to be able to harmonize [*coaptare*] this prophecy according to the explicit meaning of the surrounding letter, you still ought nevertheless to believe it to have been predicted of Christ, and to have been fulfilled in Christ."[28] In a more fundamental way, though, Richard does not see his shift from one narrative frame to another as abandoning the literal sense. Early in the treatise, he stated his intention merely to "satisfy the devotion of the faithful with a simple exposition of the literal sense."[29] Later, Richard offers this characterization of the literal, historical sense of Scripture. For him, the literal sense, especially of Old Testament texts, is always ambiguous—always, as noted above, partly revealing, partly concealing its true meaning:

Those things, therefore, which it was appropriate to conceal for a while in the sacraments of Christ were hidden partly in the veil of figures, partly in the ambiguity and obscurity of the letter itself. And, indeed, of those things which were hidden by the perplexing circumstances of the letter, certain of these kinds of things are not able to be understood concerning Christ unless they are interpreted by the Holy Spirit, such as *Out of Egypt I have called my son*. Moreover, there are certain things of this kind that from a superficial inspection seem to mean something other than Christ, but by a more diligent investigation and fuller understanding are found in no way capable of receiving some other meaning. Such surely is this place in Scripture which is greatly disputed. For where it is said, *Behold a virgin will conceive,* certain things are hinted at, certain things are added in which the truth of the meaning is veiled, [but] not entirely removed.[30]

As will be apparent below, for Richard an adequate interpretation of this text, one that satisfactorily resolves the ambiguity and obscurity of the literal sense, depends in large part on determining the best narrative context in which to read it literally.

The vocabulary Richard employs above in rejecting the local Isaiah narrative also merits attention for it reveals a crucial exegetical principle that will be central to his interpretation. To describe the exegetical act of 'squaring' a particular passage within a narrative, Richard here uses the same word, *coaptare* (translated "to harmonize"), that Augustine used in the passage cited above from *De doctrina christiana.* For Richard, such corresponding harmonies determine the best interpretation of Scripture. He is not able to find them in the narrow context of chapters 7–8 and, thus, feels compelled to seek them elsewhere.

At the outset of the *De Emmanuele,* Richard advertised the strategy he will now employ in finding such a narrative framework. Situating his project in the Augustinian-Anselmian trajectory of 'faith seeking understanding' with the standard appeal to Isaiah 7:9, he observes: "He who does not yet understand what he reads should at least believe from the heart, and thus merit to understand: *If you do not believe, you will not understand* [Is. 7:9]."[31] Such a one, approaching the text with prior faith in Christ, can begin to discern a narrative context in which Isaiah's prophecy might be rightly understood: "This [is] the most firm argument of our faith, that the prophet and the evangelist declare the same thing so harmoniously [*concorditer*]. What the prophet declared ahead of time, *Behold a virgin will conceive and bear a son, and his name shall be called Emmanuel,* is what the evangelist declared in different words, *The Word became flesh and dwelt among us* [Jn. 1:14]."[32] A christological interpretation, which links Isaiah's prophecy and the gospel account, creates the possibility for seeing harmonious correspondence between the elements in the prophetic sign and their fulfillment in the Christian understanding of salvation history.

Isaiah's Prophecy and the Genesis Account of the Fall

Richard begins his quest for a fitting narrative framework in which Isaiah's prophecy can find compelling textual resonance by aligning it with both similar and dissimilar aspects of the Genesis account of humanity's fall, arguing that the entire prophecy "points back to the original sin . . . and seems to correspond" to it.[33] Of the primal eating from the tree of the knowledge of good and evil, he notes that "here something similar is said, except that what is promised truly here [in Isaiah 7] is promised falsely there [in Genesis]."[34] In Genesis, eating resulted in guilt because it was sinful; in Isaiah, eating resulted in merit because it was virtuous. In Genesis, Adam was not able to obtain the promised knowledge by eating; in Isaiah, Emmanuel obtained the knowledge of good and evil by eating. In Genesis, humans were thrown out of paradise, forfeiting companionship with God; in Isaiah, the promised boy will be called Emmanuel, which means 'God with us.'[35] After laying out these various correspondences, he summarizes by observing the harmony of similar and dissimilar things:

> You see how man corresponds to man, woman corresponds to woman; now one way, now the other, and certain similar things seem to correspond mutually in a dissimilar way. This woman from that man alone, this man from that woman alone. Do you not see how such similar dissimilarity and dissimilar similarity teach us a certain principle of novelty or newness in these things, just as a certain principle of antiquity or oldness exists in those things? In the first man, [there is] a certain beginning of growing old in the condemnation of his posterity. In the second man, [there is] a certain beginning of renewal in the restoration of his race.[36]

For Richard, such "similar dissimilarity and dissimilar similarity" reveal a correspondence between humanity's primal fall and the sign of its future restoration, which offers a persuasive rationale for interpreting the prophecy of Isaiah 7 within a wider narrative context than that formed by chapter 8.

With this appeal to the events of Genesis, Richard has begun to recontextualize Isaiah's prophecy within the wider narrative of salvation history, allowing him to seek and find correspondences between the Genesis text and Isaiah's prophecy. Moreover, one hears an echo of Augustine's emphasis on the similarities and dissimilarities of the divine remedy in the Incarnation: "Observe, [therefore] how the character of the sign shows that it was given for the sake of taking away the first sin. See that what is said concerning Emmanuel was given as a remedy."[37] It is not simply that a correspondence exists, but the way it emerges—with similar dissimilarity or dissimilar similarity—that especially interests Richard.

Good Victorine that he is, Richard finds three aspects of loss resulting from the fall: the loss of incorruptibility, dignity, and beatitude.[38] But, in light of this threefold curse, God has provided a threefold promise of future restoration.[39] And, in conjunction with the threefold promise, God has also provided a threefold sign in the prophecy of Isaiah: "*Behold, a virgin will conceive and bear a son.* See the first sign. *And his name shall be called Emmanuel.* See the second sign. *He will eat butter and honey that he may know to reject evil and choose good.* See the third sign."[40] For Richard, the prophetic sign thus contains three elements: (1) a virgin will conceive a son; (2) his name shall be called Emmanuel; and (3) he will eat butter and honey so that he may know to refuse evil and choose the good. He proceeds to analyze each element of the sign, not only 'backward' in relation to Genesis, but also now 'forward' in relation to the Gospels. Having 'catapulted' himself out of the narrower context of the Isaiah narrative, Richard is able to move freely within the larger Christian narrative of salvation history.

Isaiah's Prophecy and Its Gospel Fulfillment

The first part of the sign is a virginal conception, which for Richard points to the recovery of incorruptibility. Having already established a link to creation and fall in Genesis, Richard now looks forward to the Gospel accounts of Christ's birth. He finds, of course, a correspondence between Isaiah's virgin and Mary, the mother of Jesus, a correspondence which had already been authoritatively sanctioned by Matthew's Gospel: "Observe, the Gospel says that the prophetic words were to be fulfilled in the blessed Mary. Who dares to contradict? There [in Isaiah] it is prophesied that a virgin will conceive; here [in the Gospel] she is said to have conceived by the Holy Spirit."[41] To Richard's satisfaction, Jerome had already proved that the Isaiah text could be interpreted to mean a virgin. But in an important sense, the Genesis-Isaiah-Matthew narrative itself provides the warrant for such an interpretation. From Richard's perspective the sign of a virginal conception in Isaiah connects not only to Christ's virginal birth from Mary but also to the Genesis story. Mary's virginal, and thus incorrupt, conception by the power of the Holy Spirit restored in her the incorruptibility that humanity had lost in Eve, which became a sign and foretaste of what all of humanity was destined to receive in Christ.[42] But it is not the mere fact of correspondences between Isaiah, Genesis, and Matthew's Gospel that warrants the connection. Richard is also keen to find a correspondence of similarities and dissimilarities:

> To be sure, if our Emmanuel had desired to be born from both sexes and if reason had required it, he would have been able to purify both [a man and a woman] so that they might beget a child together. But if Christ had assumed flesh from both sexes, he would have withdrawn further from similarity [to us] in his properties and would not have been as near to us. For he would have been dissimilar to us if he, who had only a Father in his divinity, had had both a father and a mother in his humanity. . . . But, to be sure, reason demands that just as there was one principle in the propagation of our race, so there was to be one principle in the restoration of our race.[43]

Here, Richard suggests that the sign of a virginal conception points to Mary, the singular human principle in the restoration, in a way that also corresponds to the singular primordial beginning of human beings in Adam. But the sign also points to Eve. Mary's incorrupt conception restored the incorruptibility that humanity had lost in Eve. Once again, the logic of similar and dissimilar things comes to the fore in Richard's thinking.

This text is noteworthy not only for its appeal to correspondences between similar and dissimilar things, but also in its appeal to reason as requiring this kind of correspondence.[44] It seems that there is an important link between Richard's preferred narrative framework and his sense of what is a reasonable or rational interpretation of Isaiah's prophecy.

Concerning the Sign of the Recovery of Dignity

The second sign is the name Emmanuel. Here, Richard once again uses his larger narrative context to shape his interpretation, utilizing the context to inform the meaning which he gives even to this individual word. Richard asks the grammatical question, "Is the name Emmanuel to be understood nominatively or substantively?" Is this just a name? Or does a substantial correspondence exist between the name and the boy? His argument runs as follows: According to the Gospel, Jesus was called Emmanuel nominatively. That is, he was given the name Emmanuel. But, since the name means 'God with us' and Jesus is truly and substantially God with us as the Gospel also declares, then the name is used substantially. In passing, he notes that this rules out the Jewish argument, since it presumably would not wish to assert that the boy of Isaiah 8 was substantially God.[45]

Richard's primary aim in this section is to show how the Incarnation itself, the fact that God has truly become human, is a sign of the human dignity of being made in the likeness of God, which was lost in the fall and is now recovered in Christ. Once again, his argument focuses on the correspondences of similar and dissimilar things:

> So Christ freely emptied himself, taking the form of a servant, and was found in the likeness of a human being. Now, therefore, if on humanity's behalf God was made the Son of man by nativity, why all the more is not humanity made the Son of God by God through adoption? See how that dignity of divine humiliation is granted in the sign of our future exaltation. . . . But why, I ask, did God pursue humanity all the way into exile, except that afterwards He might call human beings back into His kingdom? We have, therefore, the most certain sign of our repatriation, that intimate companionship of divine fellow-traveling on this our journey.[46]

Here, the correspondence is the traditional one, common since the patristic period, the same one on which Augustine had focused in the *De doctrina christiana:* God who is dissimilar to man is made similar to man in order that man might be made similar to God.

Concerning the Sign of the Recovery of Felicity

The third sign is the eating of butter and honey. For Richard, this sign connects to the eating in Genesis which led to the loss of felicity, since Adam and Eve were ejected from the garden, as well as to the future recovery of felicity, which also involves eating. Richard pays special attention to the butter and honey. As he sees it, butter and honey are the food—the delicacies—of insects, namely flies and bees. If the Incarnate Christ, who is the delicacy of the angels, descended all the way to the delicacies of insects, this is clearly a sign that humanity will be able to ascend all the way to the delicacies of the angels:

> See, that tremendous power, that power of eating and drinking with angels, [is] shared with humans and animals. If, therefore, the Lord of the angels was made a companion with animals on behalf of humanity, why conversely should not humanity all the more become the companion of the angels through the Lord of the angels? . . . Who, therefore, despairs of the rest, namely, that humanity is able to become a sharer in the eternal delicacies, if the Lord of majesty, as was said, descended all the way to the delicacies of the insects on behalf of humanity? See how he emptied himself for us, he who voluntarily subjected himself to such indignities. But, as was said, this self-emptying of our Redeemer was given as a sign, as the most certain argument of our future plenitude.[47]

Once again, Richard seems to be especially persuaded by the correspondence between prophecy and fulfillment.

Having analyzed in turn each component of the threefold sign, Richard pauses to summarize: "You see how the threefold sign corresponds to the threefold promise. . . . Observe how that threefold promise is confirmed in this threefold sign: In order that corruption may be a sign of incorruption, humiliation a sign of exaltation, and self-emptying a sign of future fullness."[48] In short, Richard's exegetical strategy in interpreting Isaiah's prophecy concerning Emmanuel involves seeking out a narrative framework or context in which the various features of the sign given in Isaiah 7 can find resonant correspondences which are both similar and dissimilar.

For him, such a narrative context emerges when Isaiah is linked with the opening chapters of both the book of Genesis and of Matthew's Gospel. An interpretation within this framework is, for Richard, both most fitting and most rational.

The Removal of Irony

Richard describes one last aspect of Isaiah's sign, which is simply the final dimension of the third component of the sign, "He will eat butter and honey so that he may know to refuse evil and choose good." For Richard, this reference to good and evil points back to the eating of the tree of the knowledge of good and evil in the Genesis story. But it also points forward to the promise of becoming sons of God which is begun in the Incarnation. "For this reason," he notes, "God was made like man, knowing to refuse evil and choose good, that man might become like God, knowing good and evil."[49] In this last case, Richard especially relishes the correspondence of similar and dissimilar things. He observes that in Genesis after the fall God says, "Behold, Adam has become as one of us, knowing good and evil" (Gen. 3:22), and suggests further that God said this ironically [*ironice*] and as a reproach: "See, it has been demonstrated that what was said as reproach concerning the first Adam can now be said as truth concerning the Second Adam. . . . And so Adam, glorified and transfigured thus into the divine likeness, will he not be truly as one of them from whom he heard as a reproach, *Behold Adam has become one of us?* . . . Now let the irony cease, now let it be said plainly according to its meaning."[50] Now, through the Incarnation, the irony has been removed and what was once said as a reproach can now be said plainly, according to its true meaning. In short, the same words can be said but with a different meaning.

For Richard, therefore, the threefold sign prophesied in Isaiah 7 finds its most rational and coherent interpretation within the context of the narrative of Christian salvation history. Only that narrative can adequately incorporate Isaiah's prophetic sign. Within that context, the prophecy is seen to be of Christ, revealed by the correspondences of similarities and dissimilarities that link Adam with Christ, Eve with Mary, Genesis with

Matthew's Gospel. Scholars have noted that Richard reads the biblical text *concorditer,* that is, by seeking the concordances between the two Testaments and, indeed, Richard himself uses this term in a passage quoted previously: "This [is] the most firm argument of our faith, that the prophet and the evangelist declare the same thing so harmoniously [*concorditer*]. What the prophet declared ahead of time, *Behold a virgin will conceive and bear a son, and his name shall be called Emmanuel,* is what the evangelist declared in different words, *The Word became flesh and dwelt among us* [Jn. 1:14]."[51] What has been described above is the particular texture of Richard's 'concordant' reading.

Conclusion: Richard, Student of Hugh

It is often noted that Richard's exegesis reflects the influence of his predecessor, Hugh, and Richard's interpretation of Isaiah 7 is no exception.[52] The exact outlines of Hugh's influence on the *De Emmanuele,* however, have not yet been drawn. For example, Hugh's distinction between the two works—the work of creation and the work of restoration—can be perhaps detected in Richard's concern to link creation and salvation in his exegesis.[53] Richard's interest in the literal sense could certainly stem from Hugh, as Beryl Smalley noted decades ago.[54] In this respect, one could point to the well-known metaphor for exegesis from the sixth book of the *Didascalicon,*[55] commonly called the 'edifice of exposition,'[56] which stresses the importance of the literal sense as the foundation of the subsequent spiritual senses. After introducing this metaphor, Hugh offers advice to his students which Richard seems to have taken to heart: "There are indeed many things in the Scriptures which, considered in themselves, seem to have nothing worth looking for, but if you look at them in the light of the other things to which they are joined, and if you begin to weigh them in their whole context, you will see that they are as necessary as they are fitting."[57] Hugh's exegetical wisdom here might easily have been the warrant for Richard's interest in narrative contexts as the key to his interpretation. But Richard's sensitivity to harmonious and concordant correspondences of similar and dissimilar things within a narrative framework, correspondences which have the force of rational arguments, suggests another possible, though less-noted, aspect of Hugh's influence.

In the final books of his *Didascalicon*, Hugh actually offers two metaphors for exegesis. Along with the 'edifice of exposition' just mentioned, he also offers a metaphor that seems especially pertinent to Richard's approach to Isaiah's prophecy. Earlier, in Book 5, Hugh suggests that with its various senses Scripture can be likened to a zither or lyre, a musical instrument constructed by stretching strings across a wooden frame. He notes: "On the zither and musical instruments of this type not all the parts which are handled ring out with musical sounds; only the strings do this. All the other things on the whole body of the zither are made as a frame to which may be attached, and across which may be stretched, those parts which the artist plays to produce sweet song."[58] After introducing the metaphor, he then relates it to the task of exegesis. The spiritual senses of Scripture are related to the literal sense in the same way that the strings of the lyre are related to its frame:

> All of Sacred Scripture is so suitably adjusted [*aptata*] and arranged in all its parts through the Wisdom of God that whatever is contained in it either resounds with the sweetness of spiritual understanding in the manner of strings; or, containing utterances of mysteries set here and there in the course of a historical narrative or in the substance of a literal context, and, as it were, connecting these up into one object, it binds them together all at once as the wood does which curves under the taut strings; and, receiving their sound into itself, it reflects it more sweetly to our ears—a sound which the string alone has not yielded, but which the wood too has formed by the shape of its body.[59]

Hugh suggests here that like a musician, the scriptural exegete is to 'stretch' the spiritual senses across the frame of the literal and historical narrative so that it "resounds with the sweetness of spiritual understanding in the manner of strings."[60]

Hugh's musical metaphor is instructive for understanding Richard's approach to Isaiah and his critique of the Jewish interpretation. Though Hugh introduces the metaphor in order to relate the literal and spiritual senses,

Richard seems to have adopted its logic in pursuing his own literal interpretation. For him, the Jewish interpretation of Isaiah's prophecy is insufficient because it does not yield the proper resonance; it is exegetically 'out of
tune.' The 'local' narrative framework of Isaiah 7–8 is not capable of yielding a reasonable meaning and needs to be expanded. Richard's own method,
alternatively, involves an attempt to 'tune' the exegetical instrument by ad-
justing the narrative framework—that is, by shifting to the Christian master
narrative of salvation history—so that the text can yield its fitting, that is,
its christological, sound.[61]

From the perspective of Hugh's 'lyre of exposition,' moreover, Richard's frequent references to reason (*ratio*) become more intelligible. Eileen
Sweeney has suggested that Hugh attempted to integrate a dialectical principle of *ratio* into his theology while retaining the master narrative of
Scripture.[62] Within the narrative of creation, fall, and redemption, Sweeney
finds Hugh aligning the dialectical orientation of faith (creation), seeking in
doubt (fall) a fuller understanding (redemption) of what is believed. This
is perhaps consistent with Hugh's theology, but one can also understand
his integration of dialectic and narrative from the perspective of his own
metaphor of the lyre. After introducing this metaphor in Book 5, Hugh
advises his students thus: "It is necessary, therefore, so to handle Sacred
Scripture that we do not try to find history everywhere, nor allegory everywhere, nor tropology everywhere, but rather that we assign individual
things fittingly in their own places, as reason demands."[63]

Throughout the *De Emmanuele*, Richard's exegesis reflects this Hugonian sense of the relation between narrative and reason. For Richard, the
correspondences of similar and dissimilar things between the Isaiah text
and the larger narrative of salvation history reveal the reasonableness of a
christological interpretation. He insists that his interpretation is the most
rational; and his sense of what rational means is a function of the narrative
framework, which acts as the wooden frame of his exegetical lyre. He finds
his interpretation to be the most rational because, in a sense, it alone yields
the right-sounding notes. For Richard, *ratio* is a function of *narratio*. Once
the appropriate framework is adopted, the reasonableness of an interpretation emerges from the inter-textual resonance and concordance of similar
and dissimilar things.

Notes

1. *De doctrina christiana* 1.14 (Saint Augustine, *On Christian Doctrine*, trans. D. W. Robertson [New York: Liberal Arts Press, 1958], 14–15).

2. *De doctrina christiana* 1.14 (Robertson, 15). The word used here by Augustine to describe this congruity between the medicine of the Incarnate Christ and the wounds of fallen humanity is *coaptare,* which he employs to translate the Greek word 'armonia: "coaptationem, si ita dicenda est, quam Graeci ἁρμονιαν vocant" (*De Genesi ad litteram libri duodecim* 10.21 [PL 34:425]; see also *De civitate Dei* 22.24). A *coaptatio* is a "harmonious fitting together." That it should be translated as "harmony" in the passage above is justified by Augustine's similar remark in *De Trinitate.* There he observes: "By joining therefore to us the likeness of His humanity, He took away the unlikeness of our unrighteousness; and by being made partaker of our mortality, He made us partakers of His divinity. For the death of the sinner springing from the necessity of condemnation is deservedly abolished by the death of the Righteous One springing from the free choice of His compassion, while His single [death and resurrection] answers to our double [death and resurrection]. For this congruity, or suitableness, or concord or consonance, or whatever more appropriate word there may be, whereby one is [united] to two, is of great weight in all compacting, or better perhaps co-adaptation, of the creature. For (as it occurs to me) what I mean is precisely that co-adaptation which the Greeks call 'armonia" (*De Trinitate* 4.2).

3. On Richard's exegesis generally, see Rainer Berndt, "The School of St. Victor in Paris," *The Hebrew Bible/Old Testament: The History of Its Interpretation,* ed. Magne Sæbø, vol. 1, *From the Beginning to the Middle Ages (until 1300),* 475–79; Steven Chase, *Angelic Wisdom: The Cherubim and the Grace of Contemplation in Richard of St. Victor* (Notre Dame, IN: University of Notre Dame Press, 1995); Jean Châtillon, "La Bible dans les écoles du XIIe siècle," in *Le moyen age et la Bible* (Paris: Beauchesen, 1984); Jean Châtillon, "Richard de Saint-Victor," in *Dictionnaire de spiritualité: ascétique et mystique, doctrine et histoire* 13:593–654 (Paris: Beauchesne, 1988); René Roques, *Structures théologiques, de la gnose à Richard de Saint-Victor. essais et analyses critiques* (Paris: Presses universitaires de France, 1962); Beryl Smalley, *The Study of the Bible in the Middle Ages* (Notre Dame, IN: University of Notre Dame Press, 1992); C. Spicq, *Esquisse d'une histoire de l'exégèse latine au moyen âge* (Paris: J. Vrin, 1944); J. W. M. van Zwieten, "Jewish Exegesis within Christian Bounds: Richard of St. Victor's *De Emmanuele* and Victorine Hermenuetics," *Bijdragen, Tijdschrift voor Philosophie en Theologie* 48 (1987): 327–35; Grover A. Zinn, "Personification, Allegory, and Visions of Light in Richard of St. Victor's Teaching on Contemplation," *University of Toronto Quarterly* 46 (1977): 190–214.

4. The Latin text of *De Emmanuele* (hereafter *Emman.*) can be found in PL 196:601–66.

5. This is not meant to imply a claim of Augustine's influence on Richard in this regard, but only to notice the similar nature of their arguments.

6. While the language of similarity and dissimilarity may recall the pseudo-Dionysian principle of "dissimilar similitudes," the overall approach employed by Richard does not seem especially Dionysian. See M.-D. Chenu, *Nature, Man, and Society in the Twelfth Century: Essays on New Theological Perspectives in the Latin West,* ed. and trans. Jerome Taylor and Lester K. Little (Chicago: University of Chicago Press, 1968), 130–31.

7. Richard's exegetical works include: *Mystice annotations in Psalmos* (PL 196:263–402), *Expositio in Cantica canticorum* (PL 196:405–524), *Nonulle allegorie tabernaculi federis* (PL 196:191–212), *Expositio difficultatum suborientium in expositione Tabernaculi federis* (PL 196:211–56), *Expositio catici Habacuc* (PL 196:401–4), *In visionem Ezechielis* (PL 196:527–600), *Tractatus de meditandis plagis que circa finem mundi euenient* (PL 196:201–12), *Quomodo Christus ponitur in signum populorum* (PL 196:523–28). In two other works, *De Emmanuele* (PL 196:601–66) and *Liber exceptionum* (*Liber exceptionum: texte critique avec introduction, notes et tables,* ed. Jean Châtillon [Paris: J. Vrin, 1958]), Richard offers theoretical reflections on exegesis, and in the prologue to his commentary *In visionem Ezechielis* he explains his exegetical practice.

8. See Michael Signer, "Peshat, *Sensus Litteralis,* and Sequential Narrative: Jewish Exegesis and the School of St. Victor in the Twelfth Century," in *The Frank Talmage Memorial Volume,* ed. Barry Walfish (Haifa: Haifa University Press, 1993), 1:203–11; Michael Signer, "The Land of Israel in Medieval Jewish Exegetical and Polemical Literature," in *The Land of Israel: Jewish Perspectives,* ed. Lawrence A. Hoffman (Notre Dame, IN: University of Notre Dame Press, 1986), 210–33; and Michael Signer, "King/Messiah: Rashi's Exegesis of Psalm 2," *Prooftexts: A Journal of Jewish Literary History* 3 (1983): 273–84.

9. Signer, "Peshat, *Sensus Litteralis,* and Sequential Narrative," 203–11.

10. Ibid.

11. See van Zwieten, "Jewish Exegesis within Christian Bounds"; Rainer Berndt, *André de Saint-Victor. Exégète et théologien* (Paris: Brepols, 1991) 294–301; Marianne Awerbuch, *Christlich-jüdische Begegnung im Zeitalter der Frühscholastik* (München: Chr. Kaiser, 1980); and Gilbert Dahan, *Les intellectuels chrétiens et les juifs au Moyen Age. Polémique et relations culturelles entre chrétiens et juifs en occident du XIIe au XIVe siècle* (Paris: Editions du Cerf, 1990).

12. *Hugonis de Sancto Victore Didascalicon de studio legendi: A Critical Text,* ed. Charles Henry Buttimer (Washington, DC: Catholic University Press, 1939). English translation: *The Didascalicon of Hugh of St. Victor: A Medieval Guide to the Arts,* trans. Jerome Taylor (New York: Columbia University Press, 1964). Cited hereafter as *Didasc.* followed by book and chapter, and Taylor and page.

13. The historical context of Isaiah 7–8 (also described in 2 Kings 16:1–20) is typically referred to as the Syro-Ephramite War (734–733 BCE). It is the period of the divided kingdom: Israel to the North, Judah—including the city of Jerusalem—to the South. Ahaz was the king of Judah at the time.

14. *Emman.*, *Objectiones Magistri Andreae:* "*Ecce virgo concipiet et pariet filium, et vocabitur nomen ejus Emmanuel* (Isa. VII). . . . Primo dicunt quod in Hebraico non habetur *becula*, quae vox virginem, sed *alma*, quae nunc juvenculam, nunc absconsam significat" (PL 196:601A). See also *Emman.* 1.3 (PL 196:608B).

15. *Emman.*, *Objectiones Magistri Andreae* (PL 196:602A–603A); see also *Emman.* 1.3 (PL 196:608C).

16. *Emman.*, *Objectiones Magistri Andreae* (PL 196:603B).

17. *Emman.* 1.3 (PL 196:608B).

18. *Emman.*, *Objectiones Magistri Andreae* (PL 196:603C).

19. *Emman.*, *Objectiones Magistri Andreae:* "Vos per abrupta, nos per planam incedimus viam quibus tota capituli continentia consonat; vos, tota litterae circumstantia reclamante, uni versiculo adhaeretis. Quod, ut melius pateat, ab exordio usque ad finem totum prosequimur capitulum" (PL 196:602A). See also *Emman.* 1.3 (PL 196:608C–D).

20. *Emman.*, *Objectiones Magistri Andreae:* "Ecce, inquit, omnia rationabiliter procedunt, omnia quae promittuntur fiunt" (PL 196:602B–603A).

21. *Emman.* 1.5 (PL 196:610A–D).

22. *Emman.* 1.5 (PL 196:610D–611C).

23. *Emman.* 1.6 (PL 196:612B–613B).

24. *Emman.* 1.6: "Quid ergo dicturi sunt Judaei, si dicimus Spiritum sanctum posito aequivoco sacramentum consilii sui sub verbi ambiguitate velle celari . . ." (PL 196:613B). See also *Emman.* 1.8 (PL 196:614C–615B).

25. *Emman.* 1.8: "Inveniuntur itaque quaedam similia, quaedam dissimilia, quaedam omnino contraria. Ecce de Emmanuele dicitur quia antequam puer sciat reprobare malum et eligere bonum, derelinquetur terra a facie duorum regnum suorum. Simile est quod de prophetissae filio legitur quia, antequam puer sciat vocare patrem suum aut matrem suam, auferentur fortitudo Damasci et spoila Samariae coram rege Assyriorum. De illo dicitur quod vocabitur nomen ejus Emmaneul. Diversum est autem quod de illo praecipitur, voca nomen ejus, accelara, spolia detrahe, cito praedare. Non dicit, voca nomen ejus Emmanuel. Si et hoc eum nomen habuisse contendunt, prolato Scripturae testimonio probent quod dicunt. Ibi legimus quod virgo concipiet et pariet. Omnino contrarium est quod hic invenimus, quia ex viri accessione ad eam legitur puerpera concepisse. Non dicam virgo, sed juvencula, vel abscondita" (PL 196:615B–C).

26. Emman. 1.8: "Ecce quomodo tota circumstancia litterae non nobis, ut ipsi volunt, sed illis inventa est reclamare" (PL 196:615D).

27. See Richard's *Liber exceptionum*. Here, Richard seems to follow Hugh, whose exegesis was grounded on the assumption that the whole of Scripture dealt with two things: the work of creation and the work of restoration. The opening chapters of Genesis contained the narrative of creation; the rest of Scripture, but especially the Gospels, contain the narrative of restoration. To be explored further

below is the possibility that Richard seems to be following Hugh closely here by stretching his narrative frame from Genesis to the Gospels.

28. *Emman.* 1.1: "Et hanc quidem prophetiam, etsi nunquam detur vobis secundum dictam sententiam circumjacenti litterae posse coaptare, nihilominus tamen debetis eam credere de Christo praedictam, et in Christo completam fuisse" (PL 196:606D).

29. *Emman.* 1.1: "Sufficit mihi hoc loco, si detur in simplicis litterae expositione devotioni fidelium satisfacere" (PL 196:606C).

30. *Emman.* 1.8: "Quae igitur in Christi sacramentis ad tempus oportebat latere, partim obnubilantur figurarum velamine, partim ambiguitate et obscuritate ipsius litterae. Et illorum quidem quae litterae circumjacentis perplexione obnubilantur, quaedam hujusmodi sunt ut nunquam nisi Spiritu Sancto interpretante Christum sonare intelligerentur quale est illud: Ex Egypto vocavi filium meum. Quadam autem ejusmodi sunt, ut superficie tenus inspecta videantur aliud quam Christum sonare, diligentius autem discussa et pienius intellecta inveniuntur nullo modo posse alienum sensum recipere. Talis sane est iste Scripturae locus quem modo inter manus habemus. Nam ubi dictum est: Ecce virgo concipiet, quaedam praemittuntur, quaedam subjunguntur in quibus sententiae veritas obnubilatur, non tollitur" (PL 196:614C–D).

31. *Emman.* 1.1: "Qui necdum intelligit quod legit, saltem credat ex corde, ut sic mereatur intelligere: *Si non credideritis, inquit, non intelligetis*" (PL 196:607A–B). The Hebrew text reads "He who does not believe will not remain."

32. *Emman.* 1.1: "Firmissimum argumentum fidei nostra quod idem tam concorditer nuntiant prophete et evangelistae. Quod propheta praenuntiat: Ecce virgo concipiet, et pariet filium, et vocabitur nomen ejus Emmanuel. Hoc est quod Evangelista aliis verbis enuntiat: *Verbum caro factum est, et habitavit in nobis*" (PL 196:607B).

33. *Emman.* 1.10: "Ecce totum hoc quod de Emmanuele nostro dicitur ad originalem culpam quasi ex oblique respicere et velut ex opposito respondere videtur" (PL 196:617B).

34. *Emman.* 1.10: "Hic e regione simile aliquid ponitur, nisi quod hic veraciter, quod ibi fallaciter repromittitur" (PL 196:617C).

35. *Emman.* 1.10: "Sane comestio hic ad meritum, illic fuit ad reatum, quod illic praevaricationis, hic fuit virtutis. Iste noster Emmanuel scientiam boni ac mali comedendo obtinuit, ille promissam sibi scientiam comedendo obtinere non potuit. Ibi legitur quod homo ejectus sit de paradiso, quasi de Domini contubernio atque consortio, hic de hoc nostro puero dicitur quod Emmanuel sit dictus, quod interpretatur nobiscum Deus" (PL 196:617B–C).

36. *Emman.* 1.10: "Videtis quomodo homo contra hominem, mulier contra mulierem ponitur; et modo ex oppositio, modo ordine contrario, et simili quadam dissimilitudeine sibi invicem respondere videntur. Illic femina de viro solo, hic vir

de femina sola. Ibi ex fortiori sexu fragiliori fortior fructifactur, qui utrumque reparet. Videsne tanta similitudinis dissimilitudo, dissimilitudinisque similitudo quomodo nos admonet quoddam novitatis principium in istis sicut quoddam vetustatis principium exstitisse in illis? In primo homine quaedam vetustatis inchoatio in posteritatis suae condemnatione. In secundo homine quaedam novitatis inchoatio in generis sui restaurationem" (PL 196:618A–B).

37. *Emman.* 1.10: "Ecce qualitas ipsius signi ostendit quod tollendae primae praevaricationis causa datum fuerit. Ecce quod de Emmanuele dicitur datum est ad remedium" (PL 196:618B–C).

38. "From the guilt of its sin, humanity lost the glory of incorruption [*gloriam incorruptionis*], the prerogative of dignity [*praerogativam dignitatis*], and the abundance of plenitude [*abundantiam plenitudinis*]: the glory of incorruption by which he was made immortal, the privilege of dignity by which he was made like God, the abundance of plenitude by which he was placed in the garden of delight. . . . Observe, the threefold curse in the loss of incorruptibility, dignity, and beatitude" (*Emman.* 1.11 [PL 196:618D]).

39. "In conjunction, therefore, with this threefold curse, humanity received a threefold promise from the kindness of God's mercy: the promise of recovering immortality, the promise of recovering dignity, the promise of recovering beatitude. See in this verse, the promise of the immortality to be hoped for: *Your dead will live, my dead ones will rise again* [Is. 26:19]. See next the promise of the dignity to be repaired: *I will give to them in my house and in my walls a place and a name, better than sons and daughters* [Is. 56]. Observe also the promise of the happiness to be restored: *Eye has not seen as far as you, O God, what you have prepared for those who love you* [Is. 64; 1 Cor. 2]" (*Emman.* 1.11 [PL 196:619B]).

40. *Emman.* 1.11 (PL 196:619B–C).

41. *Emman.* 1.1 (PL 196:607A).

42. *Emman.* 1.12: "Therefore, in the blessed Virgin Mary, human nature received something like a down payment or the first fruits of its future incorruptibility, the integrity, the pure wholeness of the virginal incorruption" (PL 196:619D).

43. *Emman.* 1.12: "Certe, si Emmanuel noster de utroque sexu nasci voluisset, et hoc ratio exigeret, utrumque ad mundam prolem seminandam mundare potuisset. Sed, si de utroque carnem assumeret, utique et a proprietatis suae similitudine longius recederet, et ad nostram minus appropinquaret. Proprietati enim suae esset dissimile, si patrem et matrem haberet in humanitate, qui solummodo patrem habebat in divinitate. In hoc item et nobis dissimilior esset si duos (quod nos non possumus) partes haberet" (PL 196:620C–D).

44. Moreover, Richard notes that the prophecy of a virginal conception has connection not only to Mary but also to Eve. Mary's incorrupt conception restored in her the incorruptibility which humanity had lost in Eve, making her conception the true sign of what all of humanity was destined to receive through Christ (*Emman.* 1.12 [PL 196:619D]).

45. *Emman.* 1.13: "Sed, quaero, nuncupative an substantive? Sed quis nuncupative eum Emmanuel dicit, quin potius Jesum secundum quod angelus docuit? Non igitur nuncupative, sed substantive hoc dicitur. Emmanuel autem interpretatur nobiscum Deus. Si ergo substantialiter, si veraciter hoc dictum est; ergo veraciter et substantialiter hoc est. Ergo puer hic noster substantialiter Deus est, et substantialiter nobiscum est. Si autem substantialiter nobiscum est, consequenter et Deus, et homo est. Sed quid hoc loco Judaei dicituri sunt vel quid dicere poterunt?" (PL 196:622A–C)

46. *Emman.* 1.13: "Alioquin gratis Christus semetipsum exinanivit formam servi accipiens, et habitu inventus ut homo. Nunc igitur si Deus propter homines factus est Filius hominis per nativitatem, cur non multo magis homo per Deum fiat Filius Dei per adoptionem? Ecce quomodo dignatio illa divinae humiliationis data sit in signum futurae nostrae exaltationis. . . . Sed cur, quaeso, Deus hominem prosecutus est usque in exsilium, nisi ut eum post se revocaret ad regnum? Habemus ergo certissimum repatriandi signum, familiare illud in hac nostra peregrinatione divinae cohabitationis contubernium" (PL 196:622D–623A).

47. *Emman.* 1.14: "Ecce tremenda illa potestas potestatibus angelicis comedendo et bibendo communicavit hominibus et jumentis. Si Dominus itaque angelorum propter homines factus est particeps jumentorum, cur e diverso homo per ipsum non multo magis fiat particeps angelorum? . . . Quis ergo desperet de caetero hominem posse fieri participem aeternarum deliciarum, si Dominus majestatis, ut dictum est, propter homines descendit usque ad delicias muscarum? Ecce quantum semetipsum propter nos exinanivit, qui se tali indigentiae sponte subjecit. Sed haec, ut dictum est, exinanitio nostril Redemptoris data est in signum, et certissimum argumentum futurae nostrae plenitudinis" (PL 196:623D–624A).

48. *Emman.* 1.14: "Ecce juxta triplex promissum habes et triplex signum. . . . Ecce quomodo triplex illa promissio confirmatur in hoc triplici signo: Ut sit signum incorruptio incorruptionis, humiliatio exaltationis, exinanitio futurae plenitudinis" (PL 196:624B–D).

49. *Emman.* 1.20 (PL 196:632A).

50. *Emman.* 1.21: "Ecce monstratum est per veritatem jam posse dici de Adam secundo, quod per exprobrationem prius dictum est de Adam primo. . . . Adam itaque sic clarificatus, et in divinum simile transfiguratus none veraciter erit velut unus ex illis a quibus per improperium audivit: Ecce Adam factus est quasi unus ex nobis? . . . Cesset jam ironia, dicatur jam ex sententia" (PL 196:632D–633A).

51. *Emman.* 1.1: "Firmissimum argumentum fidei nostrae quod idem tam concorditer nuntiant prophetae et evangelistae. Quod propheta raenuntiat: Ecce virgo concipiet, et pariet filium, et vocabitur nomen ejus Emmanuel. Hoc est quod Evangelista aliis verbis enuntiat: *Verbum caro factum est, et habitavit in nobis*" (PL 196:607B).

52. See, for example, Smalley, *Study of the Bible,* 178ff.; Signer, "Peshat, *Sensus Litteralis,* and Sequential Narrative," 206–11; van Zwieten, "Jewish Exegesis within

Christian Bounds," 327–31; and Grover A. Zinn, "History and Interpretation: 'Hebrew Truth,' Judaism, and the Victorine Exegetical Tradition," in *Jews and Christians: Exploring the Past, Present, and Future*, ed. James H. Charlesworth (New York: Crossroad, 1990), 100–26, esp. 106–16.

53. See note 27 above.

54. See Smalley, *Study of the Bible*, 110–11.

55. See note 12 above.

56. There Hugh compares the various senses of Scripture—for him there are three, literal, allegorical, and tropological—to the foundation, the superstructure, and the decoration or ornamentation of a building. The literal sense pertains to history, which for Hugh can mean both the deeds that have been performed in the past—what, when, where, and by whom—as well as the "first meaning of any narrative which uses words according to their proper nature" (*Didasc.* 6.3 [Taylor, 137]). Once grounded in the historical sense of the text the student may then establish the various allegorical senses—which Hugh calls the superstructure—upon the foundation of history. Then, the entire framework can be given its ornamentation through the pursuit of the tropological or moral interpretation of the text—"the house is decorated by the laying on of color" (*Didasc.* 6.2 [Taylor, 135]). Of course, this metaphor allows Hugh to demonstrate the centrality of a proper literal or historical understanding of the scriptural text, but also reveals an "aesthetic" climax of the entire exegetical project—the tropological ornamentation of both the interpretation and the interpreter. In this regard, Hugh refers to the "beauty of morality" which accrues to the fruitful interpreter of Scripture (*Didasc.* 5.6 [Taylor, 127–28]).

57. *Didasc.* 6.3 (Taylor, 137).

58. *Didasc.* 5.2 (Taylor, 120).

59. *Didasc.* 5.2 (Taylor, 121). It should be noted that in this passage Hugh uses the same Latin root *aptare* to describe the composition of Scripture which Augustine used in the passage quoted above from *De doctrina christiana* to describe the wise adaptation (*coaptare*) of the Incarnation's remedy to wounded humanity. Richard himself uses *coaptare* in the passage quoted above to describe the exegetical act of linking the prophetic sign with its antecedents and fulfillment.

60. For a fuller discussion of Hugh's exegesis in this regard, see my "*Pulchrum Esse*: The Beauty of Scripture, the Beauty of the Soul, and the Art of Exegesis in the Theology of Hugh of St. Victor," *Traditio* 58 (2003): 175–200.

61. This Hugonian metaphor of music also sheds light on another important aspect of Richard's exegetical project. It is clear that Richard intends his arguments for an already believing, if somewhat wavering, Christian audience. He does not expect his interpretation within this new narrative framework to be convincing to those who do not already believe that the Jesus born in Bethlehem was the boy about whom Isaiah prophesied. Richard's approach, therefore, assumes a prior faith

that is seeking understanding. This posture of faith seeking understanding in Richard's (and Hugh's) exegetical project can be seen as a predisposition toward a kind of textual harmony, about what is exegetically consonant as well as discordant. In a way, the rival interpretation of Andrew and the Jews sounds to Richard like an instrument played out of tune or in a minor key. For Richard, the rule of faith, the deposit of what ought to be believed, informs what 'sounds right' to his exegetical ear.

62. Eileen C. Sweeney, "Rewriting the Narrative of Scripture: Twelfth-Century Debates over Reason and Theological Form," *Medieval Philosophy and Theology* 3 (1993): 1–34.

63. *Didasc.* 5.2 (Taylor, 121).

CHAPTER SEVEN

"Following with Unequal Step"

Andrew of St. Victor, the Glossa ordinaria, *and Compilatory Exegesis in the Northern French Schools of the Twelfth Century*

Franklin T. Harkins

In her 1995 monograph, *Christians and Jews in the Twelfth-century Renaissance,* Anna Sapir Abulafia avers:

> It is the sharing of what Jews call the Hebrew Bible and Christians name the Old Testament that has lain at the root of much of the tortured relationship between the two faiths. The Old Testament for medieval Christians contained the prophecies concerning the birth, suffering, death and resurrection of Jesus Christ. They considered themselves the spiritual heirs of the Jews of the Old Testament because they recognized Jesus as the prophesied Messiah and Son of God. In their eyes, it was on account of this recognition that God had made a new covenant that superseded the old one, which had pertained only to the Jews.[1]

Much of Michael Signer's scholarly work in medieval and modern Jewish-Christian relations takes as its foundation precisely this point. As a collection of sacred texts that Jews and Christians share in common, the Hebrew Bible or Old Testament has been and remains a significant point of contact between the two religious communities and their individual members. While the history of the Jewish-Christian encounter around their common scriptural witness has been characterized generally by divisive modes of interpretation, polemics, and violence, Michael also finds in the medieval encounter sparks of interreligious respect, collaboration, and mutual learning that he hopes will illuminate the path forward for Jews and Christians together now and in the future.

Both of these Jewish-Christian trajectories—polemical and partnering—can be observed in the exegetical work of the schools of Northern France in the twelfth century: in the *Glossa ordinaria* produced at Laon and in the commentaries of Andrew of St. Victor, respectively. As Michael Signer has demonstrated, the anti-Jewish polemical trajectory is attested in the *Glossa ordinaria*, the standard authoritative gloss on the entire Vulgate Bible produced during the period c. 1080–1130 by a team of scholars led by Anselm of Laon and Gilbert of Auxerre.[2] The production of the *Glossa ordinaria* was a complicated process of gathering excerpts from patristic exegetical works (or, more properly, Carolingian compilations of these excerpts) and arranging them in the margins around the Vulgate text (marginal glosses), as well as composing brief glosses and inserting them between the lines of the scriptural text (interlinear glosses).[3] Anselm himself was certainly responsible for compiling the *Glossa* on the Psalter and the Pauline epistles, and likely for that on the four Gospels with the help of his brother Ralph. Gilbert, called "Universalis" on account of his wide-ranging learning and reputation, was a student of Anselm who compiled the *Glossa* on the Pentateuch, the Major Prophets, Lamentations, and perhaps the Minor Prophets sometime prior to his consecration as bishop of London in 1128.[4] In both its form and function, the *Glossa ordinaria* stands as a thoroughly scholastic work, aimed at providing beginners in biblical study with "an integrated and authoritative apparatus to the whole of the Vulgate."[5] In manuscript form, the entire biblical text with accompanying marginal and interlinear glosses filled nineteen to twenty-eight large volumes and was rarely found as a complete set in religious houses of the twelfth century or university libraries of the thirteenth.[6]

The original "authors" of the *Glossa*—unbeknownst to them, of course—were such preeminent patristic and early medieval scholars as Jerome, Augustine, Ambrose, Cassiodorus, Gregory the Great, and Bede.

This ancient and Carolingian exegetical material that would find its way into the *Glossa* was first edited by Rabanus Maurus, the ninth-century exegete and abbot of Fulda, in the service of his continuous commentary on nearly the entire Bible.[7] It was Rabanus' and other Carolingian compilations from which Anselm and Ralph of Laon, Gilbert the Universal, and other producers of the *Glossa ordinaria* drew in their own redactional work. Thus, E. Ann Matter has rightly noted that "the *Glossa ordinaria* shows us the last moment of the development of a tradition of compilation, done always in more concentrated form, of patristic biblical learning."[8] Similarly, Margaret Gibson has described the *Glossa* as "the hinge . . . between the old exegesis and the new, . . . the junction between traditional patristic exegesis and modern scholastic method."[9]

The exegetical work of Andrew of St. Victor (d. 1175) epitomizes the burgeoning scholastic approach to the biblical text. Furthermore, as part and parcel of his own particular approach to the Old Testament, Andrew consulted nearby Jewish scholars; as such, he and his interreligious collaborators stand as significant representatives of the positive, partnering trajectory of historical Jewish-Christian relations. Andrew's literal or historical method of scriptural reading, as a counterpoint to the predominance of allegorizing among his Christian predecessors and contemporaries, is well documented and has been an important focus of Michael Signer's scholarly work.[10] A student of Hugh (c. 1098–1141), the great Victorine master who insisted on a firm grounding in biblical *historia* as foundational for theological speculation, Andrew developed a method of reading the Old Testament that paid particular attention to its grammatical and contextual meaning.[11] Andrew describes his exegetical approach in the prologue to his commentary on the Minor Prophets:

> In my poverty, which is not always able to have either commentaries or glossed books [*vel commentarios vel libros . . . glosatos*] at hand, I consult these previous books looking for the things that are scattered and diffused among them pertaining indeed to the historical sense [*ad historicum . . . sensum*], combining them summarily and tying them together as if in one corpus. Finally, if I have been able to discover anything . . . on the Old Testament books either from the Jews or from any others who

might offer help [*vel Hebreis sive quibuslibet aliis pandentibus*], and by my own work or by divine revelation (because sometimes the Lord even understands a desire of this kind on the part of his servants), I have thought to include it so that what was usefully learned might not ruinously depart from the mind.[12]

Andrew here reveals what Michael Signer has described as his "idiosyncratic program" of scriptural exposition. First, Andrew consulted patristic commentaries, such as Jerome's *Hebraicae quaestiones in libro Geneseos* and Augustine's *Quaestiones in Genesim,* and "glossed books," that is, particular volumes of the *Glossa ordinaria,* looking for historical or literal interpretations and gathered them in his own compilation. Then, in order to clarify difficult passages, Andrew discussed the sacred text with Jewish scholars living and working near St. Victor in Paris. Finally, he made use of insights gained from personal study or given by divine inspiration.[13] What Andrew sought and gleaned from his Jewish neighbors who were familiar with the writings of northern French rabbis such as Rashi, Rashbam, Joseph ben Simeon Kara, and Eliezer of Beaugency was the *peshat* or plain meaning of the scriptural narrative.[14] Frans van Liere has argued that from his encounter with Jewish *peshat* Andrew developed a more textually oriented method of reading Scripture that was new to the Christian world of northern Europe in the twelfth century. "Establishing the meaning of the biblical text," van Liere explains, "was no longer a matter of reliance on patristic tradition or pious reflection; it had become a rational activity. . . . It had become distinct from doctrinal and theological reflection."[15]

We might well nuance van Liere's description of Andrew's approach by having recourse to the Victorine's own words in the prologue to his exposition on Isaiah. Here Andrew maintains that it is neither disrespectful nor presumptuous nor superfluous for him and other lesser interpreters of Scripture to labor in the exegetical field after the great Christian minds of antiquity have already worked the land so fruitfully. Indeed, he and his fellow contemporary exegetes are simply following Jerome and the other ancients in the same quest for finding truth in the biblical text. In deference to his predecessors, though, Andrew describes himself and other twelfth-century readers of Scripture as "following with unequal step" (*impari pede sequentes*). Continuing to hold this humble posture, Andrew leaves it to his reader to decide whether in so unevenly following his sources he has accomplished anything.[16]

The present essay, which seeks to gratefully honor Michael Signer and his many contributions to Jewish-Christian relations, aims at a comparative analysis of the compilatory exegeses found in the *Glossa ordinaria* and in Andrew of St. Victor. More specifically, in an effort to elucidate how the biblical text became a springboard for both interreligious polemic and mutual respect in the twelfth-century northern French schools, we will consider the *Glossa* and Andrew on the story of Esau and Jacob recounted in Genesis 25 and 27, a traditional scriptural flashpoint in the history of Jewish-Christian relations. Our consideration of the *Glossa* shows how Gilbert the Universal, the glossator on the Pentateuch, canonized the traditional Christian allegorical reading of Esau and Jacob as the Jewish people and the Church, respectively. Because interlinear notes first became an important element in the apparatus of the glossed Bible in the early twelfth century and therefore provide a window into the glossator's theory of compilatory exegesis (and his perspective on Jews and Judaism in this case), our treatment will give particular attention to these glosses. With this as background, we seek to demonstrate that Andrew did, in fact, rely on the patristic interpretive tradition as well as on such contemporary readings of Genesis 25 and 27 as those of his Victorine teacher, Hugh, and of the *Glossa ordinaria*. However, given his interest in the plain, literal meaning of the text and undoubtedly informed by his positive interactions with Jewish scholars around the scriptural text, Andrew followed these traditions "with unequal step." In so doing, we argue, he accomplished something quite significant: namely, he provided a Christian exegetical alternative to the anti-Jewish allegorization of the *Glossa* and thereby opened the way—even to a greater extent than had Jerome—to more positive and productive Jewish-Christian relations.

Esau and Jacob in the *Glossa ordinaria*

The story of Esau and Jacob begins in Genesis 25:21 where the newly married Isaac prays for his barren wife Rebecca, which prayer the Lord answers in Rebecca's conception of twins. The interlinear glossator interprets the patriarch's prayer for his "wife" allegorically, writing, "because the Church had not produced sons for a long time."[17] The struggle between the two children in Rebecca's womb (25:22) provides the occasion for further Christian doctrinal development as the glossator explains, "Because within the walls of the Church the elect and the reprobate feel the force of different things."[18] When Rebecca asks the Lord why it was necessary that she conceived at all if her children are already fighting *in utero,* the *Glossa* suggests the twins' life-long struggle is inborn or natural (*innati*).[19] That "quasi quid facient nati si sic luctantur innati" appears as an interlinear gloss on Rebecca's 'why' query reinforces in the reader's mind the divinely and eternally willed nature of the relationship between the Jewish people and the followers of Jesus that the glossator on Esau and Jacob goes on to elucidate.

The glossator on Genesis 25 locates the beginnings of this protracted fraternal tussle in the divine decree, "maior seruiet minori" (v. 23). Not surprisingly, he simply takes up the traditional supersessionist reading: "The older is the Jewish people, the younger is the Christian [people]."[20] The Jews have been consigned historically to servitude, the glossator goes on to explain, because they failed to "come together in unity of faith."[21] The solution to this problem of the elder's infidelity was found, however, in the birth of the younger. The interlinear gloss on Genesis 25:24a, "Now the time of giving birth had come near," reads, "in order that the Church might be expanded by means of the Gospel."[22] Gentile Christians, having heard and believed the good news of Jesus, enabled the Church to grow greatly beyond its Israelite origins, according to the glossator.

The reader of the *Glossa* on Romans 9:12, which verse repeats the Lord's affirmation that "Maior seruiet minori," finds an explicit statement legitimating the Christian allegorical reading of Esau and Jacob. "This [statement may be read]," the marginal gloss explains, "according to the letter because the Idumeans, who are from Esau who is also called Edom, were subjugated by the sons of Israel. But more is intended in this prophecy because the Jewish people who are older, that is, earlier in the worship of the one God, were going to serve the younger, that is, the later Christian [people]."[23] According to the unidentified author of this gloss, the Lord's words to Rebecca in Genesis 25 constitute not simply or even principally a historical statement concerning her actual twins, but rather a divine prophecy to be fulfilled millennia later on a much larger scale. Further-more, the Christian glossator also reads "Maior seruiet minori" meta-exegetically, i.e., in a way that moves beyond a consideration of the possible meanings inherent in the text to an authorization of his own interpretive approach. Specifically, the glossator on Romans 9:12 teaches that "the older" is the literal sense, whereas "the younger" is the allegorical. Thus, the Lord's statement "Maior seruiet minori" reveals the divine intention that the ini-tial literal or historical level of scriptural meaning should be subservient to the subsequent and higher allegorical sense.

Returning to the Genesis account, we see that the glossator on 25:24b, "and behold twins were found in her womb," makes a similar meta-exegetical move aimed at justifying Christian spiritual interpretation. The interlinear gloss reads: "Not [only] one meaning was found in the literal veil of the Law, but [rather] both a carnal and a spiritual one."[24] Our treatment thus far suggests the accuracy of E. Ann Matter's description of the *Glossa ordi-naria* as "a tool of communication admirably suited to bring the many things a biblical verse could mean into easy reach of the reader of that verse."[25] At the same time, however, it is obvious that the glossators did not believe that all meanings were created equal. Rather, they understood the Bible—both Old Testament and New—as "a tool of the Christian doctrinal enterprise," and therefore sought to privilege the spiritual or allegorical reading.[26] This Christian exegetical approach is, of course, nearly as ancient as Christianity itself, dating back at least to the Epistle of Barnabas (c. 70–150), whose principal purpose is to demonstrate that Old Testament Scriptures are, in fact, Christian Scriptures and that their real meaning is the spiritual one.[27] In the *Glossa ordinaria*, as we will see, this emphasis on Christian exegetical meaning translates to the traditional supersessionist interpretation of Esau and Jacob.

The *Glossa*'s anti-Jewish allegorical reading gains momentum with the scriptural description of Rebecca's two sons. The interlinear glossator reads Esau's hairiness (Gen. 25:25) as signaling that the first son is "accustomed only to external things," and his growth into adulthood (25:27) as denoting his "performing external action."[28] In contrast to Esau's ruddiness and hir-suteness, Jacob is described by the Vulgate text as "a simple man living in tents" (Gen. 25:27).[29] The reader finds two interlinear glosses on "vir simplex," namely, "without spot or wrinkle" and "who without deceit cuts off deceit."[30] Furthermore, the glossator understands Jacob's dwelling "in tabernaculis" as meaning that "he was eager for [or diligent in] spiritual things."[31]

As if the contrast between the brothers were not sufficiently striking from these interlinear glosses alone, the compiler of the *Glossa* on the Pentateuch bolsters it with marginal glosses strategically excerpted from Gregory the Great's *Moralia in Iob*. According to Gregory, Esau's hunting in the field "signifies the life of those who, having poured themselves out in external desires, follow the flesh."[32] The Gregorian excerpt continues: "He [i.e., Esau] is also called a farmer because the lovers of this world cultivate external things to the same degree that they leave their own internal selves uncultivated."[33] On Jacob as "simplex," by contrast, the compiler includes this interpretation of Gregory in the margin: "Because those who avoid being dissipated in external cares stand firm as simple people in meditation and in the dwelling place of conscience. For 'he lives in tents' who confines himself within the secrets of the mind and does not, while gaping for many things without and becoming estranged from meditation, retreat from his very self."[34]

Read together, the marginal and interlinear glosses on Genesis 25:27 offer a vivid allegory of Esau and Jacob. The older son signifies those whose carnal desires for the things of this world lead them to a life of sin and seemingly irretrievable dissipation. The younger son, on the other hand, represents those whose concern with the inner life enables them to remain intact appetitively and unblemished spiritually. The Augustinian influence on Gregory's tropological interpretation is unmistakable. What is equally recognizable, and more important for our purposes, is the *Glossa*'s adoption and adaption of Augustine's and other patristic exegetes' identification of Esau with the carnally minded Jewish people, on the one hand, and Jacob with spiritual Christians, on the other.

The glossator's supersessionist theology becomes conspicuously clear in his interlinear glosses on Genesis 25:28. The scriptural text here reads: "Isaac loved Esau because he [i.e., Isaac] enjoyed eating the game of his son, but Rebecca loved Jacob." By means of a number of interlinear glosses, the glossator demonstrates that the true Christian meaning is: "God the Father loved the Jewish people who were earlier in the justice of carnal observance which they were showing toward the one God, but grace through fore-knowledge was loving the younger people."[35] Here in the idea that grace foreknew and foreordained the Christian people's replacement of the Jews as God's beloved, the glossator returns to his earlier emphasis on the divinely willed nature of the interreligious relationship. This interpretation may violate in any number of ways the sensibilities of the modern biblical reader, accustomed to (if not explicitly trained in) the historical-critical approach to the Bible. What is perhaps most striking, however, is the way in which the interlinear comments here provide a powerfully anti-Jewish allegorical reading that comes to share the very space occupied by the biblical text. Indeed, by means of a series of brief interlinear glosses, Christian supersessionism is written into the very text of Sacred Scripture.

In its treatment of Esau's forfeiting his birthright (Gen. 25:29–34), the *Glossa* provides further details concerning why the Jews have been surpassed. According to the Vulgate text, Esau comes in from the field one day and says to his younger brother, who is preparing some food, "Give me some of that red food, for I am very weary" (vv. 29–30).[36] "The fool is inflamed with the desire of the palate [i.e., gluttony] around poor food," according to the first interlinear gloss on these verses.[37] The second reads: "Lentils are food for brute animals, signifying a beastly understanding of the Law, by which the unlearned Jewish people chose to be without the first place, which disappeared from them. But even now they are eager to procure it from the younger people. Having given it away for temporal things, they hope for nothing good after death."[38] Similarly, commenting on Esau's selling of the primogenital right to his younger brother (v. 33), the interlinear glossator writes, "Even now the Jew continues in foolishness; favoring temporal things, he does not care about eternal things."[39]

The portrait of Jews—both in the biblical period and at the turn of the twelfth century—offered here is that of a foolish, carnal, subhuman, irrational breed incapable of aspiring to spiritual realities and, as such, ill-equipped to retain the divine blessing. Such a characterization relies heavily on the patristic *Adversus Iudaeos* tradition. For example, the "golden-mouthed" preacher of late antique Antioch and Patriarch of Constantinople, John Chrysostom (c. 347–407), contrasts Jewish carnality with Christian spirituality thus: "In our churches we hear countless discourses on eternal punishments, on rivers of life, on the venomous worm, on bonds that cannot be burst, on exterior darkness. But the Jews neither know nor dream of these things. They live for their bellies, they gape for the things of this world, their condition is no better than that of pigs or goats because of their wanton ways and excessive gluttony. They know but one thing: to fill their bellies and be drunk."[40] John Chrysostom is notorious as an anti-Jewish polemicist, and his homilies against Judaizing Christians provide what Robert Wilken has described as "the most vituperative and vindictive attack on the Jews from Christian antiquity."[41] Whereas the caustic anti-Jewish critiques of Chrysostom and other early Christian leaders remained both temporally and textually removed from the canonical Scriptures (though related to them in various ways, of course), the *Glossa ordinaria* presents a traditional Christian supersessionist interpretation of Esau and Jacob as part and parcel of the biblical text itself. It is also noteworthy that the *Glossa* here adopts the particularly virulent strain of patristic anti-Judaism characterized by Chrysostom rather than the somewhat less vicious strain propounded by Augustine, Gregory the Great, and other western theologians.[42] This is particularly significant in light of the fact that the works of Chrysostom and other eastern Christian thinkers were just beginning to be translated into Latin in the mid-twelfth century and therefore do not appear in the *Glossa ordinaria*. In fact, the Italian jurist Burgundio of Pisa seems to have begun translating select works of Chrysostom—as a means of redeeming his son's soul from purgatory—only after his diplomatic journey to Constantinople in 1136, a full six years after the completion of the *Glossa*.[43]

In the late 1120s, as Gilbert the Universal was putting the finishing touches on the *Glossa* on the Pentateuch, Hugh of St. Victor was penning his enchiridion on sacred and secular reading. In the opening chapter of Book IV of the *Didascalicon,* Hugh defines Sacred Scriptures as "those which were produced by persons who cultivated the catholic faith and which the authority of the universal Church has included in the number of divine books and preserved to be read for the strengthening of that same faith."[44] Among these sacred texts, the Victorine master includes the writings of the early church fathers.[45] Like the Law, the prophets, and the historical writings of the Old Testament as well as the Gospels and epistles of the New, the innumerable works of "the holy fathers and doctors of the Church," Hugh explains, boldly declare the Christian faith for future generations.[46]

In its final form, the *Glossa ordinaria* grows out of and, in turn, contributes to an early scholastic milieu that enabled and even encouraged Hugh to include patristic writings in the biblical canon. Medieval Christian exegetes recognized their own inability to read and understand the scriptural text properly without having recourse to those faithful biblical readers who had preceded them. Toward this end, the Laon compilers of the *Glossa ordinaria* sought to make ancient and authoritative exegeses available to beginning theology students on the same piece of parchment as the Vulgate text. Interlinear glosses in particular entered the very space of the biblical text and, as such, came to participate in the canonical authority of the words they sought to clarify.

As such, the *Glossa* effectively canonized the traditional Christian understanding of the story of Esau and Jacob as a divine prophecy foreshadowing Jewish subservience to Christians throughout history. The interlinear glossator on Genesis 25 finds embedded in the words of Scripture the divine intention not only that the older people should serve the younger, but also that the allegorical sense of these supernatural words should surpass and subjugate the literal. Such allegorical supersessionism, in turn, legitimates the Christian supersessionism that the *Glossa* locates in the story of Esau's forfeiture of primogeniture.

Esau and Jacob in Andrew of St. Victor's *Expositio super Heptateuchum*

When the reader of the *Glossa ordinaria* takes up Andrew of St. Victor's commentary on the biblical account of Esau and Jacob, he or she discovers a radically different exposition in terms of both form and content. In contrast to the *Glossa*, which presents a more or less continuous commentary on the Vulgate text in the form of glosses between and around the very words of Scripture, Andrew pens an *Expositio super Heptateuchum*, an exegetical exposition of select passages which he understands to be particularly important or difficult.[47] Furthermore, Andrew confines himself to a strictly literal or historical reading of the narrative of Esau and Jacob that subverts the intensely anti-Jewish polemic of the *Glossa*.[48] But he does not arrive at such a reading by completely rejecting the exegetical work of his Christian predecessors—Jerome, Augustine, Hugh of St. Victor, and even Gilbert the Universal. Rather, as the following analysis seeks to show, Andrew follows them "with unequal step."

That Andrew follows the preceding Christian tradition on Esau and Jacob with unequal step is perhaps most immediately evident by quickly glancing at those passages of the biblical narrative that he chooses to and not to exposit. Several of the passages that provided the richest fodder for supersessionist allegorization in the *Glossa ordinaria*—"the older will serve the younger" (25:23), "and behold twins were found in her womb" (25:24b), "Isaac loved Esau . . . , but Rebecca loved Jacob" (25:28)—receive no treatment at all from Andrew. When he does comment on elements of the narrative that the *Glossa* takes as central to its purpose, Andrew's reading differs radically from that of the glossator. For example, whereas the interlinear glossator understands Esau's hairiness (25:25) as indicating his habituation solely to external realities (*solis exterioribus assuetus*), Andrew simply explains that the Latin *hispidus* renders the Hebrew *seir:* "Hence Esau is called 'Seir,' that is, shaggy."[49] The origin of this gloss is Jerome's *Hebraicae quaestiones in libro Geneseos,* but it also found its way into some manuscripts and the *editio princeps* of the *Glossa ordinaria.*[50] Indeed, of the four manuscripts of the *Glossa* on the Pentateuch that I examined for this study, three of them contain Jerome's literal reading.[51] Interestingly, the only one that does not have this reading is MS BnF lat. 14398, a manuscript that is known to have been in the library of the Abbey of St. Victor at the end of the twelfth century and, as such, may have been one of the "glossed books" that Andrew consulted during his work on the Pentateuch.[52] Instead of Jerome's grammatical gloss on *hispidus,* MS BnF lat. 14398 contains the allegorical "solis exterioribus assuetus" (fol. 66v).

Whereas Rainer Berndt uses the utter lack of parallels between the *Glossa* on the Pentateuch and Andrew's *Expositio* as evidence that glossed books of the Bible were not produced at St. Victor in the twelfth century, Margaret Gibson postulates the Victorine abbey as a possible institutional site for the compilation of the *Glossa* in part because Andrew's new dynamic exegetical method makes use of and advances on the static text-with-commentary form of the *Glossa ordinaria*.[53] Indeed, for Gibson, the *Glossa* is the stable hinge between traditional Christian exegesis and the new scholastic method.[54] Setting aside the question of whether glossed books of the Bible were produced at St. Victor, let us assume that Andrew did, in fact, have at his disposal and consult MS BnF lat. 14398 when compiling and composing his *Expositio*. According to his own statement of exegetical methodology discussed above, however, he consulted it looking for literal or historical glosses rather than allegorical ones. As such, Andrew glossed over the *Glossa*'s interpretation of Esau's hairiness as indicating the Jewish people's affinity for external realities, preferring instead the simple grammatical explanation that he found in Jerome's commentary.

We see Andrew making a similar exegetical move when we come to the biblical text's description of Jacob as *simplex* (25:27), which the Victorine elucidates thus: "Others say 'without deceit,' in Greek 'aplastos' (that is, not false)."[55] Here Andrew provides a very concise summary of the longer explanation offered by Augustine in his *Questions on Genesis*.[56] The fact that Andrew makes reference to the Greek *aplastos,* which Augustine explains but which is absent from the *Glossa*, reveals that he had a copy of *Quaestiones in Genesim* (or a compilation of patristic excerpts containing this Augustinian gloss) open in front of him as he compiled his *Expositio super Heptateuchum*.[57] Furthermore, the glossed book of the Pentateuch that Andrew may also have consulted, MS BnF lat. 14398, glosses Jacob as *simplex* not only with "qui sine dolo fecit dolum," but also with "Studebat in meditatione spiritualium."[58] Again, Andrew partially integrates the former gloss because he understands it to pertain to the literal or historical sense, whereas he intentionally excludes the latter presumably on account of its easy association with the traditional Christian allegorical reading of Esau and Jacob. Andrew seems to find no evidence in the scriptural text itself that Jacob "was zealous in the contemplation of spiritual realities," and so prevents this reading from entering his historical exposition.

These examples highlight the fact that Andrew's work in the *Expositio*, like that of Gilbert the Universal in the *Glossa*, is largely that of a compiler of patristic texts. Yet their respective purposes and results could not be more different. Whereas Gilbert excerpts from Gregory the Great's *Moralia in Iob* in order to read Esau's hairiness and Jacob's simplicity allegorically as Jewish carnal sinfulness and Christian interior holiness, respectively, Andrew intentionally overlooks such readings—which he undoubtedly understands as eisegetical—in favor of the simpler, less anti-Jewish interpretations of Jerome and Augustine.

In Hugh, his Victorine teacher, Andrew also finds literal readings that he prefers to the allegorical exegeses of the *Glossa*. Andrew glosses Jacob's demand that Esau sell him his birthright before obtaining some of the red stew that the younger son is cooking (25:31) as follows: "Some say that it is the firstborn of animals 'who holds onto the older by an external limb,' or [that the birthright refers to] priestly dignity. But the Law determines who the firstborns are. The dignity of the firstborn was that he should obtain from all the good things of the father double—that is, twice as much as any other from among the sons. Hence Joseph, who obtained the dignity of the firstborn among his brothers, created two tribes from himself."[59] Andrew's explanation that the birthright could refer to a more or less strict order of natural birth, as in animals, or to sacerdotal honor derives from Hugh. Indeed, Andrew's first sentence here provides a direct quotation from Hugh's *Adnotationes elucidatoriae in Pentateuchon.*[60] In his *Adnotationes,* however, Hugh makes clear, based on the subsequent scriptural narrative, that Jacob's request is not for priestly dignity: "For from the father's blessing we cannot understand this."[61] Taking his cue from Master Hugh and eliminating this possible allegorical interpretation, Andrew proceeds to explain the birthright literally as determined by the Torah. This reading, which is found in neither Jerome nor Augustine nor the *Glossa,* appears to be the fruit of Andrew's own study of the Law. If he gleaned it from personal contact with Jewish scholars or written Jewish sources, he does not reveal this to his reader as he often does.[62]

It must be noted that the literal, intertextual reading of the birthright that Andrew here provides again represents an outright rejection of the allegorical and thoroughly anti-Jewish interpretation that he found in the *Glossa*. The glossed book of the Pentateuch that Andrew likely consulted at St. Victor contains virtually the same reading of Esau's forfeiture of his birthright that we encountered earlier as attested in the *editio princeps:* "Lentils are food for brute animals, and signify a fleshly understanding of the Law, by which the unlearned Jewish people chose to be without their first place, which disappeared from them."[63] That Andrew did not integrate this gloss into his own work is not surprising given his purpose of producing a literal exposition. What is remarkable, however, is the way in which his reading stands in contradistinction to that of the *Glossa* and subverts its anti-Judaism. Indeed, whereas Gilbert the Universal understands the Jews as having lost their spiritual birthright by understanding their Law in a carnal and irrational way, Andrew himself makes use of this selfsame Law as received and understood by the Jews to clarify the meaning of the literal birthright for which Jacob asked his older brother. Thus, not only does Andrew's interpretation presuppose that the Jews throughout history have faithfully encountered God's Law, it demonstrates that the Christian who seeks to properly read the Old Testament must also approach the text with a certain basic literal and historical understanding of the Law.

Andrew's exposition of the birthright highlights the way in which he, in marked contrast to Gilbert in the *Glossa,* reads the scriptural narrative of Esau and Jacob as the literal story of two ancient Hebrew siblings and draws on his knowledge of biblical and secular history to interpret it. This general exegetical approach is also well illustrated in Andrew's treatment of two central elements of the story as recounted in chapter 27, namely, Isaac's blessing of Jacob (vv. 27–29) and the father's subsequent refusal to bless Esau (vv. 39–40). First, commenting on Isaac's words to Jacob, "May God give to you from the dew of heaven and from the fatness of the earth" (27:28), Andrew explains that dew and the fatness of the earth are necessary for the multiplication of temporal things.[64] Already his reading stands in sharp contrast to the interlinear gloss that Andrew likely read, which spiritualize the dew of heaven as the ability to "discriminatingly taste celestial realities" (for example, "to understand the sacrament of the body and blood of Christ") and the fatness of the earth as the capacity to "attend well to earthly realities."[65] For Andrew, it was precisely for the increase in *temporal things* that ancient sons struggled mightily for the paternal blessing.[66] Furthermore, whereas the *Glossa* reads Isaac's blessing of Jacob as signifying God's eternal will that Jews should serve their Christian neighbors who have rightly received their birthright, Andrew understands the blessing in very human—even haphazard—terms, as illustrated by his analogy taken from contemporary ecclesiastical life. "This blessing," Andrew explains, "is not according to intention, however, but according to the words having been spoken. Just as, if a certain bishop, supposing himself to ordain his own priest, ordains the priest of another church, that one—who came near deceitfully—is in fact ordained, not that one whom the bishop intended to ordain."[67] Andrew's use of this analogy highlights the historical concreteness and humanness of the biblical story. It removes intentionality from the divine will and even from the human father, locating it rather in the deceptive plan of the younger son. Finally, it is noteworthy that Andrew's interpretation of Isaac's conferral of the primogenital blessing on Jacob represents a summary of Hugh's longer treatment.[68] The single sentence that Andrew adds to his teacher's comments is, "Therefore in antiquity sons strove with such great effort to receive the blessing of the father," revealing his awareness of biblical and ancient Jewish history as indispensable tools for the exegetical enterprise.[69]

Andrew's particular attention to the historical reality referenced in the scriptural text can also be clearly seen in his exposition of Isaac's refusal to bless his older son after having mistakenly blessed the younger (27:39–40). On the father's words to Esau, "You will serve your brother," Andrew comments: "[I]n future generations when you cast off the yoke. This was completed when the Idumeans revolted so that they would not be under Judah."[70] This gloss is an abbreviation of Jerome, who reads the passage thus: "It signifies that the Idumeans will be enslaved to the Jews, and the time will come when they will cast the yoke of servitude off their neck and oppose the rule of the Jews. According to the seventy translators, however, who say, *But it will happen when you loosen the yoke and take it off your neck,* the sentence seems to hang in the air and not to be complete."[71] On Andrew's interpretation and his use of Jerome here, two significant observations must be made. First, following Jerome, the Victorine reads Isaac's words to Esau not in the traditional Christian allegorical way, which had become standardized in the *Glossa,* as a prophetic statement about present and future Jewish servitude to Christians. Rather, Andrew understands the text as having found its proper historical referent (i.e., its completion) in the ancient conflict between the Idumeans and the tribe of Judah. Second, a close consideration of the language of Andrew's gloss compared to that of Jerome sheds further light on how and why the Victorine followed his Christian sources "with unequal step."

Two comparative examples will suffice. First, whereas Jerome writes that this scriptural text "signifies" (*significat,* a verbal cue often signaling an imminent allegorical interpretation) future events that he proceeds to describe using future-oriented language (e.g., *seruituri sint, tempus esse uenturum*), Andrew uses neither a form of *significo* nor future-oriented verbal forms to describe events that the biblical text predicts. Rather, Andrew employs the perfect tense (e.g., *impletum est, rebellauerunt*) in an effort to show that the words of Scripture have already found their principal historical and political referent. And although this referent is surely the same for Jerome as for Andrew, where each commentator situates himself vis-à-vis the biblical narrative and its intended meaning seems significant. Jerome moves back in time from his own late-antique context, places himself within the ancient world of Isaac and his sons, and looks forward to the text's fulfillment. Andrew, by contrast, remains firmly ensconced in his own medieval milieu, from which vantage-point he knows that Isaac's words have long ago found completion (*Hoc impletum est quando*). These verbal differences between Andrew and Jerome may seem slight, particularly in light of a largely common content. Yet, the effect that Andrew's exegetical self-situating has on the reader is to reinforce that the Victorine is not providing any sort of allegorical or prophetic reading at all, but simply elucidating the text's literal and historical meaning.

Second, and relatedly, whereas Jerome understands Jacob to represent "the Jews" (*Iudaeis*) to whom the Idumeans will be enslaved, Andrew completely avoids using the term *Iudaei,* maintaining instead that the Idumeans revolted lest they be "under Judah" (*sub Iuda*). Andrew's refusal to follow his patristic source on this linguistic point highlights his intention to read the biblical text literally and non-anachronistically in light of ancient history. Furthermore, in the Christian world of twelfth-century northern Europe wherein Andrew penned his *Expositio,* the word *Iudaeus* had a far different and considerably more negative religious and cultural meaning than its original gentilic one, namely, a Judean.[72] Thus, in changing Jerome's "the Jews" to "under Judah," a phrase that medieval Christians could not have easily attributed to their neighbors who adhered to Judaism, Andrew removes a potential stumbling block from his contemporary Christian readers who might have either found confirmation for their pre-existing anti-Judaism here or fallen anew into anti-Jewish ways of understanding Scripture. We cannot know for sure whether Andrew altered Jerome's reading in this small but significant way as a result of his positive interactions around the text of Genesis with Jewish scholars in Paris. What we do know, of course, is that the language of Andrew's gloss guards against anti-Jewish thinking in a way that Jerome's simply does not. Furthermore, by following Jerome "with unequal step" and reading Isaac's statement to his elder son as finding its end in the ancient conflict between the Idumeans and the Kingdom of Judah, Andrew provides an exegetically sound alternative to the centuries-old Christian supersessionist interpretation that had recently been canonized in the *Glossa ordinaria*.

As the reader of the *Expositio super Heptateuchum* nears the end of Andrew's comments on Genesis 27, he or she plainly sees, yet again, the Victorine's emphasis on the biblical narrative as a literal story of ancient Hebrew siblings that is motivated by human intentionality. After Isaac refuses to bless Esau and instead tells him that he will serve his brother, the Vulgate text relates that Esau came to hate Jacob and said in his heart, "I will kill my brother Jacob" (27:41). The scriptural narrative affirms that "these [words] were related" (*nuntiata sunt*) to Rebecca, who quickly sent Jacob away to his uncle Laban in Haran in an effort to save his life (vv. 42–45). Postulating as to how Esau's nefarious words were related to his mother, Andrew writes, "either by divine inspiration or by some friend of Esau to whom he had revealed his secret plan."[73] This gloss appears to be a combination of what Andrew likely found in the *Glossa ordinaria* and of his own critical reflection on the narrative. Both the *editio princeps* and one of the manuscripts of the *Glossa* that I consulted contain this interlinear gloss on *nuntiata sunt*: "[B]y divine inspiration although spoken in meditation, hence it pertains to the great mystery that He [i.e., God] willed that the younger [son] be blessed instead of the older."[74] The twelfth-century glossed Pentateuch at St. Victor has the similar but simpler reading, "through the spirit of prophecy."[75] The way in which Andrew glosses over such supernatural readings, at least one of which likely appeared in a glossed Pentateuch on his desk, is significant. Whereas Andrew admits that Rebecca could have learned of Esau's sinister plan by divine inspiration, he seems to prefer the simpler, human explanation that a friend of Esau told her. Furthermore, he makes absolutely no mention of "the great mystery" that, according to the *Glossa,* underlies the divine revelation to Rebecca, namely, God's will that the younger son (read: Christian people) be blessed instead of the older (read: Jewish people). Again, considered in light of the *Glossa*'s reading, Andrew's brief and ostensibly inconsequential gloss gains a greater import. Indeed, by following the *Glossa* "with unequal step"—that is, by recognizing divine inspiration as a possibility but preferring a strictly human explanation—Andrew closes the door to an anti-Jewish reading according to which Christians have rightfully received God's singular blessing. For Andrew, the scriptural account of Esau and Jacob is a literal story of two ancient Hebrew siblings that is motivated by human intentionality, not an allegory of Christian supersessionism orchestrated by the divine will.

Conclusion

This sort of literal, reason-oriented elucidation of the biblical text that highlights human motivations is, in the works of Andrew, limited neither to the Esau-Jacob narrative nor to other stories whose ancient and medieval Christian exegetical traditions tend toward anti-Judaism. Rather, this approach characterizes Andrew's general hermeneutical method. In the Prologue to his *Expositio super Heptateuchum,* for example, Andrew takes up a question that had become customary for twelfth-century exegetes: How was Moses, the putative human author of Genesis who lived at a time long after the creation of the world, able to know how creation occurred? Andrew answers thus:

It is not surprising if the grace of the Holy Spirit, which was able to reveal to him things still in the future, was also able to reveal past events, particularly since nothing that is past falls within our realm of knowledge in this way. Nevertheless, it is not absurd [*non absurde*] to believe that the holy patriarchs and even Adam himself by frequently narrating [the story] from memory or in writing—since this is the greatest cause of divine praise [*maxima diuinae laudis causa*] and of our very love—took care to entrust the creation of the world to memory. In this way it was able to come to the attention of Moses who took care to investigate it diligently.[76]

Here Andrew does not rule out the possibility of direct divine revelation, but seems to prefer the strictly human explanation: Moses came to know how the cosmos was created by the assiduous application of his mind to the story that previous generations had learned and passed down to him. In Andrew's view, the rational mind—with its impressive ability to memorize, narrate, and investigate—is sufficient to explain what other twelfth-century exegetes could only account for by having recourse to the divine will and supernatural activity. Furthermore, the Victorine makes clear here that reading a biblical text naturally rather than supernaturally (i.e., using reason to emphasize human rather than divine motivations) in no way detracts from the praise of God; on the contrary, reason's ability to recount and elucidate the narrative of God's activity in history represents the "greatest cause" (*maxima . . . causa*) of knowing, praising, and loving God.

As we have seen, Andrew's literal approach to the biblical text flies in the face of the received tradition of Christian allegory that had recently been canonized in the *Glossa ordinaria*. Indeed, the Victorine seems quite aware that he is skating on thin exegetical ice when, as above, he prefaces his own reading of a particular text with such phrases as "[n]evertheless it is not absurd to believe. . . ."[77] Because Andrew's literal-historical exegesis was often informed by Jewish sources and even by personal encounters with Jews in Paris, several of his Christian contemporaries, including Richard of St. Victor and Nicholas of Lyra, accused him of "judaizing." Richard of St. Victor, for example, opens his *De Emmanuele* with these words: "In a certain treatise of Master Andrew in which he provided an exposition of Isaiah . . . I have found a number of things stated not carefully enough and discussed not catholically enough. For, in fact, in many places in that work the opinion of the Jews is presented as if it were not so much the Jews' but his own, and as if it were true. Moreover, on that passage, *Behold a virgin shall conceive and bear a son* [7:14], he sets forth the objections and questions of the Jews but does not answer them, and appears to give them the first-place prize since he leaves them as if they were irrefutable."[78]

For Richard and most of his Christian contemporaries, not only were the Jews refutable, they had also already been definitively and divinely refuted on account of their blind, literal reliance on the Law—even now, more than a millennium *post Christum*—for salvation. Furthermore, the biblical narrative of Esau and Jacob, as read by Richard of St. Victor and the twelfth-century school of Laon, stands as incontrovertible proof that God has withdrawn His blessing from the Jewish people and conferred it upon the Christian faithful. Richard explains:

> The story [*historia*] of how Jacob supplanted Esau with regard to the blessing of the father is well known. Isaac signifies [*significat*] God, from whom the blessing comes down on the head of the just one. Rebecca signifies mother grace [*matrem gratiam*], who advises Jacob about the desired blessing. Jacob—born later, remaining at home, [and] seeking after the blessing—denotes the Gentile people, who come to divine knowledge after the people of Israel and are nourished among themselves with the promise of mother grace. In return, they give praises to God, and they are blessed by Him in the world through grace and in heaven through glory. Esau—born earlier, devoting himself to hunting outdoors, [and] losing the blessing—signifies the people of Israel, who come to the knowledge of God earlier but strive for righteousness externally in the letter [*in littera*] and lose the blessing of heavenly inheritance.[79]

The message that both Richard and the *Glossa ordinaria* seem to speak to Andrew is quite clear: although the scriptural narrative of Esau and Jacob is *historia,* Christians are not to read it finally in a historical way. Rather, the words of the biblical text signify the sacred mystery according to which God through grace bestows (note Richard's nearly exclusive use of the present tense) His singular blessing on the Church rather than on the Jewish people. Furthermore, both Richard and the *Glossa* at least intimate that the exegete who seeks truth solely in the external letter of the text "judaizes" and may, like those whom he imitates, lose the divine blessing. And yet, in spite of warnings against "judaizing" and in spite of the fact that the school of Laon had recently compiled a ready-reference collection of authoritative excerpts of patristic allegorical interpretations, Andrew remains unshaken in his resolve to read the Old Testament historically.

The present essay has sought to investigate the different ways that Christian exegetes in the northern French schools of the twelfth century read and understood the text of the Old Testament. More specifically, we have considered how Gilbert the Universal, the compiler of the *Glossa ordinaria* on the Pentateuch, and Andrew of St. Victor engaged in compilatory exegesis in their respective readings of Genesis 25 and 27. Our analysis of the *Glossa* and Andrew on the story of Esau and Jacob has highlighted how the sacred text shared by Jews and Christians served during the early scholastic period simultaneously as a flashpoint of anti-Jewish polemic, on the one hand, and a source a positive interreligious teaching and even collaboration, on the other. By compiling select patristic texts and his own interlinear comments on the same folios of parchment containing the Vulgate text, Gilbert the Universal canonized the traditional Christian allegorical reading of Esau and Jacob according to which God has rejected the Jewish people and bestowed His singular blessing on the Church. With a copy of Gilbert's glossed Pentateuch—alongside the exegetical works of Jerome, Augustine, and Hugh of St. Victor—on his desk at St. Victor, Andrew set out to produce his own interpretive compilation. We have sought to show that Andrew, in producing a very different kind of exposition of Genesis 25 and 27, did not altogether reject the ancient and medieval Christian exegetical sources to which he was heir. Rather, he followed them—even the *Glossa ordinaria*—"with unequal step." Along his rather irregular exegetical pilgrimage, Andrew was joined by his Jewish colleagues in Paris whose insights spurred the Victorine along. The end result was a literal and historical exposition of Esau and Jacob that subverted the anti-Judaism of the *Glossa* and cleared a path for more positive and productive relations between Jews and Christians.

Notes

1. Anna Sapir Abulafia, *Christians and Jews in the Twelfth-century Renaissance* (London: Routledge, 1995), 63.

2. On anti-Judaism in the *Glossa ordinaria*, see Michael A. Signer, "The *Glossa ordinaria* and the Transmission of Medieval Anti-Judaism," in *A Distinct Voice: Medieval Studies in Honor of Leonard E. Boyle, O.P.*, ed. Jacqueline Brown and William P. Stoneman (Notre Dame, IN: University of Notre Dame Press, 1997), 591–605. On the origins of the *Glossa*, see Beryl Smalley, "La *Glossa Ordinaria.*

Quelques prédécesseurs d'Anselme de Laon," *Recherches de théologie ancienne et médiévale* 9 (1937): 365–400; Beryl Smalley, "Gilbertus Universalis, Bishop of London (1128–34) and the Problem of the *Glossa ordinaria*," *Recherches de théologie ancienne et médiévale* 7 (1935): 235–62, and 8 (1936): 24–60; and Beryl Smalley, *The Study of the Bible in the Middle Ages* (Notre Dame, IN: University of Notre Dame Press, 1964), 46–66. See also J. de Blic, "L'oeuvre exégétique de Walafrid Strabon, et le Glossa Ordinaria," *Recherches de théologie ancienne et médiévale* 16 (1949): 5–28, which summarizes the argument of Smalley, following S. Berger and others; and C. F. R. de Hamel, *Glossed Books of the Bible and the Origins of the Paris Booktrade* (Suffolk: D. S. Brewer, 1984), 1–13.

    3. M. T. Gibson, "The Place of the *Glossa ordinaria* in Medieval Exegesis," in *Ad litteram: Authoritative Texts and Their Medieval Readers,* ed. Mark D. Jordan and Kent Emery, Jr. (Notre Dame, IN: University of Notre Dame Press, 1992), 5–27, esp. 19–20; E. Ann Matter, "The Church Fathers and the *Glossa ordinaria*," in *The Reception of the Church Fathers in the West: From the Carolingians to the Maurists,* ed. Irena Backus, vol. 1 (Leiden: Brill, 1997), 83–111, esp. 85.

    4. See Smalley, *Study of the Bible,* 60–62; Smalley, "La *Glossa Ordinaria*"; and M. T. Gibson, Introduction to *Biblia Latina cum Glossa ordinaria: Facsimile Reprint of the Editio Princeps, Adolph Rusch of Strassburg 1480/81* (Turnhout: Brepols, 1992), x–xi.

    5. Jenny Swanson, "The *Glossa Ordinaria*," in *The Medieval Theologians,* ed. G. R. Evans (Oxford: Blackwell, 2000), 156–67, here 159–60.

    6. De Hamel, *Glossed Books of the Bible,* 5–10.

    7. Gibson, Introduction to *Biblia Latina cum Glossa ordinaria,* viii–ix.

    8. Matter, "The Church Fathers," 85–86.

    9. Gibson, "The Place of the *Glossa ordinaria*," 5 and 21.

    10. See, for example: Smalley, *Study of the Bible,* 120–49; Rainer Berndt, *André de Saint-Victor († 1175). Exégète et Théologien* (Paris: Brepols, 1991), 227–74; Michael A. Signer, "St. Jerome and Andrew of St. Victor: Some Observations," in *Studia Patristica* 17.1, ed. Elizabeth A. Livingstone (Elmsford, NY: Pergamon, 1982), 333–37; Michael A. Signer, "From Theory to Practice: The *De doctrina christiana* and the Exegesis of Andrew of St. Victor," in *Reading and Wisdom: The* De doctrina christiana *of Augustine in the Middle Ages,* ed. Edward D. English (Notre Dame, IN: University of Notre Dame Press, 1995), 84–98; Michael A. Signer, "*Peshat, Sensus Litteralis,* and Sequential Narrative: Jewish Exegesis and the School of St. Victor in the Twelfth Century," in *The Frank Talmage Memorial Volume,* ed. Barry Walfish (Haifa: Haifa University Press, 1993), 203–216; Michael A. Signer, "Restoring the Narrative: Jewish and Christian Exegesis in the Twelfth Century," in *With Reverence for the Word: Medieval Scriptural Exegesis in Judaism, Christianity, and Islam,* ed. Jane Dammen McAuliffe, Barry D. Walfish, and Joseph W. Goering (Oxford: Oxford University Press, 2003), 70–82; Michael A. Signer, "Polemic and Exegesis: The Vari-

eties of Twelfth-Century Hebraism," in *Hebraica Veritas? Christian Hebraists and the Study of Judaism in Early Modern Europe*, ed. Allison P. Coudert and Jeffrey S. Shoulson (Philadelphia: University of Pennsylvania Press, 2004), 21–32; Michael A. Signer, "Consolation and Confrontation: Jewish and Christian Interpretation of the Prophetic Books," in *Scripture and Pluralism: Reading the Bible in the Religiously Plural Worlds of the Middle Ages and Renaissance*, ed. Thomas J. Heffernan and Thomas E. Burman (Leiden: Brill, 2005), 77–93; Frans van Liere, "Andrew of St. Victor and the Gloss on Samuel and Kings," in *Media Latinitas: A Collection of Essays to Mark the Occasion of the Retirement of L. J. Engels*, ed. R. I. A. Nip, H. van Dijk, E. M. C. van Houts, C. H. Kneepkens, and G. A. A. Kortekaas (Turnhout: Brepols, 1996), 249–53; and Frans van Liere, "Andrew of St. Victor, Jerome, and the Jews: Biblical Scholarship in the Twelfth-century Renaissance," in *Scripture and Pluralism*, 59–75.

11. Signer, "Consolation and Confrontation," esp. 82–83.

12. My translation of Beryl Smalley's transcription from MS Paris, Bibliothèque Mazarine, 175 fol. 93r: "[M]ee paupertati, que non potest semper pre manibus vel commentarios vel libros habere glosatos consulo, que in predictis sparsim diffuseque dicta sunt libris, ad historicum quidem spectantia sensum, summatim colligens et quasi in unum corpus succinte compingens. Postremo si quid vel in prophetis quibus precipuam ob nimiam eorum obscuritatem curam impendere decrevi vel in ceteris veteris instrumenti libris, vel Hebreis sive quibuslibet aliis pandentibus, et proprio labore vel divina revelatione, quia etiam in huiusmodi desiderium sibi servientium nonnunquam Dominus exaudit, investigare potui, ne quod utiliter apprehendit dampnose mentem fugiat, interserere visum fuit" (Smalley, *Study of the Bible*, 377 lines 10–21).

13. Signer, "From Theory to Practice," 90. See also Smalley, *Study of the Bible*, 126–28.

14. See Signer, "*Peshat, Sensus Litteralis*, and Sequential Narrative"; Signer, "Consolation and Confrontation"; and Signer, "Restoring the Narrative."

15. Van Liere, "Andrew of St. Victor, Jerome, and the Jews," 73.

16. "Non est ergo quippiam derogare, non est presumere, non est perperam agere, non est otiosum vel superfluitas, quia maiores nostri in sancti expositione eloquii veritatis indagationi vacuaverunt, eiusdem investigationi in scripturarum explanatione nos minores invigilare, venerabilem itaque Ieronimum, licet impari pede sequentes, eiusdem explanationem nostre qualicumque non inmerito preponentes, in veritatis inventione, cui et ipse, et ubi totis viribus elaborabimus, lectoris arbitrio relinquentes utrum aliquid, vel non, laborando profecerimus" (transcribed from MS Paris, Bibliothèque Mazarine, 175 fol. 40r by Beryl Smalley in *Study of the Bible*, 379; see Smalley's translation at 124).

17. *Glossa ordinaria* (hereafter *GO*) on Gen. 25:21: "quia diu filios non fecit ecclesia." Unless otherwise noted, all citations from the *GO* are taken from *Biblia*

Latina cum Glossa Ordinaria: Facsimile Reprint of the Editio Princeps, Adolph Rusch of Strassburg 1480/81 (Turnhout: Brepols, 1992), which serves as the commonly used scholarly text in the absence of a critical edition. All English translations are my own.

18. *GO* on Gen. 25:22: "Quia inter parietes ecclesiae diversa sentiunt electi et reprobi."

19. *GO* on Gen. 25:22: "quasi quid facient nati si sic luctantur innati." It is noteworthy that here the Vulgate text, i.e., the biblical text of the *GO*, is quite different from the rendering found in most English translations. The pertinent part of Gen. 25:22 in the Vulgate of the *GO* reads: "[S]ed collidebantur in utero eius parvuli. Quae ait si sic michi futurum erat: quid necesse fuit concipere."

20. *GO* on Gen. 25:23: "Maior natu populus iudaicus, minor christianus."

21. *GO* on Gen. 25:23: ". . . neque ex iudeis omnis in vnitate fidei conueniunt."

22. *GO* on Gen. 25:24a: "vt ecclesia per euangelium dilataretur."

23. *GO* on Rom. 9:12: "Hoc ad litteram, quia idumei qui de esau qui et edom dicitur, subditi fuerunt; sed magis in hac prophetia intenditur quod populus iudeorum maior, id est in cultum vnius dei prior, minori id est posteriori christiano esset seruiturus."

24. *GO* on Gen. 25:24b: "Non vnus intellectus in velamine littere legis repertus est, sed carnalis et spiritalis."

25. E. Ann Matter, "The Bible in the Center: The *Glossa ordinaria*," in *The Unbounded Community: Papers in Christian Ecumenism in honor of Jaroslav Pelikan*, ed. William Caferro and Duncan G. Fisher (New York: Garland, 1996), 33–42, here 40.

26. Ibid., 40.

27. See *Early Christian Writings: The Apostolic Fathers*, rev. trans. Andrew Louth (London: Penguin, 1987), 155–84. For an overview of early Christian teaching on Jews and Judaism and the Bible as its source, see Franklin T. Harkins, "Unwitting Witnesses: Jews and Judaism in the Thought of Augustine," in *Augustine and World Religions*, ed. Brian Brown, John Doody, and Kim Paffenroth (Lanham: Rowman & Littlefield, 2008), 37–69, esp. 38–45.

28. *GO* on Gen. 25:25: "solis exterioribus assuetus"; and Gen. 25:27: "exteriorem actionem exercendi."

29. It is noteworthy that whereas the principal meaning of the Latin *tabernaculum* is "tent," the Vulgate uses this term also of the ancient Israelite "tabernacle" (e.g., Num. 7:1).

30. *GO* on Gen. 25:27: "Sine macula et ruga" and "qui sine dolo secit dolum."

31. *GO* on Gen. 25:27: "studebat in spiritualibus."

32. *GO* on Gen. 25:27: "Gregorius: eorum vitam significat qui exterioribus voluptatibus fusi carnem sequuntur" (from *Moralia in Iob*, Pt. I, Bk. V; PL 75.689D–690A).

33. *GO* on Gen. 25:27: "Agricola quoque dicitur, quia amatores saeculi tanto colunt exteriora quanto interiora sua inculta relinquunt" (from *Moralia in Iob*, Pt. I, Bk. V; PL 75.689D–690A).

34. *GO* on Gen. 25:27: "Gregorius: Quia qui curis exterioribus spargi refugiunt, simplices in cogitatione et conscientiae habitatione consistunt. [H]abitat enim in tabernaculis qui se intra mentis secreta constringit nec dum ad multa foris inhyat a se ipso cogitatione alienatus recedit" (from *Moralia in Iob*, Pt. I, Bk. V; PL 75.689D–690A).

35. *GO* on Gen. 25:28.

36. The Vulgate text of the *Glossa* reads: "Coxit autem iacob pulmentum, ad quem cum venisset esau de agro lassus, ait: Da michi de coctione hac rufa, quia opido lassus sum."

37. *GO* on Gen. 25:30: "Stultus ardescit desiderio gule propter vilem cibum."

38. *GO* on Gen. 25:30: "Lenticula esca est brutorum animalium, significans animalem legis intellectum, quo populus iudaicus illectus maluit primatu carere, quam ab eo recedere, quod etiam nunc studet a populo minore impetrare, temporalibus deditus post mortem nichil speret boni."

39. *GO* on Gen. 25:33: "Adhuc iudeus in stulticia perdurat, pro temporalibus eterna non curat."

40. *Discourse I against Judaizing Christians* 4.1, in *Saint John Chrysostom: Discourses against Judaizing Christians,* trans. Paul W. Harkins, Fathers of the Church vol. 68 (Washington, DC: Catholic University of America Press, 1979), 14. Earlier in this discourse, Chrysostom proposes Jewish irrationality as the reason for Christian replacement: "And so they [i.e., the Jews] are pitiful because they rejected the blessings which were sent to them, while others seized hold of these blessings and drew them to themselves. Although those Jews had been called to the adoption of sons, they fell to kinship with dogs; we who were dogs received the strength, through God's grace, to put aside the irrational nature which was ours and to rise to the honor of sons" (*Discourse* I.2.1, in Fathers of the Church 68, 5).

41. Robert L. Wilken, *Judaism and the Early Christian Mind: A Study of Cyril of Alexandria's Exegesis and Theology* (New Haven, CT: Yale University Press, 1971), 19.

42. See Harkins, "Unwitting Witnesses."

43. Charles Homer Haskins, *The Renaissance of the Twelfth Century* (New York: Meridian Books, 1957), 298; cf. 294.

44. *Didascalicon* (hereafter *Did.*) IV.1, my translation: "Scripturae divinae sunt quas, a catholicae fidei cultoribus editas auctoritas universalis ecclesiae ad eiusdem fidei corroborationem in numero divinorum librorum computandas recepit et legendas retinuit." Latin text taken from *Hugo von Sankt Viktor, Didascalicon de studio legendi Studienbuch,* ed. Thilo Offergeld, Fontes Christiani vol. 27 (Freiburg: Herder, 1997), 270–72.

45. *Did.* IV.2.

46. *Did.* IV.2.

47. On the various forms of twelfth-century exegesis and Andrew's approach, see Beryl Smalley, *Study of the Bible,* 120–21.

48. The incipits of several of the later (thirteenth- and fourteenth-century) manuscripts of Andrew's work describe it as an "expositio hystorica" or a commentary "ad litteram." See *Andreae de Sancto Victore Opera I: Expositionem super Heptateuchum,* ed. Charles Lohr and Rainer Berndt, CCCM 53 (Turnhout: Brepols, 1986), 4 *apparatus criticus* and x–xvii.

49. "Hispidus, in hebraeo: 'Seir.' Vnde Esau 'Seir (id est pilosus)' dicitur" (CCCM 53.74). Unless otherwise noted, all translations of Andrew's text are my own.

50. For Jerome's gloss, see CCSL 72.32.

51. The manuscripts that I inspected which contain Jerome's gloss, all from the Bibliothèque nationale de France, are MS BnF lat. 367 fol. 78v, MS BnF lat. 368 fol. 64r, and MS BnF lat. 15186 fol. 48v. I would like to thank Mark Zier for making available to me electronic versions of portions of these manuscripts as well as of MS BnF lat. 14398.

52. See Berndt, *André de Saint-Victor,* 221. Philippe Buc maintains that Andrew did have at his disposal an early as well as an amended version of the Gloss on the Pentateuch, both of which he used in the composition of his own exposition on Genesis. See Philippe Buc, *L'ambiguïté du Livre: prince, pouvoir et people dans les commentaires de la Bible au moyen âge* (Paris: Beauchesne, 1994), 72 n. 9.

53. Berndt, *André de Saint-Victor,* 221; and Gibson, "The Place of the *Glossa ordinaria,*" 20–21.

54. Gibson, "The Place of the *Glossa ordinaria,*" 21.

55. "*Simplex,* alii 'sine dolo', in graeco 'aplastos' (id est non fictus)" (CCCM 53.74).

56. See Augustine, *Quaestiones in Genesim* I.74 (PL 34.567).

57. Neither the *editio princeps* nor any of the four manuscripts of the *Glossa* that I examined contain reference to the Greek term. See MSS BnF lat. 367 fol. 78v, BnF lat. 368 fol. 64v, BnF lat. 14398 fol. 67r, and BnF lat. 15186 fol. 48v.

58. Fol. 67r.

59. "*Vende mihi primogenita tua.* . . . Hoc dicunt quidam esse primogenitum animalium, 'quae extra partem contingebant maiori', uel sacerdotalem dignitatem. Sed lex determinat, quae sint *primogenita.* Primogeniti dignitas erat, ut de omnibus bonis patris duplicia—bis scilicet—quantum quilibet alius de filius obtineret. Vnde Ioseph, qui primogeniti dignitatem inter fratres obtinuit, duae de se tribus fecit" (CCCM 53.75).

60. Hugh, *Adnotationes elucidatoriae in Pentateuchon* VII (PL 175.54B).

61. "Nam de benedictione paterna non possumus hoc intelligere" (Hugh, *Adnotationes* VII; PL 175.54B).

62. Rainer Berndt has located 248 places in the *Expositio super Heptateuchum* where Andrew provides readings from Jewish sources (whether acquired through the study of written texts or by means of personal encounter with Jewish contemporaries), often signaled by the Victorine's use of such language as "Hebrei" and "Hebreus meus." See Berndt, *André de Saint-Victor*, 221–24; and for a fuller treatment, Rainer Berndt, "Les interpretations juives dans le *Commentaire de l'Heptateuque* d'André de Saint-Victor," *Recherches augustiniennes* 24 (1989): 199–240.

63. My translation from MS BnF lat. 14398 fol. 67r.

64. "Haec duo—res scilicet et pinguedo terrae—ad multiplicationem rerum temporalium necessaria sunt" (CCCM 53.76).

65. MS BnF lat. 14398 fol. 72r contains these interlinear glosses: "ut celestia subtiliter degustes et de terrenis bene ministres" and "det tibi prudentiam intelligere sacramenta corporis et sanguinis Christi." The *editio princeps* of the GO on Gen. 27:27 provides different, but no less spiritual, glosses: "Pluuia diuini verbi; Contemplatio" and "Congregatione populorum; bonis operibus."

66. CCCM 53.76.

67. "Benedictio autem ista non secundum intentionem, sed secundum uerba fiebat. Sicuti, si aliquis episcopus, clericum suum ordinare putans, alterius ecclesiae clericum ordinaret, ille—qui fraudulenter accederet—esset reuera ordinatus, non ille, quem episcopus ordinare putauit" (CCCM 53.76).

68. Hugh, *Adnotationes* VII (PL 175.54D–55A).

69. "Ideo tanto opere apud antiquos filii benedictionem partum nitebantur accipere" (CCCM 53.76).

70. "*Fratri tuo seruies,* in posteris, quando excutias iugum. Hoc impletum est, quando rebellauerunt Idumaei, ne essent sub Iuda" (CCCM 53.76).

71. Jerome, *Hebraicae Quaestiones in Gen.* 27:40, my translation: "Significat quod Idumaei seruituri sint Iudaeis, et tempus esse uenturum, quando de collo iugum seruitutis abiciant eorumque imperio contradicant. Secundum LXX autem interpretes, qui dixerunt *erit autem cum deposueris et solueris iugum de collo tuo,* uidetur pendere sententia nec esse completa" (CCSL 72.34).

72. See *Andreae de Sancto Victore Opera VI: Expositionem in Ezechielem,* ed. Michael Alan Signer, CCCM 53E (Turnhout: Brepols, 1991), xxvii and sources cited in n. 99.

73. "*Nuntiata sunt,* uel diuinitus uel ab aliquo familiari Esau, cui arcanum suum reuelauerat" (CCCM 53.76).

74. GO on Gen. 27:42, "diuinitus quamuis in cogitatione dicta, unde ad magnum pertinet mysterium quod minorem pro maiore benedici voluit." See also MS BnF lat. 15186 fol. 52v.

75. MS BnF lat. 14398 fol. 73r: "per spiritum prophetiae."

76. "Solet quaeri, quomodo Moyses tanto tempore post conditi mundi scire potuit exordium. Non est mirum, si spiritus sancti gratia, quae ei reuelare potuit

etiam futura, potuit reuelare et praeterita; praesertim cum nihil tam nostrae subiacet cognitioni quemadmodum id, quod praeteritum est. Quamquam non absurde credi potest, sanctos antiquos patres ipsumque Adam posterorum suorum memoriae frequenti narratione uel etiam scripto—cum hoc maxima diuinae laudis causa et nostri in ipsum amoris sit—mundi creationem mandare curasse, sic ad Moysi notitiam, qui eam diligenter inuestigare curauit, peruenire potuisse" (CCCM 53.5).

77. See Smalley, *Study of the Bible*, 164–65.

78. *De Emmanuele*, Prologue, my translation: "In quemdam magistri Andreae tractatum, quem in Isaiae explanationem scripserat . . . nonnulla minus caute posita, minus catholice disputata inveni. In multis namque scripturae illius locis ponitur Judaeorum sententia quasi sit non tam Judaeorum quam propria, et velut vera. Super illum autem locum: *Ecce virgo concipiet, et pariet filium,* Judaeorum objectiones vel quaestiones ponit, nec solvit, et videtur velut eis palmam dedisse, dum eas veluti insolubiles relinquit" (PL 196.601).

79. *Liber exceptionum* Pt. II Bk. II Ch. 11: "Nota est historia quomodo Jacob Esau de benedictione patris supplantavit. Isaac significat Deum a quo descendit benedictio super caput justi. Rebecca significat matrem gratiam, que Jacob de petenda benedictione consulit. Jacob posterior natus, domi remanens, benedictionem consequens, gentilem designat populum, qui post Israeliticum populum ad cognitionem divinam venit, et intra se matre gratia vota nutrit, que reddat laudationes Deo, et benedicitur ab eo in mundo per gratiam, in celo per gloriam. Esau prior natus, foris venationi deserviens, benedictionem amittens, populum Israel significant, qui prius ad cognitionem Dei venit, sed foris in littera justitiam, querit, et benedictionem celestis hereditatis amittit" (*Richard de Saint-Victor. Liber exceptionum,* ed. Jean Châtillon [Paris: J. Vrin, 1958], 239–40).

CHAPTER EIGHT

"And Rebekah Loved Jacob," But Why?

Responses from Two Twelfth-Century Exegetes

Deborah L. Goodwin

Founder of the nation or quintessentially deceitful female? Plucky heroine or overbearing mother? The biblical matriarch Rebekah has long been viewed as an ambiguous figure, her vital role in securing Isaac's blessings for her beloved younger son Jacob a cause for embarrassment and, only rarely and more recently, for celebration. Her reputation has been rehabilitated by some contemporary, chiefly feminist, students of the Hebrew Bible, while still other feminist critics regard her equivocal status as the product of the Bible's ineluctable sexism.[1]

Historically, positive assessments of Rebekah's actions in Genesis 25 and 27 produced by most Christian and Jewish exegetes were the result of significantly rehabilitative readings. In Jewish tradition, Rebekah's role in obtaining Isaac's blessing for their younger son is explained and justified by various strategies. Her foreknowledge of Jacob's destiny is attributed to her status as a matriarch-prophet (*Gen. Rab.* 67.9), or to the instruction she received at the *bet-midrash* of Shem and Eber at the time of her troubling pregnancy (according to *Genesis Rabbah* 63.7, Shem—not the Lord—informs her that two "proud nations" struggle together in her womb).[2] The book of Jubilees minimizes Rebekah's independence, and culpability, by depicting Abraham himself guiding and directing her. The grandfather observes the characters of the twins, sees Esau's violence and impiety, and decides that the younger son must be his heir. He commands Rebekah to "watch over my son, Jacob," and blesses the boy in her presence (Jub. 19:16–30).

In the Christian tradition, Rebekah's seeming duplicity is rationalized in similar ways: she is inspired by the Holy Spirit to act on behalf of Jacob, the ancestor of David and, therefore, the ancestor of Jesus Christ in the generations descended "by faith" from Abraham.[3] Her subsequent behavior has the license of authority derived from divine inspiration. She is blameless— or better, an essential actor in salvation history. Early Christian exegetes qualify Rebekah's actions also by identifying her as a typological figure of the Church or as the Holy Spirit itself.[4] Still other commentators decline to discuss her behavior at all and focus instead on Jacob or, more rarely, Isaac. For example, in response to a query from Pope Damasus, "why was Isaac, a righteous man dear to God, allowed by God to be duped by Jacob?" Jerome replies that no mere mortal can be full of wisdom, certain of truth. God's providence ensured Isaac's physical blindness so that he would correctly bless his younger son.[5] The Bible's own record of Rebekah's initiative and her daring actions is suppressed.

In both Christian and Jewish exegetical traditions, the ambiguities of Rebekah's status are resolved by a combination of strategies: divine prompting equips her with foreknowledge which in turn absolves her from blame; the importance of her historical role overshadows or obviates discussion of her specific dubious actions; she is made to simply disappear from the narrative, replaced as an actor by Jacob (himself depicted as blameless) or a combination of Jacob and Isaac (whose actions now include those of Rebekah, rendering her superfluous to the narrative). As this brief survey indicates, she was seldom treated as a full-blown character in the story of Jacob's succession to Isaac's patrimony. Her motives and actions were not subject to sustained examination. In Christian commentaries produced in late antiquity and the early medieval period (through the eleventh and early twelfth centuries), Rebekah's role—like that of other figures in the Hebrew Bible—was reduced to that of a typological cipher, a placeholder for the fulfillment of God's promises revealed in the New Testament. Rebekah equals the Church which "mothers" the offspring of Abraham by faith, she is the personification of Patience, she "is" the Holy Spirit: typology papers over multiple difficulties stemming from her actions recorded in the biblical text.

In the twelfth century, in the Latin West, a significant number of both Jewish and Christian exegetes began to attend to scriptural narrative as a framework for interpretation. Rather than elaborating on the multivalent meanings of atomized or typological figures or events, and linking those meanings to an extrabiblical, "credal" rationale (e.g., Rebekah *is* the Church), exegetes explicated the roles of actors within the context of biblical narrative more thoroughly. The reasons for this shift in interests, and in particular the parallels between medieval Jewish and Christian exegetical methods and hermeneutical strategies, have been explored by Michael A. Signer in a number of foundational essays. As he notes, the question whether the twelfth-century "search for 'plain meaning' in Scripture" represented a "bold revolution" or continuity with older methods remains unclear as does the issue of the extent of mutual influence. Still, the parallelism between Jewish and Christian exegetical strategies, "marked by greater attention to the nature of language in Scripture, and greater effort to explain a single passage within the larger context of other passages in the Bible" has been amply demonstrated by his studies.[6]

Twelfth-century Christian exegetes such as Hugh of Saint Victor turned with renewed interest to the study of the Bible's literal and historical sense. Hugh retrieved and revived Augustine's formulation from *City of God* that some actions described in the Bible were complete in themselves (as history) while others were completed in a literal sense in the Old Testament narrative, but fulfilled spiritually in Christ, and still others would be fulfilled at the end of days.[7] Hugh urged Christian exegetes—as had Augustine—to attend to the particularities of biblical idiom and to the signifying function of events (the *res gestae*) that formed Scripture's unique vocabulary. Only in the Bible, they argued, could "things" signify as words do in ordinary texts. To understand both the proper meaning of words and the meaning of biblical events, one needed to situate both correctly within the overarching biblical narrative. Michael Signer has also demonstrated how an exegete's "mere" grammatical or literary commentary can actually constitute an intervention in the biblical text, creating a narrative superstructure that supplements, "smooths out," or redirects the narrative sequence inherent in a scriptural account. The purpose of such interventions, whether practiced by twelfth-century Jews or Christians, frequently involved the one group responding to the polemical claims of the other.[8]

This essay addresses the work of two twelfth-century exegetes, one Jewish and one Christian, both of whom commented on the role of Rebekah in the Jacob-Esau narratives: Rabbi Samuel ben Meir (Rashbam) and Peter Comestor. Each was a practitioner of the "literal," historically oriented exegesis current in his community, each was a self-conscious continuator of a rich heritage of biblical interpretation, and each was aware of the competing claims of the other community's interpretive practices. Their respective treatments of the character of Rebekah in Genesis 25–27 demonstrate that these two exegetes exercised, in their practice of literal interpretation, a careful editorial control of the story's meaning through the reconstruction of Rebekah's motives. Their works also evince some of the key qualities of twelfth-century exegesis: its increased interest in naturalistic, rational explanation; greater attention to the lexical meaning of distinctive biblical idiom (and a corresponding study of the grammar of biblical languages); and among both Christian and Jewish exegetes, an increased mutual awareness of the other's activities.[9] This essay will show how each exegete construed Rebekah's actions with a narrative sequence that served his larger theological and polemical goals.

Rashbam and Comestor were near contemporaries; the former died in 1160 and the latter is believed to have died circa 1178/9. They were geographically proximate, too: each living and working in the general Paris-Troyes axis at a time when the schools at Paris were beginning to coalesce into the university form, when the *yeshivot* of Troyes enjoyed considerable fame, and when the secular culture of the court of Champagne produced masterpieces of vernacular literature.[10] Both were members of movements responding to traditions of biblical exegesis that had emphasized "spiritual" or allegorical meanings in Scripture. Rashbam tells us that he is refining the exegetical process of his renowned grandfather, Rabbi Solomon ben Isaac of Troyes (Rashi, d. 1105), whom he had perceived as overly concerned with midrash: "However I, Samuel, the son of [Rashi's] son-in-law, Meir . . . often disputed his interpretations with him to his face. [Rashi] admitted to me that, if only he had had the time, he would have written new commentaries, based on the insights into the plain meaning of Scripture that are newly thought of day by day."[11] Avraham Grossman has argued that Rashbam's Torah commentary should be read as a kind of super-commentary to Rashi on the Pentateuch. He notes that the principal aim of Rashbam's commentary is to explain the "literal, plain meaning" of the text and, secondarily, to correct to his grandfather's presumed overreliance on more traditional midrashic explanations. Grossman points out that "Rashbam does not explain the entire text, but only 'selected' extracts, and his choice is governed by close attention to Rashi. When Rashi's interpretation seems to him 'true,' that is, in accord with the literal, plain meaning . . . he makes no comment."[12] Grossman argues further that Rashbam's "fanatical" attention to expounding Scripture's plain meaning was "strongly influenced" by interreligous debate and was intended to gainsay Christians' allegorical, christological interpretations of the Hebrew Bible.[13]

For his part, Peter Comestor's project in the *Historia Scholastica* has been classed with the exegetical projects of Hugh and Andrew of St. Victor as it seeks to lay the proper historical foundations for the study of Scripture. Beryl Smalley articulated the relation between the Victorine school and Comestor's work in *The Study of the Bible in the Middle Ages*: "The *Histories*, it has been pointed out, were really fulfilling the programme of the *Didascalicon*. Here Hugh of St. Victor had taught that theology must begin with a thorough grounding in biblical history. Peter was providing just such a groundwork. He had written a textbook for the students and an invaluable work of reference for their teachers."[14] But Comestor's achievement was not merely, as Smalley subsequently points out, the production of a textbook to fulfill the Victorines' educational objectives. In addition, she contends, he and the exegetes of his generation (gathered under the rubric of the "biblical-moral school"[15]) adopted the Victorine practice of attending closely to the literal meaning of a text in order to generate an interpretation tied to the text's historical context but open to further speculation. Since Peter Comestor's *Historia Scholastica* has been identified as a continuation or fulfillment of the Victorine exegetical project, it is worth discussing Hugh's theory of historical exegesis in some detail, the better to judge Comestor's degree of involvement in the Victorine program.

In his *Didascalicon,* Hugh of St. Victor identified three levels of textual exposition to which exegetes must attend: the letter, sense, and "deeper meaning." Each must be pondered attentively to understand its relationship to the spiritual whole of the biblical narrative. Still, as a check against unwarranted speculation, Hugh urged exegetes to bear in mind that not every passage held deeper meaning:

> Exposition included three things: the letter, the sense, and the deeper meaning (*sententia*). The letter is found in every discourse, for the very sounds are letters; but sense and a deeper meaning are not found together in every discourse. Some discourses contain only the letter and the sense, some only the letter and a deeper meaning, some all these three together. . . . [T]hat discourse in which the hearer can conceive nothing from the mere telling unless an exposition is added thereto contains only the letter and a deeper meaning in which . . . something else is left which must be supplied for its understanding and which is made clear by exposition.[16]

There is an affinity between Hugh's understanding of the "deeper meaning" of the text and Rashbam's concern for "the profundities of the plain meaning of Scripture."[17] As Martin Lockshin, Rashbam's modern editor points out, *peshat*[18] was for Rashbam "the *simplest,* most immediate level of meaning of the text [as opposed to] the midrash, which he claims is the *most important* level of meaning of the verse."[19] Hugh would agree: while a scriptural text's literal meaning must be thoroughly considered before one can turn to discerning its spiritual meaning, the process of literal exposition should not distract the exegete from the larger reality of spiritual truth: "[I]t is necessary both that we follow the letter in such a way as not to prefer our own sense to the divine authors, and that we do not follow it in such a way as to deny that the entire pronouncement of truth is rendered in it. Not the man devoted to the letter 'but the spiritual man judgeth all things.'"[20] Hugh's emphasis on the close study of textual elements—the letter, the sense, the *sententia*[21]—is linked to his emphasis on the study of biblical history: "it is not unfitting that we call by the name of 'history' not only the recounting of actual deeds but also the first meaning of any narrative which uses words according to their proper nature."[22]

The Bible's orderly unfolding of events in time is, according to Hugh, the account of the divine work devoted to the restoration of fallen humanity.[23] The exegete should study those events on three levels: the literal, the allegorical, and the tropological. In his pedagogical work the *Didascali-con*, his "handbook" of biblical hermeneutics *De scripturis et scriptoribus sacris*, and in his systematic theological work *De sacramentis christianae fidei*, Hugh discusses how the careful scholar should deploy the tools of the liberal arts in order to extract the sweetness of divine eloquence from the un-promising husks of biblical narration.[24] In the prologue to *De sacramentis*, Hugh asserts that historical study enables the scholar to achieve the neces-sary "knowledge of things," which can then be correctly correlated to "mys-tical acts done or to be done." This act of correlation is analogous to grammar's lower-level activity—correctly associating words with things as one does when analyzing non-sacred texts in which things cannot and do not signify other things.[25] Determining the aptest meaning of the biblical *res gestae* requires the exegete to interpret correctly not only the literal sense, but also the biblical idiom in which, uniquely, things or events signify other, higher-order things.

There is a kind of circularity to Hugh's approach. On one hand, he insists on the priority of historical study; without it, a student of the Bible is ludicrously ill-equipped to pronounce on its correct interpretation.[26] In the *Didascalicon*, he insists that the proper order of scriptural study begins with history before proceeding to allegory and tropology: "First you learn history and diligently commit to memory the truth of the deeds that have been performed, reviewing from beginning to end what has been done, when it has been done, where it has been done, and by whom it has been done. . . . Nor do I think that you will be able to become perfectly sensitive to allegory unless you have first been grounded in history."[27] On the other hand, it is worth pausing over the phrase "the truth of the deeds . . . from beginning to end" in relation to Hugh's subsequent comment on allegory. The "end" he has in view is, always, the restoration of the human being in the image and likeness of God. This end, goal, and purpose undergirds the spiritual meaning of historical events—the *factum* to which other *facta* allude allegorically. Allegory, he tells the reader of the next chapter, is the second foundation of the Bible's structure. It rests on the buried, some-times jumbled foundation of the literal sense, but unlike that first founda-tion, the second is smooth and seemly: "the spiritual meaning admits no opposition; in it, many things can be different from one another, but none can be opposed. . . . This foundation both carries what is placed upon it and is itself carried by the first foundation. All things rest upon the first foundation but are not fitted to it in every way. As to the latter foundation, everything else both rests upon it and is fitted to it."[28]

In other words, the exegete's ability to recognize the "*truth of the deeds done*" is conditioned by a proper orientation to the Truth itself, which is not revealed by the historical study of Scripture, but by the exegete's mastery of the higher orders of biblical scholarship: allegory and tropology. A firm grasp of the spiritual meaning, both the foundation for allegory and allegory itself, enables the exegete to traverse toward an ever-increasing "knowledge of truth and love of virtue,"[29] the purpose of Scripture study:

> The very bases of your spiritual structure are certain principles of the faith—principles which form your starting point. Truly the judicious student ought to be sure that, before he makes his way through extensive volumes, he is so instructed in the particulars which bear upon his task and upon his profession of the true faith, that he may safely be able to build onto his structure whatever he afterwards finds. For in such a great sea of books and in the manifold intricacies of opinions which often confound the mind of the student both by their number and their obscurity, the man who does not know briefly in advance, in every category so to say, *some definite principle which is supported by firm faith* and to which all may be referred, will scarcely be able to conclude any single thing.[30]

It could be argued that these instructions bear only on the study of allegory, especially since this chapter concludes with the list of biblical books Hugh judged best for the study of allegorical meaning. But recall the chapter's caution to "the man who follows the letter alone": "he cannot long continue without error. For this reason it is necessary both that we follow the letter in such a way as not to prefer our own sense to the divine authors, and that we do not follow it in such a way as to deny that the *entire pronouncement of truth is rendered in it*."[31] The process of knowledge-building outlined by Hugh proceeds not simply from the literal to the spiritual, but from an initial faithful acceptance of the narrative of restoration, to the study of biblical history's literal narrative, and then to a properly grounded study of the allegorical, whose layers of meaning are built up by studying the unique "grammar" of biblical *res gestae*.[32] The evidence from later generations of exegetes suggests that they weighed and accepted Hugh's strictures and laid a foundation of "unshaken truth" even before launching their study of the Bible's literal sense.[33]

This excursus into Hugh of Saint Victor's view of history's place in biblical study sets the stage for a discussion of Peter Comestor's role as a successor to his pedagogy. The *Historia Scholastica* can be seen as a tool to give the student "briefly in advance" an overview not only of biblical history (as has often been argued[34]), but a specific *orientation* to that history, grounded in its spiritual meaning—Hugh's "definite principle which is supported by firm faith." Events unfold in biblical time purposefully and meaningfully: the work of restoration is detectable throughout. Comestor's historical narrative is itself a work of "interpretation and commentary" that integrates the teaching of doctrine with chronology.

Two initial statements by Peter orient us to the goals of the *Historia Scholastica*.[35] One is his dedicatory letter to William, Archbishop of Sens.[36] Peter tells his noble and influential addressee that his associates (*sociorum*) have asked him to produce the work because scriptural history, read in sequence with glosses seems to them exceedingly brief, scattered, and unclear. He undertakes this work so that his brethren can acquire the truth of history they so eagerly desire. He proposes to present a continuous history from the Creation to Jesus' ascension. Peter modestly contrasts his historical rivulet (*historicum rivulum*) with the "ocean of mysteries" studied by the more learned. In his brief preface to the work as a whole, Comestor offers a variation on the "edifice" metaphor used by Hugh, Gregory the Great, Jerome, and other commentators. He describes the three mansions of the "imperial Majesty": his "assembly hall," the fullness of heaven and earth; his "bedchamber," the souls of the just in whom he rejoices; and finally, the sacred Scriptures as the Emperor's dining hall (*cenaculum*), in which "he makes his people drunk, in order to make them sober," the Psalmist's "house of God" that we entered with the throng of the wise (cf. Ps. 55:14). This hall has three parts: foundation, walls, and roof which correspond to history, allegory, and tropology, which he then defines in terms derived from Hugh of Saint Victor. Comestor summarizes the familiar metaphor telegraphically: *Prima planior, secunda acutior, tercia suavior.*[37] Note that, despite the apparent privileging of the literal and historical sense, allegory is for Peter as for Hugh the more acute, pungent, insightful form of knowledge-food dispensed by Scripture. Moreover, he closes his preface by asserting that by speaking of the "foundation" (*fundamentum*), we understand ourselves to be speaking, with God's help, of the head and origin of all things.[38]

My contention that Peter Comestor has written not just a ready reference guide for beginning students, but rather an innovative work with a distinct doctrinal purpose[39] is supported by recent research by Mark J. Clark into the association between Comestor and his teacher, Peter Lombard. In a series of recent articles, Clark has argued that the *Historia*'s links to Lombard's more speculative theological work have been underestimated. He argues that the structure of Comestor's account of Creation, which Clark insists relies extensively on Lombard's *Sentences,* represents "a structural compromise between conventional biblical commentaries and new theological works organized around theological topics."[40] Inasmuch as it constituted a move away from "strict adherence to the biblical text" as the basis for theological education, the *Historia* was innovative.[41] Regarding Comestor's text as more than a convenient biblical abridgement by an author whose program and interest were "narrow" compared to Hugh of St. Victor's[42] invites us to consider what Dominick LaCapra would term its "worklike" qualities as opposed to its "documentary" function: "The documentary situates the text in terms of factual or literal dimensions involving reference to empirical reality and conveying information about it. The 'worklike' supplements empirical reality by adding or subtracting from it. It thereby involves dimensions of the text not reducible to the documentary, prominently including the roles of commitment, interpretation, and imagination."[43] In effect, there is more than history in the *Historia.* While Clark re-examines its relationship to the emergence of "speculative" scholastic theology, I propose that we read it not only as a textbook to prepare budding exegetes, but as a skillfully constructed exegetical text in its own right, whose author engages multiple levels of scriptural meaning simultaneously, while systematically using history to affirm Christian doctrine.[44]

In Peter Comestor's exegesis of the Jacob and Esau narrative in the *Historia Scholastica* we can detect a process of constructing the story that probes its deeper meaning (the "truth of history"), while attending to the literal meaning of the text at hand. To try to get at the deeper meaning of history was not a reckless leap into allegory, but the pursuit of that meaning *did* permit the exegete to use his discretion when constructing a historical narrative. What is significant about this process is the extent to which exegetes like Comestor and Rashbam re-shape or amplify a fragmentary or scandalous biblical narrative in order to tell a coherent story. In the case of Rebekah, where adequate motivation for her actions seems to be missing in the biblical text, Comestor and Rashbam supply the needed details without contravening the literal meaning. To a certain extent, "literal meaning" in their hands came to mean "human," while the historical meaning was construed in terms of what was "plausible," both in terms of human action and theological claims.[45]

Before turning to an examination of Rashbam's and Comestor's characterizations of Rebekah, I would like to interject a modern biblical scholar's comments on the depiction of duplicitous women in Hebrew Scripture as they shed light on the generally positive results of the medieval exegeses of Genesis 25–27. In an article titled "'For I have the way of women': Deception, Gender, and Ideology in Biblical Narrative," Esther Fuchs examines female "tricksters" in the Hebrew Bible, specifically the unfolding of the character of Rachel in Genesis 31 (after she had stolen Laban's idols). Fuchs notes:

> The story of Rachel's deception dramatizes what I think distinguishes biblical tales of female deception: *the suppression of explicit indices of motivation, the suspension of authorial judgment, and the absence of closure.* As we shall see, these literary strategies create the impression that deceptiveness is somehow generic to women. By suppressing motivation, the narrator makes it difficult for the reader to exonerate the female deceiver. By suspending judgment, the narrator creates a kind of ambiguity which may lead to a paleosymbolic association of femininity and deceptiveness. The absence of closure contributes to this vagueness, suggesting that in the case of women, deception is not a problem requiring punishment or reformation. . . . In a way, the dismissal of female experience as deception is necessary for the perpetuation of the hegemony of patriarchal semiosis.[46]

In contrast to the biblical narrative that seems to condemn women who exercise power in unorthodox ways, medieval exegetes evinced a desire to explain and endorse aspects of Rebekah's behavior. This is not to say that medieval commentators tried to undermine "the hegemony of patriarchal semiosis," but simply that they acknowledged the stumbling blocks in the biblical narrative and tried to address them. Generally their explanations concentrated on rehabilitating Jacob's dubious actions by explaining them in terms of what his mother told him to do, but this is not always the case. Rashbam and Comestor, in particular, give positive and consistent portraits of Rebekah. Keeping Fuchs' three strategies in mind, we will turn to their exegeses in an attempt to see where a literal-historical reading of Genesis 25–27 can yield a resolution of tensions surrounding a duplicitous woman.

To assess our commentators' characterizations of Rebekah, we will consider their responses to passages in which Rebekah's behavior seems most questionable or her motives most obscure. Do those comments constitute part of a coherent characterization or narrative thread? If so, what role does Rebekah play in the exegete's larger interpretive scheme? These are the key passages:

1. Rebekah's response to her painful pregnancy: "If it is thus, why do I live?" (Gen. 25:22a).

2. Seeking an answer from God: "So she went to inquire of the Lord" (Gen. 25:22b).

3. The contrast between Isaac's love for Esau and Rebekah's apparently unmotivated love for Jacob: "but Rebekah loved Jacob" (Gen. 25:28b).

4. Rebekah's orders to Jacob, enjoining his cooperation in deceiving his father: "obey my word as I command you" (Gen. 27:8); "Upon me be your curse, my son, only obey my word" (Gen. 27:13).

5. Her preparation of Isaac's food and clothing Jacob in Esau's garments (Gen. 27:13–17).

6. Her anticipation of Esau's attempt on Jacob's life: "But the words of Esau her older son were told to Rebekah" (Gen. 27:42); "Now therefore, my son, obey my voice; arise, flee to Laban" (Gen. 27:43).

7. Her complaint against Esau's wives (Gen. 27:46).

Most of these passages raise the issue of Rebekah's motivation: is her question blasphemous? (Gen. 25:22a); we are told why Isaac loves Esau, but why does Rebekah love Jacob? (Gen. 25:28b);[47] why did Rebekah decide to deceive Isaac? (Gen. 27:8); what do Rebekah's actions in preparing Isaac's meal and contributing to Jacob's disguise signify? (Gen. 27:13–17); is sending Jacob to seek a wife from her family a conscious ploy to obtain Isaac's blessing for Jacob again before he leaves for Mesopotamia? (Gen. 27:46). The remaining passage, Genesis 25:22b, concerns Rebekah's dialogue with God: is it possible that Rebekah spoke directly with God or was the encounter mediated?

Rashbam does not comment on Rebekah's question (Gen. 25:22a), even though many medieval exegetes did with interpretations ranging from the naturalistic (Abraham ibn Ezra, Andrew of St. Victor) to the theological (Ramban, Rupert of Deutz). Rashbam suggests that she consulted a prophet of those days about her pregnancy, who mediated God's answer to her. But as Rashbam interprets it, God's response to her agonized query is crucial to understanding Rebekah's motivation for her subsequent behavior. He contends that the verse "the older shall serve the younger" (Gen. 25:23) is in effect a prophetic text that explains that because God loved Jacob, so did Rebekah.[48] He reinforces this point by quoting Malachi 1:2, "For it is further written 'I [the Lord] have loved Jacob,'" in support of his thesis.

Two points are noteworthy about this brief passage. First, we should bear in mind Grossman's and Lockshin's suggestions that Rashbam's Torah commentary be read as a companion to that of Rashi. Significantly, Rashi did not discuss Rebekah's actions in his comments on Genesis 25, except to reiterate midrashic commentary derived from *Genesis Rabbah*. He concentrates on the turmoil in Rebekah's womb, and on distinguishing the very different characters of Esau and Jacob apparent even *in utero:* Esau is cruel, bloodthirsty, and idolatrous, while Jacob is peaceful and pious. Rebekah's independent role is minimized, and Rashi does not attribute God's or Rebekah's love for Jacob to the phrase "the older shall serve the younger."

How, then, does Rashbam's exegesis comment on or correct Rashi's? First, while Rashi comments on all the other phrases in verse 23, Rashbam raises up the one verse he had omitted as the linchpin for his construal of the actions that follow. Rather than minimizing Rebekah's role, Rashbam aligns her motivation with God's. As we shall see, Rebekah's actions are made both consistent and laudable in Rashbam's account because she acts under the inspiration of the Spirit and in concert with the divine will. Also, the interjection of the passage from Malachi is highly significant; the verse reads in full, "I have loved you, says the Lord. But you say, 'How have you loved us?' Is not Esau Jacob's brother? Yet I have loved Jacob but I have hated Esau; I have made his hill country a desolation and his heritage a desert for jackals." God, Rebekah, and the prophet all agree: Jacob is the beloved, predestined, and fully entitled heir to the Abrahamic covenant.

When interpreting Genesis 25:28b, "and Rebekah loved Jacob," Rashbam reinforces this justification: "because she recognized his innocence [a reference to vs. 27, *veya'aqov 'ish tam*] and because of what God said, 'The older shall serve the younger.'" He notes that the text is preparing the reader to understand "that Isaac wanted to bless Esau but Rebekah acted with guile to see that Jacob would be blessed."[49] Here Rashbam exercises one of his hermeneutical rules: Scripture sometimes tells us information in advance that helps us to understand future developments in the narrative.[50] Rashbam acknowledges Rebekah's "guile" but also makes it intelligible in terms of what she knows is God's will. As a consequence of divine guidance, Rebekah is able to reassure Jacob in 27:13ff. She insists any curse of Isaac's will be upon her, not upon him. Rashbam notes, "In other words she told him, 'Do not be afraid,' for she relied on what God had told her (25:23). . . . "[51] The exculpatory nature of Rebekah's knowledge comes up in a discussion of the often-debated question of whether Isaac "confirmed" his blessing of Jacob in 27:33b: ". . . and I have blessed him?—yes, and he shall be blessed." Rashbam asserts that Isaac confirmed his blessing because he "realized that Jacob had done everything at Rebekah's suggestion and that she had recognized him to be more worthy of the blessing."[52] In Rashbam's structuring of the narrative, Rebekah emerges from the episode of Isaac's deception recognized by her husband and Jacob as a spiritual leader, an evaluation that derives from his initial discussion of *her interpretation* of the key verse, "the older shall serve the younger." Finally, in keeping with his portrait of Rebekah as a wise and insightful leader, Rashbam applauds the unspoken meaning of her complaint against Esau's Hittite wives (Gen. 27:46). It is a strategy to get Jacob out of the way while Esau's anger cools without divulging Esau's fratricidal intent and further disturbing the relations between father and elder son.[53]

Rashbam fills in just those missing elements that an analysis of this biblical text, using Fuchs' criteria, would highlight. He supplies motivation: her knowledge that the Almighty prefers Jacob makes her love him and guides all her subsequent activity, even when it runs counter to her husband's wishes. Implicitly, we understand that Rebekah is pious and wants to do God's will. Far from suspending judgment, Rashbam endorses Rebekah's chosen path and supplements her piety with wisdom. As for closure, Rashbam's comment on Genesis 27:46, that Rebekah wisely feigned fear that Jacob might take a Hittite wife to create a pretext for saving his life and for preserving family harmony, is a fitting final touch to his portrait of Rebekah. She is wise, independent, and high-minded, struggling to do right despite the shortcomings of her male relatives.

What Rashbam's account does not explain, however, is why Rebekah kept the knowledge of the prophecy to herself. Why did she withhold it from Isaac? Would life not have been simpler if she had just told him? Of course if she had, the narrative would lose all its moral ambiguity and dramatic power. Rashbam's device for explaining Rebekah's motivation serves several useful purposes while preserving the drama of the narrative. First, he provides an understanding of Jacob which minimizes any notion of Jacob's culpability.[54] Second, and by no means incidentally, Rebekah's motivation is clarified and made honorable. Third, Isaac's love for Esau is depicted as natural—it is not a deluded or beguiled father's indulgence of a wicked son as is the case in Rashi's commentary. Isaac simply did not know what Rebekah knew. Thus, according to Rashbam, he was willing to accede to her superior knowledge and judgment (see *supra,* on Gen. 27:33). The Almighty brings about the desired result in the end, but not without working through Rebekah.

The narrative of Jacob and Esau's sibling rivalry was used by medieval Christians and Jews to understand their contemporary situations. Each group saw itself as Jacob, the righteous brother, and regarded the other as Esau, the reprobate passed over by God. Christians associated the Jews with the older brother whose rights had been set aside in favor of them, representatives of a younger faith. Rabbinical tradition wove the story of Esau together with the histories and prophecies related to the nations he fathered, known variously in the Bible as Amalek, Edom, or Idumea. Esau and his descendants were understood metaphorically as Rome, and subsequently Christendom, by the Rabbis. Commenting on Genesis 25:23 ("two nations are in your womb"), *Genesis Rabbah* reports these are rulers of Edom and Israel—"Hadrian of the Gentiles and Solomon of Israel. . . . The hated of thy Creator is in thy womb, as it is written, 'But Esau I hated' (Mal. 1:3)."[55] They conceded that the Christians, figuratively understood as Esau, presently enjoyed the "fatness of the earth" as predicted in Genesis, but asserted that God would overturn this blessing at the end of days.[56] Similarly, in his Psalms commentary, Rashi affirms that despite Esau's present enjoyment of worldly power, God adopted Jacob as his firstborn, the true Israel. Ultimately, Esau will serve Jacob.[57]

Peter Comestor's depiction of Rebekah in the *Historia Scholastica* bears some striking resemblances to that of Rashbam. From the beginning of his re-telling of Genesis 25, we are alerted to Rebekah's awareness of Jacob's special status. Her private knowledge of Jacob's destiny justifies her course of action in Comestor's narrative just as it did in Rashbam's, although this point is framed very differently by Comestor.

As it was for Rashbam, Genesis 25:22a, "The children struggled within her" (*collidebantur in utero eius parvuli*) is a key passage for Comestor. His commentary on the verse is contained in a chapter headed, *De labore Rebecce in partu geminorum.* He notes the various possible interpretations of *collidebantur* derived from the Septuagint, Aquila, and Symmachus, but then abandons etymology to discuss the meaning of the disturbance. He rejects a naturalistic explanation that the maternal womb might have been too small for twins. The disturbance Rebekah experiences is testimony to the will of God, who has determined that the boys will disagree over their birthrights, and whose descendants will also disagree. The elder son's patrimony, to which he is entitled by nature, will be granted to the other son—by grace. Alluding to Paul's second letter to the Corinthians, he writes, "It is believed that Jacob was sanctified even then, in the womb, and that motion prefigured that there should not be agreement between Christ and Belial."[58] In a few swift strokes, Comestor places before the reader the classic Christian polarities of nature and grace, believer and unbeliever, spirit and flesh—and, given the highly contested identities of Jacob and Esau, Christians and Jews. Comestor's allusion to a "spiritual" meaning frames his subsequent discussion, however attentive to historical *realia* and Jewish traditions it might be.[59]

Comestor comments on Genesis 25:23 only after a lengthy discussion of how Rebekah might have consulted with the Lord—whether by sleeping at Abraham's altar and receiving a prophetic dream (induced by herbs) or by consulting Melchizedek. But in any case, he asserts, she did receive an answer from God. He interprets the prophecy in the historical sense as derived from the Hebrew Bible, not from allegory. The younger and elder signify Israel and Edom, and the Edomites will be tributaries to David. This brings us to the question of Rebekah's love for Jacob. Comestor provides a carefully parallel explanation for Genesis 25:28: "The father loved Esau, who was both the first-born and of whose game he gladly ate. But the mother loved Jacob, both by virtue of his simplicity and because of the inspiration of God."[60] It is striking to compare this to Rashbam's comment, cited above: "because she recognized his innocence and because of what God said, 'The older shall serve the younger.'"

In Comestor's version of the story, Rebekah is not the only person who learns things "in the spirit." After Jacob's spurious meal is prepared and Isaac is deceived (activities on which Comestor has no comment), we are told that Isaac confirms his blessing of Jacob in Esau's presence. Concerning Genesis 27:33, Comestor writes: "*Isaac trembled violently;* and in his terror saw in spirit from the Lord what had happened and understood the meaning of the pious fraud. He was not angry on that account, but confirming what he had done, said: '*Your brother came fraudulently and took your blessing and he will be blessed.*'"[61] In the sequel to these events the unique source of Rebekah's knowledge and the motivation for her behavior is emphasized again: she knows "in spirit" Esau's thoughts through the good offices of that same Spirit who "had intimated that Jacob should defraud his brother."[62] From the inception of the narrative, beginning when Comestor suggested that Jacob had been sanctified in the womb, Rebekah has enjoyed the privy counsel of the Spirit. This fact explains and exculpates her actions, and pointedly makes her a parallel for other—notably New Testament—mothers like Elizabeth and Mary.

Finally, Comestor interprets Rebekah's complaint regarding Esau's wives as Rashbam does: her avowed fear that Jacob will marry a Hittite woman is meant to propel Jacob on his way at his father's command and with his blessing (again). Here Comestor is also playing on a point of narrative tension raised by Josephus in the *Antiquities.* Josephus reported that Esau had married the Hittite women without his father's permission, antagonizing his parents both by his choice and by his arrogance (I.18.4). By making it seem that Jacob is obeying his father's instructions to marry a woman from Laban's household, his mother casts Jacob even more firmly in the role of "good son."[63]

Like Rashbam, Peter Comestor articulates a consistent motive for Rebekah's actions throughout his digest of Genesis 25–27. Comestor's explanation that Rebekah had always been guided by the Holy Spirit (Gen. 27:33) reinforces, and to a degree clarifies, the inferences made in his earlier comments on Genesis 25:23 and 25:28. In a sense, too, Rebekah's connection to the deeper, spiritual meaning of the events is inevitable from the moment Comestor alludes to Paul's juxtaposition of Christ and Belial. From the outset, the spiritual truth or meaning of the narrative is framed in Christian terms: what has Christ to do with Belial, or Jacob to do with Esau? Thanks to the warrant of divine inspiration, Rebekah confidently casts off her elder son's rights and engineers Jacob's succession. As had Rashbam, Peter Comestor renders a positive judgment on her actions. No blame accrues to either Rebekah or Jacob; rather Peter assiduously insulates them from blame. When Jacob replies "I am Esau your firstborn," to Isaac's question, "Who are you?" (Gen. 27:18–19), Comestor explains that Jacob is not lying—just as Christ did not lie when he called John the Baptizer "Elijah," speaking not of him personally but *in similitudine* (Mt. 17:11–12).[64] Jacob *is* Esau inasmuch as he is the true heir to the birthright. Moreover, neither he nor Rebekah can be accused of lying, since Jacob acted at his mother's direction and she through the "familiar counsel" of the Holy Spirit, an argument Comestor derives from Peter Lombard's *Sentences.*[65] To provide closure, her last recorded behavior is also "naturalized" and made coherent by the appeal to her higher, spiritual source of knowledge. Learning of Esau's bloodlust *in spiritu,* she complains about Esau's Hittite wives so that Jacob may get his father's permission to leave the household.[66]

But recall that Rashbam also had rooted his validation of Rebekah's behavior in her spiritual understanding. Without being able to assert influence or direct knowledge, it seems at least plausible to suggest that Rashbam had in mind not only the prophet Malachi's affirmation of Jacob, but also the use made of that affirmation by the Christian tradition, especially since it was repeated by Paul in Romans 9:13.[67] Even if he had no knowledge of Paul's quotation, Rashbam would surely have known of the Christian claim to be the new, true Israel, the spiritual heir to Jacob. Like Comestor, Rashbam explicated and naturalized Rebekah's actions in terms of her superior spiritual knowledge. This also provided him with an occasion to assert the Jews' status as the true heirs—spiritual and physical—of Jacob, Isaac, and Abraham. This strategy would cohere with a practice ascribed to medieval Jewish exegetes in general, and in particular to Rashi, by Michael Signer in an essay devoted to Rashi's Torah commentary.[68] There Signer demonstrates that Rashi's overarching purpose is to provide comfort to the nation in exile, to resist Christian claims, and to recall apostates from their errors: "[Rashi] would have been re-narrating the Jewish story of God's love for Israel within the specific context of a Christian environment which, in contrast to the Jewish intellectual climate under Islamic culture, required continued attention to the words, laws, and narratives of the Hebrew Bible which Christians claimed as their own. . . . [He] offers arguments that cumulatively assert that God's law and love for Israel are one and the same."[69] Rashbam's telegraphic contributions to this strategy, identified in this essay, fulfill the purposes named for *his* Torah commentary by Grossman: adding to Rashi elements of literal-based commentary that strengthen Jewish faith and which, however subtly, undermine or repudiate "the ideological message that the opposing camp claimed to find in the text."[70]

Both Rashbam and Peter Comestor preferred rational explanations to biblical puzzles; both tried to situate those explanations within a larger framework of Scripture's sequential narrative. For Comestor, as with Rashbam, Rebekah is a crucial figure whose motivation and consequence must be explicated, so that the demands of narrative plausibility and historicity can be met. Each exegete chooses to see her ambiguous presence in the narrative as an opportunity rather than a problem: neither erases her in favor of playing up the roles of Isaac or Jacob. A concern for the literal sense limits the motivations and meanings each supplies for his characters. Aware on some level of the "opposing camp's" endeavors, however, they were not solely literal- or historical-minded. The scope and import of the narrative's sequence was clearly contested. For Comestor, as for Hugh, human history gathered up in the divine work of restoration. For Rashi and Rashbam, human history bears the indelible signs of God's love for Israel.

Notes

1. A representative feminist celebration of Rebekah's qualities can be found in Danna Nolan Fewell and David M. Gunn, *Gender, Power, and Promise: The Subject of the Bible's First Story* (Nashville: Abingdon, 1993). The contrary view is maintained vigorously by Esther Fuchs in "Who Is Hiding the Truth? Deceptive Women and Biblical Androcentrism," in *Feminist Perspectives on Biblical Scholarship*, ed. Adela Yarbro Collins (Chico, CA: Scholars Press, 1985), 137–44, and more recently in *Sexual Politics in the Biblical Narrative: Reading the Hebrew Bible as a Woman* (Sheffeld: Journal for the Study of the Old Testament Supplement Series 310, 2000).

2. *Midrash Rabbah: Genesis*, trans. H. Freedman, vol. 2 (London: Soncino, 1961), 561.

3. See, for example, Hrabanus Maurus, *Commentarius in Genesim*, PL 107: 587–88, and Rupert of Deutz, *De sancta trinitate*, "In Genesim Liber Septimus," CCCM 21, 430.

4. Augustine identifies Rebekah as the Church based on her preference for Jacob, the spiritual successor to Abraham's covenant, as opposed to the Jews, his descendants according to the flesh; he contrasts the aged and blind Isaac unfavorably with her as a type of the Old Testament who preferred the elder son Esau ("Sermon on Jacob and Esau," PL 38:39). Elsewhere, in sermons against the Donatists and other schismatics, he notes that Rebekah's twins were good and evil, like the conflicting groups of Christians who claim to be the true Church. As an example, see his "On Baptism, against the Donatists," PL 43:118.

5. Jerome, Ep. 36, PL 22:459–61.

6. "*Peshat, Sensus Litteralis*, and Sequential Narrative: Jewish Exegesis and the School of St. Victor in the Twelfth Century," in *The Frank Talmage Memorial Volume*, ed. Barry Walfish (Haifa: University of Haifa Press, 1993), 203.

7. Augustine's hermeneutic of biblical history is discussed in Deborah L. Goodwin, *Take Hold of the Robe of a Jew: Herbert of Bosham's Christian Hebraism* (Leiden: Brill, 2006), 85–87.

8. "The *Glossa Ordinaria* and the Transmission of Medieval Anti-Judaism," in *A Distinct Voice: Medieval Studies in Honor of Leonard E. Boyle, O.P.*, ed. Jacqueline

Brown and William P. Stoneman (Notre Dame, IN: University of Notre Dame Press, 1997), 591–605.

9. Signer, "*Peshat, Sensus Litteralis,* and Sequential Narrative," 203–7. See also Avraham Grossman's analysis of the rise of literal exegesis among the Jewish scholars of Northern France: "The School of Literal Jewish Exegesis in Northern France," in *Hebrew Bible/Old Testament: The History of Its Interpretation,* vol. 1, pt. 2, ed. Magne Saebø (Goettingen: Vandenhoeck and Ruprecht, 2000), 321–25. Both Signer and Grossman note the debate among Jewish scholars over the question of Christian influence, and the effect of Christian polemic, on Jewish exegesis on the period but both concur with scholars such as Sarah Kamin, Frank Talmage, and Eleazar Touitou who have argued for a measure of influence, if not direct contact, between the two groups in Northern France.

10. For overviews of the historical and cultural milieu of Peter Comestor and his contemporaries, together with recent bibliography, see Agneta Sylwan, "Introduction," *Petri Comestoris Scolastica Historia: Liber Genesis,* CCCM 191 (Turnhout: Brepols, 2005); James H. Morey, "Peter Comestor, Biblical Paraphrase, and the Medieval Popular Bible," *Speculum* 68 (1993): 6–35; and Maria C. Sherwood-Smith, *Studies in the Reception of the* Historia Scholastica *of Peter Comestor,* Medium Aevum Monograph Series, n.s. 20 (Oxford: Society for the Study of Medieval Languages and Literature, 2000). Both David Luscombe's essay, "Peter Comestor," in *The Bible in the Medieval World: Studies in Memory of Beryl Smalley,* ed. Katharine Walsh and Diana Wood (Oxford: Blackwell, 1985), 109–29, and Beryl Smalley's discussion of Peter Comestor in *The Study of the Bible in the Middle Ages* (Notre Dame, IN: University of Notre Dame Press, repr. 1978) remain foundational.

11. Martin I. Lockshin, *Rabbi Samuel ben Meir's Commentary on Genesis: An Annotated Translation* (Lewiston, NY: Edward Mellen Press, 1989), 241–42. Hereafter cited as "Rashbam."

12. Grossman, "The School of Literal Jewish Exegesis," 359.

13. Ibid., 362. Rashbam's modern translator, Martin Lockshin, also suggests that Rabbi Samuel's chief purpose was to correct or adjust Rashi's commentary ("Introduction," *Rabbi Samuel ben Meir's Commentary on* Genesis, 18), although Lockshin thinks polemic against Christians was not one of R. Samuel's primary concerns ("Introduction," 15–17).

14. Smalley, *Study of the Bible,* 179.

15. Ibid., 196–97.

16. Critical text: *Hugonis de Sancto Victore Didascalicon De Studio Legendi: A Critical Text,* ed. C. H. Buttimer, Studies in Medieval and Renaissance Latin 10 (Washington, DC: Catholic University of America, 1939). English translation: *The "Didascalicon" of Hugh of Saint Victor: A Medieval Guide to the Arts,* trans. with intro. and notes by Jerome Taylor (New York: Columbia University Press, 1961). Cited hereafter as *Didasc.,* followed by book and chapter, followed by Buttimer and page; Taylor and page. *Didasc.* 6.8, Buttimer, 125–26; Taylor, 147.

17. Rashbam, 240.

18. *Peshat* or *peshuto shel miqra* is the "plain" as opposed to homiletical meaning (*derash*) of the biblical text, a definition and boundary that remains relatively fluid throughout the history of Jewish biblical interpretation. See Michael A. Signer, "How the Bible Has Been Interpreted in the Jewish Tradition," *The New Interpreter's Bible: Genesis to Leviticus*, ed. Leander Keck (Nashville: Abingdon, 1994), 66.

19. Rashbam, 242, n.1. See also "Introduction," 13, where Lockshin comments, "Midrashic exegesis, for Rashbam, does not represent the true plain meaning of the text. Yet it does not represent the primary meaning intended by the divine Author."

20. *Didasc.* 6.4, Buttimer, 122; Taylor, 144.

21. Elsewhere defined as the "deeper understanding which can be found only through interpretation and commentary" ("sententia est profundior intelligentia, quae nisi expositione vel interpretatione non invenitur") (*Didasc.* 3.8, Buttimer, 58; Taylor, 92).

22. *Didasc.*, 6.3, Buttimer, 115; Taylor, 137.

23. Grover A. Zinn, Jr., credits Hugh with "a new perspective in medieval hermeneutics, for Hugh proposed that the historical exegesis of Scripture begins by reading the Biblical narrative with an intention to understand the text *as history*, as the account of an ordered series of events" ("*Historia fundamentum est:* The Role of History in the Contemplative Life According to Hugh of St. Victor," in *Contemporary Reflections on the Medieval Christian Tradition: Essays in Honor of Ray C. Perry*, ed. George H. Shriver [Durham, NC: Duke University Press, 1974], 139).

24. He instructs the scholar to use the *trivium* to arrive at a clearer understanding of the literal meaning of history, relying particularly on the "circumstances" of rhetoric (person, place, time, number, etc.) to determine the meaning inherent in a biblical "thing's" (*res*) exterior form or interior nature (*De scripturis et scriptoribus sacris*, PL 175:21B–C). This formulation collapses the structure of inquiry laid out by Hugh in the prologue to *De sacramentis*. There, he indicates that the arts of the *quadrivium*—arithmetic, music, geometry, astronomy, and physics—should be used to study the form and nature of biblical events in terms of their allegorical or tropological significance (PL 176:185B).

25. "Unde apparet quantum divina Scriptura caeteris omnibus scripturis non solum in materia sua, sed etiam in modo tractandi, subtilitate et profunditate praecellat; cum in caeteris quidem scripturis solae voces significare inveniantur; in hac autem non solum voces, sed etiam res significativae sint. Sicut igitur in eo sensu qui inter voces et res versatur necessaria est cognitio vocum, sic in illo qui inter res et facta vel facienda mystica constat, necessaria est cognitio rerum" (PL 176:185A–B).

26. Those who claim to read Scripture without attending to its literal meaning because they are reading for its allegorical meaning are singled out for special scorn in *De scripturis* (PL 175:13B–14B).

27. *Didasc.* 6.3, Buttimer, 113; Taylor, 135–36.

28. *Didasc.* 6.4, Buttimer, 118–19; Taylor, 140–41.

29. *De Sacramentis,* PL 176:185D.

30. *Didasc.* 6.4, Buttimer, 120; Taylor, 141–42. Emphasis added.

31. *Didasc.* 6.4, Buttimer, 122; Taylor, 144. Emphasis added.

32. As Grover Zinn observed, "The very 'economy' or dispensation of sacred history becomes the integrating structural principle of order in the exposition of the truth of the Christian religion" (*"Historia fundamentum est,"* 141).

33. Beryl Smalley asserts that Stephen Langton implemented Hugh's program of study, glossing the Bible in the order recommended by Hugh. Moreover, she notes that while "Hugh advised students to read the Gospels and Epistles, where the faith was revealed plainly, in order to learn the allegorical exposition . . . Langton glossed the Gospels before he glossed the historical books of the Old Testament and the Prophets." She further observes that "Langton first prepares himself by lecturing on the *Historia Scholastica,* the Gospels, the sapiential books; then he is ready to undertake the literal and spiritual exposition of the historical books" (*Study of the Bible,* 198).

34. Previous studies give little attention to Comestor's exegetical techniques or hermeneutical principles; most, including Smalley, simply describe the *Historia Scholastica* as a "business-like textbook" (*Study of the Bible,* 200) and "convenient aid to study" (Luscombe, "Peter Comestor," 112). Louis H. Feldman suggests that Comestor's "chief interest [is] in the events of Biblical history rather than in their significance" ("The Jewish Sources of Peter Comestor's Commentary on Genesis in His Historia Scholastica," in *Begegnung zwischen Christentum und Judentum in Antike und Mittelalter,* ed. D. Koch and H. Lichtenberger [Goettingen: Vanderhoeck and Ruprecht, 1993], 101).

35. For an overview of the work's long and complex textual history, see the Introduction to the recent critical edition of the *Historia Scholastica* on Genesis by Agneta Sylwan (CCCM 191). She has identified more than 800 manuscripts dating from the twelfth through the sixteenth centuries ("Introduction," xxxi). The PL reprints the 1699 Madrid edition, with additions to the Preface that Sylwan traces to a later *Glosa in historiam scolasticum* (xxxv–xxxvi). Some of Sylwan's editorial decisions are critiqued by Mark J. Clark, "How to Edit the *Historia Scholastica* of Peter Comestor?" *Revue Bénédictine* 116:1 (2006): 83–91.

36. William held that post from 1169 to 1176; Comestor was named as the compiler of a universal history by chronicler Robert of Auxerre in 1173. Thus the work made its first appearance sometime between 1169–1173. See Saralyn R. Daly, "Peter Comestor: Master of Histories," *Speculum* 32 (1957): 67.

37. A close parallel to this phrasing is found in the *Speculum de mysteriis ecclesiae* attributed to Hugh: "In hoc enim quod in divina pagina tam rerum quam vocum necessaria est significatio artes ei subserviunt dum trivium vocum, quadrivium

physicarum rerum administrat notitiam. Significatio tamen rerum dignior est, quia allegoricus sensus acutior, tropologicus suavior est" (PL 177:375C).

38. "A fundamento loquendi sumemus principium, immo ab ipsius fundamenti principio, [d]eo iuvante qui omnium princeps est et principium" (CCCM 191, 5:27–29). "Deo" is given as a variant from one of the earliest MSS, BN lat. 16943, and is also adopted by Mark Clark in his critical edition of the first several chapters of Comestor on Genesis; see Mark Clark, "Peter Comestor and Peter Lombard: Brothers in Deed," *Traditio* 60 (2005): 85–124.

39. As Zinn remarked of Hugh's understanding of history: "History is not only the foundation of exegesis, but of the building up of doctrine as well" (*"Historia fundamentum est,"* 142).

40. He continues, "Like traditional biblical commentators, Comestor proceeded systematically through a given scriptural text, in his case through much of the Bible. Unlike traditional biblical commentators, Comestor took great freedom with Scripture to fashion a cogent historical narrative, organizing his *History* into discrete 'episodes' treated in separate chapters" (Clark, "Peter Comestor and Peter Lombard," 90).

41. Ibid., 122.

42. Luscombe, "Peter Comestor," 112–13.

43. Dominick LaCapra, "Rethinking Intellectual History and Reading Texts," in *Rethinking Intellectual History* (Ithaca, NY: Cornell University Press, 1983), 30.

44. This is in contrast to David Luscombe's summary of Peter Comestor's achievements: "He does not seek to raise theological questions, but he is far from being uncritical and uninquiring, and his method is not mere compilation. There is as much criticism, both implicit and explicit, as there is exposition. He very readily accepts that the authorities disagree, and does not hesitate . . . to record the differences he finds among orthodox Christian expositors of the Bible. . . . He read his authorities, as he read the Bible, in a literal way, and did not seek to dispel apparent inconsistencies or contradictions by the application of hermeneutical principles" ("Peter Comestor," 120).

45. Avraham Grossman has observed the frequency with which Rashbam used the phrase *derekh erez* ("the way of the world") in his Torah commentary, announcing it as a principle of interpretation at the beginning of the commentary. Grossman notes, "In Mishnaic Hebrew, the expression means proper social norms and manners, as well as worldly matters and human practices. Rashbam apparently added the meaning of 'laws of nature,' as is illustrated many times in his commentary" ("The School of Literal Jewish Exegesis," 363).

46. Esther Fuchs, "'For I have the way of women': Deception, Gender, and Ideology in Biblical Narrative," *Semeia* 42 (1988): 70. Emphasis added.

47. Fuchs comments that the lack of parallelism in the description of the parents' motives is typical of biblical accounts which disregard consideration of women's motives (ibid., 72, 76).

48. Rashbam, 134.

49. Rashbam, 136.

50. Lockshin (see Rashbam, Appendix 1); Grossman, "The School of Literal Jewish Exegesis," 360; and Signer, "*Peshat, Sensus Litteralis,* and Sequential Narrative," 208–9, all discuss Rashbam's explanation of the biblical text's use of "anticipation."

51. Rashbam, 154.

52. Rashbam, 157.

53. Rashbam, 160.

54. David Berger discusses the efforts of various medieval Jewish exegetes to preserve the moral standing of the patriarchs, noting that several, including Rashbam, insisted that Jacob paid a fair price for Esau's patrimony in addition to the lentils ("On the Morality of the Patriarchs in Jewish Polemic and Exegesis," in *Understanding Scripture: Explorations of Jewish and Christian Traditions of Interpretation,* ed. Clemens Thoma and Michael Wyschogrod [Mahwah, NJ: Paulist Press, 1987], 49–62).

55. *Genesis Rabbah* 63.7, 560–61.

56. Gerson D. Cohen, "Esau as Symbol in Early Medieval Thought," *Jewish Medieval and Renaissance Studies,* ed. Alexander Altman (Cambridge, MA: Harvard University Press, 1967), 19–48.

57. See the discussion in Goodwin, *Take Hold,* 179ff.

58. CCCM 191, 120:10–19. See 2 Cor. 6:15ff. and Gal. 4:21ff.

59. Beryl Smalley identified Peter Comestor's previously unnoticed use of Andrew of St. Victor's commentary on the Octateuch in *Study of the Bible,* 179. Since then, numerous studies have attempted to sift through the strands of Comestor's sources, and to assess whether he had direct access to contemporary Jewish exegesis (a still unprovable assertion). See the useful summary of the present state of the debate in Sherwood-Smith, *Studies,* 3–8; the most thorough attempt to identify Comestor's sources for Jewish material in Genesis is that of Feldman, "Jewish Sources," 93–121.

60. CCCM 191, 122:5–6.

61. CCCM 191, 128:35–39.

62. CCCM 191, 128–29:5–7.

63. Comestor's reliance on Josephus has been widely remarked; see most recently Sherwood-Smith, *Studies,* 4; and Feldman, "Jewish Sources," 98–101.

64. This is an addition found in most of the manuscripts consulted by Sylwan and which she believes may be authentic to Comestor himself ("Introduction," lxxvii). The PL edition classes it as a note, and indicates the homilies of Gregory the Great as its source. See Gregory's sermon on John's Gospel at PL 76:1100A.

65. CCCM 191, 128–29:5–7.

66. CCCM 191, 129:9–10.

67. Michael Signer poses the question: "Do the Rabbis develop a 'counternarrative' which might immunize the Jews from their doubts? The answer is not

easy" ("God's Love for Israel: Apologetic and Hermeneutical Strategies in Twelfth-Century Biblical Exegesis," in *Jews and Christians in Twelfth-Century Europe,* ed. Michael A. Signer and John Van Engen [Notre Dame, IN: University of Notre Dame Press, 2001], 127).

68. Ibid., 133.
69. Ibid., 129, 133.
70. Grossman, "The School of Literal Jewish Exegesis," 329–30.

CHAPTER NINE

Two Introductions by Rabbi Samuel ben Meir (Rashbam)

To the Song of Songs and Lamentations

Sara Japhet

Rashbam's Introductions

It is a common view that, unlike their colleagues in the East, the sages of the Northern France Peshat school of exegesis did not write introductions to their commentaries on biblical books.[1] A well-known exception to this state of affairs is Rashi's introduction to the commentary on the Song of Songs, the existence of which has been explained by Rashi's need to meet the challenge involved in the interpretation of this book.[2] This "common knowledge," however, should be reexamined in light of the exegetical work of Rabbi Samuel ben Meir (Rashbam), Rashi's grandson and disciple (c. 1085–after 1159).[3] While his introduction to the commentary on the Song of Songs may be regarded as following the example of Rashi, such an argument cannot hold water in relation to the other introductory passages found in his commentaries.

Rashbam wrote four introductory passages in his commentary on the Pentateuch: two of these passages form introductions to books, Genesis and Leviticus,[4] while the other two are placed at the beginning of significant sections of the Pentateuch.[5] Rashbam also wrote an introduction to

Lamentations, which so far has escaped the attention of scholars.[6] There are, however, no introductions to his other two extant commentaries, on Job and Qoheleth.[7] In the face of these observations, several questions present themselves: was the writing of introductions a regular feature of Rashbam's commentaries, or were the existing introductions the exception? Is it possible that the absence of introductions to Job and Qoheleth is a result of transmission, the introductions having been omitted by later scribes, rather than Rashbam's own decision?[8] Was the introduction to the Song of Songs indeed motivated by the example of Rashi, or was Rashbam influenced by prevalent concepts and literary examples, contemporary or earlier? We may suggest the influence of the Eastern/Spanish school of exegesis, on the one hand, and of the general intellectual milieu of Northern France, on the other,[9] but the topic needs further investigation.

In this essay, I will restrict the discussion to two of Rashbam's introductions: to the Song of Songs and to Lamentations.[10] I have already dealt to some extent with Rashbam's introduction to the Song of Songs and will use this opportunity to present the English translation of the text and my conclusions regarding its message and significance.[11] Rashbam's introduction to Lamentations will be presented and discussed here for the first time. I hope that the study of these two introductions, individually and in comparison, will add to our understanding of Rashbam's methodology, his intellectual world, and his contribution as an exegete.

Introduction to the Song of Songs[12]

Let the man of understanding be wise and lend his heart to understand
    the discourse of this book.[13]
To study and tell its plain meaning in its method and mode of expression,
As established in its position, in its phrasing.
For Agur, who gathered wisdom from all the people of the East,
Wrote his Book, and composed his Song before his Words.
His wisdom—in the ways of the world—is excellent and wonderful.
In the figure of a young woman,[14] who bemoans and mourns her lover,
    who left her and went far away,

> She recalls him and his eternal love for her; she composes a poem, and
> says:
> Such strong love my lover showed me when he was with me.
> She tells her friends and maidens: This is what my lover said to me and
> this is what I answered him.[15]

The introduction is written in an elevated style, full of allusions and rhymes. Rashbam presents here, very concisely, his view on several introductory issues: the audience of the commentary; the goal and exegetical method followed in the commentary; the identity of the author of the Song of Songs; the place of this work among the author's other compositions; the genre of the book and its central topic; its literary formulation; and the main lines of its contents.[16]

Rashbam opens his words by addressing his audience, whom he defines as "the men of understanding" (המבין).[17] "The men of understanding," "the men of reason" (המשכילים), "the lovers of reason" (אוהבי שכל) are indeed the people whom Rashbam addresses in all his works; for them he defines the intellectual activity required of his readers: "to understand," "to lend their hearts," etc.[18] The terminology is derived, with no explicit reference to the source, from the *Mahberet,* the famous dictionary of Menahem ibn Saruq,[19] but what we see here is far more than a matter of mere terminology. As E. Touitou has rightly pointed out, the address to the "learned," the "men of reason," and the like, serves to define the audience: this is the specific intellectual circle toward which Rashbam's works are targeted.[20]

The next point in the introduction is the presentation of the commentary's goal and method: "to study and tell its plain meaning, in its method and mode of expression, as established in its position, by its phrasing." These concise expressions, rhymed in the Hebrew, are constructed of characteristic "building blocks," each term belonging to Rashbam's peculiar vocabulary.[21] Rashbam presents here one exclusive goal: the explanation of the Song of Songs in its "plain meaning"—a task which is to be achieved through the characteristic components of this methodology. As becomes clear from the continuation of the introduction and from the commentary itself, Rashbam regards the Song of Songs as an allegory, but he differs from Rashi, his predecessor, and Ibn Ezra, his contemporary, in regarding the allegory itself as one aspect of the "plain meaning." In his view, when a text is written from the outset as an allegory, the tenor of the allegory is not a midrash (as it is for Rashi or Ibn Ezra, among others), but an integral aspect of the "plain meaning." Thus, the whole semantic field of "homily" is absent from his commentary on the Song of Songs. He does not make any reference to the homiletic tradition, and the verb דרש and the noun מדרש do not appear in his commentary on the Song of Songs even once.[22]

The next point in the introduction is the issue of authorship. Rashbam refers to the author as "Agur," following Proverbs 30:1: "The words of Agur son of Yakeh." Because the heading of Proverbs attributes the book to Solomon ("The Proverbs of Solomon Son of David, King of Israel"; Prov. 1:1), all the other names that appear in the book are traditionally explained as Solomon's additional names or appellatives: "Why was he called Agur (אגור)? Because he gathered (אגר) wisdom."[23] Rashbam then combines the traditional interpretation of Proverbs 30:1 with an allusion to 1 Kings 5:10, where Solomon's wisdom is described: "Solomon's wisdom surpassed the wisdom of all the people of the East" (NRSV 4:30). While the reference is unmistakable, the interpretation suggested by Rashbam here differs somewhat from the original meaning. He explains the prepositional phrase מכל (1 Kgs 5:10) not as comparative, "more than all," but as a regular preposition, "from all": these were the peoples from whom Solomon collected his wisdom.

Rashbam then turns to the three works written by Solomon: his Book, Proverbs; his Song, the Song of Songs; and his Words, Qoheleth. He also states that Solomon composed Proverbs and the Songs of Songs before Qoheleth, echoing the discussion in the homiletic tradition about the order of these works and avoiding the question of whether Proverbs preceded the Song of Songs or vice versa. He presents only the consensus view that Qoheleth was the last among Solomon's works.[24] He concludes the passage about Solomon with a characterization and evaluation of his wisdom: it was wisdom "in the ways of the world, excellent and wonderful."

"The ways of the world" (בנוהג שבעולם) is again one of the terms Rashbam uses in all his works, and is an important principle of his exegesis.[25] Solomon did not engage in the unusual, extraordinary phenomena of the world, nor in the supernatural world; he directed his attention and his intellect to the study and understanding of the regular aspects of life, "the wisdom that the world needs,"[26] what one sees around one, the ways people and nature normally behave. This is therefore the basis on which the interpretation of the Song of Songs should be carried out.

Rashbam returns to the issue of authorship in his comment on Songs 1:1, which should be seen as an extension of the introduction. There he states again that the author of the book is Solomon, but enlarges on two more matters—the linguistic basis of this ascription, and the inspiration and authority of the book. Rashbam bases the ascription of the Song of Songs to Solomon on the heading of the book, "The Song of Songs of Solomon"—a matter that may seem self-evident to a contemporary reader, but is not at all so straightforward according to traditional Jewish exegesis. The prepositional phrase לשלמה may be interpreted in three different ways: "by Solomon," "to Solomon," or "about Solomon," all three attested in the homiletic interpretations of the verse. Rashi adopts the second possibility, and combines it with the traditional view that the name Solomon is an appellative of God. According to his view, the heading of the Song of Songs does not identify Solomon as the author of the Song of Songs, but rather as the addressee of this book: "Solomon in the Song of Songs is always holy—the king whose peace is his;[27] a song which is above all the songs that were sung to God by his congregation and people, the community of Israel." Consequently, when Rashi states in his introduction to the Song of Songs that Solomon was the author of the book, he does not base this conclusion on the heading of the book but rather on tradition alone. In the commentary itself he consistently explains the references to Solomon as referring to God, never to the earthly king Solomon. Rashbam, by contrast, approaches the issue from a different standpoint. In his view the name Solomon in the Song of Songs always refers to King Solomon, and his authorship of the Song of Songs is deduced from the book's heading. With a brief linguistic analogy he compares "of Solomon" to "A prayer of Moses" (Ps. 90:1) or "a song of praise, of David" (Ps. 145:1). In the commentary itself he follows this understanding throughout, and at the level of the parable he always explains the name Solomon as referring to the human king.

In the second point regarding Solomon's authorship, Rashbam follows tradition and Rashi: Solomon wrote the Song of Songs under the inspiration of the Holy Spirit. This view has a double implication: it establishes unequivocally the authority and canonization of the Song of Songs, and it presents the book as a prophecy, intended for the future. This is the basis for the message of the Song, and I will return to it later. The concluding passage of the introduction presents a concise description of the Song of Songs: its genre, topic, main contents, and literary form. The Song of Songs is written, says Rashbam, in the figure of a young woman whose lover has left her. The woman bemoans her lover, recalls his love, and expresses her memories in a poem. The form of the poem is that of a complex dialogue, built in two stories. The first level is a dialogue between the young woman and her friends: "She tells her friends and maidens." Embedded in this dialogue is another one—between the young woman and her lover: "This is what my lover said to me and this is what I answered him." The composition of the Song of Songs is thus clearly set out: the book was composed by Solomon, in the form of a poem written by a young woman. The young woman is presented as speaking to her friends, and describing the love between herself and her lover.

This aspect of the introduction is also continued in the comment on Song 1:1. There Rashbam clarifies that the story of the young woman is an allegory, as hinted already in the introduction. The phrase "like a young woman" (כבתולה), which I represented in the translation with "in the figure of a young woman," is given an explicit explanation, which makes it abundantly clear: "King Solomon composed it under the inspiration of the Holy Spirit, for he foresaw that Israel were going to complain in their exile about the Holy One who left them, like a bridegroom who departed from his beloved, and he began to sing his song in place of the community of Israel, who is like a bride to Him."[28] The lines of the prophetical allegory are simple: the bridegroom is God, the bride is the community of Israel, and the situation is "this exile," when the people of Israel complain that God has departed. It is for this future—the actualities of Israel's existence in exile—that Solomon composed this Song of Songs. He is the spokesman for the community of Israel, "who is like a bride to Him," in their distress and exile.

The principles set out in the introduction are fully and consistently implemented in the commentary itself. Thus, the introduction is not merely a presentation of "introductory" issues or theoretical principles, but an actual blueprint for the commentary. Rashbam's views on the methodology that should be followed, on the structure, genre, topic, and message of the Song of Songs, are all put to practice and further elaborated in the actual interpretation of the book.[29]

Introduction to Lamentations

Rashbam's commentaries on two of the scrolls, Ruth and Lamentations, are among his works that did not survive. However, MS. Hamburg 32 contains, among others, three compilatory commentaries—to Ruth, Lamentations, and Esther—in which the compiler assembled and presented literal excerpts from the three most important representatives of the Peshat school in Northern France: Rashi, R. Joseph Kara, and Rashbam.[30] The largest part of the compilation consists of comments taken from the works of Joseph Kara; these are supplemented, especially at the beginning of the commentaries, by excerpts from the other two commentators.[31] In some cases the authors of the excerpts are identified by explicit notes, but this practice is not followed throughout. Whether the absence of such notes is due to the compiler's inconsistent procedure or whether it is a result of omission by later scribes is equally possible.

The passages that the compiler took from Rashbam's (and Rashi's) works are in general few in number and limited in scope. Most important among them is the introduction to Lamentations. This excerpt was explicitly identified by the compiler as Rashbam's,[32] and can be easily recognized by its contents and style. I present the introduction here in both Hebrew and English:[33]

המקונן אשר יסד מגילת קינות, אחז שיטתו לקונן בנוהג שבעולם בבני האדם. אשר האלמנה, הנשארה יחידה ובודדה שכולה וגלמודה (ו)מכל ילדיה ומאישה, קוראה למקוננות להרבות קינות עליה. ופעמ' הן מקוננות במקום האלמנה כאילו הגיעה הרעה עליה. ופעמ' הן מדברות לאלמנה בקינתן ומתאוננות עליה. ופעמ' הן מספרות קורות ואודות האלמנה לאחרים מתוך קינתן. כן יסד המקונן הזה את קינתו על ישר'. פעמ' הוא מדבר במקום כנסת ישר' ופעמ' הוא מדבר אליה. ופעמ' לאחרים עליה. ואמ' רבותי', ירמיה כתב מגילה זאת, והיא המגילה אשר שרף יהויקים מלך יהודה באש אשר על האח. ועל אותה שנשרפה הוסיף עליה דברים. שנ' "ועוד נוסף עליה דברים רבים כהמה" (ירמ' לו 32). כי מתחילה לא נכתבה כולה עד לבסוף.

The mourner who composed the scroll of Lamentations applied the method of mourning for human beings, in accordance with the ways of the world. The widow who remains by herself, lonely, bereaved and barren of all her children and her husband,[34] calls for the mourning women[35] to multiply laments for her. Sometimes they mourn in place of the widow, as though the mischief befell her.[36] Sometimes in their laments they speak to her and mourn for her. And sometimes in their laments they address other people and tell them about the widow and what happened to her. This is how the mourner composed his lament for Israel. Sometimes he speaks in place of the community of Israel; sometimes he speaks to her; and sometimes he tells others about her. Our masters said that Jeremiah wrote this scroll, and that this is the scroll which King Jehoiakim of Judah burned by fire on the brazier.[37] To the scroll that was burned he [Jeremiah] added more words, as it is said: "and many similar words were added to them (Jer. 36:32)."[38] For it was not completed at first, only at the end.

As in the introduction to the Song of Songs, Rashbam turns his attention to the issues of authorship, genre, and literary form, and outlines the main contents of the book. In contrast to his procedure with the Song of Songs, however, he does not make any statement regarding his interpretive methodology and instead turns immediately to the issue of authorship. The style of the introduction is prosaic, but its language is built of biblical components, and there are allusions to biblical and rabbinic sources.

The question of authorship is the topic of both the beginning of the introduction and its conclusion, and thus forms a kind of framework to the passage. It opens with reference to "the mourner who composed the scroll of Lamentations," and the same title—derived from Jeremiah 9:16—is repeated again later. With the title "mourner," Rashbam establishes two things: the genre of the book—"a scroll of laments," written by a professional mourner[39]—and the anonymity of its author. At this point in the introduction the author remains unidentified, with no name or even a recognized appellative. Only at the end of the introduction, after dealing with other features of Lamentations, does Rashbam return to the question of authorship, identifying the anonymous "mourner," in the wake of tradition, as the prophet Jeremiah: "Our masters said that Jeremiah wrote this scroll."

The subtle difference between the two introductions illustrates Rashbam's sensitivity to the different sources from which the information is derived. In the introduction to the Song of Songs Rashbam identifies the author as Solomon in a straightforward statement already at the beginning. He was "Agur who gathered wisdom." Rashbam does not mention the source of this information as he clearly relies on his readers' ability to recognize the well-known allusion to Proverbs 30:1. The reason for this procedure is obvious: Solomon is identified as the author of the Song of Songs already in the heading of the book, that is, in the Bible itself.[40] Lamentations, by contrast, has no heading and there is no comparable biblical testimony regarding its author. Rashbam acknowledges this fact initially by ascribing the book to an anonymous "mourner"; only later on does he refer to tradition: "Our masters said that Jeremiah wrote this scroll." The difference between these two statements is emphasized by a comparison to Rashi, whose interpretation seems at a superficial glance to be identical to that of Rashbam. Rashi too adopts the rabbinic view that Jeremiah was the author of Lamentations, and that Lamentations should be identified with the scroll burned by Jehoiakim. In Rashi's words: "Jeremiah wrote the Book of Laments, which is the scroll that was burned by Jehoiakim on the fire of the brazier." However, Rashi presents these views right away, as statements of fact, with no distinction between biblical and rabbinic evidence. He does not begin with an anonymous "mourner" and does not mention "our masters" as the source for the identification of the author.

Still, Rashbam seems not to be satisfied with the rabbinic ascription by itself, and tries to substantiate it by biblical data. For this purpose he turns to Jeremiah 36, which testifies that Jeremiah wrote a scroll, whose contents were related to the destruction of Jerusalem by the Babylonians (Jer. 36:29), and combines this datum with the identification of Jeremiah as the author of laments in 2 Chronicles 35:25. The combined biblical evidence serves to undergird the view of "our masters": that is, that the author of Lamentations, "the mourner," was the prophet Jeremiah.

Rashbam presents the process by which this scroll was composed in concise terms, following the biblical report. He passes over the first stage, in which God instructed Jeremiah: "Get a scroll and write upon it all the words that I have spoken to you—concerning Israel and Judah and all the nations—from the time I first spoke to you in the days of Josiah to this day" (36:2); following which Jeremiah did as ordered: "So Jeremiah called Baruch son of Neriah and Baruch wrote down in the scroll at Jeremiah's dictation, all the words that the Lord had spoken to him" (35:4). This scroll was burned on the fire by King Jehoiakim: "And every time Jehudi read three or four columns, [the king] would cut it up with a scribe's knife and throw it into the fire in the brazier, until the entire scroll was consumed by the fire of the brazier" (36:23). Jeremiah then received another divine command: "Get yourself another scroll, and write upon it the same words that were in the first scroll which was burned by king Jehoiakim of Judah" (36:28); "So Jeremiah got another scroll and gave it to the scribe Baruch son of Neriah. And at Jeremiah's dictation he wrote in it the whole text of the scroll which king Jehoiakim had burned; and more of the like was added" (36:32). To his concise epitome of the biblical story Rashbam adds one sentence of explanation: "For it was not completed at first, only at the end." Although the explanation is somewhat ambiguous, it seems to account for a certain discrepancy in the biblical record. God's instruction and Jeremiah's implementation mentioned that "all the words" spoken to Jeremiah were included in the first scroll. What were then "the other words" that were added to it? This is accounted for by Rashbam's qualification: the "all" refers only to the second version of the scroll, not the first one.[41]

The view of authorship presented by Rashbam—and earlier by Rashi—comprises two distinct elements: the traditional ascription of Lamentations to Jeremiah, which establishes the book's authority and canonization, and the placement of the book's origin in the time of Jehoiakim, quite some time before the Babylonian conquest of Judah and Jerusalem. According to this view the laments were prophetic proclamations, very much in advance of the actual destruction, rather than Jeremiah's response of grief to the actual historical events. Both views of the origin of Lamentations may be found in rabbinic sources, but the second is by far the more prevalent: "Since they sinned, they were exiled; and since they were exiled, Jeremiah began to mourn over them: 'Alas, lonely sits the city.'"[42] The other view is rather rare and is presupposed in the explanation of the structure of Lamentations on the basis of the story of Jeremiah 36, and on the statement: "and more of the like was added."[43] I have no answer for the question of what brought Rashbam—and Rashi before him—to prefer the view that Lamentations was a prophetic proclamation, rather than opting for the more "natural" position that it was an actual lament, spoken in the relevant historical situation.

The next statement in the introduction refers to the literary format of the laments, and can be easily recognized by its style—the appearance of Rashbam's characteristic phrases: אחז שיטתו and בנוהג שבעולם.[44] According to this statement, the laments were composed along the models of human mourning, "in the ways of the world," and this model is precisely presented. It is the model of a widow, whose whole family was exterminated. She calls for "professional women mourners" to mourn for her, and the liturgy of mourning takes on three different forms: (1) laments that are presented as the widow's own, the mourners put themselves in her place and mourn for her as if they were the ones who suffered the mischief; (2) laments in which the mourners address the widow and bemoan her fate; (3) laments in which "the mourners" address "other people" and tell them what happened to the widow and how she suffered. We may present Rashbam's three alternative forms in syntactical terms as related to the subject of the laments, the widow. The difference between the forms is in the person of the speaker; although all the laments are performed by professional mourners, they are phrased alternatively in the first, second, and third persons from the point of view of the widow.

After describing the "ways of the world"—how mourners perform their task of mourning for human beings—Rashbam turns to his view of Lamentations: "This is how the mourner composed his lament for Israel." Several issues are clarified by this statement. First, it describes the contents of the book: a "lament for Israel." Second, it elucidates the form of the text. The laments are a "composition" by "the mourner," who formulated the laments following the conventions of laments for people: "sometimes he speaks in place of the community of Israel, sometimes he speaks to her, and sometimes [he speaks] to others about her."

In establishing the format of Lamentations the principle that Rashbam applies is that of analogy: the laments for Israel are written in a form similar to that of the general genre of laments, known from "the ways of the world." Analogy is a major tool in Rashbam's exegesis, and is applied most extensively in his grammatical interpretations. As he states explicitly in his grammar book, *Dayyaqut:* "We have a short way to teach . . . how to learn about one word from another. When the grammarian errs in the analysis of one word . . . he should compare to it other, similar words that are simple for him [to understand]. From them he would understand the rule of the word in which he erred."[45] Rashbam employs here the same principle, applied to literary rather than grammatical analysis: the way to understand the different forms of the laments in Lamentations is to compare them to the known and recognized forms of mourning, those for a human widow.

The concept of Lamentations as written "in the ways of the world" is set in relief by Rashbam's earlier statement that Lamentations was an inspired work, proclaimed and written by Jeremiah. Although the author of these laments was a prophet, inspired by God, and the laments were proclaimed in advance of the historical events for which they were intended, they were nevertheless composed in accordance with the conventions of the lament genre, actualized in the practice of human "mourners" representing human widows. This is precisely the view that Rashbam presented for the composition of the Song of Songs: Solomon wrote it for the future, because he saw in a vision the suffering and the complaints of the people of Israel in exile. Nevertheless, he composed his song along the lines of the genre: "Love poems in the ways of the world" (on Song of Songs 3:5).

In the concluding statement of the introduction Rashbam returns to the issue of authorship, with which we dealt above.

Conclusion

The analysis of the two introductions highlights their similarities— similar topics, similar terminology, and similar views. There are, however, three major differences between them: different views of the literary form; the differences in handling of the issue of methodology, and the different conceptions of authorship, which I discussed above in detail. These differences are fully accounted for by the nature of the works under consideration—the Song of Songs versus Lamentations.

In the wake of a long-standing tradition, Rashbam views the Song of Songs as an allegory. For him this implies the essential existence of two levels of meaning, the meaning of the parable and the tenor. This view determines not only the structure of the commentary but also the lines of the introduction: it opens with a clear statement regarding the methodology that should be adopted in the book's interpretation, within the general methodological framework of Peshat exegesis. The introduction then presents the author of the book, the outline of its contents, and its overall literary structure. Lamentations, by contrast, is not an allegory but rather a straightforward lament for the community of Israel. It therefore does not raise methodological problems, and does not need clarification.[46] The only point in need of clarification is the literary format of Lamentations—explained by analogy to laments composed and performed "in the ways of the world."

As mentioned above, Rashbam implements the principles set forth in the introduction to the Song of Songs in the actual performance of the exegesis and enlarges further on some of these matters in the commentary. This advantage of watching Rashbam's method unfold is not offered by Lamentations, where all that has survived from the commentary is the introduction itself, along with some sporadic comments that do not touch on these matters.[47] At least for the time being, until Rashbam's lost commentary on Lamentations is somehow discovered, we must be satisfied with what we have.

I have pointed out on several occasions Rashbam's exceptional interest in literary matters—questions of authorship, modes of composition, literary structures, and the rhetorical aspects of literary works.[48] In this respect he remains unique among the Jewish biblical commentators. He was followed to some degree by his best known disciple, Rabbi Eliezer of Beaugency,[49] and his remarks on literary matters are sometimes quoted by his followers among the Tosafists. However, in the scope of his interests and in his literary acumen and penetration, he remains unique among medieval biblical exegetes. How should we interpret this aspect of his work? Was it a personal, individual feature that distinguished him against his background and environment, or was he influenced by more general intellectual currents of his time? This broad question still awaits a more thorough comparative study.

Notes

1. For the earliest development of "introductions" in Jewish biblical exegesis, see recently S. Stroumsa, "A Literary Genre as a Historical Document: On Saadia's Introductions to His Bible Commentaries," in *A Word Fitly Spoken: Studies in*

Mediaeval Exegesis of the Hebrew Bible and the Qur'an, Presented to Haggai Ben Shammai [Hebrew], ed. M. M. Bar-Asher, S. Hopkins, S. Stroumsa, and B. Chiesa (Jerusalem: Hebrew University Magnes Press and Yad Izhak Ben-Zvi, 2007), 193–204.

2. On Rashi's introduction to the Song of Songs, see S. Kamin, *Rashi's Exegetical Categories in Respect to the Distinction between Peshat and Derash* [Hebrew] (Jerusalem: Hebrew University Magnes Press, 1986), 77–86, 123–24; S. Kamin, "דוגמא in Rashi's Commentary on the Song of Songs," *Tarbiz* 52 (1983): 41–42 (= *Jews and Christians Interpret the Bible* [Hebrew] [Jerusalem: Hebrew University Magnes Press, 1991], 13–14); S. Kamin, "Rashi's Commentary on the Song of Songs and Jewish-Christian Polemic," *Shnaton: An Annual for Biblical and Ancient Near Eastern Studies* 7–8 (1983/4): 219–21 (= *Jews and Christians* [Hebrew], 32–34); S. Japhet, "Rashi's Commentary on the Song of Songs: The Revolution of the Peshat and Its Aftermath," in *"Mein Haus wird ein Bethaus für alle Völker genannt werden (Jes. 56,7)": Judentum seit der Zeit des zweiten Tempels in Geschichte, Literatur und Kult—Festschrift für Thomas Willi zum 65. Geburtstag,* ed. J. Männchen and T. Reiprich (Neukirchen-Vluyn: Neukirchener-Verlag, 2007), 202–6.

3. For his life and works, see D. Rosin, *R. Samuel b. Mëir (רשב"ם) als Schrifterklärer,* (Breslau: Verlag Wilhelm Koebner, 1880), 1–22; S. Japhet and R. B. Salters, *The Commentary of R. Samuel Ben Meir, Rashbam on Qoheleth* (Jerusalem: Hebrew University Magnes Press, 1985), 11–18; A. Grossman, "The School of Literal Jewish Exegesis in Northern France," in *Hebrew Bible/Old Testament: The History of Its Interpretation,* ed. M. Saebø, 2 vols. (Göttingen: Vandenhoeck & Ruprecht, 2000), 2:358–63.

4. In the editions of Rashbam's commentary on the Pentateuch this introduction is divided between the end of Exodus and the beginning of Leviticus. On this matter, see I. Kislev, "'Whoever Has Heeded the Words of Our Creator'—Rashbam's Methodological Preface to Leviticus and the Relationship between Rashi's and Rashbam's Commentaries" [Hebrew], *Tarbiz* 73 (2004): 225–37.

5. The longest passage forms an introduction to the section *Vayeshev,* at Gen. 37:2. On its location and function, see E. Touitou, *Exegesis in Perpetual Motion: Studies in the Pentateuchal Commentary of Rabbi Samuel ben Meir* [Hebrew] (Ramat Gan: Bar-Ilan University Press, 2003), 98–102; 112–15; 153–54. The fourth passage forms an introduction to the legal parts of the Pentateuch; it is placed at the head of the section *Mishpatim* (Ex. 21:2) and presents Rashbam's goals and methodology in these parts of the Pentateuch (see Touitou, *Exegesis,* 71).

6. See further below.

7. Rashbam wrote commentaries to most of the biblical books. Citations from his commentaries are found in *Arugat Habosem*—the commentary on the Jewish liturgical poetry by Rabbi Abraham son of Azriel. E. Urbach, the editor of this work, mentioned citations from the commentaries to Judges, Samuel, Kings, Isaiah, Ezekiel, Hosea, Joel, Amos, Nahum, Zechariah, Psalms, and Job (*Sefer Arugat*

Habosem, auctore R. Abraham b. R. Azriel, ed. Ephraim E. Urbach, SAEC 13, 4 vols. [Jerusalem: Mekitse Nirdamim, 1939–1963], 4:153–54); Touitou added to Urbach's list the books of Exodus, Jeremiah, Micah, Lamentations, and Esther. He also cited the comments in full and discussed them in detail (*Exegesis,* 208–25). Both scholars concluded that Rashbam interpreted most, if not all, of the biblical books (Urbach, *Sefer Arugat Habosem,* 4:154; Touitou, *Exegesis,* 225).

8. Rashbam's commentaries on the Pentateuch, Qoheleth, and Esther each survived in a single manuscript; among these, the manuscript of the Pentateuch (now lost) was incomplete and of particularly inferior quality. The commentary on Job survived in one complete manuscript and in a section of another. For information on these matters, see Rosin, *R. Samuel b. Mëir als Schrifterklärer,* 24–37; S. Japhet, *The Commentary of Rabbi Samuel ben Meir (Rashbam) on the Book of Job* [Hebrew] (Jerusalem: Hebrew University Magnes Press, 2000), 293–311. For the commentary on the Song of Songs, see S. Japhet, *The Commentary of Rabbi Samuel ben Meir (Rashbam) on the Song of Songs* (Jerusalem: World Union of Jewish Studies and the Rabbi David Moses and Amalia Rosen Foundation, 2008). The commentary on Esther has not yet been published.

9. For the "academic introductions" to the exegesis of Scripture in the non-Jewish literature of the twelfth century, their origin in the actual practice of teaching, and their characterization, see A. J. Minnis, *Medieval Theory of Authorship: Scholastic Literary Attitudes in the Later Middle Ages* (London: Scolar, 1984), 2, 4, 40–72. See also below.

10. Rashbam's introductions in his commentary on the Pentateuch—which are usually labeled "methodological statements" and serve as starting points for the study of his methodology, terminology, and self-understanding—have been studied extensively. See among others, Touitou, *Exegesis,* 98–105; M. Sabato, "Rashbam's Commentary on the Torah" [Hebrew], *Mahanaim* 3 (1993): 110–13; M. I. Lockshin, *Rabbi Samuel ben Meir's Commentary on Genesis: An Annotated Translation* (Lewiston, N.Y.: Mellen, 1989), 240–45; S. Japhet, "The Tension between Rabbinic Legal Midrash and the 'Plain Meaning' (Peshat) of the Biblical Text—An Unresolved Problem? In the Wake of Rashbam's Commentary on the Pentateuch," in *Sefer Moshe: The Moshe Weinfeld Jubilee Volume,* ed. C. Cohen, A. Hurvitz, and S. M. Paul (Winona Lake, IN: Eisenbrauns, 2004), 419–22. There are differences, as one might expect, between the final conclusions of the various scholars.

11. See S. Japhet, "Rashi on the Song of Songs," 207–10; S. Japhet, "Exegesis and Polemic in Rashbam's Commentary on the Song of Songs," in *Jewish Biblical Interpretation and Cultural Exchange,* ed. N. Dohrmann and D. Stern (Philadelphia: University of Pennsylvania Press, 2008), 182–95; S. Japhet, *Rashbam on the Song of Songs,* 25–27, 79–84, and 137–39.

12. Rashbam's commentary on the Song of Songs was published in 1855 by A. Jellinek from MS. Hamburg 32. Another edition of this commentary, with an

English translation, was prepared by Y. Thompson as part of his DHL dissertation, "The Commentary of Samuel ben Meir on the Song of Songs," Jewish Theological Seminary, New York, 1988. Both editions suffer from severe flaws, as does the English translation. The text of the introduction presented here is taken from our new critical edition of the commentary, without the critical apparatus(see n. 8 above). On the sources of the edition and the procedures of its editing, see Japhet, *Rashbam on the Song of Songs*, 209–30.

13. The commentary was written in medieval Hebrew and therefore the precise meaning of some words and terms is not universally agreed upon. Also, the text is not vocalized and the possible alternative vocalizations may result in different translations. In this introduction the difficulties for understanding and translation are presented by the first two sentences. The term מליצה, which I translated "discourse," is the subject of controversy, and the term שיטה seems to have a special connotation in Rashbam's usage (see below, n. 44). The word translated "to study" (ללמד) may also be rendered "to teach" (לְלַמֵּד), and both translations may be supported by adequate arguments. For some words there is no adequate equivalent in English, in particular the term פשוטו (and its synonym פשט), for which I suggest "the plain meaning." I prefer this rendering to the limited and hence inaccurate terms "literal" or "contextual" meaning. "Plain meaning" does not mean "simple," but refers to the text as is, in its obvious meaning. See also further below.

14. For this translation see below.

15. ערום יערים המבין ואת ליבו יתן להבין, לשון מליצת הספר. ללמד ולספר את פשוטו, בשיטתו ומלתו, כאשר יתכן על מכונו, בלשונו. כי אגור אשר אגר [את] החכמה מכל בני קדם, כתב ספרו, ותיקן שירו, לפני דברו. וחכמתו משובח ומופלא בנוהג בעולם. כבתולה הומה ומתאוננת על אוהבה שפירש ממנה והלך למרחקים. והיא מזכרת אותו באהבתו אותה אהבת עולם, ומשוררת ואומרת: אהבה עזה כזאת הראה לי ידידי בעדו עמדי. ומדברת ומספרת לחברותיה ונערותיה: כך וכך אמר לי דודי וכך השיבותיו.

16. These items are similar to, but not identical with, the topics included in the "academic introductions" found in non-Jewish literature of the twelfth century. Minnis mentioned the following characteristic subjects: the name of the book, the name of the author, the author's intention, the topic of the book, its literary method, the order or arrangement of the book, its benefits, and the academic discipline to which it belongs (Minnis, *Medieval Theory of Authorship*, 4). See also below.

17. The singular form should be understood as collective.

18. These terms were already pointed out by Rosin (*R. Samuel b. Mëir als Schrifterklärer*, 66, 157), and the examples he brought might be greatly multiplied. See S. Japhet, "The Commentary of Rabbi Samuel ben Meir (Rashbam) on the Song of Songs" [Hebrew], *Tarbiz* 75 (2006): 254–55.

19. Rashbam's extensive borrowing from the *Mahberet*—without the mention of the source—was pointed out by Rosin, who supported his observation with citations from both the *Mahberet* and Rashbam's commentary on the Pentateuch (*R. Samuel b. Mëir als Schrifterklärer*, 66 and n. 1). This is particularly the case in

connection with Rashbam's commentary on the Song of Songs. See Japhet, *Rashbam on the Song of Songs*, 60–63.

20. Touitou, *Exegesis*, 11–23, 101–5, and more (see the index).

21. For Rashbam's characteristic terminology and for a detailed illustration of his use of these specific terms, see Rosin, *R. Samuel b. Mëir als Schrifterklärer*, 156–58; Japhet, "The Commentary," 254–56.

22. For a more detailed analysis of Rashbam's method in the interpretation of the Song of Songs, see the works mentioned in n. 11 above, and in particular my *Rashbam on the Song of Songs*, 79–125.

23. *Song of Songs Rabbah* 1:10 (also *Tanhuma Va'era* 5; *Yalkut Shimoni* on Proverbs, section 962; Rashi on Prov. 30:1 and more). Rashbam uses this name, and the reference to 1 Kgs. 5:10, also in the heading of his commentary to Qoheleth: "Solomon is called Qoheleth because he gathered wisdom from all the people of the East and became wiser than any man; also, in one place he is called Agur because he collected wisdom, as it is said: 'The words of Agur son of Jakeh' (Prov. 30:1)" (Japhet and Salters, *Rashbam on Qoheleth*, 90).

24. See *Song of Songs Rabbah*, 1:10: "He wrote three books. . . . Which did he write first? . . . . They all admit that he wrote Qoheleth last."

25. See, among others, his comments on Job 8:9, 16:12, 26:9 and more. The phrase is derived from rabbinic literature but has a different function in Rashbam's usage. I intend to deal with this matter in more detail; see for the time being, Japhet, *Rashbam on the Song of Songs*, 100–4.

26. Rashbam on Qoheleth 2:3, 13; See Japhet and Salters, *Rashbam on Qoheleth*, 66.

27. This well-known pun does not come out very well in translation. שלמה may mean: "his peace," and thus the name is explained as an appellative of the One to whom peace belongs, that is God: המלך שהשלום שלו.

28. שלמה המלך יסדו ברוח הקוד' כי ראה שעתידין ישר' להתאונן בגלותן על הק' שנתרחק מהם. כחתן אשר נפרד מאהובתו והתחיל לשורר את שירו במקום כנסת ישר' שהיא ככלה לפניו.

29. On all these issues, see Japhet, *Rashbam on the Song of Songs*, 79–125.

30. The compilatory commentaries were published by Jellinek in 1855. See A. Jellinek, *Commentarien zu Esther, Ruth und den Klageliedern* (Leipzig: L. Schnauss, 1855), 35–36. See also S. Poznanski, *Kommentar zu Ezekiel und den XII kleinen Propheten von Eliezer aus Beaugency* [Hebrew] (Warsaw: H. Epfelberg, 1913), lxxxix.

31. A similar procedure is followed by the compiler of the commentary known as the commentary of R. Joseph Kara on Job. There, however, the compiler concealed the compilatory nature of the work and did not identify the original authors of the excerpts. See S. Japhet, "The Nature and Distribution of Compilatory Commentaries in the Middle Ages in the light of R. Joseph Kara's Commentary on Job," in *The Midrashic Imagination: Jewish Exegesis, Thought, and History*, ed. M. Fishbane (Albany: State University of New York Press, 1993), 98–130.

32. The note: ר' שמ' (Rabbi Samuel) appears at the end of the interpretation of Lamentations 1:1 and relates to the whole passage until this point, that is, the introduction and the interpretation of verse 1.

33. MS. Hamburg 32, folio 101.

34. The description of the widow is a combination of allusions to two biblical texts: "bereaved and barren" (Isa. 49:21), and "the woman was bereft of her two sons and her husband" (Ruth 1:5 RSV; NRSV: "The woman was left without her two sons and her husband"; similarly, NJPS).

35. This is certainly an allusion to Jer. 9:16 ("call for the mourning women"). I adopted the translation of the NRSV (and RSV), which preserves the specific female form of the Hebrew. The NJPS reads: "summon the dirge-singers."

36. The Hebrew is phrased along the lines of Judges 20:34, 41. I wonder whether the "her" (עליה) should not be emended to "them" (עליהם). The text would make much better sense and the change presupposes only the omission of one letter. As this is the only manuscript of the commentary, there is no way to corroborate such a proposal.

37. See Jer. 36:23.

38. Jer. 36:32, NRSV. NJPS: "And more of the like were added."

39. The Hebrew words translated "mourn" and "lament" all derive from the same root קין, which is repeated in the introduction ten times, five in verbal forms (the participle מקונן and מקוננות and the infinitive לקונן), and five in a nominal form (קינה). "Scroll of Laments" (מגילת קינות) is the traditional name of Lamentations in rabbinic sources. See e.g. BT, *Bava Batra* 15a.

40. See above.

41. This statement may also be explained in other ways. It is also possible that its general and vague phrasing is directed against the midrash, which identifies explicitly what parts of Lamentations were written in the first scroll and what parts were added later—the view adopted also by Rashi (*Lamentations Rabbah*, 3:1, and below, n. 43). From another perspective one may hesitatingly ask whether by the term "end" Rashbam refers to a much later date, that is the historical "end," the conquest of Jerusalem. This would imply a different view of the nature of Lamentations, as having been written—at least in part—after the actual events. See above.

42. *Lamentations* (כיון שחטאו גלו, וכיון שגלו התחיל ירמיה מקונן עליהם 'איכה ישבה בדד'. *Rabbah, Petihta,* end of sections 5, 6, 8, 9, 12, 13, and many more).

43. See *Lamentations Rabbah*, 3:1, and more concisely, ibid, *Petihta,* section 28. The view of the midrash is that the first scroll included Lamentations 1, 2, 4, 5, and the addition was the lament in chapter three, where the acrostic structure is tripled.

44. See, for example, Rashbam's comment to Job 39:13: למעלה אחז שטתו בחיות ועתה אוחז שטתו בעופות, על נפלאותיו שהוא מפליא להם. (also Job 13:23). The Hebrew term שיטה has several meanings in Rashbam's usage, among them category, method,

format, and perhaps also genre (see Japhet, "The Commentary," 255). The best rendition in this context seems to be: "he applied the format/method of mourning for human beings, in the ways of the world." On "the ways of the world," see n. 25 above.

45. R. Merdler, *Dayyaqut MeRabbenu Shemuel* (Jerusalem: Hebrew University Institute of Jewish Studies, 1999), 18 lines 1–4. On the use of this principle in Rashbam's grammatical anaylsis, see Japhet and Salters, *Rashbam on Qoheleth*, 37; R. Merdler, "Rabbi Samuel ben Meir and the Hebrew Grammar" [Hebrew, with English summary], Ph. D. thesis, Hebrew University, Jerusalem, 2004, 60–69.

46. If indeed the absence of introductions to Job and Qoheleth reflects Rashbam's editorial choices (see above), it may be explained along the same lines. These commentaries do not include methodological statements, and only occasional references to the "plain meaning of the text." See Japhet, *Rashbam on Job*, 54–55.

47. In addition to the sporadic excerpts in the compilatory commentary itself, one finds some comments on Lamentations in Rashbam's other works. There are altogether about fifty references to Lamentations, presenting about thirty different comments. These comments, however, are all of a linguistic nature, and their survey did not bear any fruits regarding the issues discussed in the introduction.

48. See, for instance, Japhet, *Rashbam on the Song of Songs*, 127–63.

49. See R. A. Harris, "The Literary Hermeneutic of Rabbi Eliezer of Beaugency," Ph. D. Thesis, Jewish Theological Seminary, New York, 1997; R. A. Harris, "Awareness of Biblical Redaction among Rabbinic Exegetes of Northern France" [Hebrew], *Shnaton: An Annual for Biblical and Ancient Near Eastern Studies* 12 (2000): 289–310.

CHAPTER TEN

Wandering to the End

The Medieval Christian Context of the Wandering Jew

E. Ann Matter

One of the many cogent contributions Michael Signer has made to the history of Jewish-Christian relations is his description of the ways in which Andrew of Saint Victor, the noted exegete of twelfth-century Paris, learned about Jewish interpretations for his commentary on Ezekiel.[1] Since Andrew's exegesis includes frequent references to Hebrew words and Jewish interpretations, it presents the intriguing question of whether Andrew actually could read the Bible and its Jewish interpreters in Hebrew. Signer follows the lead of scholars who doubt that Andrew had any advanced knowledge of Hebrew,[2] but nevertheless notes that in the Ezekiel commentary, when Andrew makes observations about Hebrew, he is correct.[3] So, how can this be? Signer follows Beryl Smalley's observation that Andrew's knowledge of Hebrew words and Jewish interpretation of books of the Hebrew Bible came from his conversations, in French, with the Jews of Paris.[4]

In fact, Signer describes a world of twelfth-century Jews who used French for much of their scholarly work, including reading aloud from Old French paraphrases of the Prophets in synagogue liturgies.[5] Andrew must have had opportunity to speak with Jewish scholars about many aspects of practice as well as interpretation, since he knows, for example, that one must not bend knees or cross feet during the Amida, or Standing Prayer.[6]

Andrew's use of Jewish interpretations of Isaiah earned him a rebuke from his fellow canon, Richard of Saint Victor, who accused him outright of improper messianic theology.[7] Indeed, as Signer points out: "Andrew transmitted Jewish messianic aspirations as well as their self-assurance of national restoration, [treating themes] which had been the center of Jewish-Christian argument ever since the New Testament: Jewish messianic aspirations, Jewish hope for national restoration in Israel, and the restoration of and reestablishment of the Temple cult of sacrifice and priesthood."[8]

Whether or not Richard of Saint Victor approved, Andrew was not the only twelfth-century Christian exegete who was fascinated by the role of the Jews in interpreting Old Testament messianic expectations. Sometime after 1132, somewhere in Germany, Honorius Augustodunensis, one of the most virtuosic of Christian allegorical exegetes of the twelfth century, wrote a commentary on the Song of Songs that shares some of the attitudes toward Jewish messianism that are found in the works of Andrew of Saint Victor.[9] Andrew and Honorius share some important biographical details: both were originally English, both ended up living on the Continent, both were known as gifted expounders of the biblical text.[10] Yet, as exegetes, they showed the extremes of twelfth-century Christian approaches to the Bible, from Andrew's rather literal approach[11] to Honorius's extravagant allegories.

Honorius had written a shorter commentary on the Song back in England, a work that was certainly allegorical, but had a straightforward mariological interpretation;[12] but this longer commentary, done later in his life, is a tour-de-force of allegory. Honorius sets out to interpret each verse of the Song of Songs according to the four common modes of medieval biblical interpretation: the historical, the allegorical (having to do with Christ), the tropological (or moral), and the anagogical (having to do with the End Times).[13] This pattern of four sets up his interpretation of the Song of Songs as four songs sung by Solomon to his four brides: the Daughter of the Pharaoh (Song of Songs 1:1–2:17), the Daughter of the King of Babylon (or the *Regina Austri,* the Queen of the South, 3:1–6:9), the Sunamita (6:10–7:10), and the Mandrake (7:11–8:14). Each of these Brides is associated with an age of the world, so that each of Solomon's symbolic marriages marks a new time in the unfolding of God's plan: the Daughter of the Pharaoh is the Bride of the age of the Patriarchs, the Daughter of the King of Babylon reigns in the age of the Prophets, the Sunamita is the Bride of the age of the Apostles, and the Mandrake will be the Bride of the End Times.[14] These four ages divide the text of the Song of Songs, yet each of the ages resonates within each section as well, so that the age of each Bride also bears within it the ages past and to come.

The first sense of scripture, *historia,* is not surprisingly understood as the level of the story that has to do with the Jewish people. In general, it is obvious that the first two ages (Patriarchs and Prophets) are about the revelation to the Jews, as the second two ages (Apostles and the End Times) are under the Christian dispensation. This is explicated throughout the commentary, but Honorius sets this up in his two long prologues, where he elaborates in detail on the four ages. Especially in the second prologue, which takes on the task of explaining universal history by means of the four Brides, he describes in detail how the four ages relate to the history of the Jewish and Christian peoples.[15]

In the second prologue Honorius makes it clear that it is, from the perspective of medieval Christian biblical theology, this last sense of the four, *anagogia,* upon which he will focus his commentary. Granted, this may seem odd to the contemporary reader, since the anagogical concern for Last Things seems the least relevant of possible meanings of the Song of Songs, but Honorius uses anagogy to bring home the meaning of the poems. This is not an idiosyncratic choice. Although there do not seem to have been any Christian commentaries on the Song of Songs that explicitly and exclusively interpret the love poems as relating to the Last Things or the end of the world, an apocalyptic understanding was never hidden or in any way occult, but rather was an elusive element in the tradition of Christian interpretation. After all, the Apocalypse, or Revelation to John, the last book of the New Testament, culminates in the marriage of the Heavenly Jerusalem, decked as a bride, to her husband, the Lamb of God (Apoc. 21:2–9). This passage is easily linked to the most common medieval Christian interpretation of the Song of Songs, the allegorical or ecclesiological level, since in this interpretive framework both texts speak of the mystical marriage of Christ and the Church.

This analysis gives the essential clue for why a commentary on the Song of Songs would be so interested in, even have as its goal, an understanding of the End Times. The love between Christ and the Church is the most important, the ultimate, meaning of the Song of Songs, and this mystical marriage will not be consummated until the End Times. This is why so many medieval Christian exegetes wrote commentaries on both the Song of Songs and the Apocalypse of John, that is, because they are parts of the same story.[16]

This connection between the Song of Songs and the Apocalypse became rather controversial in the fourth century when the Church, in the throes of making peace with the delayed End Times, essentially rejected chiliasm, the literal belief in Christ's return to earth to reign for a millennium. After this, Christian commentary on the Apocalypse became decidedly un-apocalyptic.[17] The shift, which began with Jerome's fourth-century editing of the first Latin Apocalypse commentary by Victorinus of Pettau, continued until the original and startlingly apocalyptic exegesis of the twelfth-century visionary Joachim of Fiore.[18] In this period, from the fifth to the twelfth centuries, Christian interpretation held to an ecclesiological framework in which the Apocalypse was understood to reveal, under the veil of allegory, the Church's history of trial and triumph.

This makes the Bride of the Last Times, the one who comes as the Mandrake in Honorius's Book Four, worthy of closer scrutiny. In this last book, Honorius is especially concerned about the Last Days, since the Mandrake—the ultimate bride of Christ—will be the manifestation of the Church that ushers in the Second Coming. Honorius explains:

> The Mandrake is a plant in the shape of a human body without a head, and it is understood to signify the multitude of the infidels. When he existed [on earth], Antichrist, the head of all evil, was the Mandrake's head. But when the head of the Mandrake was cut off, Antichrist was killed. After this killing, the bridegroom sees that the Synagogue is the conversion of the infidel [now] without the head of Antichrist. But [the Synagogue] is still lacking the head of Christ, hoping to associate herself in faith with Christ, and to take on the head of Christ. The bridegroom says: "Come, my beloved, let us go out into the fields, let us linger in the villages." (7:11)[19]

It is at this point that Christ gives the decapitated Mandrake his own head, so that Christ literally becomes the Head of the Church, that is, the decapitated

Synagogue. The text describes this as a moment of "decrepitude," the passing away of the time of earthly creation, and plunges deeply into Christian ideas of supersession over the Jews.

Who then *is* the Mandrake? Honorius approaches this question by turning to another verse of the Song of Songs, explaining that when the night of Antichrist is over, the bride and bridegroom go out into the fields to see if the vines have flowered (7:12). The vines, he says, are *Synagoga,* who will burst into flower only with Christian faith and will drink from the breast of her mother (Mother Church) when she takes in the doctrine of both the old and the new covenants.[20] Honorius turns to the allegorical sense to explain that the breasts of the mother are two revelations of the divinity of Jesus: they refer first to his encounter with the elders in the Temple at the age of twelve (Luke 2:41–49) and then, at the beginning of his public ministry, to Jesus' preaching in the synagogue of Nazareth (Matt. 13:54–58; Mark 6:1–6; Luke 4:13–30). Both stories refer to the old and new law, through which Jesus will lead *Synagoga* into the true Judea, "the home of my mother" (8:2) and the true Jerusalem, "and into her room" (8:2, var.).

Here, Honorius predicts the calling of *Synagoga,* the Church of the Jews, as the last stage of the preparation for the Eschaton. Honorius's understanding of the repeated verse, "I adjure you, daughters of Jerusalem, neither arouse nor awaken the beloved until she wishes" (8:4, with variants at 2:7 and 3:5), signifies three ages of the Church: the *Ecclesia Primitiva,* or Primitive Church, the *Ecclesia Gentium,* or Church of the Peoples ("the Gentiles" in a universal sense), and the *Synagoga Conversa,* the Converted Synagogue that will be the Church of the End Times. The Jewish people are implicated in both the first and third Churches because Christ came first for *Synagoga,* but she refused him, so the gospel message went to the Gentiles. Nevertheless, this elaborate allegory has a happy ending, because in the end *Synagoga* will also become one of the brides of Christ, when she, in the form of the Mandrake, loses the imposed head of Antichrist and instead receives the head of Christ upon her body.[21]

"Under the apple tree I aroused you," sings Song of Songs 8:5, and this, says Honorius, is where *Synagoga* will also be aroused to the true faith when she becomes the last stage of the Church on earth. The apple tree of this passage is a type for the most highly symbolic "trees" in Christian thought, the tree in the Garden of Eden and the tree of the cross of Jesus. *Synagoga* slept under the apple tree in spite of the fact that there Christ rose from death on the tree. And, Honorius says, it was there that *Synagoga* was corrupted (8:5) when she cried out "Let his blood be upon us and our children" (Matt. 27:25): just as *Synagoga* was violated when the law shifted from literal to spiritual.[22] And also there is a third possibility: "the mother, that is the Jewish people, was violated when, because of the liberation (or vindication) of the cross, she was enslaved by Titus and Vespasian."[23]

This extended allegory is an excellent example of the traditional Christian supersessionist teaching that the Jewish people (the "mother" of *Synagoga*) ignored the message of Jesus (when they slept under the tree of the cross), and so saw their Law "corrupted" by the Christian insistence on the spiritual over the literal, and were historically cast out of their own "motherland" by the Romans.

Honorius repeats this history of the Jews as outcasts at 8:10: "'I am a wall and my breasts like towers / since I am made in his presence as if finding peace.' Judah [the Jews], will have no peace with Christ and man, since he cried, 'Let his blood be upon us and our children' (Matt. 27:25). As a consequence, [Judah] serves all people under tribute [*sub tribute*], being dispersed over all the world, and all people demand recompense for the blood of Christ spilled at his hand. But after his conversion to Christ, he will have peace with all people."[24] Judah stands for the Jews and represents *Synagoga*. Judah eventually finds acceptance in the communion of the Church, so he will find full peace when he rejoices with the angels before Christ, the Prince of Peace.

Here Honorius seems to move away from allegory to a prophetic stance. He asks about the signs of the end of the world and what it will take to bring Christ's Second Coming to pass. Such a culminating event in history demands major changes in the world. On the tropological level, Honorius says, this will require the conversion of Christians to the virtues of the monastic life.[25] On both the allegorical and anagogical levels, however, it requires the conversion of history itself, the final turning of *Synagoga* toward Christianity. So, *Synagoga,* the personification of the Jewish people, finally becomes one with the Christian covenant and the New Law, and *Synagoga* becomes *Ecclesia.*

One could well ask whether this interpretation of the role of the Jewish people in the End Times resonates more with Andrew of Saint Victor or with his contemporary critic Richard. A most interesting interpretation of Honorius's attitude toward the Jews has been suggested by Jeremy Cohen, who has studied Honorius's Song of Songs exegesis for clues about Christian attitudes toward Jewish communities in the twelfth century.[26] Cohen concentrates his interpretation on Honorius's Book 3, where Solomon weds the Sunamita who comes in the four-wheeled chariot of Aminadab. Here, he suggests, Honorius shows understanding, even sympathy, for the Jewish communities whom contemporary Christian scholars and exegetes like Andrew of Saint Victor may well have known. Cohen argues that a medieval Christian could speak against the persecution of Jews because of the fact that Jews are necessary for God's plan for the world, even if the same Christian author repeats the ancient slander that Jews do behave badly and harm Christians through their usury.[27] Other scholars of medieval Christianity have agreed that Honorius's *Expositio* is one of the more positive medieval Christian portraits of the Jews, an "unusual" eschatology full of "optimistic implications."[28]

Of course, one part of Honorius's attitude toward the Jews is connected to a Christian eschatology that had long linked the legend of Antichrist to the Jewish people. For instance Hippolytus's *On the Antichrist* (c. 200) says that Antichrist was a Jew,[29] and the fourth-century Latin *Tiburtine Sibyl* says specifically that just before Antichrist arises from the tribe of Dan, "the Jews will be converted to the Lord, and his sepulcher will be glorified by all. In those days Judah will be saved and Israel will dwell with confidence."[30]

Honorius's commentary on the Song of Songs can thus give us a reason to look at Andrew of Saint Victor in a slightly different way, seeing both Honorius and Andrew as examples of a heightened twelfth-century emphasis on the conversion of the Jews as one of the signs of the Last Days. Other twelfth-century texts echo this idea. It is found, for example, in Otto of Freising's *The Deeds of Frederick Barbarosa,* in both Joachim of Fiore's Apocalypse commentary and his *Book of Figures,* and (perhaps most significantly) in the thirteenth-century Franciscan literature inspired by Joachim.[31] From this late medieval period, the idea of the conversion of the Jews as a sign of the age of Antichrist passes into Protestant Christianity, both in the Lutheran world that was directly influenced by the friars and in English millenarianism, and on into contemporary American Fundamentalism's dedication to Israel and the hope of some Christians for the building of the Third Temple in Jerusalem.[32]

And it is the Christian world of the thirteenth century that creates one of the most haunting images of the connection between the Jewish people and the Christian End Times, the Wandering Jew. The story of the Wandering Jew is a trope on the story of the *Via crucis* found in no Gospel account, canonical or apocryphal. Jesus, bowed down by the weight of the cross, at the end of his physical powers, passes the small shop, really just a booth, of a cobbler. He leans against the frame of the shop, but the shoe maker pushes him away. Jesus then curses him to wander to the end of time, without respite.[33] Although there is an earlier reference to one who smote Jesus during the Way of the Cross and lived for centuries, he is not described as a Jew.[34]

The earliest reference to the story in its classical form, at least in the West, comes from an anonymous Cistercian chronicle from Ferrara that records that in 1223, pilgrims from the Holy Land reported seeing a Jew in Armenia who had witnessed Christ going to his death. The Jew had slapped Jesus, saying "Go, you faker, get what you deserve," to which Jesus replied "I will go, but you will wait for me until I return."[35] The story is told several decades later in England by Roger of Wendover, a monk of St. Albans, who puts it in the mouth of an Armenian pilgrim who visited St. Albans in 1228.[36] Matthew Paris, who took over the chronicle of St. Albans after Roger's death in 1236, records a 1252 visit of more Armenian pilgrims to St. Albans; these pilgrims tell a similar story and name the man who insulted Jesus Cartaphile or Joseph Cartaphile.[37] Jean-Claude Schmitt reproduces a manuscript painting in an autograph manuscript of Matthew Paris where Jesus and Cartaphile speak with long scrolls: Cartaphile says, "Go, Jesus, to the judgment prepared for you," and Jesus answers "I will go, as is written of me. You, however, will wait until I come."[38]

Thirteenth-century Italian narratives about the Wandering Jew give him another name: "John the God-Smiter," that is, Joannes Buttadeus, Giovanni Bottadio, or Zan Butadio.[39] One of the early Italian narratives of Giovanni Bottadio is by the Franciscan astrologer Guido Bonatti, who died around 1300 and whom Dante places in Hell in the circle of the sorcerers and diviners.[40] Around 1415, an account by Antonio di Francesco di Andrea describes a recent apparition in Florence and in Mugello of the Wanderer, identified as "Giovanni Servo di Dio," "Buttadeo," or "Giovanni Votaddio." This version presents a positive (if whimsical) image of the Wanderer, claiming that he stays about 100 years in each place, and sometimes does good, as in the winter of 1411, when he rescued travelers caught by a sudden snowstorm in a mountain pass, appearing out of nowhere in a Franciscan habit and leading them to safety.[41] Other contemporary or successive interpretations of the legend in Italy stress that the Wandering Jew had offended Jesus and henceforth deserves eternal punishment. In some other versions, particularly the ones found in Tuscany, he possesses magical powers that can be employed for the benefit of his fellow men, like the semi-Franciscan of Antonio di Francesco di Andrea. In those versions he is not always identified as a Jew, although he maintains his gifts of ubiquity, self-transformation, and ability to foretell the future.[42]

So, over the course of three hundred years, from the exegetical works of the schools of Paris to the writings of the early Humanists, the "Eschatological Jew" had taken on an individualized form into which all of the expectations of Honorius were funneled. "You will stay until I return," Jesus says to Cartaphile, just as Honorius prophesied that *Synagoga* would find rest under the tree when she accepted the tree of the cross and became *Ecclesia*. Later forms of the Wandering Jew, especially the stories that circulated in northern Europe, where the wanderer was named Ahasverus, played on his ominous, magical powers, and came to take on more sinister tones.[43]

Of course, we need to remember that there were real wanderings of real people, especially following the expulsions of Jews from England by Edward I in 1290 and from Spain by Ferdinand and Isabella in 1492. The earlier stories of the Wandering Jew are almost a foreshadowing of the fate of the Jewish people later in the Middle Ages. The Wandering Jew takes on all of the characteristics of the whole Jewish community in Christian culture: he is a fugitive presence, punished for his treatment of Jesus, who will be an important figure in the Last Days. The Eschatological Jew has no home until the end of the world.

This is the way the figure is presented in the last text I would like to consider here, Alberto Alfireri's *Ogdoas*.[44] This is a very strange and little-known

set of eight dialogues between recently deceased members of the Visconti
and Adorno families. The *Ogdoas* was written in Caffa, a Genoese colony on
the Black Sea, by an author who describes himself as a schoolmaster and a
native Lombard, but about whom hardly anything else is known. The main
protagonist, an interlocutor in all eight dialogues, is Gabriele Maria Visconti, the illegitimate son of Gian Galeazzo Visconti. Gabriele was executed
by the tyrant of Genoa, the French governor Boucicaut, in 1408 or 1409.[45]
The internal time of the dialogues is soon after, since Gabriele arrives at the
first circle of a very Macrobian afterlife, bloodied and almost headless.[46] But
internal evidence makes it clear that the text was written in 1420 and that
one purpose of Alfieri's writing is to curry enough favor with members of
the aristocracy of Milan and Genoa to earn him a trip back to Italy.[47]

The dialogues are a series of conversations between Gabriele and other
dead Italian nobility: Gian Galeazzo and Bernabò Visconti (his father and
uncle), the Countess Caterina (his father's wife), Agnese Mantegazza (his
father's mistress and his mother), and Antoniotto Adorno, the Doge of
Genoa. Most of these discussions focus on earthly politics and the characteristics of a good ruler, on the one hand, and on the nature of the heavens
and the afterlife, on the other. But Gabriele's dialogue with Antoniotto (Dialogue 7, the longest by far) is quite different. Antoniotto, who died in 1398,
has been dead longer than any of the other interlocutors and so is just
about to forge off to another, higher sphere, when Gabriele stops him and
asks him to speak, of all things, about the city of Caffa. Antoniotto warms
to his task, regaling Gabriele with stories of the exotic peoples of the Crimea:
Greeks, Nabatheans (Arabs), and the "Scythians," probably the Tatars of
the Golden Horde, about whom he tells stories that had been passed down
from Herodotus to Marco Polo. But Antoniotto speaks first about the hor-
rors of the forthcoming ages, full of wars and tragedy for Genoa. These
catastrophes will be followed by a brief Golden Age of peace and unity, and
then by the appearance of the Wandering Jew:

> Then, at that time, a certain man will appear, called a servant of God,
> named Giovanni, who will foretell many future things. When Christ, who
> is called Jesus the savior of the world, was led to death by the impious
> Jews, this man struck the Lord with a great blow, while a great crowd of

people followed. The redeemer of the world said to him, "May you give testimony about me, go and live as long as the earthly machine will endure." He even transforms himself into various forms: now he takes the form of a youth, now that of an old gray man; now he walks invisibly; he imitates the languages of all nations; he has known all the places and towns of the habitable regions. Who speaks to him today does not recognize him tomorrow. He will tell many things about the princes and the popes of the Christian people. Some will call him a saint, some the Lord, some a demon. Nevertheless, he was a Jew, and he comes from the age of that eternal judge from whom he secured grace. What shall I say about this one, who now is in Genoa, now Paris, now Venice, now in Scythia, now in Egypt? He is faster than the soul that has departed from the body and escaped from bondage. He assumes a most honest appearance. He is blessed with eloquence and sanctity. He is also a most true witness of the Christian faith. Neither Proteus, spoken of in fables, nor Thetis, once the goddess of the sea, were described in such a way as this man will be by the most upright voice of men.[48]

Alfieri's description of the Wandering Jew has many familiar elements: he is ubiquitous, mysterious, a foreteller of future havoc. He can predict the future and is known as John Servant of God. His eternal wandering is punishment for a cruel act toward the Savior on the way to Calvary. He will be sometimes invisible and sometimes mistaken for a saint, the Lord, or the devil.

Yet, Alfieri's Giovanni is by no means a totally negative character, since throughout the centuries he will remain a true witness to the Christian faith. The fact that the Wandering Jew was a witness of Christ casts him in a positive image, but the fact that he offended Jesus and was condemned to wander till the end of time is certainly negative. By those themes, Alfieri voices the conflicting Christian attitude toward the Jews, who were seen at once as impious enemies of Jesus and, at the same time, as valuable testimony to his revelation.

Alfieri's description of the character of the Wandering Jew shows the maturation of a medieval legend. As we have seen, contemporary and successive interpretations of the legend in Italy share many characteristics of Alfieri's Wandering Jew. In some other versions, particularly the ones found in Tuscany, he possesses magical powers employed for the benefit of his fellow men. In those versions he is not always identified as a Jew (as, indeed, Alfieri takes his time in mentioning this detail). According to Morpurgo, there were other reports of Giovanni Buttadeo visiting Siena in the first decades of the fourteenth century. This is interesting because it is close to the time when the prediction of Antoniotto would take place, that is, in the internal time of the *Ogdoas*. Morpurgo shows that there was clearly an increasing interest in the legend in fifteenth-century Italy, with different characteristics in different parts of the peninsula.[49] Even though Alfieri could not have read some of these texts in Caffa because they were written after his departure for Crimea, he must have read some of their sources since he certainly has a good grasp of the main tradition.

In the *Ogdoas*, the apparition of the Wandering Jew is a sign of impending calamities. According to Antoniotto, that disquieting presence will be accompanied by recurrences of smallpox, plague, and famine in the Genoese eastern colonies. At this point Alfieri may speak from direct experience, referring to the current situation in Caffa. That the plague would appear in Genoa is also accurate, since cases of the disease were recorded in Italy around 1420.[50]

It is a long wander from twelfth-century Paris to fifteenth-century Caffa, and along the way Christian attitudes about the role of Jews in the End Times underwent a subtle series of changes. The twelfth-century context is crucial since it is here that we can witness the development of the Eschatological Jew. Andrew of Saint Victor and Honorius Augustodunensis both felt that the survival of the Jewish people was necessary until the End Times because their conversion to Christianity would be one of the signs of the end. Nevertheless, other scholars, like Richard of Saint Victor, wanted to make it absolutely clear that the messianic aspirations of the Jews were in error and that Christians should not be fooled into forgiving Jewish theological blindness and obstinacy just because they were necessary for the Eschaton. In the following century, this attitude contributed to the legend of the Wandering Jew, a symbolic representation of the Jewish people, punished because he did not recognize Jesus (and, indeed, insulted him), and condemned to wander until the End.

In the Wandering Jew of Alberto Alfieri's *Ogdoas,* we find that the legend has turned a corner, and has turned into something else. All of the familiar elements are there, but this Giovanni, only incidentally a Jew, is more of a Merlin-like wonder-worker than a harbinger of the End Times. What is striking about Alfieri's Wandering Jew is the extent to which he is connected to calamities on earth, during human times, with no reference to his importance for the Eschaton. This Wandering Jew is a tragic figure, and he comes in times of tribulation, but he is, perhaps, no longer an Eschatological Jew; he seems instead to be the official prophet of the Genoese state. It is no accident that the one who tells the story of the Wandering Jew in the *Ogdoas* is the former Doge of Genoa, since for Antoniotto Adorno, as much as for Alfieri and many other Humanist authors, the End of the World is a political event.

Notes

1. *Andreae de Sancto Victore opera 6: Expositio in Ezechielem,* ed. Michael Alan Signer, CCCM 53E (Turnhout: Brepols, 1991), xii–xxxvii.

2. A. Saltman, "Pseudo-Jerome in the Commentary of Andrew of St. Victor on Samuel," *Harvard Theological Review* 67 (1974): 195–253.

3. Signer, CCCM 53E, xxiii–xxv.

4. Signer, CCCM 53E, xxvii–xxx: Beryl Smalley, *The Study of the Bible in the Middle Ages* (Notre Dame, IN: University of Notre Dame Press, 1964), 155.

5. Signer, CCCM 53E, xxii.

6. Andrew of Saint Victor, *Expositio in Ezechielem* 1:7 (CCCM 53E.13); see also CCCM 53E, xxx.

7. Richard of Saint Victor, *De Emmanuele* (PL 196.601–666).

8. Signer, CCCM 53E, xxxii–xxxiii.

9. Honorius Augustodunensis, *Expositio in Cantica canticorum* (PL 172. 347–496).

10. For the life of Andrew of Saint Victor, see R. Berndt, *André de Saint-Victor (+1175). Exegete et théologien* (Paris: Brepols, 1991); for Honorius, see Valerie Flint, "The Commentaries of Honorius Augustodunensis on the Song of Songs," *Revue bénédictine* 84 (1974): 196–211.

11. Andrew was the hero of Smalley's thesis that medieval exegesis became gradually more literal; her several learned articles on the topic were summarized in the chapter on Andrew in *Study of the Bible,* 112–95.

12. Honorius Augustodunensis, *Sigillum Beatae Mariae ubi exponuntur Canticum canticorum* (PL 172.485–513); English translation by Amelia Carr, *The Seal of the Blessed Mary by Honorius Augstodunensis* (Toronto: Peregrina, 1991).

13. The four senses of Scripture, originating from John Cassian, are the focus of an intricate study by Henri de Lubac, *Exégèse médiévale: Les quatres sens de l'écriture*, 4 vols. (Paris: Aubier, 1959–1964). For a version of this story as it applies to Honorius, see E. Ann Matter, *The Voice of My Beloved: The Song of Songs in Western Medieval Christianity* (Philadelphia: University of Pennsylvania Press, 1990), 49–85.

14. See Matter, *The Voice of My Beloved*, 64, for a chart of how these and several other levels of interpretation fit together.

15. For a synopsis of the two prologues, see ibid., 60–70.

16. E. Ann Matter, "The Love Song of the Millennium: Medieval Christian Apocalyptic and the Song of Songs," in *Scrolls of Love: Ruth and the Song of Songs,* ed. Peter S. Hawkins and Lesleigh Cushing Stahlberg (New York: Fordham University Press, 2006), 228–43; see p. 351 n. 7 for a list of exegetes who wrote on both texts.

17. See E. Ann Matter, "The Apocalypse in Early Medieval Exegesis," in *The Apocalypse in the Middle Ages,* ed. Richard K. Emmerson and Bernard McGinn (Ithaca, NY: Cornell University Press, 1992), 38–50 for a more detailed discussion of this shift and the "unapocalyptic" nature of early medieval Apocalypse exegesis.

18. Many of Joachim's works are not in modern editions, but see *Liber figurarum,* ed. L. Tondelli, M. Reeves, and B. Hirsch-Reich (Turin: Società editrice internazionale, 1953), and *Abbot Joachim of Fiore: Liber de concordia Noui ac Veteris Testamenti,* ed. E. Randolph Daniel (Philadelphia: American Philosophical Society, 1983), as well as the selected English translations of Bernard McGinn in *Apocalyptic Spirituality: Treatises and Letters of Lactanius, Adso of Montier-en-Der, Joachim of Fiore, the Franciscan Spirituals, Savonarola* (New York: Paulist Press, 1979), 97–148, and his *Visions of the End: Apocalyptic Traditions in the Middle Ages* (New York: Columbia University Press, 1979, 1998), 126–41. There is more literature on the (heterodox) Franciscan followers of Joachim than on the Calabrian Cistercian himself, but see Randolph Daniel, "Joachim of Fiore: Patterns of History in the Apocalypse," in *The Apocalypse in the Middle Ages,* 72–88.

19. Honorius Augustodunensis, *Expositio in Cantica canticorum* (PL 172. 471B–C).

20. Ibid. (PL 172.472C–D).

21. Ibid. (PL 172.474D–475C).

22. Ibid. (PL 172.481B).

23. "Vel genitrix, videlicet Judaica gens est violata, quando ob vindictam crucis a Tito et Vespasiano est captivata" (Honorius, *Expositio;* PL 172.481C).

24. Honorius, *Expositio* (PL 172.488C–D).

25. Honorius, *Expositio* (PL 172.476A–477A).

26. Jeremy Cohen, "*Synagoga Conversa*: Honorius Augustodunensis, the Song of Songs, and Christianity's 'Eschatological Jew,'" *Speculum* 79 (2004): 309–40.

27. Jeremy Cohen, *Living Letters of the Law: Ideas of the Jew in Medieval Christianity* (Berkeley: University of California Press, 1999), 243. Cohen is basing this argument on a reading of Bernard of Clairvaux's Letter 363.

28. Bernard McGinn, *Antichrist: Two Thousand Years of the Human Fascination with Evil* (San Francisco: HarperSan Francisco, 1994), 118.

29. Ibid., 60–61.

30. McGinn, *Visions of the End*, 49.

31. See ibid., 118, 134, 138, and 191 (the fascinating case of Roger Bacon's writings on the coming "angelic pope").

32. See McGinn, *Antichrist*, 217–18. For the Lutheran adaptation of Franciscan Joachite ideas, see David Todd Heffner, "*Eyn Wunderliche Weyssagung von der Babstums*": *Medieval Prophecy into Reformation Polemic*, Ph.D. dissertation in History of Art, University of Pennsylvania, 1991. For Protestant Fundamentalist ideas of the Jews and the End Times, see Lawrence Wright, "Letter from Jerusalem: Forcing the End," *The New Yorker* (July 20, 1998): 42–53; and for the stout of heart, Tim LaHaye and Jerry Jenkins, *Left Behind: A Novel of the Earth's Last Days* (Wheaton, IL: Tyndale House, 1995) and sequels.

33. For the history of the Wandering Jew, see Gaël Milin, *Le cordonnier de Jérusalem: la veritable histoire du Juif Errant* (Rennes: Presses Universitaires de Rennes, 1997); and Jean-Claude Schmitt, "La genese médiévale dela légende et de l'iconographie du Juif Errant," in *Le Juif Errant: un témoine du temps*, ed. Pierre Birnbaum (Paris: Musée d'Art et d'Histoire du Judaïsme, 2001), 55–75. The latter is the catalogue of an exhibition of representations of the Wandering Jew.

34. In *The Spiritual Meadow* of John Moschos, a Syrian monk who lived at the turn of the seventh century, the culprit is an Ethiopian. Compare Milin, *Le cordonnier de Jérusalem*, 14.

35. *Ignoti monachi Cisterciensis S. Mariae de Ferraria Chronica*, cited in Milin, *Le cordonnier de Jérusalem*, 18, by Schmitt, "La genese médiévale," 58.

36. Roger of Wendover, *Flores historiarum*, ed. Henry G. Hewlett in *Scriptores rerum britannicarum*, 3 vols. (London: Rolls Series, 1889), vol. 2, 352–55; Milin, *Le cordonnier de Jérusalem*, 19.

37. Matthew Paris, *Chronica majora*, in *Scriptores rerum britannicarum*, 7 vols., ed. Henry G. Hewlett (London: Rolls Series, 1872–1883), vol. 3, 161–63; Milin, *Le cordonnier de Jérusalem*, 21. It is interesting that the three earliest Western versions of the story mention Armenia—perhaps there is an earlier version of the wandering Jew in Armenian sources.

38. Cartaphile: "Vade, Jhesu, ad judicium tibi preparatum." Jesus: "Vado sicut scriptum est de me. Tu vero expectabis donc veniam" (Schmitt, "La genese médié-

vale," 63). The manuscript is Cambridge, Corpus Christi College 16, fol. 70v. It is an autograph of Mattthew Paris dated between 1240–1253. See Nigel Morgan, *Early Gothic Manuscripts [I] 1190–1250* (Oxford: Harvey Miller, Oxford University Press, 1982), 136.

39. See Milin, *Le cordonnier de Jérusalem*, 37–48, for a careful discussion of Joannes Buttadeus in his various forms. For the wandering Jew in Italy, see also Simone Morpurgo, *L'Ebreo errante in Italia* (Florence: Dante, 1891, repr. Sala Bolognese: Arnaldo Forni, 1983).

40. Guido Bonatti, *Introductorius ad judica stellarum* (Augsburg, 1491), cited by Milin, *Le cordonnier de Jérusalem*, 37–38; Dante, *Divina Commedia, Inferno,* Canto XX, 118–20. Milin cites the French translation of Dante by A. Masseron (Paris, 1947).

41. Printed in full by Morpurgo, *L'Ebreo errante in Italia*, 15–40; cf. Milin, *Le cordonnier de Jérusalem*, 44–48.

42. Morpurgo (*L'Ebreo errante in Italia*, 7 n. 2) quotes Mariano da Siena, *Viaggio in Terrasanta fatto e descritto da Ser Mariano da Siena nel secolo XV (1431)* (Florence: Stamperia Magheri, 1822), as an early fifteenth-century author who had mentioned the Wandering Jew.

43. Maurice Kriegel, "La lancement de la légende ou la courte description et histoire d'un Juif nomme Ahasvérus," in *Le Juif Errant,* 77–89; Milin, *Le cordonnier de Jérusalem,* 65–105. For a study of the genesis and development of the legend, see George Anderson, *The Legend of the Wandering Jew* (Providence, RI: Brown University Press, 1965), esp. 11–27. Joseph Gaer, *The Legend of the Wandering Jew* (New York: New American Library, 1961) is a more general survey of the spread of the legend with minimal attention to its promulgation in Italy during the Renaissance. *The Wandering Jew: Essays in the Interpretation of a Christian Legend,* ed. Galit Hazan-Rokem and Alan Dundes (Bloomington: Indiana University Press, 1986) offers a series of essays by different authors on the topic. In this collection, R. Edelmann's "Ahasuerus, the Wandering Jew: Origin and Background," 1–10, focuses on a later German interpretation of the legend and shows how, with the passing of time and the progression toward the north of Europe, the legend assumes more sinister tones.

44. See the forthcoming edition and translation of Carla P. Weinberg and E. Ann Matter, *Education, Civic Virtue, and Colonialism in Fifteenth-Century Italy: The* Ogdoas *of Alberto Alfieri* (Tempe, AZ: Medieval and Renaissance Texts and Studies, 2010). The text has been printed once: Antonio Ceruti, "L'*Ogdoas* di Alberto Alfieri: episodi di storia genovese nei primordii del secolo XV," *Atti della società ligure di storia patria* 17 (1885): 255–320.

45. The traditional year of Gabriele's death is 1408, but this has been disputed by Vito Vitale, *Breviario della Storia di Genova,* I (Genova: Società ligure di storia patria, 1955), 151, who gives 1409 as the date.

46. For the Macrobian context of the *Ogdoas,* see E. Ann Matter, "The Afterlife as a Mirror of Princes: Macrobius in the Quattrocento," in *Mind Matters: Studies*

of Medieval and Early Modern Intellectual History in Honour of Marcia Colish, ed. Cary J. Nederman, Nancy Van Deusen, and E. Ann Matter (Turnhout: Brepols, 2009), 233–54.

47. This is discussed at length in the introduction of Weinberg and Matter to *Education, Civic Virtue, and Colonialism.*

48. Ceruti, "*L'Ogdoas,*" 308, translation of Weinberg and Matter.

49. Morpurgo, *L'Ebreo errante in Italia,* 7–10.

50. Domenico Gioffré, *Il mercato degli schiavi a Genova nel secolo XV* (Genoa: Bozzi, 1971), 68, 71 n. 9.

CHAPTER ELEVEN

Hugh of St. Cher and Medieval Collaboration

Lesley Smith

In an essay in honor of a friend and scholar who has so often worked so fruitfully with others, I would like to consider the case of Hugh of St. Cher and the question of medieval collaboration. Hugh was one of the first friars working at the new Dominican house of study in Paris, the city whose university was the most important school for theologians in medieval Europe. He was a prolific and important writer, as well as a prominent ecclesiastical administrator; but there is a question mark over the authorship of his most famous work, the *Postilla in totam bibliam,* which has somewhat blighted his reputation.[1] Some scholars have judged it simply impossible that Hugh could have fitted everything he is credited with doing into a single lifetime and have declared the *Postilla* to be not by Hugh himself, but the product of a team of young Dominicans under his control. Others credit him with even less involvement. In this essay, I would like to consider this question of authorship, partly for its own sake, but mostly to use Hugh's case to suggest that the way we have studied the thinkers and writings of the early schools has done violence to a fuller understanding of what the participants themselves thought they were doing—and so to our historical picture of the time.

Hugh was born, we estimate, around 1190, in southeastern France, in the area around Lyons. There is no evidence for his family or connections, although they are commonly described as decent but unknown.[2] He is traditionally thought to have been a master of canon law, possibly at Paris, possibly teaching canon law in the city.[3] He may well have met Dominic, who was in and out of Paris until his death in 1221. On 22 February 1225 or 1226 (the sources differ), Hugh joined the Dominican Order, again most likely in Paris. By then, he may already have been a bachelor of theology or close to it, and he was certainly well on the way to his mastership in theology in 1229 when he lectured on the *Sentences* of Peter Lombard, the primary textbook of the Paris schools. By the time he was awarded the theology doctorate around 1230, he had probably already served as prior provincial of France (from 1227 to 1230), the first of his many administrative roles. His rise in the Order was swift.

The Dominicans had settled in Paris because it was the best place in Europe to study theology, and so Hugh's qualifications were of the highest academic caliber. From 1230 to 1236 he lectured in the Order's school at their Paris house on the rue St. Jacques. Nevertheless, his academic talents did not protect him from having to take administrative posts as prior of the St. Jacques house (1235–36) and a second term as prior provincial (1236–44).[4] He must have been a likely candidate to be Minister General (the Dominicans' top dog), had he not been made cardinal of Santa Sabina, Rome, in 1244—the first cardinal from the Order. Hugh was a notably active and reforming cardinal: *inter alia,* he championed the introduction of the feast of Corpus Christi, conducted a campaign against pluralism, supported the poverty arguments of the mendicants against their detractors, and worked on a reform of the Carmelite Rule. He died in Orvieto in March 1263.

Although engaging in his own right, Hugh is even more interesting as the archetype of an early Dominican, a perfect example of the sort of man the founder wished to recruit. New religious orders were forbidden by canon thirteen of the Fourth Lateran Council, but the way of life of Dominic's Preachers had been accepted as valid by Innocent III in 1215, as long as they lived under the Augustinian Rule.[5] Unlike the early Franciscans, the Preachers were animated by the organizational vision of their founder and in short order had put in place a program geared to producing trained, disciplined, itinerant clergy, ready and able to care for souls throughout Christendom. Dominic had begun his mission with Bishop Diego of Osma in and around Toulouse in southern France, but his aims soon led him to gravitate to the university towns of Bologna and Paris so that he could recruit educated men as his friars, and so that his friars could work with students. Intelligent men thinking about their faith and their future were just the sort of people Dominic was keen to influence.

It is clear from the beginning that Dominic had a strategy for recruitment—a clear picture of whom he wanted as a brother and whom he did not, in contrast to his contemporary, Francis of Assisi. We have no stories of Francis tracking down and enticing men to join him, but Dominic is depicted as setting his sights on men he wanted and running them to earth: "I was greatly astonished and still wonder by what instinct he called me in this way and clothed me with the habit of the Friar Preachers. For never before had I spoken with him of my entering religion. I think it was through an inspiration or revelation from God."[6] Maturity, experience, and education were all high on Dominic's list of desirable (and necessary) characteristics for his recruits. Francis urged his brothers to avoid learning because it could so easily tempt his Minors to pride, but Dominic positively commanded it for the formation of his Preachers. The earliest Dominican Constitutions (1220) impose a fundamental obligation to study, and Paris was made the first Dominican *studium,* a school for the higher education of friars from across the Order. By 1228, each province had the right to send three students to the St. Jacques house to study for three years. With none of the vacations enjoyed by the students at the secular schools, this made for an intensive program.[7]

The friars did not go to Paris so that they could study in the nascent university: this was forbidden. A statute of the Council of Paris, held under Cardinal Legate Robert Courçon in 1213, banned religious from leaving their cloisters to go to the schools.[8] The schools had, in some sense, to come to them. The Dominicans reached Paris in 1218, and by 1221 had been given a house on the rue St. Jacques by John of St. Albans, dean of St. Quentin. John was a master of theology and taught the friars himself in the house that was now their convent. One of the first students at St. Jacques was Roland of Cremona, who became a master of theology himself in 1229, giving the Dominicans their first university chair; shortly after, in 1230, he was joined by John of St. Giles, already a teaching master, who interrupted his sermon to step down from the pulpit and take up the habit, resuming his preaching as a Dominican.[9] In Bologna, too (the hub of legal teaching), the Order was attracting clever men: three professors of law and philosophy, along with numerous students, joined Dominic's brothers.[10] Master Reginald of Orleans, a renowned professor of canon law, took the habit and was sent immediately to Bologna to strengthen the house there. He was successful as a preacher and recruiter of talent, and in 1219 was sent back to the new Paris house before his subsequent death.[11]

How does Hugh fit into this picture of the ideal Dominican? For the Order, he was a marvelous combination of scholar and practical man, distinctly someone they would have wanted to headhunt. By the time he joined, probably a qualified lawyer and already studying theology, he must have been about thirty-five years of age. His talents easily account for his rise to offices of responsibility: he understood the milieu of the schools and studying, and he knew how to argue persuasively; he was clever, organized, very energetic, with a lawyer's pragmatism. Was he also an obviously spiritual man? We can only suppose so. Most importantly, as we shall see, when the Order got Hugh, it got a terrific team player. As a leader of the French province, he was a learned man looking to train a learned Order; he took stock, calculated what was needed for the education of the brethren in preaching and pastoral work, and set about producing it.

Hugh and his confrères realized very quickly the need for a set of textbooks from which to teach. Since Dominican studying was for a purpose, and this purpose required not only a thorough and sophisticated knowledge of the Bible but also the ability to be able to *use* the Bible effectively in pastoral situations beyond the convent and the schools, it gave a manifest slant for what materials should be provided for its pursuit; and provide them Hugh did. On top of his commentary on the *Sentences* of Peter Lombard, his apprentice-piece for becoming a master of theology (part of which circulated as a manual for confessors), Hugh wrote: a commentary on the *Historia Scholastica* of Peter Comestor (the Bible for beginners); around three hundred known sermons, most now surviving in something like point form, probably *reportationes,* as models for others to learn from; a treatise on the Mass, the *Speculum ecclesiae;* and a series of *quaestiones* on important contemporary theological and ecclesiological issues, such as pluralism.[12] In addition, he was probably involved in producing or directing the production of both a concordance to the Bible and a set of corrections to the biblical text.[13] We might note in passing that, while working on these projects, Hugh and his brethren seem to have revolutionized book layout and production in Paris, importing the pecia method of copying, using the seven-point page layout, and adding biblical cross-references.[14] Already, this output is impressive; but Hugh's name is most closely linked not to these works but to a multi-volume commentary on the entire Bible, running to hundreds of pages in early printed editions, known as his *Postilla* or *Postillae in totam bibliam*. Indeed, the word *Postilla* appears to have been invented to describe Hugh's commentary, and it became the standard title for commentaries thereafter.

This is indeed a substantial body of work, and we must add to it everything Hugh produced as a cardinal and administrator. This total alone has led scholars to argue that Hugh could not really have written all of it himself. In particular, they question the extent of his involvement in the *Postilla*, the very work that made his name. Rather, they say, Hugh was the director of a group of scholars, Dominican brothers at St. Jacques, who produced the work with him; he is the *éminence grise* but not the *onlie begetter*. It is unusual to say that a medieval author worked collaboratively, and Hugh's status as a writer and thinker, particularly in relation to the *Postilla*, is undermined in the eyes of some scholars since he is no longer seen as a brilliant individual, stamping his personality on his material, but more as an efficient organizer with others to do the work. While Hugh is discussed by historians alongside other early Dominicans such as Albert the Great and Thomas Aquinas, or even Raymond of Peñafort and Humbert of Romans, his is seen as a subsidiary role in the beginnings of the Order. Why might this be? It seems that the collaborative label has reduced his stature. But what does collaboration mean in this context, and how and why might Hugh have set about producing his works? I should like to consider the question of Hugh's authorship of the *Postilla*, before looking more widely at the context of authorship in the Middle Ages and how historians of Christian theology have approached it.

In an article from 2004, Robert E. Lerner records Riccardo Quinto (1999), Louis Bataillon (1997), Philippe Buc (1994), and Beryl Smalley (1985, and elsewhere), as all stating that Hugh of St. Cher produced the *Postilla* in collaboration with others.[15] This is certainly a formidable line-up. But what firm evidence is there for the idea that Hugh was not the sole author of the *Postilla*? The idea of Hugh working collaboratively dates back, I think, to a suggestion in a 1949 article by Smalley on the Sapiential Books: "We know that the *correctoria* and concordance . . . were the fruit of team work. Perhaps he prepared his *Postilla*, too, in collaboration with a group of *fratres adiutores*, each one provided with paste and scissors."[16]

Her proposal was taken up in an article of 1952 on thirteenth-century ideas of the Beatific Vision by Hippolyte Dondaine.[17] In this, Dondaine notes that Hugh's *Postilla* contains two differing opinions on a particular question on the Vision, taken from the Latin translation of John Chrysostom on the subject. The *Postilla* on Isaiah determines the question in one way, that on John in another. The conclusion in Isaiah accords with contemporary orthodoxy, while that in John does not (although, of course, orthodox opinion on this matter did change). Having noted these variant opinions, Dondaine speculates about the oversight Hugh might have been able to give to his work:

> Dans quelle mesure la Postille sur saint Jean engage-t-elle maître Hugues? Il est difficile de le dire. L'authenticité ne fait pas question. . . . Mais quelle y est la part de Maître Hugues? Il est arraché aux études dès 1236 par de lourdes charges: provincial de France (1236–1244), cardinal en 1244; déjà provincial en 1227–1230, on se demande où il a pris le temps de mener à bien l'énorme encyclopédie biblique de ses Postilles. Quelle est la part de ses collaborateurs?[18]

This is the extent of his discussion of the matter, and clearly he himself is not sure; like Smalley, he is making a suggestion, not proposing a definite conclusion. Note, too, that Dondaine is referring solely to the *Postilla* on John, not to the whole work: if, as Smalley notes, Hugh probably postillated the Bible in order, John would have been near the end of his labors— and thousands of words distant from Isaiah.

Smalley based her suggestion on the size of the *Postilla* and the evidence that Hugh had employed his fellow friars to construct two particular biblical works—a set of textual corrections (the *correctorium*) and a con-

cordance. We shall consider his role in these works later. Following Dondaine's report of the inconsistency he finds in the doctrine of the Beatific
Vision, in subsequent work, Smalley continues her note of scholarly caution:
". . . we do not know the extent of Hugh's responsibility for the scissors-
and-paste business of compilation."[19] Lerner, however, is positive: "Hugh
of St. Cher the great Dominican commentator on Scripture is a figment of
bibliographers' imaginations. . . . 'Hugh' was never really one author but
always a consortium."[20] Lerner is convinced that the *Postilla* is simply too
big to be the work of any one author. His own investigation into two works
(known by their *incipits* as *Vidit Jacob* and *Aser pinguis*) which each at
some time circulated as Hugh of St. Cher's *Postill* on the Book of Revelation, points up their differences, *Aser pinguis* professing much more radical ideas than *Vidit Jacob*. For Lerner, these differences mean that Hugh
could not have written them both and his solution is that both must have
been compiled by a group of Dominicans at St. Jacques, possibly but not
necessarily overseen by Hugh: ". . . individual friars [had] leeway to work
as they liked; yet some direction existed to produce a modicum of common
outlook within a given postill; yet this direction need not always have been
that of the real Hugh."[21] Indeed, for Lerner Hugh becomes 'Hugh'; and he
is followed in this by Quinto.[22]

There is one further step. In his 2004 article on Hugh, Lerner quotes
Quinto's 1999 article in support of the argument that the *Postilla* was a collaboration. But Quinto says this only because he is quoting Lerner in 1985.
So from scholars with a depth of knowledge about Hugh and his output,
proposing cautious theories about working methods in a particular milieu,
we have proceeded seamlessly to the assured description of a practice over
which Hugh had little or no oversight. The great Dominican commentator
can no longer even be referred to by name:

A point worth emphasizing here is how Dominican teamwork can explain some of the characteristics of Hugh's works, particularly of the
very long biblical *Postilla*. As Robert E. Lerner (and Beryl Smalley before
him) have noted, we should probably put Hugh's name in quotation
marks in front of some of 'his' *Postills*: what goes under 'Hugh's' name
is the product of quite a large Dominican team, and the attitude of the

'author' towards 'his' sources can change radically from one part of the commentary to another . . . our cardinal can say: "My name is Legion, for we are many. . . ."[23]

Smalley's "perhaps" has become a definite "is"; Hugh is no longer an author but an "author," supposedly following Smalley's lead; the *fratres adiutores* of the *correctorium* and concordance have become "quite a large Dominican team" for the *Postilla;* and finally, the "author" is accused of inconsistency toward his sources (Quinto's actual interest), although what that exactly means is not made clear and evidence for any or all of these points is in short supply. Here, then, is a reason why the question of collaboration matters: the idea that Hugh might not have been the sole producer of the *Postilla* can result in a not-so-subtle denigration of his reputation; he becomes "a figment of bibliographers' imaginations."

Viewing Hugh in this way, as a somehow "failed" author, misunderstands the context and purpose of his work for and in the earliest Dominican school and neglects to consider how other, later Dominican authors may have worked. Hugh's assumed collaborative method renders him second rate; yet even if he did work with others as part of a team, the judgment of the work and its purpose seems to be made on modern rather than medieval principles. So we need now to attempt to assess the evidence that Hugh worked in a collaborative team, and to discover, if he did, what sort of oversight he might have exercised on the *Postilla*—was he an involved *chef d'équipe* or an absentee landlord?

As we have seen, modern arguments for Hugh's having worked collaboratively fall into two categories: first, that "it is inconceivable that a single individual could have accomplished such a vast amount of work by himself while also attending to weighty . . . responsibilities";[24] and second, that there is an inconsistency in the arguments presented in the text. Are these, together or separately, strong enough to be decisive? The argument from size is particularly difficult to make in the medieval context when many writers have left us huge quantities of written work. Prolixity is, indeed, almost a defining characteristic of medieval scholarship. The Franciscan biblical commentator Nicholas of Lyra, working a century after Hugh, produced an even bigger set of *Postilla* on the whole Bible on top of his administrative and teaching load, but it has never been suggested that they were written by "Nicholas of Lyra." J. H. H. Sassen, writing of Hugh's period as a cardinal, described the unquenchable energy he brought to the role, and if this was the case then it does not seem unreasonable to suggest that he might have been equally energetic in every part of his life and vocation.[25] Hugh may simply have been one of those people with energy to burn. There are other historical examples of almost unbelievably prolific individuals: J. S. Bach, W. E. Gladstone, A. W. N. Pugin, John Ruskin—each has left a body of work that would seem to belie the finite number of hours in a day.

Second, the fact that the *Postilla* is not always internally consistent cannot, I think, be judged to be determining evidence—in fact, in so large a work it is perhaps more surprising that so few inconsistencies have been detected. The doctrine of the Beatific Vision was relatively new and complex, and, as Dondaine's article was designed to show, in a state of flux in the thirteenth century. Whether we see Hugh as sole author or as editor of a team production, we may explain this inconsistency as the nodding of Homer. Lerner, however, has more strenuous objections to the idea that Hugh can have taken any part in some of the *Postilla*'s books. His argument relies on both Revelation *Postillae, Aser pinguis* and *Vidit Jacob*, being identifiable as Hugh's work. But there is another possible explanation for the divergence: that *Aser,* and indeed the whole alternative "short" version which exists for most of the *Postilla,* should not be associated with Hugh at all. "[L]e toilettage de cette nouvelle édition a été beaucoup plus sommaire (pourquoi?)," asks Carra de Vaux, and his query pinpoints the implausibility of the inferior "short" version having been written by or overseen by Hugh.[26] If Hugh was not responsible for the short edition *Postilla,* then the contrasts between the two versions are explicable, and the changes Lerner details between the two Revelation *Postillae* are the result of the new author(s), who took Hugh's work as one of the sources of his (or their) own.

Recent work on the manuscripts of the *Postilla* by Patricia Stirnemann has only added to the complexity of the question.[27] Stirnemann characterizes her research so far as "très provisoire," but it is clear that the manuscripts of the short version do not appear until around ten to twenty years later than those of the long, and more importantly that the very first copies of the *Postilla* do not cover the entire Bible. Further work on the distribution of the biblical books and the dating of the manuscripts will bring more evidence—if not necessarily more clarity—to the problem.

It has long been known that some manuscripts and early printed copies of the *Postilla* have attributions to other authors, especially for the Psalms. Because of this, Quétif and Échard's eighteenth-century conspectus of Dominican writings reflects a debate as to what should be included. Nonetheless, having considered the materials, they themselves are inclined to be inclusive: "It might have been enough to give this general indication, were it not for those who removed certain items from him and fathered them on others; for that reason, we decided to list them individually by their first and last words, citing too the ancient manuscripts on whose authority the reader may be persuaded of which are his genuine productions."[28]

On the other side, there are positive arguments for Hugh as the author of the *Postilla*. His close contemporaries and successors do not suggest that he was not responsible for the work. Stephen of Salagnac, for instance, writing before 1291 on Dominican luminaries, puts him first on the list of *fratres illustres in scriptis et doctrinis;* being Dominicans, these men are second only to the Order's martyrs in the hierarchy of illustrious friars. Hugh is not at the top of this list for being a cardinal, for he is first on that (separate) list, too, as well as being third in the list of Masters of Theology at Paris.[29] Stephen is judging the men on his lists in terms of specific characteristics and achievements, and Hugh is included for his writing on matters of Christian knowledge. Moreover, Stephen appears careful to differentiate between different sorts of writing. He says that Raymond of Peñafort "*compilavit*" his works on canon law—a case book and a set of decretals. Hugh, however, is not described as a "*compilator*" or "*commentator*"; he is said to "make treatises, books, and postills" (*Qui tractatus et libros et postillas fecit*).[30]

There is medieval evidence that Hugh worked on some projects with other friars. Sometime before 1247, the Dominicans at St. Jacques created the first of three concordances to the Bible that are associated with them. Although not the best or most successful of the three, this first pioneering publication paved the way for the others to follow. According to Bartolomeo of Lucca, it was organized and overseen by Hugh, but the donkey work was done by a group of junior friars: "*primas concordantia super bibliam cum suis fratribus adinvenit.*"[31] We know this was how it was done because four quires, each in a different hand and containing different parts of the alphabet, have been recovered from the bindings of manuscripts from St. Jacques. They appear to be the final draft to be checked and edited before the fair copy was written out. A manuscript of the concordance notes: "*Incipiunt capitula . . . concordantiarum veteris et novi testamenti quas utilitate multorum fratres predicatores compilaverunt.*"[32] A concordance is precisely the type of undertaking that is done better by a group, working to tight rules. Once the basics are laid down by a director, the work benefits from less rather than more individual thought.

Another massive St. Jacques project was the *Correctorium* of the text of Scripture, a list of improvements to the biblical text drawn from early Bible manuscripts and patristic quotation, which attempted to render it more literally accurate. Richard and Mary Rouse judge the first *correctorium* to have been made by William of Sens, but the Dominicans produced at least two more versions, one by a group overseen by Hugh between about 1256 and 1263 when he was already a cardinal.[33] Their evidence for linking Hugh with these productions is limited, although as prior provincial one of his tasks was the supervision and organization of study. Collaborative working on tasks like these would not be unusual; indeed, it would be the most sensible and practical course to take.

Can the same be said of the *Postilla?* More than a biblical commentary, the *Postilla* is essentially a massive updating of the *Glossa ordinaria,* a phrase-by-phrase compendium of interpretation of the Bible. On any given lemma, Hugh quotes or paraphrases the exposition and opinion of the most important patristic commentators, and adds the views of important *moderni,* such as Hugh of St. Victor, Stephen Langton, William of Auxerre, and Bernard of Clairvaux.[34] Hugh must have started (as all commentators at the time did) with a copy of the *Glossa* open beside him, and alongside this he would have wanted the works of the moderns he incorporates. Why would he not have had Dominican helpers working for him, gathering material and sorting out what he was to deal with next? If Hugh was indeed a lawyer, working with clerks who provided his material would have been second nature to him.

Yet the *Postilla* is not only a conglomeration of interpretation thrown together with little order or purpose. Smalley characterizes the *Postilla* as a "mosaic . . . like walking into a house furnished at random from a second-hand furniture store."[35] But although she describes Hugh as a great exponent of the scissors-and-paste method, nevertheless the *Postilla* has a definite identity and distinct virtues, chief among which are clarity and organization. Indeed, this is so much the case that the best way to understand either the *Glossa* or Nicholas of Lyra's great and ubiquitous fourteenth-century *Postilla* is often to read the same lemma first in Hugh; he is generally excellent at explaining the context, stating the issues, and showing what possible solutions have been advanced. And the work is not bland: it collates, but it also disagrees, comments, and decides. We should also note the *Postilla*'s use of Bernard for the mystical exposition of the text. Up to this point, Bernard was not a commonly cited source in scholastic theology; the *Postilla* in effect rescues him from monastic bookshelves. Very unusually, Hugh names his modern sources as well as his patristic ones; this may be another sign that he was trained as a lawyer, since we know that lawyers were more likely to cite all their sources than were theologians.[36] Walter Principe describes Hugh as "masterful in his presentation of the *status questionis,* his summaries, and exposition...."[37] Other readers agree: Hugh is an "organisateur réaliste et efficace"; the *Postilla* "apporte sans cesse des éléments nouveaux"; they have "rien d'une compilation impersonelle."[38] I do not think it is stretching the facts to see these as essentially a lawyer's virtues and to imagine Hugh bringing his legal training to his biblical scholarship.

Have these considerations brought us any closer to knowing whether or not Hugh worked collaboratively on the *Postilla?* In fact, the more we know, the more difficult the questions become. Given the present state of our knowledge of the manuscript tradition, of the two sets of *Postilla,* and of the St. Jacques school, I do not think it is possible to know for certain who wrote what, or supervised what, when. To move the story forward, we will need a modern collaboration far beyond the scope of this essay, between manuscript scholars, experts in the text, and historians of the early Dominican institutions. If we accept that we cannot yet (and perhaps never will) know quite how Hugh was involved in the *Postilla,* might we nonetheless consider some working hypotheses to allow us to look more fruitfully at the question of Hugh's work, to illuminate the nature of his labor and of the *Postilla* itself?

Let us begin by imagining that Hugh was not "a figment," but was indeed involved as the controlling mind in writing and producing the *Postilla* at St. Jacques. Let us further imagine that he worked using Dominican *fratres adiutores* to research and assemble patristic and modern materials for each of the various biblical books. Hugh used some of these materials to give a series of lecture courses on books of the Bible; in the fashion of the schools, he and/or his helpers wrote up or edited these lectures into a version of the *Postilla,* covering much of the Bible.[39] Time and the demands of the syllabus and the Order prevented him from treating the whole text in lectures, but this was clearly desirable, and so the brothers continued to assemble material for Hugh to work into shape. So far, so good: Hugh took the *Glossa ordinaria* of the twelfth century and brought it up to date, not as a controversialist, but as a recorder. His work meant that the Dominicans did not have to rely on having a library of other books in their houses, and the *Glossa,* looking distinctly old-fashioned after almost a hundred years of use, was revisited and given new life in the *Postilla.*

We do not know if Hugh, as prior provincial, thought out for himself what the *studium* needed, or whether he was working to a centrally ordered program, planned by a leadership group. Whichever it was, the work we associate with Hugh provided the Dominicans with their own biblical textbook, along with a set of aids such as *correctoria* and concordances, for better understanding their key working text, the Bible. They could make copies of these themselves (or pay scribes to copy them) and circulate them round the Order; and the *Postilla* was so useful that non-Dominicans wanted it as well. It is possible to set up a comprehensive library of biblical study for a Dominican house with just the few volumes of Hugh's works. This would be very important for a religious order dedicated to learning for the sake of pastoral work, but which was also vowed to poverty, and which valued mobility and wide coverage across European Christendom. How could they make such a combination work? The answer was to provide the materials for their own *bibliotheca.*[40] Hugh's works gave a group of men without the resources of, say, the library of St. Victor, the means to carry through their vocation.

Let us further imagine that Hugh did not write or supervise the later, scrappier form of the *Postilla,* generally (not quite accurately) known as the short version. It exists in far fewer manuscript copies than the earlier version and is not the version printed in early copies; and what we know of it seems at odds with, or to render incorrectly the exegesis in, the earlier set. There is no obvious answer as to why Hugh would have been involved (after he became a cardinal, given the dates of the earliest surviving manuscripts of the text) in producing a botched, abbreviated edition, with added chunks of the redundant *Glossa ordinaria*. If we absolve him from responsibility for the short form, we also remove the need to explain away the inconsistencies between the two.

Now let us think about Hugh working collaboratively: why might he do it and what might it mean for his reputation? All of Hugh's life and work speaks of his practical bent. As a Dominican, he was part of a religious order that thought of itself as truly fraternal, each working for the good of the whole rather than for himself. The entire schema of production at St. Jacques was aimed at the better fulfillment of the Dominican vocation. Evidence for the practical intention of the *Postilla* can be found in the tone and content of Hugh's exegesis. He never loses sight of his audience. Much of what he writes is directed to telling or reminding preachers who they are and how they should act. For example, he uses a memorable variety of metaphors to describe preaching itself: "first the bow [of the rainbow] is bent in study, and then the arrow loosed in preaching"; the preacher is like a cloud, raining doctrine, thundering warnings, or like a deer leaping over thorns, which are riches to be despised. He lists nine properties of preachers, from subtlety in understanding to purity of intention. He tells the brethren to remember who it is to whom they are preaching. He chides those brothers who insist on preaching in Latin even when it is clear that their audience is more comfortable understanding French. (He has the same rebuke for those who refuse to listen to a sermon if it is not in Latin, despising the vernacular.)[41] The *Postilla* is generally laid out in a particularly functional way, in point form, with examples, with a clear taxonomy of the problem, with usable jokes, biblical *distinctiones,* and proverbs: in short, perfect sermon material. Much of the time, the *Postilla* does not read like biblical exegesis for its own sake, but material recounted for a direct purpose. Stephen of Salagnac, describing Hugh's work, reports: "*Qui tractatus et libros et postillas fecit* valde utiles . . . ."[42] Mulchahey says that the *Postilla* was "every bit as much a tool for Dominican preachers as it was a necessary accompaniment to the study of Scripture."[43] This is right, but also wrong; it is *more* useful for preachers than for scholars, because it is the Preachers, and not the "pure" scholarly community, at whom it is aimed.

We must think about this sense of purpose when we consider Hugh's use of *fratres adiutores* and his personal reputation as an author, for it can be too easy for modern scholars to look at medieval works without considering their context. Particularly in the case of authorship, there is a tendency to wear Romantic spectacles, employing the notion of the author, be it of a text, a picture, a sculpture, or any piece of creative work, as an individual (and preferably tortured) genius. This is surely inimical to the medieval view of authorship, which was focused strongly on purpose, rather than on creation for its own sake. In the historiography of medieval religion, the ideal of the single author of genius has had a strong following, culminating in a strand which conceived of the history of the Middle Ages substantially as the History of Christian Philosophy. In this, theology was equated with philosophy (that is, with speculative rather than, say, mystical or pastoral theology), and history of thought in the Middle Ages was conceived of as a kind of Whig History of Thomism: here, Aquinas was the perfection of medieval systematizing, and all other thinkers were judged in terms of his achievement. This history is a history of progress, reaching Aquinas as its peak.

But the cult of the author—a single name to attach to every work—is problematical for the Middle Ages in more ways than one. Leaving aside the enigma of anonymity, in which so many works are shrouded, the technique and structure of some types of medieval material make individual examples hard to distinguish from one another. A great deal of twelfth- and thirteenth-century biblical commentary, for instance, especially that made in Gloss form, is similar to the point of verbatim quotation. Prevailing values favored tradition over novelty, so that Kilian Lynch has argued that the question of originality has no meaning in the Middle Ages.[44] Even where there is no verbal identity, works use the same authoritative quotations, structure, and arguments. Some of these commentaries are so alike as to seem to be different revisions of one work, and textual scholars have attempted to put them in order of redaction.[45] Yet it is not clear that such texts all belong to a single author; some may well be lecture notes, written up and revised by pupils (perhaps for use by a student-turned-teacher). They cannot exactly be called a work by the teacher, but they are not exactly a work by the pupil either. We can see a related issue in exegesis attributed to a single named author. Andrew of St. Victor's Commentary on Jeremiah, for instance, is at least ninety percent verbatim Jerome.[46] The selection (since large swathes of Jerome's commentary are omitted) is certainly Andrew's, and it is not arbitrary, since it sits alongside additional (though rare) comments by Andrew himself or selections from his other, mostly Hebrew, sources. Can this really be regarded as an authorial work by Andrew of St. Victor, even within the reflexive genre of biblical commentary, rather than notes for a commentary that was never completed? Medieval authorship is tightly linked to the notion of *auctoritas*—the authority carried by the writer and transferred to his writings and opinions. Here it is Andrew's *auctoritas* that makes him the author even of such a derivative work; the same, perhaps, can be said for Hugh.

Can we produce another, more medieval model of collaborative work? We need to think of a pattern of individuality and authorship, identity and anonymity, which is very different from our own. In our era, the prizes are given for named authorship and originality; modesty is a rare academic virtue and not useful in institutional, monetary terms. In the Middle Ages, the picture was more complicated. In medieval art, for instance, we are generally unaware of the names of individual makers, and we take it for granted that "an artist" was a group or school of crafts- and tradesmen, with pupils of the master working alongside him. Indeed, some medieval techniques such as fresco required the practice of more than one craft simultaneously to be accomplished successfully, necessarily involving a team at work together. This is a model of working practiced in modern research laboratories, with a leading investigator inevitably supported by a team of junior assistants. For such scientists, collaboration is not a sign of failure, but a practical means of undertaking massive projects; those fortunate enough to be surrounded by assistants are those well funded enough to be judged a success.

So we need to be clear by whose standards—medieval or modern—we are judging these authors and their works. Using modern criteria of authorship and originality will lead us to look at medieval works from the wrong angle. Critics of Hugh's *Postilla* say that it is the product of cut-and-paste, that it is made up of a wide variety of other sources, that it has very little that is novel or unusual in it, that the structure is derivative, and that he did not write every word of it himself. But looked at as fulfilling the immediate needs of a new and growing Order, within the traditions of interpretation and using the resources of manpower available, the *Postilla*'s approach has to be seen in a more favorable light. Placing stress on the Dominican context of production and use helps us to understand what the *Postilla* is and is not trying to be and do, so we can judge it on its own terms. A writer like Hugh was, I would argue, as central to the Dominicans in his time as Thomas Aquinas and Albert the Great were in theirs. In fact, in terms of the Order's growth, development, and status at the crucial early stages of its life, one can argue that Hugh's provision for biblical scholarship and its dissemination throughout the Order as an aid to preaching was even more important. It helped establish the Dominicans from their very beginnings in Paris as a force to be reckoned with, as a group who could achieve their missionary goals unaided, and with scholarly credentials. This surely is how Hugh himself would ask to be judged: not as an innovative philosophical theologian, but as a servant of the Order.

Looking at the material in this way asks us to think about something else, too. All Dominicans traveled in twos—they had a *socius,* a friend or fellow-traveler, who lived and worked alongside them. It is an idea taken from the Gospel, when Jesus sends the disciples out two by two. Who exactly counted as a *socius* and what they did has been little studied.[47] Perhaps the most famous of them was Reginald of Piperno or Priverno, *socius* to Thomas Aquinas and generally referred to nowadays as his "secretary." This term suggests the passive role of someone who simply wrote down what the great man said—Watson to Thomas's Holmes; this is again an imposition of the "great artist" model on a different time and relationship. Yet we know that Reginald taught in his own right after Thomas's death, and to have worked so closely with Thomas for so many years, he cannot have been without intelligence of his own. Yves Congar has considered the meaning of *socius* for Albert the Great, who seems to have used the word in a number of ways, as referring to all his brothers, to his pupils, and to fellow-researchers.[48] It would not be impossible to imagine that the "social" working practices of the Dominicans, perhaps even pioneered by Hugh at St. Jacques, were taken up a little later by the Franciscans in Paris, when they established their *studium:* Bonaventure, too, speaks of *socii* who are, at least, notetakers: "*alii quidem duo socii mecum notabant.*"[49]

I would suggest that, rather than Hugh being the odd man out for working in concert with other friars, his was the common pattern, and historians have erred in preferring not to think of the great Mendicant scholars of the later thirteenth century as anything other than solitary geniuses. They too were likely to have worked in groups, directing those friars who prepared material for them and contributed to the larger work. Congar notes in particular for Albert how often he refers to his work as "*commune bonum intuens,*" and James of Asti, another of Thomas's *socii,* says they took notes "*ad utilitatem fratrum Ordinis nostri.*"[50] These men took their satisfaction not from personal reputation but from the fulfillment of their duty to the Order.

At the present state of our knowledge, we cannot solve the problem of how and with whom Hugh produced some or all of the *Postilla in totam bibliam.* We may never illuminate the situation fully, but to get further will certainly involve modern collaboration between scholarly disciplines to look at different facets of the work in its context. In the meantime, even if we accept the *Postilla* as a collaborative production, we should not on that account dismiss Hugh as a scholar. He was reflecting—perhaps he even invented—the common Mendicant pattern of working. Rather, we should reconsider the working practices and productions of Hugh's later brethren and begin to think of them not as solitary geniuses but as leaders of fraternal *équipes.*

This is a question where the past has been judged by standards other than its own. Of course, we can, and sometimes must, do this, but only when we can first be sure that we understand the material in its own terms, when we have climbed inside its skin and walked around in it. The Thomistic history of medieval theology, or any history of medieval theology that sees it as a branch of philosophy, has limited our view of the medieval intellectual world. This has had implications for all non-speculative theology, which has until recently barely been studied. Similarly, it has led to neglect of the Aquinas who was a pastoral physician and a preacher, or to lament for the

Bonaventure who left the schools to become Minister General of his Order. But first and foremost, both were friars, and to understand them fully we must see them, as we must see Hugh, in the context of service to their Mendicant vocation. Hugh and his *Postilla* need to be judged as part of a whole Dominican picture, not simply as a commentator working in the schools, relegated to the second rank for his fraternal virtuous circle. In scholarship then, as in scholarship today, working together was likely to bring benefits that were more than the sum of the parts. This volume is proof that Michael Signer has shown us the truth of that statement for our own time.

Notes

1. Unfortunately, there is no modern edition of the *Postilla*, but it is available in a number of early printed copies. There is a list in B. Carra de Vaux, "La Constitution du corpus exégétique," Annexe 1, in L.-J. Bataillon, G. Dahan, and P.-M. Gy, *Hugues de Saint-Cher († 1263): Bibliste et théologien* (Turnhout: Brepols, 2004), 43–63, at 56–57. This collection is the only modern, wide-ranging consideration of Hugh and his work and is an excellent launching pad for research.

2. See, most recently, P.-M. Gy, "Hugues de Saint-Cher Dominicain," in Bataillon et al., *Hugues de Saint-Cher*, 23–28, with bibliography.

3. The first note of Hugh as a lawyer is in J. Quétif and J. Échard, *Scriptores Ordinis Praedicatorum*, 2 vols. (Paris: Ballard & Simart, 1719–21), 1.194–202, at 195, but there is no contemporary documentary evidence to support or deny this. From the interest in law shown in the *Postilla*, I am inclined to think that Hugh was a lawyer; see also A. Boureau, "Hugues de Saint-Cher commentateur des *Sentences*. Le cas du sacrement du mariage," in Bataillon et al., *Hugues de Saint-Cher*, 427–64. Lyons, near to which Hugh was born and where he was buried, was noted for the study of law (although it never achieved university status). Although Honorius III banned the teaching of civil law in Paris in 1219 (to encourage the study of theology), canon law was still allowed, but Paris declined as a center of legal teaching in consequence.

4. Gy, "Hugues de Saint-Cher," is dubious that he was prior provincial, 1227–1230.

5. However, Honorius III refers to "*fratres ordinis Praedicatorum*" as early as 1220: see H. Denifle and E. Chatelain, *Chartularium universitatis Parisiensis*, 2 vols. (Paris: Delalain, 1889–91), 1.95. n. 36.

6. Witness from the process of Dominic's canonization, quoted in M.-H. Vicaire, *Saint Dominic and His Times* (New York: McGraw Hill, 1964), 275.

7. A. H. Thomas, ed., *Constitutiones antique ordinis Fratrum Predicatorum,*
in *Die oudste Constituties van de Dominicanen: Voorgeschiedenis, Tekst, Bronnen,
Onstann en Ontwikkeling (1215–1237)* (Leuven: R. H. E. van de Bureel, 1965), Dist. II,
c. 28, pp. 361–62.

8. J.-D. Mansi and P. Labbe, *Sacrorum conciliorum nova et amplissima collectio,* 53 vols. (repr. Graz: Akademische Druck- u. Verlagsanstalt, 1961), 22.838.

9. Hinnebusch says that John of St. Albans was engaged to teach the brothers by Dominic himself: see W. A. Hinnebusch, "Foreign Dominican Students and
Professors at the Oxford Blackfriars," in *Oxford Studies Presented to Daniel Callus,*
Oxford Historical Society, n.s. 16 (Oxford: Clarendon Press, 1964), 101–34. The
question of how the Dominican Roland could become a master in the schools and
the status of the St. Jacques' *studium* vis-à-vis the theology faculty is much debated:
see M. M. Mulchahey, "The Dominican *Studium* System and the Universities of
Europe in the Thirteenth Century," in *Manuels, Programmes de Cours et Techniques
d'Enseignement dans les Universités Médiévales,* ed. J. Hamesse (Louvain-la-Neuve:
Institut d'Études Médiévales de l'Université Catholique de Louvain, 1994), 277–324,
at 290–95, with a good bibliography of the debate.

10. Bologna had higher faculties of law, medicine, and arts, but not of theology; the Dominican *studium* there functioned as a *de facto* theology faculty until
the university established its own in 1364; see W. A. Hinnebusch, "Foreign Dominican Students," 102, n. 2. For Reginald and Bologna, see Vicaire, *Saint Dominic,*
268–75.

11. S. Tugwell, "Notes on the Life of St. Dominic III," *Archivum Fratrum
Praedicatorum* 66 (1996): 5–200, at 50. Since 1995, Tugwell has contributed a substantial article to every volume of *AFP* detailing evidence for the life of Dominic
and the early history of the Order.

12. For Hugh's works see P. Glorieux, *Répertoire des maîtres en théologie de
Paris au XIIIe siècle,* 2 vols. (Paris: Librairie philosophique J. Vrin, 1933), 1.43–51;
T. Kaeppeli, *Scriptores Ordinis Praedicatorum Medii Aevi,* 4 vols. (Rome: Ad S. Sabinae, 1970–93), 2.269–81; and Bataillon et al., *Hugues de Saint-Cher, passim.* I do not
think it likely that Hugh was the author of *De doctrina cordis:* see N. F. Palmer, "The
Authorship of the *De doctrina cordis,*" in *A Companion to* The Doctrine of the Hert:
Latin and Vernacular Contexts, ed. D. Reveney and C. Whitehead (Exeter: University of Exeter Press, forthcoming 2010).

13. See R. H. and M. A. Rouse, "The Verbal Concordance to the Scripture,"
Archivum Fratrum Praedicatorum 44 (1974): 5–30; eidem, *Preachers, Florilegia and
Sermons: Studies on the* Manipulus florum *of Thomas of Ireland* (Toronto: Pontifical Institute of Mediaeval Studies, 1979), 7–36; G. Dahan, "La critique textuelle dans
les correctoires de la Bible du XIIIe siècle," in *Langages et philosophie: Hommage à
Jean Jolivet,* ed. A. de Libera et al. (Paris: J. Vrin, 1997), 365–92; M. M. Mulchahey,

"First the Bow is Bent in Study . . .". Dominican Education before 1350 (Toronto: Pontifical Institute of Mediaeval Studies, 1998), ch. 7.

14. R. H. Rouse and M. A. Rouse, "The Dissemination of Texts in Pecia at Bologna and Paris," in *Rationalisierung der Buchherstellung im Mittelalter und in der frühen Neuzeit,* ed. P. Rück and M. Boghardt (Marburg an der Lahn: Institut für Historische Hilfswissenschaften, 1994), 69–77; eidem, *Manuscripts and Their Makers: Commercial Book Producers in Medieval Paris, 1200–1500,* 2 vols. (Turnhout: H. Miller, 2000), 1, ch. 3. The design and layout of books altered in favor of those who wanted to fillet books for information rather than read them continuously from beginning to end for spiritual edification.

15. R. E. Lerner, "The Vocation of the Friars Preacher: Hugh of St. Cher between Peter the Chanter and Albert the Great," in Bataillon et al., *Hugues de Saint-Cher,* 215–31; R. Quinto, "Hugh of St.-Cher's Use of Stephen Langton," in *Medieval Analyses in Language and Cognition,* ed. S. Ebbesen and R. L. Friedman (Copenhagen: Royal Danish Academy of Sciences and Letters, 1999), 281–300; L.-J. Bataillon, "L'Activité intellectuelle des Dominicains de la première génération," in S. Lusignan and M. Paulmier-Foucart, *"Lector et compilator". Vincent de Beauvais, frère prêcher* (Grâne, France: Créaphis, 1997), 9–19; P. Buc, *L'Ambiguité du livre: prince, pouvoir, et peuple dans les commentaires de la Bible au Moyen Age* (Paris: Beauchesne, 1994); B. Smalley, *The Gospels in the Schools c. 1100–c. 1280* (London and Ronceverte, WV: Hambledon Press, 1985), ch. 4; and see Lerner, "Poverty, Preaching, and Eschatology in the Revelation Commentaries of 'Hugh of St. Cher,'" in *The Bible in the Medieval World: Essays in Memory of Beryl Smalley,* ed. K. Walsh and D. Wood (Oxford and New York: Blackwell, 1985), 157–89.

16. B. Smalley, "Some Thirteenth-Century Commentaries on the Sapiential Books," *Dominican Studies* 2 (1949): 318–55, at 345. Smalley had written on Hugh before this, but with no suggestion that the *Postills* were anything other than his own work, e.g., see "A Commentary on Isaias by Guerric of Saint-Quentin, O.P.," *Studi e Testi* 122 (1946): 383–97. She does, however, seem to have been aware of the possibility of inconsistency, noting (at 395), that "[i]t is doubtful whether he really thought out the implications of his interpretations of the prophecies."

17. H.-F. Dondaine, "L'Objet et le 'medium' de la vision béatique chez les théologiens du XIIIe siècle," *Recherches de Théologie Ancienne et Médiévale* 19 (1952): 60–130.

18. Ibid., 83, and n. 83.

19. Smalley, *Gospels,* 120.

20. Lerner, "Poverty, Preaching, and Eschatology," 157 and 181.

21. Ibid., 183.

22. Quinto, "Hugh of St.-Cher's Use of Stephen Langton"; Philippe Buc removes Hugh's name entirely and refers to "la *Postille dominicaine sur le Lévitique,*"

". . . *sur I Petr.*," or "*Postille dominicaine in I Cor.*": Buc, *L'Ambiguité du Livre*, e.g., 145, 148.

23. R. Quinto, "Hugh of St Cher's Use of Stephen Langton," 290–91.

24. Lerner, "The Vocation of the Friars Preacher," 1.

25. J. H. H. Sassen, *Hugo von St. Cher, seine Tätigkeit als Kardinal 1244–1263* (Bonn: Peter Hanstein, 1908); and A. Paravicini Bagliani, *Cardinali di curia e familiae cardinalizie: dal 1227 al 1254*, 2 vols. (Padua: Antenore, 1972).

26. Carra de Vaux, "La Constitution" (here at 54), considers the two versions and notes the contradictions between them; these differences are noted by a number of other essays in the Bataillon volume, e.g., those by Morard, Lerner, and Stirnemann. I use "short" in quotation marks here because the later version of the *Postills* is not always shorter, but it is always less careful and finished.

27. P. Stirnemann, "Les Manuscrits de la *Postille*," in Bataillon et al., *Hugues de Saint-Cher*, 31–42.

28. "Sat forsan fuisset sic generatim indicare, nisi essent qui ei quaedam auferrent aliisque supponerent: unde visa sunt sigillatim ex principio et fine recensenda additis codd. MS antiquis ex quorum fide qui sint ipsius genuini foetus lector convincatur" (Quétif and J. Échard, *Scriptores*, 1.198b). I am grateful to Dr. Leofranc Holford-Strevens for advice on eighteenth-century Latin. In effect, as far as it is possible to tell, they attribute the "long" version of the *Postilla* to Hugh, with the exception of the *Postilla* on Revelation, where they include *Aser pinguis* rather than *Vidit Jacob*. Quétif and Échard's evidence is reflected in F. Stegmüller, *Repertorium biblicum medii aevi*, 12 vols. (Madrid: Instituto Francisco Suárez, 1940–1980), nos. 3621–3773 (Hugo de S. Caro).

29. *Fratres viri illustres in scriptis et doctrinis* in *De quatuor in quibus Deus praedicatorum ordinem insignivit Stephanus de Salaniaco et Bernardus Guidonis*, ed. T. Kaeppeli (Rome: Institutum Historicum Fratrum Praedicatorum, 1949), 31, 48, 125.

30. Kaeppeli, *De quatuor*, 31 (Hugh), 32 (Raymond). Medieval writers of this period were not unaware of the different status of different kinds of work. Most famously, Bonaventure divides writers into four types, *scriptor, compilator, commentator, auctor*, depending on the amount of their own material and wording they supplied, and this distinction was one that was familiar to contemporaries, not something Bonaventure had invented. See A. J. Minnis, *Medieval Theory of Authorship: Scholastic Literary Attitudes in the Later Middle Ages*, 2nd ed. (Aldershot: Scolar Press, 1988).

31. Bartolomeo of Lucca, *Historia ecclesiastica nova*, 22.2, quoted in Rouse and Rouse, "The Verbal Concordance," 7; they note, however, that Hugh is not associated with the concordance in other Dominican catalogues.

32. MS Troyes, MAT, 2019. R. H. and M. A. Rouse, *Authentic Witnesses: Approaches to Medieval Texts and Manuscripts* (Notre Dame, IN: University of Notre

Dame Press, 1991), 224–25; and eidem, "The Verbal Concordance," 11, n. 25 (here the number of quires is given as five).

33. M. A. and R. H. Rouse, "The Book Trade at the University of Paris, ca. 1250–ca. 1350," in *La Production du livre universitaire au moyen âge. Exemplar et pecia*, ed. L.-J. Bataillon, B. G. Guyot, and R. H. Rouse (Paris: Éditions du Centre national de la recherché scientifique, 1988), 41–114; Dahan, "La critique textuelle"; Mulchahey, *First the Bow*, ch. 7.

34. Sources are listed by Smalley, *Gospels*, 125–43; Dahan, "L'exégèse de Hugues," and A. Sylwan, "Pierre le Chantre et Hugues de Saint-Cher. Contribution à l'étude de leurs sources," in Bataillon et al., *Hugues de Saint-Cher*, 65–99, and 197–212.

35. Smalley, "A Commentary on Isaias," 395.

36. See, for example, J. Warichez, "Les *Disputationes* de Simon de Tournai," *Spicilegium Sacrum Lovaniense* 12 (1932): xviii–xix.

37. W. H. Principe, *Hugh of Saint-Cher's Theology of the Hypostatic Union* (Toronto: Pontifical Institute of Mediaeval Studies, 1970), 20.

38. Carra de Vaux, "La Constitution" (at 51); Dahan, "L'exégèse" (at 99); M. Morard, "Hugues de Saint-Cher, commentateur des Psaumes" (at 129), in Bataillon et al., *Hugues de Saint-Cher*.

39. For evidence for at least some of the *Postilla* being given as lectures see Smalley, *Gospels*, 125.

40. Master-General Humbert of Romans gives a list of books that every conventual library should contain; see K. W. Humphreys, *The Book Provisions of the Mediaeval Friars, 1215–1400* (Amsterdam: Erasmus Booksellers, 1964), Appendix C and ch. 2.

41. *Postilla* on Gen. 9; Gen. 49; Ps. 18 (19); Ps. 134 (135); but the lemmata where he finds a way to talk about preaching and preachers are very numerous.

42. Kaepelli, *De quatuor*, 31, emphasis mine.

43. Mulchahey, *First the Bow*, 500.

44. Lynch is quoted in A. Boureau, "Hugues de Saint-Cher, Commentateur des *Sentences*: le cas du sacrement du mariage," in Bataillon et al., *Hugues de Saint-Cher*, 427–64, here at 429. Boureau adds: "Certes, le souci de la singularité, de l'écart individuel n'a guère de place dans la culture théologique du moyen âge . . . ."

45. C. Mews, "Orality, Literacy, and Authority in the Twelfth-Century Schools," in *Exemplaria* 2 (1990): 475–500, has some interesting examples of this for Peter Abelard.

46. I am grateful to Ms. Christine Feld, whose work on Andrew brought this statistic to my attention.

47. See W. A. Hinnebusch, *The History of the Dominican Order*, 2 vols. (Staten Island, NY: Alba House, 1966–73), 1.57 (Humbert of Romans) and 364.

48. Y. Congar, "'In dulcedine societatis quaerere veritatem'—Notes sur le travail en équipe chez les Precheurs au XIIIe siècle," in *Albertus Magnus Doctor*

Universalis 1280/1980, ed. G. Meyer and A. Zimmerman (Mainz: Matthias Grüne-wald, 1980), 47–57. Congar also gives references to Aquinas and his *socii.*

49. Bonaventure, *Collationes in Hexaëmeron,* quoted in Congar, "'In dulcedine societatis,'" 52.

50. Congar, "'In dulcedine societatis,'" 47–48, 55.

CHAPTER TWELVE

Wessel Gansfort's (1419–1489) Use of Hebrew

Arjo Vanderjagt

It is a truism that the most important, constant, and indeed self-defining issue in Christianity down through the ages from its first beginnings in the New Testament to our contemporary twenty-first century has been its relation to Judaism and the Old Testament. More cogently and certainly more urgently, this might be rephrased in personal terms as the relationship between Jews and Christians, between the text of the Old Testament and its reception. According to the Gospel of Matthew 5:17, Jesus himself establishes such a connection as the foundation of his mission: "Think not that I have come to abolish the law and the prophets; I have come not to abolish them but to fulfill them" (RSV). As arrogantly painful as this imperative must be for Jews, Jesus here does not cast his birthright aside but he posits it as fundamental to his mission. The Christian churches—Catholic as well as Protestant—have, however, in their very bosom an apparent, strong anti-Semitic streak. We have only to refer to medieval pogroms for example in the Rhine valley, to Luther's rabid hatred of the Jews, to the nineteenth-century background of the great disaster of the Shoah in the twentieth, and to the far too mild protests against it by many, often "leading" Christians.

Much of this anti-Semitism—focused especially on Judaism but also on Islam—down through the ages was based on and even intellectually defended by formalist and conceptualist theologies; but the last half century has seen the beginnings of a new point of departure in interreligious dialogue. Risto Jukko has shown that during the second half of the twentieth century beginning with the Second Vatican Council (1962) and extending afterward through the offices of the Secretariat for Non-Christians (SNC) and the Pontifical Council for Interreligious Dialogue (PCID) general, abstract concepts of man's nature and place in reality have given way to approaches concerned with the concrete unity of people as they appear in the world and within history.[1] Influenced by existentialism, phenomenology, and personalism, theology generally has come to emphasize anthropology and "the human being as an existential person, as a 'Thou.'" Christian theology has not hereby become less sure of its origins and faith, as is demonstrated aptly by the words of Pietro Rossano, undersecretary and secretary of the SNC/PCID, quoted by Jukko.[2] But through this new "anthropological" theology, Christians may just possibly be more open to personal interfaith dialogue with Jews and Muslims than when they engage in systematic theology based upon general and formalist theoretical foundations. Much of Michael Signer's work in this important arena has grown out of his own personal experiences and dialogues with Christian friends such as the writer of this piece in his honor.[3] But all of this is not easy. That even a foundational personal attitude is more often than not prone to failure is clear from the vicissitudes of a comparable intellectual movement in the fifteenth century.

In fifteenth-century Europe there was in many religious circles a turning away from scholastic theology and from what was often seen as dry and useless speculation. Berndt Hamm has designated this movement as "Frömmigkeitstheologie" (theology of piety). According to Hamm, this

> 'theology of piety' saw a high degree of simplification and reduction, or 'centering', in comparison to complex scholastic theology and speculative mysticism. Theological knowledge and spiritual experience were boiled down and reduced to those elements considered primary to the didactics of 'piety'. . . . [P]roponents of the 'theology of piety' shared basic assumptions about their task and method, evident in their reduction and simplification of the material with the common aim to provide guidance which was focused almost exclusively on that which aided devotion and led to salvation.[4]

This 'normative centering' put great emphasis on the individual personal piety which was to lead to salvation instead of on intellectual scholastic analysis which yielded general theological knowledge.

This shifting away from systematic theology and toward piety is demonstrated by two very different scholars and pious men of the fifteenth century, both students of Hebrew as well: Giannozzo Manetti (1396–1459), renaissance humanist of Florence, and Wessel Gansfort (1419–1489), northern humanist of Groningen and the IJssel Valley of the northeastern Low Countries.[5] Their knowledge of Hebrew and of the Old Testament was extraordinary for Christians of their time, and it was closely connected to personal pious devotion especially as evinced from their love for the Psalms as Jesus' own voice.[6] One might thus have expected that they had some inclination toward dialogue at least with their teachers of Hebrew if not with other Jews. But nothing is further from the truth. Manetti stigmatizes Jews as willfully misrepresenting the Old Testament—even in Hebrew grammar itself—and for being blind to its fulfillment in the New. Moreover, he considers that since Jews did not choose to understand the New Testament as the *rational* continuation of the Old, they could not be regarded even as possessing human dignity, for which, of course, rationality was seen as a principal requisite.[7] The same attitude holds for Wessel Gansfort. He regards Jews as "enemies of our faith" and goes so far as to claim that much of the Old Testament was divinely written in tropes in order to prevent its Jewish readers from destroying the truth of their own Law and Prophets.[8]

In contemporary scholarship relatively much attention has been given to Manetti's knowledge and use of Hebrew but far less to Wessel Gansfort's.[9] In fact, Gansfort's name, inasmuch as it is known at all, is rarely associated with Hebrew. His learned biographer Maarten van Rhijn discusses Gansfort's love for the Hebrew Bible and in a footnote gives a list of places in his works where Gansfort cites Hebrew sources.[10] Heiko Oberman has importantly given attention to Gansfort's use of Hebrew in his exegetical efforts and in connection with his piety; and, finally, there are three articles by the present author in which Gansfort has a place.[11] This volume honoring Michael Signer, who is very involved with Jewish-Christian dialogue and also highly interested in theology—both activities intrinsically stemming from his sense of piety with regard to both God and fellow human beings—

seems an appropriate place to discuss systematically for the first time all the places where Gansfort uses his knowledge of Hebrew for his own pious reading and even correction of Christian tradition. First a short sketch will be given of Wessel Gansfort's biography; this will be followed by a discussion of the places in his works where he uses Hebrew.

The Life of Wessel Gansfort

Born around 1419 in the very heart of the city of Groningen in the northern Low Countries to a baker's family with just enough money to send him to St. Martin's Latin school, Gansfort was a gifted student.[12] Soon, however, the family fell on hard times and would have been forced to send him out to work had not the burgomaster's wife, Oda Jarges, heard about his plight. She paid for his schooling and then with her own son sent him south to Zwolle on the IJssel River around 1432 to continue his studies at the Latin school there and with the Brethren of the Common Life, with whom the young scholar lived. A quick-witted student, Wessel soon became a master himself, meanwhile striking up an intimate friendship with Thomas à Kempis (1379/80–1471), the author of the mystical work *Imitatio Christi,* which emphasizes personal piety. The devotional practice of the modern devouts attracted Gansfort, but a thirst for scholarship and dialectical precision led him initially to opt for a career of learning. In 1449 he matriculated as a student at the University at Cologne.[13] Taking his degree as *Magister artium* in 1452, he possibly visited Paris soon afterward and certainly taught at Cologne and Heidelberg until about 1460, occasionally visiting Zwolle. In the 1460s he may have spent time in the French towns to which he refers in his writings: Lyon, Limoges, Poitiers, and Vienne.[14] Increasingly disenchanted with scholastic "realist" generalizing systematics, Gansfort hovered around nominalist approaches which had more affinity with individuals and what has been called "experienced reality."[15] His vacillations earned him the sarcastic title "magister contradictionis" before he turned away from the academy to a life of devotion in the service, among others, of the sisters of a convent in Groningen, whose rector he became.[16]

The first references to Gansfort's knowledge of Hebrew derive from a letter written by his compatriot and friend of humanist fame, Rudolph

Agricola (1444–1485), to Johannes Reuchlin (1455–1522), the first great German Hebrew scholar, and from the testimony of Reuchlin to Melanchthon mentioned by the latter in his life of Agricola of 1539, but which he must have heard before the former's death in 1522. Reuchlin is said to have told Melanchthon that while he was studying at Basel between 1474 and 1477, Gansfort privately tutored him there in theology, Greek, and Hebrew. Sometimes called a doctor of theology in the fifteenth century, no record of that degree attached to Gansfort's name has hitherto been found. As for his knowledge of Hebrew, the facts are only slightly less uncertain. According to Van Rhijn, who bases his conjecture on Hardenberg's life of Gansfort, Wessel began to learn Hebrew upon his arrival at Cologne in the early 1450s.[17] Of course it is telling that Reuchlin, in his greatness as a Hebraist, later deigns to remember Gansfort at all as his earliest teacher of Hebrew, who, as we will see, dissuaded him from making a career of it. Clearly, Gansfort possessed more than the not uncommon smattering of a few Hebrew words learnedly displayed by some of the more astute scholastic theologians and devout brethren of the fourteenth and fifteenth centuries such as Nicholas of Cusa.

On 9 November 1484, Agricola from Heidelberg sent a letter, written partly in Greek, to the younger Reuchlin in reply to two letters from him which have not survived.[18] The major theme of this correspondence was the value of a knowledge of Hebrew. Agricola had apparently decided to study Hebrew in the course of 1479, and he had then defended his decision to his medical friend Adolph Occo thus: "I see the Holy Writ as being the most honourable study for my old age, and you know how helpful Hebrew can be to me in this respect. Unless I am simply being too self-indulgent, it will perhaps be the right thing for me to engage in theology in a more sophisticated way, and better equipped with letters than the common run of people. . . . "[19] This demonstrates well the emphasis on piety in the intellectual circles in which Agricola and Gansfort moved, as well as Agricola's disdain for scholastic theologians. In the spring of 1484, Agricola was learning Hebrew from an erudite, converted Jew, whose name is unknown, at the court of Bishop von Dalberg in Heidelberg.[20] It seems that Reuchlin, who had then not yet mastered Hebrew—Gansfort's lessons to him at Basel in the mid-1470s may in hindsight have gained importance in his mind toward the end of his life—was aware of Agricola's venture and wrote him expressing his belief that it was a waste of time (which seems particularly curious in light of his own later interests). Ironically, Agricola countered:

> As you must know, I do not make mistakes without reason, even though it is for the wrong reason. For I think that great men like yourself, who have acquired a famous and illustrious reputation from more distinguished studies [e.g., Greek], can easily account for your lives without studies such as Hebrew.... But ... what will I have to defend my studies from being labeled a form of inertia if I do not try my hand at something more impressive than the common herd?

Agricola reiterated what he had written to Occo and to an Antwerp friend, Jacobus Barbirianus, that he intends to spend his old age studying Holy Writ, adding that Wessel Gansfort had "acriter" encouraged him to learn Hebrew, however much Reuchlin says that the latter had dissuaded him. It seems that Agricola had made enough progress in his Hebrew studies by the end of 1485 and gained some reputation in them for Reuchlin to write him urgently on a matter much debated at that time, namely, the interpretation of God's name in Psalm 54.[21] An answer, if one was written at all, has not survived, and Agricola died on 27 October 1485, four years before his older friend Wessel Gansfort.

But Gansfort's vivid interest in Hebrew can be demonstrated best and more colorfully perhaps by a story he himself enjoyed telling. Possibly during a visit to Florence, Gansfort had struck up a friendship with Francesco della Rovere, Minister General of the Franciscans from 1464 and the cardinal of San Pietro in Vincoli at Rome from 1467.[22] After Francesco's elevation as Pope Sixtus IV in 1471, Gansfort visited him at Rome perhaps around 1473 and sermonized the former Franciscan on his spiritual duties, apparently appalled by the latter's question concerning what worldly goods he might desire and no doubt also aware of the pope's unbridled nepotism and the venality of office under his reign. Pressed by the Holy Father to demand at least something, to his surprise Gansfort had merely asked for Greek and Hebrew Bibles from the Vatican library. These books he had with him when he returned to Zwolle and Groningen around 1477.[23] This story juxtaposes the great tireless *Restaurator Urbis,* the patron of Pinturicchio,

Ghirlandaio, Perugino, and Botticelli, the builder of the Sistine Chapel, in short the universal constructor of papal aesthetic, with the pious *reductor* of human activity to the simple personal perusal and ethical implementation of the dual fount of faith, the Hebrew and Greek testaments.

Gansfort's Use of Hebrew

Without discussing them, Maarten van Rhijn in a note lists the most important places in Gansfort's writings where he treats and puts to use his reading of the Hebrew original of the Bible.[24] An examination of these and a few other closely related citations shows that Gansfort is restrained in demonstrating his scholarship and ingenuity, limiting himself strictly to what he thinks might benefit what elsewhere he calls the salvific *ministerium* of piety.[25] His seems to have been a different sensibility than that of his contemporary humanist friends who gladly touted their learning. In fact, his discussions of the Old Testament are almost invariably connected to the New or to the Psalms, regarded as the "voice" of Jesus through David. In Gansfort's view, the Church's *ministerium* of piety must be founded entirely and directly on the Gospels and the Apostles, thus simultaneously leaving the Old Testament in its own right behind and vaulting over later ecclesiastical papal interpretations back to the New Testament. To be found there is the fount of piety itself. The truth of the Gospel, for example, with regard to the implications and connotations of the second word of the Lord's Prayer, "noster"—most importantly that all our knees must bow to God the Father—is, according to Wessel, so universal—holding for Jew, Christian, and Muslim alike—that it is indirectly found in both "Thalmud & Alcoranus."[26]

Even though the length and the intricate rhetoric of piety of his *De oratione et modo orandi*, the *Scala meditationis,* and *De dispensatione Verbi incarnati et magnitudine passionis* initially suggest otherwise, these works of Gansfort concentrate almost entirely on the salvific devotion which their author derives directly from the Gospels, the book of Psalms, and the Prophets, always using a lucid, expository, and explanatory style.[27] Time and again, Gansfort insists that the first and only rule of faith for any

Christian believer in whatever circumstance is the Gospels and what was handed down by the Apostles. In the early sixteenth century, Albert Hardenberg in his biography of Gansfort writes that to that purpose he, as much as anyone could at that time, sought out the Greek—and by extension—the Hebrew sources in order to understand the meaning of the original texts.[28]

Gansfort's use of Hebrew is concentrated in three of his major works that are still extant. What follows is a list of references. The page numbers given here are from the text of the *Opera;*[29] they indicate the first occurrence of a Hebrew term and its Gansfortian explanation in a given section, which may go on for a page or two.

De oratione Dominica (On the Lord's Prayer)[30]
Liber 3, cap. 5, p. 59
Liber 3, cap. 10, p. 71
Liber 3, cap. 11, p. 74
Liber 3, cap. 13, p. 78
Liber 4, cap. 6, p. 85
Liber 5, cap. 6, p. 97
Liber 5, cap. 10, p. 102
Liber 7, cap. 1, p. 125
Liber 8, cap. 7, p. 149

De causis incarnationis: de magnitudine et amaritudine Dominicae passionis (On the Incarnation: on the magnitude and bitterness of the Lord's Passion)[31]
Cap. 4, p. 419
Cap. 11, p. 437
Cap. 10 (*De magnitudine* etc.), p. 471
Cap. 11, p. 472
Cap. 15, p. 482
Cap. 16, p. 484
Cap. 27, p. 510
Cap. 31, p. 515
Cap. 40, p. 541
Cap. 54, p. 565
Cap. 71, p. 600

De sacramento Eucharistiae (On the Eucharist)[32]

Cap. 8, p. 674

Cap. 8, p. 675

Cap. 10, p. 679

Cap. 14, p. 684

Cap. 14, p. 687

In addition there is a list of passages on the Passion of Christ collected by Gansfort from Scripture; here he quotes the Hebrew text on p. 744.

We are now ready to summarize Gansfort's use of Hebrew and the unconventional insights he had for his time. We are particularly concerned to show how Gansfort applied his knowledge of Hebrew to the explication of those passages from the New Testament that were central to his theological interests and his devotion. To my knowledge, only George Moore, Heiko Oberman, and I have given specific attention to the use which Gansfort makes of his knowledge of Hebrew.[33] It thus seems useful to me to sum up these observations in this contribution so that there might be a single reference point for others interested in further pursuing these studies. Some additional points will also be made.

From the titles of the works in which Gansfort cites Hebrew texts it is already evident that he is seeking to enhance his knowledge of the very crux of his piety, and that he is trying to help his readers along on the same path of the imitation of Jesus. These writings—often in a high rhetorical style— treat Jesus' prayer in Gethsemane, his Passion, and the Eucharist in which he is celebrated. This explains why these treatises and the others in Gansfort's *Opera*—his only surviving works—are not scholastic systematic theology but highly personal, devotional exercises. Gansfort is seeking to understand—indeed, almost to endure—the Passion of Christ. This is certainly true not only for his *Scala meditationis,* a very large work in which he does not quote Hebrew, but also for the writings cited above in which he does.[34] Often, then, his literary style here is not cast in third-person propositions but in first- and second-person performatives. Even when he uses propositional forms, Gansfort's seriatim employment of words such as "noster" draws his reader into a pious exercise—for, in fact, that is what it is. In this context there are three main concatenations of meaning in which Gansfort's knowledge of Hebrew stands central and drives home the point he is making.

The first one is his analysis of Psalms 25:6 in the context of his discussion of the Lord's Prayer.[35] He points out that the Vulgate Latin translates the Hebrew words "rechem" and "chesed" with a single concept, "miserationes/misericordiae." But to understand this passage in the terms of the ordinary Latin meaning of "misery" would be incomplete.[36] Moreover, the Vulgate ignores the fact that "rechem" refers to the motherly womb and that it can be interpreted to signify maternal love, whereas "chesed" means paternal care and love. Gansfort then concludes "quia sicut Deus nobis pater, sic mater est." Therefore, the third scale of the love of God toward us becomes, to quote the medieval Dutch, that of "moederlike goedertierenheit doer welke god tot ons beweecht wort recht als een moeder tot dat kindekijn hoer lichaems."[37] This is an important theme to Gansfort and he employs it as well in his *De causis incarnationis,* in *De sacramento eucharistiae,* and in *De providentia Dei,* albeit without directly citing the Hebrew in these works.[38] Gansfort's remarks on this maternal and paternal affection in connection with the Eucharist and God's providence are especially poignant. In the Eucharist as well as outside it, Jesus is said to burn not merely with human love but with the love of a mother, even a mother with child, for every individual for whom he suffered.[39] Incidentally, this passage also shows that Gansfort likes to move from the general—"human"—to the particular—"mother" in this case, and even more specifically to the very heart of motherhood itself. In *De providentia Dei* (again, more of a personal devotional treatise than a scholastic exposition), Gansfort in first-person anguish cries out: "[I know that God is] my father and mother in all the vital relations of parent and son; I know that the Word incarnate is my brother and sister; I know and admit that the eternal Spirit of the Father and the Son is my friend, my beloved. In spite of this, I am cold, dull, and devoid of affection!"[40] This despondency will not be lifted from Gansfort even in the course of his performative writing. His great consolation comes finally at the end of the treatise: this weakness of feeling hopeless will be removed from him by God when He chooses to do so, and He will not impute it a sin that is as yet not taken away.[41]

Embellishing on this insight into God as both Father and Mother, Gansfort returns in other places to cognates of "rechem." In Chapter 27 of *De magnitudine passionis,* he departs from a discussion of Psalms 108(109):4–5, where "the Prophet speaks in the person of the Lord Jesus: '[i]n return for my love they accuse me . . . , [s]o they reward me evil for good' [RSV]."[42] Gansfort imputes this hatred for Jesus to the Jews, but he continues that yet "[n]ecesse igitur dilectionem Domini Iesu in eis non perfunctoriam fuisse, aut, ut dici solet, superficialem." He compares this love to the sad words of Paul in Romans 9:3, where the Apostle demonstrates his great love for his brethren, the Jews, by exclaiming that he could even desire to be cut off from Jesus for their sake. And Gansfort poses the question of whose love is greater, that of Paul or of Jesus. The answer is obvious: Paul's love has a difficult choice to make between either his brethren or Christ; but Christ's love, "for all and therefore also for me," is as boundless as the sand on the seashore. In conclusion, Gansfort then quotes the beginning of Psalm 18(17), "Diligam te, Domine," putting it in his readers' mouths. He points to the Hebrew "Archamcha Jehovah," and describes his love for God in the first person singular, in feminine, maternal terms: "hoc est, matercaliter amabo te Domine; vel, matercaliter movebor in te; aut, matercaliter miserabor tui Domine."[43] That Gansfort's insight into the feminine aspect which he reads in the Hebrew is extraordinary for his time can be seen from the commentary on the same Psalm by his Italian contemporary, Pico della Mirandola, a great Hebrew scholar, who ignores it.[44] And yet this high, very personal, devotional insight leaves Gansfort with little charity toward Jews (as is clear from the above), even though Christ's love transcends that of Paul (who chooses Christ rather than his Jewish brethren) by encompassing everyone universally "etiam pro singulis." Apparently Gansfort has here landed in an irresolvable "spagato."

The second cluster of meaning in which Gansfort's knowledge of Hebrew comes to the fore concerns the name of God. For Gansfort a study of the names of God is not merely a philological exercise, and neither is that name "only" a name.[45] Just as the sun is reflected in an ordinary mirror, albeit on a smaller scale, so also our thinking minds always reflect "a small God."[46] This simple, general, and direct knowledge that we have of God, Gansfort in *De oratione et modo orandi* calls "the name of God": "Nomen ergo Dei notitia est, qua Deus cognoscitur."[47] We are duty bound to develop our knowledge of this name, and the best and most efficient way to do this is by taking seriously the Bible, especially the words of Jesus himself. Hence

Gansfort castigates the Jews as liars who, according to Jesus' own words in John 8:48–59, do not know the Father because they do not recognize him. Immediately after Gansfort has mentioned the universality of "*Our* Father," adducing the Talmud and Koran (as we have seen above), he discusses the Trinity in Hebrew terms. His point in this section is that Our God and Lord loves and enjoys (*amat et gaudet*) being called "Pater noster"; the Word, "frater noster"; and God the Holy Spirit, "amator noster."[48] In the Hebrew of the Old Testament, Gansfort sees these same meanings in three names used for God: "ita in Hebraeo germana etiam sunt nomina, *Abim, Ahinu, Abahim.*" Obviously for anyone with even a sprinkling of Hebrew, something is quite wrong with Gansfort's understanding of these terms. He seems to be grasping at the correct forms "Avinu" (our Father), "Ahinu" (our Brother), and a form of "Ahav" (our Lover). Moore has pointed out this problem with Gansfort's Hebrew as it is printed in the text of 1614 and attributes it, correctly it seems to me, to the printer of that volume.[49]

Similarly, Gansfort gives much attention to other words denoting (the name of) God.[50] Oberman has written about Gansfort's remarks about God's self-revelation in Exodus 3:4, traditionally given in English as "I am who I am"—rendered in the Latin Vulgate as "Ego sum qui sum."[51] The Hebrew, insists Gansfort, is "ehejeh asher ehejeh" and this translates into the Latin in the future tense: "'Ero qui ero' and without the pronoun 'Ego.'"[52] He thus undermines the philosophy and theology of being which is underwritten by the scholastics, in which God is the supreme Being: [God] "semper erit quod non comprehendant."[53] Interestingly, too, Gansfort formulates an understanding of the Trinity in this context, and also a history of hermeneutics in which he defends the 'classic' translation of "Ego sum qui sum" by St. Jerome and the doctors of the Church. However, now that Christian doctrine has been firmly established, it is important to make known the truth of the Hebrew original in order to stem the ridicule of the Jews.[54]

Throughout his works, Gansfort continues to discuss this and various other Hebrew names of God.[55] That he distinguishes these names carefully for theological purposes but also for a better devotional understanding is clear from a short debate with Bernard of Clairvaux on the passion of Christ.[56] Wessel says that Bernard's interpretation of Isaiah 6:1 ("vidi

Dominum sedentem": I saw the Lord sitting upon a throne [RSV]) is incorrect "cum tamen originalis Hebraica veritas non *Adonaj* habeat, sed *Iohavah* tetragrammaton, absolutum naturae Dei nomen, absque ulla dominationis connotatione."[57] This is important because in this passage Gansfort stresses obedience issuing from love—the implication of the name of God *par excellence*—and not the aspect of domination and its connotations. It should be pointed out here as well that Gansfort's phrase "Dei nomen" is significant, too. He once again suggests hereby, as we have seen above, that God Himself cannot be seen but only reflected as "name."

This entire point of the names and the naming of God is of great importance to Gansfort in the context of his theology of piety—or perhaps better said, of his devotional directives. His concept of God is not that of a highest Being, whether as defined and discussed by the scholastics or by Aristotle and Averroes. The problem is that God so conceived can have no personal relationship with human beings. He can by definition have no real contact with the world; He cannot love what He Himself has created; He cannot will anything outside Himself.[58] For Gansfort, God is not an Absolute Being —"I am who I am," an ultimate *Esse* or even *Non Esse;* rather He is: "Shall be who shall be," "Ero qui ero." Or, as Oberman has succinctly phrased it, He is always "ahead," beyond human grasp. To this must be added that God thus leads the way individually and personally for everyone and everything in His creation and is intimately attached to each of them.

Closely connected to 'the name of God' are other unexpected insights which Gansfort gleans from his knowledge of Hebrew and his interpretation of the Old Testament in connection with the New. He puts forward the idea that the word "ruach" at the root of the name of the Holy Spirit denotes an element of fragrance.[59] Coming to the second Person of God, he notes that the second word of the *titulus* of the Cross might be read "HaNozri," or in Latin "Floridus," allowing him to exclaim to Jesus, "Esto mihi rex, o floridi rex."[60] Gansfort's is also the sympathetic idea that Christ, the consolation of the faithful, came to save not only human beings but also animals, a notion which he discusses in the context of his interpretation of the name "Maher Shalal Hash Baz" (Isaiah 8:3).[61] In general Gansfort's work is not dry and distanced scholarship; rather it is normatively centered around his pious concerns as well as those of his readership and the practitioners of his devotional method. Hence, it is often worded directly and insistently in the first- or second-person performative language of faith, not in third-person declarative expository learning.

The third clutch of interpretations of terms from the Old Testament which demonstrates Gansfort's knowledge of Hebrew is directly related to his views on Christ and the Eucharist. Although I have discussed this point elsewhere, it must at least be mentioned here because it is so central to his ideas of salvific devotion.[62] In this context, Gansfort repeatedly quotes Psalm 110(111):4–5: "Escam dedit timentibus se"—"He [i.e., God] provides food for those who fear him" (RSV).[63] Thus in *De magnitudine passionis* Gansfort points out that the meaning in the Psalm text of the Hebrew "Thereph" (= taraph), translated into Latin as "esca," is not only that of "food": "He does not provide mere food but rather meat torn by a wild animal: He provides '*Thereph*' for those who fear Him."[64] This point is important because it connects the Psalm directly to Hebrews 13:11–12 by way of Leviticus 6:23 and Exodus 22:13: Jesus is the lamb who was torn apart for his people outside the city gates—the "hostia," a telling word in Catholic theology, of course, as Exodus has it in the Latin more correctly than the "esca" of the Latinized Psalm—and at the same time he is the high priest in eternity.[65] Thus Gansfort explains in *De sacramento Eucharistiae* that Jesus' body is food for salvation for the faithful and food for condemnation for the unfaithful, whom Gansfort identifies in the first instance as the Jews.[66]

In conclusion, Gansfort uses his knowledge of Hebrew almost exclusively in the context of these three central points of Christian doctrine. There are only a few other places where he quotes Hebrew words.[67] Most of Gansfort's extant writings are written in a very personal, non-scholastic style. As noted at the beginning of this essay, we might thus expect that he would have had an eye for 'conversation' with those outside the Christian community, especially in view of the fact that Jews preserved the very texts with which Gansfort had to engage in order to better understand and develop his own theology of piety and devotion. Regrettably this was not the case. We are sad that in the early twenty-first century our exciting, moving, and deeply religious conversation with Michael Signer has come to an end.[68]

Notes

1. Risto Jukko, *Trinity in Unity in Christian-Muslim Relations: The Work of the Pontifical Council for Interreligious Dialogue* (Leiden: Brill, 2007), ch. 2, "Philosophical and Theological Influences on a Dialogic Roman Catholic Attitude," esp. 77–91.

2. Ibid., 78–79.

3. See e.g., Michael A. Signer, "*Speculum Concilii:* Through the Mirror Brightly," in *Unanswered Questions: Theological Views of Jewish-Christian Relations,* ed. Roger Brooks (Notre Dame, IN: University of Notre Dame Press, 1988), 105–27); and the introduction to the present volume by Franklin T. Harkins.

4. Berndt Hamm, "Normative Centering in the 15th and 16th Centuries," in *The Reformation of Faith in the Context of Late Medieval Theology and Piety,* ed. Robert J. Bast (Leiden: Brill, 2004), 1–50, here 19–20; see also my "Wessel Gansfort (1419–1489) and Rudolph Agricola (1443?–1485): Piety and Hebrew," in *Frömmigkeit— Theologie—Frömmigkeitstheologie. Contributions to European Church History. Festschrift für Bernd Hamm zum 60. Geburtstag,* ed. Gudrun Litz, Heidrun Munzert, and Roland Liebenberg (Leiden: Brill, 2005), 159–72.

5. Much of what follows in the next three pages is based on several articles I have authored, namely: "Wessel Gansfort (1419–1489)"; "Mediating the Bible: Three Approaches. The Cases of Giannozzo Manetti (1396–1459), Wessel Gansfort (1419–1489), and Sanctes Pagninus (1470–1556)," in *Cultural Mediators: Artists and Writers at the Crossroads of Tradition, Innovation, and Reception in the Low Countries and Italy 1450–1650,* ed. Annette de Vries (Leuven: Peeters, 2007), 23–40; and "*Ad fontes!* The Early Humanist Concern for the *Hebraica veritas,*" in *Hebrew Bible/ Old Testament. The History of Its Interpretation,* vol. 2, *From the Renaissance to the Enlightenment,* ed. Magne Saebø (Göttingen: Vandenhoeck & Ruprecht, 2008), 154–89.

6. See Vanderjagt, "*Ad fontes!*" and the bibliography given there.

7. Ibid., 172–73.

8. Heiko A. Oberman, "Discovery of Hebrew and Discrimination against the Jews: The *Veritas Hebraica* as Double-Edged Sword in Renaissance and Reformation," in *Germania Illustrata,* ed. Andrew C. Fix and Susan C. Karant-Nunn (Kirksville: Northeast Missouri State University Press, 1992), 19–34, at 32.

9. On Manetti see especially Paul Botley, *Latin Translation in the Renaissance: The Theory and Practice of Leonardo Bruni, Giannozzo Manetti, and Erasmus* (Cambridge: Cambridge University Press, 2004) and the literature cited there. For a careful linguistic analysis of Manetti's labors, see Christoph Dröge, *Giannozzo Manetti als Denker und Hebraist* (Frankfurt am Main: Peter Lang, 1987); cf. Vanderjagt, "*Ad fontes!*"

10. Maarten van Rhijn, *Wessel Gansfort* (The Hague: Nijhoff, 1917), 66–68, 89–93. That this important and engagingly written book was published in Dutch

was no doubt an important obstacle to the reception of Gansfort in the English-speaking scholarly world. Some fifteen years later, Van Rhijn published a set of follow-up essays (also in Dutch): *Studiën over Wessel Gansfort en zijn tijd* (Utrecht: Kemink, 1933).

11. Oberman, "Discovery of Hebrew," and his "Wessel Gansfort: Magister con-tradictionis," in *Wessel Gansfort (1419–1489) and Northern Humanism,* ed. Fokke Akkerman, Arjo Vanderjagt, and Gerda C. Huisman (Leiden: Brill, 1993), 97–121. For my own articles see note 5 above. As this essay was going to press I happily found an older, insightful article on some aspects of Gansfort's knowledge of Hebrew, apparently not known to Oberman either: George F. Moore, "Notes on the Name יהוה," *The American Journal of Semitic Languages and Literatures* 28.1 (1911): 56–62, for Gansfort especially 61–62. Although Moore does not consider Gansfort's knowledge of Hebrew very profound, he sees it as valuable for his attempt—one of the earliest in the Renaissance—at pronouncing the Tetragrammaton.

12. This is a slightly revised version of several paragraphs in my "Wessel Gansfort (1419–1489)." For a full biography see Van Rhijn, *Wessel Gansfort,* 23–155, and the important corrective update in Jaap van Moolenbroek, "Wessel Gansfort as a Teacher at the Cistercian Abbey of Aduard," in *Education and Learning in The Netherlands, 1400–1600: Essays in Honour of Hilde de Ridder-Symoens,* ed. Koen Goudriaan, Jaap van Moolenbroek, and Ad Tervoort (Leiden: Brill, 2004), 113–32; and his "The Correspondence of Wessel Gansfort: An Inventory," *Dutch Review of Church History* 84 (2004): 100–30. A seminal study on Gansfort and a translation of some of his works into English is Edward W. Miller and Jared W. Scudder, *Wessel Gansfort: Life and Writings. Principal Works,* 2 vols. (New York: Knickerbocker Press, 1917); unfortunately, especially the first volume is marred by many errors.

13. Erich Meuthen, *Kölner Universitätsgeschichte,* Band I: *Die alte Universität* (Cologne: Böhlau, 1988), 205–6; on the attraction of Cologne for scholars from Groningen, including Rudolph Agricola: 93–94, 213–14.

14. Van Moolenbroek, "The Correspondence of Wessel Gansfort."

15. For Gansfort's relation to "realism" and "nominalism," see Henk A. G. Braakhuis, "Gansfort between Albertism and Nominalism," in *Wessel Gansfort (1419–1489) and Northern Humanism,* 30–43; Maarten J. F. M. Hoenen, "*Albertistae, thomistae* und *nominales:* die philosophisch-historischen Hintergründe der Intellekt-lehre des Wessel Gansfort (+1489)," in *Wessel Gansfort (1419–1489) and Northern Humanism,* 71–96; see also Oberman, "Wessel Gansfort," esp. 100–3.

16. Wessel Gansfort's extant works were published at Groningen on the occa-sion of the founding of the university in 1614: *M. Wesseli Gansfortii Groningensis rarae & reconditae doctrinae viri, Qui olim Lux Mundi vulgò dictus fuit, OPERA,* ed. Joachim Altingh and Petrus Pappus à Tratzberg (Groningen: Sassius, 1614; facsimile reprint: Nieuwkoop: B. de Graaf, 1966). Some of his work was translated: see Miller and Scudder, *Wessel Gansfort,* vol. 2.

17. Van Rhijn, *Wessel Gansfort*, 66–68. It must, however, be noted here that Hardenberg's memory is not always to be trusted.

18. Rudolph Agricola, *Letters*, ed. Adrie van der Laan and Fokke Akkerman (Assen: Van Gorcum, 2002), Letter 41, 226–31.

19. Ibid., Letter 18, 144–46.

20. Ibid., Letter 38, 216–17; Agricola was acquainted with a number of Jews and Jewish converts to Christianity, among them the well-known Flavius Wilhelmus Raimundus Mithridates, later teacher of Pico della Mirandola; cf. Letter 47, 246–47. On Mithridates, see Franz J. Worstbrock, "Die Brieflehre des Konrad Celtis. Textgeschichte und Autorschaft," in *Philologie als Kulturwissenschaft. Festschrift Karl Stackmanm*, ed. Ludger Grenzmann, Hubert Herkommer, and Dieter Wuttke (Göttingen: Vandenhoeck & Ruprecht, 1987), 242–65, here at 257ff.; and especially Chaim Wirszubski, *Pico della Mirandola's Encounter with Jewish Mysticism* (Jerusalem: Israel Academy of Sciences and Humanities, 1989).

21. Agricola, *Letters*, Letter 52, 256–57; cf. Vanderjagt, "*Ad fontes!*"

22. Van Rhijn, *Wessel Gansfort*, 90ff., 103ff. Wessel Gansfort is not mentioned in recent studies on Sixtus IV, e.g., *Un pontificato ed una città: Sisto IV (1471–1484)*, ed. Massimo Miglio et al. (Vatican City: Scuola Vaticana di Paleografia, Diplomatica e Archivistica, 1986), and Egmont Lee, *Sixtus IV and Men of Letters* (Rome: Storia e letteratura, 1978).

23. Gansfort's Greek Bible has probably been lost; he must have had his Hebrew text with him at the Cistercian St. Bernard Abbey at Adwert near Groningen after 1477, for there is a contemporary account that the younger monks laughed at the strange sounds the pious master made while reading from it aloud. It seems some leaves from this Bible were still extant in the early seventeenth century. Recently a folio of Hebrew (Joshua 21:7–38 and 17:6–18:21), probably written in Italy in the twelfth century, was extracted from the covers of a collection of Bonaventure's works (printed in 1495) once in the Franciscan library at Groningen. It is difficult to imagine that Christians other than Gansfort in this northern city would have then been able to read Hebrew. Still, chances are slim that this is indeed part of Gansfort's Bible because the text is Aramaic in Hebrew characters; cf. *Hel en Hemel*, ed. Egge Knol, Jos. M. M. Hermans, and Matthijs Driebergen (Groningen: Museum, 2001), 83–84.

24. Van Rhijn, *Wessel Gansfort*, 67; this list has twenty-four items. Gansfort often cites from the Old Testament but apparently does not always need the Hebrew to clarify his thought. Only a part of Gansfort's writings is extant; it is likely that there was more Hebrew in the large notebook which he always carried with him (he called it his "Mare Magnum") and in other writings which were destroyed soon after his death, allegedly by friars who were afraid that these contained heterodox theological opinions.

25. Gansfort, *Opera: De sacramento poenitentiae*, 892.

26. Gansfort, *Opera: De oratione dominica*, 71.

27. Gansfort, *Opera: De oratione et modo orandi*, 3–192; *Scala meditationis*, 193–412; *De dispensatione Verbi incarnatio et magnitudine passionis*, 457–654. Although Miller and Scudder, *Wessel Gansfort*, claim that they translate Gansfort's "Principal Works," they do nothing of the sort. By "principal works" they mean those writings of Gansfort which can be brought to bear directly on Reformed doctrine and what is seen as its proto-history. Hence they leave many of Gansfort's works, including the last two just mentioned, untranslated.

28. Albert Hardenberg, *Vita Wesseli Groningensis*, in Gansfort, *Opera*, **[1v]: "sed quaesivit fontes quantum omnino potuit pro tempore illo."

29. Gansfort, *Opera*.

30. Ibid., 3–192.

31. Ibid., 413–654.

32. Ibid., 655–708.

33. See the works cited in notes 5, 8, and 11 above.

34. Gansfort, *Opera*, 194–412.

35. Gansfort, *Opera: De oratione*, 59–61; cf. the Dutch vernacular translation of this work (c. 1500) edited by Anne J. Persijn, *Wessel Gansfort. De oratione dominica in een Dietse bewerking* (Assen: Van Gorcum, 1964), 113–14; see also the discussion of this point in Oberman, "Discovery of Hebrew," 28–29, and in his "Wessel Gansfort," 114–16; cf. Vanderjagt, "*Ad fontes!*" 62–63.

36. Gansfort, *Opera: De oratione*, 59: "Unde & in Hebraeo Deus non misericors a sensu miseriae, aut misereri dicitur; sed vel gratificare, vel materno affectu tractare, vel paterna in filium paternitate profluere potius quam misereri."

37. Persijn, *Wessel Gansfort: De oratione*, 117; cf. Gansfort, *Opera: De oratione*, 61: "Viscera, seu pietas materna, qua sicut mater super puero uteri sui, ita super nobis afficitur."

38. Gansfort, *Opera*, 453, 697, 721.

39. Gansfort, *Opera: De sacramento Eucharistiae*, 697: "Quis dubitabit, ita posse hoc simul tempore fieri extra Eucharistiam, sicut in Eucharistia? Quis ad singulos, pro quibus passes est, non humano dico, sed materno, quin & matricio eum flagrare affectu?" Compare Miller and Scudder, *Wessel Gansfort*, vol. 2, 58.

40. Gansfort, *Opera: De providentia Dei*, 721; cf. Miller and Scudder, *Wessel Gansfort*, vol. 2, 90.

41. Gansfort, *Opera: De providentia Dei*, 733.

42. Gansfort, *Opera: De magnitudine passionis*, 508–11.

43. Ibid., 510–11. The Hebrew word has the light connotation of a mother's womb. In his *De sacramento eucharistiae* (*Opera*, 679–80), Gansfort issues these words of the Psalmist from the Virgin's mouth, comparing her love for Jesus with that of the Magdalene. It must be noted here that the printer of the 1614 edition of Gansfort's works makes a mistake by printing "Ar(c)hanicha," obviously confusing "ni" for a handwritten "m".

44. Pico's commentary on this phrase reads: "Erchomcha significat amare et diligere, quod Septuaginta sequuti sunt, et hoc modo potissimum exponunt Hebrei. Significat etiam supplicare, sed, cum potius victoria sit, non supplicat sed agit gratias." See Ioannis Pici Mirandula, *Expositiones in Psalmos,* ed. Antonio Raspanti (Florence: Olschi, 1997), 132.

45. Van Rhijn, *Wessel Gansfort,* 164–71.

46. Gansfort, *Opera: Scala meditationis,* 222.

47. Gansfort, *Opera: De oratione,* 88.

48. Ibid., 72.

49. Moore, "Notes on the Name," 62; as I have noted (note 43 above) the printer is responsible for a similar error in another context.

50. Ibid. Moore discusses Gansfort's statement in *De oratione,* 102–3, to which the latter returns a number of times in other places as well: "Manifeste Salomon, Proverb. 8, quando dicit, *Iehaiiel ohabe Ies,* ponit *Ies* nomen Dei substantivum, sicut *Ehola, Iah,* & *Iohavah.* Sunt ergo praeter pluralia de *El* & *Eloha,* sex nomina substantiva apud Hebraeos: *El, Eloha, Elohim, Iah, Ies, Iohavah, Eheje, Aser, Ehejeh.*" (Incidentally, it seems to me that the last three words, which are in fact a single Hebrew phrase, were separated with commas by the unlearned printer; if those commas are removed and the "*El*" heading the list is not counted—it has already been mentioned just before—the number of six in Gansfort's text also makes sense.) In addition, Moore points out how Gansfort struggles with the transliteration of the Tetragrammaton, uniformly writing "Iohavah," as, for example, in the quotation given here and in a number of other places.

51. For discussions of this point see Oberman, "Discovery of Hebrew," 29–30, and his "Wessel Gansfort," 104–5; cf. Vanderjagt, "Wessel Gansfort (1419–1489)," 171–72; cf. also a remark by Moore, "Notes on the Name," 62.

52. Gansfort, *Opera: De oratione,* 74–75; *De causis incarnationis,* 419–21.

53. Gansfort, *Opera: De causis incarnationis,* 421.

54. Ibid., 419.

55. Gansfort, *Opera: De oratione,* 72, 74–78, 85, 97–98, 101–3; *De causis incarnationis,* 419–20, 436–37.

56. Gansfort, *Opera: De magnitudine passionis,* 483–84.

57. This also demonstrates that Gansfort's manuscript text was one of many that for this passage in Isaiah indeed used the Tetragrammaton instead of the "Adonai" of our modern printed editions. Moreover, it shows that Gansfort had carefully compared the Latin and the Hebrew texts on this point.

58. Gansfort, *Opera: De causis incarnationis,* 420, 548; cf. Van Rhijn, *Wessel Gansfort,* 159.

59. Gansfort, *Opera: De oratione,* 125. Moore, "Notes on the Name," 62, castigates Gansfort for reputedly transliterating "Ruach" and "Eloah" as "Rucha" and "Eloha," "a mistake a man would hardly make who had had even elementary

instruction in pronunciation from a Jewish teacher." It is, however, highly likely that Gansfort was instructed in Hebrew at Cologne by a Jewish teacher. The error in our printed text would again seem to be the printer's; alternatively, Gansfort may be using an Aramaic text (which would comport with the manuscript leaves discovered a few years ago; see note 23 above).

60. Gansfort, *Opera: De causis incarnations,* 403; *De magnitudine passionis,* 472–73.

61. Gansfort, *Opera: De magnitudine passionis,* 589–90: "Grandis igitur consolationis verbum est nomen Iesu *Maher Salal Chabaz* omnibus hominibus bonae voluntatis, quantumlibet imperfectis: quia propter parvulos parvulus factus non solum parvulus esse voluit, sed insuper in praesepio reclinari, vere spoliator velox, vere festinus praedator, quando non solos homines, se & jumenta salvat. Quid enim divino consilio virgineis maternis manibus in praesepe ponitur in stabulo Iesus, nisi quia jumenta salvare venit?" Note here, too, Gansfort's usage, "*nomen* Iesu" (my italics). For these three examples, cf. Vanderjagt, "Wessel Gansfort (1419–1489)," 172.

62. Vanderjagt, "Wessel Gansfort (1419–1489)," 172, and Vanderjagt, "*Ad fontes!*" 163–64; I have not used the following passage in these earlier articles.

63. Gansfort, *Opera,* 149, 515–29, 541, 684–88.

64. Gansfort, *Opera: De magnitudine passionis,* 541.

65. Ibid., 541–42: "*Thereph,* quoniam ab impijs lacerata. Sacerdos, quia constitutus a Deo. Iustitiam igitur indutus est super omnes. Erit igitur et ipse cibus, ipse hostia, ipse Sacerdos, ipse Deus, ipse panis propositionis, ipse nutriens, roborans, confortans, transformans. Et quia tulit infirmitates nostras, ipse est medicina nostra."

66. Gansfort, *Opera: De sacramento Eucharistiae,* 684–89. Gansfort entirely excludes the Jews even to the extent of calling them unclean by his explanation of the Old Testament injunction upon which he founds his exegesis of Hebrews 13 (689; the English translation is from Miller and Scudder, *Wessel Gansfort,* vol. 2, 41): "It is as though he [i.e., God] said: 'The sin offering shall be offered outside the camp and not in the tabernacle, because, being torn to pieces by wild beasts, to the Jews it shall be unclean; but since it is made outside the synagogue, to the nations it shall be as offered in a clean place.'"

67. E.g., in Gansfort, *Opera: De sacramento eucharistiae,* 674–75 (derivations of the so-called "Bread of Faces" and of the word for "faith"); *De magnitudine passionis,* 482 (exegesis of Psalm 17:5) and 656 (the meaning of "testamentum"); *De magnitudine passionis,* 744 (exegesis of Psalm 89).

68. I am grateful to my friend and colleague Wout van Bekkum, Professor of Semitics at the University of Groningen, for his keen eye and constructive criticisms in matters of Hebrew language and exegesis.

CHAPTER THIRTEEN

"The Guardian of Israel neither Dozes nor Sleeps"

*Exegesis, Polemics, and Politics in the
Late Medieval Jewish-Christian Encounter*

Jeremy Cohen

A brief chapter in Solomon ibn Verga's early-sixteenth century Hebrew work *Shevet Yehudah* (The Staff of Judah) presents a fitting opportunity to pay tribute to a dear friend and colleague. For the substance and ramifications of ibn Verga's text intersect with both the scholarly and personal interests of Michael Signer: biblical interpretation, both Jewish and Christian; cooperation and hostility between Jews and Christians both during the Middle Ages and in modern times; concern with fostering mutual understanding between the two religious communities; and, not least, the love of a good story itself.

Our text reads as follows:

> It happened in Spain, when the non-Jews reported that they had found a corpse in the home of a Jew, that one of the king's advisors spoke incriminatingly against the Jews. Then the people declared forcefully to the king that, if he would not administer justice, they would avenge the dead man of their own accord.

The king said: "Praise and exalt the true ruler and righteous judge, a faithful God, never false! Now I shall expose your lie and my courtier's evil counsel. All this you should behold and recount to those who follow you."

He then ordered that all the Jews be brought before him, and when they assembled, he asked: "What is the meaning of David's words, 'See, the guardian of Israel neither dozes (*yanum*) nor sleeps (*yishan*)' (Psalm 121:4)?[1] For if he does not doze, then it goes without saying that he does not sleep, since in Hebrew, as I have heard, sleeping (**shenah**) exceeds [and therefore would be subsumed within] dozing (*tenumah*)." The Jews replied: "Our commentators explained it to mean simply that he does not doze, and *a fortiori* that he does not sleep."

The king said: "That answers the question with the question itself! They have not understood what Scripture intends to say, whereas here is its meaning, as I have witnessed with my own eyes. Last night I could not rest or sleep at all, and thus I arose from my bed, went into the outer hall, and peered with my head out the window. The moon was bright, and I saw people running—one with what looked like a human figure on his shoulder. And I sent three men to follow them at a distance, to determine carefully whether it was a dead person or something else, and to report to me. My servants proceeded as I instructed; they lay in waiting, saw that it was a dead person, and recognized two of the men transporting the corpse—as they are here to testify themselves." They came and so testified, and the king's counselor asked them: "Why did you not apprehend those men?" They responded: "Because they went quickly, threw the corpse in the Jew's courtyard, and ran away; moreover, they bore weapons while we had none, since the king had not ordered us to capture them but only to investigate." The king then returned to the matter at hand and said: "When Scripture says, 'See, he neither dozes nor sleeps,' it means that neither does he [God] doze nor does he allow him who protects the people of Israel to sleep."

All [the Jews' detractors] then left disappointed, while he [the king] punished the conspirators.[2]

The motif of the rescue of Jews from a slanderous libel owing to the sleeplessness of their king spans the long history of Jewish folklore. It has roots in the biblical book of Esther; and one finds the invocation of Psalm 121:4 in tales of ritual murder accusations in diverse contexts, ranging from anthologies like the early modern Yiddish *Ma'aseh Buch* on the one hand, to present-day internet sites where the story is simply attributed to *Ma'asei ha-Tzadikim,* or tales of the righteous, on the other hand.[3] As Eleazar Gutwirth has shown with reference to the inquisitorial records of Segovia, a notably similar version of the story already circulated among Spanish conversos as early as the 1460s.[4] Yet I propose here to focus on the rendition of the story in *Shevet Yehudah,* where it numbers among an array of accounts of blood libels that threatened the stability and very survival of medieval Jewish communities.[5]

Largely complete by around 1520, though not published until the mid-1560s, *Shevet Yehudah* was one of the most popular Hebrew books of its day. It captivated many a Jewish reader with some six dozen stories of trial and tribulation endured by the Jews, from the destruction of the Second Temple in the first century CE to the persecution of Spanish-Portuguese Jewry in the fifteenth and sixteenth centuries, and the resolute survival of the nation of Israel despite such suffering. *Shevet Yehudah* and its author prove no less fascinating for the present-day historian, both for their preservation of collective memories of old and for the dimensions of a critical, transitional phase in Jewish history that they illuminate.

Exiled from Spain in 1492 and presumably baptized against his will in Portugal before the turn of the century, Solomon ibn Verga numbered among the conversos who subsequently left Portugal after the Lisbon Massacre of 1506. His life thus witnessed the downfall of Iberian Jewry—the largest, most colorful, and perhaps most self-conscious of Jewish communities in medieval Europe—and the dispersion of Sephardic Jews throughout various areas in Christian Europe, Muslim North Africa and the Middle East, and the Ottoman Empire (that from 1516 incorporated the land of Israel). He experienced the highly problematic phenomenon of Marranism, the crypto-Judaism of tens of thousands of Iberian Jewish converts to Christianity, in all of its religious, social, and cultural complexity—both in his relationship with the conversos of Spain before the expulsion of 1492 and in his own experiences in Portugal. He evidently died (perhaps in Northern Europe) en route from Western Christendom to Ottoman Turkey, and he therefore tasted of the dynamic multidimensional processes whereby conversos reassumed their Jewish identities and ultimately reentered the Christian West on a qualitatively new basis. Perhaps most interestingly, in its ideas no less than in the biography of its author, *Shevet Yehudah* bridges the divide between the world and values of the Middle Ages and those of early modern times. The work appears to break out of its medieval milieu, challenging regnant assumptions, offering new solutions to age-old problems, hinting at modern, enlightened ideas, and seeking a viable basis for Jewish survival in an essentially hostile non-Jewish world. *Shevet Yehudah* accordingly offers the historian a treasure trove of insights into the precarious, transitional situation of the Jews and their worldview on the eve of modernity—and the particular perspective of one Jewish intellectual grappling with the changing world around him.[6]

Our story from *Shevet Yehudah* appears to take shape around three overlapping concerns:

1. *The ritual murder accusation.* As noted, such accusations figure repeatedly in ibn Verga's collection of stories, and I have recently dealt with the place and significance of the blood libel in *Shevet Yehudah* at some length.[7] Suffice it to note here that, while the conspiracy to condemn the local Jewish community for the murder of a Christian encases the narrative at hand, neither does the story record actual historical events[8] nor does it evince significant interest in the phenomenon of the blood libel itself. The narrator tells us nothing about the murder or its victim. No one hints at any ritual dimension to the crime of the Jews; we learn nothing about the specific locale or the time of year (Purim? Passover? Easter?) in which the events supposedly occurred or the reasons for the antagonism between Jews and Christians. The crime of the murder is never resolved, and the story therefore lacks tension or suspense. No one debates or ever wonders seriously whether Jews in fact commit ritual murder, as medieval European Christians might have done, nor does the story seek to refute the ritual murder accusation in general. Rather, the characters appear simply to fulfill their predetermined roles. Those actually responsible for the murder habitually seek to incriminate the Jewish community by bringing the corpse to a Jewish home. The wicked counselor of the king exploits the opportunity to attack the Jews; he incites the mob against them; and the mob threatens to undermine the stability of the regime by taking justice into its

own hands. For his part, the king never for a moment doubts the falsity of the libel, which his insight and insomnia allow him to expose, thereby mollifying the public pressure exerted upon him.[9]

2. *Exegetical discussion and debate.* Indeed, far more interesting and noteworthy than the blood libel in this tale is the exegetical discussion sparked by the king's insomnia, which results in his rescue of the Jewish community from disaster. Within the narrative itself, in other words, the anti-Jewish conspiracy serves simply as an excuse for the king to engage the Jews on the implications of sleeplessness in Hebrew Scripture. Before revealing his proof of the Jews' innocence, he summons them to court, confronting them with the following challenge:

> "What is the meaning of David's words, 'See, the guardian of Israel nei-
> ther dozes (*yanum*) nor sleeps (*yishan*)' (Psalm 121:4)?" For if he does not
> doze, then it goes without saying that he does not sleep, since in Hebrew,
> as I have heard, sleeping (**shenah**) surpasses [and therefore would be
> subsumed within] dozing (*tenumah*)."

Why the redundancy? Why, asks the king, does the psalmist state twice in one sentence that God does not sleep? And to the Jews' (technically correct) reply that the verse simply wishes to make its point more emphatically, the king objects that their answer merely reiterates his question. The king proceeds to explain how his own sleeplessness has enabled him to save the Jews from their enemies, and he then returns to the exegetical issue that interests him even more. "When Scripture says, 'See, he neither dozes nor sleeps,' it means that neither does he [God] doze nor does he allow him who protects the people of Israel to sleep." When God does not doze, he prevents the true guardian of Israel—*none other than the king himself*—from sleeping.[10]

The entertaining nature of this exegetical consultation notwithstanding, the interpretation-history of Psalm 121:4 in both Jewish and Christian traditions[11] certainly nourished—and gave expression to—the often antagonistic encounter between them during the Middle Ages, and it therefore bears directly on the depth and significance of our story in *Shevet Yehudah*. The psalm itself numbers among the pilgrimage psalms or "songs of ascents,"[12] as it assures Israelite wayfarers, whether en route to the temple in Jerusalem or simply traversing the difficult course of life, that the God of creation and of Israel will protect them with unceasing vigilance.

> I turn my eyes to the mountains; from where will my help come?
> My help comes from the Lord, maker of heaven and earth.
> He will not let your foot give way; your guardian will not slumber.
> *See, the guardian of Israel neither slumbers/dozes*[13] *nor sleeps!*
> The Lord is your guardian; the Lord is your protection at your right hand.
> By the day the sun will not strike you, nor the moon at night.
> The Lord will guard you from all harm; He will guard your life.
> The Lord will guard your going and coming now and forever.[14]

Although modern biblical scholars have debated over a dozen possible understandings of the historical context or *Sitz im Leben* in which Psalm 121 originally took shape,[15] the basic import of the verse, part of a response to the opening (perhaps somewhat plaintive) question of the psalm's opening words, appears clear enough: genuine blessing and protection will come to the Israelite not from the mountains or any other source, but solely from the divine creator of heaven and earth. On the heels of the preceding verses, as biblical scholar Arthur Weiser noted, the assertion that "the guardian of Israel neither dozes nor sleeps" testifies to the truth that "creation and history, past and present, are welded into a unity. . . . History is not something past and complete in itself; it is an activity of God which in a significant way extends into the present. This is why the individual, too, as a member of his people has a share in its history and in the God who is at work in it. . . . The saving will of the Creator-God is also directed to him personally, and thus he comes to trust in his care in all circumstances."[16] As such, Psalm 121:4 would seem relatively straightforward, confronting its readers with few blatant exegetical difficulties. Medieval and modern commentators concerned with the primary meaning of the biblical text have occasionally dwelled upon the different terms employed to denote God's slumber/ dozing and sleep. Raising what appear to be the obvious questions, they have noted the fullness, the perfection, of divine providence emphasized by the verse, and they have understandably associated the verse with Israel's yearning for divine redemption.[17]

Removed from the immediate context of Psalm 121, however, "the guardian of Israel neither dozes nor sleeps" evoked an extensive array of noteworthy concerns among rabbinic and ecclesiastical scholars alike. Jewish homilists, for instance, cited our verse in wrestling with the implications of God's unrelenting sleeplessness. God rules over sleep, just as he rules over other negative qualities like jealousy; and sleep, like eating and drinking, characterizes the inferior realm of human beings in contrast with the superior realm of the deity.[18] God is never unaware of what befalls his creatures. His perpetual wakefulness shows how the prophet's cry, "then would I weep day and night for the slain of my poor people" (Jeremiah 8:23, and see also 14:17), can refer only to God himself; no human being could weep constantly, since "it would be impossible not to eat, drink, and sleep."[19] Echoing an ancient midrash, a thirteenth-century liturgical commentary related that because the first human being created by God was "so beautiful, the angels sought to declare 'Holy, holy, holy' before him, and God cast a deep sleep [Gen. 2:21] upon him so as to say, 'Not so! See, it is the guardian of Israel that neither dozes nor sleeps.'"[20] And just as they beheld sleeplessness as a distinguishing characteristic of God, so did the rabbis extrapolate from our verse regarding the singular protection afforded by the "guardian of Israel" to his chosen people.[21] Divine providence, suggested some, was in principle Israel's alone and extended to other peoples only secondarily, as a byproduct of God's care for the Jews.[22] This unflinching divine guardianship could well explain the pointlessness in the Moabite king Balak's insistence that Balaam curse the Israelites in the desert of Midian.[23] It oversaw the rise and fall of nations, kingdoms, and empires over the course of human history in the utmost detail, ensuring that foreign powers would not rule over Israel.[24] And it even preserved the integrity of critical class distinctions within the people of Israel itself (priests, Levites, Israelites, etc.). One midrash asked in this vein,

> By what parable may the verse [Psalm 121:4] be illustrated? By the parable of a mortal king who was sitting on his throne, in front of him a golden salver on which were figs, grapes, pomegranates, nuts, dates, dried figs,

apples, and citrons. Sitting over them, he sorted them, putting the figs apart, the dried figs apart, the citrons apart, and so on. And as he turned away to other matters, the wind came up and mixed all the fruit together again. Thereupon sitting to the task again, he sorted them once more, putting the figs apart, the grapes apart, the pomegranates apart, the nuts apart, the dates apart, the dried figs apart, and the apples apart. And again as he turned away to other matters, the wind came up and mixed up the different fruits all over again.

Just as this human king kept his fruits sorted, so does the divine king of Israel keep the classes within his people separate and distinct. For "had the Holy One let go of Israel for two or three successive generations, the ten different classes would have freely intermarried, and Israel would have become [mixed] like the peoples of the world."[25]

Yet did such an idyllic picture—of a Jewish people free of foreign domination, its ideal internal class distinctions preserved intact—exceed the bounds of credibility? Rabbinic preachers themselves had experienced the harsh realities of exile and dispersion, foreign rule, religiously motivated discrimination against their people, and the despondency in which these could result. Didn't circumstances "on the ground" often suggest that God had actually fallen asleep, that his commitment to protect Israel had perhaps lapsed? Or, homiletically, if "the guardian of Israel [in fact] neither dozes nor sleeps," why did the psalmist implore him (Psalm 44:24), "Rouse yourself, why do you sleep, O Lord?" Had God made good on the promise of Psalm 121, the poet of Psalm 44 would not have to supplicate, "Awaken, do not reject us forever!" Some rabbis suggested that the description of a sleeping God was not genuine but illusory (*kivyakhol, ke-ilu, nidmeh*), the expression of a temporary state in which the Jewish people (especially outside the Land of Israel) suffered in exile under foreign rule and the Gentiles prospered.[26] But as the Spanish king declared in Solomon ibn Verga's blood libel tale, such an answer may simply have reformulated the question: for the time being, the guardian of Israel may well have dozed off. Others invoked the biblical contrast between "a time for protecting and a time for discarding" (Ecclesiastes 3:6) to suggest that the natural rhythm of human history mandated such periods of rise and decline in the destiny of Israel: "A time for protecting, as Scripture states, 'See, the guardian of Israel neither dozes nor sleeps'; and a time for discarding, as Scripture states, 'He cast them into another land [as is still the case]' (Deuteronomy 29:27)."[27] Still other homilists strove to explain that God's sleepless vigilance on Israel's behalf ostensibly fluctuated according to their compliance with his will. "Is there truly sleep in the divine realm?! Rather, when Israel sins, God makes it appear as if he sleeps, as Scripture states, 'Rouse yourself, why do you sleep?' But when the Jews do God's will, 'See, the guardian of Israel neither dozes nor sleeps.' "[28] The travails of Jewish experience, however, kept any of these explanations from laying the matter permanently to rest. In the wake of the downfall of Iberian Jewry, thus did Rabbi Isaac Yavetz poignantly explicate the poet's predicament at the opening of Psalm 121: "Behold, in my exile I was like a person standing between two mountains, when a robber approached him and sought to kill him. Seeing that there was no one to rescue him, he lifted his eyes to the mountains, to see from where help might come."[29]

Christian exegetes read Psalm 121:4 in a manner instructively similar to that of their Jewish counterparts. While any attempt to trace the influence of one commentator on another lies beyond the purview of this essay, a brief, comparative overview will serve our purposes well. Just as the rabbis did, patristic authors—and the medieval churchmen who followed them—viewed both the sleeplessness and the protective vigilance attributed to God in our verse as emblematic of his divinity. As Augustine wrote in his commentary on Psalms, "God is never asleep: If you wish to have a guardian who never sleeps, choose God as your guardian. . . . So do not seek to rely on any human being; for every human slumbers and will sleep. When does he slumber? When he bears the flesh of infirmity. When will he sleep? When he shall be dead."[30] The absence of divine protection accordingly renders any human protection worthless. God is the protector par excellence, and the term guardian (*custos*) actually numbers among the names of God. Inasmuch as the Hebrew word Samaritan (**Shomer**oni) includes the Psalm's word for guardian (**shomer**), commentators like Epiphanius Latinus followed Origen and Augustine before him in citing our verse to identify the proverbial good Samaritan (Luke 10) as none other than Christ himself, who mercifully tended to a wounded traveler after a priest and Levite had ignored him.

Thus a Samaritan going that way and seeing him was filled with mercy. Such is not stated of the priest and Levite—that they were filled with mercy. For the law is not one of mercy, but of justice and vengeance. So let us make our way to our Samaritan. This Samaritan is our Lord, to whom the blaspheming Jews said, "You are a Samaritan and have a demon" [John 8:48–49]; and when he responded, saying "I have not a demon," he did not deny that he is a Samaritan. For Samaritan means guardian. He who descended from heaven to protect and save our souls is therefore our Lord—of whom the prophet had previously foretold: "See, the guardian of Israel neither dozes nor sleeps."[31]

And as Chromatius of Aquileia (d. 406–407) explained Jesus' walking on the water of the stormy sea toward his disciples' ship precisely during the fourth watch of the night (Matthew 14:22–23), God's protection of his elect extends continuously over the course of terrestrial history:

We should attend to the significance of this fourth watch, in which God approached his disciples as they endured the storm. The first watch of this night—that is, of the present age (*saeculi praesentis*)—is understood to extend from Adam to Noah. The second watch extends from Noah to Moses, through whose agency the law was given. The third watch extends from Moses to the coming of the Lord the savior. In these three watches, even before the Lord came incarnate, he used his vigilant angels to defend the camp of his saints from the attacks of their enemies, the devil and his angels who from the creation of the world have plotted against the welfare of the just. . . . The fourth watch is understood as the present age, from the time when the son of God saw fit to be born and suffer according to the flesh. During this everlasting watch he promised his disciples and church following his resurrection, "I am with you always, to the close of the age." David, too, understood this eternal protection of the Lord when he said: "See, the guardian of Israel neither dozes nor sleeps."[32]

Like rabbinic interpreters of Scripture, Christian exegetes felt obliged to address the problematic implications of divine slumber and wakefulness.

John Cassian cited both "Rouse yourself, why do you sleep, O Lord?" (Psalm 44:24) and "the guardian of Israel neither dozes nor sleeps" to consider the issue of divine anthropomorphism in Scripture and to conclude that "without horrible profanity these things cannot be understood literally of him who is declared by the authority of Holy Scripture to be invisible, ineffable, incomprehensible, inestimable, simple, and uncompounded."[33] How, then, should one explain particular attributions of sleep to Jesus, as well as to God the Father? Using Psalm 121:4 to postulate that God never sleeps, some churchmen distinguished between the humanity of Christ, to which sleep did appertain, and his divinity.[34] Some agreed that the impression of divine sleep amounted to human illusion.[35] And others explained references to God's sleeping as metaphoric, effectively transferring the attribution of sleep from the deity to humans. Ambrose put it quite simply: "He who guards over you does not sleep, so long as he does not find you asleep."[36] In a similar vein, Cassiodorus commented on Psalm 121 that "people speak of the Lord slumbering when we grow lukewarm in our belief in him. . . . If we abandon contemplation of him, he too withdraws himself from protecting us, as happened in the ship when the disciples grew careless, and the Lord slept [Mark 4:35-41]. But when their faith was roused, the Lord too rose from sleep and at once shifted the perils of the deep from them."[37] Simply put, spiritual slumber resides in the faithlessness of skeptical Christians and the hearts of infidels, who entertain the false impression that God sleeps. In scenes such as that mentioned by Cassiodorus—when Jesus slept during a storm while on the boat with his disciples—such an impression can have a positive function, prodding doubters to call out to God, and thus rousing them from their own slumber.[38]

The most forceful Christian resolution of the seeming contradiction between allusions to divine slumber and the declaration that "the guardian of Israel neither dozes nor sleeps" echoed rabbinic interpretation in asserting that God's role as an ever vigilant, provident guardian applies to Israel and not to others. Yet Israel for the churchman entailed not the biological descendants of Abraham but his spiritual progeny, God's elect,[39] or, as patristic tradition (that derived from Philo the Jew of Alexandria) interpreted the Hebrew *Yisra'el,* those that truly see God. Augustine thus instructed the Christian faithful,

"See, the guardian of Israel neither dozes nor sleeps." For Christ guards over Israel, so be you Israel. What is Israel? Israel means one who sees God. And how is God seen? First through faith, then through actual sight. If you cannot yet actually see him, then see him in your faith. If you cannot behold his face, inasmuch as this is what actual sight would entail, then behold his back. This is what was said to Moses by God (Exodus 33:20–23): "You cannot see my face, [but] you will see my back when I shall pass by."[40]

Here Augustine echoed Hilary of Poitiers before him in explaining the term "Israel" in our verse, while Prosper of Aquitaine, Cassiodorus, Julian of Toledo, Gerhoch of Reichersburg, and others followed in their wake.[41] The sleeplessness of God prevents true believers from dozing or wavering in their faith; as the twelfth-century Gerhoch of Reichersburg noted, "He sleeps, to be sure, for the slumbering, indolent servant, while he stands guard for the good, vigilant servant."[42] Or, as the Jesuit Robert Bellarmine put it centuries later, "He who guards his very own people—which is meant by Israel, and which includes all those wayfarers who live in this world and hasten to ascend to their heavenly fatherland—never slumbers or sleeps."[43]

3. *Interreligious polemic.* Allowing for essential differences between the beliefs of Jews and Christians, the sources we have considered manifest extensive similarity in the way that rabbinic and ecclesiastical exegetes, ancient and medieval, interpreted the statement that "the guardian of Israel neither dozes nor sleeps." Yet the ritual murder accusation figuring prominently in *Shevet Yehudah* evolved against the background of theologically grounded debate, competition, and antagonism so characteristic of Jewish-Christian interaction during the Middle Ages.[44] Psalm 121:4 also had applications for the Jewish-Christian debate—owing to its designation of God as the guardian of the chosen people on the one hand, and the homiletic transference of ostensibly divine sleep to the imperfect realm of human beings and their misperceptions on the other hand—and these, too, must inform our appreciation of the tale that Solomon ibn Verga has brought us.

Polemical overtones reverberate, for example, in a rabbinic midrash on the biblical book of Esther, which expounded the malicious appeal of the Jews' archenemy Haman to the Persian king Ahasuerus: "There is (*yeshno*) a certain people, scattered and dispersed among the other peoples in all the provinces of your realm, whose laws are different from those of any other people and who do not obey the king's laws; and it is not in your majesty's interest to tolerate them" (Esther 3:8). The homilist drew from the likeness between the Hebrew word for "there is," *yeshno,* and that for "he sleeps," *yashen,* and thus interpreted Haman's affront to God: "The holy one, blessed be he—of whom Haman has suggested, 'the Lord (that) is one' has fallen asleep for his people—declares: Sleep does not at all pertain to me, as is written in Scripture, 'the guardian of Israel neither dozes nor sleeps'; and yet you have dared to say that I sleep! By your life, I shall rise as from sleep against that very person (*oto ha-ish*) and eliminate him from the world!"[45] Haman has evidently concluded from the present circumstances of the Jews that their God has fallen asleep, that he has proven remiss in guarding them, and that one can therefore crush the Jewish people quite readily. God, however, responds that his vigilant protection of Israel endures and that he will obliterate Haman's presence altogether. Such a rabbinic protest against the presumption that the God of Israel has forsaken his people suggestively echoes the patristic claim—expressed, as elsewhere, in commentaries on Esther—that God has transferred his covenant from the old Israel of the flesh to the new Israel of the spirit. And the image of Haman, eventually hanged for plotting against the Jews, frequently evoked that of the crucified Jesus, straightforwardly in Jewish lore and more indirectly—even subliminally—in Christian tradition.[46] This particular midrash renders such a reading virtually unmistakable by referring to Haman as "that very person" (*oto ha-ish*), a term whereby rabbinic Jews have typically denoted Jesus, whose name they have preferred not to utter. God, as this homily would have it, will yet rise to destroy the crucified Jesus and his Church, saving his people Israel from ruin.

For Jewish polemicists of the Middle Ages, Christian use of our verse to allege that God had ceased to protect Israel perhaps led understandably to their own refutation of Jesus' divinity on similar grounds. One of the earliest Jewish anti-Christian treatises of the period, *The Book of Nestor the Priest,* challenged believers in Jesus in precisely such fashion:

> Do you not know that Jesus fell asleep in a boat and a great storm arose upon them, until his disciples woke him up and he awoke and called to the Lord and the storm was quieted? Furthermore, he slept at a wedding

of a groom and he got drunk, but the verse states, "Woe to those who are heroes at drinking wine, etc." In the village of Simon he was sleeping again, and a Samaritan harlot came and fell at his feet. He slept until they woke him up. I wonder how you could command me to worship a God who sleeps all the time. Did not David say, "See, the guardian of Israel neither dozes nor sleeps"?[47]

Some two hundred years later, *Sefer Niẓẓaḥon Yashan* (*Nizzahon Vetus*) reiterated this message more succinctly in criticizing the gospels' report that Jesus slept while sailing during that tempestuous evening (Mark 4, Matthew 8): "It says that he was asleep; but if he were God, how could he sleep? It is, after all, written, 'See, the guardian of Israel neither dozes nor sleeps.'"[48] In a word, our verse demonstrates that the true God does not fall asleep.

Christian writers incorporated Psalm 121:4 just as directly into their own *Adversus Judaeos* polemics. In understanding Jeremiah 14:9 to foresee the transfer of God's covenant from Jews to Gentiles and from Temple to Church, Jerome wrestled with the Septuagint's rendition of the verse: "Why are you [God] like a man who sleeps, like a warrior who cannot prevail," and to the similar words of Psalm 44:24, "Rouse yourself, why do you sleep, O Lord?" Jerome cautioned: "This does not mean that God sleeps, concerning which it is written, 'See, the guardian of Israel neither dozes nor sleeps'; but it does mean that to those whom he has deserted he seems to sleep."[49] He who had once guarded the Jews with ever sleepless vigilance now appears to them to slumber. But Jerome did not stop with attributing a false impression of divine slumber to the Jews; God had in fact withdrawn his protection from them, such that Psalm 121:4's promise concerning the guardian of Israel no longer applied to them. Commenting on the words of Isaiah 1:8 that "Zion is left like a booth in a vineyard, like a hut in a cucumber field," Jerome noted that "Israel as a whole is designated a vineyard," just as Psalm 80:9 addresses God: "You plucked up a vine from Egypt; you expelled nations and planted it." But this same psalm then cries out (vv. 13–14): "Why did you breach its wall, so that every passerby plucks its fruit, wild boars gnaw at it, and creatures of the field feed upon it," and Jerome explained: "As long as this vine bore copious fruit, it had the Lord as its keeper, as is written: 'See, the guardian of Israel neither dozes nor sleeps. . . .' Yet when such fruits will have been removed, only bowers of thorns and huts [will] remain, inasmuch as the caretaker, having nothing more to guard, will leave. Thus the omnipotent God has forsaken his temple and rendered his city deserted. It is not necessary to prove this at length, especially not to ourselves, who see Zion deserted, Jerusalem overturned, the temple consigned to utter ruin."[50]

Isidore of Seville intertwined different strands of Jerome's interpretation of Psalm 121:4 in his influential polemical work *De fide catholica contra Iudaeos* in a chapter "On the Ruin of Jerusalem." Deprived of God's protection, "Zion will be torn apart by its adversaries." The divine promise then concludes: "I shall destroy its walls so that it will lie open before its enemies, and I will command the clouds to drop no rain upon it."[51] And just as rabbinic homilists did, Richard of St. Victor glossed the book of Esther's description (6:1) of the king's insomnia as referring not to the Persian Ahasuerus but to God himself, since "the guardian of Israel neither dozes nor sleeps." Here began the dramatic reversal of fortune that culminated in the salvation of Israel and their defeat of their enemies, which for Richard had striking contemporary relevance: "Thus the pride of the Synagogue is defeated, and the humility of Ecclesia exalted; thus the persecutors of the church and the faith are reduced to naught, and the confessors of Christ glorified throughout the world."[52]

Within the framework of the Jewish and Christian interpretation-history of Psalm 121:4, our blood-libel story in *Shevet Yehudah* assumes meaning and importance, both for Solomon ibn Verga and his sixteenth-century Jewish readership. Ibn Verga, surely, did not create this folk tale, which, as we have seen, circulated in many Jewish communities over the course of centuries. But, directly concerned with the Jewish-Christian debate of the Middle Ages, he did put the tale to use in conveying his own appraisal of the Jewish condition in his day.[53] The rivalry between Jews and Christians focused in large measure on identifying precisely who had inherited the Bible's promises of divine election, blessing, and redemption to Israel. And, in this polemical and theological context, Psalm 121:4 and its exegetical history certainly had a role to play—a role that did not figure in most other attestations of the folk tale.[54]

The affirmation that "the guardian of Israel neither slumbers/dozes nor sleeps" notwithstanding, the late medieval persecutions and expulsions of Iberian Jewry in the name of Christianity understandably triggered skeptical ruminations and resentful protests on the part of numerous Jewish writers concerning the efficacy of their God's protection. One liturgical poet, for instance, passionately reproached God,

> Who is the father who raises children
> to take vengeance on them,
> to pour anger on them,
> with great and fuming wrath?

And when God responds that he has simply punished the Jews for their stubbornness and sin, the poet quickly retorts,

> But even if we have sinned, where are your mercies?
> If in anger you expelled us, tell us wherein the children sinned,
> whose kindnesses we have seen
> with our own eyes.[55]

Other voices resounded with similar cries, and *Shevet Yehudah* itself tells of one Jewish exile whose wife and children died as they fled their Spanish homeland. Left to perish in an uninhabited place by a merciless ship captain, he rose to his feet and exclaimed: "Lord of the universe! You do the utmost so that I should forsake you. But know full well that in spite of the will of those that reside in heaven, I am a Jew and will remain a Jew, no matter what you have done or may yet do to me!"[56] Or as Solomon ibn Verga himself declared: "When a person ponders over all these misfortunes [endured by the Jews], he will be astounded and say, 'Why this immense divine wrath? God has not done this to any other people, even those guilty of more sins than the Jews!'"[57] Put more simply, many Iberian Jews of the late fifteenth or early sixteenth century could easily have concluded—or at least been tempted to conclude—that their eternally vigilant, protective God had at least dozed off, if not fallen soundly asleep.

Against such a backdrop, our story's almost quaint reassertion that the guardian of Israel never dozes or sleeps could not but have struck an ironic note. Indeed, the ironic juxtaposition of traditional belief and practice on the one hand with contemporary reality on the other hand might well help to understand Solomon ibn Verga's intent in recounting this popular folk-tale as he did. As noted, the tale as rendered in *Shevet Yehudah* focuses primarily on the exegetical discussion convened by the Spanish king, in which he has ordered the Jews to participate. This discussion easily reminds one of the interreligious disputations of the Middle Ages, in which Christian clerics and Jewish rabbis—frequently at the insistence of the secular Christian prince—convened to debate the respective claims of their rival communities. Debate typically focused on the exposition of biblical verses that pertained to the true beneficiaries of divine election and salvation, just as Psalm 121:4 pertained to these issues, and each side claimed these promises for itself. Augustinian doctrine actually mandated the preservation of a Jewish presence in Christendom in order to facilitate the effective pursuit of such debate, allowing for the assertion of Christian doctrine through the negation of the beliefs of the Jewish "other."[58] Although ecclesiastical authorities often repudiated it, the ritual murder accusation ultimately derived from this *Adversus Judaeos* tradition, offering popular testimony to the pernicious presence of Jews in Christian society—Jews constructed so as to exemplify everything that Christian believers, often identified collectively as the body of Christ, did not.

At the same time, *Shevet Yehudah*'s rendition of our folk tale suggests that the traditional medieval basis for Christian-Jewish coexistence and interaction was no longer viable. Reversals of traditional roles and assumptions characterize the description of the brief *disputatio* more than anything else. The Christian king, not a cleric as one might expect, challenges the received Jewish exegesis of the biblical text under discussion. Yet in doing so, his tone of voice lacks hostility. And his preferred interpretation of Psalm 121:4 pertains directly to the political realm of this world and identifies Israel as the Jews, precisely the terrestrial sort of reading that typified the Jews and Judaism in Christian imagination—and the opposite of what one would expect of a Christian disputant. Moreover, the king's claim that he, the earthly king and not God, is the true guardian of Israel in this psalm contravenes both Jewish and Christian tradition, ostensibly removing the deity from an active providential role in worldly affairs.[59] Moreover, as we have noted above, just as the exegetical repartee deviates from age-old forms and expectations, so too does the ritual murder accusation lack any theological or ideological justification. This blood libel story manifests no concern whatsoever for what Jews do or do not do to Christians in their various rituals—a concern at the center of the libels surrounding Simon of Trent (1475) and the Holy Child of LaGuardia (1490–1491) with which Solomon ibn Verga must have been familiar—but rather with what Christians do to them.

Our folk tale in *Shevet Yehudah*, I suggest, expresses ibn Verga's determination to leave the Jewish-Christian encounter of the Middle Ages behind him and advance into a qualitatively new era. In this new post-expulsion, post-medieval reality,[60] traditional frameworks for Jewish-Christian interaction, ranging from the religious disputation to the blood libel, have lost their intrinsic meaning and much of their power. The violence often deemed characteristic of medieval justice has, in our tale, given way to a more rational form of judicial inquiry, in which the eyewitness testimony of the king's unarmed servants ensures the exoneration of the innocent and the conviction of the guilty. And the eternally vigilant, sleepless, providential God of Scripture, though surely not read out of the picture, has been relegated to a back seat, assuming a more transcendent, indirect role in the supervision of human affairs. Ibn Verga's insomniac guardian of Israel is here a human being, a non-Jew. At the end of the day—literally and otherwise—the people of Israel can no longer rely on the miraculous and extra-terrestrial, as they once did, for ensuring their safety in this tempestuous world.

Notes

Research for this project has been supported by the Israel Science Foundation (grant 245/08), the Abraham and Edita Spiegel Family Foundation Chair for European Jewish History at Tel Aviv University, and a grant from Tel Aviv University's Vice President for Research.

1. Here and below, translations from the Hebrew Bible generally follow *Tanakh: A New Translation of the Holy Scriptures according to the Traditional Hebrew Text* (Philadelphia: Jewish Publication Society of America, 1985), and from the New Testament the Revised Standard Version. While these and other translations typically translate the verb of *yanum* (*nym*) as "slumber," I have usually rendered it "doze," in keeping with the import of the story.

2. Solomon ibn Verga, *Shevet Yehudah* [Hebrew], ed. Azriel Shochat and Yitzhak Baer (Jerusalem: Mosad Bialik, 1947), ch. 16, 62–63; unless indicated otherwise,

translations are my own. Cf. also the partial translation in Yosef Hayim Yerushalmi, *The Lisbon Massacre of 1506 and the Royal Image in the Shebet Yehudah, Hebrew Union College Annual* Supplements 1 (Cincinnati: Hebrew Union College–Jewish Institute of Religion, 1976), 46–47.

3. On this "type" of folktale, see Dov Noy, "Alilot-Dam be-Sippure ha-Edot," *Mahanayim* 110 (1967): 35 and n. 13, 36, 45–46. Different versions appear in *Ma'aseh Book: Book of Jewish Tales and Legends,* trans. Moses Gaster, 2 vols. (Philadelphia: Jewish Publication Society of America, 1934), 2:400–401; http://www.imaadama.co.il/religions/kabbala/week_chapters/week_chapter_hrikeren33b_behukutay.htm (last accessed 3 January 2008); and in the tales found in the Israel Folktale Archives Named in Honor of Dov Noy at the University of Haifa, type AT *730E, stories 00996, 03625, 05471, 08804, 09107, 10276, IFA339 (all of which include explicit reference to Psalm 121:4), and cf. also 02964, 09522, 10017. I am grateful to Idit Pintel-Ginsberg, Academic Coordinator of the Archive, for her kind assistance.

4. Eleazar Gutwirth, "The Expulsion of the Jews from Spain and Jewish Historiography," in *Jewish History: Essays in Honour of Chimen Abramsky,* ed. Ada Rapaport-Albert and Steven J. Zipperstein (London: P. Halban, 1988), 141–61, esp. 153–55. The inquisitorial document in question appears in Carlos Carrete Parrondo, ed., *Fontes Iudaeorum Regni Castellae,* 8 vols. (Salamanca, 1981–1998), 3:69.

5. The difference between the ritual murder (often ritual crucifixion) and blood (or ritual cannibalism) libels will prove inconsequential in this context, owing largely to ibn Verga's own lack of interest in such a distinction. I shall therefore use "ritual murder libel" and "blood libel" virtually interchangeably. By contrast, see Cecil Roth, "The Medieval Conception of the Jews," in *Essential Papers on Judaism and Christianity in Conflict,* ed. Jeremy Cohen (New York: New York University Press, 1991), 305ff.; and Gavin I. Langmuir, *Toward a Definition of Antisemitism* (Berkeley: University of California Press, 1990), esp. ch. 11.

6. On *Shevet Yehudah* and its author, see (among others): Yitzhak Baer, *Untersuchungen über Quellen und Komposition des Schebet Jehuda* (Berlin: C. A. Schwetschke & Sohn, 1923), and "New Notes on Shebet-Yehuda" [Hebrew], *Tarbiz* 6 (1934): 152–79; J. D. Abramski, *Al mahuto u-tekhano shel "Shevet Yehudah": Deyokan shel Sefer* (Jerusalem: Yedidi, 1943); Abraham A. Neuman, "The *Shebet Yehuda* and Sixteenth Century Historiography," in *Louis Ginzberg Jubilee Volume,* ed. Saul Lieberman (New York: American Academy for Jewish Research, 1945), 253–73; Meir Benayahu, "A New Source Concerning the Spanish Refugees in Portugal; Their Move to Saloniki after the Edict of 1506; Concealment and Discovery of the Book *Sefer ha'Emunot*" [Hebrew], *Sefunoth* 11 (1967–1973): 233–65; Yerushalmi, *The Lisbon Massacre,* and *Zakhor: Jewish History and Jewish Memory* (Seattle: University of Washington Press, 1982), ch. 3; Gutwirth, "The Expulsion of the Jews from Spain," 141–61, and "Italy or Spain? The Theme of Jewish Eloquence in 'Shevet Yehudah,'" in *Daniel Carpi Jubilee Volume* (Tel Aviv: Tel Aviv University, 1996), 35–67; José Faur,

In the Shadow of History: Jews and Conversos at the Dawn of Modernity (Albany: State University of New York Press, 1992), ch. 9; Margarete Schlüter, "Zuchtrute und Königszepter; zur Frage der Komposition des 'Shevet Yehuda,'" in *Jewish Studies in a New Europe,* ed. Ulf Haxen et al. (Copenhagen: C. A. Reitzel A/S International Publishers, 1998), 712–31; and Joseph Dan, *Jewish Mysticism* (Northvale, NJ: Jason Aronson, 1999), ch. 2 (*"Shevet Yehudah:* Past and Future History").

7.   Jeremy Cohen, "The Blood Libel in Solomon ibn Verga's *Shevet Yehudah,*" in *Jewish Blood: Reality and Metaphor in History, Religion, and Culture,* ed. Mitchell B. Hart (New York: Routledge, 2009), 116–35.

8.   On the historicity of this tale (and others like it) in *Shevet Yehudah,* see the notes of Azriel Shochat in ibn Verga, *Shevet Yehudah,* 184; Faur, *In the Shadow of History,* esp. 178ff., and "Imagination and Religious Pluralism: Maimonides, Ibn Verga, and Vico," *New Vico Studies* 10 (1992), 43ff.; and Eli Yassif, *The Hebrew Folktale: History, Genre, Meaning,* trans. Jacqueline S. Teitelbaum (Bloomington: Indiana University Press, 1999), 298ff. Cf. also Joseph Hacker, "The Sephardi Sermon in the Sixteenth Century: Between Literature and Historical Source" [Hebrew], *Pe'amim* 26 (1986): 108–27.

9.   On the far-reaching social and cultural ramifications of the blood libel (and related anti-Jewish slanders) in medieval Christendom, see—among many others—Joshua Trachtenberg, *The Devil and the Jews: The Medieval Conception of the Jew and Its Relation to Modern Anti-Semitism* (New Haven, CT: Yale University Press, 1943); Langmuir, *Toward a Definition,* esp. pt. 4; Christopher Ocker, "Ritual Murder and the Subjectivity of Christ: A Choice in Medieval Christianity," *Harvard Theological Review* 91 (1998): 153–92; Miri Rubin, *Gentile Tales: The Narrative Assault on Late Medieval Jews* (New Haven, CT: Yale University Press, 1999); Lee Patterson, "'The Living Witnesses of Our Redemption': Martyrdom and Imitation in Chaucer's *Prioress's Tale,*" *Journal of Medieval and Early Modern Studies* 31 (2001): 507–60; Israel J. Yuval, *Two Nations in Your Womb: Perceptions of Jews and Christians in Late Antiquity and the Middle Ages,* trans. Barbara Harshav and Jonathan Chipman (Berkeley: University of California Press, 2006), esp. chs. 3–4.

10.   As Noy explains in "Alilot Dam," 35, the Bible's doubling of the first letter of the Hebrew *yyšn* in Psalm 121:4 allows for the vocalization of the phrase to mean either "he will not sleep" or "he will not cause to sleep."

11.   The message of the verse figured in classical Muslim tradition as well. See Sura 2:255 of the Qur'an, trans. N. J. Dawood, *The Koran,* 4th ed. (Harmondsworth: Penguin Books, 1974), 360: "Neither slumber nor sleep overtakes him."

12.   On this genre of Psalms 120–134, see, among others: Joseph Freund, "'Esa 'Enai el he-Harim': 'Iyyun be-Shirei ha-Ma'alot," in *Haim M. I. Gevaryahu Memorial Volume* [Hebrew], ed. Ben-Zion Luria (Jerusalem: Ha-Ḥevrah le-Ḥeker ha-Mikra be-Yisra'el 'a.y. Kiryat Sefer, 1989), 215–22; Daniel Grossberg, *Centripetal and Centrifugal Structures in Biblical Poetry,* Society of Biblical Literature Monograph Series 39 (Atlanta: Scholars Press, 1989), 15–54; Loren D. Crow, *The Songs of Ascents (Psalms*

120–134): *Their Place in Israelite History and Religion,* Society of Biblical Literature Dissertations Series 148 (Atlanta: Scholars Press, 1996); and Nisim Ararat, "'A Song of Ascents': A Poem from the Period of the Ascent to Zion" [Hebrew], *Beit Mikra* 44 (1998): 83–90. I am grateful to Edward Greenstein for his suggestions in this regard.

    13. See above, n. 1.

    14. *Tanakh,* 1261–62.

    15. See, among others: John T. Willis, "Psalm 121 as a Wisdom Poem," *Hebrew Annual Review* 11 (1987): 435–51; Anthony R. Ceresko, "Psalm 121: A Prayer of a Warrior," *Biblica* 70 (1989): 496–510; Manfred Weippert, *Jahwe und die anderen Götter: Studien zur Religionsgeschichte des antiken Israel in ihrem syrisch-palästinischen Kontext,* Forschungen zum Alten Testament 18 (Tübingen: Mohr Siebeck, 1997), ch. 6 ("Ecce non dormitabit neque dormiet qui custodit Israhel: Zur Erklärung von Psalm 121,4"), 99–107; Armin Schmitt, "Zum literarischen und theoligischen Profil von Ps 121," *Biblische Notizen* 97 (1999): 55–84; and Leonard P. Maré, "Some Remarks on Yahweh's Protection against Mythological Powers in Psalm 121," in *Psalms and Mythology,* ed. Dirk J. Human, Library of the Hebrew Bible/Old Testament Studies 462 (New York: T. & T. Clark, 2007), 170–80.

    16. Artur Weiser, *The Psalms: A Commentary,* trans. Herbert Hartwell (London: SCM Press, 1962), 748.

    17. See, for example, the commentaries ad loc. of Abraham ibn Ezra, David Kimchi (*The Commentary on the Fifth Book of the Psalms, CVII–CL* [Hebrew], ed. Jacob Bosniak [New York: Jewish Theological Seminary of America, 1954], 157), Menachem ha-Meiri (*Commentarius libri Psalmorum* [Hebrew], ed. Joseph Cole [Jerusalem: Mekize Nirdamim, 1936], 253), Obadiah Seforno (*Kitvei Rabbi Ovadyah Seforno,* ed. Ze'ev Gottlieb [Jerusalem: Mossad ha-Rav Kook, 1983], 232), and Solomon Attiyah (*Sefer Tehillim* [Venice: Justinian Press, 1549], 55a). Citations to medieval Christian commentators appear in the notes below. For a small sampling of modern commentators, see the works cited in the previous notes, as well as Sigmund Mowinckel, *Psalmenstudien,* 6 pts. in 2 vols. (1921–1924; repr., Amsterdam: P. Schippers, 1966), 1, 2:170–71; Walter Eichrodt, *Theology of the Old Testament,* trans. J. A. Baker, 2 vols. (Philadelphia: Westminster Press, 1961), 1:214; Hans-Joachim Kraus, *Psalms 60–150: A Commentary,* trans. Hilton C. Oswald (Minneapolis: Augsburg, 1989), 426–30; and James Luther Mays, *Psalms* (Louisville: John Knox Press, 1994), 389–92.

    18. *Mechilta d'Rabbi Ismael* [Hebrew], ed. H. S. Horowitz and I. A. Rabin, 2nd ed. (Jerusalem: Bamberger & Wahrmann, 1960), 226; *Midrash Haggadol on the Pentateuch* [Hebrew] ad Deuteronomy 5:9, ed. Mordecai Margulies et al., 5 vols. (Jerusalem: Mossad Harav Kook, 1947–1975), 5:107; and Bahya ben Joseph ibn Paquda, *Sefer Torat Ḥovot ha-Levavot* 4.2, ed. Joseph Kafah (Jerusalem: Feldheim, 1973), 195.

    19. *Midrash Lamentations Rabbah* 1.16; cf. also ibid. 1.52, and *Pesikta Rabbati: Midrasch für den Fest-Cyclus und die auzgezeichneten Sabbathe* [Hebrew] 29, ed. Meir (Ish-Shalom) Friedmann (Vienna: J. Kaizer, 1880), 136b.

20. Eleazar ben Judah, *Perushei Siddur ha-Tefilah la-Rokeah*, ed. Moshe Hershler and Yehudah A. Hershler, 2 vols. (Jerusalem: H. Vagshal, 1992), 2:499; cf. *Genesis Rabbah* 8.10, and see Jeremy Cohen, *"Be Fertile and Increase, Fill the Earth and Master It": The Ancient and Medieval Career of a Biblical Text* (Ithaca, NY: Cornell University Press, 1989), 89ff.

21. For example: *Exodus Rabbah* 34.3; *Song of Songs Rabbah* 2.1; Moses ben Nachman, *Perush ha-Torah* ad Exod. 19:5, ed. Charles B. Chavel, 2 vols. (Jerusalem: Mossad Harav Kook, 1959–1960), 1:383.

22. *Sifre on Deuteronomy* [Hebrew] 40.12, ed. Louis Finkelstein (1939; repr., New York: Jewish Theological Seminary of America, 1969), 80; *Midrash Haggadol* ad Deuteronomy 11:12, 5:202; *Midrash Alfa Beta* 3, in *Batei Midrashot* [Hebrew], ed. Sholomo Aharon Wertheimer and Abraham Joseph Wertheimer, 2nd ed., 2 vols. (1950–1953; repr., Jerusalem: Mossad Harav Kook, 1968), 2:425.

23. *Numbers Rabbah* 20.20; *Midrash Tanhuma* (Balak 14, Nitzavim 3), and *Midrash Tanhuma he-Kadum veha-Yashan* (Balak 22), ed. Solomon Buber, 6 pts. in 2 vols (1885; repr., Jerusalem: Ortsel, 1964), 2,5:72b.

24. *Seder Olam Rabbah* 28, ed. M. Y. Weinstock, 3 vols. (Jerusalem: Metivta Torat Hesed, 1956–1962), 3:431–32; *Mechilta d'Rabbi Ismael*, 208; *Siphre ad Numeros* 40 [Hebrew], ed. H. S. Horowitz (1917; repr., Jerusalem: Wahrmann Books, 1966), 44.

25. *Seder Eliyahu Rabba* [Hebrew] 18, ed. Meir (Ish-Shalom) Friedmann (Vienna: Achiasaf, 1902), 100; trans. William G. Braude and Israel J. Kapstein, *Tanna debe Eliyahu: The Lore of the School of Elijah* (Philadelphia: Jewish Publication Society of America, 1981), 260–61.

26. Tosefta *Sotah* 13.9; Babylonian Talmud *Sotah* 48a; Palestinian Talmud *Ma'aser Sheni* 5.5, 56d, and *Sotah* 9.11, 24a; *Esther Rabbah* 10.1; Eleazar ben Judah, *Perushei Siddur ha-Tefilah*, 2:499; and elsewhere.

27. *Kohelet Rabbah* 3.2; *Midrash Zuta 'al Shir ha-Shirim, Rut, Ekhah ve-Kohelet* ad Eccl. 3:12, ed. Solomon Buber (Berlin: Hevrat Mekitse Nirdamim, 1894), 122.

28. *Midrash Panim Acherim* B.6, in Solomon Buber, ed., *Sammlung agadischer Commentare zum Buche Esther* [Hebrew] (Vilna: Wittwe et Gebrüder Romm, 1886), 74. Cf. also *Mechilta d'Rabbi Ismael*, 134; *Midrash Tanhuma*, Beshalah 15; and *Seder Eliyahu Rabba* 21, 123; and elsewhere.

29. See Isaac Yavetz's commentary "Torat Hesed" ad loc., in *Sefer Kehillot Moshe*, 4 vols. (Amsterdam: M. Frankfurt, 1724–1727), 4:93a; cf. the commentary of David ibn Yachya, ibid.

30. Augustine, *Enarratio in Psalmos* 120.6, CCSL 40:1790–1792.

31. Epiphanius Latinus, *Interpretatio Evangeliorum* 50, PLS 3:926. Cf. Origen, *Homiliae in Lucam* 34, GCS 49:192, and *Commentarii in Ioannem* 20.36, GCS 10:375; Augustine, *In Iohannis evangelium tractatus* 43.2, CCSL 36:373–74, and *Sermo* 171.2, PL 38:934; Caesarius of Arles, *Sermo* 161, CCSL 104:660–63; Heiricus Autissiodorensis, *Homiliae per circulum anni*, pars hiemalis 56, CCCM 116A:532–44; Radulph

Ardens, *In epistolas et evangelia dominicalia homiliae* 44, PL 155:1824; and Thomas Aquinas, *Catena aurea in Lucam* 10.9, in *Opera omnia*, ed. Roberto Busa, 7 vols. (Stuttgart: Frommann-Holzboog, 1980), 5:322 (in the name of Augustine).

32. Chromatius of Aquileia, *Tractatus in Matthaeum* 52, CCSL 9A:457–58.

33. John Cassian, *De institutis coenobiorum et de octo principalium uitiorum remediis* 8.3, CSEL 17:152, trans. Select Library of Nicene and Post-Nicene Fathers 2,11:347.

34. See Didymus of Alexandria, *De trinitate* 3, PG 39:912; Epiphanius of Salamis, *Ancoratus* 31.2, GCS 25:40; and Anselm of Laon, *Enarrationes in Evangelium Matthaei* 8, PL 162:1324, among others.

35. See, for examples, the *Postillae* of Nicholas of Lyra in *Biblia sacra cum glossis*, 6 vols. (Venice, 1588), 3:277r.

36. Ambrose, *Expositio psalmi cxviii* 52, CSEL 62:182. Cf. the like-minded exhortation of Origen, *Commentariorum in Matthaeum series* 90, GCS 38:207.

37. Cassiodorus, *Expositio psalmorum* 120.3–4, CCSL 98:1146–47; trans. P. G. Walsh, *Cassiodorus: Explanation of the Psalms*, Ancient Christian Writers 53 (New York: Paulist Press, 1991), 267. Cf. the earlier comments of Basil the Great, *Homiliae in Psalmos* 29.2, PG 29:308; and Eucherius, *Instructiones ad Salonium* 1.54, CSEL 31:100–101.

38. Peter Chrysologus, *Sermo* 21, CCSL 24:122–27; Bede, *In Marcum* 2, CCSL 120:489–91.

39. For instance, Bruno the Carthusian, *Expositio in Psalmos* 120, PL 152:1317.

40. Augustine, *Enarratio in Psalmos* 120.6, CCSL 40:1790–91. On the Philonic foundations of this tradition, see Ellen Birnbaum, *The Place of Judaism in Philo's Thought: Israel, Jews, and Proselytes*, Brown Judaic Studies 290 and *Studia Philonica Monographs* 2 (Atlanta: Scholars Press, 1996).

41. Hilary of Poitiers, *Tractatus super Psalmos* 120.10, CSEL 22:565; Prosper of Aquitaine, *Expositio Psalmorum* 120.4, CCSL 68A:126–27; Cassiodorus, *Expositio Psalmorum* 120.4, CCSL 98:1147; Julian of Toledo, *Interrogationes* 72, PL 96:627–28, among others.

42. Gerhoch of Reichersburg, *Expositio in Psalmos* 120.3, PL 194:844. Cf. *Enarrationes in Psalmos* attributed to Remigius of Auxerre, 120, PL 131:770; and Bruno the Carthusian, *Expositio in Psalmos* 120, PL 152:1317.

43. Robert Bellarmine, *Explanation in Psalmos* 120.4, Appendix to *Commentarii in Sacram Scripturam* of Cornelius à Lapide (London: Pelagaud, 1855), 499. Unfortunately, the commentaries of Denis the Carthusian were unavailable in Israel for my examination.

44. On the multifaceted connections, see the works cited above, n. 9, and below, n. 58.

45. *Esther Rabbah* 7.12, translated somewhat freely to convey the polemical thrust of the midrash.

46. On the long-standing linkage between the Purim story, its arch villain Haman, and the blood libels, see Cecil Roth, "The Feast of Purim and the Blood Accusation," *Speculum* 8 (1933): 520–26; James Frazer, *The Golden Bough, 6: The Scapegoat* (New York: Macmillan, 1935), 360ff., 392–423; Edgar Wind, "The Crucifixion of Haman," *Journal of the Warburg Institute* 3 (1938): 245–48; Katrin Kogman-Appel, "The Tree of Death and the Tree of Life: The Hanging of Haman in Medieval Jewish Manuscript Painting," in *Between the Picture and the Word: Manuscript Studies from the Index of Christian Art*, ed. Colum Hourihane, Index of Christian Art Occasional Papers 8 (Princeton, NJ: Index of Christian Art, 2005), 187–208; Yuval, *Two Nations in Your Womb*, 163–74; and Elliott Horowitz, *Reckless Rites: Purim and the Legacy of Jewish Violence* (Princeton, NJ: Princeton University Press, 2006), esp. chs. 4, 6. I am grateful to Israel Yuval for his helpful suggestions in this regard.

47. Daniel J. Lasker and Sarah Stroumsa, ed., *The Polemic of Nestor the Priest* (Jerusalem: Ben-Zvi Institute, 1996), 115–16 (with slight modifications in Lasker's translation).

48. David Berger, ed. *The Jewish-Christian Debate in the High Middle Ages: A Critical Edition of the* Nizzahon Vetus (Philadelphia: Jewish Publication Society of America, 1979), 183 (with slight modifications in Berger's translation).

49. Jerome, *In Hieremiam prophetam* 3.30.3, CCSL 74:139; and see his *Tractatus in Psalmos* 120.10, CSEL 22:564–65.

50. Jerome, *Commentarii in Isaiam* 1.1.8, CCSL 73:13–14.

51. Isidore of Seville, *De fide catholica contra Iudaeos* 2.10.5, PL 83:516.

52. Pseudo-Hugh of St. Victor, *Allegoriae in Vetus Testamentum* 9.1, PL 175:737; on Richard of St. Victor's authorship see Rebecca Moore, "Hugh of St. Victor and the Authorship of *In Threnos Ieremiae*," *Journal of Religious History* 22 (1998): 256 n. 2.

53. See above, n. 3; and see also Yassif, *The Hebrew Folktale*, 298ff.

54. Precisely here lies the novelty in ibn Verga's singular adaptation and rendition of the story; cf. the implications of the earlier version of fifteenth-century conversos discussed by Gutwirth, "The Expulsion of the Jews from Spain," 153–55.

55. Herman P. Salomon, "Two Elegies on the Expulsion of the Jews from Spain," *The Sephardi Scholar* 3 (1977): 37–47 (quotation on 43). See also A. M. Habermann, "Two Elegies on the Expulsion of the Jews from Spain," *Tesoro de los Judios Sefardies* 5 (1962): 11–16; Dan Pagis, "Dirges on the Persecutions of 1391 in Spain" [Hebrew], *Tarbiz* 37 (1958), 355–69; and, more generally, the important study of Joseph Hacker, "The Responses of the Exiles to the Spanish Expulsion and to the Forced Conversion in Portugal" [Hebrew], in *Jews and Conversos at the Time of the Expulsion*, ed. Yom Tov Assis and Joseph Kaplan (Jerusalem: Zalman Shazar Center for Jewish History, 1999), 223–45.

56. *Shevet Yehudah*, 122.

57. Ibid., 127.

58. See, among others, Jeremy Cohen, *Living Letters of the Law: Ideas of the Jew in Medieval Christianity* (Berkeley: University of California Press, 1999); and *The Friars and the Jews: The Evolution of Medieval Anti-Judaism* (Ithaca, NY: Cornell University Press, 1982), esp. ch. 1.

59. See the important comments of Yerushalmi, *The Lisbon Massacre,* 47–48, n. 121, who adduces other examples of *Shevet Yehudah*'s attributing biblical epithets to non-Jewish secular rulers. Yerushalmi interprets the story we have discussed as expressive of a pro-monarchic political ideology, while I have read it as calling for a new perspective on Jewish-Christian relationships. I believe these two readings to be complementary and not at all mutually exclusive.

60. See Faur, *In the Shadow of History,* 204–7, where Solomon ibn Verga is dubbed "the harbinger of the postmodern society."

II. MODERN PERSPECTIVES: THEOLOGY, PRAXIS, AND PERCEPTIONS OF THE OTHER

CHAPTER FOURTEEN

"To Get to Know, to Understand, and to Respect Each Other"

Guidelines Old and New

Peter von der Osten-Sacken

Ancient Jewish tradition relates the meaningful encounter between an inquisitive Gentile student and Hillel. Promised by the Gentile that he would convert to Judaism if Hillel would teach him the whole Torah while he—the Gentile—stood on one foot, Hillel answered: "That which is odious to yourself, do not do to your neighbor; for this is the whole Torah."[1] The fellow who comes to Hillel in this story seems to be somewhat lazy, yet he might be a bit embarrassed at the same time. He obviously is impressed by Judaism, otherwise he would not ask to know its essence. Nevertheless, he seems to be a little confused and perplexed by its variety and the number of rules which guide its life. Thus he might feel like we do at certain moments in our life when we start a new period, entering little-known terrain.

Sometimes it is just one sentence or one point which is underlined, as in the case of the so-called Golden Rule noted by Hillel. Sometimes it contains three points, as in the summary of the prophetic message formulated by the prophet Micah (6:8): "He has told you, O mortal, what is good; and what does the Lord require of you but to do justice, and to love kindness, and to walk humbly with your God?" And sometimes there is a bit more to learn as is the case with the Ten Commandments, which are a summary for orientation as well. Yet they are a somewhat long summary. Most of the summarizing rules of life are much shorter. The community of the Dead Sea Scrolls chose the one sentence of the prophet Micah just cited, enriching it with two or three terms of their own.[2] Jesus chose a sentence close to that of Hillel and interpreted the Golden Rule as a form of the commandment to love one's neighbor (Matt. 7:12; 22:34–40), as did ancient Jewish tradition in general.[3] The Gospel of Matthew underlined justice, mercy, and faith (23:23); the Apostle Paul chose faith, love, and hope (1 Cor. 13:13). A real treasure of summarizing, guiding rules is the Mishnah tractate *The Sayings of the Fathers* (*Pirké Abot*). It connects every early teacher with at least one guiding principle; for example, the first teacher mentioned in this tractate, Simon the Just: "On three things does the world stand: On the Torah, and on worship, and on deeds of loving kindness."[4] This tractate is an impressive testimony to the fact that not only students, like Hillel's Gentile, need to learn guidelines. Indeed, every teacher is obliged not only to offer important material to students, but also to formulate and to live an ethical orientation that helps the next generation to take part in building its future in a humane way.

Because it is the task of every generation to find its own leading rules, it would be an interesting undertaking to follow the footsteps of those who have done so since ancient times. Of course this would be impossible here. Thus we now make a large leap, bringing us nearer to the present. The decade of the 1880s was a very hard time for Jewish communities in Russia and Germany, bringing with it persecutions in Russia as well as an anti-Semitic movement in Germany, especially in Berlin. The hostility also spilled over into the German army and influenced the relationship between Christian and Jewish soldiers. In this situation one of the rabbis in the army proclaimed the motto with which I have titled this brief essay: "What we need," he said, "is to get to know, to understand, and to respect each other."[5]

Since first reading this motto twenty years ago, I have found it to be of the same clarity and the same helpfulness as those sentences which I mentioned at the outset and which are rooted in biblical and rabbinical times. "What we need is to get to know, to understand, and to respect each other." This guideline seems to be helpful for the relationship between Christians and Jews, and of course for the adherents of other religions as well. It is also a helpful guideline for our personal conduct in daily relationships and for our social and political behavior. It may be especially urgent today when we are aware of a growing alienation between cultures—in a time when even the farthest neighbor on the other side of the world is only a few hours away (and only a few seconds away by means of the internet). Not long ago, a present-day rabbi moved in the same direction as his nineteenth-century forerunner and advocated for the Jewish-Christian dialogue thus:

> I do not know what will come of this [Jewish-Christian] encounter, but it is clearly worthwhile. In the twentieth century walls have been built between peoples more often than bridges, and of late the urgent work of understanding the other has been neglected or abandoned. Some say that dialogue is passé, but I would argue the opposite: if we want to live together on this bruised planet without more butchery, we must seek and create more moments of connection.[6]

"To get to know, to understand, and to respect each other"—this motto is not the solution to our problems, but rather an invitation, a guideline which can help us to find a way, a path, in our relationships. It may be helpful to think more deeply about the three phrases that constitute this motto and how they might be related. On the one hand, there may very often be a three-step process: to get to know each other in the beginning, to understand each other on the basis of this acquaintance, and then to respect each other. On the other hand, it seems important to maintain that one can view these three points like the three sides of a triangle as well, for we owe each other a basic respect as human beings even if we have not yet come to know and understand each other.

Let us now ponder the issue as we have to do as students and teachers, that is, let us question the whole thesis. Is this really a generally possible guideline—to get to know, to understand, to respect each other? Are there no situations where this movement will not function? Moreover, are there no situations where to understand might be wrong, or impossible, or at least narrowly limited? Here, I shall hint at three of these. The first and the second one have to do with the danger of understanding, the third is of another nature.

Our understanding of one another might easily turn into conflict as soon as we go beyond an exchange of ideas, especially when someone's deeds have evil consequences. Understanding arises in the process of accepting the other person. However, there are deeds which may be *explained,* but are *not* to be *understood.* I think that especially Judaism, as a religion that insists on and enables repentance, has been aware of this aspect from the beginning, as has Christianity on the basis of our common Bible.

The fact that understanding always occurs in the process of accepting the other includes another factor which could be viewed as dangerous. The more I understand the other, the more I might be attracted to his way of life, to his religion, to his ideology. And at the end there might be the strong wish on my part not only to accept the other and to respect him, but also to be like him. Even if we have to respect every honest personal decision, we all surely agree that this is not the kind of understanding our anonymous Jewish military chaplain had in mind.

As indicated above, there is still another kind of limit to the way we understand each other, and I think it is this direction which the chaplain had in mind. What I am thinking of has been circumscribed by the famous Jewish religious thinker Martin Buber. He said with regard to dialogue that both sides, Jews and Christians, are centered around a mystery which in its deepest core remains a mystery to the other person. But what we can do is to acknowledge the other in this mystery as he or she is, to share what we know about our common ground and our common hope, to try to be what we should be, and to try to do what we should do.[7]

The phrase of the nineteenth-century rabbi with which I have titled my essay testifies to his nobleness. In his time, hostile reactions came from the majority in the army, that is, from soldiers with a Christian background. However, he did not say, "What we need is that *you* get to know *us,*" but rather, "What we need is to get to know . . . *each other.*" It was a similar experience of nobleness which greatly impressed me when, after an incomparably desolate period in my own country and church, I went to Israel in 1960 for the first time. I had the same experience again twenty years later when contact between Los Angeles and Berlin was established by Professor Lewis Barth, first in Berlin, and some years later in Los Angeles, together with Professor Michael Signer, Dr. Neil Sandberg from the American Jewish Committee, and, last but not least, Rabbi Sanford Ragins.

I am sure that the Gentile with whose question to Hillel we began was not only a bit lazy, curious, and somewhat confused, but that he also thought it was especially clever to try to embarrass Hillel. Yet the great teacher seems to have been one step ahead of him. He answered that the Golden Rule is the whole Torah. He then continued, and one can well imagine that he smiled as he added: "The rest is commentary—go and learn."[8] Perhaps our whole life can be understood in this sense as a commentary on Hillel's rule. Go and learn. And may God bless us, Jews and Christians, as we go and learn together.

Notes

1. Babylonian Talmud, Tractate *Schabbat* 31a. Present circumstances unfortunately preclude my preparing a fitting contribution in honor of our friend and colleague, Michael Signer. Hence I have chosen to offer the following essay, which is based on my commencement address to the graduates of Hebrew Union College–Institute of Jewish Religion in Los Angeles in May 2006. The essay deals with much of what has motivated Michael's inestimable and indefatigable efforts to build relationships between Jews and Christians on a new and sound foundation. It is with particular joy and gratitude that I recall the classes that I have been privileged to co-teach with Michael and our invigoratingly controversial wrestling with the common biblical heritage shared by Jews and Christians. I am grateful to Dr. Roger Aus and Dr. Thomas Day for their help in revising the English text.

2. 1QS 5:3–4; 8:2. See *The Dead Sea Scrolls: Hebrew, Aramaic, and Greek Texts with English Translations*, Vol. 1: *Rule of the Community and Related Documents*, ed. James H. Charlesworth (Tübingen: Mohr, 1994), 20–21 and 34–35.

3. See *Midrash Bereshit Rabba: Critical Edition with Notes and Commentary*, ed. J. Theodor and C. Albeck (Jerusalem: Wahrmann Books, 1965), note on Par. 24.7 on Gen. 5:1, pp. 236–37.

4. Mishnah, Tractate *Pirke Avot* 1:2. For further material see T. Söding, *Die Trias Glaube, Hoffnung, Liebe bei Paulus* (Stuttgart: Verlag Katholisches Bibelwerk, 1992).

5. This quote was part of an exhibition of the Federal German Army (*Bundeswehr*) about Jews in the German Army (*Wehrmacht*) during the nineteenth and twentieth centuries. The traveling exhibition was shown in many cities. I saw it in May 1988 on the North Sea island of Sylt. Some years ago, the Ministry of Defence could not fulfill my request to document this citation since the exhibition had already been dismantled.

6. Sanford Ragins, "A Meeting between a Christian and Jew: A Rabbi and a Pfarrerin Study Bonhoeffer Together," in *Momente der Begegnung. Impulse für das*

christlich-jüdische Gespräch. Bertold Klappert zum 65. Geburtstag, ed. Michael Haarmann, Johannes von Lüpke, and Antje Menn (Neukirchen-Vluyn: Neukirchener Verlag, 2004), 315–18, here 315. According to Rabbi Ragins, the citation was first published in the Leo Baeck Temple Bulletin for January 1997.

7. Martin Buber, "Kirche, Staat, Volk, Judentum," in *Der Jude und sein Judentum. Gesammelte Reden und Aufsätze* (Köln: Joseph Melzer Verlag, 1963), 558–70, esp. 567–68.

8. See n. 1.

CHAPTER FIFTEEN

Biblical and Historical Perspectives on "the People of God"

Angela Kim Harkins

More than forty years ago, the Second Vatican Council's Dogmatic Constitution on the Church, *Lumen Gentium,* described the Church as the *populus Dei,* "the people of God."[1] While the model of *populus Dei* continues to serve as an important ecclesial image of the post-conciliar Church and as a critical counterpoint to *Corpus Christi mysticum,* it remains an ambiguous phrase.[2] Since the term is theological and not historical, it means different things to different people. Norbert Lohfink described the phrase well as "sweet to some and sour to others."[3] This study examines the phrase "the people of God" from both biblical and historical perspectives and considers the implications of its complexity for Jewish-Christian relations today.

I seek to critique the Second Vatican Council's use of the expression "the people of God" from the perspective of Jewish-Christian relations. From the interreligious standpoint, there are two significant problems with the Council's references to biblical Israel in *Lumen Gentium.* First, the language of "the people of God" is not a term that ancient Israel would have used as a ready reference to itself. Instead, it is a Christian theological construct that speaks more about Christian understandings of Jews than about actual Jews. Second, the Council presents ancient Israel with biblical references that highlight exclusivity and position Israel as a contrasting type to the Church. Within the context of *Lumen Gentium's* theological understanding of the eschatological inclusion of all of humanity, such exclusivity may be perceived as negative. In addition to the problematic ways that *Lumen Gentium* presents Israel, the expression "the people of God" is complicated by the difficult social and political context in which this expression first appeared in modern biblical scholarship.

Terms and Taxonomy: General versus Specific Terms for Israel

As powerful vehicles for constructing meaning, terms are always worth examining, especially one as significant as "the people of God." Hans Küng, a *peritus* at the Second Vatican Council, acknowledges the theological power of this expression when he affirmed that "the concept of the People of God is at the heart of Judaism."[4] Such statements presume that the simple meaning of the term "the people of God" points to biblical Israel and that it is an obvious identification; however, this is simply not the case. Writing not long after the Council convened, Küng stated that "specific references are superfluous for an idea which runs through the whole Old Testament."[5] So too, Yves Congar maintained that "the notion people of God has its own rich meaning which comes from the Old Testament."[6] The words of these theologians, both influential at the Second Vatican Council, are telling in light of the fact that this expression is not a stereotypical phrase that ancient Israel would have used for itself. In fact, the exact Hebrew equivalent for the expression "the people of God" (עַם אלהים) appears only once in the Hebrew Bible, specifically in 2 Samuel 14:13.[7]

What is striking about Küng's discussion of the biblical phrase is how readily he reads the phrase eschatologically and how easily he sees its interchangeability with other titles like "Israel" and "ekklesia of God."[8] In fact, any and all references to "people" are wrongly assumed to reference the biblical idea of "the people of God." Küng writes: "The phrase 'people of God' is used over and over again (λαός θεου) and the old-fashioned and solemn word λαός has the same overtones even if the genitive θεου is not added."[9] While the scarcity of the phrase "the people of God" in the Old Testament did not appear to trouble Küng who was writing in the 1960s, it should be considered more thoughtfully by biblical scholars and theologians today. The term does not clearly point to an actual social institution from the biblical period. Instead, the Council fathers' references to biblical Israel point to a theological construction of biblical Israel—one that serves the purpose of Christian theology but that is not useful for Jewish-Christian relations.

Norbert Lohfink remarks that the specific term "the people of God," highlighted at the Second Vatican Council, was in fact not a typical expression used by biblical Israel to refer to itself:

> We might begin by asking what the relationship was of "the people of God"—in the original sense of the expression—to the structures and institutions of Israel. . . . Today we use the phrase "the People of God" to describe the Church. Thus we place the Church, which comes from Jesus of Nazareth and is attested by the New Testament, in continuity with the Israel of the Old Testament. In doing this we assume that Israel designated itself "the People of God." But it is precisely at this point that we must begin to question common convictions. . . . A correction that must be made—not the most important, but well worth noting—is that the exact expression is "the people of Yahweh" and not "the People of God."[10]

Lohfink's point is that the phrase "the people of God" is rarely attested in the Hebrew Bible and altogether absent from the passages that are cited in *Lumen Gentium.* So *Lumen Gentium* does not cite Old Testament biblical references to "the people of God," but instead cites references to "the assembly of YHWH" (קהל יהוה). *Lumen Gentium* states: "Just as the people of Israel in the flesh, who wandered in the desert, were already called *the church of God* (see 2 Esd. 13:1; Num. 20:4; Deut. 23:1), so too, the new Israel, which advances in this present era in search of a future and permanent city (see Heb. 13:14), is also called the church of Christ (see Mt. 16:18)" (§9). This translation of *Lumen Gentium* uses the phrase "the church of God" for a phrase that may be rendered from the Hebrew as, "the assembly of YHWH."

The phrase cited by *Lumen Gentium* is not a common biblical expression for ancient Israel. Many other terms appear with greater frequency in the Hebrew Bible. One of them is the expression "the assembly of Israel" (קהל ישראל) which appears thirteen times in the Hebrew Bible.[11] A similar word, "congregation" (עדה), also appears in a number of combinations to refer to the community's special covenantal status. For example, we find in the Hebrew Bible the two expressions, "the congregation of Israel" (עדת ישראל)[12] and "the congregation of the children of Israel" (עדת בני ישראל),[13] with the latter appearing some twenty-seven times. Both of these words, "assembly" and "congregation" (קהל and עדה), point to a social group that is somehow delimited and hint at an exclusive covenant status, but neither term exhausts the many ways that biblical Israel describes itself in the Hebrew Bible.[14] Also, while the Hebrew words for "assembly" (קהל) and "congregation" (עדה) are similar in meaning, they should not be thought of as equivalents. Instead, these different ways of referring to biblical Israel point to distinct ways of referring to ancient Israelite communities. Another community term that comes close to the idea of "the people of God" in the Hebrew Bible is "the people of YHWH." The expression "the people of YHWH" (עם יהוה) appears fewer than ten times.[15] In all of these combinations, the basic sense of the Hebrew word "people" (עם) does not carry the general inclusive sense that comes with our English word. The Hebrew word עם is generally used to refer to the particular nation of Israel and may or may not appear with various modifiers.[16]

It is instructive to observe the great diversity of references for biblical Israel throughout the Hebrew Scriptures. Roman Catholic theologians should consider carefully the diversity of terms for biblical Israel when referring to Judaism in antiquity because they are reminders of the diverse expressions of Israel. Using the phrase "the people of God" as a general reference to biblical Israel ignores the wide variety of terms that are attested for the different groups that laid claim to this idea in the Bible and leads to the problematic misconception that biblical Israel was more stable, that is, more uniform and recognizable, than it actually was. Much more is known about Judaism in antiquity now almost fifty years after the Second Vatican Council. Today biblical scholars readily recognize that there was no monolithic Israel or Judaism in antiquity. In fact, this is perhaps one of the most important conclusions of twentieth-century biblical scholarship, and it has significant implications for contemporary Jewish-Christian understanding. New considerations of taxonomy and terminology reflect the changes in historical awareness of Judaism's great diversity. Today scholars speak of

"Early Judaism," which spanned from roughly 450 BCE–650 CE, instead of "Late Judaism." Early Judaism differed in many respects from the biblical Israelite religion that preceded it. Martin Jaffee is correct to caution against using the traditional language of Intertestamental Judaism and Late Judaism to describe the Judaisms of the Second Temple period (520 BCE–70 CE) when he writes:

> The flaws in this way of imagining Judaism are clear. Late Judaism is a way of naming a religion in the process of decay, a process redeemed only by a new religion, Christianity. To call the Judaism of our period 'late,' in other words, is to affirm traditional Christian claims to have displaced Judaism as the true covenantal community. Not all contemporary Christians—and, obviously, few Jews—wish to affirm this. But those who do must recognize that such judgments are grounded in theological judgments rather than in the interests of critical historical understanding. Indeed, the continued vitality of Judaic worlds for centuries after the emergence of Christianity as its own family of religious worlds reminds us that what is late Judaism for Christian Theology is just the beginning for the history of Judaism.[17]

Jaffee's critique of traditional (Christian) biblical terminology and taxonomy is an example of how recent scholars have used historical knowledge about the diverse and distinct experiences of historical Jewish communities in antiquity to reflect critically upon the Christian theological underpinnings of long-accepted statements about Jews and Judaism.

Current scholarly understanding of ancient Judaism allows for far more diversity and dynamism than scholarship recognized more than forty years ago at the time of the Council. This includes a greater appreciation for the Jewish context of Jesus.[18] In contrast to Küng who moves quickly from theological statements about biblical Israel to the new eschatological Israel, Edward Schillebeeckx, writing more than twenty years after the Council, considers more carefully and deliberately the Jewish context of the earliest Christian communities and thus the relationship between the two communities. The contrast between the two theologians may be seen in the following passage from Schillebeeckx's 1989 book on the Church:

Despite a whole variety of common forms, there were particular elements which now and then led to tensions, just as people had known more internal tensions within Judaism and continue to do so. For the first Christians, who were all Jews, it was clear that the death of Jesus was the consequence of the action of a particular group, not of the Jewish people as such. It was Jews who, on the basis of the crucifixion of Jesus and their faith in the resurrection, were converted and accepted the message of the gospel. But gradually there were more disputes between Jews who rejected Jesus and Jews who recognized Jesus as their saviour. Initially, however, this was basically a controversy within Judaism.[19]

What may be detected in Schillebeeckx's words is a more nuanced understanding of the complexity of Judaism in antiquity and of Christianity's relationship to these ancient expressions of Judaism. This is in contrast to Küng who describes Christianity in the following way: "The new Israel, the new people of God, was founded as such before it described itself as such."[20] Thus, while Küng, writing in the 1960s, easily collapses all of biblical Israel into "the people of God" and understands Christianity as the "new people of God," Schillebeeckx, writing twenty years later, offers a more careful construction of Judaism and Christianity in antiquity. This is likely a consequence of the biblical scholarship that had emerged during the years that elapsed between the two publications.

What may be seen in Schillebeeckx's presentation reflects contemporary scholarly consideration of the relationship between ancient Judaism and Christianity which tends to move away from broad generalizations that mask differences within Judaism in favor of emphasizing the diversity and distinctiveness of religious groups in antiquity. Many of these insights have come from the study of the Dead Sea Scrolls, which offer a wealth of information about actual Jews during the time of the Second Temple and provide a window onto the complexities of Judaism in antiquity. The use of the Scrolls by scholars interested in the origins of Christianity is instructive for our present discussion. The general model of linear development from Second Temple Judaism branching neatly into the two forks of Christianity and Rabbinic Judaism has been roundly criticized as overly simplistic and not true to the actual diversity that was present among these groups in antiquity. The first generation of Scrolls scholars was far more likely to conceptualize the Qumran sect as a prototype of Christianity, with some even claiming to have identified Christian documents among the Qumran manuscripts![21] Today, sixty years after the discovery of the Scrolls, contemporary understanding of the evidence for the varied and richly diverse groups during this exciting period known as the Second Temple quickly recognizes the inadequacy of early Scrolls scholarship and its simplistic generalizations about the ancient period.

In light of the developments in contemporary biblical scholarship, which strives to speak with care about the great diversity within ancient Judaism, the tendency of the Council and of Catholic theologians not long after the Council to refer to biblical Israel with sweeping generalizations is all the more striking. By collapsing the diverse references to biblical Israel into a single collective term, "the people of God," these theologians project a false understanding of the stability and uniformity of ancient Israel. Unlike the term *verus Israel, populus Dei* represents neither a simple retrieval of a biblical self-understanding nor an exegetical appropriation of a Jewish idea, for neither Jews in antiquity nor today would use the language of "the people of God" as a stereotypical reference to themselves. It is not a historical term that Jews in antiquity would have turned to as a ready reference to themselves, but rather a modern Christian theological term intended to describe biblical Israel. As a Christian construct, it aims to describe Jews and Judaism for the purpose of Christian theology. As such, the phrase complicates any actual encountering of real Jews on their own terms.

Biblical Israel as a Contrasting Type to the Eschatological People of God

Lumen Gentium's references to biblical Israel in its section on "the people of God" are problematic for Jewish Christian relations today. Here biblical passages are cited that underscore the exclusive nature of Israel's experience of salvation, which passages make Israel a contrasting type to the inclusive and universalistic conceptualization of the eschatological people of God. It is also the case that the document's citation of Third

Isaiah presumes a particularly Christian reading of this book that Jews would not share. The Council exaggerates the universalistic tendencies of this biblical text.

It has already been noted that *Lumen Gentium* does not provide actual biblical references to "the people of God," but rather cites references to "the assembly of YHWH" (קהל יהוה). This phrase is one that serves to evoke the idea of the communal rather than the individual experience of salvation. In the original Latin of *Lumen Gentium,* the phrase appears as *Dei Ecclesia* or "the church of God," but the Hebrew of Numbers 20:4 and Deuteronomy 23:2–4 is more accurately rendered as "the assembly of YHWH" (קהל יהוה). The Latin comes directly from the Greek Septuagint which reads the Hebrew word for "assembly" (קהל) as ἐκκλησία.[22] Remarkably, five of the ten instances of "the assembly of YHWH" (קהל יהוה) that appear in the Hebrew Bible are found in Deuteronomy 23:2–4.[23] These verses emphasize exclusion by listing the many types of people who may not be permitted in the "assembly of YHWH": "And the wounded one who has a crushed or severed male member may not approach the assembly of YHWH. The illegitimate one may not approach the assembly of YHWH, not even the tenth generation may approach the assembly of YHWH. The Ammonite and the Moabite may not approach the assembly of YHWH, not even their tenth generation may approach the assembly of YHWH." Among the excluded are the physically impaired, the illegitimate, and specific ethnic groups. Deuteronomy's understanding of the ideal community demanded a level of cultic purity that would not permit such people in the assembly.

The Council's decision to choose these references to Israel ("assembly of YHWH") is telling. While associations with a cultic context make the typological leap from the "assembly of YHWH" to the idea of the Church an easy one, these passages from Deuteronomy emphasize the exceedingly exclusive nature of Israel's corporate experience. By using the language of "Church" (Hebrew "assembly of YHWH" or Greek "ekklesia"), the Council succeeds in highlighting the idea that salvation is experienced by a religious community; unfortunately the citations chosen by the authors of *Lumen Gentium* reveal little about the political or national aspects of Israel's experience.

Once the document moves to a more expansive and universal idea of the people of God, biblical Israel's exclusive experience of election functions as a contrasting type. *Lumen Gentium* moves from the specific community or an ecclesial idea of biblical Israel (i.e., "the assembly of YHWH" [קהל יהוה]) to a broader and more inclusive idea of "the people of God" in section 13. There the totality of the Church's understanding of the eschatological people of God is described: "All women and men are called to belong to the new people of God. This people therefore, whilst remaining *one* and unique, is to be spread throughout the whole world and to all ages in order that the design of God's will may be fulfilled: he made human nature *one* in the beginning and has decreed that all his children who were scattered should be finally gathered together as *one*. . . . The *one* people of God is accordingly present in all the nations of the earth, and takes its citizens from all nations, for a kingdom which is not earthly in character but heavenly" (emphasis mine). The Council makes a theological move toward the universal when it expresses the expectation that the Church itself "is mindful that it must gather in along with that king to whom the nations were given for an inheritance (see Ps 2:8) and to whose city they bring gifts and offerings (see Ps 71 [72]:10; Is 60:4–7; Apoc 21:24)." This is the hope that all of humanity will be brought together in the eschatological "people of God." The document not only describes the Church as being gathered in as the nations were gathered to Israel, but also claims that the Church comes to fully participate in Israel's election. Here in section 13, the common nature of the experience is underscored by the "one-ness" and singularity of the new "people of God."

Isaiah 60:4–7 is offered in section 13 as one of the Old Testament scriptural warrants for this theological idea of ingathering. It is important to note that the Council's understanding of this text reflects a Christian reading of Isaiah that Jews would not share. According to *Lumen Gentium,* the eschatological "people of God" will be united into a new single community; yet this is not quite the idea expressed in the Isaian passage. Isaiah 60:4–7 describes how at the time of Zion's restoration, many nations will participate in her restoration. But there is always a careful distinction made between Israel and the non-Israelite peoples. The nations (אֻמִּים) and the Gentiles (גוֹיִם) remain distinct from Israel (עַם). In Third Isaiah, there is neither the expectation that Israel will merge into a single community with the nations nor a sense that the nations will become a part of Israel. At the same time, there is no expectation that Israel will dissolve or cease to be at the moment of restoration. In a recent study on election theology, Joel Kaminsky is correct to note that Christian appeals to Isaiah as support for a universalism exaggerate the meaning of the biblical text.[24] In fact, the theology of Isaiah suggests that restoration brings with it an ever deepening sense of the distinctiveness of Israel. Kaminsky notes that Christianity's generally positive evaluation of the universal (Christianity) and negative evaluation of the particular (Judaism) reflects a deeply rooted supersessionism.[25] Similarly, Joseph Blenkinsopp has explained: "The term 'universalism,' with its antonym 'particularism,' is one of those slippery words the precise meaning of which is rarely defined. In biblical theology it tends to recur in discussions of opposite trends in early Judaism, and especially where Judaism is contrasted unfavorably with early Christianity. The categories themselves are a relic of the Enlightenment with its postulate that true religion must be in conformity with the universally valid laws of reason and a universally accessible moral law derived from them."[26] There is no universalism in this passage from Third Isaiah, even though it is offered as a scriptural support for the Council's understanding of the universalism of the new "people of God." It must be noted that the characterization of Third Isaiah as having a universalizing tendency does not arise from a simple reading of the biblical text.

References to biblical Israel in *Lumen Gentium*'s discussion of "the people of God" may be problematic for Jewish-Christian relations today insofar as they cast biblical Israel as a contrasting type to the eschatological universal people of God. Given the many different possible choices for referring to ancient Israel's corporate experience of salvation, the Council's portrayal of ancient Israel in such starkly exclusivist terms, e.g., by means of the Deuteronomic prohibitions discussed earlier, reinforces a negative perception of Judaism, particularly in light of the positive understanding of the Christian universal eschatological "people of God." In short, the progressive development from the exclusive (biblical Israel) to the inclusive (Roman Catholic Church) to the universal (the eschatological "people of God") sets up a problematic relationship between Judaism and Christianity. Furthermore, *Lumen Gentium*'s reference to Third Isaiah as support for the singularity of the universal people of God exaggerates the restoration theology in that biblical book and overlooks Israel's deep self-understanding of distinctiveness.

The Complicated Context of "the People of God"

In addition to the problematic way the Council makes reference to biblical Israel, there are other aspects of the phrase "the people of God" that represent challenges for contemporary Jewish-Christian relations. In this section, I will contextualize the expression "the people of God" in twentieth-century biblical scholarship in order to reveal the complexity of this expression.

Norbert Lohfink notes but does not discuss one of the earliest modern appearances of the term "the people of God" when he gestures to the title of Gerhard von Rad's (1901–1971) published dissertation, *Das Gottesvolk im Deuteronomium* (*The People of God in Deuteronomy*), which was published by W. Kohlhammer in 1929.[27] Von Rad was a remarkable scholar and theologian who lived in one of the most pivotal Jewish-Christian contexts of the twentieth century, namely Germany prior to and during the Holocaust.[28] Given the notable infrequency of this phrase in the Hebrew Bible, it is significant that von Rad chose to employ it in his study of the book of Deuteronomy.

Particularly within a contemporary American social context, the idea of "the people of God" suggests the idea of democratization. However, within the German context of the mid-twentieth century, the expression would have had very different associations. Not long after von Rad's publication of *The People of God in Deuteronomy,* Germany fell under the rule of the Nazi Party in the 1930s and 1940s. At this time, ideological discourse about "people" and "race" (*Volk*) came to the fore in Germany. In her work on the German Christian movement in Nazi Germany, Doris Bergen notes that people-oriented language was particularly strong: "The German Christian theory of race depended on a particular vocabulary. German Christians made heavy use of the words *Volk, Volkstum,* and *völkisch.* These terms are difficult to translate into English because they combine aspects of ethnicity, race, and culture. . . . The problem of translating these terms highlights the alien nature of German Christian thought outside the context of Nazi Germany. We cannot recapture in another language, another time, and another setting all of the messages intrinsic in German Christian utterances on race."[29] The German Christian movement sought to purge Hebraic and Jewish elements, including the Old Testament, from all aspects of the experience of Christianity. While resistance to these movements found expression in the Confessing Church (*Bekennende Kirche*), Bergen and others propose that its struggle against the German Christians had more to do with ecclesial control of the Protestant church in Germany than with political opposition to Nazi ideology.[30]

As a member of the Confessing Church, Gerhard von Rad rightly opposed the German Christian movement and its attempt to eradicate all Jewish elements from Christianity. For him, the Old Testament was essential to Christianity. As a scholar and pastor, von Rad's expertise was far ranging, but his interest was held fast by the book of Deuteronomy. In a recent study, Bernard Levinson and Douglas Dance show well that von Rad's interpretation of Deuteronomy reflected more the extreme political context of his academic career than the biblical book itself.[31] In a classic study on the book of Deuteronomy, von Rad proposed that its genre was not a law book but a sermon.[32] This represented, according to Levinson, his attempt to preserve the Old Testament as meaningful Christian Scriptures, a status that had been seriously undermined by the German Christians. Levinson and Dance write:

> At many points, von Rad positioned the Bible in such a way as to resist the discipline of theology from being co-opted by National Socialism and to maintain the discipline's autonomy. Deuteronomy, with its affirmation of law as the foundation of God's covenant with his nation, Israel, inevitably brought this issue to the forefront. The moment Deuteronomy was viewed simply as "law," it became a Jewish rather than a Christian text. It could therefore play no meaningful, let alone redeeming, role within the Church. Von Rad's intellectual response to these crises was to redefine these shared elements as inherently—if not exclusively—Christian. Von Rad rehabilitated Deuteronomy. He reclaimed it as a vital expression of Christian theology. His work took the form of positioning the Old Testa-

ment, and Deuteronomy in particular, not as Jewish *nomos* but as a foundational Christian text preaching salvation. Its form is not dead letter but rather live sermon or *kerygma*. Its content reflects not Jewish legalism but Christian grace.[33]

Levinson's and Dance's study of the political and ideological influences on the biblical scholarship of von Rad convincingly shows that von Rad's interest in Deuteronomy in particular was motivated by a Christian theological concern to rehabilitate the legalism of the book in ways appropriate to the political context of his day.

Although the expression "the people of God" made its first appearance on the biblical scholarly horizon in Gerhard von Rad's study of the book of Deuteronomy in 1929, its influence is still felt today. The publication date of this work clearly predates the Nazi control over Germany (1933–1945) and the *Kirchenkampf* of the 1930s. Obviously these events could not have influenced von Rad's scholarship. Yet the language of *Das Gottesvolk* that he introduced would have been heard with powerful associations in the context of the growing discourse about *Volk* in Germany—a discourse that particularly characterized the German Christian and Nazi movements—whether or not von Rad intended to participate in that discourse.

Von Rad's career unfolded in a dire political and social context. His commitment to the scholarly study of the Old Testament in the service of the Church may explain why von Rad was attracted to the language of "the people of God": it was a phrase that would have resonated well with his Christian audience both in the classroom and in the pew. It is recognizably Christian, appearing in the New Testament in 1 Peter 2:9–10: "But you are a chosen race, a royal priesthood, a holy nation, God's own people, in order that you may proclaim the mighty acts of him who called you out of darkness into his marvelous light. Once you were not a people, but now you are a *people of God;* once you had not received mercy, but now you have received mercy" (emphasis mine). In this familiar passage, a number of references that were formerly applied to biblical Israel are now applied to the Christian hearers of this letter.

Von Rad's interest in the book of Deuteronomy and his attempt to preserve its importance within a believing Christian community succeeded in making the law book of biblical Israel relevant to spiritual Israel (i.e., Christians). The phrase "the people of God" would have been a recognizably Christian phrase that was being employed within the context of the book of Deuteronomy for a Christian theological purpose, and it is one that would have been readily recognized by his Protestant German-speaking audience. In his Letter to the Romans, Paul distinguishes between the earthly Israel (Jews) and the spiritual Israel (Christians). The German text of Romans 9–11 makes explicit what is often implicitly understood by Christian readers. Consider the text of Romans 9:6 in the Greek and German:

Greek:

German:

Ούχ οἷον δέ ὅτι ἐκπεπτωκεν ὁ
λόγος τοῦ θεοῦ, οὐ γαρ πάντες οἱ
ἐξ Ισραὴλ οὗτοι Ισραήλ.

Es ist undenkbar, daß Gottes Wort
hinfällig geworden ware. Aber nicht
alle Israeliten gehören zu Gottes Volk.

But it is not as though the Word of
God had failed. For not all those who
are from Israel will belong to *Israel.*

It is unthinkable that the Word of
God had failed. For not all of the
Israelites will be called to *the people*
of God.

Here, by changing the second occurrence of "Israel" to "the people of God," the German translator makes explicit what is often read into the text of Romans 9:6. In this way, the theological transformation of earthly Israel into spiritual Israel is written into the German text of Romans 9:6. Von Rad's preference for this expression illustrates the use of a Christian spiritual understanding of Israel and comes from this German theological rendering of Romans.

Commenting on the significance of von Rad and his work, Manfred Oeming recently stated: "Without doubt Gerhard von Rad is one of the most important and most influential OT scholars of the twentieth century."[34] In light of von Rad's significance, the phrase "the people of God" must be situated within the complex historical context of the scholarly career of Gerhard von Rad. The context in which this phrase appears in twentieth-century biblical scholarship contributes to the complexity of the phrase "the people of God" for Jewish-Christian relations today.

The expression "the people of God" is not primarily an ancient Jewish self-description; rather, it is a modern Christian notion of biblical Israel that was constructed for Christian theological purposes. What may be seen in the German translation of Romans 9:6 is the classic Christian presentation of biblical Israel in the familiar role of the carnal Israel which then serves as a type for the spiritual Israel, "the people of God." The use of the phrase "the people of God" by Christian scholars and theologians reflects a classic Christian desire to situate itself in continuity with the promises made to biblical Israel by claiming the eschatological fruits of that covenant relationship. But the expression would not have been recognized by Jews in antiquity nor is it recognized by Jews today as a ready reference to themselves.

Conclusion: Implications of Christian Theological Constructions of Jews and Judaism

The Council's use of the expression "the people of God" reflects a desire to anchor the idea of the Church in the biblical narrative of salvation history by drawing upon an association with biblical Israel. Hans Küng affirmed that "the concept of the People of God is at the heart of Judaism," but then went on to write that the consideration of these "specific references is superfluous" since it is "an idea which runs through the whole Old Testament."[35] Contrary to the dated views expressed by systematic theologians like Küng, it is important to consider seriously the diverse terms that reflect the distinct expressions of ancient Judaism in the Hebrew Bible. Overlooking historical insights into the great diversity of Judaism in antiquity could lead to the conceptualization of Jews as "types" famously portrayed in Christian theology as the "hermeneutical Jew," a phrase formulated by Jeremy Cohen.[36] For much of the history of Christianity, references to Jews and Judaism were primarily theological and decidedly ahistorical as attested in the dangerous supersessionist *Adversus Iudaeos* tradition.[37] It is important that bishops and Christian theologians draw upon a sound historical understanding of actual Jews and Jewish self-understandings when they construct their theologies of Jews and Judaism or of the Church in relation to the Jewish people. Israel was in the biblical period and remains today a living religion with many diverse and particular expressions. Christians today should be ever conscious of creating hermeneutically crafted Jews for the purpose of Christian theological discourse. Oftentimes the Jew who is thus constructed primarily serves the purpose of Christian discourse and resembles little of the actual Jew whom it purportedly represents. Bishops and theologians should also not silence the diversity of ancient Jewish communities by projecting a more stable and unified idea of Judaism than existed during that time.

It must be reiterated that this essay does not aim to undermine the Second Vatican Council's desire to offer the Church a new and important self-understanding as "the people of God." From a purely ecclesiological perspective, the expression *populus Dei* has introduced significant and welcome advantages for the Church's self-understanding in the modern world. Rather, this study seeks to encourage a more nuanced understanding of this idea from a biblical and historical perspective that takes seriously the important work of Jewish-Christian relations. Bishops and theologians today would do well to note the ahistorical and theological ways in which Jews are described in the Council documents and to remember that few Jews, from either the past or the present, would welcome being associated with the idea of "the people of God" as it is formulated in *Lumen Gentium.*

Today, almost fifty years after the Council, the Catholic Church's ambivalent attitude toward Jews and Judaism continues. This topic was recently engaged by Michael Signer who offered an important critique of the Church's use of the expression "the people of God" from the perspective of Jewish-Christian relations. On the Church's use of this expression in paragraph 840 of the *Catechism of the Catholic Church,* Signer wrote: "Two elements in this paragraph require careful attention because they place Judaism in a pre-Vatican II position. First is the term 'God's People of the Old Covenant' to describe Jews, and 'new People of God' to describe Christians. Some theologians would claim that 'God's People of the Old Covenant' is a positive expression of the church's esteem for the Old Covenant, which has never been revoked. However, when this expression is placed in the context of 'the new People of God' it acquires a more negative tone, as if the 'new' supersedes the 'old.'"[38] Signer has noted well the problematic aspects of the expression "the people of God" from the perspective of Jewish-Christian relations and he is correct to point them out within the larger context of the Church's ambivalent attitude toward the Jewish people. This ambivalent attitude can be seen in recent discussions by the United States Conference of Catholic Bishops about revising the language of the *U.S. Catholic Catechism for Adults* concerning God's covenant with the Jews. In August 2008, the USCCB voted to ask the Vatican to approve the removal of the sentence that reads, "Thus the covenant that God made with the Jewish people through Moses remains eternally valid for them." The Conference has proposed replacing this clear statement affirming the irrevocable nature of the divine covenant with Israel with a markedly less clear and more Christian-oriented one, namely: "To the Jewish people, whom God first chose to hear his word, 'belong the sonship, the glory, the covenants, the giving of the law, the worship and the promises; to them belong the patriarchs, and of their race, according to the flesh, is the Christ.'"[39] This change is striking because it obfuscates the nature of God's covenant with the Jewish people on its own terms. Michael Signer's voice has been steady in pointing out the ambivalence of the Church toward the Jews in this and similar past situations, and this work needs to be continued in the future. It is a great honor for me to offer this essay on the ambiguity of the expression "the people of God" to such an esteemed scholar who has spent a lifetime working to transform relations between the two religious communities.

Notes

It is a true honor to be a part of this collection honoring Michael A. Signer. A much shorter version of this essay was presented at the Catholic Theological Society of America annual meeting in 2007, and I am grateful to Michael for discussing it with me during that time. I would also like to thank Elena Procario-Foley for inviting me to present my work on that CTSA panel. I am also grateful to the following individuals for their insights and conversation about the far-ranging topics covered in this essay during its various stages: Nancy Dallavalle, John Thiel, and Franklin Harkins, and I wish to thank both Elizabeth Groppe and Paul Lakeland in a special way for sharing with me their insights into Vatican II.

1. References are to the translation by Austin Flannery (ed.), *Vatican Council II: The Basic Sixteen Documents—Constitutions, Decrees, Declarations* (Northport, NY: Costello, 1996), 1–95, esp. 12–25.

2. Norbert Lohfink, S.J., "The People of God: The Old Testament and the Central Concept of the Council's Verbal Fireworks," in *Great Themes from the Old Testament,* trans. R. Walls (Edinburgh: T & T Clark, 1982), 117–133, quote at 117.

3. Ibid., 118.

4. Hans Küng, *Die Kirche* (Freiburg: Herder, 1967); all citations are taken from the English translation, *The Church* (Garden City: Image Books, 1976), here 159.

5. Ibid.

6. "The People of God," *Vatican II: An Interfaith Appraisal. International Theological Conference at the University of Notre Dame, March 20–26, 1966,* ed. John H. Miller (Notre Dame, IN: University of Notre Dame Press, 1966), 197–207, here 200.

7. There is one instance of "the people of the God of Abraham" (עם אלהי אברהם) in Ps. 47:10; and "the assembly of the people of God" (קהל עם־האלהים) in Judg. 20:2. Lohfink offers different calculations since he is including these other collocations in his count of "the people of God" (see "The People of God," 119).

8. Küng, *The Church,* 155.

9. Ibid., 158.

10. Lohfink, "The People of God," 118–19.

11. Lev. 16:17; Deut. 31:30; Josh. 8:35; 1 Kgs. 8:14 (twice), 22, 55; 12:3; 1 Chr. 13:2; 2 Chr. 6:3 (twice), 12, 13.

12. The specific expression "congregation of Israel" (עדת ישראל) appears eleven times: Exod. 12:3, 6, 19, 47; Lev. 4:13; Num. 16:9; 32:4; Josh. 22:18, 20; 1 Kgs. 8:5; 2 Chr. 5:6.

13. The specific expression "the congregation of the children of Israel" (עדת בני ישראל) appears twenty-seven times: Exod. 16:1, 2, 9, 10; 17:1; 35:1, 4, 20; Lev. 16:5; 19:2; Num. 1:2, 53; 8:9, 20; 13:26; 14:5, 7; 15:25, 26; 17:6; 19:9; 25:6; 26:2; 27:20; 31:12; Josh. 18:1; 22:12.

14. See also Pancratius Beentjes, "'Holy People': The Biblical Evidence," in *A Holy People: Jewish and Christian Perspectives on Religious Communal Identity,* ed. M. Poorthuis and J. Schwartz (Leiden: Brill, 2006): 3–15.

15. Num. 11:29; 17:6; Judg. 5:11; 1 Sam. 2:24; 2 Sam. 1:4; 6:21; 2 Kgs. 9:6; Ezek. 36:20; Zech. 2:10.

16. When referring to Israel, some modifiers include: "holy people" (עם קדש) in Deut. 7:6 (3 times), "people of the holy ones" (עם קדושים) in Dan 8:24; "the Holy People" (עם הקדש) in Isa. 62:12; 63:18; Dan. 12:7; and "a treasured people" (עם סגלה) in Deut. 7:6; 14:2; 26:18. When the word "people" is used to refer to non-Israelites, there is a modifier attached to the word—e.g., "foreign people" (עם נכרי) in Exod. 21:8, or "another people" (עם אחר) in Deut. 28:32; or "all people," i.e., all of humanity (עם אחד) in Gen. 11:6.

17. For distinctions between the earliest historical periods of Judaism and their taxonomy, see Martin S. Jaffee, *Early Judaism* (Upper Saddle River, NJ: Prentice Hall, 1997), 1–23, quote at 16. Jaffee was not the first to make this criticism; see too

the earlier discussion by Charlotte Klein, *Theologie und Anti-Judaismus* (München: Kaiser Verlag, 1975); all references are to the English translation, *Anti-Judaism in Christian Theology*, trans. Edward Quinn (Philadelphia: Fortress Press, 1978), 15–38.

18. It was not uncommon for New Testament scholars to go to great lengths to disassociate Jesus from his Jewish context; see Klein, *Anti-Judaism in Christian Theology*, 11–12. In more recent years, there have been several excellent scholarly attempts to situate Jesus historically within ancient Judaism. These studies seek to avoid two extremes: (1) overemphasizing the uniqueness of Jesus over and against the Judaism of his time by retrojecting later theological debates and apologetics into first-century Palestine; and (2) overemphasizing the Jewishness of Jesus by separating him from the emergence of Christianity which then becomes seen as a Pauline invention. See E. P. Sanders, *Jesus and Judaism* (Philadelphia: Fortress Press, 1985); and the study by John P. Meier, *A Marginal Jew: Rethinking the Historical Jesus*, 3 vols. (New York: Doubleday, 1987–2001).

19. Edward Schillebeeckx, *Mensen als verhaal van God* (Baarn: Nelissen, 1989); all citations are according to the English translation, *Church: The Human Story of God*, trans. John Bowden (New York: Crossroad, 1994), here 148.

20. Küng, *The Church*, 155.

21. Scholars who suspected or identified the Qumran group as Christian include: André Dupont-Sommer, *The Dead Sea Scrolls: A Preliminary Survey* (Oxford: Basil Blackwell, 1952); Edmund Wilson, "The Scrolls from the Dead Sea," *The New Yorker* (May 1955): 45–131; Herbert Braun, *Qumran und das Neue Testament* (Tübingen: J. C. B. Mohr, 1966); and Jose O'Callaghan, "Papiros neotestamentarios en la cueva 7 de Qumran?" *Biblica* 53 (1972): 91–100. See the summary discussion by James C. VanderKam, "The Dead Sea Scrolls and Early Christianity, Part One: How Are They Related?" *Bible Review* 7 (1991): 14–21, 46–47 and "The Dead Sea Scrolls and Early Christianity, Part Two: What They Share," *Bible Review* 8 (1991): 16–23, 40–41; repr. as "The Dead Sea Scrolls and Christianity," in *Understanding the Dead Sea Scrolls*, ed. Herschel Shanks (New York: Random House, 1992), 181–202.

22. The same root that is translated here as "assembly" appears in the title of the Hebrew book, *Qoheleth*. The ecclesial associations with this root are transparent in the Latin name for this book, *Ecclesiastes*.

23. Deut. 23:2 (MT) and Num. 20:4. The expression "the assembly of YHWH" also appears in Mic. 2:5 and 1 Chr. 28:8. Note that the numbering of the MT verses for this passage in Deut. differs from the numbering in *Lumen Gentium*.

24. Joel S. Kaminsky, *Yet I Loved Jacob* (Nashville: Abingdon Press, 2007). Kaminsky proposes three categories of people in Jewish election theology: the elect (Israel), the non-elect (other nations), and the anti-elect (the damned). The category of the non-elect participates in God's plan for salvation in their own way without being damned. The nations who participate in Israel's restoration in Third Isaiah do so while maintaining their distinct status (see p. 5).

25. Ibid.

26. Joseph Blenkinsopp, "YHWH and Other Deities: Conflict and Accommodation in the Religion of Israel," *Interpretation* 40 (1986): 354–66, here 360.

27. Lohfink, "The People of God," 117.

28. See Rudolf Smend, "Gerhard von Rad," *From Astruc to Zimmerli: Old Testament Scholarship in Three Centuries* (Tübingen: Mohr Siebeck, 2007), 170–97.

29. Doris L. Bergen, *Twisted Cross: The German Christian Movement in the Third Reich* (Chapel Hill: University of North Carolina Press, 1996), 22–23. Bergen's study is important for the nuanced way she examines the complex relationship between the German Christian movement and the Nazi Party.

30. Ibid., 12. That the church struggle of the 1930s was primarily about ecclesial power in Germany is also the conclusion of Shelley Baranowski, who notes the ambivalence of the Confessing Church to get involved politically in matters concerning the treatment of non-baptized Jews. See Shelley Baranowski, "The Confessing Church and Anti-Semitism: Protestant Identity, German Nationhood, and the Exclusion of Jews," in *Betrayal: German Churches and the Holocaust*, ed. Robert P. Ericksen and Susannah Heschel (Minneapolis: Fortress, 1999), 90–109, esp. 99.

31. Bernard M. Levinson and Douglas Dance, "The Metamorphosis of Law into Gospel: Gerhard von Rad's Attempt to Reclaim the Old Testament for the Church," in *Recht und Ethik im Alten Testament*, ed. B. M. Levinson and E. Otto with assistance from W. Dietrich (Münster: LIT Verlag, 2004), 83–110. The substance of this essay reappears in shorter form in B. M. Levinson, "Reading the Bible in Nazi Germany: Gerhard von Rad's Attempt to Reclaim the Old Testament for the Church," *Interpretation* (July 2008): 238–54.

32. G. von Rad, *Deuteronomium-Studien* (Göttingen: Vandenhoeck & Ruprecht, 1947); English translation, *Studies in Deuteronomy* (London: SCM Press, 1953).

33. Levinson and Dance, "The Metamorphosis of Law into Gospel," 87. The authors note how von Rad remarks too about the "protestant atmosphere" that pervades the book of Deuteronomy. See von Rad, *Deuteronomium-Studien,* 47; *Studies in Deuteronomy,* 68.

34. Manfred Oeming, "Gerhard von Rad as a Theologian of the Church," *Interpretation* 62 (2008): 231–37, here 231. Von Rad's most important works include: *Theologie des Alten Testaments. BD I, Die Theologie der geschichtlichen Überlieferungen Israels* (Munich: Chr. Kaiser Verlag, 1957); English translation, *Old Testament Theology*, vol. 1: *The Theology of Israel's Historical Traditions*, trans. D. M. G. Stalker (New York: Harper & Row, 1962); and the influential *Theologisches Wörterbuch zum Neuen Testament* (Stuttgart: W. Kohlhammer, 1932), which he edited with Gerhard Kittel (an open supporter of the Nazi Party). These were included among the many standard sources cited in Hans Küng's work on the Church.

35. Küng, *The Church,* 158, 159.

36. Jeremy Cohen coined the expression "hermeneutical Jew" in "Anti-Jewish Discourse and Its Function in Medieval Christian Theology," paper presented to the New Chaucer Society in August 1992; and in "The Muslim Connection: On the Changing Role of the Jew in High Medieval Theology," presented at the Herzog August Bibliothek in Wolfenbüttel, Germany, October 1993, later published in *From Witness to Witchcraft: Jews and Judaism in Medieval Christian Thought,* ed. J. Cohen (Wiesbaden: Harrassowitz, 1996), 141–62. See also his *Living Letters of the Law: Ideas of the Jew in Medieval Christianity* (Berkeley: University of California Press, 1999). Other important studies are Robert A. Markus, "The Jew as a Hermeneutical Device: The Inner Life of a Gregorian *Topos,*" in *Gregory the Great: A Symposium,* ed. John C. Cavadini (Notre Dame, IN: University of Notre Dame Press, 1995), 1–15; and Franklin T. Harkins, "Nuancing Augustine's Hermeneutical Jew: Allegorical and Actual Jews in the Bishop's Sermons," *Journal for the Study of Judaism* 36 (2005): 41–64.

37. See Rosemary Radford Ruether, "The *Adversus Judaeos* Tradition in the Church Fathers: The Exegesis of Christian Anti-Judaism," in *Essential Papers on Judaism and Christianity in Conflict: From Late Antiquity to the Reformation,* ed. Jeremy Cohen (New York: New York University Press, 1991), 174–89. The ahistorical depiction of Jews is so common that special note is made of Agobard (769–840), the archbishop of Lyons, who was the first Christian thinker to write at length about *actual* Jews in his time. See Cohen, *Living Letters of the Law,* 130–31.

38. Michael A. Signer, "Jews and Judaism in the New Catechism of the Catholic Church—An Intervention," in *Coming Together for the Sake of God: Contributions to Jewish-Christian Dialogue from Post-Holocaust Germany,* ed. Hanspeter Heinz and Michael A. Signer (Collegeville, MN: Liturgical Press, 2007), 63–68, quote at 65. Paragraph 840 of the New Catechism is: "And when one considers the future, God's People of the Old Covenant and the new People of God tend toward similar goals: expectation of the coming (or the return) of the Messiah. But one awaits the return of the Messiah who died and rose from the dead and is recognized as Lord and Son of God; the other awaits the coming of a Messiah whose features remain hidden till the end of time; and the latter waiting is accompanied by the drama of not knowing or of misunderstanding Jesus Christ."

39. See "U.S. Bishops Seek Clarity on Jewish Covenant," *America* 199.5 (2008): 6–7.

CHAPTER SIXTEEN

Rabbi Hayim David Halevi on Christianity and Christians

An Analysis of Selected Legal Writings of an Israeli Authority

David Ellenson

One of the greatest joys and blessings in my life has been my thirty years of relationship with my irrepressible and brilliant friend Michael Signer. For more than a decade, I was privileged to be his faculty colleague at Hebrew Union College–Jewish Institute of Religion in Los Angeles, and not a single day passed during those years that Michael and I did not speak with—often for hours—and learn from one another about intellectual, spiritual, and personal matters. While I felt his departure from HUC-JIR to become the Abrams Professor of Jewish Thought and Culture at the University of Notre Dame as a great loss, I remain grateful that the chord that links us has remained unbroken. I take such pride in all he has accomplished in his current position and am thankful that the Jewish community has such a learned, passionate, and committed scholar-rabbi in the highest international and national circles of Catholic-Jewish dialogue and academic discourse.

Michael has modeled so many things for me, foremost among them that profound scholarship is linked to the deepest existential commitments that a person possesses. I will review some of those commitments as a way of introducing the present essay in honor of Michael. Raised as I was with so many traditional teachers, the Jewish voice as contained in the legal tradition of my people continues to inform my soul at some very deep level. I continue to be attracted to the genre of Jewish legal literature labeled "responsa" and this genre continues to represent for me—all the issues raised by post-modernism regarding "essentialist postures" notwithstanding—a powerfully authentic Jewish language to which I have devoted many hours of research.

For the uninitiated in this literature, responsa can best be understood as technical legal documents—case discussions and their "holdings," in modern Western jurisprudential nomenclature—that rabbis throughout the centuries have used to apply the insights, meanings, norms, and precedents provided by the literary and legal texts of the Jewish past (namely, Bible, Talmud, codes of law, and other responsa) to the issues of the age. Simply put, for over a thousand years leading rabbinic jurist-legislators have employed responsa to issue authoritative renderings of Jewish law to rabbinic colleagues for application in particular cases. A single responsum must be seen as part of a vast body of Jewish case law that stretches over the centuries. It is the crossroads where text and context meet in the ongoing tradition of Jewish legal hermeneutics. Responsa constitute a distinctively idiomatic mode of Jewish discourse.

I have always loved discussing this literature with Michael and have profited immeasurably from the empathic yet critical insights his conversations and observations on this material have yielded. It is therefore with a great sense of gratitude to Michael for our ongoing friendship and ties that I here provide an analysis of a legal writing authored by Rabbi Hayim David Halevi (1924–1998) on the relationship between Judaism and Christianity. Rabbi Halevi was the outstanding pupil of the famed Chief Sephardic Rabbi of Israel Ben Zion Meir Hai Ouziel and studied with his mentor for many years at the prestigious *Yeshivat Porat Yosef* in Jerusalem. He later served as Chief Sephardic Rabbi of Tel Aviv–Jaffa and he was one of the most prolific and famous rabbinic authorities in Israel during his lifetime.

The legal writing under consideration in this essay reveals the complex attitudes this traditional Israeli Sephardic rabbi, who received no formal secular education, possessed regarding the Church and Christians. The changes in positions Rabbi Halevi adopted toward Christians and the Church are contained in various parts of his nine-volume collection of responsa entitled, *'Aseh l'kha rav.* While I will focus in particular on a responsum entitled, "Concerning the Relationships between Jews and Non-Jews," I will also contextualize this particular writing by placing it against the backdrop of several other responsa that both Rabbi Halevi and a major rival, Rabbi Ovadiah Yosef, former Chief Sephardic Rabbi of Israel and founder and head of the Israeli Shas political party, wrote relating to this broad topic.[1]

To provide a framework for comprehending the nature and for illuminating the significance of the positions Rabbi Halevi advanced in his responsum, I turn to a distinction Michael has drawn in a lecture, "Body and Soul: Interreligious Dialogue in the Theology of Abraham Joshua Heschel," that he delivered in Warsaw on 7 June 2008.[2] In his lecture, Michael offers an analysis of a letter that Rabbi Heschel sent to Augustine Cardinal Bea on 22 May 1962, as well as the 1966 address, "No Religion Is an Island," that Heschel delivered as his Inaugural Lecture as Henry Emerson Fosdick Visiting Professor at Union Theological Seminary.

At the conclusion of his remarks, Michael noted that Heschel called for "a revolution in language" in interreligious discourse. He pointed out that Heschel called for Jews and Christians in interreligious dialogue "to be of 'help to one another.'" In explicating the meaning of this phrase, Michael called for "a shift in the discursive style that Jews and Christians have addressed their communication to one another." He concluded: "The political power of either flattery or refutation moves humans to split their communicative patterns into an inner and outer discourse. The inner discourse is one of triumph while the outer discourse is purely utilitarian and aims at manipulating the other."

This distinction between "inner" and "outer" modes of Jewish discourse is both provocative and suggestive, though not absolute. As such, it provides an illuminating starting point for comprehending the writings under consideration in this essay. In his legal work, Rabbi Halevi clearly engages in an "inner discourse" in an idiomatic Jewish legal genre. However, we will see that his work ultimately reflects neither "manipulation" nor "triumph." On the contrary, it bespeaks an evolving understanding of and even the development of an attitude of appreciation for Christians and the Church. The complexity of the positions he advances demonstrates that even in an

internal mode of discourse, a sensitive religious leader can come to understand that both Jews and Christians are commanded to recognize that God
addresses Jew and Gentile alike in a manner that asks members of both
faith traditions "to demand justice, to promote compassion, and to develop
an empathy for those who struggle to remain faithful to the living God." As
Michael observes, quoting Heschel, "Religion is not an end, but a process."
The legal writings presented in this essay capture this ethos of development
and progression as they sometimes appear even in the most traditional pre-
cincts of the modern Jewish world.

Background to Rabbi Halevi's Mature Views

In the first volume of his responsa collection, *'Aseh l'kha rav,* Responsum 59, Rabbi Halevi was asked by a Jewish tourist who "came to visit in a
church" whether Jewish "entry into a church was permitted for purposes of
a visit only."[3] In order to comprehend the answer that Rabbi Halevi offered
in this instance, it is necessary to understand that the Christian belief in
the Trinity is theologically problematic from a Jewish perspective. Judaism
requires that Jews affirm a belief in the "Absolute Oneness" (*Achdut*) of God.
The Trinitarian conception of the deity—as the Father, the Son, and the
Holy Spirit—was therefore understood by no less an authority than Maimonides as a form of idolatry,[4] for Maimonides held that the doctrine of
the Trinity compromised the standard of *Achdut* that Judaism establishes
as necessary for a faith to be defined as monotheistic.[5]

Rabbi Halevi was aware of this Maimonidean stance concerning Christianity. At the same time, he knew that other rabbinic authorities took a
less severe stance on this question. These authorities would not consign
Christianity to the category of idolatry, nor would they accept a definition
of Christians as idol-worshippers. In a comment on *Sanhedrin* 63b, Rabbi
Isaac of late twelfth-century France, the nephew of Rabbenu Tam, spoke
of Christians and Christianity in the following terms: "Although they [i.e.,
Christians] mention the name of Heaven, meaning thereby Jesus of Nazareth, they do not at all events mention a strange deity, and moreover, they
mean thereby the Maker of Heaven and Earth too; and despite the fact that

they associate the name of Heaven with an alien deity, we do not find that it is forbidden to cause Gentiles to make such an association . . . since such an association (*Shituf*) is not forbidden to the sons of Noah [i.e., Gentiles]."[6]

In adopting this position, Rabbi Isaac adopted a perspective that removed Christians from the category of "idol-worshippers." While Trinitarianism remained a forbidden theological posture for Jews, adherence to this notion by Christians was deemed an acceptable form of monotheism as this doctrine fell under the rabbinic category of *Shituf* (Associationism). Indeed, Rabbi Menachem Ha-Me'iri of early fourteenth-century Provence expanded upon this doctrine and stated explicitly that contemporary Christians "recognize the Godhead" and "believe in God's existence, His unity and power, although they misconceive some points according to our belief."[7] He further declared that his Christian peers did not fall under the category of "idol-worshippers" and stated, "Now idolatry has disappeared from most places."[8] This trajectory found later expression in Jewish legal writings and Rabbi Yehuda Ashkenazi, writing on Christians and Christianity in his commentary on the *Shulhan Aruch, Yoreh De'ah* 151:2, asserted, "In our era . . . when the Gentiles in whose midst we dwell . . . [speak of God], their intention is directed towards the One Who made Heaven and Earth, albeit that they associate another personality with God. However, this does not constitute a violation of Leviticus 19:14, 'You shall not place a stumbling block before the blind,' for non-Jews are not warned against such Associationism (*Shituf*)."[9]

Returning to the responsum itself, Rabbi Halevi—despite the various postures displayed in Jewish law toward Christianity—held that Jewish law on the question of whether a Jew could enter a church for purposes of a tourist visit was nonetheless clear: entry into a church was absolutely forbidden. He maintained that this was because a Jew is forbidden to enter "a house of idol worship even after the idolatry is removed."[10] In advancing this ruling, Rabbi Halevi indicated that he relied upon Maimonides. He observed that the Mishneh Torah held that a Jew was prohibited from entering a city where there was a house of idol worship. Halevi reasoned that if it was forbidden to even enter a city where such a building exists, then it was surely forbidden to enter the church itself. Indeed, Rabbi Halevi asserted that the only exception to such entry into a church for a Jew was when life itself was at stake—that is, one could enter a church in order to save a life.[11]

Rabbi Halevi further stated that he did not believe, as his questioner did, that the rabbinic principle, "on account of the ways of peace" (*mipnei darkhei shalom*), should constitute grounds for easing this prohibition. While the Talmud and early rabbinic literature had ruled that this principle could be evoked to demand, among other things, that a Jew care for Gentile poor, eulogize and bury Gentile dead, and offer comfort to Gentiles who were engaged in mourning,[12] Rabbi Halevi did not believe that this principle could be extended to justify Jewish entry into a church.[13]

Rabbi Halevi explained his stance by advancing the following argument. He acknowledged that contemporary Christians were not idolaters, as Christians—unlike Jews—are not commanded concerning the absolute Unity and Oneness of God (*Achdut*). Rather, they are required to affirm the existence (*Metziut*) of God alone. Consequently, *Shituf* (Associationism) was permitted them as a form of monotheism. However, *Shituf* is not permitted Jews. For Jews, *Shituf* constitutes idolatry as it violates the standard of affirming the "Absolute Oneness" (*Achdut*) of God that Jewish tradition requires of Jews.[14]

Rabbi Halevi then asserted that the specific issue of whether a Jewish tourist could enter a church for purposes of "enjoyment" rather than "ritual worship" depended entirely upon the uses that contemporary Christians make of the church. Citing *Avodah Zarah* 3 as precedent, he noted that the Talmud permitted a Jew to enter a bath where there was a statue of Aphrodite that was intended only for beautification, not worship. Therefore, Rabbi Halevi reasoned by analogy that a Jew could enter a museum or private home where crosses and other Christian artifacts stand, for these ritual items are intended for aesthetic purposes alone. However, if the church was employed for contemporary Christian worship, then it was forbidden for a Jew to cross the threshold of the church, for a Christian house of worship was—for a Jew—idolatrous.[15]

In making these statements, Rabbi Halevi indicated that he did not agree that the refusal of a Jew to enter a church used for Christian worship should be regarded as an insult to Christians or Christianity. Rabbi Halevi therefore asked why this failure to enter a church used for Christian worship should be construed as injuring or insulting anyone. He asked, "If a Jew refuses to eat non-kosher food, does this injure anyone?"[16] Having presented this example, Rabbi Halevi therefore contended that he saw no reason why a Jew should be required, "on account of the ways of peace," to surrender "his faith and his principles" and enter the church. He insisted that the prohibition against Jewish entry into a church used for Christian worship entailed no act of "religious or national discrimination" against Christianity or Christians and only allowed the Jew to affirm the integrity of the Jewish theological position regarding monotheism for Jews.[17] With this observation, his first responsum came to an end.

Years later, Rabbi Halevi was asked once again whether a Jew was allowed to enter a church that was not used for ritual purposes. Here the questioner asked Rabbi Halevi whether it was permissible to enter into a church as a tourist, "as one who goes into a museum."[18] He ruled once again that it was certainly not forbidden for a Jew to enter a church for purposes of tourism. However, this time he added another consideration. He cited another authority who stated, "There is no prohibition against praying in a structure where idol worship took place, even if such worship was fixed."[19] Consequently, inasmuch as "temporary prayer" was allowed in a building that had formerly been used for "forbidden worship," he contended that it was certainly permitted to enter a church for purposes of appreciating its architectural structure. In moving from Rabbi Halevi's first to second responsa on this subject, one observes a slight softening of his view of a church as "a house of idolatry" for Jews, an evolution that would be—as will be shown below—more fully developed in later years. Had the beginnings of this change not been evidenced here, Rabbi Halevi could not have even countenanced the possibility that a Jew could recite "temporary prayer" in a church.

Before turning to the responsum, "Concerning the Relationships between Jews and Non-Jews," that represents the attitudes that the fully mature Rabbi Halevi adopted on the question of the relationship between Judaism and Christianity, it will be instructive to examine the ruling that his chief rival, Rabbi Ovadiah Yosef, put forth on the same question of whether a Jew could visit a church. The posture Rabbi Yosef assumed on this matter and the contrasts between his reasoning and citations and those of Rabbi Halevi—despite overlaps between them—will provide an important framework not only for appreciating the slightly changed tone that marked Rabbi Halevi's later ruling on this question, but also for illuminating the precise nature of the positions that Rabbi Halevi put forth in his final responsum on the subject.

In his responsa collection, *Y'haveh Da'at* 4:45, Rabbi Yosef was asked the exact question, "Is it permissible for a Jew to visit a Christian church," that had been put to Rabbi Halevi. In his response, Rabbi Yosef began by observing that the Talmud (*Avodah Zarah* 17a) states that it is forbidden to even approach the entrance of a house of idol-worship. Furthermore, Maimonides, commenting on the Mishnah found on *Avodah Zarah* 11b, says— as we saw above—that all non-Jewish houses of prayer in Gentile cities are by definition "houses of idolatry."[20] Ideally, Jews should not even live in such cities. However, "on account of our sins, we are compelled against our will to dwell in the lands of idol worshipers."[21] If the law is such that we should not even live in such cities, then it is certainly forbidden—where Jews are not compelled to do so—for Jews to enter a church,[22] for Christians, he ruled, basing himself upon Maimonides in *Hilchot Ma'acha'lot Asurot* 11, are idolaters. Entry into their churches constitutes entering a house of idolatry, and it is therefore forbidden for a Jew to enter a church under any conditions.

To underscore this point, Rabbi Yosef turned to the writings of Judah the Pious (12th–13th centuries), who, in his *Sefer Hasidim* 435, told the following story. Judah wrote, "A Gentile owed a Jew a financial debt, and when the Jew attempted to collect the debt, the Gentile fled to his house of worship [in order to escape the Jew, as the Jew would not follow him there as his house of prayer was a place of idolatry that it was forbidden the Jew to enter]."[23] However, once the Jew, Rabbi Judah reported, did follow after him and entered the church in order to collect the debt. The Jew then repented this deed and approached a Sage to ask what he should do as an act of repentance for this violation. The Sage told him that he should fast each year on the anniversary of his having entered the church as an act of remorse, and this he did all his days.[24]

Rabbi Yosef then cited other authorities to further bolster his stance. Among them were Rabbi Hayyim Palagi of Izmir, Turkey (d. 1873), who ruled in his responsa collection (*Hayyim Ba-yad* 26) that "there was a severe prohibition against entering their houses of worship," and Rabbi David Zilberstein who (in his *Sh'vilei David* 145) ruled that entry into a Christian church was an *"issur torah,"* a prohibition decreed by the Torah itself.[25] Indeed, Rabbi Yosef stated that Rabbi Zilberstein held that a Jew could not enter into a church even when there was a fear that this would arouse enmity (*eivah*) on the part of Gentiles against Jews. And when Rabbi Eliezer Deutsch of Hungary (1850–1916) was asked, in his *Pri Hasadeh* 2:4, whether it was appropriate that Jews of public prominence had entered a church to attend a memorial ceremony for a non-Jewish national leader, he asserted that even this act of respect for a deceased Gentile violated a "grave prohibition" (*issur hamur*).[26] Rabbi Yosef also ruled, as Rabbi Deutsch had, that the prohibition was so great that it could not be waived even in a place where "enmity" would result. Indeed, Rabbi Deutsch, Rabbi Yosef approvingly reported, contended that Jews who had entered a church for any reason needed to engage in an act of repentance. Rabbi Yosef therefore concluded that it was absolutely forbidden for a Jew to enter a church under any conditions, and that Jewish tourists should not be swayed by any lenient ruling on this question and enter either past or present Christian houses of worship.[27] The uncompromising positions Rabbi Yosef put forth in this responsum only underscore the contrast between his posture and that of the fully mature Rabbi Halevi on the issue of Judaism's attitudes toward Christianity and Christians.

Rabbi Halevi's Mature Views on Christians and the Church

In Kislev 5748 (December 1987), Rabbi Halevi delivered what would be his definitive statement on Christians and Christianity, "Concerning the Relationships between Jews and Non-Jews." At the outset, he asserted that he deliberately chose not to focus in the traditional way on the halakhic category, "on account of the ways of peace," as a warrant for an inclusive approach to this topic.[28] Rabbi Halevi did this because he contended that most of the laws that fall under this category are irrelevant for deducing a proper Jewish attitude toward Christianity and Islam and Christians and Muslims for contemporary Jews who live in the sovereign Jewish State of Israel.[29] This was because the bulk of laws that fall under the category, "on account of the ways of peace," addressed Jewish life under the conditions of the Diaspora, conditions under which the Jewish community was reduced to a distinct and sometimes powerless minority. As a result, the directives that fell under this category and often instructed Jews to behave in charitable ways toward their Gentile neighbors were often primarily motivated by pragmatic considerations that would allow the Jew to live in harmony with more powerful Gentile neighbors. Rabbi Halevi did not dismiss such pragmatic motivations as frivolous or unimportant. However, it is clear that he wanted to discover a moral as opposed to a pragmatic posture to undergird a present-day Jewish attitude toward the other Abrahamic faiths and their adherents. Rabbi Halevi desired to affirm a stance that was consonant with both the politically sovereign status Jews now enjoyed as a majority population in the State of Israel and the ethos contained in the Israeli Declaration of Independence that stated, "Complete social and political equality will be established among all her citizens regardless of religion, race, or sex."[30] Rabbi Halevi embraced this affirmation and asserted that Israel must be committed to all its citizenry, including Gentiles, and must extend all the same rights to them that were granted to Jews.[31]

This does not mean that Rabbi Halevi totally ignored the category, "on account of the ways of peace." Indeed, he turned to Maimonides, *Hilchot Avodah Zarah* 9:5, where it states that Gentile poor are to be supported along with Jewish poor "on account of the ways of peace."[32] Rabbi Halevi also took note of the fact that the law immediately following, contained in *Hilchot Avodah Zarah* 9:6, seemed to circumscribe the application of this principle because Maimonides stated there that these directives based on the principle, "on account of the ways of peace," applied only when Jews dwelt as a minority in the midst of a majority culture or when Gentiles had sovereignty in the Land of Israel. As Maimonides wrote, "These rules only apply when the people Israel are exiled among the nations, or when the Gentiles have power over the people of Israel. However, when Israel has power over them, it is forbidden to allow Gentiles to dwell among us."[33]

However, Rabbi Halevi asserted that these last strictures contained in 9:6 of the Rambam were not applicable in the contemporary setting and that the instructions found in 9:5 that called upon the Jewish community to offer support to the poor "on account of the ways of peace" were actionable in the present-day State of Israel. While one might suppose that these obligations would not be incumbent upon Jews in contemporary Israel inasmuch as Israel was now a sovereign nation, Rabbi Halevi contended that that was not so. He said that those who make this claim were mistaken since the western world of democracy in which Israel participates has at its foundation the notion of equal rights among all persons. Rabbi Halevi stated that there is no place in a democratic state for religious discrimination and added that the world would simply not tolerate such behavior from the State of Israel. Consequently, Jews cannot be said to possess absolute sovereignty anywhere—even in the State of Israel. The ruling in *Hilchot Avodah Zarah* 9:6 was "non-actionable" in the present setting.[34]

However, Rabbi Halevi was not content to rest his argument upon what might be labeled a *realpolitik* approach. He further stated that all the decrees forbidding kindness and social interaction and support with Gentiles found in ancient and medieval rabbinic tradition did not apply to contemporary Gentiles for other reasons as well. Everything stated above in Maimonides and elsewhere in classical rabbinic sources applied only to those who were genuinely "idolaters," i.e., people who actually worshipped "statues and monuments."[35] Yet, contemporary Muslims and Christians who live in the State of Israel obviously did not fall into this category. Islam was a form of pure monotheism and Muslims no less than Jews worshipped the one God "Who created heaven and earth." Rabbi Halevi felt no need to engage in a lengthy discussion concerning the monotheistic status of Islam and did nothing more than advance the position that Muslims were not "idolaters."[36]

In regard to Christianity, Rabbi Halevi acknowledged that it might be possible to define Christianity as "idolatry." However, he asserted that that was not so in the contemporary era. To be sure, Rabbi Halevi introduced his discussion with a few general observations. He pointed out that Judaism has a "long and piercing account with Christianity as a religion."[37] This is not only because much Jewish blood has been spilled in the name of Christianity. Rather, it is because Christianity "perverted the foundations of Judaism beyond recognition."[38] The concept of the Trinity distorted the pure monotheism of Judaism with its belief that "God is One and God's Name is One." At a single blow, Christianity also uprooted those commandments and Jewish ways of life that served as the basis for the covenant that God established with the people Israel when Israel left Egypt.[39] His indictment of Christianity here at the outset of his discussion was certainly a strong one.

At the same time, Rabbi Halevi observed, Judaism is not a missionary religion. It pays no attention to any other faith. However, this is not the case with Christianity, which engages in vigorous proselytizing. Rabbi Halevi asserted that while Christianity may have denied any allegiance to the commandments, Jews should clearly appreciate Christianity. Through its missionary efforts, Christianity uprooted idolatry from the world and spread a permitted form of monotheism for Gentiles throughout the world. Rabbi Halevi therefore drew a distinction between Christianity as a faith, on the one hand, and Christians, on the other. With Christianity as a religion, Jews have had a long and painful history. However, this is not so with the Christian man or woman. In fact, Judaism maintains, along with Ben Azzai, that its adherents ought to interact with Christians according to the great principle of the Torah ("You shall love your neighbor as you love yourself") since all humanity is created in the image of God (*Avot* 3:14).[40]

Having opened his remarks in this way, Rabbi Halevi then continued with a lengthy discussion of whether Jewish law still regarded Christianity as a form of "idolatry." He acknowledged that there were surely elements of what could be labeled as "*avodah zarah*" (idolatry) in Christianity—faith in the Trinity, for example, stands in opposition to belief in the unity of God. Furthermore, the multiplicity of icons and statues of saints and crucifixes could admittedly be regarded as "idolatrous." However, Rabbi Halevi insisted that the concept of "idolatry" had to be regarded in a nuanced and multi-layered way. Indeed, he contended that what classical Jewish law condemned so uncompromisingly (*b'humrah rabah*) as "idolatry" was distinct from the Christian worship of God.[41]

Rabbi Halevi defended this position by constructing the following argument. He contended that the Talmud itself had already begun to develop the "first signs of greater moderation in later generations" that allowed for the creation of a novel legal category that would exempt many non-Jews from the category of "idol worshipper."[42] Thus, in *Hullin* 13a, the Talmud, commenting upon the ruling that meat slaughtered by an "idol-worshipper" is ritualistically impure and unfit for sale, distinguished between Gentiles who are committed to idolatry in principle and Gentiles who are not "genuine idolaters" but rather ones "who have inherited customs from their ancestors" (*she-minhag avoteihem b'y'deihem*).[43] Halevi claimed that the logic that even Maimonides put forth in his commentary on this *Hullin* passage should have compelled him to acknowledge that a logical distinction must be made between persons who hold a principled commitment to idol-worship and attribute divinity and power to their idols, on the one hand, and those who simply follow the practices and customs that their Sages instructed them to follow, on the other; and Halevi stated that this latter group constitutes the majority of Gentiles in the world.[44] Of these persons, as Rabbi Jochanan said, "Gentiles outside the Land of Israel are not actually idolaters. Rather, the custom of their ancestors is in their hands."[45]

Rabbi Halevi then followed this line of reasoning by noting that the *Tur, Yoreh De'ah* 148,[46] states that all the prohibitions that are prescribed for Jews toward idolaters are not applicable in "our age" (*ha-idana*).[47] He based this upon the Rashbam who cites Rashi, who states, "All is permitted, for they are not idolaters and they do not come and confess."[48] The *Bet Yosef*[49] also stated there that all the prohibitions listed in this chapter of the *Tur* are no longer in force, "as Gentiles outside the Land are not idolaters."[50] Rather, they fall under the category of those in whom "the customs of their ancestors are in their hands."[51] Finally, in the *Shulchan Aruch, Yoreh De'ah* 148:12, Caro wrote, "At this time, they are not steeped in the nature of idolatry. Therefore, all is permitted."[52]

From all this, Rabbi Halevi concluded, "And if this is said regarding those who genuinely worship idols, i.e., those who worship icons and statues, it is all the more so in relationship to Christianity."[53] For Trinitarianism does not constitute idolatry for Gentiles. It is a form of monotheism (*Shituf*) permitted to non-Jews. "No Christians in our day," Rabbi Halevi wrote, "are actually idol worshippers as were the Gentiles whom the Talmud condemned during the Talmudic era."[54] Moreover, he claimed that a literal belief in the Trinity had weakened among many Christians, and that there were many Christians who understand this form of faith as nothing more than allegory.[55] Consequently, contemporary Christians clearly fall within the legal category of "the customs of their ancestors are in their hands." They were not and are not "idolaters." While Rabbi Halevi conceded that Maimonides refused to make this distinction, he also contended that Maimonides was virtually the only medieval legal authority not to apply the category of "the customs of their ancestors are in their hands" to contemporaneous Christians and he looked to specific rulings issued by a variety of rabbis on a host of particular issues to demonstrate the correctness of this claim.[56]

In making this argument, Rabbi Halevi was grounding this part of his responsum on a particular traditional Jewish legal approach that Hebrew University professors Moshe Halbertal and Avishai Margalit have pointed out "involves changing the status of Christians without changing the status of Christianity."[57] It is an approach that asserts that "the Christians were not devoted adherents of their religion but were simply following the customs of their ancestors. There is no change in the status of Christianity as an idolatrous religion; only the status of the Christians as loyal practitioners of this religion changed."[58] While this approach was clearly more tolerant than one that simply labeled Christians as "idolaters," Rabbi Halevi was not content with this position and in the final pages of his responsum advanced another posture that represents his views in their full development.

In *Idolatry*, Halbertal and Margalit point out that the great Provençal scholar Rabbi Menachem ben Solomon Meiri (1249–1316) (Ha-Me'iri) advanced a Jewish position regarding Christianity that was distinct from the one discussed above. While that stance involved "changing the status of Christians without changing the status of Christianity," the posture Ha-Me'iri put forth reflected "a change in the status of Christianity itself."[59] As Halbertal and Margalit view it, "The change in attitude toward Christianity stemmed not from the claim that Christians have monotheistic metaphysical beliefs but from a renewed understanding of idolatry as a lawless lifestyle."[60] By creating a distinction "between monotheists and idolaters," Ha-Me'iri created "a new distinction between nations that are law-abiding and nations that are not."[61] By putting forth this new mode of categorization, Ha-Me'iri was able to distinguish "Christians from the idolaters to whom the laws in tractate *Avodah Zarah* and in other parts of the Talmud apply."[62] It is the matter of "degenerate lifestyle," not issues of "metaphysics," that defines "idolatry." Inasmuch as Christians "insist upon a moral lifestyle," Christianity is "a nonidolatrous religion."[63]

Halbertal and Margalit are undoubtedly correct in identifying the approach that Ha-Me'iri adopted toward Christianity as "a nonidolatrous religion" as a novel one in the Jewish legal tradition. Indeed, we will see that

Rabbi Halevi justified his own approach to Christianity on the basis of Ha-Me'iri's teachings. At the same time, an examination of the final arguments he put forth in this responsum went beyond issues of "Christian lifestyle," and his presentation of Ha-Me'iri on this topic reflected a "metaphysical appreciation" of Christianity as well.

In a number of sections in his responsum dealing with various Talmudic interdictions against Jewish interactions with "idolaters," Rabbi Halevi asserted, based on his reading of Ha-Me'iri, that none of these prohibitions were in force in regard to Christians. Citing the opinions of Ha-Me'iri contained in his commentary on the first tractate of *Avodah Zarah*, Rabbi Halevi contended, "In our times, all [interactions with Gentiles] are permitted, as [these prohibitions issued by the rabbis of the Talmud] applied only to their time . . . when they (i.e., non-Jews) worshipped the hosts of heaven—sun, moon, and stars."[64] While it is true that Ha-Me'iri claimed that Christians "erred" (*mishtabshin*) in regard to certain issues of faith, he also asserted that they nevertheless believed in the existence of God—His Unity and Power. Christian faith bore no resemblance to pagan religion, in which "idols of stone and wood" were worshipped. Contemporary Christians worshipped the God "Who created Heaven and Earth."[65] Rabbi Halevi could therefore assert that Christians believe in "the Exodus from Egypt, the renewal of the world, and in the fundamental principles of faith. Their every intention is toward the One who made Heaven and Earth."[66] His reading of Ha-Me'iri caused Rabbi Halevi to assume an attitude toward Christianity that did far more than simply acknowledge that Christians adopted a "moral lifestyle" incumbent upon all persons. His own theological sensibility allowed him to appreciate, as he felt Ha-Me'iri had, the "metaphysical truths" contained in the Christian faith as well.

Rabbi Halevi further contended that countless other Jewish legal authorities—among them Ovadiah Bartenora, Tosafot Yom Tov, and Moses Isserles—subsequent to Ha-Me'iri developed their teachings on Christianity in relationship to these theological understandings that Ha-Me'iri had advanced. These rabbis therefore asserted that the Christians in whose midst they dwelt were absolutely not "*ovdei avodah zarah*" (idol worshippers). In the words of Isserles in his note on *Orah Hayyim* 126, "We are obligated to pray for their welfare."[67]

Rabbi Halevi went on to claim that instances of positive interaction with Christians in all facets of life constituted acts of *"Kiddush hashem"* (sanctification of the Name of God) that "adorn Israel." Rabbi Halevi cited numerous responsa by diverse rabbinical authorities who described specific deeds of charity and goodness toward Christians as *ma'asei Kiddush hashem,* actions that sanctified the Name of God in the world.[68]

Rabbi Halevi even asserted that Jews should accord Christians and Muslims the same treatment they would extend to Jews in areas of ethical obligation and concern. Based on the reasoning of Ha-Me'iri, Rabbi Halevi concluded his responsum by stating, "The legal category of 'idolater' does not apply to Gentiles of our day. [Therefore], even if Israel was completely sovereign, we are in no way obligated to act towards contemporary Gentiles as if the category of 'idolater' applied to them."[69] Furthermore, while "all relations between Jews and Gentiles, whether in Israel or in the Diaspora, whether in societal relationship as a State to her Gentile citizens, or whether in personal relationship between the Jew and his Gentile neighbor or friend" must be conducted with fairness and integrity, this should not be based on the prudential halakhic category of "on account of the ways of peace" as some rabbis might maintain.[70] Rather, "the maintenance and support of Gentiles, visiting their sick, burying their dead, comforting their mourners, and all other duties" can and should be performed, Rabbi Halevi maintained, on the basis of an overarching teaching of "human ethical obligation" (*hovah enosheet musarit*) that animates and informs all of Jewish religious tradition.[71] In making this last point, Rabbi Halevi clearly extended his teachings beyond what Ha-Me'iri had advanced and held that Judaism possessed a universal moral posture that was consonant with the democratic ethos that marked the modern world. The expansiveness of his thought was clearly profound.

It is noteworthy that, in an addendum to his responsum, Rabbi Halevi reported that Professor Menachem Elon, the Justice of the Israeli Supreme Court and the great student of Jewish law, objected to the position Rabbi Halevi had advanced in his presentation. While Justice Elon conceded that the approach of Ha-Me'iri did remove Christians "altogether from the category of idolaters," he nevertheless stated that Ha-Me'iri was alone in adopting this general stance.[72] Indeed, Elon asserted that no other rabbinic authority did so, even though in specific instances they did rule leniently, as Rabbi Halevi correctly pointed out. Therefore, he asked, "How can we arrive at the overarching Jewish conclusion that Christians in our day can be removed from the category of 'idolaters?'"[73]

To this, Rabbi Halevi responded that it might be true that Ha-Me'iri was alone among all Jewish legal authorities in explicitly advancing an overarching position that removed Christians altogether from the category of "idolaters." However, Ha-Me'iri was hardly a minor authority. Furthermore, Rabbi Halevi would not concede that Rabbi Meiri was unique in his assertion that Christians do not fall within the category of "idolaters." He stated that countless rabbis, writing on particular issues, had asserted over and over again and in diverse sources drawn from different lands and times that Christians were not idolaters. Therefore, asked Rabbi Halevi, "What prevents us—on the basis of the same legal logic—from expanding these specific *hetarim* (permissions) and establishing the general principle that Ha-Me'iri had, one that affirms that Christians are not idolaters?"[74] Therefore, Rabbi Halevi concluded, "I stand by my position" regarding Christians and Christianity.[75]

Conclusion

In summarizing and assessing the content and nature of the legal stances Rabbi Halevi put forth in his writings on Christians and Christianity, it is instructive to turn to a commentary that Avi Ravitsky of Hebrew University has written on the major responsum under consideration in this essay. A consideration of Ravitsky's commentary illuminates not only the broader dynamics at play in Rabbi Halevi's approach to Jewish law but also the significance of the latter's positions on this particular issue. In his article, "'Ways of Peace' and the Status of Gentiles according to the Rambam: An Exchange of Letters with Rabbi Hayyim David Halevi," Ravitsky observes that Rabbi Halevi prefers to interpret classical halakhic sources "according to their straightforward meaning."[76] He does not attempt to impose upon them novel interpretations, "*midrash hadash.*" However, Ravitsky also notes that this "legal fundamentalism" does not prevent "R. Halevi from displaying flexibility and halakhic innovation. Indeed, exactly the opposite is the case. He 'neutralizes' the source and negates its contemporary relevance and authority."[77] The rabbinic interpreter must understand the meaning of the source precisely as it is and then determine carefully whether it is actually applicable in the contemporary situation.

Ravitsky defines this approach that characterizes Rabbi Halevi as one of "conservative audacity."[78] Indeed, his "legal fundamentalism"[79] and his refusal to provide "a new midrash" on the sources before him often allow him not only to "neutralize the earlier source," but "to display halakhic flexibility in response to a new [social-political-religious] reality."[80] Precedents contained in earlier writings are often deemed "irrelevant" as the circumstances that surrounded the source are completely different from those that obtain in the current situation. The vitality of Jewish law provides the rabbinic decisor with broad discretionary powers as the rabbi has the right to assert that as "the contours and circumstances of life change," so the application of the Law must change as well.[81]

In the examples presented in this essay, Rabbi Halevi therefore acknowledges that the sources do speak of "idolatry." There is no question that the Talmud and rabbinic tradition have stringent views on the topic. However, his analysis of these sources permits Rabbi Halevi to assign and limit the applications of these sources to a past when persons actually worshiped statues and masks. They do not refer to Gentiles in our day, and they certainly cannot be applied to contemporary Muslims and Christians. In effect, his legal methodology facilitates innovation even as it affirms a fidelity to the tradition.

In Ravitsky's opinion, this is precisely what is most significant about his writings on Christians and Christianity. Indeed, his approach allowed Rabbi Halevi to contend that care for Christians and Muslims—indeed, all humans—stems from a worldview of "ethical human obligation" inherent in the tradition. This sense of moral obligation allows for a correction of the formal Jewish law beyond the pragmatic considerations inherent in the category, "on account of the ways of peace." Furthermore, this belief that Jewish tradition countenanced a spirit of "ethical human obligation" provided the basis for expanding the recognition of obligations toward Gentiles in a broad and inclusive way not limited by specific matters defined in the Talmud. By asserting that "ethical human obligations" constitute an integral and overarching principle—a meta-principle—that informs and guides the Jewish legal tradition, Rabbi Halevi offered a "*hiddush hilchati*" (an halakhic innovation), and he had Judaism speak in a contemporary ethical voice that held, as Ravitsky puts it, "that universal obligations exceed the bounds of the halakhic formal command."[82]

In concluding this analysis of Rabbi Halevi and his writings on Christians and Christianity, the overarching developments that took place in the Sephardic Sage's attitudes toward Christians and Christianity are noteworthy. While Rabbi Halevi "did not hesitate to rule that [Christian believers] were akin to idolaters in every way" in his earlier writings, he ultimately came to affirm that contemporary Christians "were not idolaters."[83] As Ravitsky states in his summation of Rabbi Halevi's work, "Over the passage of years there was a significant evolution in his opinions on these matters."[84] This essay certainly concurs in that assessment. Through an analysis of this Jewish mode of "internal discourse," we have seen that religious tradition, in the hands of a sensitive and bold interpreter, can be supple. The task of developing "empathy for those who struggle," in all religions, "to remain faithful to the living God" is an ongoing challenge for us all. In attempting to meet this challenge, I remain especially grateful that we have figures like Rabbi Halevi and my friend Rabbi Signer to guide us.

Notes

1. Two significant English language articles on R. Halevi are Marc Angel, "Rabbi Hayyim David Halevy: A Leading Contemporary Rabbinic Thinker," *Jewish Book Annual* 52 (1994): 99–109; and Zvi Zohar, "Sephardic Religious Thought in Israel: Aspects of the Theology of Rabbi Haim David Halevi," in *Critical Essays on Israeli Society, Religion, and Government,* ed. Kevin Avruch and Walter Zenner (Albany: SUNY Press, 1997), 115–36. In addition, I have written three essays in the past decade on elements of his thought. See David Ellenson, "Interpretive Fluidity and P'sak in a Case of *Pidyon Sh'vuyim:* An Analysis of a Modern Israeli Responsum as Illuminated by the Thought of David Hartman," in *Judaism and Modernity: The Religious Philosophy of David Hartman,* ed. Jonathan Malino (Jerusalem: Shalom Hartman Institute, 2001), 341–67; "Jewish Legal Interpretation and Moral Values: Two Responsa by Rabbi Hayyim David Halevi on the Obligations of the Israeli Government towards its Minority Population," *Central Conference of American*

Rabbis' Journal 48 no. 3 (Summer 2001): 5–20; and "A Portrait of the *Posek* as Modern Religious Leader: An Analysis of Selected Writings of Rabbi Hayyim David Halevi," in *Jewish Religious Leadership: Image and Reality,* vol. 2, ed. Jack Wertheimer (New York: Jewish Theological Seminary, 2004), 673–93. Two books on Rabbi Halevi have also appeared. The first, an important and comprehensive book of essays, is *A Living Judaism: Essays on the Halakhic Thought of Rabbi Hayyim David Halevi* [Hebrew], ed. Zvi Zohar and Avi Sagi (Jerusalem: Shalom Hartman Institute and the Faculty of Law, Bar Ilan University, 2005). The second is written by Marc D. Angel with Hayyim Angel, *Rabbi Haim David Halevi: Gentle Scholar and Courageous Thinker* (Jerusalem: Urim Publications, 2006). Recent years have also seen two major scholarly works appear on Rabbi Yosef that bear attention: Benjamin Lau, *From "Maran" to "Maran": The Halakhic Philosophy of Rav Ovadiah Yosef* [Hebrew] (Tel Aviv: Miskal-Yedoth Ahronoth Books and Chemed Books, 2005), and Ariel Picard, *The Philosophy of Rabbi Ovadya Yosef in an Age of Transition* [Hebrew] (Ramat-Gan: Bar-Ilan University Press, 2007).

2. I would like to thank Michael for sharing this as yet unpublished lecture with me in typescript. In that lecture, Michael reports that the letter between Rabbi Heschel and Cardinal Bea is being prepared for publication by Susannah Heschel. The Heschel essay, "No Religion Is an Island," appears in Abraham Joshua Heschel, *Moral Grandeur and Spiritual Audacity,* ed. Susannah Heschel (New York: Farrar, Straus and Giroux, 1996), 235–50.

3. *'Aseh l'kha rav* 1:59, p. 178.

4. See Maimonides, *Mishneh Torah, Hilchot Akum* 9:4 and *Peirush Hamishnah, Avodah Zarah* 1:3.

5. Moshe Halbertal and Avishai Margalit in *Idolatry* (Cambridge, MA: Harvard University Press, 1993), 110–12, provide a philosophical explanation as to why Maimonides regarded the Christian concept of the Trinity as an unacceptable standard of monotheism for Jews. As they explain, Jewish belief "in the oneness of God [is] not merely denial of polytheism." Rather, the belief in *Achdut* as a requirement of monotheism for Jews demands the rejection of "Multiplicity," i.e., "not only the [rejection of the] belief in many gods," but the rejection of "an error that concerns God himself, which may be called 'internal polytheism.' The strict demand on unity implies a rejection of corporeality," for corporeality assumes that God is divisible, thus "vitiat[ing] God's perfection." After all, "the idea of matter is associated with decay, and it is also conceptually connected with finitude," and "decay and finitude" cannot be combined "with the idea of a perfect God." Moreover, "corporeality entails divisibility, and hence the notion of a corporeal God undermines God's unity."

6. The text of Rabbi Isaac can be found in the *Tosafot* to *Sanhedrin* 63b and *Bekhorot* 2b. The translation is taken from Jacob Katz, *Exclusiveness and Tolerance: Jewish-Gentile Relations in Medieval and Modern Times* (New York: Schocken, 1969), 35.

7. This translation from Ha-Me'iri is found in Katz, *Exclusiveness and Tolerance*, 36.

8. Ibid., 121.

9. The translation of Rabbi Ashkenazi is mine.

10. *'Aseh l'kha rav* 1:59, p. 178.

11. Ibid., 178–79.

12. See Jerusalem Talmud, *Gittin* 5:9; *Demaii* 4:6; *Avodah Zarah* 1:3; and Babylonian Talmud, *Gittin* 63a; as well as Maimonides, *Mishneh Torah, Hilchot Melachim* 10:12

13. *'Aseh l'kha rav* 1:59, p. 180.

14. Ibid., 181.

15. Ibid.

16. Ibid., 180.

17. Ibid.

18. *'Aseh l'kha rav* 4:53, p. 280.

19. Ibid.

20. *Y'haveh Da'at* 4:45, p. 235.

21. Ibid.

22. Rabbi Yosef goes on to cite numerous authorities—the Rashba, the Ritba, and the Rosh—who also all rule in this fashion on this matter.

23. *Y'haveh Da'at* 4:45, pp. 235–36.

24. Ibid. The phrasing here is mine.

25. Ibid., 237, where Rabbi Yosef cites both Rabbi Palagi and Rabbi Zilberstien.

26. Ibid.

27. Ibid.

28. Another treatment of this responsum is found in Marc Angel, *Rabbi Haim David Halevi*, 190–93.

29. *'Aseh l'kha rav* 9:30, p. 61.

30. Ibid.

31. Ibid.

32. Ibid., 62.

33. Ibid.

34. Ibid., 63.

35. Ibid.

36. Ibid.

37. Ibid.

38. Ibid., 64.

39. Ibid.

40. Ibid., 64–65.

41. Ibid., 65.

42. Ibid.

43. Ibid., 65–66.

44. Ibid., 66–67.

45. *Hullin* 13b.

46. The *Tur* is the great legal code of Rabbi Jacob ben Asher (1270–1340).

47. *'Aseh l'kha rav* 9:30, p. 66.

48. The Rashbam is Rabbi Samuel ben Meier, the grandson of Rashi and a medieval commentator on the Bible and the Talmud.

49. A commentary on the *Tur* written by Rabbi Joseph Caro between 1522–1544.

50. *'Aseh l'kha rav* 9:30, p. 66.

51. Ibid.

52. The *Shulchan Aruch* is the premiere code of Jewish law completed in 1564 by Joseph Caro.

53. *'Aseh l'kha rav* 9:30, p. 66.

54. Ibid., 67.

55. Ibid.

56. Halevi devotes a considerable number of pages to establishing this point and cites numerous authorities who issue *hetarim* (permissions) for Jews to interact with Christians on matters ranging from business dealings to selling them homes, from returning lost objects to them to praying for their health. However, R. Halevi concedes that the justification for these "leniencies" are based primarily either on the essentially pragmatic principle of "on account of the ways of peace," or as a result of the legal category, "the ways of their ancestors are in their hands." See his summations of these issues on pp. 67–72 of his responsum.

57. Halbertal and Margalit, *Idolatry,* 211.

58. Ibid., 211–12.

59. Ibid., 212.

60. Ibid.

61. Ibid.

62. Ibid.

63. Ibid., 212–13.

64. *'Aseh l'kha rav* 9:30, p. 68.

65. Ibid., 68 and 71.

66. Ibid., 71.

67. Ibid., 69 and 71.

68. Ibid., 70.

69. Ibid., 72.

70. Ibid., 73.

71. Ibid.

72. Ibid., 74.

73. Ibid.

74. Ibid., 75.

75. Ibid.

76. Avi Ravitsky, "'Ways of Peace' and the Status of Gentiles according to the Rambam: An Exchange of Letters with Rabbi Hayyim David Halevi," in Zohar and Sagi, *A Living Judaism,* 255–85, here 264.

77. Ibid.

78. Ibid., 260.

79. Ibid., 264.

80. Ibid., 260.

81. Ibid., 265.

82. Ibid., 258.

83. Ibid., 257.

84. Ibid., 258.

CHAPTER SEVENTEEN

Michael Signer's Theological Philosophy of the Plain Sense

Peter Ochs

Michael Signer's text-historical scholarship on medieval plain-sense commentary embodies a more general theological philosophy of the plain sense. This philosophy introduces a model, at once, for text-historical studies and for reparative work in the Jewish and Christian communities today. The purpose of this essay is, through a brief overview of Michael's work and through illustrative readings of several of his essays, to provide evidence of this model and to outline its defining elements. In a first draft, I added "I believe" to almost every sentence since Michael does not draw attention to his work in this way and since I cannot therefore be sure that he or fellow scholars would agree with my reading and modeling. To have mercy on the reader, I have removed all but one of the "I believe"s, but please note that this disclaimer remains. And one more thing: The reason I offer this account is that I believe Michael's philosophy of the plain sense answers an urgent need in both the academy and the religious communities today.

Once Over: An Overview

By the end of this essay, I hope to squeeze the defining elements of Michael's philosophy into something like an algorithm. First, I offer this warm up: a less disciplined overview of four broad areas of Michael's work—and that means work, at once, in academy and society.

Attention to scriptural commentary as an axiological window: Michael studies Jewish and Christian medieval scriptural commentary. While he focuses on the twelfth century and while he refuses to overgeneralize, there are more general lessons to learn from his studies of Rashi and the Tosafot and of Hugh and the Victorines. The first lesson is that a study of scriptural commentary reveals a lot about a tradition's defining values (what I will label its "axiology").[1] When, therefore, Michael examines Rashi's or the Rashbam's approach to plain sense, there are lessons not only about a particular set of scriptural passages or of rabbinic commentaries or of medieval interpretations of both of these. There are also more general lessons about such issues as: why plain sense is not enough; but why midrash is also not enough; why, therefore, Rashi and his descendants return to the plain sense but in a new way; how this return illumines the character and needs of the medieval Jewish communities; but how it may also speak deeply to the needs of our contemporary Judaism; and what, finally, this approach to plain sense tells us about the power of scripture and about the strengths and limitations of classical rabbinic midrash.

Attention to medieval Jewish commentary within its own context, but also to medieval Christian commentary within its context, and to what we may learn if we examine both of these at once: Reading Michael's studies of Rashi and the Victorines, one is first treated to a broad and deep education in these patterns of medieval Jewish and Christian reading. Soon, however, one realizes that Michael is also uncovering some surprising lessons about the relationship between Jewish and Christian commentaries. One lesson is that medieval Jewish commentary responds in part to an antagonistic Christian environment. Michael shows how, for example, Rashi and the Rashbam offer their studies of plain sense, in part, to respond to christological readings of biblical narratives. Michael also shows, with poignancy, how Rashi's attention to the tropes of "God's love for Israel" addresses his community's tragic experience, as if to say "Living in exile and under constant threat in these Christian lands, how can we remember God's love for us and how can we look forward to God's bringing us home?" Another lesson is that some medieval Christian commentary serves the goal of supersessionism, arguing that the people Israel lost God's affection, which turned instead to the Church. At the same time, Michael shows how, within its own context, medieval Christian commentary also addresses concerns that parallel those of the Jewish commentators: the realities of tragic life for Christian congregants, as well, and thus the need for commentaries that preach hope and remind members of the Church that they are destined for a better world. A third lesson is of equal significance: the degree to which Christian and Jewish exegetes know of and are influenced by each other's hermeneutical practices and strategies. A fourth highly significant lesson is that, for some reason, these twelfth-century parallels speak deeply to the contexts of Jewish-Christian relations today.

Attention to Jewish-Christian relations today, hermeneutical, theological, and social: Here, the first image that comes to mind is not Michael's writing, but Michael's flying, back and forth, between South Bend and Poland and Israel and Germany and the Vatican and New York and on and on. Attached to this is the image of Michael face-to-face, here with Christian scholars and religious leaders, here with Jewish congregants, there with Jewish and Christian scholars, and on and on. A first lesson is from Michael as scholar-pragmatist: that study moves from words written on the page to words spoken face-to-face, in the flesh. This means that religious texts respond both to other texts and to the issues and crises that cut through everyday life. This also means that religious commentary is not fully read until its effects are traced into the world of face-to-face relations, which means until its readers participate directly in such relations. In these terms, the Michael Signer who flies to Poland to engage Catholic theologians is the same Michael Signer who writes about Rashi and the Victorines. Hermeneutical and interreligious practices both implicate and require one another. This is how I knew Michael as co-participant in *Dabru Emet* and the Jewish-Christian dialogues surrounding it and how, more recently, I know Michael as co-participant in the inter-Abrahamic activities of Scriptural Reasoning.

A theological philosophy of plain sense: Whether or not it is explicit in his writing, there is a theological philosophy of plain sense implicit in the activity that binds Michael's studies of medieval commentary to his work today within and between communities of belief. The rest of this essay outlines the defining characteristics of this philosophy as culled from a representative sampling of his writings. These characteristics are numbered as if they represented an ordered series. I hope the numbering will help readers see this philosophy as a portable model to be applied, reshaped, and tested in a variety of different contexts; and I hope it will help readers identify just which characteristics may or may not work for them in a certain way and which in some other way.

Over Again: Signer's Theological Philosophy of the Plain Sense

(1) *Presupposing the plain sense.* This philosophy's first general assumption is that it is helpful to access each scriptural tradition by examining how reading communities understand the plain sense of their scriptures. For starters, Michael understands "plain sense" the way the Amoraic writers do: the intra-literary meaning of a text, the way scriptural words display their meaning in relation to the words that directly surround them, for example, within a given verse, within a given pericope, within a given narrative or book, and so on. This plain sense is the sense out of which all other meanings, including all conflicting interpretations, will arise. One could call it the grammatical sense. One could call it the least common denominator of all other readings. Or one could define it in contradistinction to both the "interpreted meaning" and the "literal sense." Here, "interpreted meaning" refers to what happens after the plain sense is offered. "Literal sense" refers to what some readers *misunderstand* as the plain sense: they take this literal sense to mean something like "what the text is talking about out there in the world." In the words of Hans Frei, these readers are referring to the text's "ostensive reference," or the way it refers outside of itself to something in the empirical world of events and experiences or in the ideal world of ideas. For Michael, however, the plain sense is an initial identity marker for participants in a given tradition, the "alphabet" in terms of which the tradition talks about itself. As we will see, a "return to plain sense" may therefore have to do with a non-reductive[2] effort to *recover a tradition's simple identity* as opposed to the various levels of meaning or stereotype that accumulate around the tradition. In these terms, to return

to the plain sense is to recover elemental features of one's own identity and to get a fairer appreciation of basic elements of the neighbor's identity.

(2) *Presupposing the limits of plain sense and the need for interpreted senses: an interpretive dialogue.* The mishnaic sage Rabbi Ishmael cautioned, famously, "A verse does not (that is, should not) depart from the plain sense" (*eyn mikre yotse midei peshuto*).[3] With these words he communicated two rabbinic presuppositions: that the scriptural text speaks, in fact, by way of its many interpreted meanings and that this speaking must not subvert or supersede the plain sense of the text. As it functions in Michael's work, Rabbi Ishmael's injunction implies that the scriptural text does not by itself direct religious behavior and belief. It directs only by way of the many interpreted senses to which it gives rise, each of which displays the force of the text as it speaks, by way of the text tradition, to the specific context of its reception—and specific in every way, historically, socially, ethically, and existentially. Since one text gives rise, over time and place, to many meanings, this also means, as Rabbi Ishmael cautions, that the plain sense remains the font of these many meanings, one amidst the many.[4]

Meaning is in this sense a dialogue between plain and interpreted senses. As Michael writes in "'These Are the Generations'": "We can compare Rashi's effort to bring together two layers of sediment.... One layer is the biblical text Rashi has before him. The second layer is constituted by the rabbinic explanations that he could gather from the Talmud and other rabbinic texts. Neither of these layers was homogeneous, but they were composed of fragments that appeared to look coherent. However, upon closer examination, they required careful examination in order to align them with one another. This is precisely what Rashi attempted to do."[5] While Michael applies the term "dialogue" primarily to exchanges between different communities of reading, there is strong precedent for extending the term, as well, to the relation Michael perceives between the plain and interpreted senses within Rashi's commentary. One precedent is set in the literary-philosophic work of Mikhail Bakhtin, as helpfully summarized in the following review of Bakhtin's work:

> For Bakhtin, the situated act of dialogic discourse, the *utterance,* is where the being of language resides. "The entire life of language, in any area of

its use . . . is permeated with dialogic relationships."[6] . . . An utterance is constrained by a dialogical relation with other utterances handed down through a tradition of discourse. Moreover, each utterance responds to utterances that have come before it, such that it "refutes, affirms, supplements, and relies on the others, presupposes them to be known, and somehow takes them into account."[7] . . . An utterance . . . also speaks to future possible utterances. This is because "from the very beginning, the utterance is constructed while taking into account possible responsive reactions, for whose sake, in essence, it is actually created."[8] Bakhtin is referring [to] the utterance's "quality of being directed to someone, its *addressivity*."[9] We construct our utterance in anticipation of the other's active responsive understanding.[10]

Within recent scholarship in rabbinics, this use of the term "dialogue" appears, for example, in Steven Fraade's study of *Sifre Deuteronomy:*

> Ancient scriptural commentaries . . . even as they closely scrutinize the particles of the text to which they attend, are always about that text as a *whole*. By this I mean that they not only seek for the text to be held in high regard by its interpretive community, but for the interpretive community to regard *itself* in relation to that text as mediated by its commentary. In other words, such a commentary is not simply a series of declarative assertions about the meanings of words . . . in a text but an attempt to *effect* a relationship between that text overall and those for whom it is "scripture," predicated on the assumption not only that the text needs and deserves to be interpreted, but that the community for whom it needs to be interpreted itself needs to be engaged in that activity of interpretation to understand itself and *transform* itself into what it ought to be.[11]

Fraade adds that the text and its students are thereby "transformatively brought toward each other, while never fully merged, so as to confront each other through the double-dialogue of commentary. By *double dialogue* I mean that the commentary simultaneously faces and engages the text that it interprets and the 'society' of readers for whom and with whom it interprets. I employ the term *dialogue* here somewhat fictively. . . . I intend the term to denote the dynamic and inter-relational ways in which the commentary creates and communicates meaning."[12]

(3) *Why there is a need to "return" to the plain sense without losing the interpreted sense and why there are different levels of interpretive dialogue.* Within Fraade's text-historical scholarship, there is a "double-double dialogue": between scriptural plain sense and rabbinic commentary, between rabbinic commentary and contemporary historical commentary, and—within each commentary—between text-tradition and a contemporary society of readers. Michael's scholarship adds another layer of doubling since medieval commentary sits between rabbinic midrash and contemporary historical commentary. This means that Michael attends to a second level of plain sense. There is the plain sense of scripture as the Rabbis saw it, and there is the plain sense of scripture to which the medieval commentators returned after the epoch of midrash. Even if it belongs to the same Hebrew canon, this second plain sense is not the same as the first. The difference has to do with the historical consciousness that emerges in medieval commentary and with the text-historical science that takes notice of this emergence. Michael writes: "When Rashi wrote his commentary, . . . he insisted that a comment must take into account the primary meaning of the words within their biblical context, and only then integrate the teachings of the Rabbis. . . . The creation of this commentary . . . would be a process of careful observation, thinking, and only then an effort to establish the meaning."[13] Michael sees in the commentaries of Rashi and his descendents an effort to recover a layer of plain sense that lies behind rabbinic midrash. In some ways suggestive of what Paul Ricoeur labeled "second naïveté," this plain sense is neither an unselfconscious reading of the scriptural text as direct "window" to its meaning (or to God's will and intention), nor the fruit of a "hermeneutics of suspicion," according to which the text is not what it claims to be. It is, instead, a reconsideration of what else the text may have to say after its apparent contradictions and ambiguities have stimulated some form of allegorical, metaphoric, or midrashic re-reading. Might these re-readings smooth-over textual gaps or conundrums that bear meanings or messages that have yet to be heard? Or has the proliferation of so many interpretive readings covered-over the unity of the text as divine

word? Or covered-over lexical, grammatical, semantic, or historical details that would otherwise address and supply even more contexts of future reading? Or details that would simply reveal more of what simply is the case? If textual gaps may have stimulated the Rabbis' interpretive re-readings, then questions like these may have stimulated the medieval scholars' plain-sense re-reading.

Michael's scholarship shows how all four of these questions may underlie the medieval commentaries and how two, in particular, contribute both to a historical account of medieval theology and to a historically grounded model for contemporary theologies of the plain sense of Scripture. Michael shows, for example, how Rashi and his confreres re-examine the grammar and linguistics of the scriptural base-texts in a way that was immanent in much rabbinic midrash but also obscured through the creative and apologetic constructions of the later generations of rabbinic interpreters. He shows, furthermore, how the return to plain sense offers medieval commentators a means of reaffirming the unity of God's Word amid the multiplicity of its readings. At the same time, Michael also shows to what degree the return to plain sense is a symptom of the commentators' turn toward historical and textual science for its own sake. This is a mark of the medieval Renaissance, as first the Muslims, then their Abrahamic confreres, rediscovered Aristotle and pursued the literal sense as the proper object of scriptural science. This was, first, a pursuit of "science," as a discipline of inquiry that may be applied to the scriptural text as well as to other literatures and other fields of knowledge, including the created world. It was, second, a pursuit of history and thus the introduction of historical consciousness into scriptural exegesis. The classic rabbinic sages' plain sense was for the most part ahistorical, a sense for the inner world of the text in a way that made it available to future readers as a source for self-understanding rather than for situating themselves against a different past. Rabbinic midrash more fully contemporized the text, albeit in a way that offered readers an ideally smooth passage from one context of social and religious life to another. The Rabbis' scripture thereby displayed several layers of meaning, at least one layer of which could be situated in another time and place. Nonetheless, the other layers were disclosed as if through direct perception of that synchronic "now" that was truly as much of the "time" of the base text as of the "time" of the midrash. The Rabbis' dual reading is thus of a then-and-now that is different from the then-and-now, for example, of Rashi's Bible commentary. Rashi's historical sense overlaps in part with that of modern historical science and the *Wissenschaft des Judentums.*

Michael's historical scholarship attends to that place of overlap, and that is why it speaks so well to the context of contemporary theology. Like the medieval *pashtan,* or plain-sense commentator, contemporary theologians inherit and respect the need for both a historian's attention to context and chronology and a pastor's and homilist's attention to the burdens, aspirations, and understandings of his or her contemporary community and society of readers and practitioners. I mention "community" here to refer to environments of relatively coherent belief and practice; I mention "society" to refer to the relatively heterogeneous polities within which such communities operate and within which individual readers may pay various sorts of allegiances to more than one community. Michael's work helps uncover the place of scriptural commentary in both environments and in both the medieval and contemporary settings.

(4) *Yet another layer of dialogue: parallels between the reparative strategies of both medieval Jewish and Christian plain-sense commentaries.* In "Restoring the Narrative: Jewish and Christian Exegesis in the Twelfth Century" and in "God's Love for Israel," Michael displays the central claim of his historical scholarship: the Jewish and Christian commentators employ parallel methods and strategies of plain-sense reading, including parallel ways of defending each tradition's claims against the other. Here, by way of illustration, are three of these parallels:

Hermeneutical consciousness of the limits of derived or figural reading. Michael notes that "Jewish and Christian exegetical literatures manifest consciousness of the distinction between "plain meaning [*peshat* or *sensus literalis*] and derived or figural meaning [*derash* or *sensus spiritualis*]."[14] In the "cultural environment of the twelfth century . . . Jews and Christians read the Rabbis or the Fathers and discovered that these works put them at greater distance from the line of biblical text."[15] For both traditions, furthermore, there is "a fecundity of imaginative readings for the biblical text. However, many of the classical rabbinic texts make no attempt to provide a link between successive verses in the biblical text itself. In the same way, patristic writings offer little guidance to the student who wanted to track the verses of scripture in their own order."[16]

A corrective turn from metaphoric to metonymic interpretation. "In 'metaphoric reading' each word in the Bible provides an occasion to enter the entire thought world of the Rabbis or Fathers. By contrast, Rashi and the Victorines will offer what Northrop Frye calls a 'metonymic' reading that provides a link between each word of the biblical sentence in proper order."[17] This way, each word speaks by way of its relations to proximate words in the biblical verse, text segment, or book.

Metonymic commentary as "return" to a coherent scriptural narrative that also "fends off" potential criticisms from the other commentary tradition(s). Metonymic commentaries "recover" a second-level of plain sense whose narrative order and whose message serve to reassure readers that their scripture is whole and true and, therefore, that criticisms of their religion are false. Michael notes, for example, how Rashi's commentary on Song of Songs reassures his readers that, despite "their fall from glories of the biblical past," they could look forward to "the rewards that God would restore in the world to come." He adds that "this effort by Rashi to restore the broad context of the biblical narrative has a strong resonance [that is, a "similarity in approach . . . rather than (explicit) interaction"] in the biblical commentaries written by High and Andrew of St. Victor."[18] The Victorines' plain sense "fused biblical text and ancient traditions" in a way that reassured "Christians [who were] experiencing confusion about their future directions of their sense of religious community and the fragmentation of theological knowledge."[19] As Franklin Harkins reports in his introduction to this volume, these parallel strategies for reassuring the home community were at times the flip-side of parallel efforts to delegitimate the other community. Thus, on the one hand, "Michael demonstrates how the standard scriptural gloss used by twelfth- and thirteenth-century schoolmen conveys and even intensifies certain themes found in the ancient *Adversus Iudaeos* tradition."[20] On the other hand, Michael shows how the plain-sense readings of Abraham Ibn Ezra and others provided a way to wrest the scriptural text from Christian figural readings—even at the cost of wresting it, in a more modest way, from rabbinic figuration or midrash.[21]

(5) *The reparative force of plain sense inquiry today: how contemporary historiography serves as well as sees.* In "Community and the Other," Michael identifies two contemporary crises that may represent the reparative context for his historical scholarship: (1) "schism and division within the Jewish

community" today; and (2) rupture and hope in Jewish-Christian relations and, more recently, in inter-Abrahamic relations.[22] First, let me explain these hairy terms. I have in mind the American pragmatists' notion that intellectual inquiry is verifiable (and worth the time and effort) when it responds to identifiable challenges to human well-being—what John Dewey labeled "problematic situations" and Charles Peirce labeled settings of "doubt" or "irritation." (If the response contributes to some reduction in suffering or some increase in well-being, then it was worth the time and effort.) So, "reparative context" refers to some problematic situation that could be repaired through inquiry. Signer's overall project is reparative—and pragmatic—in this sense, because he offers his academic inquiry as a contribution both to learning for its own sake and to the work of responding reparatively to these two crises. As for Michael's historical scholarship, I mean to suggest both that Michael offers a historical account of the setting and force of medieval plain-sense commentary and that he draws on this account as if it served the following two directives:

(a) To help repair "schism and division within the Jewish community," try this: examine the plain-sense practices of Rashi and company; consider what practice of reading today may be analogous to these (see below); and propose ways of adopting such a practice as adapted to academic and to intra-communal settings of inquiry and conduct.

The pragmatic hypothesis here is that plain-sense reading is a reparative practice that helps restore not only the literary unity of Tanakh but also the "unity of dialogue" that is supposed both to guide and be strengthened by Jewish text study. Jewish text study, in turn, is supposed to guide and be strengthened by the complementary practices of Jewish liturgy and Jewish social work (or ethical conduct).

(b) To repair "rupture and hope in Jewish-Christian and in inter-Abrahamic relations," try this: examine the plain-sense practices of medieval Jewish and Christian (and also Muslim) exegetes; consider what practice of reading today may be analogous to these (see below); and propose ways of adopting such a practice as adapted to academic and to inter-communal settings of inquiry and conduct.

The pragmatic hypothesis here is that plain-sense reading is a reparative practice that helps not only to restore unity to intra-communal practices of study and encounter but also to introduce a new "unity of dialogue" among the communities, at least within the contexts of inter-communal study and socialization. Jewish text study, in turn, is supposed to guide and be strengthened by the complementary practices of Jewish liturgy and Jewish social work (or ethical conduct).

Over Yet Again: Signer's Reparative Hermeneutic

As introduced in the previous section, Michael's theological philosophy of plain sense both observes and hosts a dialogue between plain and interpreted senses, between historiography and tradition(s), and between Jewish and Christian plain-sense commentary. Enacting one more level of reflection, this final section re-describes Michael's overall practice as a "reparative hermeneutic." Readers may detect some modest repetition here, since it is only as it turns round and round that what may otherwise look like a "method" of inquiry or a "set of claims" re-appears as a practice, at once at the desk, across the table, and in the world. This is a "hermeneutical" practice since it involves reading and interpreting text traditions as well as symptoms and signs in the world. It is a "reparative" practice since its ultimate goal is to make a difference, specifically by recommending ways of repairing schisms inside and outside the Jewish communities today. The goal here is to provide an overview of some defining features of Michael's reparative and hermeneutical practice.

Michael examines how the medieval exegetes put a science of plain sense to the service of a reparative hermeneutic. Michael argues that the metonymic practice of linear text reading—what he labels "sequential narrative"—constitutes a literary science and that this science may, as a whole, serve a context-specific communal purpose.[23] In this case, he argues that the purpose is to provide a source of religious unity at a time of social and spiritual confusion or disunity. Michael's careful studies, for example, of Rashi's commentary illustrate how Rashi may read the plain sense one way as opposed to another in order to lend narrative coherence to his community's sacred text and, thereby, to its religious cosmos. This claim of Michael's is all the more striking because he reads Rashi's pragmatic reading (for the sake of communal unity) as within the bounds of plain-sense science. This suggests that his analysis is not defined by the modern binaries of objective versus subjective reading or science versus confession. He appears to assume, instead, that the practice of science—here, literary science—includes what Gadamer dubs "prejudice," others call "pre-understanding" and what, I believe even more helpfully, Charles Peirce and some subsequent philosophers of science call "abductive reasoning" or the process of hypothesis formation. In terms of Continental hermeneutics, this is an activity that may fall between the alternatives of "understanding" (*Verstehen*) and "explanation" (*Erklärung*). Michael does not insist on a hard and fast disjunction but intimates that there are moments where "subjective choice" contributes to an account of the facts and where "science" serves as an instrument of subjective or communal needs.

In one essay, Michael reads Rashi's prologue to his commentary on Song of Songs as an account of this pursuit of religious unity through narrative interpretation:

> [Rashi] begins the prologue with a deliberate imitation of the *proem* or opening statement that is utilized in the homiletical Midrashim, citing Psalm 62:12, "God has spoken once, we have heard it twice." Rashi applies this verse to the process of interpreting Scripture, "a scriptural verse may have many meanings, but the final result is that no scriptural verse goes beyond its context (*mashm'a*)."[24] The link between the Psalm verse and application builds a framework for the act of interpretation. Divine revelation is a unified whole but human beings "hear" (*shm'*) as multi-voiced. Rashi grants that any verse in scripture may have many meanings, but the act of interpretation requires that the context (*mashm'a,* the way the verse is "heard") set the boundary for understanding. This statement about *mashm'a* indicated the metonymic dimension of Rashi's commentary. It is the 'broad context' or horizontal relationship between the words and verses that follow the verse in question that sets the horizons for the interpretative activity.[25]

Here, Rashi situates his plain-sense practice in a rabbinic practice, citing midrash as warrant for his own assumptions about the multi-vocality of scripture. At the same time, Rashi adds something to the classic midrash and to the rabbinic practice of reading itself. In his commentary to Exodus 20:8, Rashi reads Psalm 62:12—"Once has God spoken, twice do I hear"— in the sense of the midrash *Mekhilta* (*Bachodesh* 7) that "God has spoken one word, but we hear two [or thus many]."[26] But in his commentary on Song of Songs—cited by Michael—Rashi reads the verse in the manner of the phrase we previously cited from Rabbi Ishmael, "A verse does not depart from its plain sense (*peshuto*)."[27] Rashi varies the phrase, however, "A verse does not depart from its *context* (*mashm'a*)." I take Michael's citation to suggest that Rashi advances here his own medieval understanding of "plain sense" as including perhaps not only the intra-scriptural literary context (as in earlier rabbinic usage of the term *peshat*), but also what Michael identifies as "the broad context or horizontal relationship between the words and verses that follow the verse."[28] Michael cites an example from Rashi's prologue that further illustrates this second sense: "Even though the prophets spoke in types of figures (*dugm'a*) one must explain their types according to the order and characteristics of the verse, just as the scriptural verses follow one after the other."[29] As Michael suggests, the classical rabbinic "plain sense" may include but is not restricted to Rashi's metonymic reading.[30] Rashi's science is in this sense stricter: interpretation is bound not only by the base-text in general but also by the specific sequence of words in the base-text.

Why does Rashi add this restriction? Michael's defining claim is that Rashi thereby provides his readers with a heightened sense that scripture offers a rhetorically coherent narrative and that rabbinic interpretations that follow from this narrative therefore rest on a (more) coherent reading of the unity of scripture and, thereby, of the unity of God's voice. Shall we say, therefore, that Rashi's version of plain sense is overly beholden to these subjective needs of his religious community, or shall we say to the contrary that Rashi's pastoral judgments are over-constrained by the literal sequence of words and verses on the page? Michael's reading overcomes the binary standards that underlie these two questions, and he suggests something else: that Rashi does within the medieval context what Michael does in the contemporary context, which is to recognize that scripture actually speaks with several voices and that one of these is the voice that restores unity to a divided and troubled Jewish community. This means that scripture's polyvalence is not a product of what readers impose on it; it is a dimension of the text itself. This means, furthermore, that among the many voices, the particular voice that provides unity is one that links the sequential order of verses to the medieval Jewish community's specific needs for religious coherence. Michael shows that there is a science specific to this particular kind of plain-sense reading, but that this science also has a particular social context. Lest you wonder how "science" could serve a social purpose without losing its status *as* science, think of the various scientific laboratories in the United States of America that receive government funding because a particular kind of medical/biological or intergalactic inquiry is judged to have social merit. There is subjective interest here and there is scientific discipline; the two may contribute equally to the prosecution of what we call "objective inquiry." I read Michael to be saying this about plain-sense science.

Why, finally, would Rashi (and Michael) imagine that a metonymic science would help repair the Jewish community's sense of disorder? Michael's answer is that metonymic reading "restores the biblical narrative" and that restoring the narrative is a way of restoring the reading community's sense of religious (and that includes cosmic) order. The repair here is of classical rabbinic hermeneutics itself: "We can observe in Rashi's [prologue to the Song of Songs] a powerful restoration of a unifying narrative. The rabbinic traditions on the book provided a rich assembly of images. However, their patterns of organization were too fragmented. It is the order of biblical verses and chapters which sets the structure for the rabbinic exegetical work."[31] The implication of Michael's last sentence is that Rashi locates his reparative principle directly within the rabbinic discourses that are the source of both the wisdom that underlies medieval Judaism and the sense of disorder that burdens it. The principle is "the order of biblical verses and chapters." The source of disorder is that rabbinic literature's "rich assembly of images" is not fully ordered by this standard. This standard is employed only to order the sequence of chapters and commentaries in the classic collections of rabbinic midrash, such as the midrash on the Song of Songs. But Rashi observes that this order is not applied in any systematic or consistent way to the classic scriptural commentaries themselves. Rashi thereby discerns an area of work that the Rabbis warrant but have not yet undertaken. He appears to reason that if he accepted this work as his own responsibility, then he might achieve a rabbinically warranted means of uncovering a narrative coherence that the Rabbis did not themselves fully uncover. Since it had not yet been fully tried, this work of uncovering might therefore provide just what the medieval Jewish community was lacking.

One confirmation of Michael's reading of Rashi is Rashi's tendency to interpret various scriptural verses as displaying God's love for Israel and in particular God's love for her despite exile and suffering. Michael devotes an entire essay to this topic: "God's Love for Israel: Apologetic and Hermeneutical Strategies in Twelfth-Century Biblical Exegesis." Setting the context, Michael writes: "'Blessed are You O God who chooses His People in Love.' This liturgical formulation of God's election of Israel in love constitutes the principle theme of community formation for the Jewish populations in Northern Europe during the Middle Ages. They lived in Christian lands where ecclesiastical buildings proclaimed the message that God's love for Israel had been extended to another people. . . . How would it be possible [in such an environment] to maintain the continuity of Jewish communal identity grounded in God's freely chosen election of the Jewish people in love?"[32] Michael's essay then examines many cases in which Rashi reads the plain sense of the five books of Moses as reassuring Israel of his love. So, for example, on Leviticus 1:1, "And God called Moses," Rashi comments "All of God's words, statements, and commandments were preceded by 'calling.'" This "call" is an expression of affection, for this is the way the ministering angels expressed themselves in Scripture, "They called to one another" (Isa. 6:3). Or, commenting on the first sentence of Deuteronomy, "These are the words," Rashi "indicates that all of the place names [enumerated in Deut.] are a deliberate attempt to preserve Israel's honor." In sum, Rashi reads these words of "God's love" as one of the voices in the plain sense, and he attends to this voice for the sake of restoring his community's sense of divine unity. Homilies about love therefore serve the same purpose as commentaries that reinforce the narrative coherence of God's Word.

Until now, I hope I have not burdened this account with my own pet models of inquiry. If Michael were, however, to accept my account of his reading in the last paragraph, then I would imagine that he might also feel comfortable if I dressed him in my pet model of pragmatic inquiry. One might say that Michael reads Rashi as a "rabbinic pragmatist," at least in the following sense: that among the several voices of the plain sense itself, Rashi observes that one voice (the metonymic one) would speak to his community of readers with reparative effect. In these terms, Rashi would be pragmatic because he both interpreted his base-text for the sake of repairing something within his community of reading and also located a reparative voice within the text itself rather than in something he brought to the text eisegetically.

Michael locates a model for reparative reading today within the medieval practice of plain-sense reading. Here I am interpreting one half step beyond Michael's explicit claims. Between the lines, he offers his history of medieval commentary as a resource for reparative theological work today. This means that, like Rashi, he too works as a "rabbinic pragmatist," offering his textual science as also a reparative inquiry on behalf of contemporary communities of readers. In this regard, I might read Michael's brief comments on "Communal Identity and the Other" as a prologue to his own reparative inquiry.[33] He writes, "The past 30 years have witnessed a growing sense of schism and division within the Jewish community."[34] He notes that the schism is of crisis proportions: "Jews from all age groups are attracted to [these] polarities, and there is a growing sense that the divisions can no longer be easily bridged."[35] But, Michael adds, the rabbinic tradition that undergirds modern Judaism remains a resource for repairing the crisis in this Judaism. Michael writes, "The rabbinic dictum, 'Any argument that is for the sake of heaven will endure in the end,' may indeed point toward a hermeneutical framework for discussions which can bring Jews together to engage with one another. As they discuss a text from the Bible or rabbinic literature, members of Jewish communities can learn the discursive models that might bring them back into conversation with the 'other within.'"[36] As he suggests further on in his text, these "models" refer for the most part to the standards of interpretation we have just examined in Rashi. I take this to mean that Michael would gather contemporary communities of Jewish readers around the Rabbis' plain sense of scripture as linked to their midrashic commentaries and as brought to coherence, finally, in relation to the metonymic plain sense. To introduce contemporary readers to this tripartite model is, we might add, also to introduce them to the form of contemporary scholarship that is illustrated in Michael's work. At least as a temporary marker, we might label this work as I have in the title to this essay "A Theological Philosophy of the Plain Sense." Perhaps we would do better with something like "Jewish reparative reasoning" or "Jewish history as reparative reasoning." This would refer to scholarship that integrated text-historical science with reparative interpretation. As in the example of Michael's work, this would be a quadratic inquiry, integrating studies in rabbinic plain sense, midrash, medieval plain sense, and the reparative Jewish history that integrates these three with the needs of the contemporary academy and the contemporary Jewish community. Michael's scholarship integrates rigorous text-historical science with an acute sense of why we have reason to listen attentively today to the narrative coherence of Jewish text-history. The analogue to Michael's reparative inquiry is, therefore, not some contemporary imitation of Rashi's Bible commentary, but Michael's plain-sense history of medieval plain-sense commentary.

For Michael, the "scripture" that would guide Jewish reparative inquiry today is not merely Tanakh ("Hebrew Scripture") nor rabbinic or medieval commentary, but the entire project of Jewish text-history. He looks to the metonymic order of Jewish text-history as a standard of coherence to guide Jewish reparative inquiry today. The purpose of this inquiry is to recommend practices of study through which Jewish readers may heal the inner schisms that threaten Jewish communities today. This study represents a practice, at once, of science, fellowship, and repair.

Michael models his science, in part, on the Rabbis' plain-sense reading of scripture. Like scripture for the Rabbis, Jewish text-history has a kind of sacrality and authority within contemporary Jewish self-understanding. This implies that Jewish self-understanding must never "ignore" the plain sense of history. But it also implies that the actual norms of Jewish belief and conduct today cannot be located in plain-sense history alone. History is mute until, on the analogy of rabbinic midrash, it stimulates a reparative inquiry that finds its context and purpose within the specific burdens of Jewish life today. Here, there is more than an analogy with rabbinic midrash, since both Tanakh and midrash remain ineradicable dimensions of Jewish text-history. Scripture still speaks, midrash still re-reads, but there are also two other dimensions of Jewish text-history: the plain-sense commentary of Rashi and his descendants, and modern plain-sense history. These represent both literal curricula within plain-sense text-history and models of two additional aspects of the practice of plain-sense text-historiography.

Just as Rashi found rabbinic midrash inadequate as an exclusive source of Jewish self-understanding, so too Michael finds that the previous generations' reparative inquiries cannot serve by themselves as models of reparative inquiry today. While today's Jewish community relies first on its sense of history, this history is also a source of pain, confusion, and sharp disagreement within contemporary Jewish society. Michael's message of hope is that this dolorous history begins to repair itself when it offers the bare fact of its narrative order as a ground for societal dialogue and therefore for trust that "my Redeemer lives" (Job 19:25) though as yet we see him not.

Jewish reparative inquiry is built on the metonymic ground of Jewish text-history. But how? Through a fellowship of reparative study.

In Michael's vision, reparative inquiry is and will be undertaken by decentralized fellowships of study. While we cannot pre-judge the contents of reparative inquiry, Michael's account indicates its form. It will be a decentralized practice of study, operating at once among many different fellowships of study, each addressing its own regional challenges through a distinctive community of dialogue. Michael's recommendation is that each community include text-historians, that is, scholars and interpreters of scripture, midrash, plain-sense commentary, and plain-sense history, and representatives of the relevant societal institutions. While the historian's distinctive contribution is plain-sense text-historiography, the historian's work is also shaped by the fact that it will be received by these fellowships. This means that its fruits will be measured not only by members of some academic guild, but also by other citizens of everyday society, along with members of many other guilds in and out of academe.

Reparative inquiry crosses the borders of tradition and community. In his introduction to this volume, Franklin Harkins provides a fitting overview of Michael's contribution to Jewish-Christian dialogue. At the center of that contribution is Michael's observation that "[t]he history of scriptural interpretation provides a significant point of entry for understanding the nature of the relationship between Judaism and Christianity during the past two millennia."[37] Michael shows both that "the interpretation of Scripture was at the heart of the separation"[38] between Judaism and Christianity, and that "the most productive dialogue between Jews and Christians is grounded on face-to-face studies of texts in the Hebrew Bible through the lenses of pre-modern interpretations in both traditions."[39] As Harkins has shown and as we have seen in this survey of Michael's reparative hermeneutic, these observations across the borders of Judaism and Christianity belong to an integrative and embodied practice of movement both within and across those borders. The reparative hermeneutic is, to a great extent, a dialogic hermeneutic, and that hermeneutic is present wherever Michael is present: when reading plain sense and midrash, or medieval and rabbinic and patristic commentary, or Rashi and the Victorines, or narrative and science, or plain-sense commentators and contemporary text-historians, or *Nostra Aetate* and *Dabru Emet;* or when speaking with Jew and Jew, or Christian and Jew, or now Muslim, Christian, and Jew. It is not *all* dialogue, mind you, since it is also plain-sense science (of history and of text), and this science sees when and where there is not dialogue, but exclusion, supersessionism, and hatred. But Michael's distinctive virtue is to see and then know when it is time to turn from seeing and turn to doing, and the doing is dialogue again, now reparative dialogue.

Reparative Inquiry is measured by its fruits. This "ultimate" measure of the "coherence" of historical narrative is religious and societal peace.

This is the pragmatic test of inquiry: how it helps repair the societal disorder and religious schism that gives rise to it.

Notes

1. Michael does not essentialize, by which I mean he would not say something like "commentary reveals the essence of a tradition."

2. I will clarify this later, but I wanted to indicate right away that I do not mean some "foundationalist" or obsessive and presumptuous drive to isolate the "essence" or "fundaments" or "defining rules" of the tradition. The goal, instead, is more like a rule of thumb or an initial sense of the tradition's identity for those who claim it.

3. *Yevamot* 24a. But there are exceptions when the reading does depart from its plain sense (Cf. Saadya Gaon, *Emunot v'Deot* 7:1).

4. As Michael writes, "[M]edieval commentaries constitute an important resource for understanding how Jews understood themselves and their ancestors.

They approached the text of the Torah as a treasure house with infinite meanings." This quotation is taken from an earlier unpublished version of Michael Signer, "'These Are the Generations': Reasoning with Rabbi Samuel ben Meier," in *Crisis, Call,* and *Leadership in the Abrahamic Traditions,* ed. Peter Ochs and William Stacy Johnson (New York: Palgrave Macmillan, 2009), 73–83.

5. Signer, "'These Are the Generations,'" 4.

6. Mikhail Bakhtin, *Problems of Dostoevsky's Poetics,* ed. and trans. C. Emerson (Minneapolis: University of Minnesota Press, 1984), 183.

7. Mikhail Bakhtin, *Speech Genres and Other Late Essays,* ed. C. Emerson and M. Holquist, trans. V. McGee (Austin: University of Texas Press, 1986), 91.

8. Ibid., 94.

9. Ibid., 96.

10. J. Allan Cheyne and Donato Tarulli, "Dialogue, Difference, and the 'Third Voice' in the Zone of Proximal Development," *Theory and Psychology* 9 (1999): 5–28.

11. Steven Fraade, *From Tradition to Commentary: Torah and Its Interpretation in the Midrash Sifre to Deuteronomy* (Albany: State University of New York Press, 1991), 13.

12. Fraade, *From Tradition to Commentary,* 13–14. Among the resources for this notion of dialogue, Fraade cites Peter Brooks' claim that "Meaning is not simply in the text nor wholly the fabrication of a reader (or a community of readers) but comes into being in the dialogical struggle and collaboration of the two, in the activation of textual meanings in the process of reading" (Peter Brooks, "The Idea of a Psychoanalytic Literary Criticism," *Critical Inquiry* 13 [1987]: 343; cited on p. 183 n. 47).

13. Signer, "'These Are the Generations,'" 5.

14. Michael Signer, "Restoring the Narrative: Jewish and Christian Exegesis in the Twelfth Century," in *With Reverence for the Word: Medieval Scriptural Exegesis in Judaism, Christianity, and Islam,* ed. Jane Dammen McAuliffe, Barry D. Walfish, and Joseph W. Goering (Oxford: Oxford University Press, 2003), 70–82, here 71.

15. Ibid., 71.

16. Ibid., 72.

17. Ibid., 4, citing Northrop Frye, *The Great Code* (New York: Harcourt, Brace, Jovanovich, 1982), 5–27.

18. Signer, "Restoring the Narrative," 16.

19. Ibid., 22.

20. Harkins, in the "Introduction" to this volume, citing Michael A. Signer, "The *Glossa ordinaria* and the Transmission of Medieval Anti-Judaism," in *A Distinct Voice: Medieval Studies in Honor of Leonard E. Boyle, O.P.,* ed. Jacqueline Brown and William P. Stoneman (Notre Dame, IN: University of Notre Dame Press, 1997), 591–605.

21. See Michael Signer, "Hearing, Speaking, Reading: The Inscription of Communal Identity in Medieval Northern Europe" (unpublished manuscript), 30–35.

22. Michael Signer, "Community Identity and the Other," paper delivered to Center of Theological Inquiry Research Group on Scriptural Reasoning, Princeton, NJ, May 2006, 7.

23. See Michael A. Signer, "The Land of Israel in Medieval Jewish Exegetical and Polemical Literature," in *The Land of Israel: Jewish Perspectives,* ed. Lawrence A. Hoffman (Notre Dame, IN: University of Notre Dame Press, 1986), 210–33, here 213. And see the discussion of "sequential narrative" in the editor's "Introduction" to this Festschrift.

24. Signer notes that this text is cited from the edition by Judah Rosenthal, *Perush Rashi al Shir HaShirim* in *Sefer Yovel Likhvod Shemu'el Kalman Mirky,* ed. S. Bernstein and G. A. Churgin (New York: 1958), 130–88, with comparisons to another transcription.

25. Signer, "Restoring the Narrative," 74.

26. *Mekhilta of Rabbi Ishmael* 2:252, ed. and trans. Jacob Lauterbach (Philadelphia: Jewish Publication Society, 1976).

27. *Yevamot* 24a.

28. Signer, "Restoring the Narrative," 74.

29. Ibid.

30. Ibid., 76.

31. Ibid.

32. Michael A. Signer, "God's Love for Israel: Apologetic and Hermeneutical Strategies in Twelfth-Century Biblical Exegesis," in *Jews and Christians in Twelfth-Century Europe,* ed. Michael A. Signer and John Van Engen (Notre Dame, IN: University of Notre Dame Press, 2001), 123–49, here 123.

33. Signer, "Communal Identity and the Other."

34. Ibid., 5.

35. Ibid., 6.

36. Ibid.

37. Michael Signer, "Searching the Scriptures: Jews, Christians, and the Book," in *Christianity in Jewish Terms,* ed. Tikva Frymer-Kensky, David Novak, Peter Ochs, David Fox Sandmel, and Michael A. Signer (Boulder, CO: Westview Press, 2000), 85–98, here 87; cited in Harkins, "Introduction."

38. Signer, "Searching the Scriptures," 89; cited in Harkins, "Introduction."

39. Michael A. Signer, "Tradition in Transition: Approaches to Jewish-Christian Relations," in *Jews and Christians in Conversation: Crossing Cultures and Generations,* ed. Edward Kessler, John Pawlikowski, Judith Herschcopf Banki, and Barbara Ellen Bowe (Cambridge: Orchard Academic, 2002), 123–40, here 134; cited in Harkins, "Introduction."

CHAPTER EIGHTEEN

Can We Speak of a Theological Bond between Christians and Jews?

A Dialogue with Michael Signer

John T. Pawlikowski, O.S.M.

Michael Signer has written extensively on the theological relationship between Judaism and Christianity. His ideas are found in a number of essays in edited volumes.[1] Since he has never written a single volume bringing together the ideas outlined in these disparate essays, one must try to draw together his overall perspective from these varied contributions. In addition, as one of the four authors of the much discussed Jewish statement on Christianity *Dabru Emet* (Speaking the Truth),[2] originally published in the *New York Times,* the affirmations found in this groundbreaking document can be understood as part of Signer's overall understanding of the Jewish-Christian theological nexus. A careful reading of these essays yields a number of theses central to his theological outlook on the Jewish-Christian relationship.

A central focal point of Signer's perspective is the basic texts of each tradition, particularly the biblical tradition, though he also gives considerable play to the Jewish mystical tradition. For Signer the biblical tradition is essentially the Hebrew Scriptures which he sees as an inescapable starting point for any theological discussion between Jews and Christians. In one essay he writes, "[W]hat the violence of the past millennium does demand is that we look to the Hebrew Scriptures for the key to our mutual bond of community and non-community. To diminish its role makes us deaf to the divine call to choose life for our communities and for one another."[3] In the same essay, originally presented at a conference at the Tantur Ecumenical Institute in Jerusalem in 1997, Signer argues that by reason of the link provided through the sharing of the Hebrew Scriptures Jews are part of "the extended household of Christians," a notion he attributes to Martin Buber as well.[4] This assertion about a shared book between Judaism and Christianity also appears in point two of *Dabru Emet*. However, it is only in the Tantur address that Signer uses this language of "extended household" which seems to imply on his part an explicit bond between Jews and the Christian community.

From conversations with several of the authors of *Dabru Emet* I know that this statement about "Jews and Christians seeking authority from the same book" was one of the most difficult in terms of group consensus. It was also one of the statements most strongly critiqued by some Jewish scholars such as Jon Levenson.[5] In fact, the discussion about "Hebrew Scriptures" versus "Old Testament" has been an ongoing scholarly debate for some years. The controversy has not followed an easy Jewish-Christian fault line. Both Jewish and Christian scholars have argued that because of the arrangement of the books as well as the theological use made of these writings, which significantly differ in the Church and in the Jewish community, one cannot see them as creating a genuine link between the two. The authors of *Dabru Emet*, while not denying these differences, nonetheless are prepared to argue, as Michael Signer has also done in several of his individual essays, that there is enough correspondence in their roles in the two faith communities to make them a positive link between Jews and Christians.[6]

In a presentation at a Christian-Jewish conference at Cambridge University in March 2001 Signer expanded on his vision of the Hebrew Scriptures as the central locus for the contemporary Jewish-Christian conversation. In that presentation he put forth the idea that the three major parts of the Hebrew Canon (Torah/Pentateuch, Neviim/Prophets, and Ketuvim/Other Writings) can serve as a basic model for interreligious dialogue. The joint discussion on each section of the Hebrew canon can certainly draw on modern forms of biblical scholarship. But for Signer as primarily a medieval scholar, pre-modern forms of biblical interpretation may prove even more mutually enriching: "The disclosures that emerge from reading Augustine and the rabbis or Rashi and Hugo of St. Victor allow for deep and nuanced discussions of the commonplaces and differences of Jews and Christians."[7] Signer had made the same point in an earlier lecture at a conference held at Chicago's Catholic Theological Union in 1998: "For Jews and Christians to return to their interpretive traditions of the Hebrew Bible would fulfill the idea that Abraham Joshua Heschel claimed: that great reformulations of Judaism and Christianity begin with a study of the Hebrew Bible. To follow the diverging paths of interpretation throughout our history together, and doing this in the living presence of one another, will provide both an atmosphere of dialogue and its contents."[8]

In the concluding paragraph in his "The Rift That Binds" essay Signer insists that discussions between Jews and Christians should not focus only on the variety of influences that shaped the relations between Church and Synagogue in the first centuries. While such information certainly has its place in determining the contemporary Jewish-Christian relationship it cannot provide "a corrective norm for our mutual explorations of how we might care for one another."[9] Christians and Jews must make clear the fundamentally different lens that influences the biblical text we share: the centrality of Christ in the Christian tradition and the collected works that constitute oral Torah in Judaism.

Michael Signer is also consistent in maintaining that a common spirituality is nourished in the dialogue between Christians and Jews through in-depth, face-to-face differences in interpreting the common texts of the Hebrew Scriptures. It is through recognition of the "rift" between the faith communities that a measure of bonding is generated. So his view might be described as paradoxical: unity through an understanding of difference. His strong emphasis on having this process take place through personal exchange rather than merely written commentary from each side creates in my view a measure of what I would term "spiritual bonding" that in the end might be more important than a stress on objectively similar beliefs. I want to emphasize that the term "spiritual bonding" is my interpretation of his "rift that binds" terminology. He himself never employs the term. But clearly throughout the collection of his writing on the Jewish-Christian relationship there is a continuing emphasis on difference rather than similarity.

We find this repeated in a response Signer delivered to a paper by Professor Karl-Josef Kuschel at the third Crown-Minow conference at the University of Notre Dame. Professor Kuschel maintained that as the diverse interpretation of Father Abraham caused deep divisions in the Abrahamic family of Jews, Christians, and Muslims, so a new reappropriation of their common linkage may be the key path to a new constructive and enriching relationship today. Signer sees possibilities in such an approach, but he underlines the need for such study in the presence of the other ("When we study our texts together we embody them") and not only through literary analysis.[10] He then goes on to stress the importance of continuing differences in the way in which the three faith communities appropriate their Abrahamic inheritance: "Our witness compels us to strive for peace in the communities of Abraham. However, the unity of that peace must allow for the unique embodiments which Judaism, Christianity and Islam have nurtured through the centuries. It must be a peace of the many who seek the One in their unique ways."[11]

Signer expanded on his emphasis regarding the use of the varied interpretations of the Hebrew Scriptures as the foundation for Christian-Jewish dialogue in his contribution to the volume that accompanied the release of *Dabru Emet*. Once more he underlines the fact that the two major modes of interpretation—allegorical for the Christians and mystical for the Jews—result in quite dissimilar understandings. But for Signer, looking at the situation from the Jewish perspective, if Jews can come to appreciate the allegorical method classically employed within the Church he is convinced they will grasp more profoundly "what binds the Christian community to biblical Israel and its progeny—the Jewish people." Through the experience of the dialogue Signer is convinced that Christians on their side can come to engage in allegorical interpretation of the Hebrew Scriptures that is authentic to their faith perspective but does not lead to "oppressive proselytizing." This experience will also enable Jews to recognize Christianity "as a profound exploration—or *derash*—of the way God operates among humanity." Signer concludes this essay with reflections that echo the perspective he laid out in his "The Rift That Binds":

> Once we pass over the threshold of the core tradition of allegory or *derash*, the mystical tradition differs because the intimate symbolism of each tra-

dition excludes the possibility of the other. However, it is precisely the inability to grasp the whole Scriptures' meaning that can create a spirit of collaboration between our two communities, and so even here there is promise. No single tradition can or ought to dominate the other. The ability to share our readings of "spirit" or *derash* may be the model for a future reconciliation that recognizes both our profound differences and the imperative to become partners in understanding the divine word to be a blessing to the entire world.[12]

Finally, in a presentation to a trilateral Jewish-Christian-Muslim program sponsored by the Rotko Chapel in Houston in February 2006,[13] a program in which I also spoke, Signer listed the four critical dimensions of authentic Christian-Jewish encounter. The first is "mysterium," which is emphasized in chapter four of Vatican II's *Nostra Aetate*. For Signer this characteristic of the encounter ensures that Christians understand Judaism as integral to their basic self-understanding without reducing either religious tradition to a simplistic common core.

The second characteristic Signer terms "patrimonium." For most of two millennia Christians and Jews claimed exclusive control of their Abrahamic inheritance. But *Nostra Aetate* broke through that exclusivity from the side of the Church. It spoke of a "common inheritance," a notion subsequently reaffirmed in the writings of Pope John Paul II.[14] Signer adds that in his view this is also a patrimony shared with Muslims though he would likely still hold to his point about the distinctive interpretations of this Abrahamic inheritance he made in his response to Professor Kuschel cited above.

A third dimension of the contemporary Christian-Jewish relationship is "dialogue." As he sees it, *Nostra Aetate* profoundly altered the nature of the conversation between Jews and Christians by insisting that the creation of a permanent relationship was more fundamental than differences in belief. The relationships created in the spirit of *Nostra Aetate* have been sustained over several decades despite some deeply conflictual situations such as the Auschwitz convent controversy.

Finally, the Jewish-Christian relationship is marked by "mutual respect." This is far more than "toleration," as Signer presents it. It involves two interrelated aspects: respect for the other as person and respect for the fundamental religious perspective of the other. The 2001 Pontifical Biblical Commission document[15] (including the Introduction by the then Cardinal Joseph Ratzinger) argues, contrary to what had been the dominant view in Christianity for centuries, that the Jewish religious perspective and its distinctive interpretation of the Hebrew Scriptures continues to have authentic meaning from the Christian viewpoint. This assertion creates a fundamentally new dynamic in the relationship.

Signer's overall perspective on the Christian-Jewish relationship certainly deserves strong commendation. I especially appreciate its rootedness in fundamental texts, particularly the biblical tradition, and in personal relationships. I would agree with him that both remain central to the ongoing dialogue if it is to acquire genuine depth and sustained vitality. But given the fact that his perspective has never been developed into a comprehensive study of the Jewish-Christian relationship (something that I would hope he might take on in the future), I do believe there are important questions that can be addressed to him in the spirit of the mutual respect he underscored in his 2006 Houston address.

The first question would have to do with the role of the Hebrew Scriptures or Old Testament which in all of his essays acquire a foundational status for authentic Christian-Jewish dialogue. As was indicated above, Signer sees the possibility of a certain bondedness emerging from the study of how the two faith communities of Judaism and Christianity have interpreted these scriptures in quite different—one might even say, contradictory—ways over the centuries. As a scholar deeply immersed in the medieval tradition, Signer knows the Jewish and Christian schools of exegesis developed in this period and beyond inside and out. There is little question that Christian and Jewish religious scholarship interpreted the books of the Hebrew Scriptures–Old Testament in quite different ways. And Signer is correct in my judgment in arguing that through an understanding of the diverse interpretive paths taken by the Church and the Jewish community we today can come to a richer appreciation of the faith perspective of "the other" in the Christian-Jewish relationship.

My concern is that Signer's viewpoint seems to lock the dialogue today into the dominance of the classical interpretation of the Hebrew Scriptures–Old Testament. This is not so great a problem on the Jewish side, provided one does allow some room for modern scientific exegesis, but it poses considerable difficulty on the Christian side. While as a Christian scholar I do believe an appreciation of the classical medieval approach retains value, it must give way in terms of priority to the modern scientific approach. Let me be clear. I do not wish to accord modem scientific exegesis an absolute priority. Some parts of it have taken biblical studies down an unproductive road. But, unlike Signer, I would definitely assign it a priority in understanding the biblical tradition in our time and in providing a scriptural basis for the contemporary Christian-Jewish dialogue. In my view, Signer is overly positive on the value of the classical form of exegesis. While I would certainly not wish to label it anti-Judaic at its core, this exegetical approach clearly contributed to the development and the integration of anti-Jewish views into the heart of Christian faith expression that often had dire consequences for the Jewish community on the ground. So I think Signer is obligated to confess the dark side of the classical exegetical outlook in Christianity far more than he does in the essays we have examined, even though I know he is personally painfully aware of the legacy of Christian anti-Semitism. The classical form of interpretation of the Old Testament in the Christian churches ultimately undercut any continuing validity for the Hebrew Scriptures except as a foretaste of Christian faith. In so doing the Jewish biblical tradition was reduced to an empty shell for Christian scholars, a reduction that ultimately had a disastrous impact on the perception of the value of the Jewish people in political society.

Signer's discussion of the Hebrew Scriptures–Old Testament as the crucial resource for the development of Jewish-Christian mutual respect in our day fails to take into account some of the changing attitudes regarding the Old Testament in Christian circles. While the classical approach retains some strength within the churches—as is evident in some of the key periods of the liturgical year such as Advent with its strong emphasis on Jesus as the fulfillment of messianic prophecies, in the Easter Vigil where the texts of the Old Testament are presented as being in darkness, and in the overall Easter season where in the Catholic lectionary readings from the Old Testament are not included as the Church relates its origins—Christian biblical studies and some church pronouncements appear to be moving in a somewhat new direction that assigns greater continued value to the Old

Testament for Christian faith today. There is growing recognition that the Hebrew Scriptures stood at the heart of Jesus' own spirituality. He did not know an "Old Testament," only "the Scriptures" which he drew upon in great depth in presenting his spiritual and ethical vision. To fail to include the "Hebrew Scriptures" in the core of Jesus' message is in fact seriously to truncate that message in my perspective. The Hebrew Scriptures–Old Testament, call them what you will, must assume central significance in contemporary Christian theology and spirituality as constructive elements and not just as foil or foretaste for New Testament perspectives. We still have a long way to go in achieving this concretely in the Christian churches, but it is an emphasis we must continue to promote in light of the increasing thrust in biblical scholarship and key documents on Christian-Jewish relations issued in the last forty years or so by various church bodies (e.g., the 1985 Vatican *Notes* on Christian-Jewish relations). The 2001 Pontifical Biblical Commission document which Signer cites very positively at the close of his Houston talk seems to move in the same direction with its argument that Jewish messianic interpretations based in the Hebrew Scriptures remain valid.

It is somewhat ironic to bring this out, but there appears to be some contradiction between the Michael Signer of *Dabru Emet* and the author of the various essays I have drawn upon in this chapter. *Dabru Emet's* strong emphasis on the Hebrew Scriptures–Old Testament as a common foundation for Jews and Christians, an assertion that has elicited considerable fire from some Jewish scholars such as Jon Levenson of Harvard, is very much in line with the change of perception I have just described in Christian circles. Yet many of Signer's writings on the topic of the Christian-Jewish relationship seem to undercut this assertion with their strong insistence on the importance of the fundamental interpretive difference. While it is true that one might distinguish between foundational text and diverse interpretations of that text, any negative interpretation of the foundational text which is largely the situation in Christian exegesis of the Old Testament would seem to undercut the basic value of the text itself.

Another area where Signer's perspective requires further elaboration is the role of the New Testament in forging a link between Church and the Jewish people today. British Christian scholar James Aitken, in responding to the challenge of *Dabru Emet,* argues that the current dialogue must begin with the upfront acknowledgment of the basic irreconcilable difference between Jews and Christians: "Christians know and serve God through Jesus Christ . . . ."[16] He adds that the New Testament is far more crucial for Christian self-identity than the Old Testament, though he in no sense means to disparage the value of the Old Testament for contemporary Christianity. He thus is critical by implication of Signer as one of the four authors of *Dabru Emet,* a criticism that he would no doubt extend to Signer's personal writings since they too are marked by such an omission.

Such misrepresentations in Aitken's view are likely intended to render Christianity more understandable to Jews. In a response to a question regarding *Dabru Emet*'s silence with regard to Jesus at the 2001 Cambridge University conference, Signer indicated that the document's authors felt that the Jewish community was not yet ready for an in-depth conversation in this area. But in failing to bring out the fundamental basis of the irreconcilable difference between Judaism and Christianity they in fact, according to Aitken, present Jews with a distorted image of Christian belief that ultimately renders the dialogue simplistic. He sums up his position in the following terms: "An honest appreciation of Christianity would have been preferred, one in which the Trinity, one of the elements of Christianity that Jews often express as being the hardest to accept or to recognize as monotheistic, should be given full weight. The need is for Jews to say that they may not understand Christianity, they may not be able to accept the divinity of Jesus, but that they understand that Christians believe in it, and that the Christian belief in the Trinity is a wrestling with the complexity of revelation, while holding onto a monotheistic belief."[17]

In one sense Aitken and Signer do not stand all that far apart, despite Aitken's incisive critique. Though Aitken does not speak to the question directly, it would seem he and Signer are on the same wavelength that any bonding between Jews and Christians today comes through a constructive appreciation of the theological rift that separates the two faith communities. But for Aitken any such bonding requires a clear appreciation of the fundamental gap in theological perception generated by Christianity's adherence to the notion of Christ's divinity. The "rift" will not become a constructive link if its description is restricted only to the differences between

Jewish and Christian interpretations of the Hebrew Scriptures–Old Testament as Signer posits. For Aitken we cannot bypass the New Testament and its portrayal of Jesus as *Dabru Emet* and Signer have done.

Another point of agreement probably also exists between Aitken and Signer albeit implicitly. Aitken at one point in his essay speaks of past attempts to portray Jesus as a Jew while avoiding any mention of Christian understandings of his divinity. For Aitken this represents a basic circumvention of the principal irreconcilable difference. While Signer does not refer to the modern Jewish attempts to present Jesus as a "liberal" Jew who stood far closer in a positive sense to the Jewish tradition than the "distorted" presentations of his teaching by most Christian scholars, an effort amply documented in a new study by Matthew Hoffman,[18] knowing his work as I do I definitely think Signer would be on the same page as Aitken in rejecting such an approach. On this point I would find myself concurring with Aitken and Signer.

Overall I find myself in partial agreement with Aitken's analysis but also in significant disagreement both with Aitken and Signer. Aitken is quite correct in his insistence that any authentic dialogue between Jews and Christians today cannot relegate the theological discussion of the "Jesus question" to the sidelines. This question is simply too central for Christian identity. Reversing the injunction of the 1974 Vatican Guidelines which stresses the importance of Christians understanding Jews as they define themselves and hence not creating "straw Jews," Jews must come to understand Christians as they define themselves and not create "straw Christians."

Where I find myself in substantive disagreement with Signer and Aitken has to do with their shared insistence on "difference" as the core of bonding between Jews and Christians, even though they define that difference in dissimilar ways. Clearly differences must be kept on the front burner in any authentic dialogue and I do not regard the limited positive approaches to the Jesus question by nineteenth-century Jewish scholars such as Heinrich Graetz and Abraham Geiger as of much help for our present-day discussions. But, on the other hand, neither can we ignore the profound re-evaluation of Jesus' relationship to the Jewish community of his time that has emerged in Christian biblical scholarship over the past several decades.

The contrast between the description of Jesus' relationship with the Jewish community by scholars who dominated the world of biblical interpretation only a few decades ago (and whose work still vibrates in some quarters of Christianity) and the view that is gaining rapid ascendancy today is like day and night. It truly represents a total about-face. Scholars such as Martin Noth and Rudolf Bultmann maintained a strong separation between Jesus and the Jewish community of his day. Noth, for example, whose *History of Israel* became a standard reference for students and professors alike, described Jesus as standing apart from the history of Israel: "In him the history of Israel had come, rather, to its real end. What did belong to the history of Israel was the process of his rejection and condemnation by the Jerusalem religious community."[19]

In the latter part of the twentieth century and continuing into the twenty-first scholars such as James Charlesworth, John Meier, W. D. Davies, E. P. Sanders, Douglas Hare, Daniel Harrington, Clemens Thoma, Bruce Chilton, and Robin Scroggs, to name only a few, have moved New Testament interpretation in directions directly opposite that advanced by Noth and Bultmann. Jesus is now seen as an integral part of first-century Judaism and as having drunk deeply from its spiritual well. These scholars have also raised serious doubts whether Jesus himself ever envisioned a new religious community totally severed from Judaism. This new viewpoint has even taken hold in more official Christian circles. Cardinal Carlo Martini, S.J., the retired Archbishop of Milan and a prominent exegete in his own right, has written that "Without a sincere feeling for the Jewish world, and a direct experience of it, one cannot fully understand Christianity. Jesus is fully Jewish, the apostles are Jewish, and one cannot doubt their attachment to the tradition of their forefathers."[20] And the 1985 Vatican *Notes* on preaching and teaching about Jews and Judaism declares that "Jesus was and always remained a Jew. . . . Jesus is fully a man of his time, and his environment—the Jewish Palestinian one of the first century, the anxieties and hope of which he shared."[21]

Signer is surely aware of these developments in biblical interpretation and official statements, but he does not appear thus far to incorporate their implications in his reflections on the Jewish-Christian relationship. In my judgment he needs to do so. While certainly not eliminating a basic gulf between the two faith communities they do provide a positive basis for communal bonding that simply did not exist previously. These ground-breaking developments cannot be ignored. They represent a much different substantive approach to the "Jesus as Jew" question than that found in nineteenth-century Jewish liberal scholarship. Jesus cannot be seen any longer as only a "barrier" in Christian-Jewish relations. He must now also be recognized as a "bond."

At this point I need to make it quite clear what I am proposing in my argument that Jesus must now be recognized as a "bond" between Jews and Christians. I am definitely not advocating support for those movements such as "Jews for Jesus" or the "Jewish Messianic Fellowship" nor the "de-Christianized" understanding of Jesus promoted by certain liberal Jewish scholars in the nineteenth and early twentieth centuries. In this sense I know I stand with Michael Signer in rejecting such efforts. The Jewish Jesus cannot be totally divorced from the christological overlay attached to him by the Christian churches. Hence "Jesus as the Christ" remains a barrier to Christian-Jewish bonding even though "Jesus the Jew" provides a certain linkage.

I also realize that there is some basis for Jewish apprehension in terms of stressing Jesus as an authentic son of Judaism. Given the fact that the Christian churches have tended to push the issue of proselytizing Jews under the carpet in recent decades without grappling with the question front and center, many in the Jewish community remain suspicious that any emphasis on Jesus' ties to Judaism is merely intended to make Christianity far more palatable to Jews and hence make them more open to conversion. This is certainly not my intent nor that of the many Christian biblical scholars and certain ecclesial documents that have been highlighting Jesus' personal embodiment of central teachings of Judaism prevalent in his day. But until Christian leadership explicitly stipulates that there is no requisite need to proselytize Jews as Cardinal Walter Kasper said some years ago[22] and the ecumenical Christian scholarly document *A Sacred Obligation*[23] subsequently reaffirmed, it will remain difficult for many in the Jewish community to regard Jesus as a bond between Church and Synagogue.

The more difficult question we face is whether the Church's christological proclamations make it virtually impossible to view Jesus as a limited bond between Jews and Christians. Without question they constitute a gulf between the two faith communities. But is this gulf totally impassable? On the whole it is and will remain so in my judgment. For one, as the noted Jewish theologian Eugene Borowitz remarked when he and I shared a platform on this topic at the University of St. Thomas in St. Paul, Minnesota, some years back, very few Jews have any interest whatsoever in christological understandings of the person and work of Jesus. But even here I see some new openings that will definitely not eliminate the essential gulf but might create some new understanding and hence some new appreciation of bondedness. The prevailing view within Judaism has been that the notion of Incarnational Christology is totally foreign to Jewish self-understanding. Expressed in largely Greek philosophical categories as Incarnational Christology has been over the centuries since the patristic era, this prevailing Jewish perspective is certainly valid. But a few Jewish and Christian scholars have begun to explore the roots of Incarnational Christology in certain parts of the Jewish religious tradition in Jesus' day. I think here of the work of the German Christian theologian Franz Mussner who proposed that what he termed "Son Christology" had some resonance with aspects of first-century Jewish thought[24] and biblical scholar Bruce Chilton who speaks of Jesus' intimacy with God in the context of the Jewish kabbalistic tradition of the time[25] as well as Jewish scholars such as Michael Wyschogrod[26] and Elliot Wolfson[27] who have engaged the issue of the Incarnation with some seriousness. These efforts are very much exploratory and may not in the end achieve widespread scholarly endorsement, but they at least suggest that what has been regarded traditionally as an impassable barrier may yet contain some minimal seeds of bondedness. I believe Michael Signer needs to look at these efforts as he continues to explore the Christian-Jewish relationship in his own work.

Another recent scholarly development that has to enter into any contemporary discussion of Jewish-Christian bonding relates to the new perceptions of the separation between Christianity and Judaism in the first centuries. The prevailing view both in scholarly circles and in the public perception has been that by the time Jesus died the Church had been firmly established as a distinct religious entity apart from Judaism. It has been further argued that Paul, in his missionary journeys, further split the two communities both theologically and in terms of religious observance by allowing converts to bypass certain central Jewish legal obligations. We now know that this picture of Paul is rather simplistic and that he may have had a much more positive regard for the Jewish legal tradition than previously imagined even though he was willing to grant dispensations for those coming to the Church without a Jewish background. Likewise the so-called definite split between Church and Synagogue that supposedly took place at the Council of Jerusalem on the Christian side and at the Synod of Jabneh on the Jewish side was not as thorough as once believed. Jewish and Christian scholars such as Robert Wilken, Wayne Meeks, Alan Segal, Amy Jill-Levine, Daniel Boyarin, and Anthony Saldarini have demonstrated that the separation between Judaism and Christianity was a process that took a number of centuries to complete, especially in the East. Christians and Jews continued to interact on a regular basis in a number of important places such as Antioch. The exact nature of this interaction lacks sufficient documentary evidence, but it clearly appears to be something desired by both communities. Clearly the Jewish tent was wide enough to embrace the "followers of the Way," as Christians were sometimes called, for several centuries until the patristic "adversus Judaeos" theology began to gain strength and influence the political climate in a negative way for the Jewish community.

This sense of an inherent component of Judaism in the Christian soul has been restored to Christian thinking in recent years, in part through a new recognition that in fact it has been there for many centuries though often submerged beneath the more overt anti-Jewish theology. The Italian historian Anna Foa makes this point in a recent essay: "With Gregory the Great, at the end of the sixth century, the Western Church definitely opted for the presence of Judaism in its midst, basing its theological pronouncements concerning the Jews on the theories of Paul and Augustine."[28] Pope John Paul II reaffirmed this perspective during his papacy on several occasions, including during his historic visit to the synagogue in Rome when he spoke the following words: "The Church of Christ discovers her 'bond' with Judaism by 'searching into her own mystery' (cf. *Nostra Aetate*). The Jewish religion is not 'extrinsic' to us, but in a certain way is 'intrinsic' to our own religion. With Judaism, therefore, we have a relationship which we do not have with any other religion."[29] More recently, from the Protestant side, a 2001 document *Church and Israel* published in English and German by the Association of Reformation Churches in Europe known as the Leuenberg Church Fellowship argues that the interrelationship between the Church and Israel is not a marginal issue for Christianity. Rather it represents a central dimension of ecclesiology. The relationship with Israel is seen in this document as an indispensable foundation of Christian faith. The Church is required to reflect on its relationship with Judaism because of its profound linkage to the Jewish community in its beginnings. The biblical texts referring to these "beginnings," according to this document, "do not only speak of the historical origin of the Church and thus of the historical relation with Israel; they also form the starting point and critical point of reference (*fons* et *iudex*) for all theological reflection."[30]

The question posed by the new understanding of the gradual nature of the Jewish-Christian separation as well as by the reaffirmation of Christianity's profound Jewish roots by Foa, Pope John Paul II, and the Leuenberg Church Fellowship presents challenges both for Michael Signer and myself. On the one hand I know we would be in agreement that neither of us would opt for some sort of restored Jewish Christianity. Christian self-understanding has developed in quite different ways from Jewish self-understanding for a variety of reasons and on account of profoundly divergent experiences based *in part* in the tremendous political inequality of the our two faith communities over the centuries. But at the minimum the new scholarship reaffirms a persistent measure of bondedness at the beginning which in my judgment requires some reaffirmation of continuing bondedness today as the above Christian declarations have underlined. I believe it is incumbent upon Signer, as he develops his thought further on the Christian-Jewish relationship, to address this challenging question from the side of Judaism. Would he in any way affirm these statements of linkage? Or, in his perspective, is Christianity going it alone with such a perspective?

The final point I would raise for consideration in terms of Christian-Jewish bonding relates to the Holocaust. Has the experience of the Holocaust undermined covenantal certitude on both sides of the interreligious divide between Jews and Christians, something Irving Greenberg, Emil

Fackenheim, and Emmanuel Levinas have argued? If so, can a post-Holocaust covenantal awareness arise only through theological interaction between the two faith communities? Greenberg first addressed this issue in his groundbreaking essay at the first major international conference on the Holocaust held at the Cathedral of St. John the Divine in New York City in 1974.[31] Fackenheim spoke to this question in the following words: "[A]fter the neo-pagans had perpetrated such an assault upon our two faiths, Judaism and Christianity, it was unavoidable that whatever had divided us in the course of almost two millennia had to come to an end. A new Jewish-Christianity reality had to be born, a new link between the two covenants, the Jewish and the Christian one, between what, decades later, the Protestant theologian Roy Eckardt would call the elder and the younger brother."[32] And Emmanuel Levinas has argued that "the religious amplitude [of the Shoah] is destined to mark the world forever."[33]

Certainly Michael Signer has made the Holocaust a central dimension of his own scholarly work over the years. There is no question on this score. In addition, he organized a major international conference on the Holocaust at Notre Dame in response to the Vatican's 1998 document on the Shoah[34] as well as continuing events through the Notre Dame Holocaust project. His more recent involvements in theological discussions and student conferences in Germany and Poland, something that has become very central to his life in the last years, have been undertaken in the shadow of the Holocaust.[35] But, up till now, Signer has not grappled personally in a comprehensive way with the Holocaust's implications for Jewish-Christian bonding today. Grappling more profoundly with the Holocaust would demand some modification of Signer's thesis about the rift in biblical interpretation as the sole source of linkage between Jews and Christians in our time. Would he agree with Fackenheim and Greenberg that the Holocaust has rendered previous covenantal understandings both in Judaism and Christianity in need of significant revision? If so, do Christianity and Judaism share common ground in recognizing a need to rebuild covenantal understanding today and to do so, at least in part, as a common effort? I believe this to be the case and I would hope that Signer too might come to this important conclusion in an explicit way.

The above challenges to my friend and soulmate Michael Signer are not intended so much as critiques as a summons to continue his reflections in an expanded fashion. Having encountered his thinking in his formal writings, in platforms we have shared, and in informal conversations over coffee in the near-Loop location in Chicago where I reside and the Signers have an in-city condo, I have come to recognize a yet not fully tapped richness in his soul on the issue at hand. I am convinced that he has the ability to offer a comprehensive interpretation of Christian-Jewish bonding that would incorporate his already meaningful reflections on the rift that binds into a wider understanding of our bonding that would continue to respect fully the gulf that we will never fully bridge and will amplify the significance of his cryptic statement quoted earlier in this essay about Christians living in the household of Israel.

Notes

1. Michael Signer's principal writings on this topic include the following: "One Covenant or Two: Can We Sing a New Song?" in *Reinterpreting Revelation and Tradition: Jews and Christians in Conversation,* ed. John T. Pawlikowski and Hayim Goren Perelmuter (Franklin, WI: Sheed & Ward, 2000), 3–23; "The Rift That Binds: Hermeneutical Approaches to the Jewish-Christian Relationship," in *Ecumenism: Present Realities and Future Prospects,* ed. Lawrence S. Cunningham (Notre Dame, IN: University of Notre Dame Press, 1998), 95–115; "Tradition in Transition: Approaches to Jewish-Christian Relations," in *Jews and Christians in Conversation: Crossing Cultures and Generations,* ed. Edward Kessler, John Pawlikowski, Judith Herschcopf Banki, and Barbara Ellen Bowe (Cambridge: Orchard Academic, 2002), 123–39; "Abraham: The One and the Many," in *Memory and History in Christianity and Judaism,* ed. Michael A. Signer (Notre Dame, IN: University of Notre Dame Press, 2001), 204–12; "Searching the Scriptures: Jews, Christians and the Book," in *Christianity in Jewish Terms,* ed. Tikva Frymer-Kensky, David Novak, Peter Ochs, David Fox Sandmel, and Michael A. Signer (Boulder, CO: Westview Press, 2000), 85–98; and "Many Religions, One Destiny: Religions for a Better Humanity," unpublished address delivered at the Rotko Chapel, Houston, Texas, February 7, 2006.

2. The text can be found in *Christianity in Jewish Terms,* ed. Fryer-Kensky et al., xvii–xx.

3. Signer, "The Rift That Binds," 113.

4. Ibid., 96.

5. Cf. Jon D. Levenson, "How Not to Conduct Jewish-Christian Dialogue," *Commentary* 112.5 (December 2001): 31–37; for a response by the authors of *Dabru Emet* and others, cf. "Jewish-Christian Dialogue: Jon D. Levenson and Critics," *Commentary* 113.4 (April 2002): 8–21.

6. Roger Brooks and John J. Collins, ed., *Hebrew Bible or Old Testament: Studying the Bible in Judaism and Christianity* (Notre Dame, IN: University of Notre Dame Press, 1990).

7. Signer, "Tradition in Transition," 134.

8. Cf. Signer, "One Covenant or Two," 19–20. One may note also his reference to Abraham Joshua Heschel's remark that "great reformulations of Judaism and Christianity begin with a study of the Hebrew Bible," 18.

9. Signer, "The Rift That Binds," 113.

10. Signer, "Abraham," 211.

11. Ibid., 212.

12. Signer, "Searching the Scriptures," 98.

13. "Many Religions, One Destiny," 4–9.

14. Cf. Eugene J. Fisher and Leon Klenicki, ed., *Pope John Paul II on Jews and Judaism* (Washington, DC: United States Catholic Conference, 1987); Pope John Paul II, *Spiritual Pilgrimage: Texts on Jews and Judaism 1979–1995*, ed. Eugene J. Fisher and Leon Klenicki (New York: Crossroad, 1995). Also cf. Byron L. Sherwin and Harold Kasimow, ed., *John Paul II and Interreligious Dialogue* (Maryknoll, NY: Orbis, 1999).

15. The Pontifical Biblical Commission, *The Jewish People and Their Sacred Scripture in the Christian Bible* (Vatican City: Libreria Editrice Vaticana, 2002). Also cf. Donald Senior, "Rome Has Spoken: A New Catholic Approach to Judaism," *Commonweal* 130 (31 January 2003): 20–23; also cf. articles by Mary Boys, Leslie Hoppe, Michael O'Connor, John T. Pawlikowski, and Amy-Jill Levine in *The Bible Today* 41.3 (May 2003): 141–72.

16. James K. Aitken, "What Does Christianity in Jewish Terms Mean?" in *Challenges in Jewish-Christian Relations,* ed. James K. Aitken and Edward Kessler (New York and Mahwah, NJ: Paulist, 2006), 212.

17. Ibid.

18. Cf. Matthew Hoffman, *From Rebel to Rabbi: Reclaiming Jesus and the Making of Modern Jewish Culture* (Stanford, CA: Stanford University Press, 2007).

19. Martin Noth, *The Law in the Pentateuch and Other Stories* (Edinburgh: Oliver and Boyd, 1966).

20. Carlo Maria Martini, S.J., "Christianity and Judaism: A Historical and Theological Overview," in *Jews and Christians: Exploring the Past, Present, and Future,* ed. James H. Charlesworth (New York: Crossroad, 1990), 19.

21. The *Notes* may be found in *In Our Time: The Flowering of Jewish-Catholic Dialogue,* ed. Eugene J. Fisher and Leon Klenicki (New York and Mahwah, NJ: Paulist, 1990), 38–50.

22. Cardinal Walter Kasper, "Christians, Jews, and the Thorny Question of Mission," *Origins* 32.28 (19 December 2002): 464.

23. Note #7, *A Sacred Obligation*. The full text of the statement may be found in *Seeing Judaism Anew: Christianity's Sacred Obligation*, ed. Mary C. Boys (Lanham, New York, and Oxford: Rowman & Littlefield, 2005), xiii–xix.

24. Franz Mussner, *Tractate on the Jews: The Significance of Judaism for Christian Faith* (Philadelphia: Fortress, 1984); Franz Mussner, "From Jesus 'the Prophet' to Jesus 'the Son,'" in *Three Ways to the One God: The Faith Experience in Judaism, Christianity, and Islam*, ed. Abdold Javad Falaturi, Jacob J. Petuchowski, and Walter Strolz (New York: Crossroad, 1987), 76–85.

25. Bruce Chilton, *Rabbi Jesus: An Intimate Biography—The Jewish Life and Teaching That Inspired Christianity* (New York, London, and Toronto: Doubleday, 2000), 195.

26. Michael Wyschogrod, "A Jewish Perspective on Incarnation," *Modern Theology* 12 (1996): 197ff.

27. Elliot R. Wolfson, "Judaism and Incarnation: The Imaginal Body of God," in *Christianity in Jewish Terms*, ed. Frymer-Kensky et al., 239–54. Also cf. Randi Rashkover, "The Christian Doctrine of the Incarnation," ibid., 254–61.

28. Anna Foa, "The Difficult Apprenticeship of Diversity," in *The Catholic Church and the Jewish People: Recent Reflections from Rome*, ed. Philip A. Cunningham, Nobert J. Hofman, and Joseph Sievers (New York: Fordham University Press, 2007), 42.

29. Cf. Pope John Paul II, *Spiritual Pilgrimage*, 63.

30. Cf. The Leuenberg Church Fellowship, *Church and Israel: A Contribution from the Reformation Churches in Europe to the Relationship between Christians and Jews* (Frankfurt am Main: Verlag Otto Lembeck, 2001), 1.3 and 3.1. Also cf. the papers from the Jewish-Christian Discussion Group of the Central Committee of German Catholics, *Coming Together for the Sake of God: Contributions to Jewish-Christian Dialogue from Post-Holocaust Germany*, ed. Hanspeter Heinz and Michael A. Signer (Collegeville, MN: Liturgical Press, 2007).

31. Irving Greenberg, "Cloud of Smoke, Pillar of Fire: Judaism, Christianity, and Modernity after the Holocaust," in *Auschwitz: Beginning of a New Era? Reflection on the Holocaust*, ed. Eva Fleischner (New York: KTAV, the Cathedral of St. John the Divine, and the Anti-Defamation League, 1977), 7–55; Irving Greenberg, *For the Sake of Heaven and Earth: The New Encounter between Judaism and Christianity* (Philadelphia: Jewish Publication Society, 2004); "Judaism and Christianity: Covenants of Redemption," in *Christianity in Jewish Terms*, ed. Frymer-Kensky et al., 141–58.

32. Emil Fackenheim, *Jewish-Christian Relations after the Holocaust: Toward Post-Holocaust Theological Thought*, The Joseph Cardinal Bernardin Lecture (Chicago: Archdiocese of Chicago, Spertus Institute of Jewish Studies, the Jewish Federation of Metropolitan Chicago, and the American Jewish Committee, 1996), 15.

33. Emmanuel Levinas, *Difficult Freedom: Essays on Judaism* (Baltimore, MD: Johns Hopkins University Press, 1990), 12.

34. The papers from this conference were published as *Humanity at the Limit: The Impact of the Holocaust Experience on Jews and Christians,* ed. Michael A. Signer (Bloomington and Indianapolis: Indiana University Press, 2000).

35. Michael A. Signer, "Dialogue out of the Ashes: Jewish-Catholic Dialogue in Germany," in *Coming Together for the Sake of God,* ed. Heinz and Signer, 148–55.

CHAPTER NINETEEN

Philosemitism and "Judaizing" in the Contemporary Church

David Fox Sandmel

In the preamble to *Dabru Emet: A Jewish Statement on Christians and Christianity,* Michael Signer, along with Tikva Frymer-Kensky, David Novak, and Peter Ochs, writes:

> In recent years, there has been a dramatic and unprecedented shift in Jewish and Christian relations. Throughout the nearly two millennia of Jewish exile, Christians have tended to characterize Judaism as a failed religion or, at best, a religion that prepared the way for, and is completed in, Christianity. In the decades since the Holocaust, however, Christianity has changed dramatically. An increasing number of official Church bodies, both Roman Catholic and Protestant, have made public statements of their remorse about Christian mistreatment of Jews and Judaism. These statements have declared, furthermore, that Christian teaching and preaching can and must be reformed so that they acknowledge God's enduring covenant with the Jewish people and celebrate the contribution of Judaism to world civilization and to Christian faith itself.[1]

The premise of this essay is that the dramatic changes Signer and his colleagues acknowledged as "merit[ing] a thoughtful Jewish response" are reflected not only in public statements and the works of post-Holocaust

Christian theologians, but also in what might be called a "Christian reclamation of Judaism." This complex phenomenon manifests itself in a number of ways within the diverse world of contemporary Christianity.[2] In what follows, I intend to give some examples of this phenomenon, suggest a number of factors that contribute to it, and reflect on its implication for Jewish-Christian relations. This is a preliminary, exploratory effort; the phenomenon itself, as well as any conclusions at which I arrive, will require further, more comprehensive research. If this phenomenon is as widespread as this initial exploration suggests and if it is growing, it will have significant implications for Jewish-Christian relations.

Some Selected Examples

The following section contains a brief selection of examples of what I am calling the Christian reclamation of Judaism. In and of themselves, some of these may not seem particularly significant; however, taken together, I believe they indicate a broad trend within Christianity toward the incorporation of Jewish traditions and practices into Christian worship and spirituality.[3]

It is worth noting that while Jewish-Christian relations and Jewish-Christian dialogue have historically taken place primarily among Jews, mainline Protestants, and Roman Catholics, the location of the most enthusiastic "reclamation," at least in terms of Jewish ritual, appears to be in the evangelical community. This aspect of the phenomenon demands further exploration. The following statement is found on the website of the New Life Christian Center, a non-denominational church in San Antonio, Texas, whose founding pastor is also the San Antonio coordinator for Christians United for Israel. It contains many of the components that will be discussed in more detail below. Dr. Vaughan writes:

> Walk anywhere on our campus and you will sense a strong Jewish influence. From our majestic Sea of Galilee replica, or our beautiful western wall replica, or the alternating American & Israeli flags encircling the campus, the Jewish impact is clearly evident. Join us for a worship service and

you might experience Israel day/Banner day: a service honoring the God, Word, People, and Land of Israel, or enjoy Davidic song & dance, or pray using a Tallit during midnight prayer, or witness our tithing worship in our replica of the Ark of the Covenant. As a visitor to New Life, you might wonder why we embrace Israel and the Jewish culture. First and foremost let me assure you that anything you see at New Life always has a scriptural basis. We believe in the entire Bible from Genesis to Revelation. The [B]ible describes the plight of the Jewish people from Egypt to the promised Land of Israel. In Exodus, God gave the Jewish people the Torah (first five books). The Torah provides guidelines and instructions for living—often referred to as the law. Fast-forward several hundred years into [the future,] we see Jesus complete the messianic prophecies. Jesus was born a Jew. Our Lord studied and lived his life according to the guidelines and instructions of the Torah. In our quest to learn more about JESUS, we embrace his roots, heritage, and culture. We study the Torah. We embrace Jewish history and customs. We sing Hebrew songs. We travel to Israel and we pray daily for her. I firmly believe that the God of Israel, His Word, Land, and His people are inseparable. To understand one, we must study and embrace them all. Revelation says that in the last days the body of Christ is supposed to embrace Israel. At New Life, we make a concerted effort to support and align ourselves with Israel—the apple of God's eye.[4]

Some additional examples include:

1. *The use of Hebrew terms and songs.* Jewish religious terminology in Hebrew and Jewish music are finding their way into Christian worship. Presbyterian, United Methodist, and Episcopalian hymnals contain the song "Shalom Chaverim."[5] A music CD entitled "25 Bible Action Songs" can be purchased from worshipmusic.com and includes "Onward Christian Soldiers," "I Am A C-H-R-I-S-T-I-A-N," and "Hineh Mah Tov."[6] When Katherine Jefforts Schori was invested as the Episcopal Church's twenty-sixth Presiding Bishop, she preached her inaugural sermon on "shalom," which she described as a "wonderful Hebrew word"; in the course of her sermon she used the term over a dozen times. She closed her sermon by saying "Shalom chaverim, shalom my friends, shalom." The transcript then

adds "The Congregation responded: Shalom."[7] Indeed, the use of the word "shalom" is apparently so ubiquitous in Protestant circles that Martin Marty, in an essay on an unrelated topic, takes a swipe at "the mainline Protestant churches with their incessant talk about the Prince of Peace and shalom and reconciliation."[8] Other Hebrew terms are now regularly used in Christian settings, among them "tikkun olam" (repairing the world) and "teshuvah" (repentance). The use of the name "Yeshua" for Jesus is becoming more common, primarily among conservative Protestants. Finally, some Christians are starting to refer to the Holocaust with the Hebrew word, "Shoah."

2. *The purchase and use of Jewish ritual items.* Christian websites and catalogs that offer Jewish ritual items for sale abound. ChristianBook.com, the Internet arm of Christian Book Distributors, Inc., describes itself as "the world's largest distributor of Christian products." Christian Book Distributors does not market to a Jewish audience, yet it offers numerous Jewish ritual items (e.g. menorahs, shofars, mezuzot) for sale, including a tallit (prayer shawl) imprinted with the Lord's Prayer in English and Hebrew. Christians who visit Israel often buy Jewish ritual items.

3. *Christian bar mitzvah.* The bar mitzvah ceremony is also being adapted for Christian usage. Craig Hill has written a book called *Bar Barakah: A Parent's Guide to a Christian Bar Mitzvah.* He argues that the "parental blessing of children at the time of puberty to release them to adulthood" is "not a Jewish tradition or a primitive ceremony" but an "ancient path" that has been lost and deserves to be restored. He then describes a "Jewish friend" whose bar mitzvah was "the most important day of his life" and states: "I would like to suggest that as believers in Yeshua (Jesus) the Messiah, we should call our children passing through such a ceremony a 'Bar Barakáh' (bar ber-aw-káw) or 'Bat Barakáh' (bot ber-aw-káw) which is in Hebrew a 'Son of the Blessing,' or a 'Daughter of the Blessing.'"[9] Hill outlines a course of study and provides an outline format for such ceremonies.

Another example of the self-conscious use of the model of bar/bat mitzvah in a Christian setting is Rite 13, which was started at an Episcopal church in 1990 and, according to a 2005 *Time* article, is found in over 1,300 churches.[10] The "Rite-13 Liturgy Guide" refers to bar and bat mitzvah several times, either drawing parallels between Rite 13 and the Jewish ceremony or making distinctions between it. It is clear, however, that Rite 13 is a conscious adaptation of the Jewish rite: "It is very similar to a Bar Mitzvah or Bat Mitzvah in the Jewish tradition."[11] The Guide also invokes the bar mitzvah as a familiar point of departure to help participants understand Rite 13 as a "ritual that allows us to celebrate together the transition from childhood to manhood or womanhood." In a lesson plan for parents, it states: "Our Jewish brothers and sisters have been doing this for centuries in the Bar/Bat Mitzvah. For many cultures, this age marks the transition from being a child to being a man or a woman and is accompanied by various initiation rites. The average age of menarche—the beginning of menstruation—today in young women in North America is eleven years and ten months."[12]

4. *Christian seders.*[13] Perhaps the most prevalent example of the Christian reclamation of Judaism is the contemporary Christian Passover seder. This is not the same as an interfaith seder or model seder designed to teach those who are not Jewish about the Jewish festival of Passover. A Christian seder may include elements of teaching about Judaism, but it is, at its core, a form of Christian worship, including prayers that invoke Jesus, readings from the New Testament, and reinterpretation of the symbols of the seder in christological terms. In an article entitled "Introduction to a Christian Seder: Recovering Passover for Christians,"[14] Dennis Bratcher, after explaining that the Last Supper was a Passover seder, writes: "Our goal here in presenting a Christian adaptation of Passover is to retain the theological, confessional, and educational dimensions of the service. That is, it is presented as a way for people of Christian Faith to express that faith in the context of a gathered community by participating symbolically in the story of salvation. It is presented very deliberately and purposefully as a Christian service, with no apologies."[15] He continues: "Yet, there has also been a deliberate attempt to preserve the spirit of the Jewish traditions and experience in the service, and to respect the faith journey of Israelites and Jews across the centuries. For that reason, apart from the fact that it will likely be Christians who are participating in the service, the thoroughly Christian dimension will come at the end of the service. After all, that is really how God chose to work in history: to the Jew first, and then also to the rest of us!"[16]

The seder ritual that this author is describing reserves the "thoroughly Christian dimension" until the end. Other Christian seders and Hagaddot interpret every aspect of the ritual in Christian terms such as we find in an article called "How the Passover Reveals Jesus Christ": "Christian symbolism in the Passover occurs early in the Seder (the Passover dinner). Three matzahs are put together (representing the Father, Son, and Holy Spirit). The middle matzah is broken, wrapped in a white cloth, and hidden, representing the death and burial of Jesus. The matzah itself is designed to represent Jesus, since it is striped [*sic*] and pierced, which was prophesized by Isaiah, David, and Zechariah. Following the Seder meal, the 'buried' matzah is 'resurrected,' which was foretold in the prophecies of David."[17]

Factors Influencing the Christian Reclamation of Judaism

The phrase "Christian reclamation of Judaism" consciously echoes the phrase "Jewish reclamation of Jesus," used most notably by Donald Hagner in the title of his 1984 book.[18] As Hagner, Susannah Heschel,[19] Jonathan Brumberg-Kraus,[20] and more recently, Matthew Hoffman[21] have shown, during the nineteenth and twentieth centuries attitudes toward Jesus among Jews in the West shifted away from the classical negative view of Jesus as renegade Jew who brought untold misery to his people. In its stead, a new Jesus emerged in the Jewish imagination, a Jew of whom Jews could be proud, a "brother."[22] The Jewish reclamation of Jesus, however, as Hagner notes, is limited to the fully human Jewish Jesus; it does not encompass Jesus as the risen Christ, the Jesus who is the object of Christian faith. In that regard, it is found wanting by some Christian scholars.[23] Similarly, the Christian reclamation of Judaism is selective and often filtered through a specifically Christian lens. If for Jews the reclamation of Jesus requires stripping Jesus of any christological aspects, the Christian reclamation of Judaism often involves the addition of Christology in one form or another. When this involves ritual, what may have had its origins in Judaism is transformed into a form of Christian piety.

This "reclamation" is noteworthy because it is in stark contrast to the teachings and attitudes that viewed Jews and Judaism in opposition to the Church and to Christianity which characterized the Church until the modern era. The Church was "of God," and Jews were, to quote the Gospel of John, "of your father, the devil" (Jn. 8:44). "Judaizing," the performance of Jewish rituals by both Jewish and Gentile Christians, most notably circumcision and the dietary regulations, was one of the central conflicts in the early church. This conflict is found in the New Testament itself, for example, at the "Jerusalem Synod" described in Acts 15, and in Paul's Epistle to the Galatians (2:1–10). The appeal of Judaism for Christians remained a concern for church authorities such as Ignatius of Antioch, Justin Martyr, and John Chrysostom. Indeed, despite official condemnation, there is evidence of an ongoing attraction to Jewish practice among Christians during this period. John Gager explains: "[P]opular Christianity was not nearly as convinced as were its leaders that the beliefs and practices of Judaism had been rendered powerless by the appearance of Christianity. . . . For significant numbers of Christians in late antiquity, Judaism continued to represent a powerful and vigorous religious tradition. Unlike their ecclesiastical and theological superiors, they saw no need to define themselves in opposition to Judaism or to cut themselves off from this obvious source of power."[24]

Recent studies have shown that the boundary between Judaism and Christianity, and therefore between Jews and Christians, remained fluid much longer than was previously acknowledged. The parting of the ways is now understood to have been a process, rather than an event, that took centuries and which developed at different speeds depending on both geographic and social location.[25] However, as Christianity progressed from diversity toward orthodoxy, the relationship with Judaism became increasingly oppositional, leading eventually to the institutionalization of the teaching of contempt and persecution of Jews under Christian political domination. It is only in the modern era and especially after the Holocaust that a profound and dramatic shift in Christian attitudes toward Jews and Judaism emerges.

Among the factors influencing the Christian reclamation of Judaism are the increasing appreciation by Christians of the Jewishness of Jesus, a claim to kinship with the Jewish people, the impact of the Holocaust on Christians' self-understanding as seen in post-Holocaust Christian theology, the existence of the state of Israel, the emergence of Christian Zionism, and the influence of Jews for Jesus and other such groups, at least among evangelical Christians.[26]

The Jewish Jesus

If classical Christianity viewed Jesus as opposed to Judaism rather than part of it, critical scholarship has firmly rooted Jesus in the context of first-century Judaism. Critical scholarship over the last century and a half has convincingly made the case that Jesus can only be understood as a Jew who was fully part of the Jewish world of early first-century Palestine. Today, the suggestion that Jesus was fully Jewish is widely accepted among the general public. One example that shows just how far the concept of the Jewish Jesus has penetrated into popular culture is the bumper sticker that states, "My boss is a Jewish carpenter." One website offers not only bumper stickers, but also t-shirts, sweatshirts, tracksuits, mugs, hats, and tote bags emblazoned with this message.[27] The Christian who puts this on his or her car may not be well informed about Jewish-Christian relations or biblical scholarship. However, this message not only assumes that others will understand the reference, but actually accepts and celebrates the Jewishness of Jesus. Indeed, many Christians also identify Jesus as a rabbi and use that identity as a bridge to relating to Jews and Judaism.[28] Jesus is now understood to have been an observant Jew who followed Jewish law and celebrated the Sabbath and Jewish festivals. Contemporary Jewish rituals, to the extent that they preserve aspects of Second Temple Judaism, are sometimes seen by Christians as a window into the life of Jesus. The historical development of Judaism here is often overlooked, resulting in an anachronistic conflation of first-century Judaism with the rabbinic Judaism that followed it.

The Jews as "Family"

The embracing of the Jewish Jesus is mirrored by an embracing of the Jews themselves as part of the extended family through which Jews and Christians are related. Again, what was once seen as opposed is now seen as part of a greater whole. At one extreme is the view in the Gospel of John that the Jews are descended from Satan or the Augustinian concept that the Jews are the enemies of the Church whose miserable existence is a demonstration of God's graciousness to the Church. Now, many Christians view Jesus as a devout and loyal Jew who loved his people, an attitude that, they believe, should serve as a model for Christians today. Some Christians rely on Romans 11 to portray Jews as God's people to whom Christians are related through the common fatherhood (one of the flesh and one of the spirit) of Abraham; Christians are "grafted in" to the family of Abraham *along with,* rather than in place of, the Jews. This transformation of the relationship has been aptly described as "from 'other' to 'brother.'"[29] John Paul II famously referred to the Jews as "elder brother" when, in 1986, he became the first pope to visit the synagogue in Rome, and this kind of relational language has become common for many Christians today.

The Holocaust

Irving Greenberg has described the Holocaust as a revelatory event for Christianity;[30] it is also a significant factor in the Christian reclamation of Judaism. As Christians have come to understand the ways that Christian teaching and Christians themselves contributed to the Holocaust, they have been moved to respond to it in official statements such as the Declaration of the Evangelical Lutheran Church in America to the Jewish Community[31] and the 1998 Vatican document "We Remember: A Reflection on the Shoah," each of which acknowledges the connection between Christian attitudes and teaching and the Nazi Final Solution.[32] It is worth noting the use of the Hebrew word "Shoah" not only in the title of the Vatican document but throughout, as well as the use of the "teshuvah" to define the act of repentance that the document calls upon the Church to perform. Using the sacred terminology of the "other," or better, "brother," in a document such as this serves not only as an act of contrition, but also as a statement of solidarity and identification.[33]

In addition to being the subject of official church statements, the Holocaust is increasingly being memorialized ritually by Christians and Jews, and often others, in interfaith observances. Additionally, some Christians are choosing to memorialize the Holocaust in Christian-only circles. For example, the Lutheran School of Theology at Chicago and McCormick Seminary (affiliated with the Presbyterian Church/USA) co-sponsor an annual "Service of Remembrance & Commitment" in commemoration of Kristallnacht. The liturgy used at the 2007 event included the communal singing of two songs in Hebrew and the chanting of *El Male Rachamim* (a traditional memorial prayer) by a Jew. Though this event was open to the public, it was planned and targeted specifically at the seminary community as a worship experience for Christians. The Christian memorialization of the Holocaust appears to be motivated, at least in part, by the sincere desire to disavow publicly—and ritually—those aspects of Christian teaching and tradition that contributed to the Shoah. This includes identifying with the Jewish victims as human beings and as "brothers and sisters." This can be seen in the following excerpt from a proposed liturgy contained in a Roman Catholic document, "God's Mercy Endures Forever: Guidelines on the Presentation of Jews and Judaism in Catholic Preaching":

> On the Sunday closest to Yom ha Shoah, Catholics should pray for the victims of the Holocaust and their survivors. The following serve as examples of petitions for the general intercessions at Mass:
>
> For the victims of the Holocaust, their families, and all our *Jewish brothers and sisters,* that the violence and hatred they experienced may never again be repeated, we pray to the Lord.
>
> For the Church, that the Holocaust may be a reminder to us that we can never be indifferent to the sufferings of others, we pray to the Lord.
>
> For our *Jewish brothers and sisters,* that their confidence in the face of long-suffering may spur us on to a greater faith and trust in God, we pray to the Lord.[34]

The State of Israel

The establishment of the State of Israel, and especially travel to Israel, has provided another avenue for Christians to connect to Jews and Judaism. Christian tourism to Israel accounts for as much as a quarter of Israel's tourist industry[35] and the Israeli Ministry of Tourism actively courts the Christian market, as do private tour operators. Many churches offer Holy Land tours. Though Christian tours may focus primarily on Christian holy sites associated with Jesus and the early church, even limited exposure to Jewish history and Jewish life in Israel can have a profound impact on Christian understandings of, and identification with, Jews and Judaism, especially when it is part of religious travel or pilgrimage, not merely secular tourism. Christian tourists in Israel often purchase Jewish ritual items such as prayer shawls or mezuzot as souvenirs or gifts that remind them of the spiritual experience of their pilgrimage and connect them both to the Jewish people and to the Jewish Jesus.

The International Fellowship of Christians and Jews (IFCJ) was founded by a rabbi "to promote understanding and cooperation between Jews and Christians and to build broad support for Israel and other shared concerns." It claims to have "provided millions of dollars to help Jews make aliyah (immigrate to Israel), supply emergency aid in times of crisis in Israel, and support needy Jewish children, families and elderly in distress around the world." Though its top leadership includes both Jews and Christians, its target audience is exclusively Christian and its programs all have a focus on Israel. In addition to its fundraising efforts, the IFCJ offers tours to Israel and its website has a "Store" that features a "Fellowship Connection . . . bringing Israel to your home." One can purchase Israeli products, flags, and "Judaica and Worship Items" including Kiddush cups, menorahs, prayer shawls, shofars, and Torahs.[36]

For some in the evangelical Christian community the establishment of the state is seen in eschatological terms as a prerequisite for the Second Coming of Jesus. According to Christians United for Israel: "Christian Zionism can be defined as Christian support for the Zionist cause—the return of the Jewish people to its biblical homeland in Israel. It is a belief among some Christians that the return of Jews to Israel is in line with a biblical prophecy, and is necessary for Jesus to return to Earth as its king. These Christians are partly motivated by the writings of the Bible and the words of the prophets. However, they are also driven to support Israel because they wish to 'repay the debt of gratitude to the Jewish people for providing Christ and the other fundamentals of their faith,' and to support a political ally. . . ."[37] Christian Zionists express their belief by celebrating, visiting, and praying for Israel, by mobilizing political support for Israel, and in some instances by promoting the adaptation of Jewish forms of worship.

"Messianic Jews"

There is a close relationship between various "messianic Jewish" organizations (e.g., Jews for Jesus, Messianic Judaism)[38] and some churches, especially Christian Zionists or those, like the Southern Baptists, who maintain an active mission to the Jews.[39] On the one hand, messianic Jewish organizations often rely on churches as sources of funding. On the other hand, churches turn to messianic organizations to provide educational programs and conduct Christian seders. Since messianic Jewish worship makes use of Hebrew terminology, Jewish music, and Jewish ritual items, it stands to reason that Christians who have come into contact with these organizations and their ideology, which also stresses the Jewishness of Jesus, have been influenced by them.

Many of the factors and indicators that are enumerated above are apparent in the following statement from the Hebraic Christian Global Community, a non-profit religious and research organization based in Atlanta, Georgia, aimed at promoting the restoration of the Judaic heritage of the Christian church.[40] Explicitly and implicitly, it refers to a rejection of the teaching of contempt, to the Holocaust, and to connecting with the Jewishness of Jesus:

> Something truly amazing is happening right now before our eyes! What can only be seen as a sovereign work of the Holy Spirit is breaking forth as Christians around the world are working to restore the Hebrew foundations of Christianity. After being marred for more than eighteen centuries by Judaeophobia, anti-Judaism, and anti-Semitism, Christianity is being impacted by a revolution of restoration. Scholars, clergy, and laity from virtually every nationality, ethnicity, and denomination are reconnecting their faith in Jesus with its historical Hebraic roots.[41]

Conclusions

The new Christian relationship to Judaism to which *Dabru Emet* responds has affected more than just attitudes. It has led some Christians to adapt aspects of Jewish culture and ritual as expression of kinship both with Jesus and with Jews. In antiquity, the church fathers taught anti-Judaism and sought to root out "judaizing." Today many Christians reject anti-Judaism and anti-Semitism, embrace Jews as brothers and sisters, and, to varying degrees, see Jewish practice as a resource that can be used to enhance Christian spirituality and identity. This is especially the case among some evangelical Christians.

Some Christians have told me that these Jewish practices seem more "authentic" to them than their own traditional Christian practices, which they now understand not to be rooted in the life and experience of Jesus but are later developments of the Church. In a way, then, the Christian reclamation of Judaism and Jewish ritual in part serves to bridge a gap that has been opened by contemporary scholarship on Christian origins between the religion of Jesus and the religion about Jesus.

The adoption and adaptation of Jewish rituals in a Christian setting has already raised concerns within the Jewish community and among some Christians as well. Some Jews might see this as an indication of a positive attitudinal shift among Christians that therefore is to be welcomed. Others, however, react negatively to what is perceived to be yet another example of two thousand years of Christian disregard for the sanctity of the Jewish tradition and Jewish sensibilities. The phenomenon might also be seen in terms of Christian cultural imperialism, or supersessionism—since Christianity has replaced the Jews as God's covenantal partners, Jewish tradition itself can be mined for Christian purposes without concern about the reactions of Jews. Some Christians, as seen in the ELCA document referenced above, are concerned about Jewish sensibilities,[42] while others will view the importation of Jewish rituals in terms of the classical understanding of judaizing.

There is much about the phenomenon of the Christian reclamation of Judaism that remains to be explored. How widespread is the phenomenon, especially outside Western, English-speaking Christian communities? Are there debates about it within the Christian world and, if so, what are they? How is the Jewish community reacting to it? What are its implications for Jewish-Christian relations? I hope to be able to address these and other questions in the future.

Notes

1. The text can be found on www.jcrelations.net, a site owned and operated by the International Council of Christians and Jews.

2. Almost all the examples I bring are from the North American context. The extent to which this phenomenon is found in Europe or other parts of the world remains to be explored.

3. None of the examples, to the best of my knowledge, is from messianic "Jewish" organizations or individuals. However, the influence of messianic "Judaism" is significant and will be discussed below.

4. The text can be found at www.christiancenter.com under "Jewish Connection" on the About Us menu.

5. *The Presbyterian Hymnal: Hymns, Psalms, and Spiritual Songs* (Louisville: Westminster–John Knox Press, 1990); *The United Methodist Hymnal: Book of United Methodist Worship* (Nashville: United Methodist Publishing House, 1989); *The Hymnal 1985 According to the Use of the Episcopal Church* (New York: Church Hymnal Group, 1985). It is worth noting that while this song is quite popular in Jewish settings, it is a secular children's song and not usually used by Jews liturgically.

6. The music CD is available from www.worshipmusic.com.

7. The sermon is archived at www.episcopalchurch.org/78703_79214_ENG _HTM.

8. Martin E. Marty, "Fighting Words," *Christian Century*, July 12, 2005.

9. Craig Hill, *Bar Barakah: A Parent's Guide to a Christian Bar Mitzvah* (Littleton, CO: Family Foundations International, 1998), 9. Hill accepts without question the anachronistic view that bar mitzvah ceremonies were held in Jesus' day. He also states that it was customary for Jewish fathers to pronounce, "This is my beloved son in whom I am well pleased," as a blessing over the son (p. 16). There is no evidence that this phrase, which in the synoptic Gospels God speaks over Jesus at his baptism (and which for Hill is a model of parental blessing), was ever used in Jewish liturgy. Hill also recommends that "[t]here should be as much planning and preparation, as much money spent, and as many people invited to the Bar Barakah ceremony as there would be to your child's wedding" (p. 49).

10. The article is available at www.time.com/time/magazine/article/ 0,9171,1088734-3,00.

11. Copyright 1996–2008, St. Philip's Episcopal Church, Durham, NC.

12. Ibid.

13. Jews often have a negative reaction to Christian seders; however, this does not fall within the scope of this essay. I will make some general comments about Jewish reaction to the Christian reclamation of Judaism in the conclusion.

14. See the article by Dennis Bratcher at www.crivoice.org/seder. The identification of the Last Supper as a Passover seder is an anachronism, since the seder ritual emerges only after the destruction of the Second Temple in 70 CE and thus post-dates Jesus. However, as will be discussed below, the retrojection of later Jewish practice into the time of Jesus is a common feature of the Christian reclamation of Jewish ritual. Amy-Jill Levine addresses the Christian seder in *The Misunderstood*

Jew: The Church and the Scandal of the Jewish Jesus (San Francisco: HarperSan-Francisco, 2006), 206–10. The Evangelical Lutheran Church of America warns its members: "Although attendance at Seders in Jewish homes or synagogues is to be preferred, 'demonstration Seders' have been held rather widely in Christian churches and can serve a useful educational purpose, in which both common roots and significant differences can be learned. This should be approached with caution, however, and with the awareness that this might be considered 'trampling on the other's holy ground.' If such demonstrations are done, they should be done carefully, preferably in consultation with, or hosted by, a local rabbi." The Guidelines are available at www.elca.org under WhoWe Are.

15. Bratcher article.

16. Ibid.

17. See www.godandscience.org/apologetics/passover.

18. Donald Hagner, *The Jewish Reclamation of Jesus: An Analysis and Critique of the Modern Jewish Study of Jesus* (Grand Rapids, MI: Zondervan, 1984).

19. Susannah Heschel, "Jesus as Theological Transvestite," in *Judaism Since Gender,* ed. Miriam Peskowitz and Laura Levitt (New York: Routledge, 1997), 188–99.

20. Jonathan Brumberg-Kraus, "A Jewish Ideological Perspective on the Study of Christian Scripture," *Jewish Social Studies* n.s. 4.1 (1997): 121–52.

21. Matthew Hoffman, *From Rebel to Rabbi: Reclaiming Jesus and the Making of Modern Jewish Culture* (Stanford, CA: Stanford University Press, 2007).

22. Schalom Ben-Chorim, *Brother Jesus: The Nazarene through Jewish Eyes,* trans. Jared S. Klein and Max Reinhart (Athens and London: University of Georgia Press, 2001).

23. Hagner, *The Jewish Reclamation,* 14, 27.

24. John Gager, *The Origins of Anti-Semitism: Attitudes toward Judaism in Pagan and Christian Antiquity* (New York: Oxford University Press, 1983), 133.

25. See, for example, Adam H. Becker and Annette Yoshiko Reed, ed., *The Ways That Never Parted* (Tübingen: J. C. B. Mohr, 2003); and *Jewish Christianity Reconsidered,* ed. Matt Jackson McCabe (Minneapolis: Fortress Press, 2007).

26. This is by no means an exhaustive list. There are broader social currents, such as pluralism and multiculturalism, and other more specific phenomena, such as interfaith marriage between Jews and Christians, that would have to be considered in a more in-depth study of this phenomenon.

27. These items may be found at www.cafepress.com/ralley.

28. There is a historical problem with this identification. Most scholars agree that though the term "rabbi" as an honorific title was widespread in the time of Jesus and is applied to him in the New Testament, it is unlikely that Jesus was ordained as a rabbi or that rabbinic ordination per se even existed at that time. See Shaye J. D. Cohen, "Epigraphic Rabbis," *Jewish Quarterly Review* 72 (1981–82): 1–17.

29. Rabbi Jan Katzew of the Union coined this phrase for Reform Judaism.

30. Irving Greenberg, *For the Sake of Heaven and Earth: The New Encounter between Judaism and Christianity* (Philadelphia: Jewish Publication Society, 2004), 15, 23, 130.

31. The Declaration is available at www.elca.org under Who We Are.

32. The document may be found at the Vatican website www.vatican.va.

33. Other instances of the use of Hebrew by Christians as an aspect of reclamation will be discussed below.

34. Bishops' Committee on the Liturgy, National Conference of Catholic Bishops, "God's Mercy Endures Forever: Guidelines on the Presentation of Jews and Judaism in Catholic Preaching" (September 1988), section 29, emphasis added.

35. Noga Collins-Kreiner, *Christian Tourism to the Holy Land: Pilgrimage during Security Crisis* (Aldershot: Ashgate, 2006), 14.

36. This is but one example of the marketing of Israeli and, more specifically, Jewish religious items to Christians.

37. The article by David Krusch may be found at www.cufi.org.

38. I am drawing a distinction here between, on the one hand, "messianic Jewish," understood as organizations whose outreach is targeted at the Jewish community and whose worship is based on Jewish modes of expression, and, on the other hand, Christian churches whose primary mission is not to Jews and whose worship is more "traditionally" Christian, though perhaps containing some Jewish elements. The distinction between these groups may be becoming blurred, one consequence of "reclamation" that requires further research.

39. For a history of Christian mission to Jews, see Yaakov Ariel, *Evangelizing the Chosen People: Missions to the Jews in America 1880–2000* (Chapel Hill: University of North Carolina Press, 2000).

40. See hebraiccommmunity.org.

41. Ibid.

42. In this regard, see the distinction between appropriation and expropriation discussed by George Lindbeck in his article, "What of the Future? A Christian Response" in *Christianity in Jewish Terms*, ed. Tikva Frymer-Kensky, David Novak, Peter Ochs, David Fox Sandmel, and Michael Signer (Boulder, CO: Westview Press, 2000), 357–66.

CHAPTER TWENTY

Contempt for the Jews and Disregard for the Old Testament

The Re-establishment of the Tridentine Rite in German Perspective

Hanspeter Heinz
translated by Johanna Schmid

One of the greatest gifts of my life has been my encounter with Judaism. It has enriched and deepened my faith. It has even freed me from an arrogant view that Christians often have of their religion. Some think that Christianity constitutes a set of higher moral principles than Judaism because Christians are obliged to love their enemies; others imagine that the Christian liturgy is more spiritual and more personal than Jewish services; still others believe that Christianity is radically founded on faith and grace, whereas Judaism is a religion focusing on laws and obedience to them. I have learned that such stereotypical views do not stand up to thorough scrutiny, and I believe that we Christians cannot and must not maintain our identity at the expense of the Jews.

While studying theology in Rome, I had the privilege of seeing the Second Vatican Council with my own eyes, even the dramatic struggle over *Nostra Aetate,* paragraph 4, the declaration on the Jews. *Nostra Aetate* is the shortest document of the Council, but the most courageous one and the one that has had the most far-reaching consequences. It has overcome (or at least has irrevocably begun to overcome) the fundamental schism of the Church, that is, the un-Christian rejection of Judaism, the religious soil in which Christianity is permanently rooted. It was not until later, however, that I discovered the implications of this crucial turning point. This discovery came through my encounter with Judaism as it is lived today, through my personal interactions with Jews, some of whom are as close to me as my best Christian friends. Hence, I know Judaism not only from the many books I have read as a scholar, but even more profoundly from sustained, sometimes painful face-to-face interactions with my Jewish friends engaged in the dialogue.

I was present in 1980 when Pope John Paul II met the representatives of the Central Council of Jews (*Zentralrat der Juden*) and the Rabbinic Conference (*Rabbinerkonferenz*) at Mainz. This meeting became a decisive experience for me. In his speech, the pope expressed a ground rule for Catholic theology: "The first dimension of this [Jewish-Christian] dialogue, that is, the meeting between the people of God of the Old Covenant, never revoked by God, and that of the New Covenant, is at the same time a dialogue within our Church, that is to say, between the first and the second part of her Bible."[1] With these words, John Paul II acknowledges that the Old Testament has theological value, "since this value is not wiped out by the later interpretation of the New Testament."[2] In the same speech, he continues: "A second dimension of our dialogue—the true and central one—is the meeting between present-day Christian Churches and the present-day people of the Covenant concluded with Moses. It is important here that Christians—to continue the post-conciliar directives—should aim at understanding better the fundamental elements of the religious tradition of Judaism, and learn what fundamental lines are essential for the religious reality lived by the Jews, according to their own understanding."[3]

My Friend Michael

Michael Signer is one of my closest friends. I got to know him in 1989 when I, together with my colleagues Professors Klaus Kienzler and Jakob J. Petuchowski, held a theological symposium in Augsburg. Petuchowski's former students, Professors David Ellenson and Michael Signer, also took part in the symposium. Within the first few days, Michael and I had established a friendship. Anyone who knows Michael knows that he is not only an excellent scholar of the Jewish tradition; he also understands Christianity and its history, and can even see it from an insider's perspective in some significant ways. Michael is also good at making friends; he has established friendships with Jewish and Christian colleagues in the United States and Canada as well as in Israel, Germany, and Poland. Personally I admire how he remains in close contact with young people, particularly his students. They are our hope for continuing the Jewish-Christian dialogue in the next generation and beyond.

Since 1989, Michael and I have met at least once a year when he, on his way to or from Israel, has been passing through Germany. We have met in Berlin for the Summer Academy founded by our Protestant colleague, Professor Peter von der Osten-Sacken, and for conferences and lectures in Munich, Aachen, and Bamberg. In 2003, for example, Michael delivered a groundbreaking lecture at the Catholic Academy of Bavaria entitled "The Jewish Perspective on Jesus"; in 2005 he presented a critical analysis of *Nostra Aetate* 4 in Aachen. It is Michael's talent for language that made him so daring as to give two lectures in German in 2007. Furthermore, together with Betty Signer, our program coordinator and "chief rabbi," Michael and I have held international seminars with Jewish and Christian participants at Auschwitz, Cracow, Nuremberg, and Lublin. Our main goal has been to win undergraduate and graduate students as well as established scholars for the Jewish-Christian dialogue and to educate them on topics pertinent to it. I am also grateful for Michael's help during my sabbatical year in the United States in connecting me with many Jewish and Christian experts with whom I continue to work.

Steps Forward in Spite of Obstacles

Michael has been the most important Jewish partner in the dialogue between Jews and the Catholic Church in the United States for decades. He believes that during the last several decades the relationship between the

Christian churches and the Jews has made such positive strides that he and his co-authors of *Dabru Emet* took the bold step of inviting Jewish scholars and rabbis to answer it.[4] In spite of such progress, there have been obstacles in our way again and again, which call into question all our efforts.

When we held our international seminar at Auschwitz in 2000, Michael was very disappointed that the Vatican document *Dominus Iesus* had been published simultaneously with *Dabru Emet*. He became discouraged upon realizing that *Dominus Iesus* had apparently "forgotten" that Judaism remains a valid religious path by virtue of the fact that God has not revoked His covenant with the Jewish people.

I am also reminded of the simultaneous beatification of two popes, Pius IX (1846–1878) and John XXIII (1958–1963), by John Paul II in September 2000. The two pontiffs seemed to serve two opposing tendencies within the Church. Whereas John XXIII convened the Second Vatican Council and worked personally for a renewed relationship between the Church and the Jews, Pius IX, the pope of the First Vatican Council, engaged in overt anti-Jewish discourse and actions.[5]

Another obstacle to progress in the Jewish-Christian dialogue was the 2005 release of Mel Gibson's film, *The Passion of the Christ*.[6] The Jews and their Christian friends who publicly criticized the movie unfortunately garnered support neither from the Catholic bishops nor from the Vatican. Some members of and advisers for the Bishops' Committee for Ecumenical and Interreligious Affairs (BCEIA), a committee of the United States Conference of Catholic Bishops (USCCB) that deals with—among others— issues concerning the relationship of the Church to the Jewish people, were bitterly disappointed when their head, Cardinal William H. Keeler, did not think it necessary to hold a consultation on this significant media event.

The latest setback, with which the present essay is concerned, is Pope Benedict XVI's *motu proprio* rescript entitled *Summorum Pontificum* regarding the Tridentine rite and its wider re-admission.[7] In spite of often being deeply disappointed and hurt, Michael has not given up; he has always gathered enough courage to continue on the road of dialogue and reconciliation. His Jewish and Christian friends, who also have not lost hope, play a decisive role in his perseverance. Additionally, Michael's extraordinary sense of humor sustains him. Those of us engaged in the dialogue gratefully acknowledge the efforts of Pope John Paul II in renewing the Jewish-Christian relationship. He did more than all of his papal predecessors put together. Nevertheless, we do not put all our hope for sustainable reforms in Jewish-Christian relations in popes and bishops alone. Rather, we also trust in scholars, priests and ministers, rabbis, religious educators, and centers for Jewish-Christian dialogue to make innovative decisions, to prepare groundbreaking documents, and to pave the way for their positive reception.[8]

The Announcement of the *Motu Proprio* and a Warning Signal from Germany

Shortly before Easter 2007, an official announcement by the Holy See's Secretary of State, Cardinal Tarcisio Bertone, confirmed that Pope Benedict XVI was going to allow the wider use of the 1962 Latin Missal. After rumors spread for weeks, the situation began to become clear. On April 4, the discussion group "Jews and Christians" of the Central Committee of German Catholics (*Zentralkomitee der deutschen Katholiken*) published a statement in anticipation of the *motu proprio;* an English translation was immediately published by the Center for Christian-Jewish Learning at Boston College.[9] The statement, in part, reads:

> The discussion group "Jews and Christians" of the Central Committee of German Catholics, presently composed of sixteen Catholics and fourteen Jews, unanimously expressed the following serious objections against this prospect [of Pope Benedict issuing a *motu proprio* that would more generally allow the celebration of the pre-conciliar Mass of the 1962 Roman Missal].
>
> 1. The *Missale Romanum* of 1962 contains the Good Friday Intercession "for the conversion of the Jews" (*pro conversione Iudaeorum*). Although this rite no longer includes the denigrating descriptions of the Jews as acting "perfidiously" (*perfidus*) and/or as "perfidious" (*perfidia*), the Good Friday Intercession otherwise expresses the overall [demeaning] perspective of the text as it has been prayed in the Liturgy of Good Friday since the Middle Ages. The intercession speaks of the "blindness"

(*obcaecatio*) of the Jewish people and says that the Jewish people walk "in darkness" (*tenebrae*). This contradicts in a striking way the conciliar declaration *Nostra Aetate,* which states in chapter 4: "Sounding the depths of the mystery which is the church, this sacred council remembers the spiritual ties which link the people of the new covenant to the stock of Abraham. . . . [T]he apostle Paul maintains that the Jews remain very dear to God, for the sake of the patriarchs, since God does not take back the gifts he bestowed or the choice he made (see Romans 11:28–29; *Lumen Gentium* 16). . . . [T]he Jews should not be spoken of as rejected or accursed as if this followed from Holy Scripture. Consequently, all must take care lest in catechizing or in preaching the word of God they teach anything which is not in accord with the truth of the Gospel message or the spirit of Christ."

To revive the 1962 Missal with the old Good Friday intercession means the denial of a substantial theological paradigm-shift made by the Council: namely, the biblically-justified new understanding of the relationship of the Church to Judaism with the accompanying change to the Church's own self-understanding. The traditional Good Friday intercession still beseeched categorically that the Jews would acknowledge "our Lord Jesus Christ, the light of truth." The post-conciliar revised version is more open: it recognizes the way of salvation of the Jews founded upon God's design, even if it asks that the Jews may 'arrive at the fullness of redemption.'

2. The pre-conciliar Roman Missal is also inseparably connected to the old lectionary. In its sequence of about sixty diverse formularies for the celebration of Mass for Sundays and holy days, there is no reading from the Old Testament for each Sunday except in only three cases: Isaiah 60:1–6 on the Feast of the Epiphany, Hosea 6:1–6 and Exodus 12:1–11 on Good Friday, as well as twelve Old Testament readings in the liturgy of the Easter Vigil, which were reduced during the re-organization of 1951–55 to four (Genesis 1; Exodus 14:24–15:1; Isaiah 4:2–6; and Deuteronomy 31:22–30). This is blatant Marcionism, which devalues the first part of the two-part Christian Bible—namely the Bible of Israel—to insignificance. With the rejection of Marcion, however, the Church already in the middle of the second century said "Yes" to the Old Testament!

3. The theology and spirituality of the *Missa Tridentina*, in particular regarding the doctrine of the Church, also contradicts much that was theological[ly] central to the Second Vatican Council. This concerns, not least, the unique relationship between the Church and Judaism (see *Lumen Gentium* 16 and *Nostra Aetate* 4).

The demand for the reinstatement of the Tridentine rite concerns such fundamental theological questions and is not really a question about the celebration of the Mass in Latin. This already is easily possible always and everywhere according to the post-conciliar Roman Missal (third edition, Rome 2002)! It is clearly obvious what ensues with the reacceptance of the Tridentine Missal: a lasting disruption to the Catholic-Jewish Dialogue that began so hopefully at the Second Vatican Council. Many dedicated personal and also theological efforts on both sides would be intentionally damaged. We hope that Pope Benedict XVI will not permit this injury to Christian-Jewish relations to occur.[10]

To summarize the objections: the proposed *motu proprio* favors contempt for the Jews and disregard for the Old Testament, and it contradicts the ecclesiology of the Second Vatican Council.

What, one might well ask, is the nature and purpose of this German discussion group, of which Michael Signer has been a part for a number of years? He joins them for their conferences and actively participates in their meetings as a corresponding member. The discussion group "Jews and Christians" has been in existence for thirty-five years. Since 1979 it has authored several theological publications that are widely read in Germany and acknowledged internationally among experts. The group has the courage to discuss delicate topics related to the dialogue and to publish its insights. The discussion group, organized by the Central Committee of German Catholics, is a unique theological forum for Jews and Christians. Unlike other groups of its kind, which are actively involved in most German cities in adult education and public relations, "Jews and Christians" publishes theological statements. Although there is a sub-commission for relations with the Jews within the German Bishops' Conference, which has the task of writing theological and pastoral statements on Jewish-Christian relations, it has no Jewish experts. The Central Council of Jews in Germany supports the Jewish population in matters of political, cultural, and public concern, but does not become involved in religious issues. In contrast to all other initiatives, the discussion group of the Central Committee is neither a political lobby for Jewish interests nor a sponsor of educational events. As a national organ for theological dialogue, it is the only Jewish-Christian committee of its kind in Europe. Since 1974 I have been the head of the group and Professor Ernst Ludwig Ehrlich served as its co-leader until his death in October 2007.[11]

An Echo of Our Document

We were content with how our statement was reported and discussed in the media. We heard from many people in agreement with us, even from abroad. Furthermore, we received an answer from Cardinal Walter Kasper, to whom we had faxed the document before it was published. In reply, he sent us a copy of his letter to Professor John Pawlikowski dated April 3.[12] Here Cardinal Kasper writes:

> Already before receiving your letter, I had spoken with Cardinal Castrillón Hoyos, who is responsible for this aspect, expressing the concerns of many people engaged in the Jewish-Christian dialogue. After a long conversation, it was reiterated that the use of the Missal does not represent principally a new situation insofar as its use has been permitted over time in particular cases. The 1962 Missal does not have the term 'perfidious Jews.' I 'was unable to obtain a clear answer with regard to the prayer for the Jews. While I do not know what the Pope intends to state in his final text, it is clear that the decision that has been made cannot now be changed.

Kasper's letter is not a sign of resignation or neglected vigilance, but rather a sober acknowledgment of his limited influence within the Curia; in this case, Cardinal Hoyos possesses an inordinate degree of power and responsibility. What we see here is not a problem deriving from persons, but rather from structures. We can, according to Hans Maier, "compare the pontifical way of governing the church to date with that of the European monarchs of the late-18th century."[13] The pope asks the head of a particular Vatican department for advice. When the person is put in charge of a task, he is not obliged to cooperate with his colleagues; his single-handed efforts can pass without feedback or correction. Instead of this kind of lone-ranger approach, "the heads of departments must coordinate and harmonize their efforts concerning church policies supposed to have an effect in our complex world. All those persons participating must take on their share of the responsibility for the decision made and support or justify it according to the principle of collegiality."[14]

This antiquated way of governing employed by the pope leads to many unfortunate mishaps when writing and publishing documents concerning the universal Church. Many arguments necessary to the appropriate presentation of a particular topic are neither presented nor taken seriously, nor are the foreseeable public reactions properly anticipated and addressed. Subsequent corrections added "to clarify misunderstandings" subsequently attempt to minimize the damage done. Futhermore, Benedict XVI's personnel policy reinforces a general lack of sensitivity to the world outside the Vatican; he appointed Tarcisio Bertone, a canonist, the Holy See's Secretary of State, whereas Bertone's predecessors, Agostino Casaroli, Giovanni Benelli, and Angelo Sodano, had been experienced diplomats.

As we learned, Cardinal Karl Lehmann wrote a long letter to Pope Benedict some months before the *motu propio* was published, expressing the misgivings of the German Bishops' Conference about the wider use of the Tridentine rite. The only answer he got was a curial secretary acknowledging receipt of his letter. In my view, the principle of collegiality among the bishops should be implemented differently. Even after Vatican II, bishops and bishops' conferences are obviously treated as servants and delegates of the pope rather than as successors of the apostles with the authentic and original mission to lead as pastors and to spread the gospel as teachers of faith, as was (re-)affirmed by the Council.[15]

On June 28, Professor Ehrlich and I received the following answer from Cardinal Tarcisio Bertone:

Your statement has been brought to the attention of this administration by being published on the committee's website. The document deals with three critical topics concerning the planned new *motu proprio* on the use of the 1962 Missal.

On his Holiness's instructions, I am taking the liberty to give the following explanations:

1. The 1962 Missal has never been abrogated and can be used with the local bishop's permission; if the local bishop authorizes its use, it still has its place in the liturgy. According to the indult by Pope John Paul II, the communities under the jurisdiction of the pontifical committee "Ecclesia Dei" use this Missal. With the new *motu proprio* the opportunities to use the Missal are not essentially extended. Basically, the document's attempt is to simplify the existing canonical norms and to clarify them.

2. According to the new *motu proprio,* during the Easter Triduum only the Missal promulgated by Pope Paul VI can be used in the parishes. The communities under the jurisdiction of the pontifical committee "Ecclesia Dei" have used the Missal of Pope John XXIII since 1988. As you know, this pope abolished the expression 'pro perfidis Judaeis.' In conclusion, the new *motu proprio* does not change anything concerning the Easter Triduum.

3. Claiming that the 1962 Missal is founded on an essentially different theology than that from 1970 is incorrect and untrue. In the history of the liturgy we can certainly speak of development but never of 'rupture.' It is the so called 'Levebrians' whose position includes talking about 'rupture.'

I hope that this clarification contributes to [your] gaining an objective view and avoiding scare-mongering, which would be completely unreasonable.[16]

Before proceeding, three formal observations must be made. First, Cardinal Bertone emphasizes that he is writing "on instruction," which means that Pope Benedict is aware of our misgivings. So, being completely cognizant of our concerns, the pope refuses to address the issue directly. Second, Cardinal Bertone learned of our statement via the internet, which indicates just how poor the communication between him and Cardinal Kasper is. Third, we, unlike Cardinal Lehmann, received a comprehensive answer from Rome, suggesting that a published statement leaves a deeper impression or is more effective than a personal letter to the pope written by the head of a bishops' conference.

On June 29, Professor Ehrlich and I answered Cardinal Bertone thusly:

> The discussion group, who discussed your letter on June 25, anticipates our Holy Father's decision with great concern. Our motive for raising objections to extending the use of the 1962 Missal was not irrational scaremongering, as you called it, but grave theological and pastoral concerns. Your letter could not remove these in any way. First, as we said in our document, the Good Friday intercession in the 1962 Missal contradicts the theology of Vatican II, even if Pope John XXIII did eliminate the words 'perfidis' and 'perfidiam.' According to the Council and to the teaching of Pope John Paul II this contempt of the Jews is unacceptable. . . .
>
> Second, the sequence of liturgical readings in the 1962 Missal contradicts the directives of the Council due to its disregard for the Old Testament. As you did not refer to our arguments against the sequence [of readings] in your letter, we conclude that you share our theological objections. . . . Third, we interpret your clarification in such a way that in the future the 1962 Missal may exclusively be used by the communities of "Ecclesia Dei," but in any other case it will not be allowed. . . . If this were not the case, there would be different interpretations of the principle of "lex orandi—lex credendi" concerning the Roman Catholic rite; both interpretations, which contradict each other, could be legitimate.
>
> You write in your letter that the 1962 Missal has never been abrogated and can be used by the communities under the jurisdiction of "Ecclesia Dei" if the local bishop has granted indult. We see this usage sanctioned by an indult as a measure deriving from pastoral zeal, but not at all from a fundamental decision for the 1962 Missal. That is why, taking all the aforementioned theological reasons into consideration, we think that its use must remain restricted! Concerning the communities under the jurisdiction of "Ecclesia Dei" and their use of the 1962 Missal, we demand use of the Good Friday intercession as it is formulated in the Missal by Pope Paul VI; otherwise we would have no defense against those who reproach us as being the enemies of the Jews.

We hope that our objections, which we have brought forward out of a sense of responsibility for the Church and for Christian-Jewish relations, will be addressed in the publication of the *motu proprio*. . . .

Unfortunately, the *motu proprio* issued by Pope Benedict XVI has only confirmed our objections. Shortly before the *motu proprio* was issued, a book strongly defending traditionalism and directed against the statement issued by our discussion group was published.[17] This publication is noteworthy for its several well-documented statements by Cardinal Joseph Ratzinger supporting the pre-conciliar liturgy and objecting to the liturgical reform of Pope Paul VI. One such statement reads: "It is impossible to see what could be dangerous or unacceptable about that [i.e., the old rite]. A community is calling its very being into question when it suddenly declares that what until now was its holiest and highest possession is strictly forbidden and when it makes the longing for it seem downright indecent. Can it be trusted any more about anything else? Will it not proscribe again tomorrow what it prescribes today?"[18] Cardinal Ratzinger also writes:

> In order to raise an appropriate awareness of the liturgy it is also important to stop defaming the liturgy in the form used until 1970. Those persons committed to this form of liturgy or participating in it are treated like lepers; all tolerance comes to an end here. . . . This has never happened in all of history; it also means banning and condemning the entire tradition of the Church. How should we trust her in the present when this is the case? I admit that I also do not understand why so many of my brothers in the episcopal office acquiesce in that directive demanding intolerance, which impedes without reason the reconciliation necessary within the Church.[19]

As a cardinal within the Curia, Ratzinger encouraged the friends of the old rite. He celebrated Mass at their conferences according to the old Missal, and he has never severed ties with the followers of Archbishop Marcel Lefebvre, who was excommunicated in 1988. For years those people attached to the traditional liturgy have been urging him—and continue to do so now that he is pope—to be true to his word and to allow the Tridentine rite to be celebrated generally.

The *Motu Proprio* of 7 July 2007
and "Clarifications" from the Vatican

The meaning of the *motu proprio* for the reform of the liturgy, a process which is always taking place, is certainly a topic worthy of treatment in its own right, but one that I cannot here explore.[20] In what follows, therefore, I will discuss its importance for the Jewish-Christian relationship up to 1 January 2008.

First, I must say that neither the text itself nor the pope's accompanying letter to the bishops utters a single word suggesting concern for the relationship with the Jews and how it may be damaged. Pope Benedict, fully aware of the grave objections to his rescript, neglected the topic altogether. Personally, I found Article 2 of the *motu proprio* especially irritating. It avers that every priest celebrating "Mass without people" is free to use the 1962 Missal "every day, except during the Paschal Triduum."[21] This is nothing new, as the rubrics of the 1962 Missal forbade private Masses on Good Friday. But Article 2 raises a critical question: namely, if this ban which eradicates the offense of the old Good Friday intercession is valid for private Masses, is it not necessary that it must be valid for all Masses with a community or lay people present? This question is addressed in the *Communiqué* published by the Pontifical Commission for Religious Relations with the Jews on 21 July 2007. It clarifies that the communities under the jurisdiction of "Ecclesia Dei" are still allowed to celebrate the Good Friday liturgy according to the 1962 Missal, but notes that "the problem of the Prayer for the Conversion of the Jews requires further reflection." The document concludes by affirming the Commission's commitment to search for an appropriate solution that accords with *Nostra Aetate*.[22] Whereas we might have hoped for a binding directive, the Vatican has given nothing more than this vague statement of intent. If, in fact, correcting the shortcomings of the *motu proprio* is important for Pope Benedict, we can understand neither why he himself did not do so before publishing the rescript nor why the issue still awaits clarification even now.

Second, I take issue with a statement in Cardinal Bertone's letter to our discussion group: "[W]ith the new *motu proprio* the opportunities to use the [1962] Missal are not essentially extended. Basically, the document's attempt is to simplify the existing canonical norms and to clarify them." This is simply not true. The usage of the pre-conciliar Missal is, indeed, essentially extended; furthermore, its status is elevated. Instead of being restricted by the indults of 1984 and 1988, it is promoted to a *forma extra-ordinaria* of the liturgy.

There is no reason to doubt Pope Benedict's attempts to do everything in his power to reconcile the persons and groups favourably disposed toward the traditional liturgy with the wider Catholic community. He understands the lines of development that have led to separation and disruption after the Council, and he desires to resolve the conflicts and overcome the community divisions without revoking the Second Vatican Council. Toward this end, he offers the opportunity to celebrate Mass according to the 1962 Missal. This is now sanctioned as an extraordinary liturgical form and not merely a form to be implemented by indult, i.e., special permission. As a theologian, Benedict XVI remains faithful to his long-held conviction that the Second Vatican Council was an act of substantial continuity. The Council, he maintains, allowed elements that neither veered from nor contradicted the great Catholic tradition. Some people see the Second Vatican Council and its consequences as a break with the past, as a disruption of Catholic continuity. In my view, they are simply mistaken. Vatican II is part of an organic developmental process. By holding to this view, Pope Benedict wants to distance himself from the main argument used by those defending the old liturgical rite. Whether they are satisfied with his concessions remains to be seen. Those defending the old rite not only disagree with the liturgical reform of the Council; they also take issue with its ecclesiology, which opens the Catholic Church to the contemporary world, to other Christian communities, and to dialogue with Judaism and other religions.

Third, the new *motu proprio* makes the liturgy of the 1962 Missal, like that of the Missal of Paul VI, an authentic expression of the principle "lex orandi—lex credendi" (Art. 1). In his letter accompanying the rescript, Pope Benedict claims that there is no contradiction between the two editions of the Roman Missal: in the history of the liturgy there is growth and progress, but no rupture. This cannot be affirmed of the Good Friday intercession and the sequence of readings for Sunday Mass, as the contempt for the Jews and disregard for the Old Testament in the rite of 1962 clearly contradict *Nostra Aetate* and the obligatory liturgical reform introduced by Pope Paul VI. Here it is not continuity but discontinuity which must be considered, as the Second Vatican Council broke with the 2,000-year-old theology of anti-Judaism. According to the Lord's word, "But from the beginning it has not been this way" (Mt. 19:8). *Nostra Aetate* rejected the un-Christian ecclesial tradition and went back to the original good news according to St. Paul's letter to the Romans, chapters 9–11. To continue praying that the Jews may be freed from their blindness and delivered from their darkness in spite of all the conciliar and post-conciliar efforts in Jewish-Christian relations is a scandal! Perhaps some will object that *Nostra Aetate* rejected only the traditional charge of deicide and the claim that the Jews have been forsaken and cursed by God, maintaining that the Church may continue to compare the blind *Synagoga* with the triumphant *Ecclesia*. This comparison, too, is theologically erroneous and has had disastrous consequences!

We cannot in any way conclude from the *motu proprio* that Pope Benedict does not support *Nostra Aetate* 4 and the numerous declarations issued by his predecessors, particularly John Paul II. His speeches at the Cologne synagogue on World Youth Day in 2005 and at Auschwitz in 2006, as well as his book, *Jesus of Nazareth*, where he explicitly distances himself from the anti-Judaism of early Christian theologians, bear sufficient witness. I regret, however, that in the great opus of Joseph Ratzinger I am unable to find a Christian theology developed 'in the presence of the other,' especially of the Jews. I regret even more that Pope Benedict favors making allowances for traditional Catholic groups more than showing consideration for the Jews.

German Episcopal Regulations for Applying the *Motu Proprio*

"I very much wish to stress that these new norms do not in any way lessen your own authority and responsibility [as bishops], either for the liturgy or for the pastoral care of your faithful. Each bishop, in fact, is the moderator of the liturgy in his own diocese."[23] With these words in his letter accompanying the *motu proprio*, Pope Benedict affirms that the local bishops are responsible for the liturgy and its order in their respective dioceses. With these words in mind, I wrote to Cardinal Lehmann on behalf of the discussion group on 10 July 2007:

> The scandalous Good Friday intercession in the 1962 Missal must not be allowed to be used in the parishes in any case. . . . Otherwise we would be unable to defend ourselves against the reproaches of those who view us as enemies of the Jews. . . . Furthermore, we explicitly ask the bishops' conference to fulfill its pastoral duty for the Catholic Church in Germany by allowing only the new sequence of liturgical readings [to be used] in the dioceses. According to the 1962 Missal, the Old Testament does not play any role in the Sunday readings. Readings from the Old Testament are only to be found on the holy days of Epiphany, Good Friday, and at the Easter Vigil. This kind of disregard for the Old Testament, which constituted the Scriptures of Jesus, contradicts the principle of Catholic theology that Pope John Paul II formulated in the presence of the representatives of the Central Council of Jews and the Rabbinic Conference at Mainz in 1980: "The first dimension of this [Christian-Jewish] dialogue is the encounter between the people of God of the Old Covenant, the covenant never revoked by God, and that of the new Covenant. At the same time it is a dialogue within our Church, between the first and second part of her Bible." This desideratum can easily be fulfilled by a synopsis of the sequences of readings.

Although we did not receive a reply from Cardinal Lehmann, the German bishops apparently made our demands their own and sent them to Pope Benedict. But obviously no German bishop is courageous enough to use his authority, derived from his being a successor to the apostles, to enforce our demands in his diocese. Article 8 of the guidelines for *Summorum Pontificum* established by the German Bishops' Conference on 28 September 2007 even says that the sequence of readings from the 1962 Missal is authorized for celebrating Mass in extraordinary form. As did the bishops in France, Poland, Austria, and Switzerland, the German bishops agreed that there are only small groups of Catholics in the country who are interested in the older liturgy. As these groups represent a rather marginal minority, the issue has been addressed on a case-by-case basis. In terms of practical implementation, certain ways of celebrating Mass are offered which do not dodge the post-conciliar liturgy reform and which should not confuse the great majority of worshippers. Those in authority seem content only with controlling the damage done.

A New Intercession—But the Old Spirit Still Prevails

Following its April 2007 statement on the wider usage of the Tridentine rite, our discussion group again considered the different versions of the Good Friday prayer for the Jews and adopted the following statement on 29 February 2008:

> On 4 February 2008, Pope Benedict XVI promulgated the Good Friday prayer 'For the Jews' in the extraordinary rite [Tridentine] version, which unleashed international protests from Jews and Christians. It struck that nerve, which touches a historic trauma for Jews irrespective of their religious orientation: conversion to believing in Jesus Christ! Ever since the Middle Ages the prayer for the Jews on Good Friday has led to harsh, humiliating, and dangerous excesses against the 'perfidious' and 'blind' Jews. Although this vocabulary of traditional enmity toward Jews does not occur in the new intercession, old Jewish fears are evoked by the language that Christians hope for the enlightenment of the hearts of the Jews and their acknowledgment of Jesus Christ.
>
> The new text authorized by Pope Benedict reads:
>
>> Let us also pray for the Jews. That our Lord and God may enlighten their hearts, that they may acknowledge Jesus Christ as the Savior of all men. (Let us pray. Let us kneel. Let us stand.)
>>
>> Almighty and ever-living God, who wills that all men be saved and come to the knowledge of the Truth, graciously grant that all Israel may be saved when the fullness of the nations enters into your Church. Through Christ Our Lord. Amen.

Irritating questions are raised by this prayer. If the Tridentine rite of 1570 (last revised in the Roman Missal of 1962) spoke of blindness and darkness, and now, however, the new intercession prays for 'enlightenment,' the question arises whether this is merely a friendlier sounding rephrasing of the same thing. If the Jews are to arrive at the realization and thus acknowledgment of Jesus Christ as the Savior of all humanity, do they then have to convert to believing in Jesus Christ during the course of history? Or will they see the Savior of the world when history, which is the time of faith, has come to an end? Is the Jews' acknowledgment of Jesus Christ—when and however it takes place—a condition for their salvation? Or are there two ways of salvation: one for the peoples entering into the Church, and another for Israel without the Church? Does the Church continue hoping and praying for Israel to be saved, leaving it ultimately to God? Or must the Church feel obliged to invite the Jews by evangelization—certainly without any coercion or compulsion—to believe in Jesus Christ and the Gospel? Pope Paul VI's Good Friday liturgy, renewed in the spirit of the council, has not raised such questions and fears. . . .

What makes these prayers different is obvious. On the one hand, in the prayer of 1970, which is said on Good Friday in the ordinary rite of the Roman Catholic Church almost everywhere, the Church expresses unequivocally her appreciation for the dignity of Israel, God's chosen people, to whom God has given the promises and a covenant that was never revoked and will never be revoked (cf. Rom. 9:4 and 11:29 and *Nostra Aetate* 4). On the other hand, the Church acknowledges that the Jews who are faithful to God's covenant and live in the love of His name are on the path to salvation. She asks that God lead Israel to fulfillment along this path. The Church does not speak here of a Jewish confession of Jesus Christ as a condition for salvation because she trusts that their being faithful to God's covenant will lead the Jews to their salvation. . . .

Comparing the two prayers, it becomes overwhelmingly clear that the prayer of Pope Benedict XVI is a step backward from the prayer of Pope Paul VI and from the groundbreaking words and gestures of Pope John Paul II. We are disappointed and dismayed that Pope Benedict did not use the formulation of the 'ordinary form' of the Missal of 1970 verbatim for the 'extraordinary form' of the rite. The *motu proprio* of July 2007, which permits the extended use of the Tridentine rite, states that the post-conciliar rite of 1970 is the norm, while the rite of 1962, although now permitted for general use, is only the exception. But it also emphasizes that both forms of the rite testify authentically to the faith of the church (*lex orandi—lex credendi*). The authorization of two forms weighs particularly heavy on such a historically burdened topic as the Good Friday prayer for the Jews. The ambiguity of having two authorized forms of the prayer for the Jews irritates Catholics and has greatly damaged the growing trust between Catholics and Jews.

It was also felt that unnecessary damage to this trust and further annoyance was caused by the fact that Pope Benedict, as far as we know, neither before the publication of the *motu proprio* last year nor before the promulgation of the new Good Friday prayer consulted with Jewish dialogue partners to discover whether the new Good Friday intercession would hurt their religious feelings. Numerous letters and public statements—for instance, the statement of our discussion group of April 2007—had made the volatility of the proposal unmistakably clear. What is difficult to understand is that the new Good Friday prayer for the Jews was implemented without official comment. The subsequent explanation of Cardinal Kasper, that the excitement was based on misunderstandings since the text only expresses the Church's eschatological hope, was hardly convincing.

We hope and ask that Pope Benedict revise his decision and permit only the Good Friday prayer of 1970 for the entire Roman rite.

The new intercession cannot be improved; it must be revoked because it is inconsistent with the intercession of the 1970 Missal and can be easily misunderstood. In spite of urgings in this direction by Christians and Jews and even by the German Bishops' Conference, however, Pope Benedict appears unwilling to rescind the prayer.

The Problematic Silence of the Pope

Urged by divergent perspectives on the new intercession, some cardinals and German bishops issued public statements. At the beginning of

March 2008, Bishop Mussinghoff, head of the subcommittee for relations with the Jews, was the first to remark that he was "unhappy about the phrasing" of the prayer, expressing his hope for a meeting with the rabbis of Germany to clarify the matter. One month later, Cardinal Lehmann, who among the German bishops is supposed to be the strongest advocate for the relationship with the Jews, similarly voiced his concern. But instead of entering the discussion and answering questions, Lehmann simply warned that some accusations might be immoderate and tried to pacify those making them.

In his article in the *Frankfurter Allgemeine Zeitung* (*FAZ*) on 20 March 2008, Cardinal Kasper treated the new intercession extensively. Kasper tried to justify the new prayer for the Jews theologically; unfortunately, however, in so doing, he neither raised the obvious question of why Pope Benedict had not decided to use the intercession as it was written by Pope Paul VI nor mentioned any specific objection to it. Kasper interpreted the new intercession as the Church's confession of its eschatological hope whose fulfillment remains entirely in the hands of God, thereby precluding any notion that the Jews are to be proselytized. Similarly, Cardinal Lehmann wrote: "By no stretch of the imagination can I detect any appeal to convert the Jews, directly or indirectly."[24] By contrast, Cardinal Schönborn of Vienna published an article in the English newspaper "The Tablet" on March 29 favoring evangelization. He claimed that reading the biblical text through the lens of the contemporary world calls for proselytizing the Jews. Unfortunately, this assessment fails to take the tragic history of the Church's relationship with the Jewish people into account.

And what did the official spokesman of Pope Benedict, Cardinal Bertone, say in his communiqué of April 4, just two months after the new intercession had been promulgated? Nothing—except to assert that the Holy Father was faithful to the Second Vatican Council and that the Church's position concerning the Jews had not changed. Benedict had Bertone announce that the text would remain as is and that questions would not be answered.[25] Why, we might ask, was the intercession by Pope Paul VI, which is generally accepted, not implemented in the extraordinary rite? Is the new prayer for the Jews, as Cardinal Kasper maintains, to be understood eschatologically? Or does Cardinal Schönborn's view reflect the thinking and intention of Pope Benedict? Cardinal Bertone's statement simply does not reveal Pope Benedict's position on the documents of liturgical reform written since Vatican II.

What is indeed problematic is that Benedict remains silent, hearing all of these diverging episcopal interpretations of the new intercession without comment. Using pontifical power in this way has done great damage to the pope's authority, but there is no effective remonstrance against or remedy for it in Catholic canon law. So, what are those of us who are deeply committed to the often difficult work of transforming Jewish-Christian relations to do?

Outlook

However serious and enduring the current disturbance from Rome may be, for Michael and me and many of our Jewish and Christian friends, it is not a reason to question our continuing work toward a better relationship between Jews and Christians, which relationship has grown strong over the past forty years and has become stable enough to withstand some burdens. Although stumbling blocks seemingly litter the path, we feel called to continue down the road along which we have journeyed together. We must continue to cultivate and improve our relationship by establishing contacts among Jews and Christians and by discussing theological topics together. There was a panel discussion concerning the controversy over the new intercession at the Ninety-seventh German Catholic Conference in Osnabrück in 2008. Before the meeting, a volume of essays written by Jewish and Catholic authors, including Michael and me, entitled ". . . *damit sie Jesus Christus erkennen"—die neue Karfreitagsfürbitte in der Diskussion,* was published.[26]

For many centuries the Good Friday intercession for the Jews was the key element in the liturgy that mirrored the unspeakable Christian contempt for the people whom God first chose as His own. Christians even went so far as to pervert the reconciling gift of Jesus on the cross, wickedly twisting it into a charge of deicide against the Jews. Since the Second Vatican Council, every pope has been well advised to teach the new people of

God to stand up for their elder brothers and sisters who have long been oppressed and maltreated, to intervene in thought, word, and deed on their behalf, and to show them honor and respect. That this may be done now and for all time, "let us pray."

Notes

1. Pope John Paul II, *Spiritual Pilgrimage: Texts on Jews and Judaism 1979–1995,* ed. Eugene J. Fisher and Leon Klenicki (New York: Crossroad Herder, 1995), 15.

2. Ibid.

3. Ibid.

4. In *Dabru Emet* the Jewish response takes the form of an agenda of theological questions that Jews want to discuss with Christians critically and constructively.

5. See "Pope Pius IX and the Jews. A Statement of the Discussion Group 'Jews and Christians' of the Central Committee of German Catholics—July 21, 2000," in *Coming Together for the Sake of God: Contributions to Jewish-Christian Dialogue from Post-Holocaust Germany,* ed. Hanspeter Heinz and Michael A. Signer (Collegeville, MN: Liturgical Press, 2007), 108–11.

6. The movie has been criticized for its simplistic, black-and-white character development, its lack of historical accuracy and anachronistic tendencies, and its reinforcement of traditional anti-Jewish hostilities.

7. Masses following the pre-conciliar rite are often called "Tridentine rite" or "the Tridentine liturgy." The texts are taken from the liturgical books edited by the Council of Trent in 1570. They have been revised several times, with notable changes to the liturgical calendar and the participation of the faithful. Concerning the participation of the faithful, it is noteworthy that the first edition of the Tridentine Roman Missal made no provision for lay participants to receive Communion.

8. In recent church history, we have been encouraged by various developments in ecumenism, biblical studies, the liturgy, and lay apostolates, which not only set the stage for the Second Vatican Council but also have further benefited from the Council's official documents and determinations.

9. See http://www.bc.edu/research/cjl.

10. Concerning the discussion group's first point, it may be helpful to provide the full text of the Good Friday intercession for the Jews according to each Missal. From the 1962 Missal: "For the conversion of the Jews: Let us pray also for the Jews that the Lord our God may take the veil from their hearts and that they also may acknowledge our Lord Jesus Christ. Almighty and everlasting God, you do not refuse your mercy even to the Jews; hear the prayers which we offer for the blindness of that people so that they may acknowledge the light of your truth, which is

Christ, and be delivered from their darkness." From the 1970 Missal: "For the Jews: Let us pray for the Jewish people, the first to hear the Word of God, that they may continue to grow in the love of his name and in faithfulness to his covenant. Almighty and eternal God, long ago you gave your promise to Abraham and his posterity. Listen to your church as we pray that the people you first made your own may arrive at the fullness of redemption."

11. Professor Ehrlich, who had served during Vatican II as a Jewish counselor for Cardinal Augustin Bea and had worked on *Nostra Aetate*, became well known for his attempts to reconcile Jews and Christians throughout Germany, Europe, and around the world.

12. Another copy was sent to the Coordinating Committee for Christian-Jewish cooperation (*Koordinierungsausschuss für christlich-jüdische Zusammenarbeit*) in Austria. On April 26 the Koordinierungsausschuss had sent Cardinal Kasper a document with an argument similar to that of the German discussion group.

13. See Hans Maier, "Braucht Rom eine Regierung?" *Stimmen der Zeit* 219 (2001): 147–60, here 152.

14. Ibid., 155.

15. See Vatican II, *Lumen Gentium* 3.

16. A copy of this letter was also sent to the German Coordinating Council of Committees for Christian-Jewish Cooperation (*Deutscher Koordinierungsrat der Gesellschaften für Christlich-Jüdische Zusammenarbeit, DKR*) in response to its previous letter to Pope Benedict dated May 8. On two subsequent occasions, June 30 and August 31, the *DKR* wrote again to the Holy Father without receiving an answer.

17. Heinz-Lothar Barth, *Ist die traditionelle lateinische Messe antisemitisch? Antwort auf ein Papier des Zentralkomitees der deutschen Katholiken* (Altötting: Sarto-Verlag, 2007).

18. Joseph Cardinal Ratzinger, *Salt of the Earth* (San Francisco: Ignatius Press, 1997), 176–77.

19. Joseph Cardinal Ratzinger, *Aus meinem Leben. Erinnerungen, 1927–1977* (München: Wilhelm Heyne Verlag, 2000), 173. Albert Gerhards, Professor of Liturgy at the University of Bonn, disagrees. He writes: "When the Council of Trent decided to reform the liturgy, the result was not less rigorous than the reform of Vatican II" (A. Gerhards, "Die 'alte' und die 'neue' Messe. Versuch einer Sondierung der Positionen," *Gottesdienst* 41 [2007]: 57–59, here 57).

20. See Andrea Grillo, "Ende der Liturgiereform, Das Motuproprio *Summorum pontificum*," *Stimmen der Zeit* 225 (2007): 730–40; and Gerhards, "Die 'alte' und die 'neue' Messe," 57–59.

21. This statement is not clear. Neither is the expression in Cardinal Bertone's letter to us that in the parishes the Missal promulgated by Paul VI "could exclusively" be used for the Paschal Triduum. We asked for clarification—whether this

constitutes a directive that can be or must be followed. As Vatican officials know how to put their ideas into words precisely, the question of why neither Pope Benedict nor Cardinal Bertone did so at this critical point arises.

22. For the complete text of the *Communiqué* and related documents, including the *motu proprio* itself, see www.jcrelations.net.

23. Benedict's letter accompanying the *motu proprio* with reference to Vatican II, *Sacrosanctum Concilium* 22.

24. *Mainzer Kirchenzeitung,* 6 April 2008.

25. See www.jcrelations.net, under "NewsNotes."

26. ". . . *damit sie Jesus Christus erkennen"—die neue Karfreitagsfürbitte in der Diskussion,* ed. Walter Homolka and Erich Zenger (Freiburg: Herder, 2008).

Publications of Michael A. Signer

1970s

"Andrew of St. Victor and the Authorship of the Glossae in Ezechielem in MS. B.N. Lat. 14432." *Manuscripta* 22 (1978): 20–21.

"Barmherzigkeit." In *Theologische Realenzyklopadie.* Vol. 5, 227–32. Berlin: Walter de Gruyter, 1979.

1980s

Shared Searching: A Report on the First Year of the Outreach Programs. Palm Springs, CA: Pacific Association of Reform Rabbis, 1981.

Spinoza's Earliest Publication? The Hebrew Translation of Margaret Fell's A Loving Salutation to the Seed of Abraham Among the Jews, Wherever They Are Scattered Up and Down Upon the Face of the Earth, by Margaret Askew Fell Fox and Benedict Spinoza. Coedited with Richard Popkin. Wolfeboro, NH: Van Gorcum, 1987.

"The Aims and Objectives of Judaeo-Christian Studies—A Jewish Response." In *Defining a Discipline: The Aims and Objectives of Judeo-Christian Studies, Papers Presented at the First Bronstein Colloquium, November 7–8, 1983,* edited by Jakob J. Petuchowski, 73–82. Cincinnati: Hebrew Union College–Jewish Institute of Religion, 1984.

"*Communitas et Universitas:* From Theory to Practice in Judaeo-Christian Studies." In *When Jews and Christians Meet,* edited by Jakob J. Petuchowski, 59–83. Albany: State University of New York Press, 1988.

"Exégèse et Enseignement: Les Commentaires de Joseph ben Simeon Kara." *Archives Juives* 18.4 (1982): 60–63.

"King/Messiah: Rashi's Exegesis of Psalm 2." *Prooftexts: A Journal of Jewish Literary History* 3.3 (1983): 273–78.

"The Land of Israel in Medieval Jewish Exegetical and Polemical Literature." In *Land of Israel: Jewish Perspectives*, edited by Lawrence A. Hoffman, 210–33. Notre Dame, IN: University of Notre Dame Press, 1986.

"Preaching and Sermons, Jewish." In *Dictionary of the Middle Ages*. Vol. 10, edited by Joseph R. Strayer, 73–75. New York: Charles Scribner's Sons, 1982–1989.

"*Speculum Concilii*: Through the Mirror Brightly." In *Unanswered Questions: Theological Views of Jewish-Catholic Relations*, edited by Roger Brooks, 105–27. Notre Dame, IN: University of Notre Dame Press, 1988.

"The *Speculum Ecclesiae* by Honorius Augustodudensis on Jews and Judaism: Preaching at Regensburg in the Twelfth-Century." In *Crossroads of Medieval Civilization: The City of Regensburg and Its Intellectual Milieu*, edited by E. DuBruck and K. H. Goller, 121–37. Detroit: Michigan Consortium for Medieval and Early Modern Studies, 1984.

"St. Jerome and Andrew of St. Victor: Some Observations." *Studia Patristica* 17.1, edited by Elizabeth A. Livingstone, 333–37. Elmsford, NY: Pergamon Press, 1982.

"Texts in Context: Hebraica in the Vatican Library as a Resource for Jewish-Christian Relations." In *A Visual Testimony: Judaica from the Vatican Library*, edited by Philip Hiat and Philip E. Miller, 20–26. Miami: Center for the Fine Arts, 1987.

"Thirteenth-Century Christian Hebraism: The 'Expositio' on Canticles in MS Vat lat 1053." In *Approaches to Judaism in Medieval Times*. Vol. 3, edited by David R. Blumenthal, 89–100. Atlanta: Scholars Press, 1988.

"To See Ourselves as Others See Us: Circumcision in Pagan Antiquity and the Christian Middle Ages." In *Berit Mila in the Reform Context*, edited by Lewis M. Barth, 113–27. New York and Los Angeles: Berit Mila Board of Reform Judaism, 1990.

1990s

Andreae de Sancto Victore Opera 6: Expositio in Ezechielem. CCCM 53E. Turnhout: Brepols, 1991.

The Hebrew Renaissance. Coedited with Michael Terry and Deeana Copeland Klepper. Chicago: Newberry, 1997.

"*Adversus Judaeos (Against the Jews)*" and "Jews and Judaism." In *Augustine through the Ages: An Encyclopedia*, edited by Allan D. Fitzgerald, 12–14 and 470–74. Grand Rapids, MI: William B. Eerdmans, 1999.

"Andrew of St. Victor's Anti-Jewish Polemics." In *The Bible in the Mirror of Its Interpreters,* edited by Sara Japhet, 412–20. Jerusalem: Magnes Press, 1993.

"Bible, Jewish interpretation of." In *Medieval France: An Encyclopedia,* edited by William Kibler, 123–26. New York: Garland, 1995.

"Bundeserneuerung." *Das Prisma: Beiträge zu Pastoral, Katechese, und Theologie* 10 (1999): 23–27.

"Crossing the Threshold of Reconciliation: John Paul II and the Jews." *Reform Judaism* (Spring 1995): 36–40.

"Defining a Discipline: Jakob J. Petuchowski's Contribution to Jewish-Christian Relations." In *Memorial Tributes to Jakob Josef Petuchowski,* 33–40. Privately published by Aaron M. Petuchowski, 1993.

"Dies Domini: Jewish Observations on a Papal Document." Coauthor with Lawrence Hoffman. *Worship and Music* (Spring 1999): 46–57.

"Do Jews Read the 'Letter': Reflections on the Sign (אות) in Medieval Jewish Biblical Exegesis." In *The Quest for Context and Meaning: Studies in Biblical Intertextuality in Honor of James A. Sanders,* edited by Craig A. Evans and Shemaryahu Talmon, 613–24. Leiden: Brill, 1997.

"Fleisch und Geist: Opfer und Versöhnung in den Exegetischen Traditionen von Judentum und Christentum." In *Versöhnung in der jüdischen und christlichen Liturgie,* edited by David Ellenson, Hanspeter Heinz, Klaus Kienzler, and Jakob Petuchowski, 197–219. Freiburg: Herder, 1990.

"Foreword: The Spiritual Journey to Recovery through Torah." In *Renewed Each Day: Daily Twelve Step Recovery Meditations Based on the Bible.* Vol. 1, *Genesis & Exodus,* edited by Kerry M. Olitzky and Aaron Z., xiii–xvii. Woodstock, VT: Jewish Lights, 1992.

"From Theory to Practice: The *De doctrina christiana* and the Exegesis of Andrew of St. Victor." In *Reading and Wisdom: The* De doctrina christiana *of Augustine in the Middle Ages,* edited by Edward D. English, 84–98. Notre Dame, IN: University of Notre Dame Press, 1995.

"The *Glossa Ordinaria* and the Transmission of Medieval Anti-Judaism." In *A Distinct Voice: Medieval Studies in Honor of Leonard E. Boyle, O.P.,* edited by Jacqueline Brown and William P. Stoneman, 591–605. Notre Dame, IN: University of Notre Dame Press, 1997.

"Honour the Hoary Head: The Aged in the Medieval European Jewish Community." In *Aging and the Aged in Medieval Europe,* edited by Michael Sheehan, 39–48. Toronto: Pontifical Institute of Mediaeval Studies, 1990.

"How the Bible Has Been Interpreted in the Jewish Tradition." In *New Interpreters Bible.* Vol. 1, *Genesis to Leviticus,* edited by Leander Keck, 42–73. Nashville: Abingdon, 1994.

"An Irresistable Choice: On the Canonization of Edith Stein." *Reform Judaism* (Spring 1999): 25–31.

"Jewish-Christian Relations in Poland: A Personal Reflection." *European Judaism* 30.1 (1997): 93–100.

"Jewish Deliberations." *Journal of Ecumenical Studies* 27 (1990): 66–68.

"Judaism as Interpretation: Text and Spirit." In *Bits of Honey: Essays for Samson S. Levey,* edited by Stanley F. Chyet and David H. Ellenson, 277–87. Atlanta: Scholars Press, 1993.

"Konversion [Judentum]." In *Theologische Realenzyklopädie.* Vol. 19, 563–66. Berlin: Walter de Gruyter, 1990.

"Landed Ethics." *Tikkun* 5 (1990): 81–82.

"*Peshat, Sensus Litteralis,* and Sequential Narrative: Jewish Exegesis and the School of St. Victor in the Twelfth Century." In *The Frank Talmage Memorial Volume,* edited by Barry Walfish, 203–16. Haifa and Hanover, NH: Haifa University Press, 1993.

"The Poetics of Liturgy." In *The Changing Face of Jewish and Christian Worship in North America,* edited by Paul F. Bradshaw and Lawrence A. Hoffman, 184–98. Notre Dame, IN: University of Notre Dame Press, 1991.

"Positive Stellungnahmen der Päpste nicht berücksichtigt." In *Juden und Judentum im neuen Katechismus der Katholischen Kirche: Ein Zwischenruf,* 32–40. Zentralkomitee der deutschen Katholiken Dokumnetation, 1996.

"Rashi as Narrator." In *Rashi et la Culture Juive en France du Nord au Moyen Age,* edited by Gilbert Dahan and G. Nahon, 103–10. Leuven: Peeters, 1997.

"Restoring the Balance: Musings on Miracles in Rabbinic Judaism." In *Miracles in Jewish and Christian Antiquity: Imagining Truth,* edited by John C. Cavadini, 111–26. Notre Dame, IN: University of Notre Dame Press, 1999.

"The Rift That Binds: Hermeneutical Approaches to the Jewish-Christian Relationship." In *Ecumenism: Present Realities and Future Prospects,* edited by Lawrence S. Cunningham, 95–115. Notre Dame, IN: University of Notre Dame Press, 1998.

2000–

Christianity in Jewish Terms. Coedited with Tikva Frymer-Kensky, David Novak, Peter Ochs, and David Fox Sandmel. Boulder, CO: Westview Press, 2000.

Coming Together for the Sake of God: Contributions to Jewish-Christian Dialogue from Post-Holocaust Germany. Coedited with Hanspeter Heinz. Collegeville, MN: Liturgical Press, 2007.

The Exorbitant: Emmanuel Levinas Between Jews and Christians. Coedited with Kevin Hart. New York: Fordham University Press, 2010.

Humanity at the Limit: The Impact of the Holocaust Experience on Jews and Christians. Bloomington: Indiana University Press, 2001.

Jews and Christians in Twelfth-Century Europe. Coedited with John Van Engen. Notre Dame, IN: University of Notre Dame Press, 2001.

Memory and History in Christianity and Judaism. Notre Dame, IN: University of Notre Dame Press, 2001.

The Way into the Relationship between Jews and Non-Jews: Searching for Boundaries and Bridges. Woodstock, VT: Jewish Lights, 2007.

"Abraham: The One and the Many." In *Memory and History in Christianity and Judaism,* edited by Michael A. Signer, 204–12. Notre Dame, IN: University of Notre Dame Press, 2001.

"Blindness or Insight? The Jewish Denial of Jesus Christ." In *Who Do You Say That I Am? Christians Encounter Other Religions,* edited by Calvin E. Shenk, 187–206. Notre Dame, IN: University of Notre Dame Press, 2004.

"Building toward Teshuvah." *Catholic International* 13.2 (2002): 5–6.

"Can Jews Trust Catholics?" *Commonweal* 128.1 (2001): 12–14.

"Community and Education in Premodern Judaism." In *Educating People of Faith: Exploring the History of Jewish and Christian Communities,* edited by John Van Engen, 132–49. Grand Rapids, MI: William B. Eerdmans, 2004.

"Consolation and Confrontation: Jewish and Christian Interpretation of the Prophetic Books." In *Scripture and Pluralism: Reading the Bible in the Religiously Plural Worlds of the Middle Ages and Renaissance,* edited by Thomas J. Heffernan and Thomas E. Burman, 77–93. Boston and Leiden: Brill, 2005.

"*Dabru Emet:* A Contextual Analysis." *Theologiques* 11.1–2 (2003): 187–202.

"*Dabru Emet:* A Jewish Statement on Christians and Christianity." Coauthored with Tikva Frymer-Kensky, David Novak, and Peter Ochs. First published as a full-page advertisement in *The New York Times* on September 10, 2000; reprinted in *Christianity in Jewish Terms,* edited by Tikva Frymer-Kensky, David Novak, Peter Ochs, David Fox Sandmel, and Michael A. Signer, xv–xviii. Boulder, CO: Westview Press, 2000.

"Dialogue out of the Ashes: Jewish-Catholic Dialogue in Germany." In *Coming Together for the Sake of God: Contributions to Jewish-Christian Dialogue from Post-Holocaust Germany,* edited by Hanspeter Heinz and Michael A. Signer, 148–55. Collegeville, MN: Liturgical Press, 2006.

"*Dor dor vedorshav:* Of Fathers and Sons." In *History and Literature: New Readings of Jewish Texts in Honor of Arnold J. Band,* edited by William Cutter and David C. Jacobson, xxxiii–xxxvi. Providence, RI: Program of Judaic Studies, Brown University, 2002.

"God's Love for Israel: Apologetic and Hermeneutical Strategies in Twelfth-Century Biblical Exegesis." In *Jews and Christians in Twelfth-Century Europe,* edited by Michael A. Signer and John Van Engen, 123–49. Notre Dame. IN: University of Notre Dame Press, 2001.

"Jews and Judaism in the New Catechism of the Catholic Church—An Intervention." In *Coming Together for the Sake of God: Contributions to Jewish-Christian Dialogue from Post-Holocaust Germany*, edited by Hanspeter Heinz and Michael A. Signer, 63–68. Collegeville, MN: Liturgical Press, 2007.

"Juden und Christen in postmoderner Gesellschaft." *Zur Debatte* 34 (2004): 26–27.

"One Covenant or Two: Can We Sing a New Song?" In *Reinterpreting Revelation and Tradition: Jews and Christians in Conversation*, edited by John T. Pawlikowski and Hayim Goren Perelmuter, 3–23. Franklin, WI: Sheed and Ward, 2000.

"Polemic and Exegesis: The Varieties of Twelfth-Century Hebraism." In *Hebraica Veritas? Christian Hebraists and the Study of Judaism in Early Modern Europe*, edited by Allison P. Coudert and Jeffrey S. Shoulson, 21–32. Philadelphia: University of Pennsylvania Press, 2004.

"Rabbi and *Magister*: Overlapping Intellectual Models of the Twelfth-Century Renaissance." *Jewish History* 22.1–2 (2008): 115–37.

"Rabbinic Literature." Coauthored with Susan L. Graham. In *Handbook of Patristic Exegesis: The Bible in Ancient Christianity*. Vol. 1, edited by Charles Kannengiesser, 120–44. Leiden: Brill, 2004.

"Rashi's Reading of the Akedah." In *Memoria-Wege jüdischen Erinnerns: Festschrift für Michael Brocke zum 65. Geburtstag*, edited by Birgit Klein and Christiane E. Müller, 613–25. Berlin: Metropol, 2005.

"Relationships and Obligations: The Future of Jewish-Christian Dialogue." *Midstream* (January 2003): 6–8.

"Restoring the Narrative: Jewish and Christian Exegesis in the Twelfth Century." In *With Reverence for the Word: Medieval Exegesis in Judaism, Christianity, and Islam*, edited by Jane Dammen McAuliffe, Barry D. Walfish, and Joseph W. Goering, 70–82. New York: Oxford University Press, 2003.

"The Role of the Local Bishop in Catholic-Jewish Relations." In *Unfailing Patience and Sound Teaching: Reflections on Episcopal Ministry in Honor of Rembert G. Weakland, O.S.B.*, edited by David A. Stosur, 133–49. Collegeville, MN: Liturgical Press, 2003.

"Searching the Scriptures: Jews, Christians, and the Book." In *Christianity in Jewish Terms*, edited by Tikva Frymer-Kensky, David Novak, Peter Ochs, David Fox Sandmel, and Michael A. Signer, 85–98. Boulder, CO: Westview Press, 2000.

"Seeing, Tasting, Telling: How the Jews Celebrate Passover." *America* 196.12 (2007): 22–23.

"Sic et Non." *Begegnungen—Zeitschrift für Kirche und Judentum* 3 (2004): 8–11.

"'These Are the Generations': Reasoning with Rabbi Samuel ben Meier." In *Crisis, Call, and Leadership in the Abrahamic Traditions*, edited by Peter Ochs and William Stacy Johnson, 73–83. New York: Palgrave Macmillan, 2009.

"Tradition in Transition: Approaches to Jewish-Christian Relations." In *Jews and Christians in Conversation: Crossing Cultures and Generations*, edited by Edward

Kessler, John Pawlikowski, Judith Herschcopf Banki, and Barbara Ellen Bowe, 123–40. Cambridge: Orchard Academic, 2002.

"Trinity, Unity, Idolatry? Medieval and Modern Perspectives on *Shittuf.*" In *Lesarten des jüdisch-christlichen Dialoges: Festschrift zum 70. Geburtstag von Clemens Thoma,* edited by Silvia Käppeli, 275–84. Bern: Peter Lang, 2002.

"Vision and History: Nicholas of Lyra on the Prophet Ezechiel." In *Nicholas of Lyra: The Senses of Scripture,* edited by Lesley Smith and Philip D. W. Krey, 147–71. Boston: Brill, 2000.

"What of the Future? A Jewish Response." Coauthored with Tikva Frymer-Kensky, David Novak, Peter Ochs, and David Fox Sandmel. In *Christianity in Jewish Terms,* edited by Tikva Frymer-Kensky, David Novak, Peter Ochs, David Fox Sandmel, and Michael A. Signer, 366–73. Boulder, CO: Westview Press, 2000.

"Die Würde des Judentums und des Jüdischen Volkes Achten." *Kirche und Israel* 22.2 (2007): 161–70.

Index

www.ingramcontent.com/pod-product-compliance
Lightning Source LLC
Chambersburg PA
CBHW020351100426
42812CB00001B/19